BATMAN GORDON OF GOTHAM

BATMAN GORDON OF GOTHAM

Chuck Dixon   Dennis O'Neil
writers
Klaus Janson   Jim Aparo   Bill Sienkiewicz   Dick Giordano
artists
Kevin Somers   Ian Laughlin   Pam Rambo   Jamison
colorists
John Costanza   Clem Robins
letterers

Klaus Janson
collection cover artist
BATMAN created by **BOB KANE**

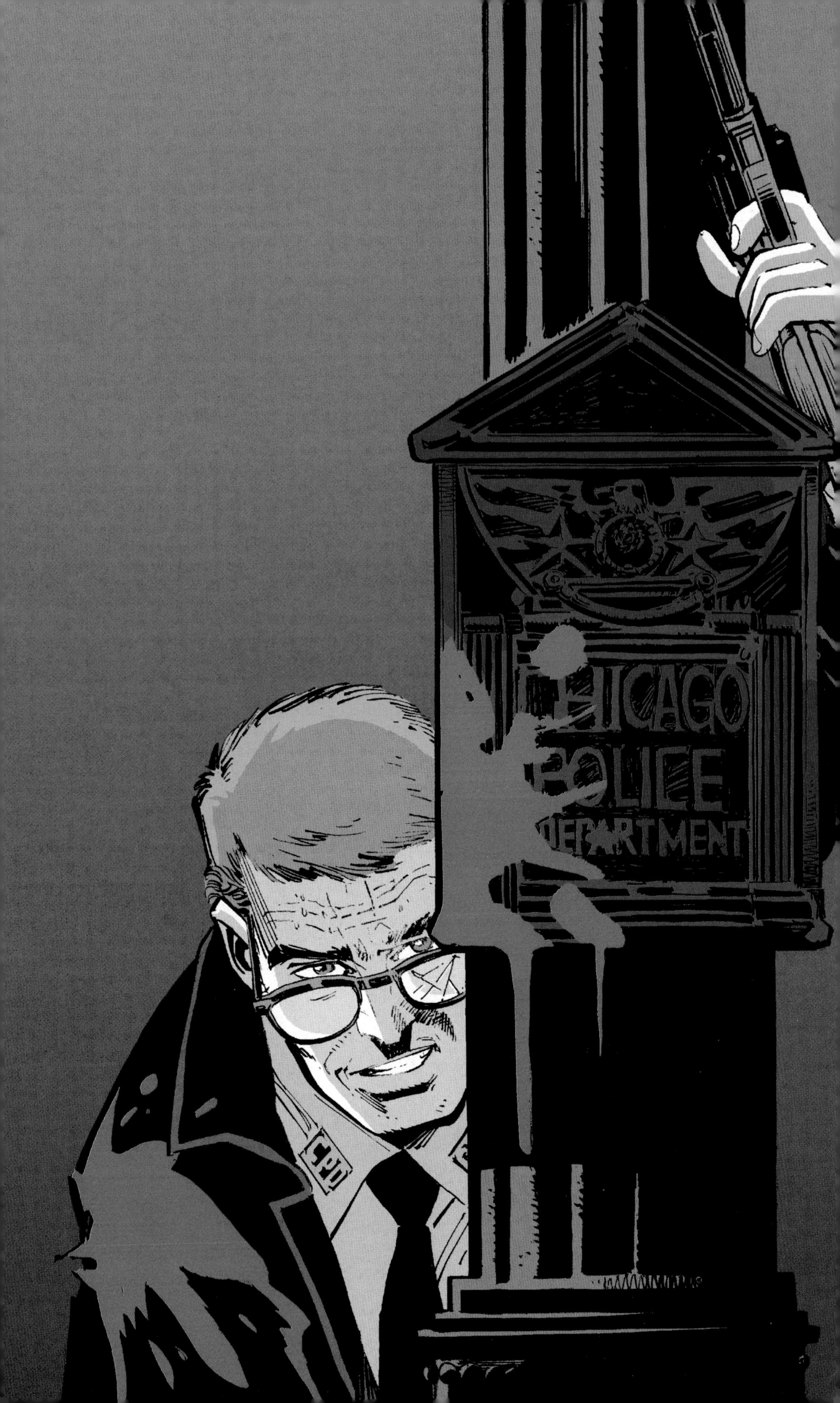
ICAGO
OLICE
DEPARTMENT

SCOTT PETERSON Editor – Original Series   DARREN VINCENZO Associate Editor – Original Series   RACHEL PINNELAS Editor
ROBBIN BROSTERMAN Design Director – Books   SARABETH KETT Publication Design

BOB HARRAS Senior VP – Editor-in-Chief, DC Comics

DIANE NELSON President   DAN DIDIO and JIM LEE Co-Publishers   GEOFF JOHNS Chief Creative Officer
AMIT DESAI Senior VP – Marketing & Franchise Management   AMY GENKINS Senior VP – Business & Legal Affairs
NAIRI GARDINER Senior VP – Finance   JEFF BOISON VP – Publishing Planning   MARK CHIARELLO VP – Art Direction & Design
JOHN CUNNINGHAM VP – Marketing   TERRI CUNNINGHAM VP – Editorial Administration   LARRY GANEM VP – Talent Relations & Services
ALISON GILL Senior VP – Manufacturing & Operations   HANK KANALZ Senior VP – Vertigo & Integrated Publishing
JAY KOGAN VP – Business & Legal Affairs, Publishing   JACK MAHAN VP – Business Affairs, Talent
NICK NAPOLITANO VP – Manufacturing Administration   SUE POHJA VP – Book Sales   FRED RUIZ VP – Manufacturing Operations
COURTNEY SIMMONS Senior VP – Publicity   BOB WAYNE Senior VP – Sales

BATMAN: GORDON OF GOTHAM

Published by DC Comics. Copyright © 2014
DC Comics. All Rights Reserved.

Originally published in single magazine form in
BATMAN: GORDON'S LAW 1-4, BATMAN: GCPD 1-4,
AND BATMAN: GORDON OF GOTHAM 1-4. Copyright
© 1996, 1997, 1998 DC Comics. All Rights Reserved.
All characters, their distinctive likenesses and
related elements featured in this publication are
trademarks of DC Comics. The stories, characters
and incidents featured in this publication are
entirely fictional. DC Comics does not read or accept
unsolicited ideas, stories or artwork.

DC Comics, 1700 Broadway, New York, NY 10019
A Warner Bros. Entertainment Company.
Printed by RR Donnelley, Salem, VA, USA. 8/22/14.
First Printing.
ISBN: 978-1-4012-5174-1

Library of Congress Cataloging-in-Publication Data

O'Neil, Dennis, 1939- author.
  Batman : Gordon of Gotham / Dennis O'Neil, Chuck
Dixon, Klaus Janson.
    pages cm
  ISBN 978-1-4012-5174-1 (paperback)
  1. Graphic novels. I. Dixon, Chuck, author. II.
Janson, Klaus, illustrator.
III. Title. IV. Title: Gordon of Gotham.
  PN6728.B360535 2014
  741.5'973—dc23
                                2014011712

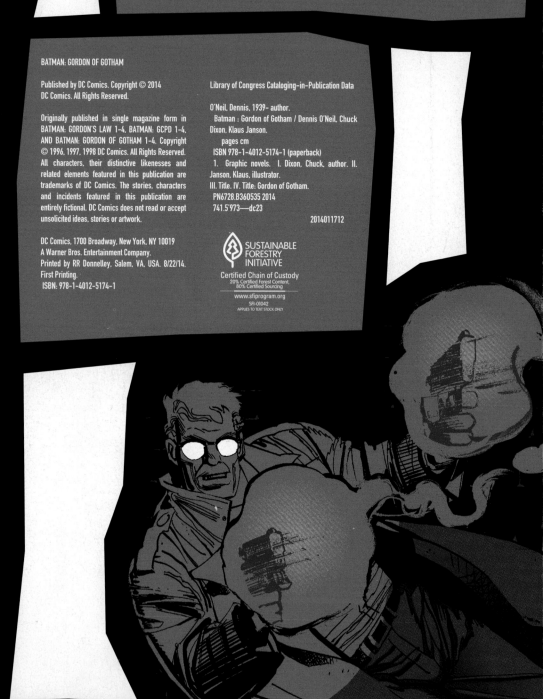

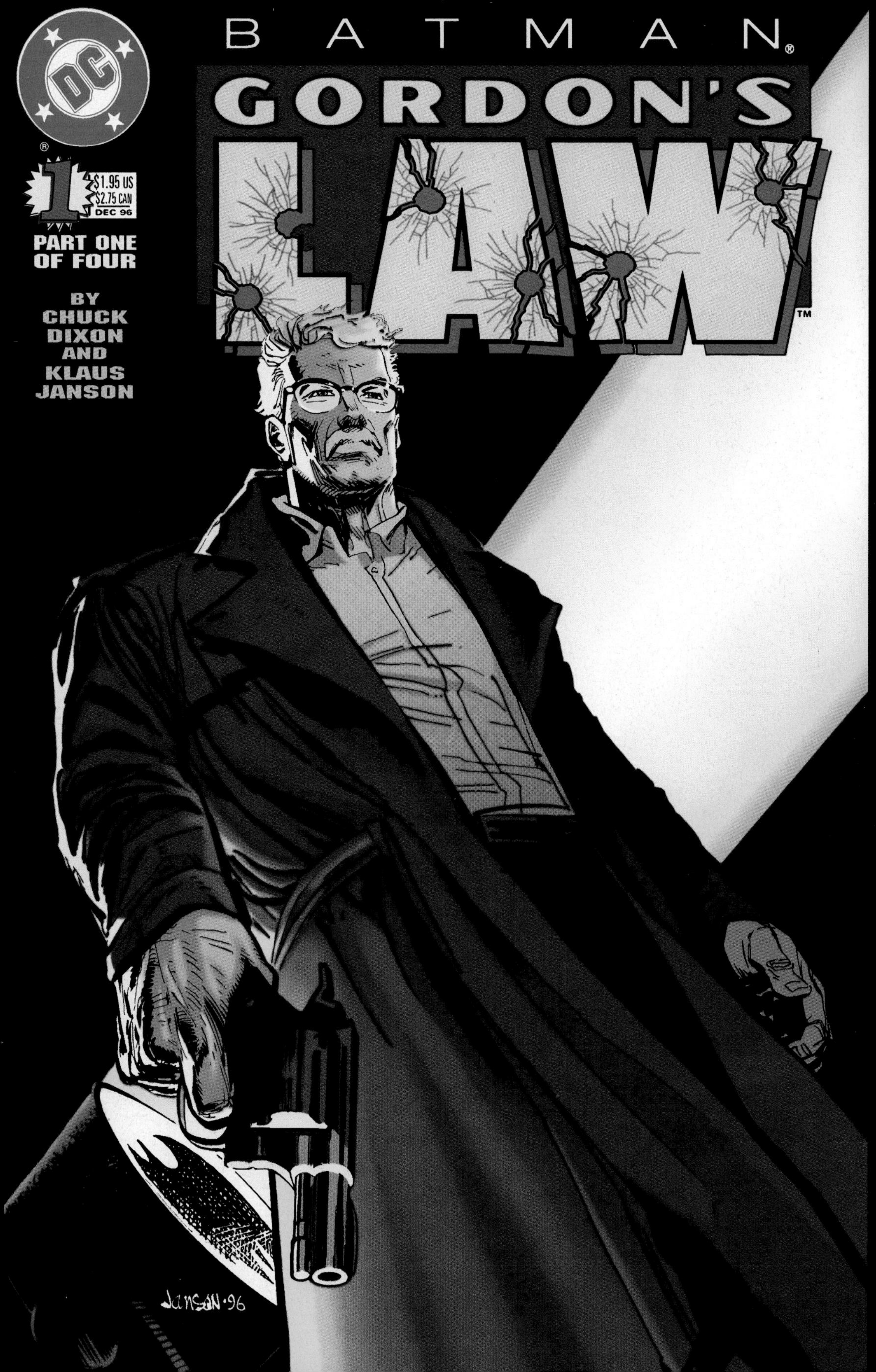
BATMAN®
GORDON'S LAW™
1 $1.95 US $2.75 CAN DEC 96
PART ONE OF FOUR
BY CHUCK DIXON AND KLAUS JANSON
JANSON·96

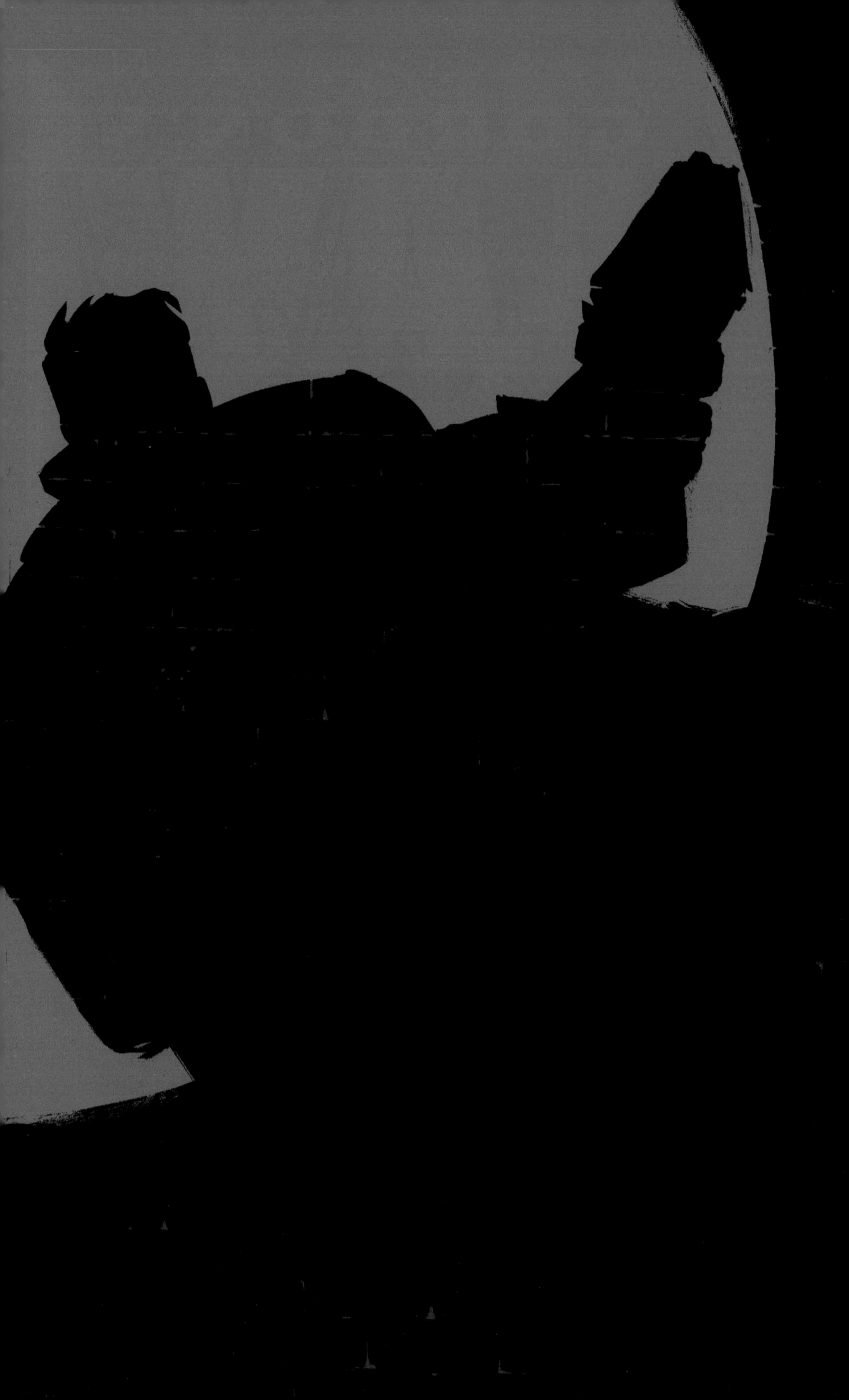

DIRTY DEAL

Chuck Dixon-writer
Klaus Janson-artist
Kevin Somers-colorist
John Costanza-letterer
Darren Vincenzo-assoc. editor
Scott Peterson -editor

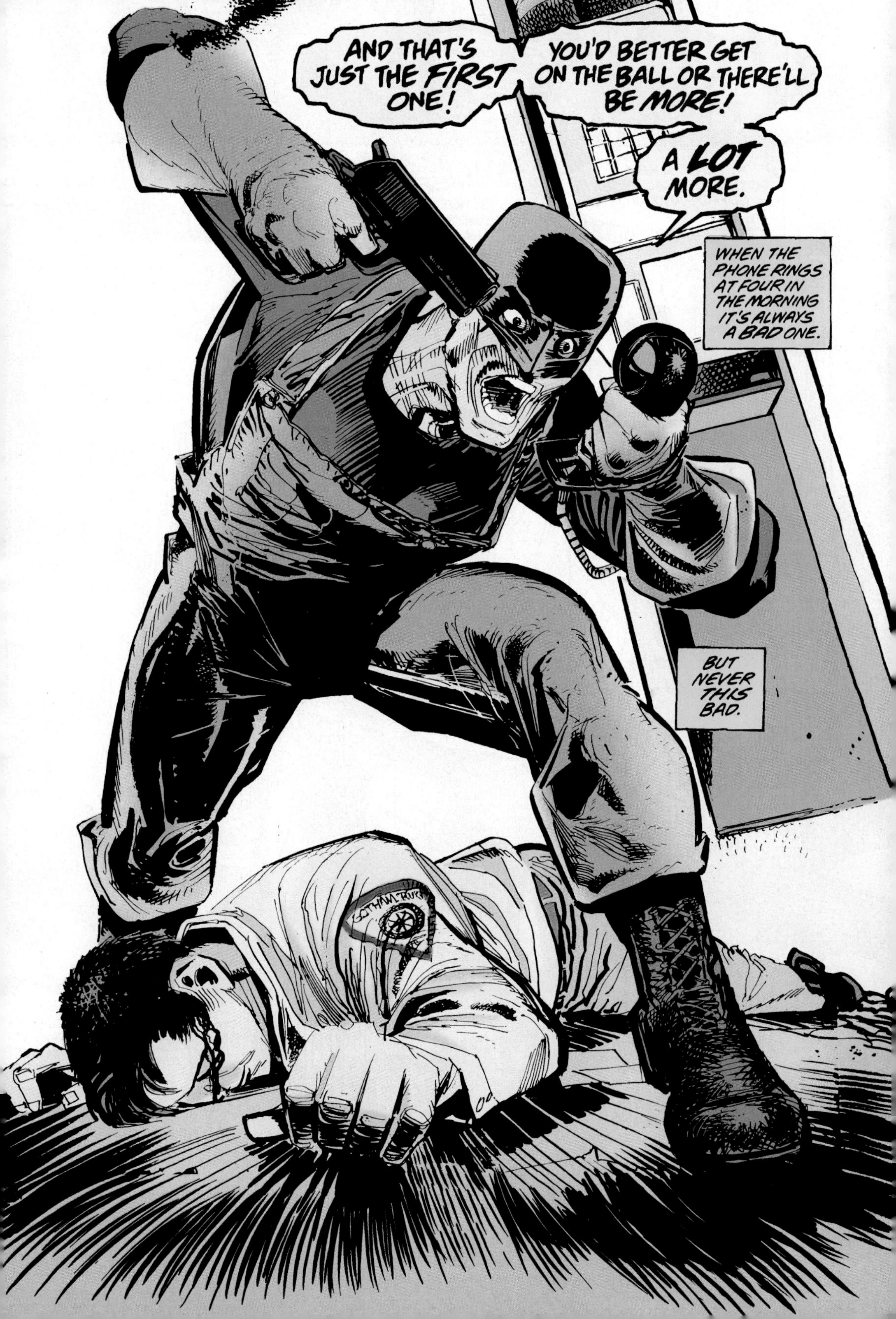

AND THAT'S JUST THE FIRST ONE!
YOU'D BETTER GET ON THE BALL OR THERE'LL BE MORE!
A LOT MORE.
WHEN THE PHONE RINGS AT FOUR IN THE MORNING IT'S ALWAYS A BAD ONE.
BUT NEVER THIS BAD.
GOTHAM CAB

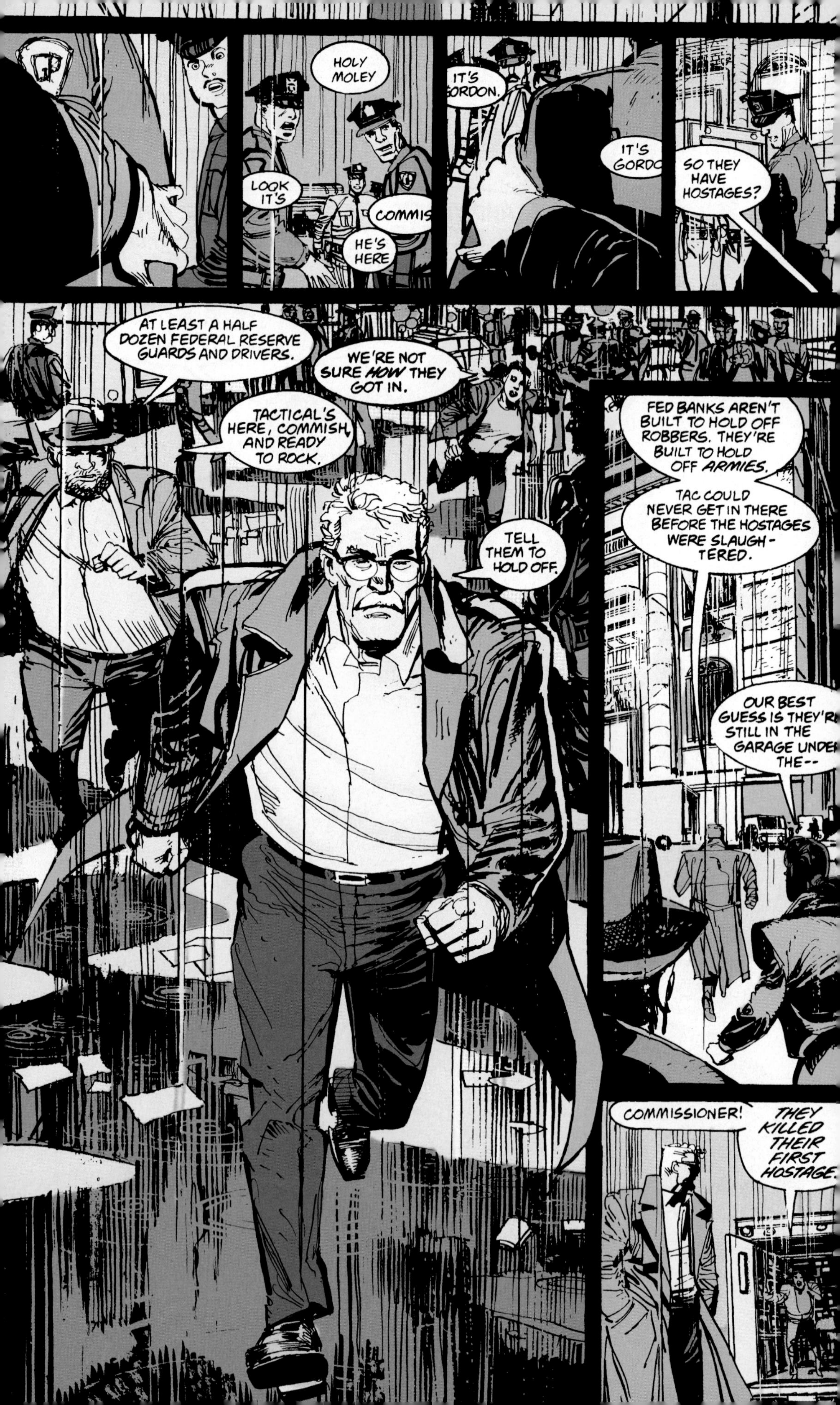
HOLY MOLEY
LOOK IT'S
COMMIS
HE'S HERE
IT'S GORDON.
IT'S GORDO
SO THEY HAVE HOSTAGES?
AT LEAST A HALF DOZEN FEDERAL RESERVE GUARDS AND DRIVERS.
WE'RE NOT SURE HOW THEY GOT IN.
TACTICAL'S HERE, COMMISH, AND READY TO ROCK.
TELL THEM TO HOLD OFF.
FED BANKS AREN'T BUILT TO HOLD OFF ROBBERS. THEY'RE BUILT TO HOLD OFF ARMIES.
TAC COULD NEVER GET IN THERE BEFORE THE HOSTAGES WERE SLAUGH-TERED.
OUR BEST GUESS IS THEY'R STILL IN THE GARAGE UNDE THE--
COMMISSIONER!
THEY KILLED THEIR FIRST HOSTAGE.

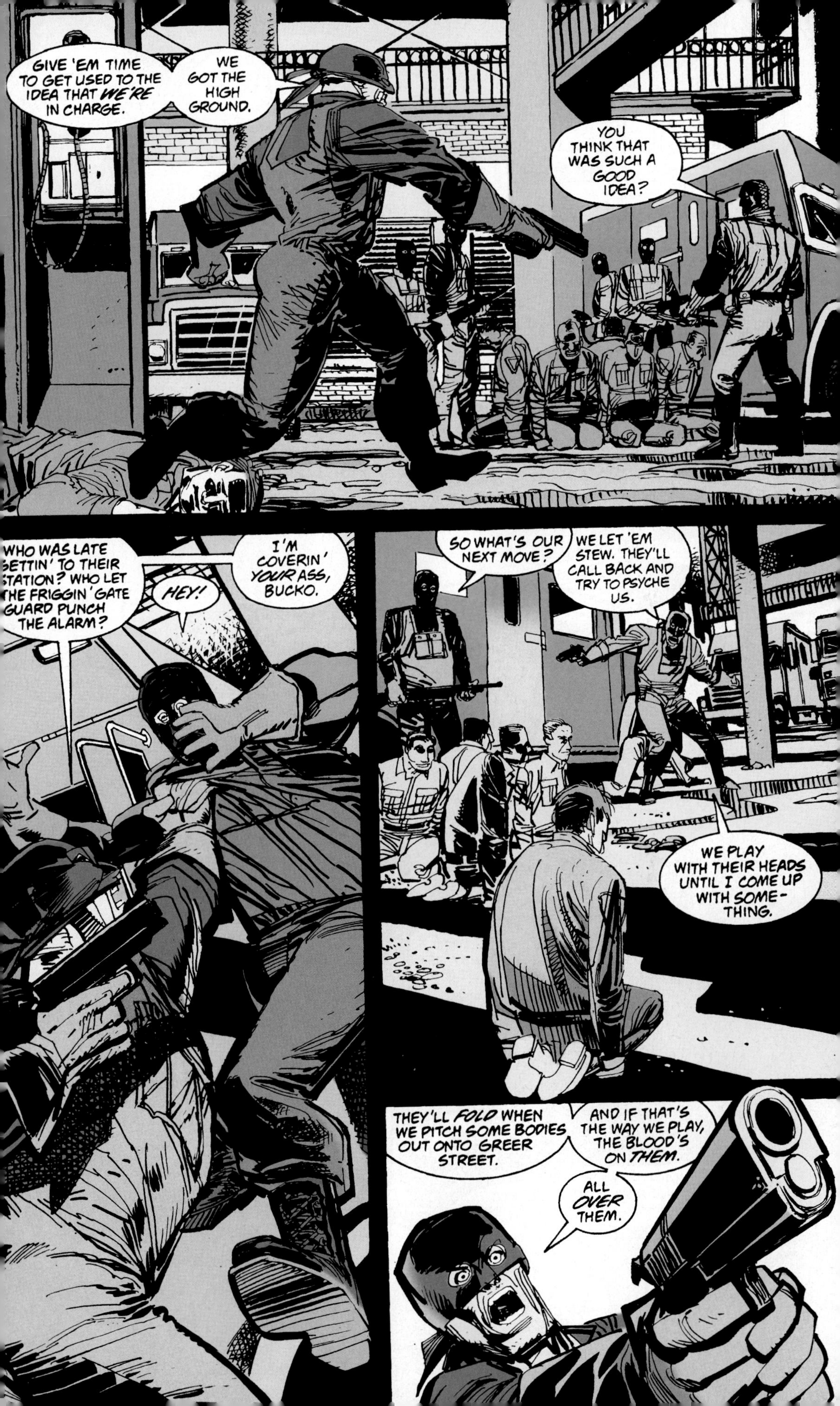
GIVE 'EM TIME TO GET USED TO THE IDEA THAT WE'RE IN CHARGE.
WE GOT THE HIGH GROUND.
YOU THINK THAT WAS SUCH A GOOD IDEA?
WHO WAS LATE GETTIN' TO THEIR STATION? WHO LET THE FRIGGIN' GATE GUARD PUNCH THE ALARM?
HEY!
I'M COVERIN' YOUR ASS, BUCKO.
SO WHAT'S OUR NEXT MOVE?
WE LET 'EM STEW. THEY'LL CALL BACK AND TRY TO PSYCHE US.
WE PLAY WITH THEIR HEADS UNTIL I COME UP WITH SOME-THING.
THEY'LL FOLD WHEN WE PITCH SOME BODIES OUT ONTO GREER STREET.
AND IF THAT'S THE WAY WE PLAY, THE BLOOD'S ON THEM.
ALL OVER THEM.

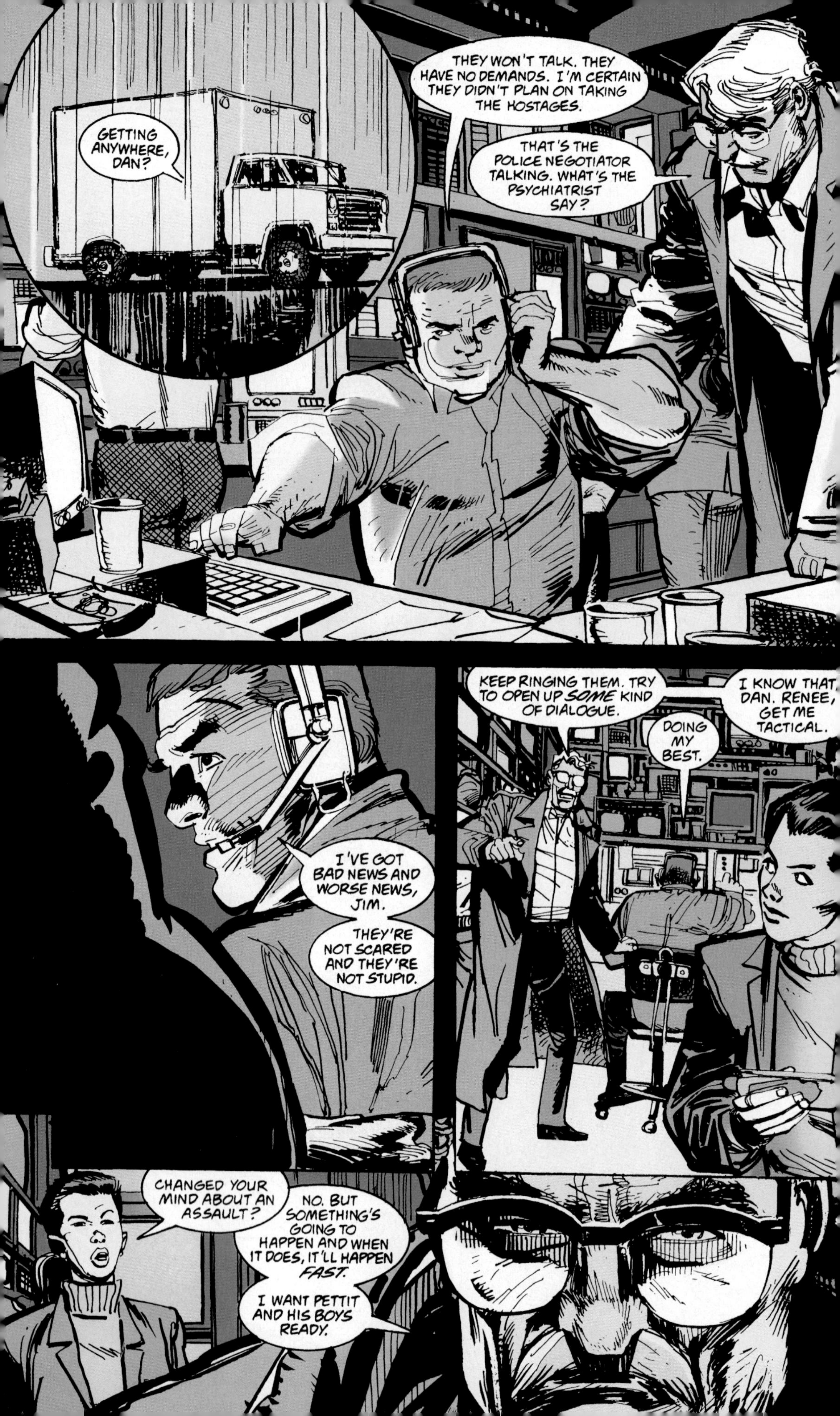
GETTING ANYWHERE, DAN?
THEY WON'T TALK. THEY HAVE NO DEMANDS. I'M CERTAIN THEY DIDN'T PLAN ON TAKING THE HOSTAGES.
THAT'S THE POLICE NEGOTIATOR TALKING. WHAT'S THE PSYCHIATRIST SAY?
I'VE GOT BAD NEWS AND WORSE NEWS, JIM.
THEY'RE NOT SCARED AND THEY'RE NOT STUPID.
KEEP RINGING THEM. TRY TO OPEN UP *SOME* KIND OF DIALOGUE.
I KNOW THAT, DAN. RENEE, GET ME TACTICAL.
DOING MY BEST.
CHANGED YOUR MIND ABOUT AN ASSAULT?
NO. BUT SOMETHING'S GOING TO HAPPEN AND WHEN IT DOES, IT'LL HAPPEN *FAST*.
I WANT PETTIT AND HIS BOYS READY.

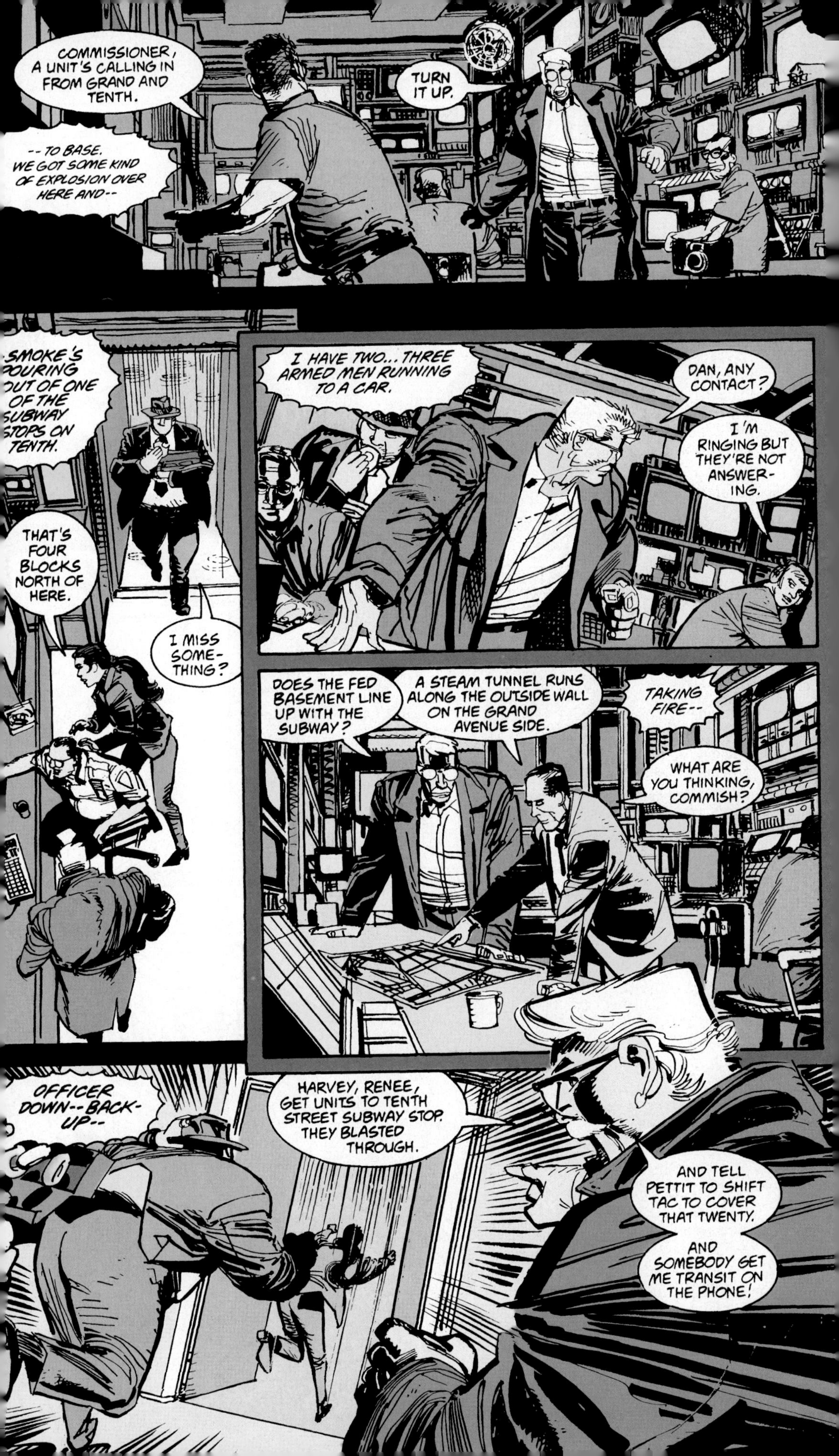
COMMISSIONER, A UNIT'S CALLING IN FROM GRAND AND TENTH.
TURN IT UP.
-- TO BASE. WE GOT SOME KIND OF EXPLOSION OVER HERE AND--
SMOKE'S POURING OUT OF ONE OF THE SUBWAY STOPS ON TENTH.
THAT'S FOUR BLOCKS NORTH OF HERE.
I MISS SOME-THING?
I HAVE TWO... THREE ARMED MEN RUNNING TO A CAR.
DAN, ANY CONTACT?
I'M RINGING BUT THEY'RE NOT ANSWER-ING.
DOES THE FED BASEMENT LINE UP WITH THE SUBWAY?
A STEAM TUNNEL RUNS ALONG THE OUTSIDE WALL ON THE GRAND AVENUE SIDE.
TAKING FIRE--
WHAT ARE YOU THINKING, COMMISH?
OFFICER DOWN--BACK-UP--
HARVEY, RENEE, GET UNITS TO TENTH STREET SUBWAY STOP. THEY BLASTED THROUGH.
AND TELL PETTIT TO SHIFT TAC TO COVER THAT TWENTY.
AND SOMEBODY GET ME TRANSIT ON THE PHONE!

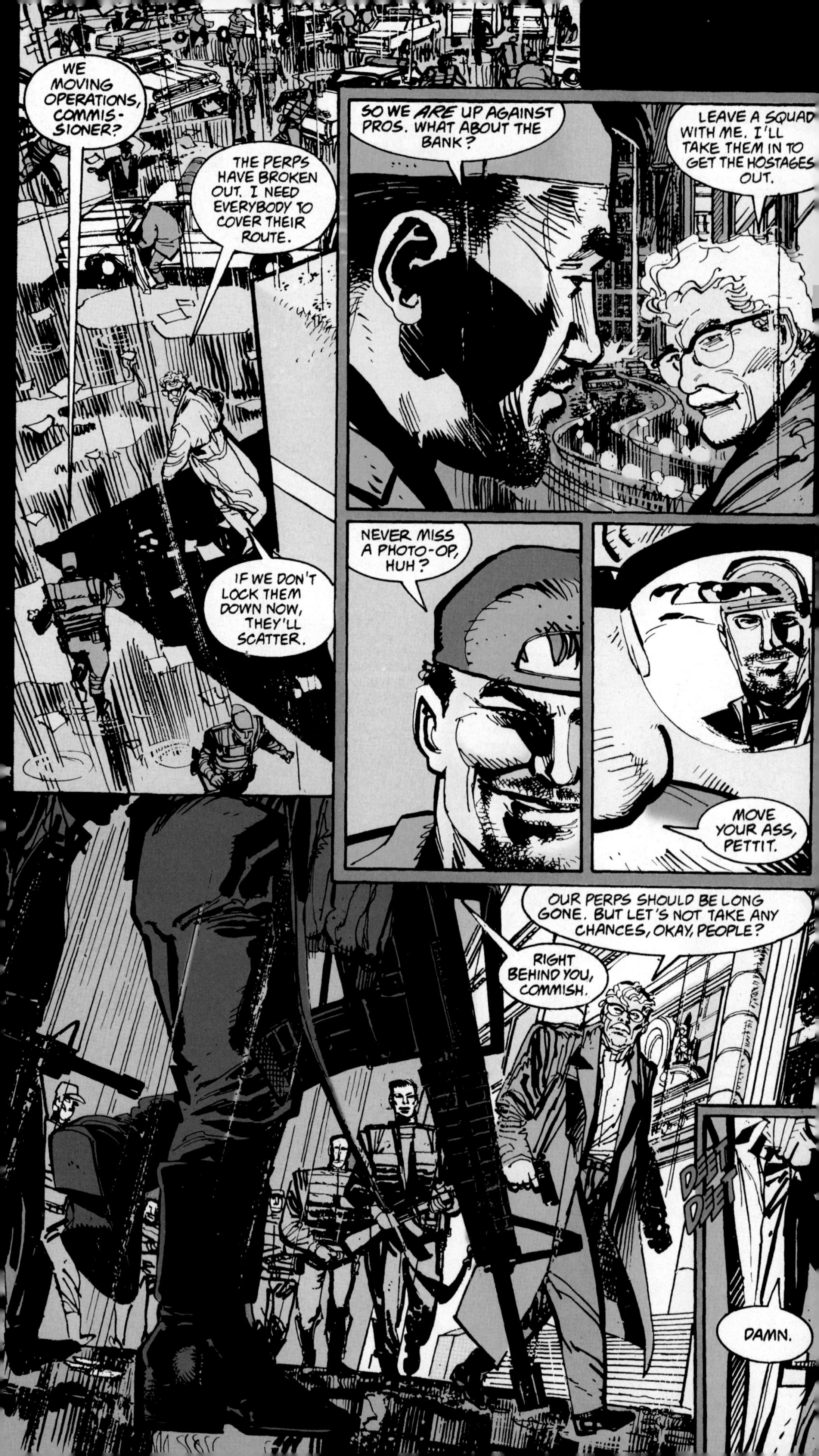
WE MOVING OPERATIONS, COMMIS-SIONER?
THE PERPS HAVE BROKEN OUT. I NEED EVERYBODY TO COVER THEIR ROUTE.
IF WE DON'T LOCK THEM DOWN NOW, THEY'LL SCATTER.
SO WE ARE UP AGAINST PROS. WHAT ABOUT THE BANK?
LEAVE A SQUAD WITH ME. I'LL TAKE THEM IN TO GET THE HOSTAGES OUT.
NEVER MISS A PHOTO-OP, HUH?
MOVE YOUR ASS, PETTIT.
OUR PERPS SHOULD BE LONG GONE. BUT LET'S NOT TAKE ANY CHANCES, OKAY, PEOPLE?
RIGHT BEHIND YOU, COMMISH.
DEET DEET
DAMN.

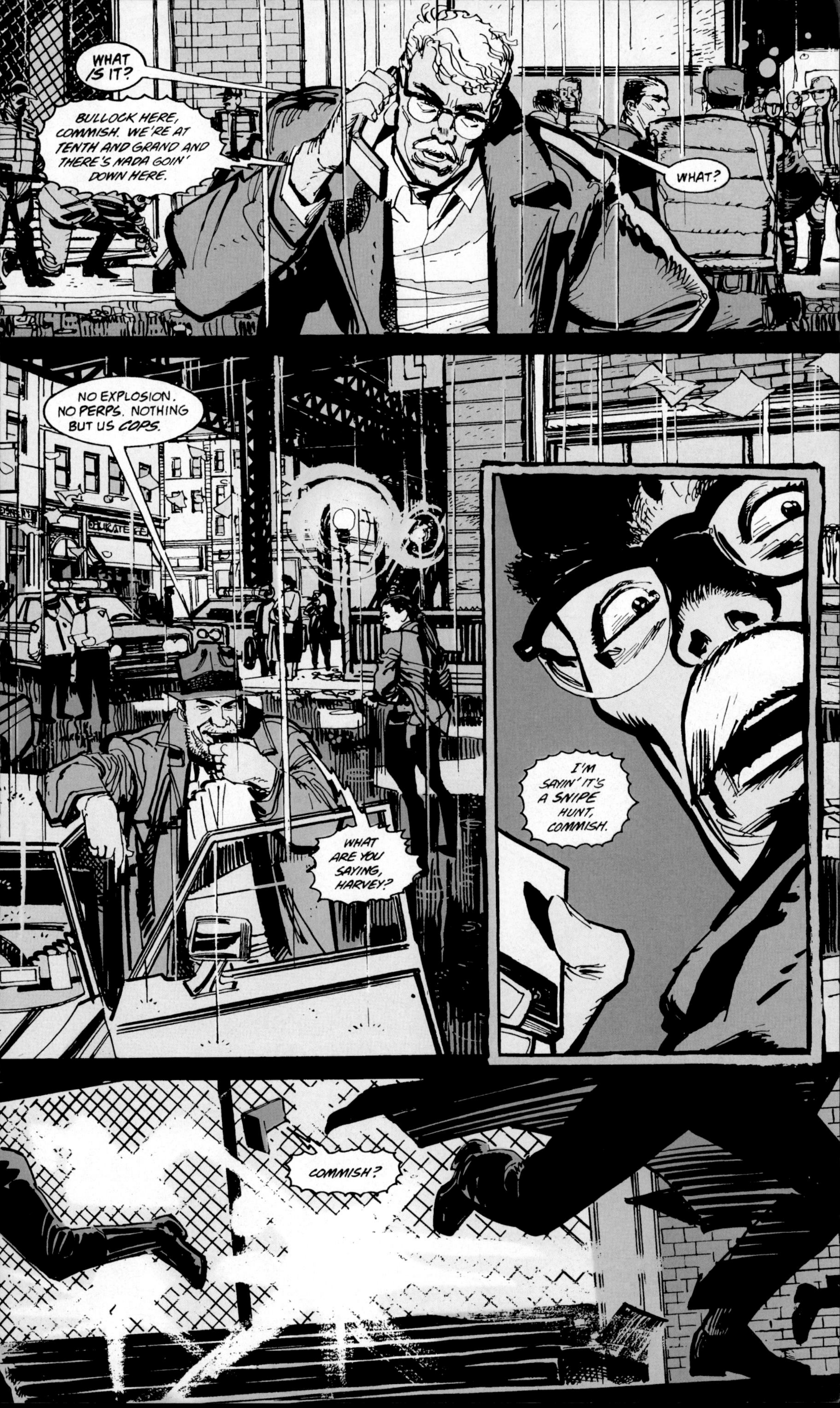
WHAT IS IT?
BULLOCK HERE, COMMISH. WE'RE AT TENTH AND GRAND AND THERE'S NADA GOIN' DOWN HERE.
WHAT?
NO EXPLOSION. NO PERPS. NOTHING BUT US COPS.
WHAT ARE YOU SAYING, HARVEY?
I'M SAYIN' IT'S A SNIPE HUNT, COMMISH.
COMMISH?

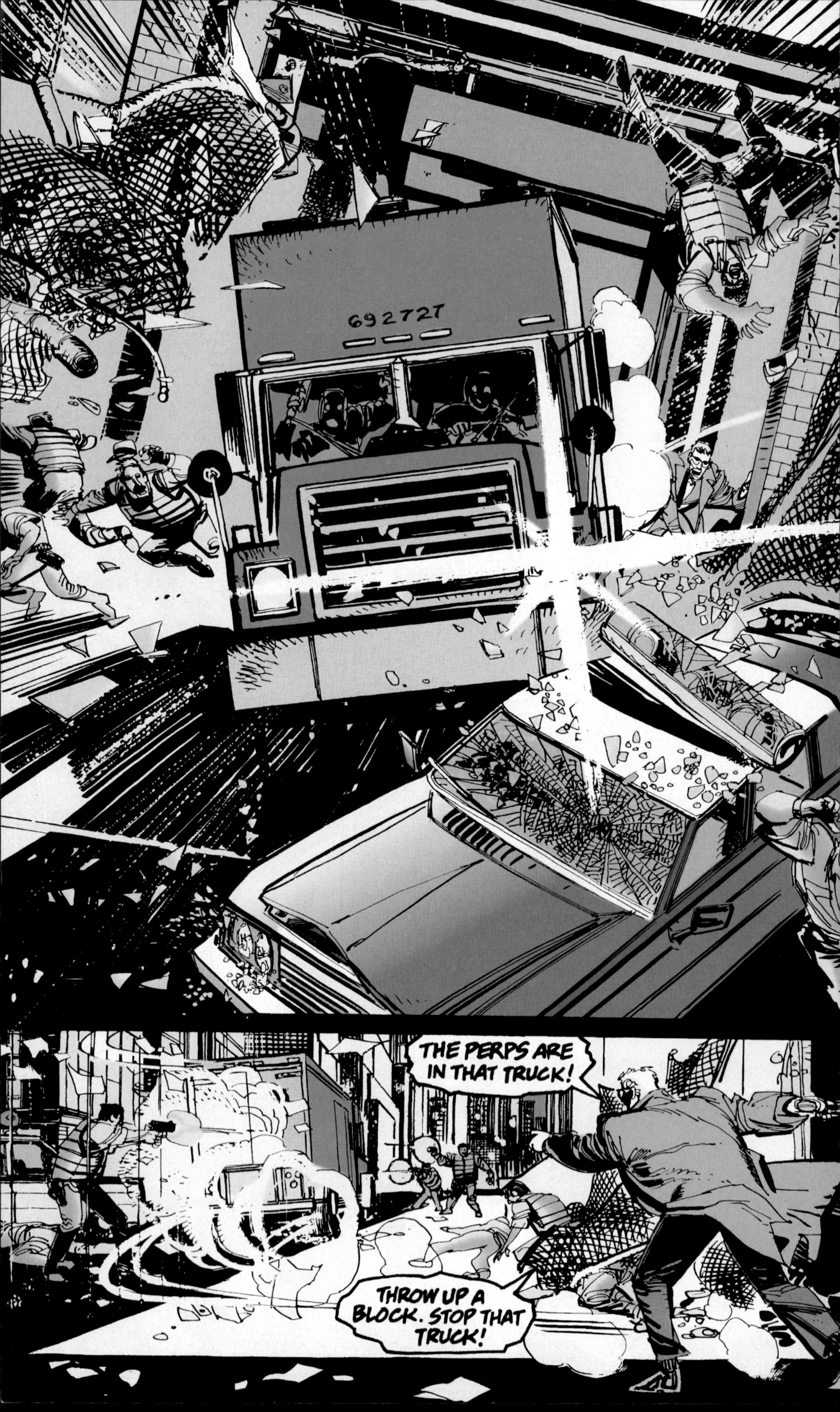
692727
THE PERPS ARE IN THAT TRUCK!
THROW UP A BLOCK. STOP THAT TRUCK!

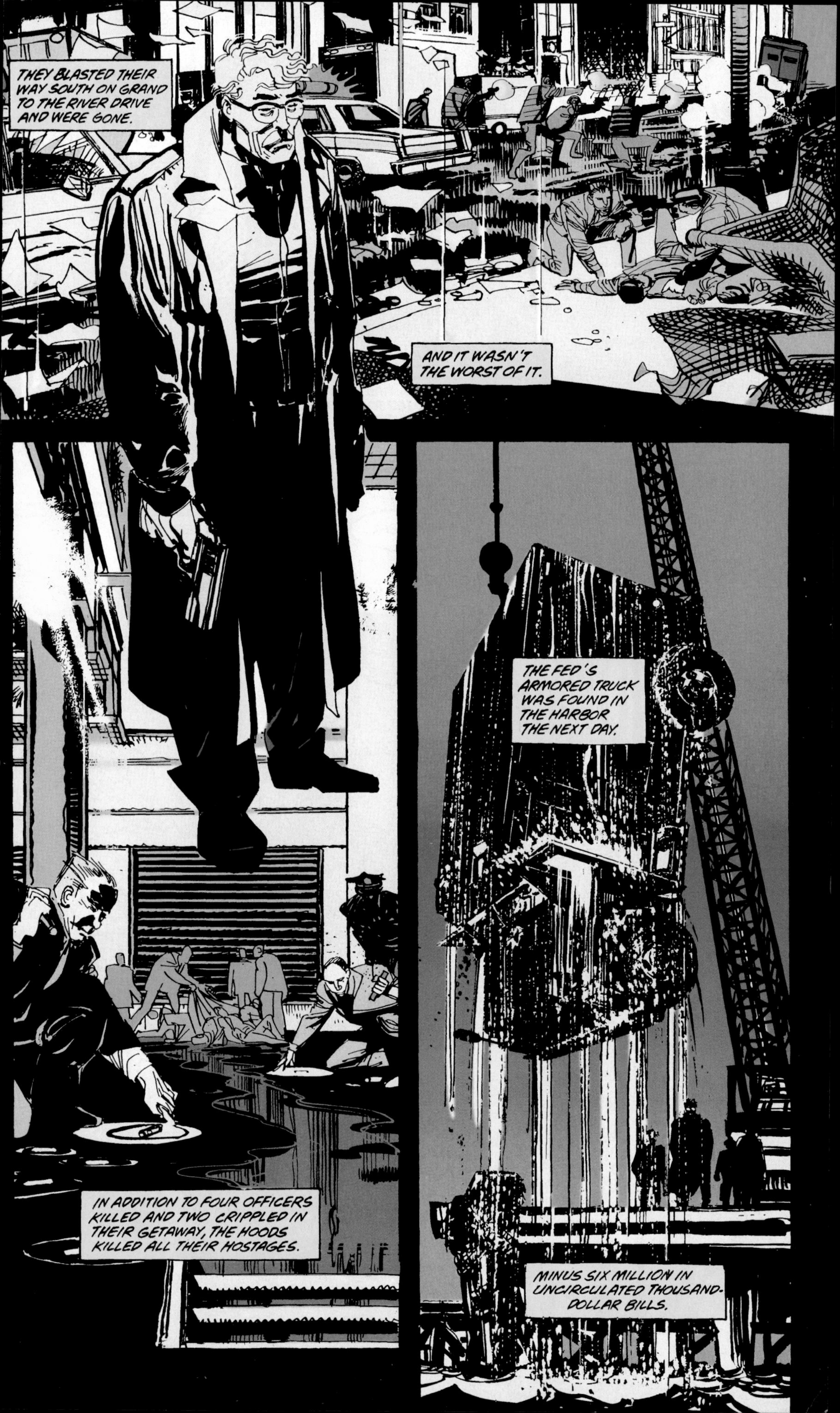
THEY BLASTED THEIR WAY SOUTH ON GRAND TO THE RIVER DRIVE AND WERE GONE.
AND IT WASN'T THE WORST OF IT.
IN ADDITION TO FOUR OFFICERS KILLED AND TWO CRIPPLED IN THEIR GETAWAY, THE HOODS KILLED ALL THEIR HOSTAGES.
THE FED'S ARMORED TRUCK WAS FOUND IN THE HARBOR THE NEXT DAY.
MINUS SIX MILLION IN UNCIRCULATED THOUSAND-DOLLAR BILLS.

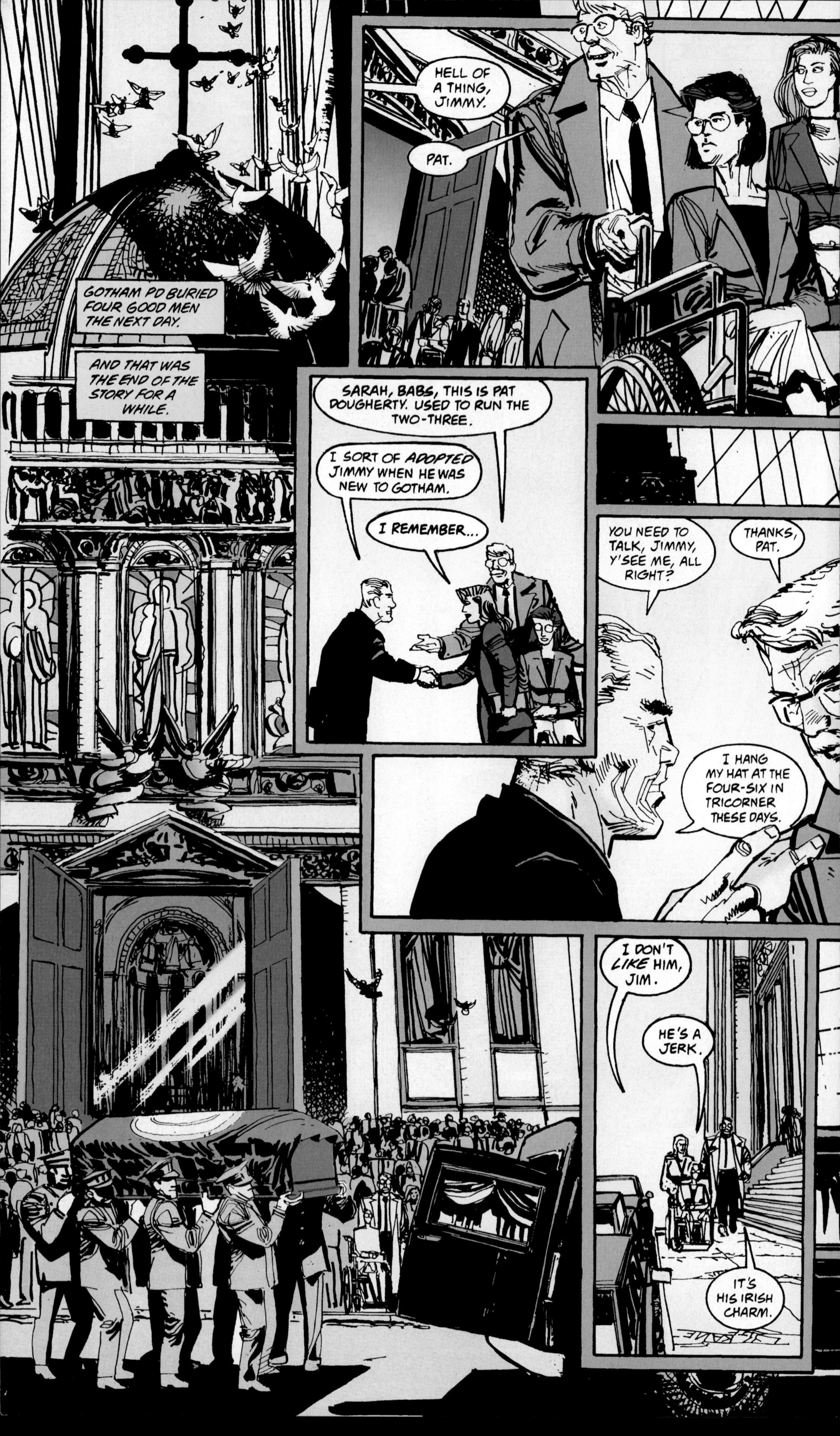
GOTHAM PD BURIED FOUR GOOD MEN THE NEXT DAY.
AND THAT WAS THE END OF THE STORY FOR A WHILE.
HELL OF A THING, JIMMY.
PAT.
SARAH, BABS, THIS IS PAT DOUGHERTY. USED TO RUN THE TWO-THREE.
I SORT OF ADOPTED JIMMY WHEN HE WAS NEW TO GOTHAM.
I REMEMBER...
YOU NEED TO TALK, JIMMY, Y'SEE ME, ALL RIGHT?
THANKS, PAT.
I HANG MY HAT AT THE FOUR-SIX IN TRICORNER THESE DAYS.
I DON'T LIKE HIM, JIM.
HE'S A JERK.
IT'S HIS IRISH CHARM.

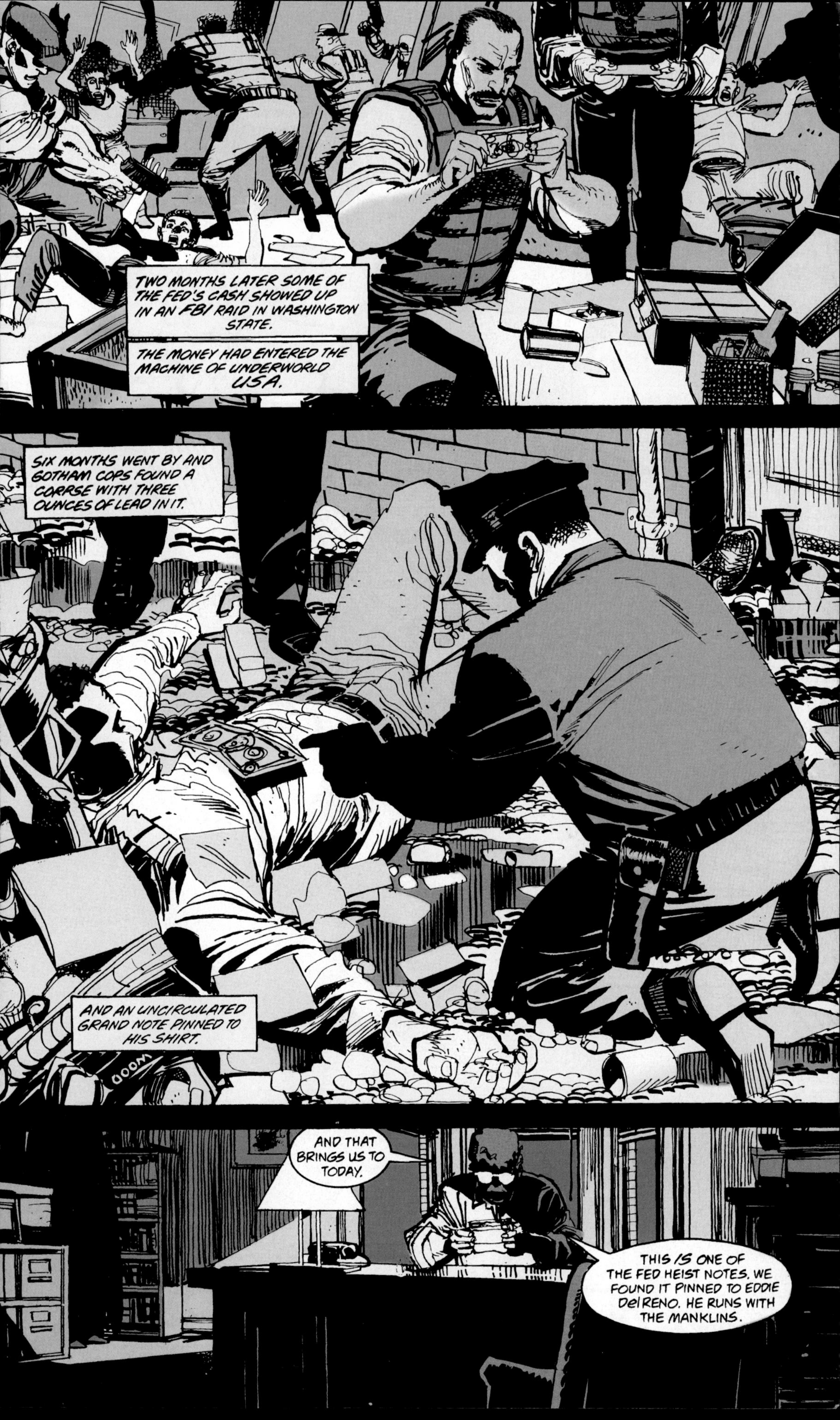

TWO MONTHS LATER SOME OF THE FED'S CASH SHOWED UP IN AN FBI RAID IN WASHINGTON STATE.
THE MONEY HAD ENTERED THE MACHINE OF UNDERWORLD USA.
SIX MONTHS WENT BY AND GOTHAM COPS FOUND A CORPSE WITH THREE OUNCES OF LEAD IN IT.
AND AN UNCIRCULATED GRAND NOTE PINNED TO HIS SHIRT.
AND THAT BRINGS US TO TODAY.
THIS IS ONE OF THE FED HEIST NOTES. WE FOUND IT PINNED TO EDDIE DelRENO. HE RUNS WITH THE MANKLINS.

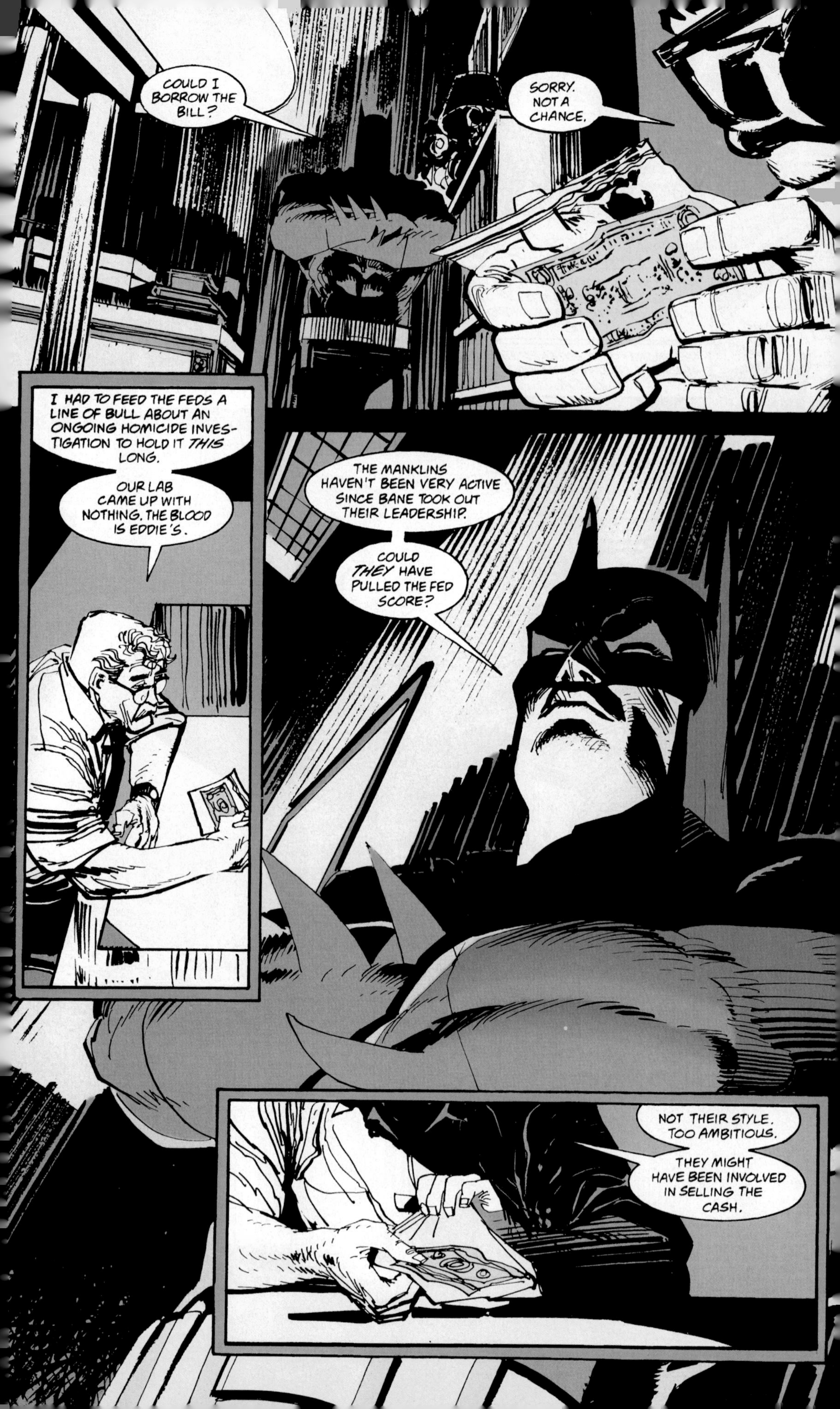

COULD I BORROW THE BILL?
SORRY. NOT A CHANCE.
I HAD TO FEED THE FEDS A LINE OF BULL ABOUT AN ONGOING HOMICIDE INVESTIGATION TO HOLD IT THIS LONG.
OUR LAB CAME UP WITH NOTHING. THE BLOOD IS EDDIE'S.
THE MANKLINS HAVEN'T BEEN VERY ACTIVE SINCE BANE TOOK OUT THEIR LEADERSHIP.
COULD THEY HAVE PULLED THE FED SCORE?
NOT THEIR STYLE. TOO AMBITIOUS.
THEY MIGHT HAVE BEEN INVOLVED IN SELLING THE CASH.

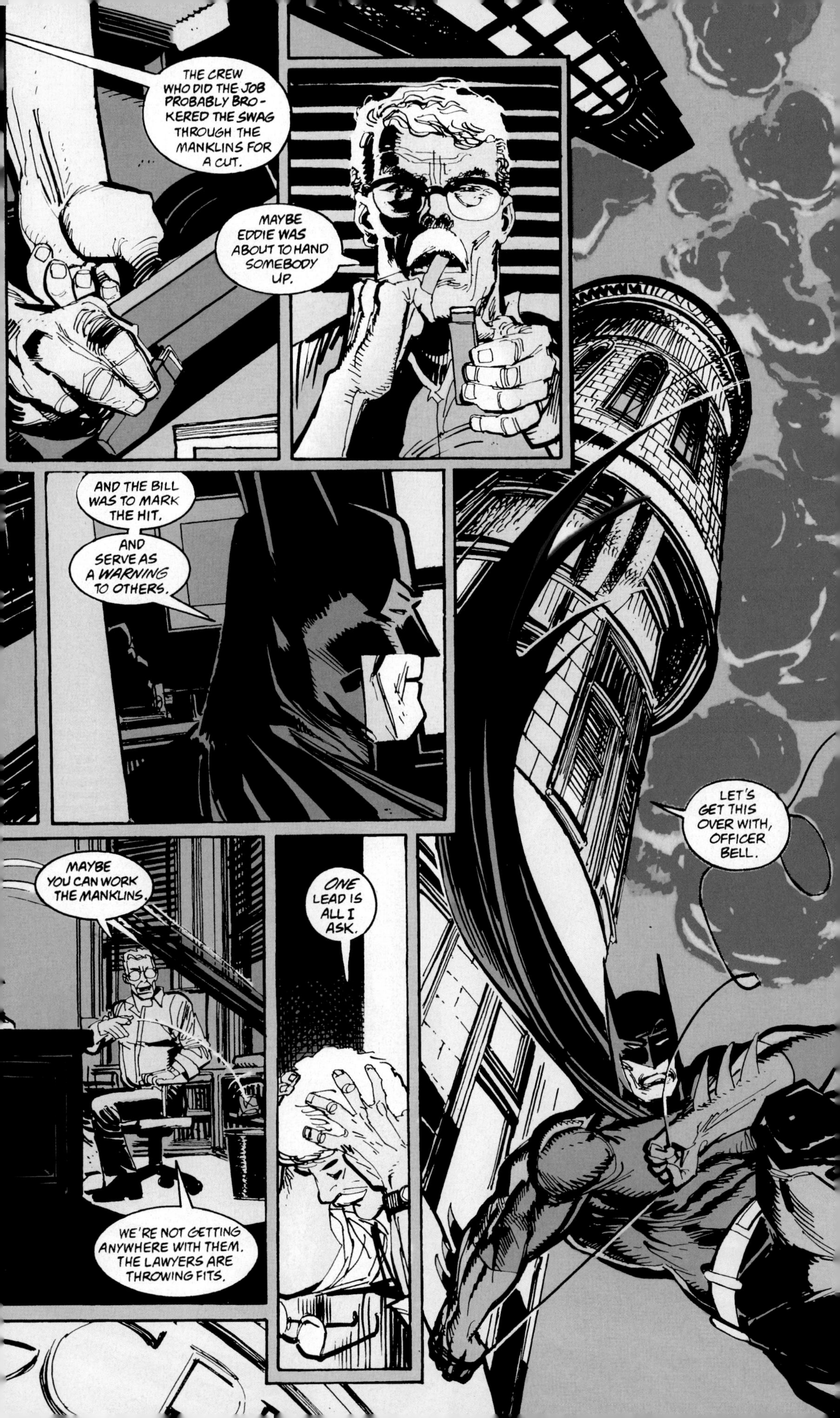
THE CREW WHO DID THE JOB PROBABLY BRO-KERED THE SWAG THROUGH THE MANKLINS FOR A CUT.
MAYBE EDDIE WAS ABOUT TO HAND SOMEBODY UP.
AND THE BILL WAS TO MARK THE HIT.
AND SERVE AS A WARNING TO OTHERS.
LET'S GET THIS OVER WITH, OFFICER BELL.
MAYBE YOU CAN WORK THE MANKLINS.
ONE LEAD IS ALL I ASK.
WE'RE NOT GETTING ANYWHERE WITH THEM. THE LAWYERS ARE THROWING FITS.

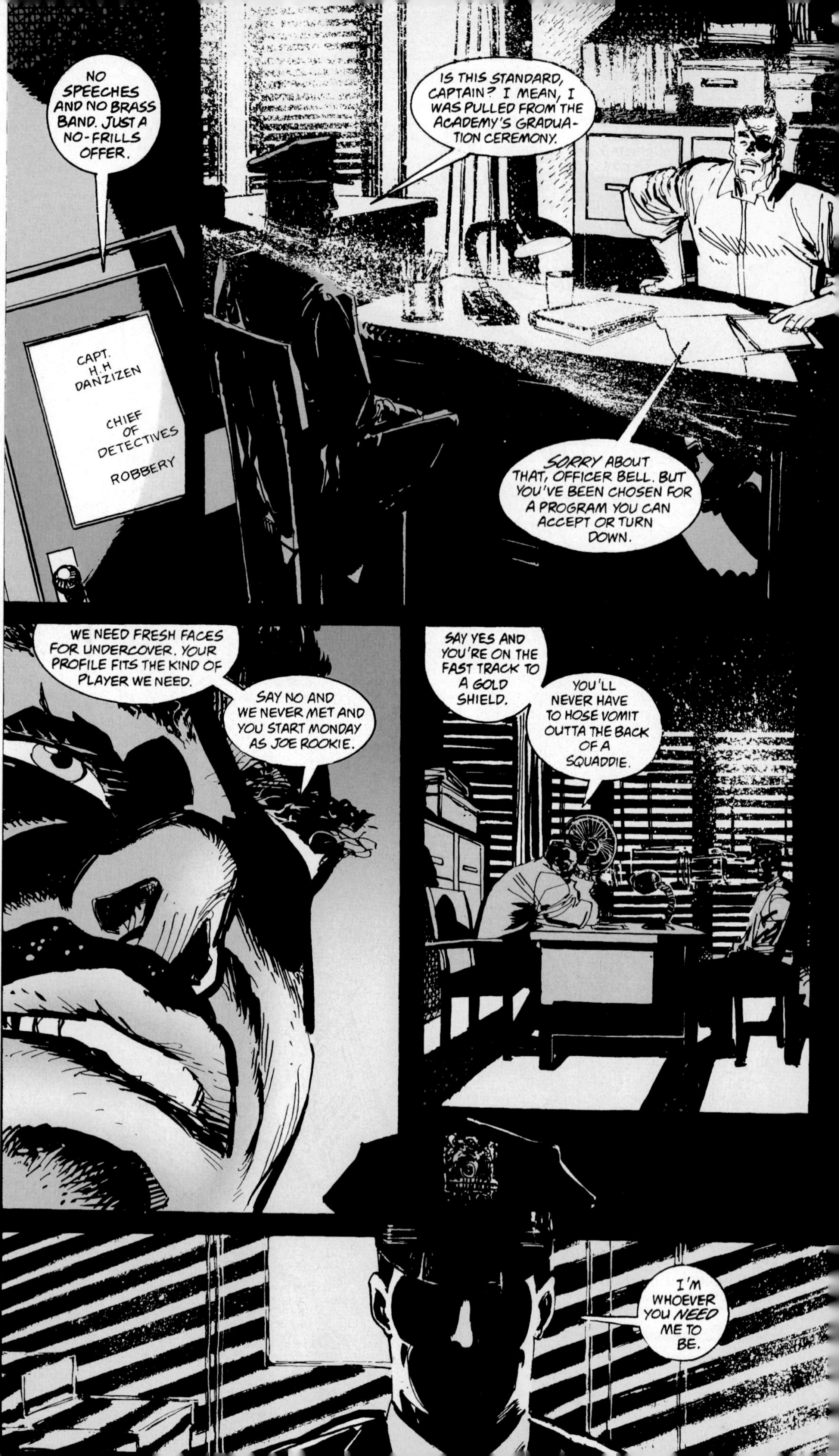

NO SPEECHES AND NO BRASS BAND. JUST A NO-FRILLS OFFER.
IS THIS STANDARD, CAPTAIN? I MEAN, I WAS PULLED FROM THE ACADEMY'S GRADUATION CEREMONY.
CAPT. H.H DANZIZEN CHIEF OF DETECTIVES ROBBERY
SORRY ABOUT THAT, OFFICER BELL. BUT YOU'VE BEEN CHOSEN FOR A PROGRAM YOU CAN ACCEPT OR TURN DOWN.
WE NEED FRESH FACES FOR UNDERCOVER. YOUR PROFILE FITS THE KIND OF PLAYER WE NEED.
SAY NO AND WE NEVER MET AND YOU START MONDAY AS JOE ROOKIE.
SAY YES AND YOU'RE ON THE FAST TRACK TO A GOLD SHIELD.
YOU'LL NEVER HAVE TO HOSE VOMIT OUTTA THE BACK OF A SQUADDIE.
I'M WHOEVER YOU *NEED* ME TO BE.

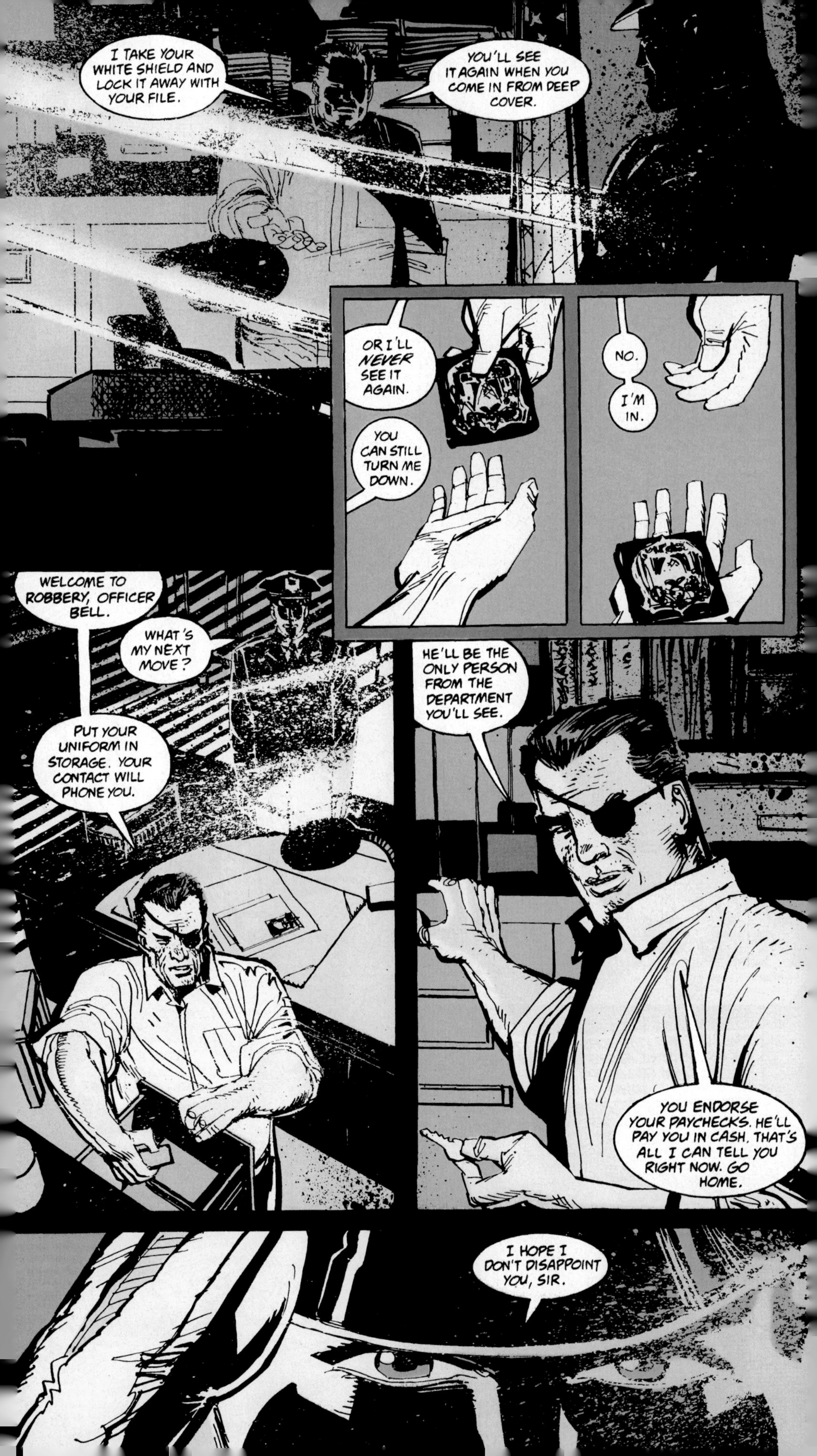
I TAKE YOUR WHITE SHIELD AND LOCK IT AWAY WITH YOUR FILE.
YOU'LL SEE IT AGAIN WHEN YOU COME IN FROM DEEP COVER.
OR I'LL *NEVER* SEE IT AGAIN.
YOU CAN STILL TURN ME DOWN.
NO.
I'M IN.
WELCOME TO ROBBERY, OFFICER BELL.
WHAT'S MY NEXT MOVE?
PUT YOUR UNIFORM IN STORAGE. YOUR CONTACT WILL PHONE YOU.
HE'LL BE THE ONLY PERSON FROM THE DEPARTMENT YOU'LL SEE.
YOU ENDORSE YOUR PAYCHECKS. HE'LL PAY YOU IN CASH. THAT'S ALL I CAN TELL YOU RIGHT NOW. GO HOME.
I HOPE I DON'T DISAPPOINT YOU, SIR.

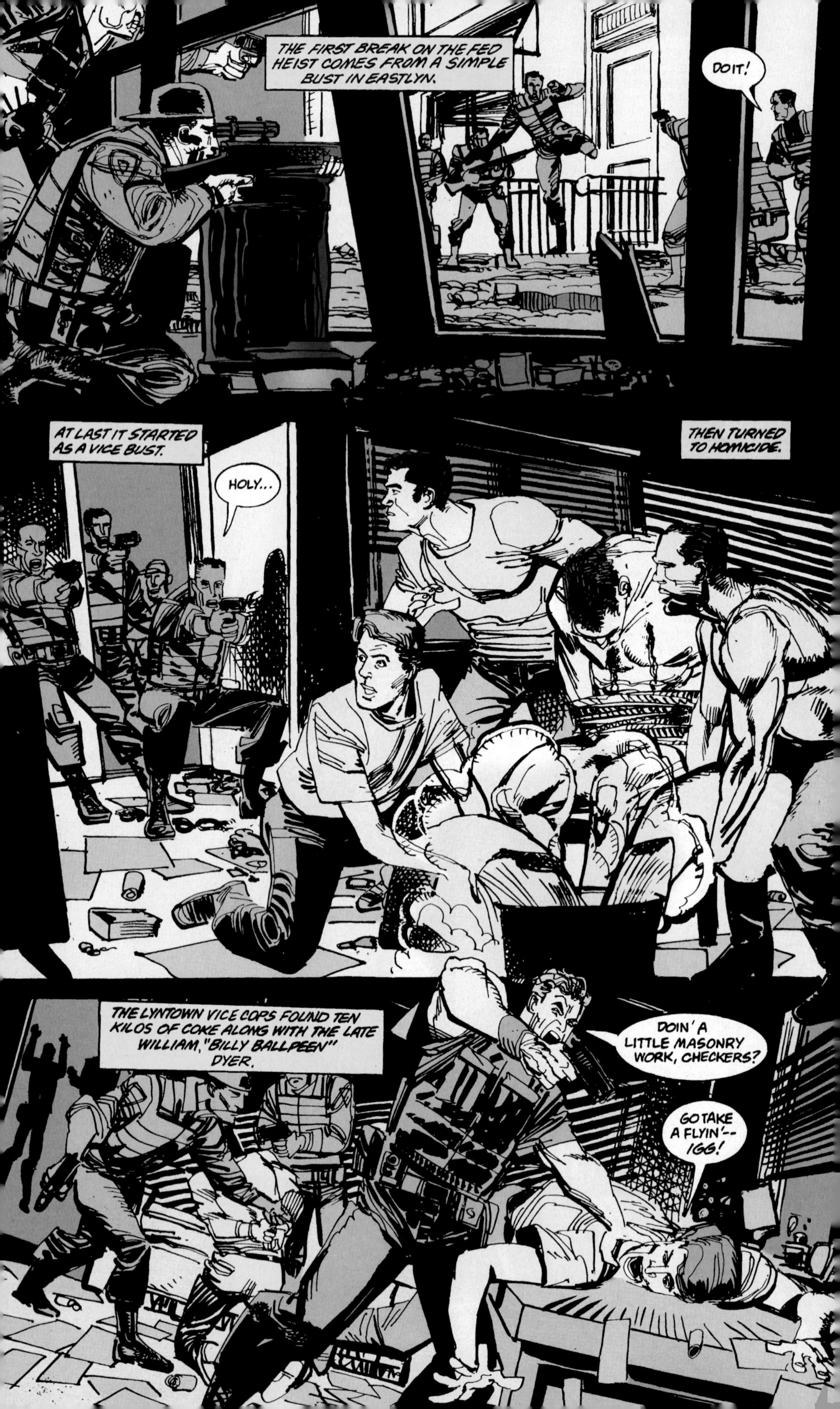

THE FIRST BREAK ON THE FED HEIST COMES FROM A SIMPLE BUST IN EASTLYN.
DO IT!
AT LAST IT STARTED AS A VICE BUST.
HOLY...
THEN TURNED TO HOMICIDE.
THE LYNTOWN VICE COPS FOUND TEN KILOS OF COKE ALONG WITH THE LATE WILLIAM, "BILLY BALLPEEN" DYER.
DOIN' A LITTLE MASONRY WORK, CHECKERS?
GO TAKE A FLYIN'-- IGG!

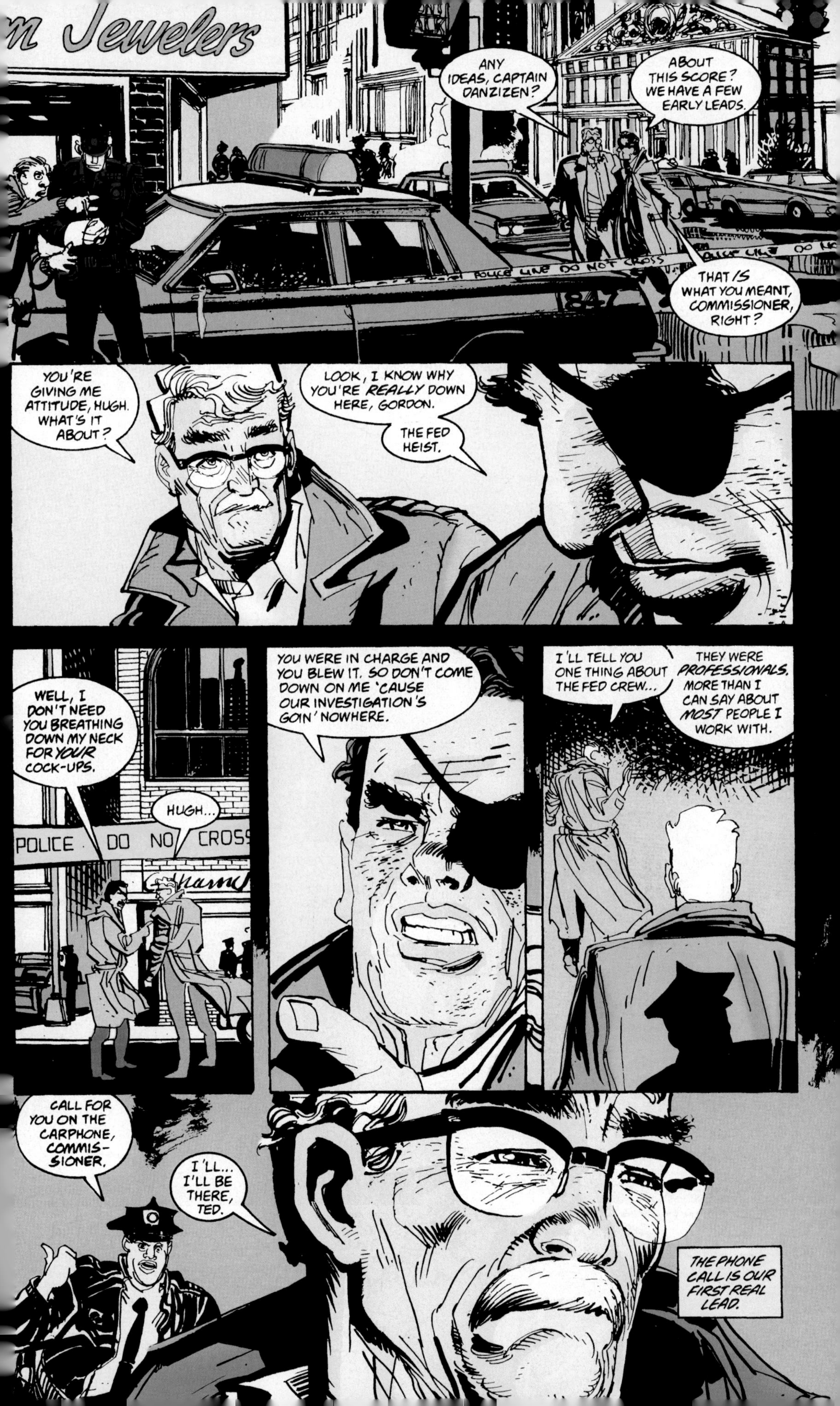

n Jewelers
ANY IDEAS, CAPTAIN DANZIZEN?
ABOUT THIS SCORE? WE HAVE A FEW EARLY LEADS.
POLICE LINE DO NOT CROSS
THAT IS WHAT YOU MEANT, COMMISSIONER, RIGHT?
YOU'RE GIVING ME ATTITUDE, HUGH. WHAT'S IT ABOUT?
LOOK, I KNOW WHY YOU'RE REALLY DOWN HERE, GORDON.
THE FED HEIST.
WELL, I DON'T NEED YOU BREATHING DOWN MY NECK FOR YOUR COCK-UPS.
HUGH...
POLICE DO NO CROSS
YOU WERE IN CHARGE AND YOU BLEW IT. SO DON'T COME DOWN ON ME 'CAUSE OUR INVESTIGATION'S GOIN' NOWHERE.
I'LL TELL YOU ONE THING ABOUT THE FED CREW...
THEY WERE PROFESSIONALS. MORE THAN I CAN SAY ABOUT MOST PEOPLE I WORK WITH.
CALL FOR YOU ON THE CARPHONE, COMMIS-SIONER.
I'LL... I'LL BE THERE, TED.
THE PHONE CALL IS OUR FIRST REAL LEAD.

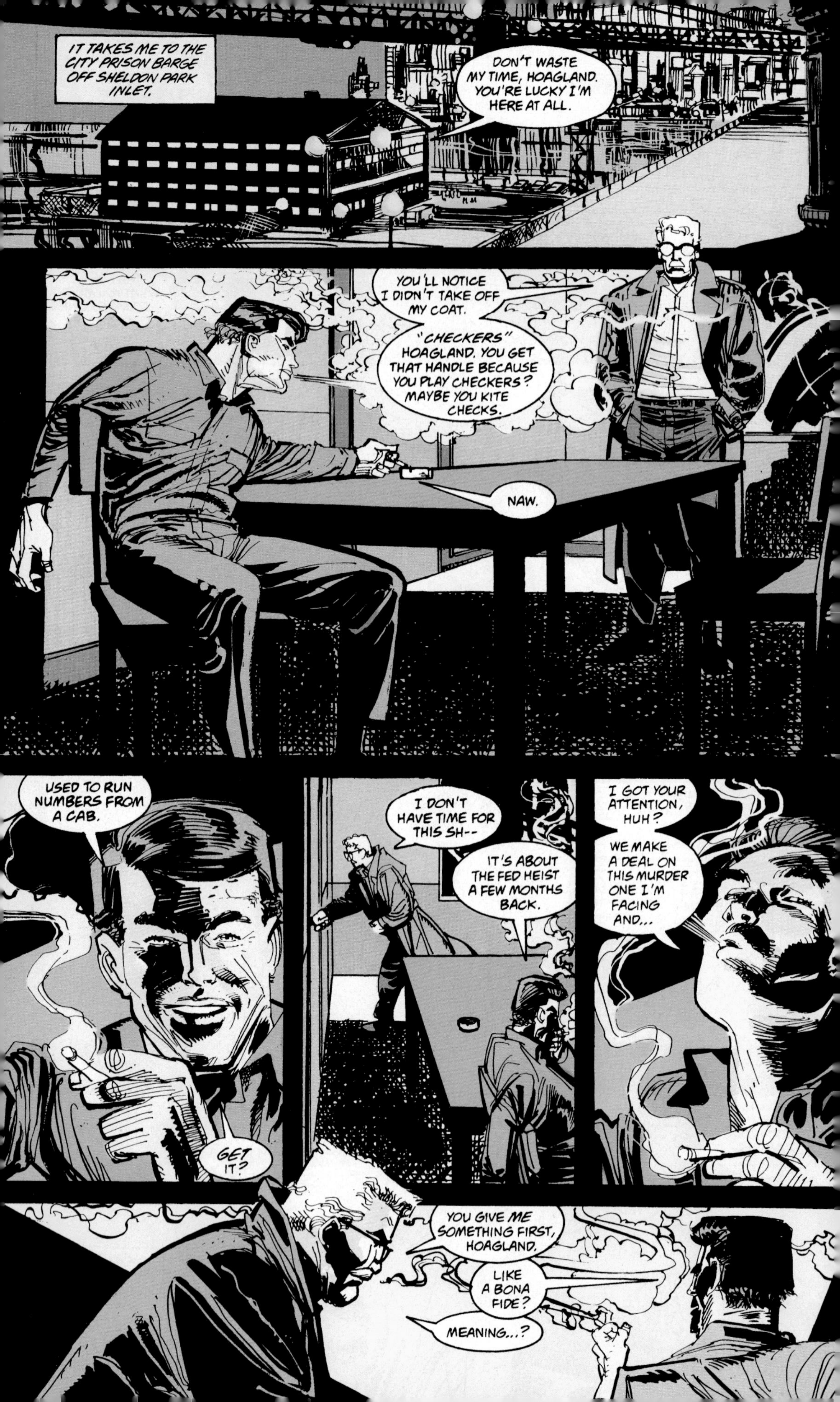
IT TAKES ME TO THE CITY PRISON BARGE OFF SHELDON PARK INLET.
DON'T WASTE MY TIME, HOAGLAND. YOU'RE LUCKY I'M HERE AT ALL.
YOU'LL NOTICE I DIDN'T TAKE OFF MY COAT.
"CHECKERS" HOAGLAND. YOU GET THAT HANDLE BECAUSE YOU PLAY CHECKERS? MAYBE YOU KITE CHECKS.
NAW.
USED TO RUN NUMBERS FROM A CAB.
GET IT?
I DON'T HAVE TIME FOR THIS SH--
IT'S ABOUT THE FED HEIST A FEW MONTHS BACK.
I GOT YOUR ATTENTION, HUH?
WE MAKE A DEAL ON THIS MURDER ONE I'M FACING AND...
YOU GIVE ME SOMETHING FIRST, HOAGLAND.
LIKE A BONA FIDE?
MEANING...?

THE HOTEL PHILLIPE IN KINGSTON SQUARE. THEY'RE HOLDING AN ENVELOPE IN THEIR SAFE FOR ME.

YOU LOOK IN THERE AND THEN WE'LL TALK.

WHY'RE YOU SHOWERING ME WITH ALL THESE FAVORS?

YOU'RE A BASTARD, GORDON.

BUT YOU'RE AN *HONEST* ONE.

I'M NOT SURE WHAT MAKES ME FOLLOW UP ON THIS.

SOMETHING IN HOAGLAND'S EYES.

HIS BONA FIDE.

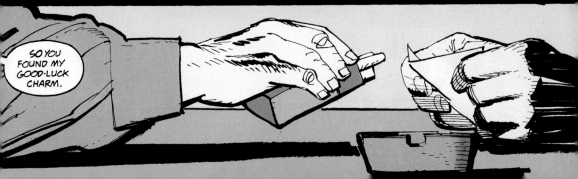

SO YOU FOUND MY GOOD-LUCK CHARM.

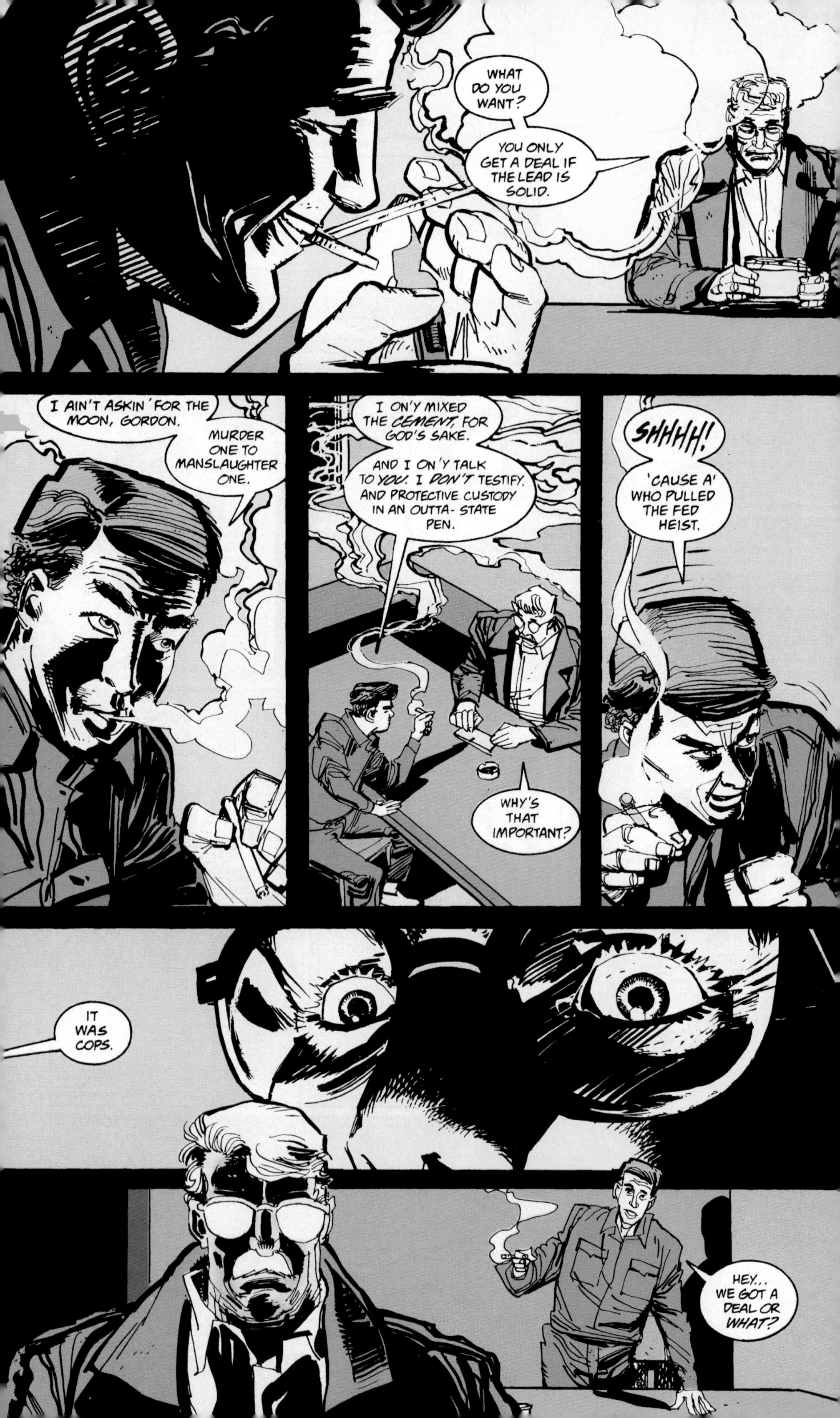
WHAT DO YOU WANT?
YOU ONLY GET A DEAL IF THE LEAD IS SOLID.
I AIN'T ASKIN' FOR THE MOON, GORDON.
MURDER ONE TO MANSLAUGHTER ONE.
I ON'Y MIXED THE CEMENT, FOR GOD'S SAKE.
AND I ON'Y TALK TO YOU. I DON'T TESTIFY. AND PROTECTIVE CUSTODY IN AN OUTTA- STATE PEN.
WHY'S THAT IMPORTANT?
SHHHH!
'CAUSE A' WHO PULLED THE FED HEIST.
IT WAS COPS.
HEY... WE GOT A DEAL OR WHAT?

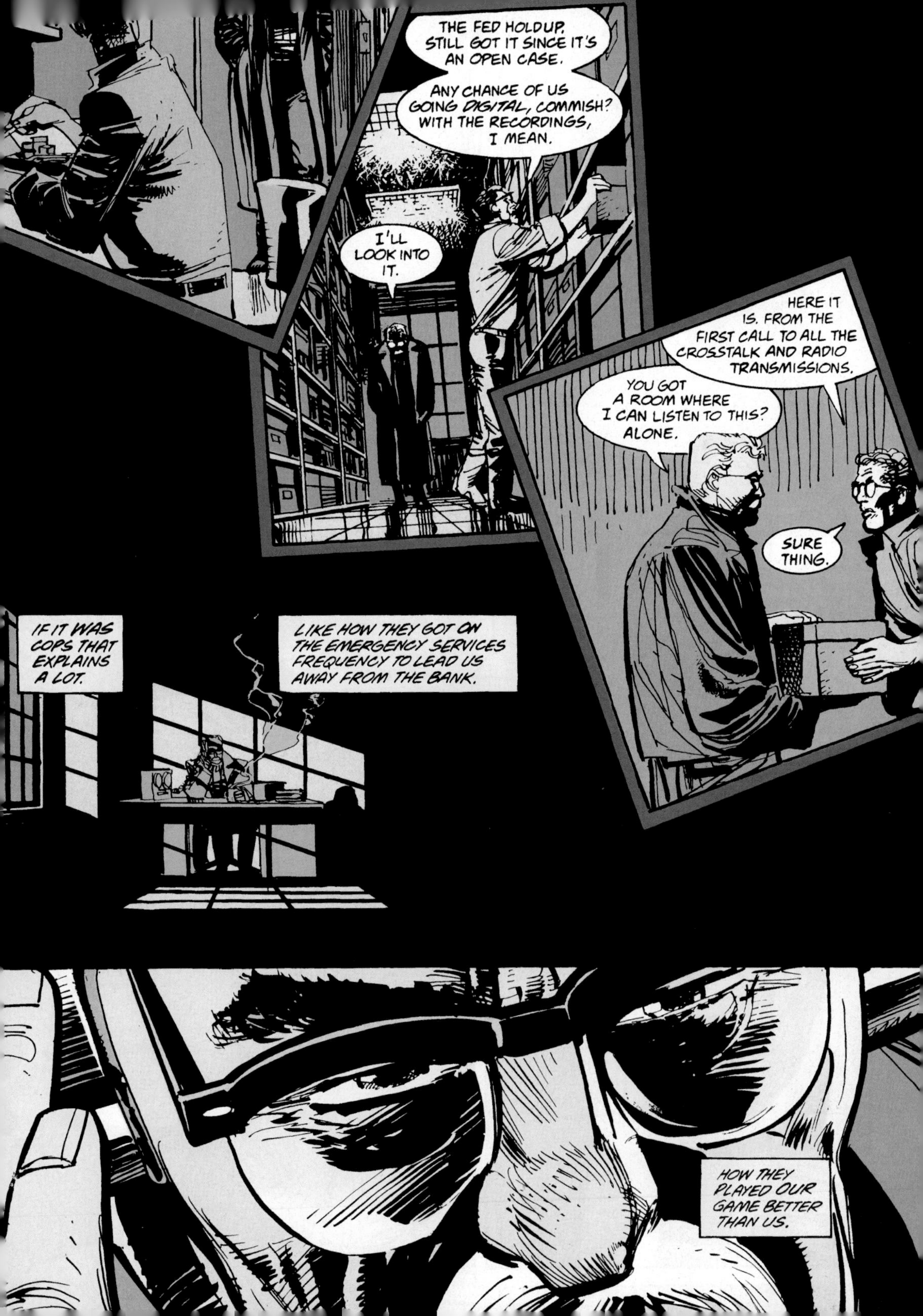
THE FED HOLDUP. STILL GOT IT SINCE IT'S AN OPEN CASE.
ANY CHANCE OF US GOING DIGITAL, COMMISH? WITH THE RECORDINGS, I MEAN.
I'LL LOOK INTO IT.
HERE IT IS. FROM THE FIRST CALL TO ALL THE CROSSTALK AND RADIO TRANSMISSIONS.
YOU GOT A ROOM WHERE I CAN LISTEN TO THIS? ALONE.
SURE THING.
IF IT WAS COPS THAT EXPLAINS A LOT.
LIKE HOW THEY GOT ON THE EMERGENCY SERVICES FREQUENCY TO LEAD US AWAY FROM THE BANK.
HOW THEY PLAYED OUR GAME BETTER THAN US.

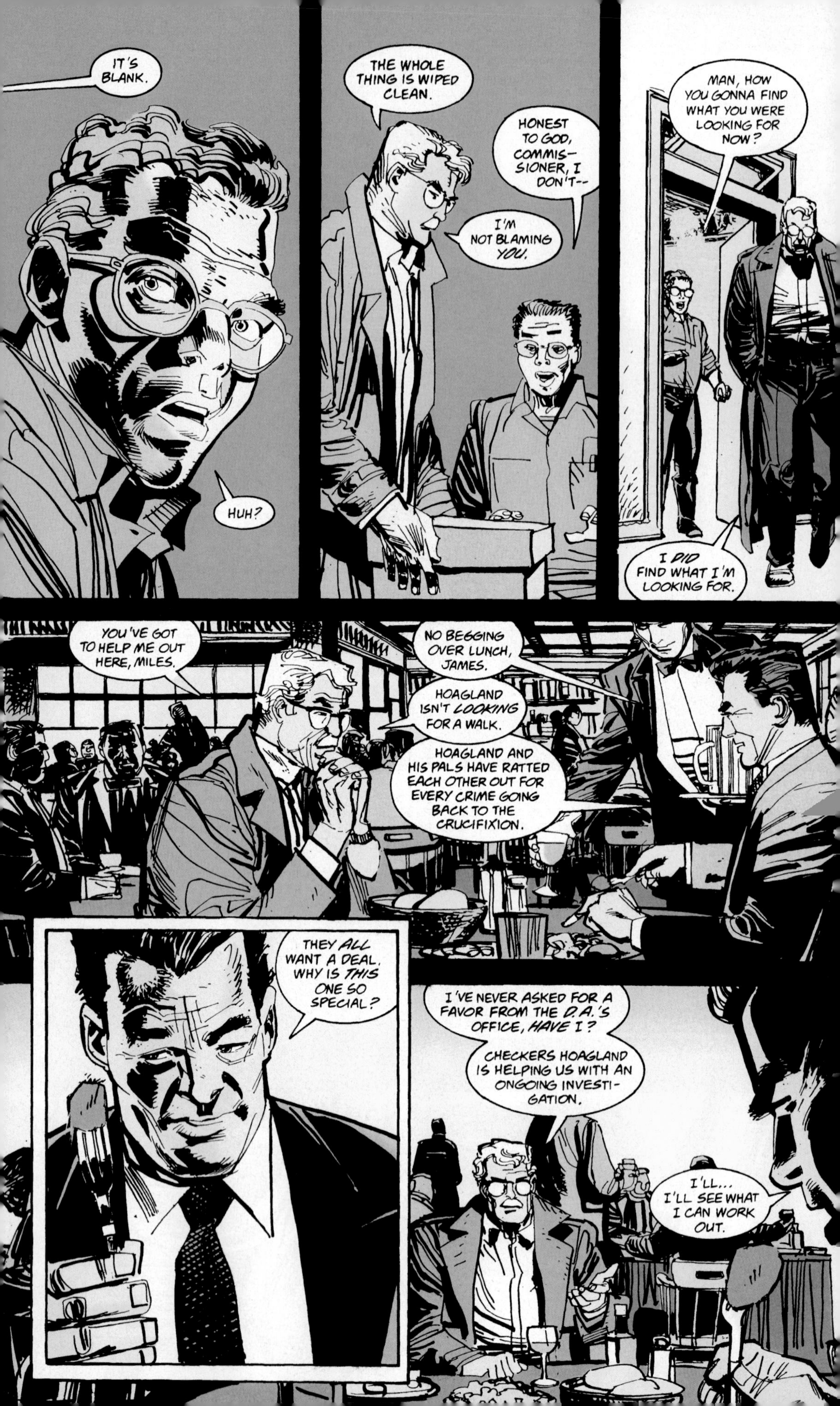
IT'S BLANK.
HUH?
THE WHOLE THING IS WIPED CLEAN.
HONEST TO GOD, COMMIS-SIONER, I DON'T--
I'M NOT BLAMING *YOU.*
MAN, HOW YOU GONNA FIND WHAT YOU WERE LOOKING FOR NOW?
I *DID* FIND WHAT I'M LOOKING FOR.
YOU'VE GOT TO HELP ME OUT HERE, MILES.
NO BEGGING OVER LUNCH, JAMES.
HOAGLAND ISN'T *LOOKING* FOR A WALK.
HOAGLAND AND HIS PALS HAVE RATTED EACH OTHER OUT FOR EVERY CRIME GOING BACK TO THE CRUCIFIXION.
THEY *ALL* WANT A DEAL. WHY IS *THIS* ONE SO SPECIAL?
I'VE NEVER ASKED FOR A FAVOR FROM THE D.A.'S OFFICE, *HAVE* I?
CHECKERS HOAGLAND IS HELPING US WITH AN ONGOING INVESTI-GATION.
I'LL... I'LL SEE WHAT I CAN WORK OUT.

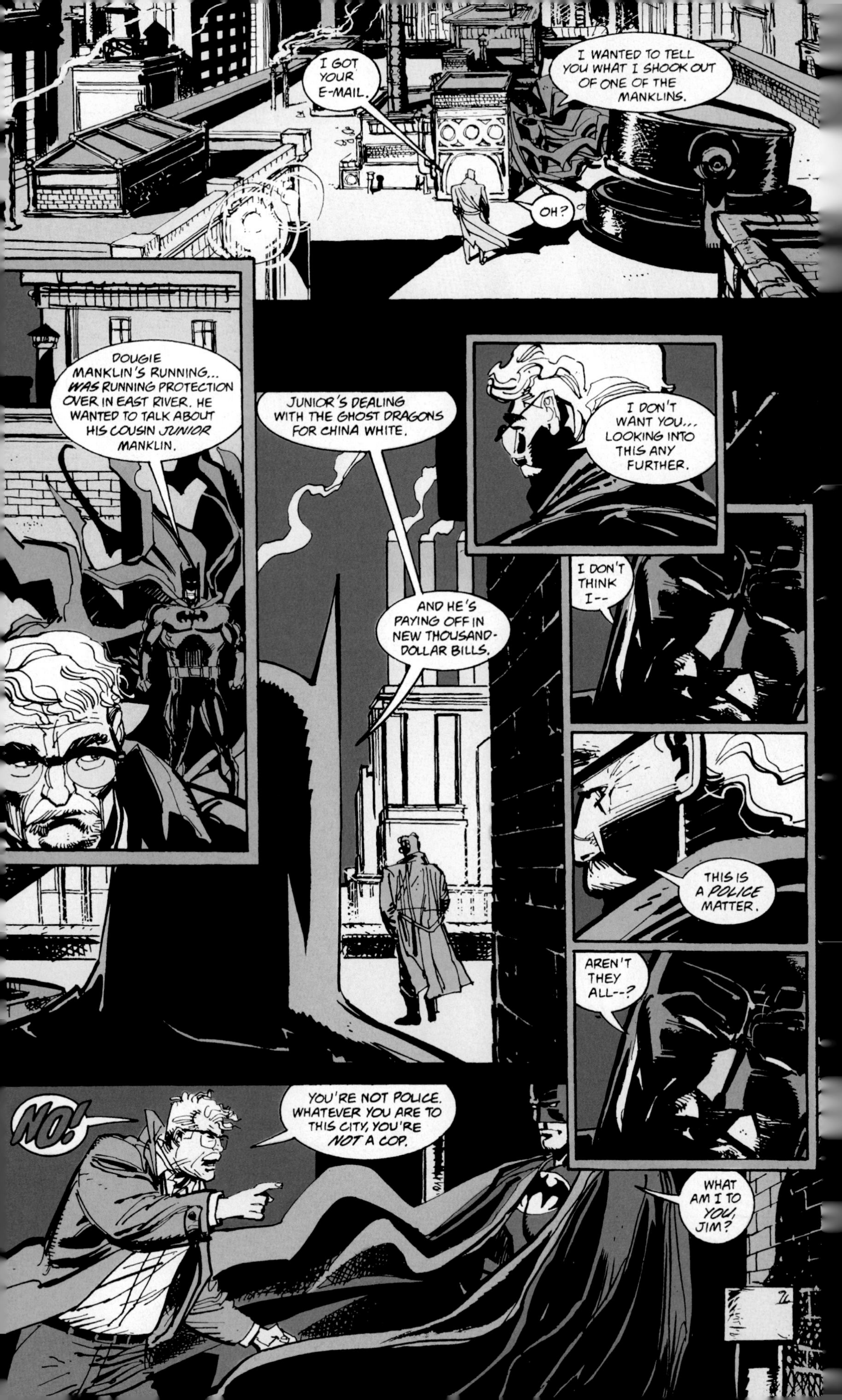
I GOT YOUR E-MAIL.
I WANTED TO TELL YOU WHAT I SHOOK OUT OF ONE OF THE MANKLINS.
OH?
DOUGIE MANKLIN'S RUNNING... WAS RUNNING PROTECTION OVER IN EAST RIVER. HE WANTED TO TALK ABOUT HIS COUSIN JUNIOR MANKLIN.
JUNIOR'S DEALING WITH THE GHOST DRAGONS FOR CHINA WHITE.
AND HE'S PAYING OFF IN NEW THOUSAND-DOLLAR BILLS.
I DON'T WANT YOU... LOOKING INTO THIS ANY FURTHER.
I DON'T THINK I--
THIS IS A POLICE MATTER.
AREN'T THEY ALL--?
NO!
YOU'RE NOT POLICE. WHATEVER YOU ARE TO THIS CITY, YOU'RE NOT A COP.
WHAT AM I TO YOU, JIM?

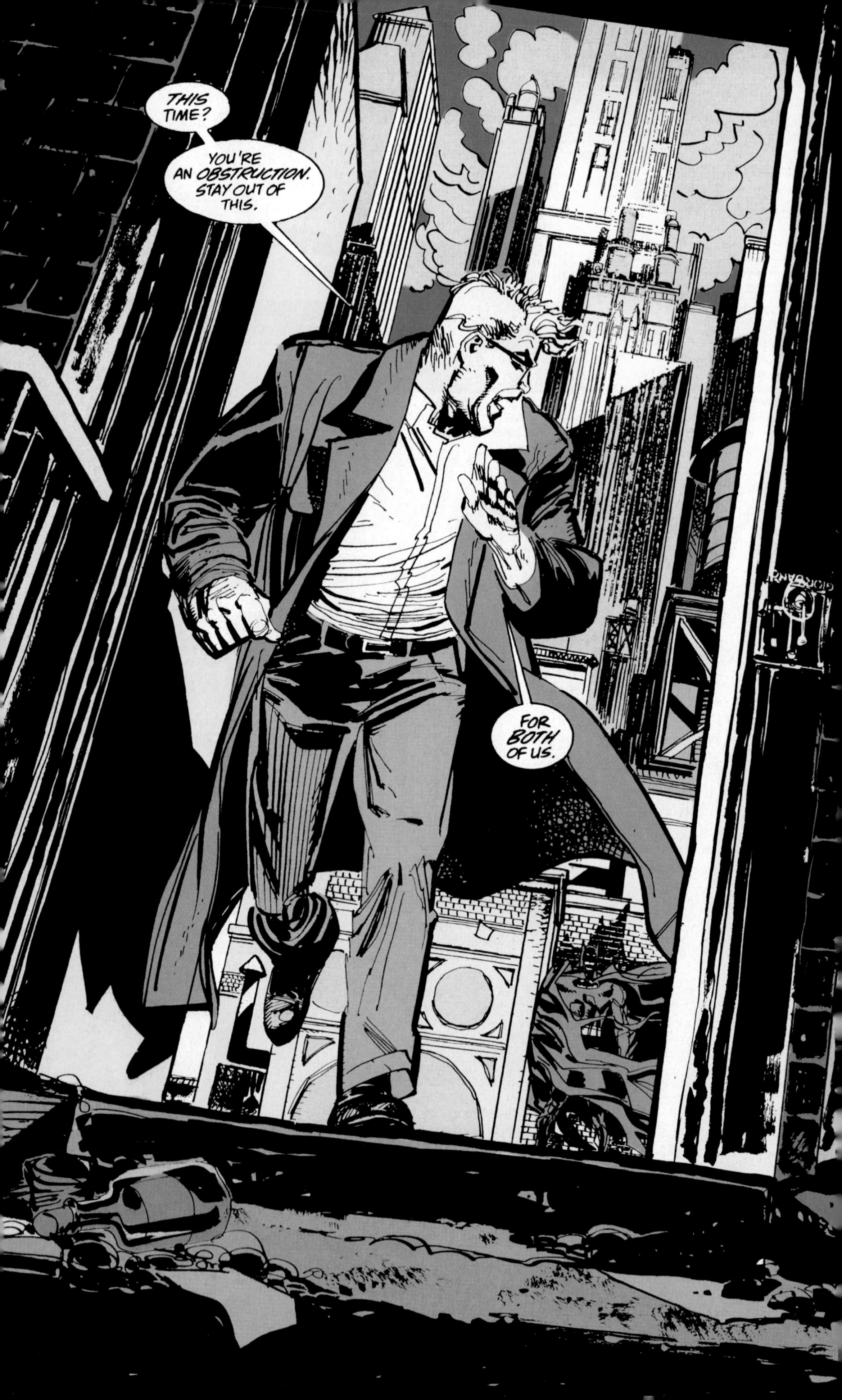
THIS TIME?
YOU'RE AN OBSTRUCTION. STAY OUT OF THIS.
FOR BOTH OF US.

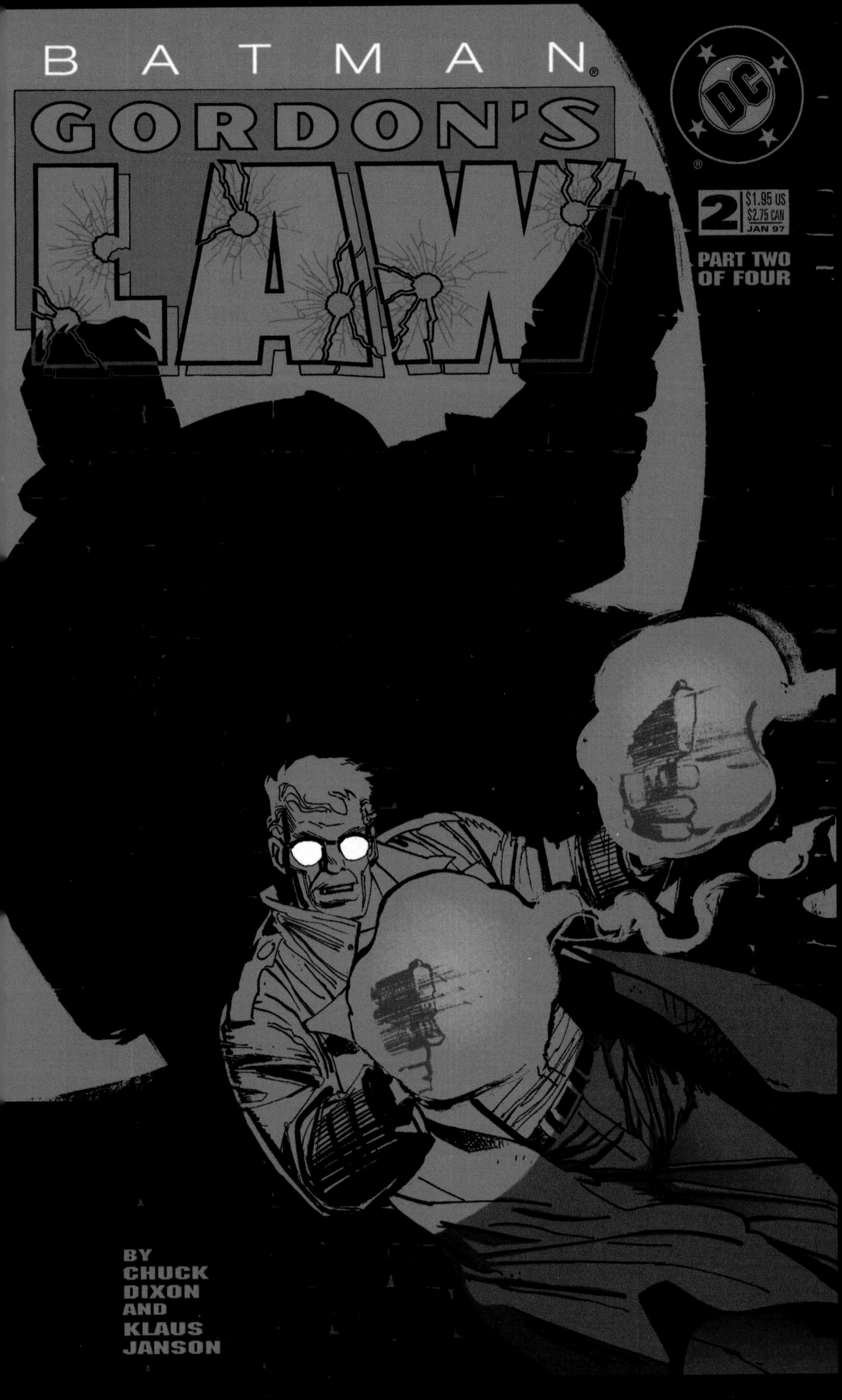
BATMAN
GORDON'S
LAW
DC
2
$1.95 US
$2.75 CAN
JAN 97
PART TWO
OF FOUR
BY
CHUCK
DIXON
AND
KLAUS
JANSON

Suspicious Minds

Chuck Dixon–writer
Klaus Janson–artist
Kevin Somers–colorist
John Costanza–letterer
Darren Vincenzo–assoc. editor
Scott Peterson–editor

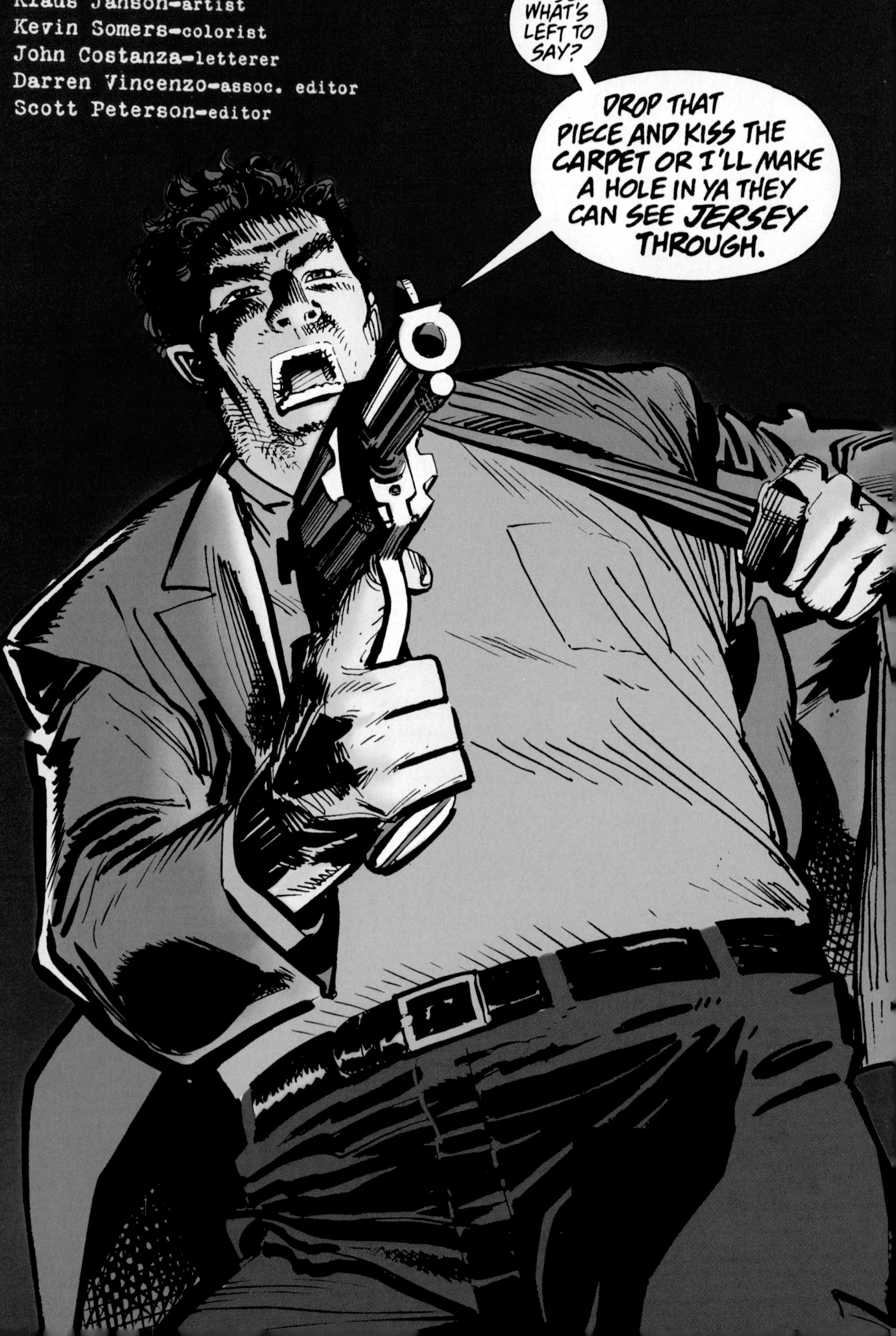
SO WHAT'S LEFT TO SAY?
DROP THAT PIECE AND KISS THE CARPET OR I'LL MAKE A HOLE IN YA THEY CAN SEE JERSEY THROUGH.

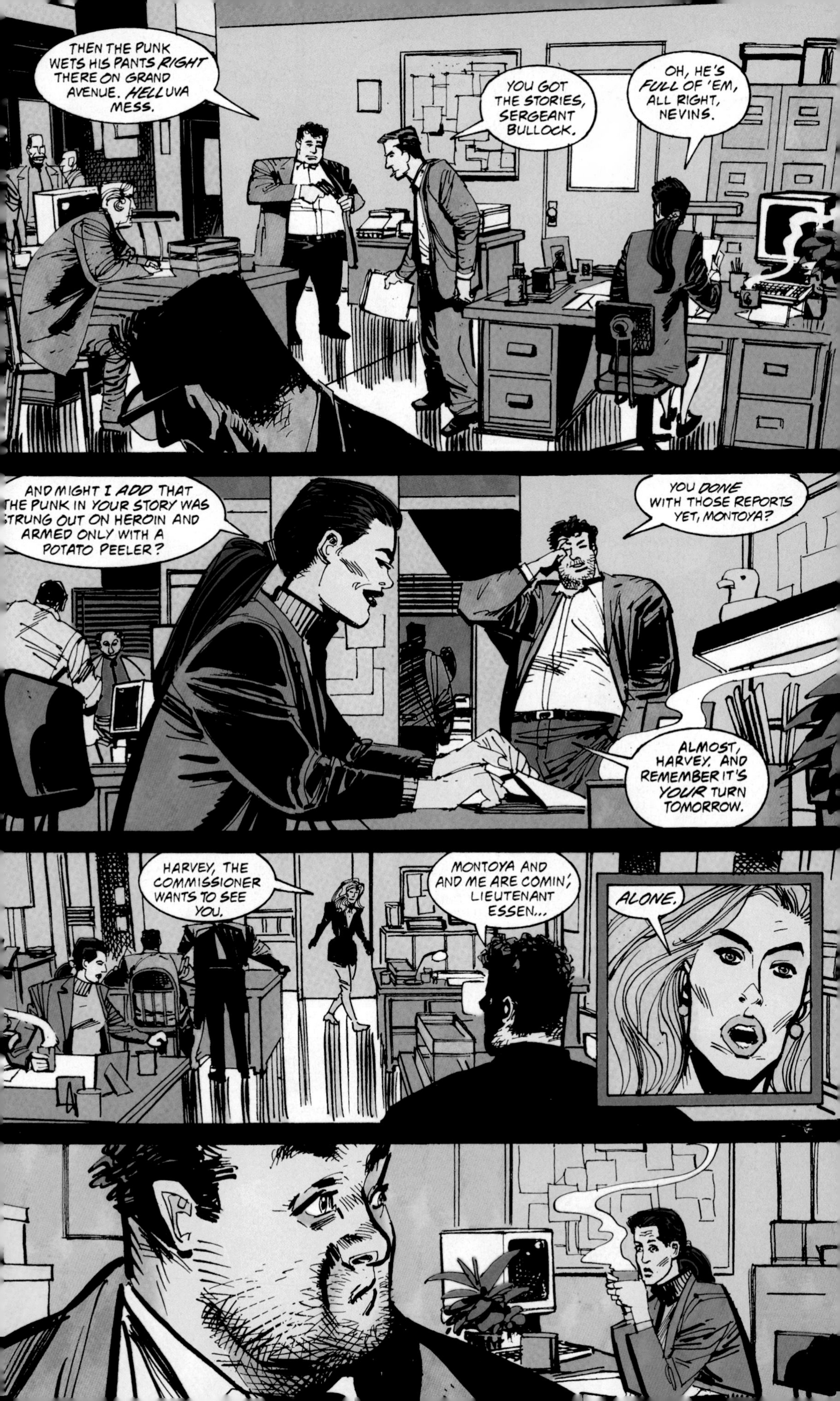
THEN THE PUNK WETS HIS PANTS RIGHT THERE ON GRAND AVENUE. HELLUVA MESS.
YOU GOT THE STORIES, SERGEANT BULLOCK.
OH, HE'S FULL OF 'EM, ALL RIGHT, NEVINS.
AND MIGHT I ADD THAT THE PUNK IN YOUR STORY WAS STRUNG OUT ON HEROIN AND ARMED ONLY WITH A POTATO PEELER?
YOU DONE WITH THOSE REPORTS YET, MONTOYA?
ALMOST, HARVEY. AND REMEMBER IT'S YOUR TURN TOMORROW.
HARVEY, THE COMMISSIONER WANTS TO SEE YOU.
MONTOYA AND AND ME ARE COMIN', LIEUTENANT ESSEN...
ALONE.

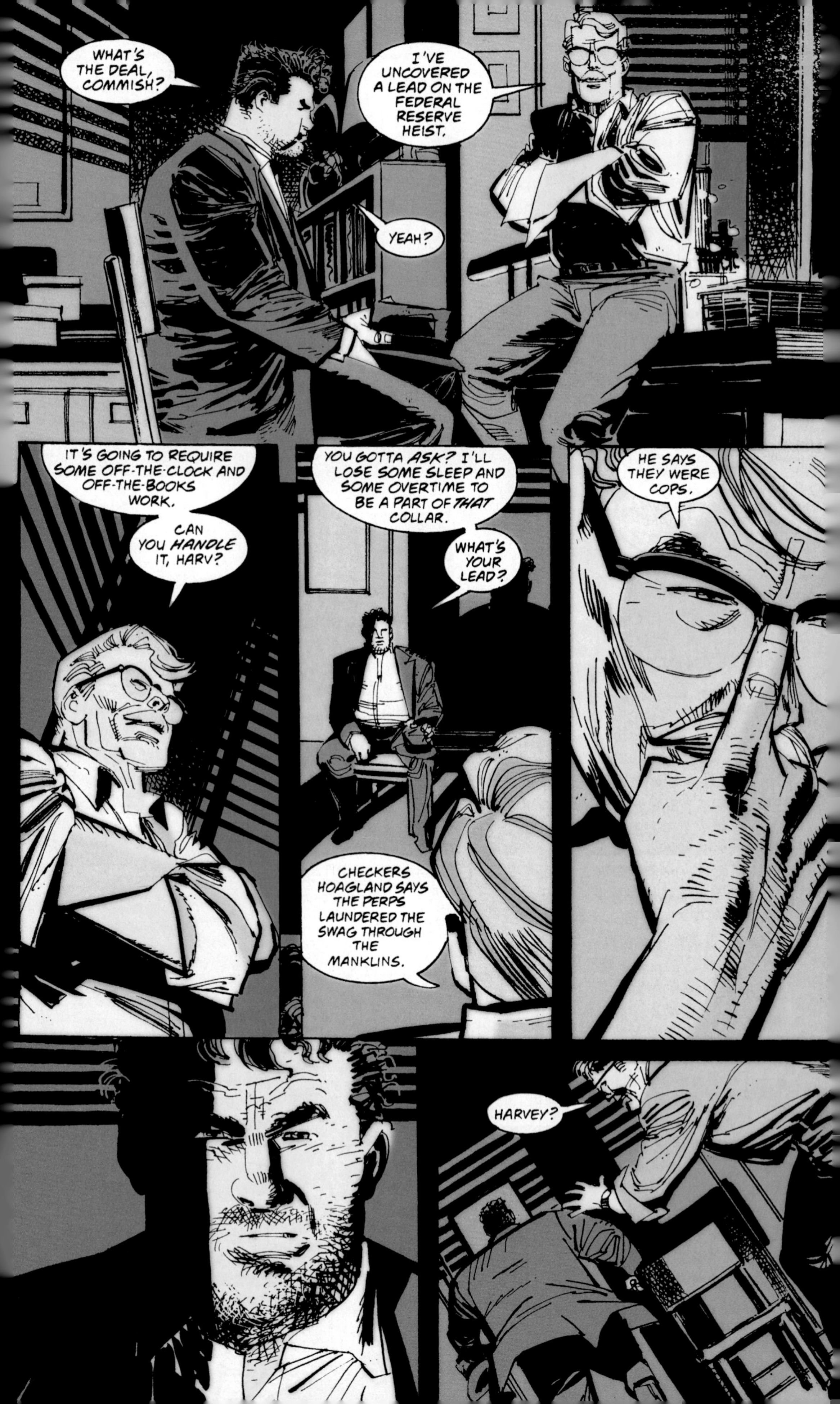
WHAT'S THE DEAL, COMMISH?
I'VE UNCOVERED A LEAD ON THE FEDERAL RESERVE HEIST.
YEAH?
IT'S GOING TO REQUIRE SOME OFF-THE-CLOCK AND OFF-THE-BOOKS WORK.
CAN YOU HANDLE IT, HARV?
YOU GOTTA ASK? I'LL LOSE SOME SLEEP AND SOME OVERTIME TO BE A PART OF THAT COLLAR.
WHAT'S YOUR LEAD?
CHECKERS HOAGLAND SAYS THE PERPS LAUNDERED THE SWAG THROUGH THE MANKLINS.
HE SAYS THEY WERE COPS.
HARVEY?

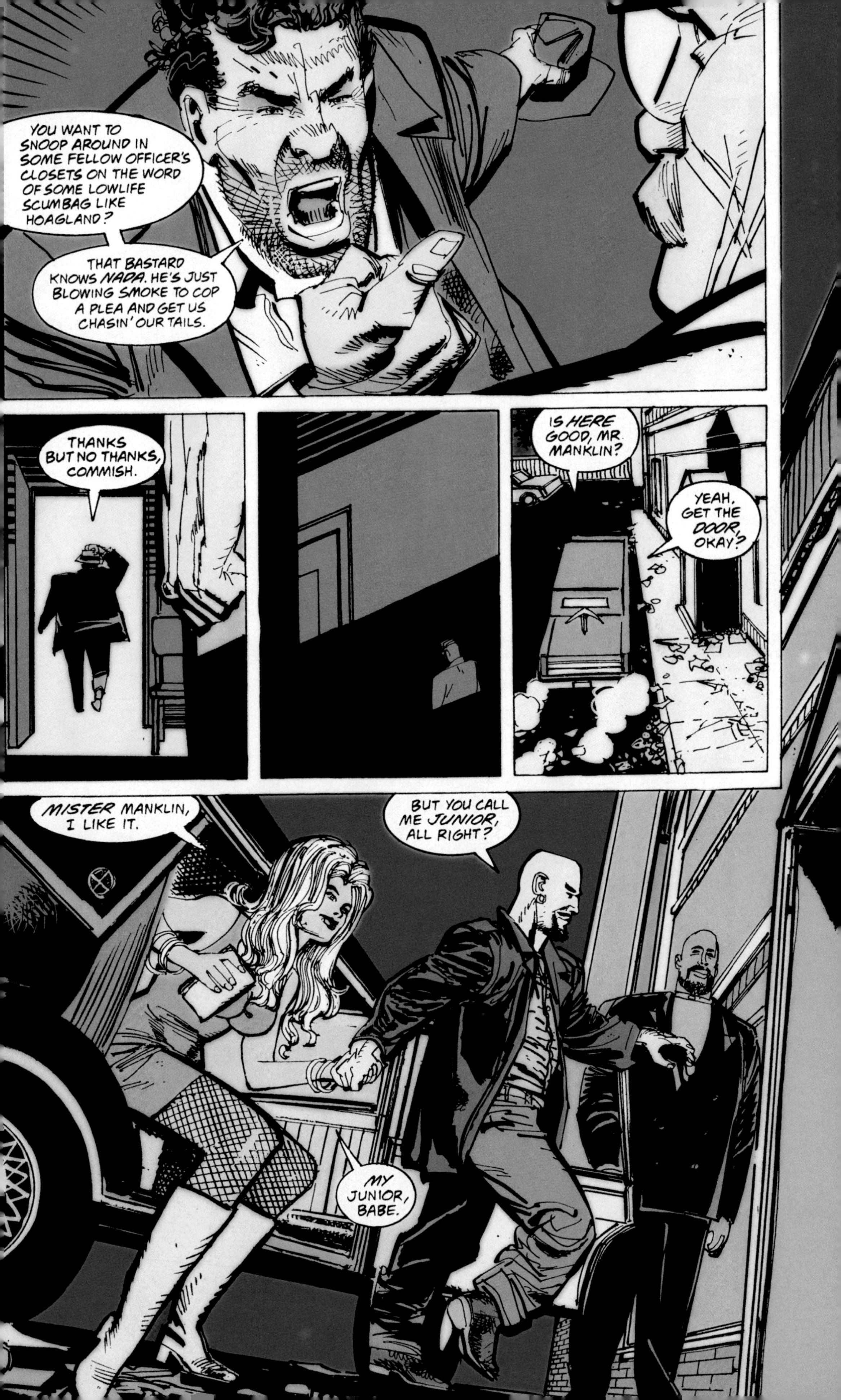
YOU WANT TO SNOOP AROUND IN SOME FELLOW OFFICER'S CLOSETS ON THE WORD OF SOME LOWLIFE SCUMBAG LIKE HOAGLAND?
THAT BASTARD KNOWS NADA. HE'S JUST BLOWING SMOKE TO COP A PLEA AND GET US CHASIN' OUR TAILS.
THANKS BUT NO THANKS, COMMISH.
IS HERE GOOD, MR. MANKLIN?
YEAH. GET THE DOOR, OKAY?
MISTER MANKLIN, I LIKE IT.
BUT YOU CALL ME JUNIOR, ALL RIGHT?
MY JUNIOR, BABE.

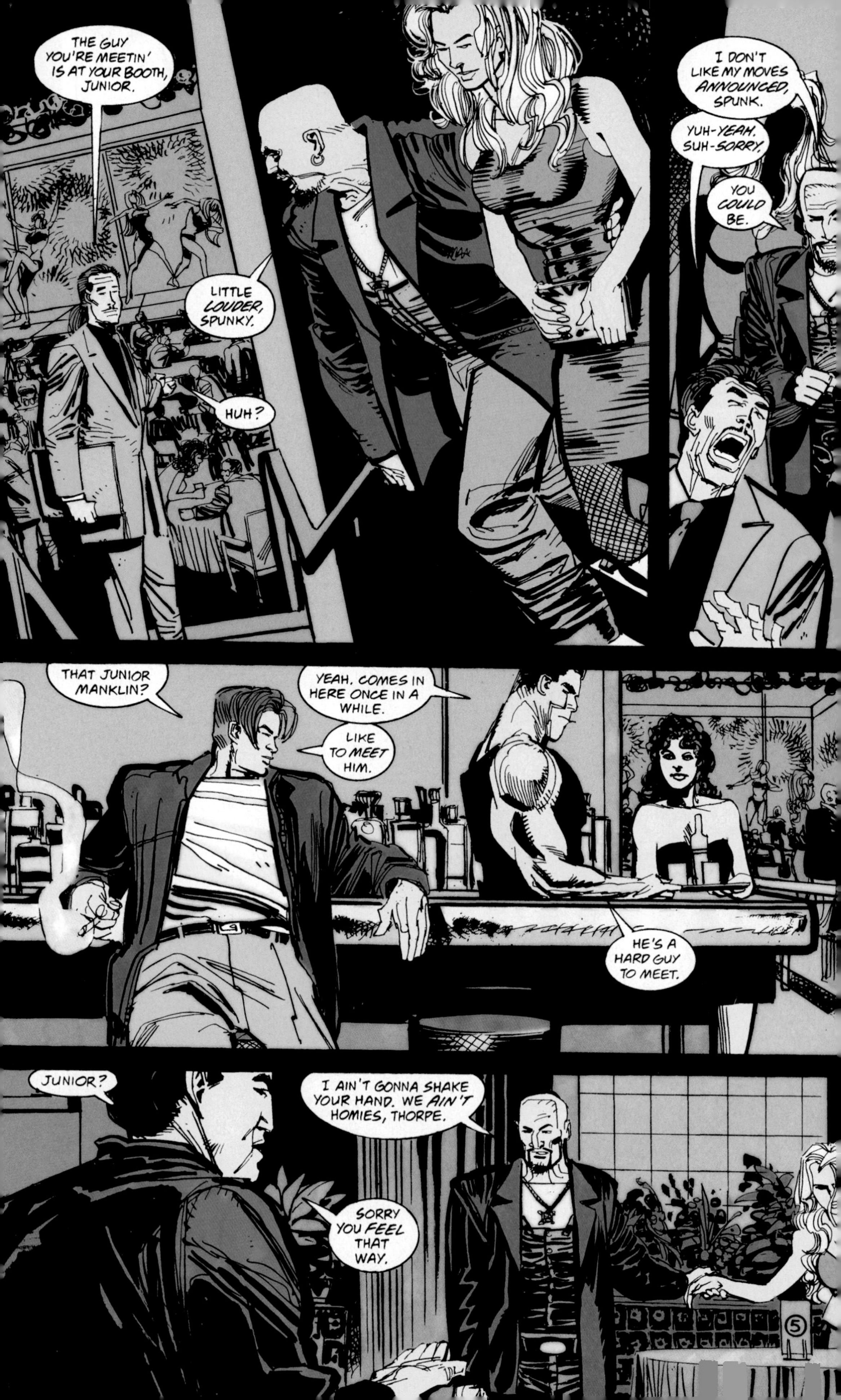
THE GUY YOU'RE MEETIN' IS AT YOUR BOOTH, JUNIOR.
LITTLE LOUDER, SPUNKY.
HUH?
I DON'T LIKE MY MOVES ANNOUNCED, SPUNK.
YUH-YEAH. SUH-SORRY.
YOU COULD BE.
THAT JUNIOR MANKLIN?
YEAH. COMES IN HERE ONCE IN A WHILE.
LIKE TO MEET HIM.
HE'S A HARD GUY TO MEET.
JUNIOR?
I AIN'T GONNA SHAKE YOUR HAND. WE AIN'T HOMIES, THORPE.
SORRY YOU FEEL THAT WAY.
5

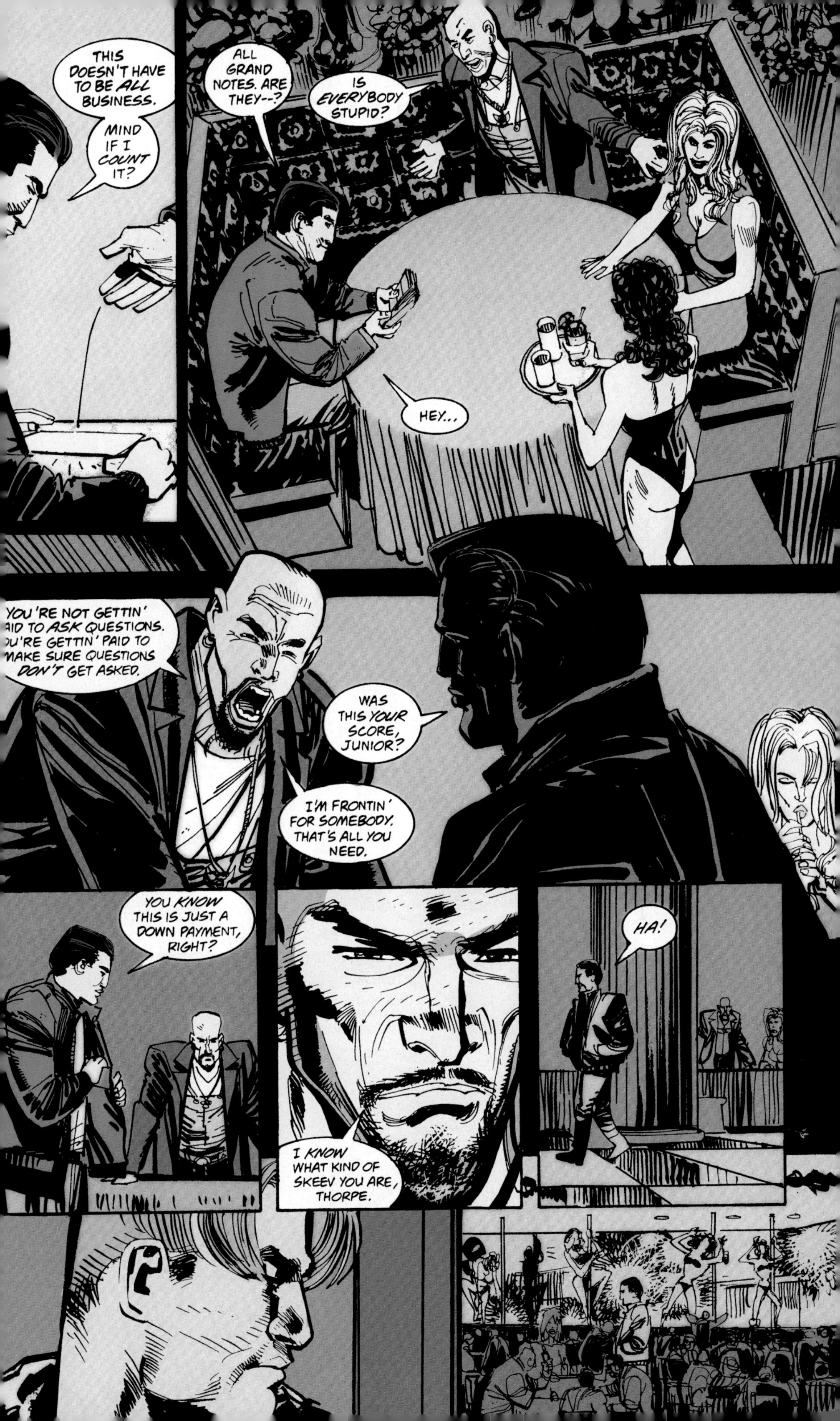

THIS DOESN'T HAVE TO BE ALL BUSINESS.
MIND IF I COUNT IT?
ALL GRAND NOTES. ARE THEY--?
IS EVERYBODY STUPID?
HEY...
YOU'RE NOT GETTIN' PAID TO ASK QUESTIONS. YOU'RE GETTIN' PAID TO MAKE SURE QUESTIONS DON'T GET ASKED.
WAS THIS YOUR SCORE, JUNIOR?
I'M FRONTIN' FOR SOMEBODY. THAT'S ALL YOU NEED.
YOU KNOW THIS IS JUST A DOWN PAYMENT, RIGHT?
I KNOW WHAT KIND OF SKEEV YOU ARE, THORPE.
HA!

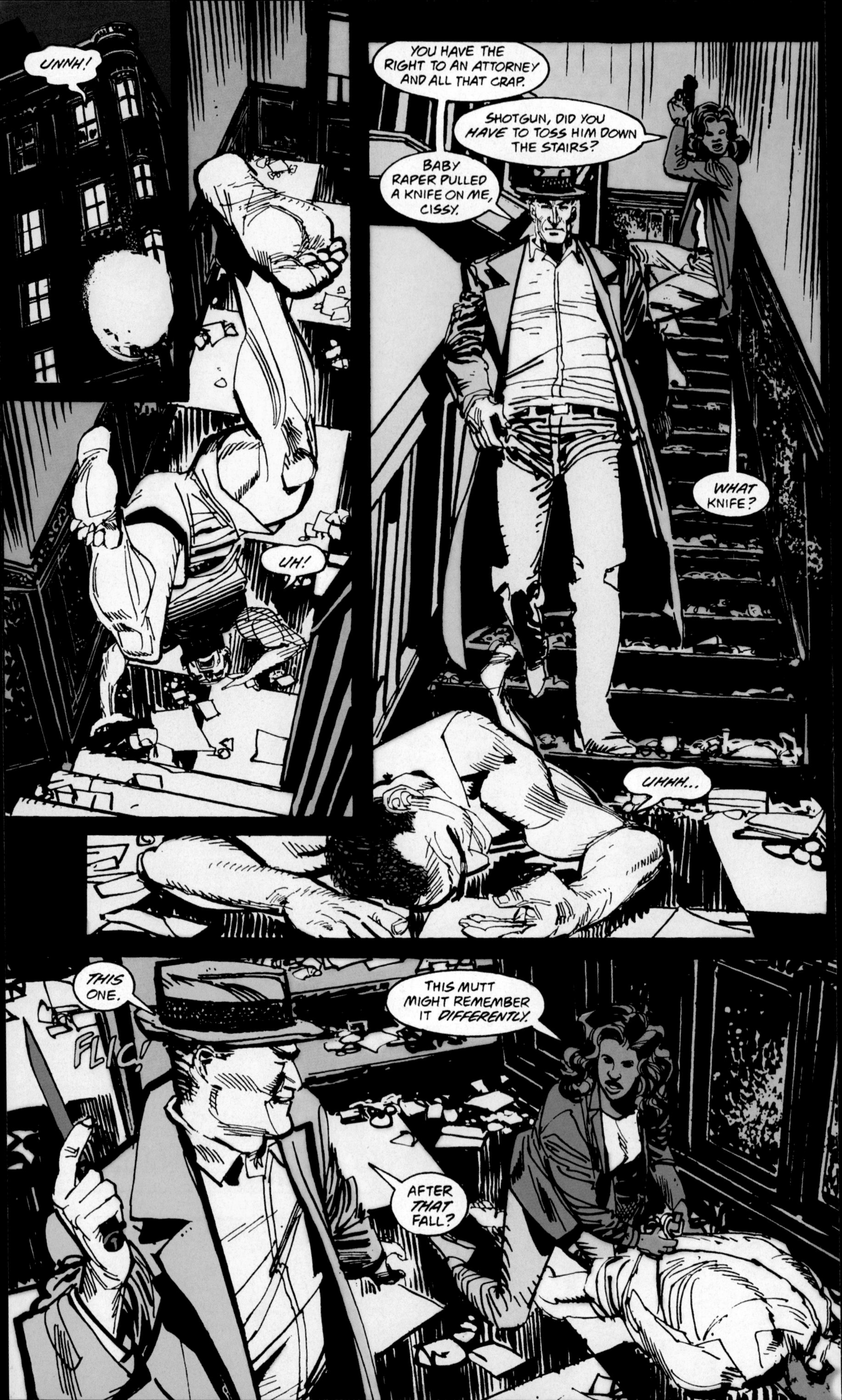
UNNH!
UH!
YOU HAVE THE RIGHT TO AN ATTORNEY AND ALL THAT CRAP.
SHOTGUN, DID YOU *HAVE* TO TOSS HIM DOWN THE STAIRS?
BABY RAPER PULLED A KNIFE ON ME, CISSY.
WHAT KNIFE?
UHHH...
THIS ONE.
FLIC!
THIS MUTT MIGHT REMEMBER IT *DIFFERENTLY.*
AFTER *THAT* FALL?

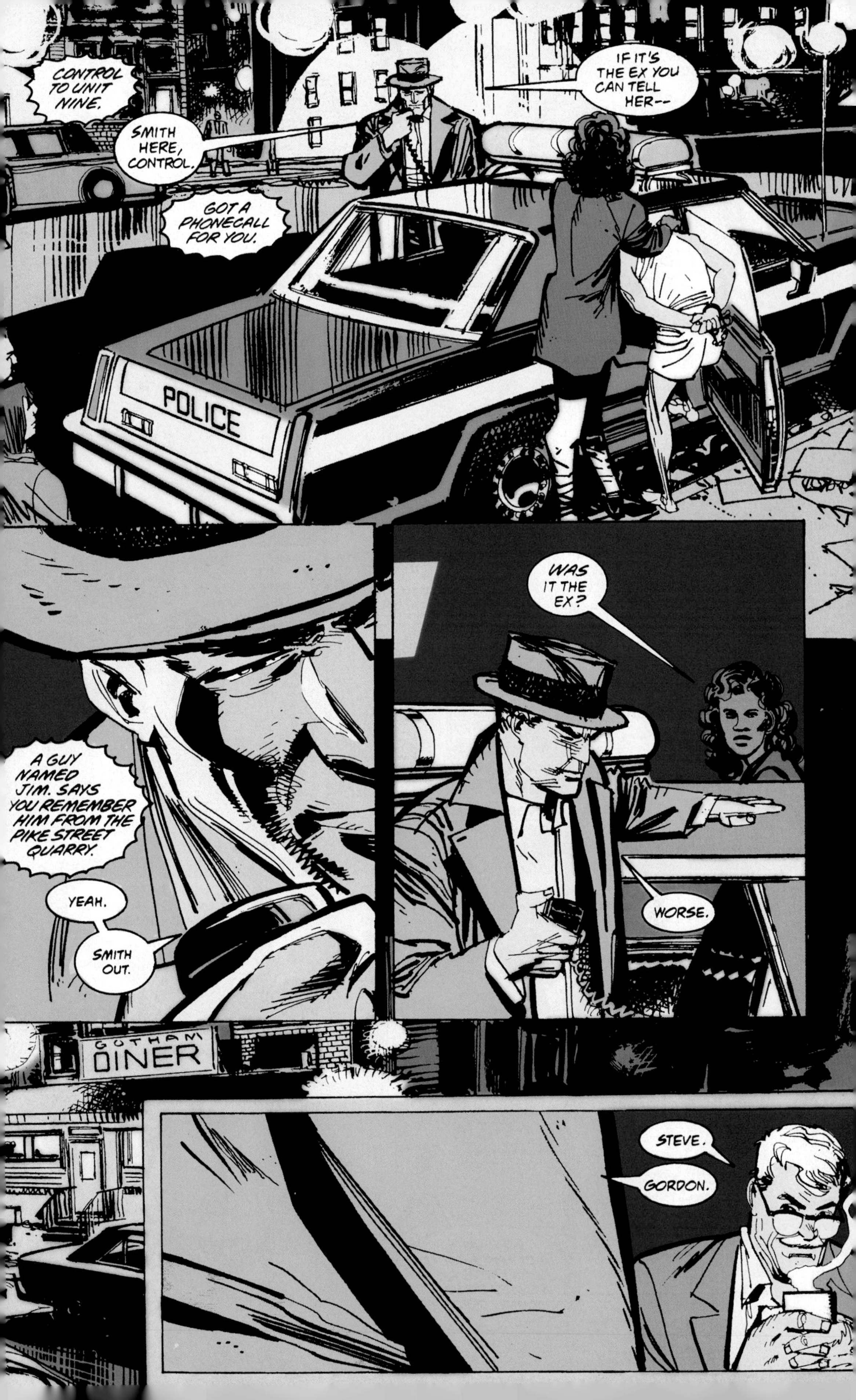
CONTROL TO UNIT NINE.
SMITH HERE, CONTROL.
IF IT'S THE EX YOU CAN TELL HER--
GOT A PHONECALL FOR YOU.
POLICE
A GUY NAMED JIM. SAYS YOU REMEMBER HIM FROM THE PIKE STREET QUARRY.
YEAH.
SMITH OUT.
WAS IT THE EX?
WORSE.
GOTHAM DINER
STEVE.
GORDON.

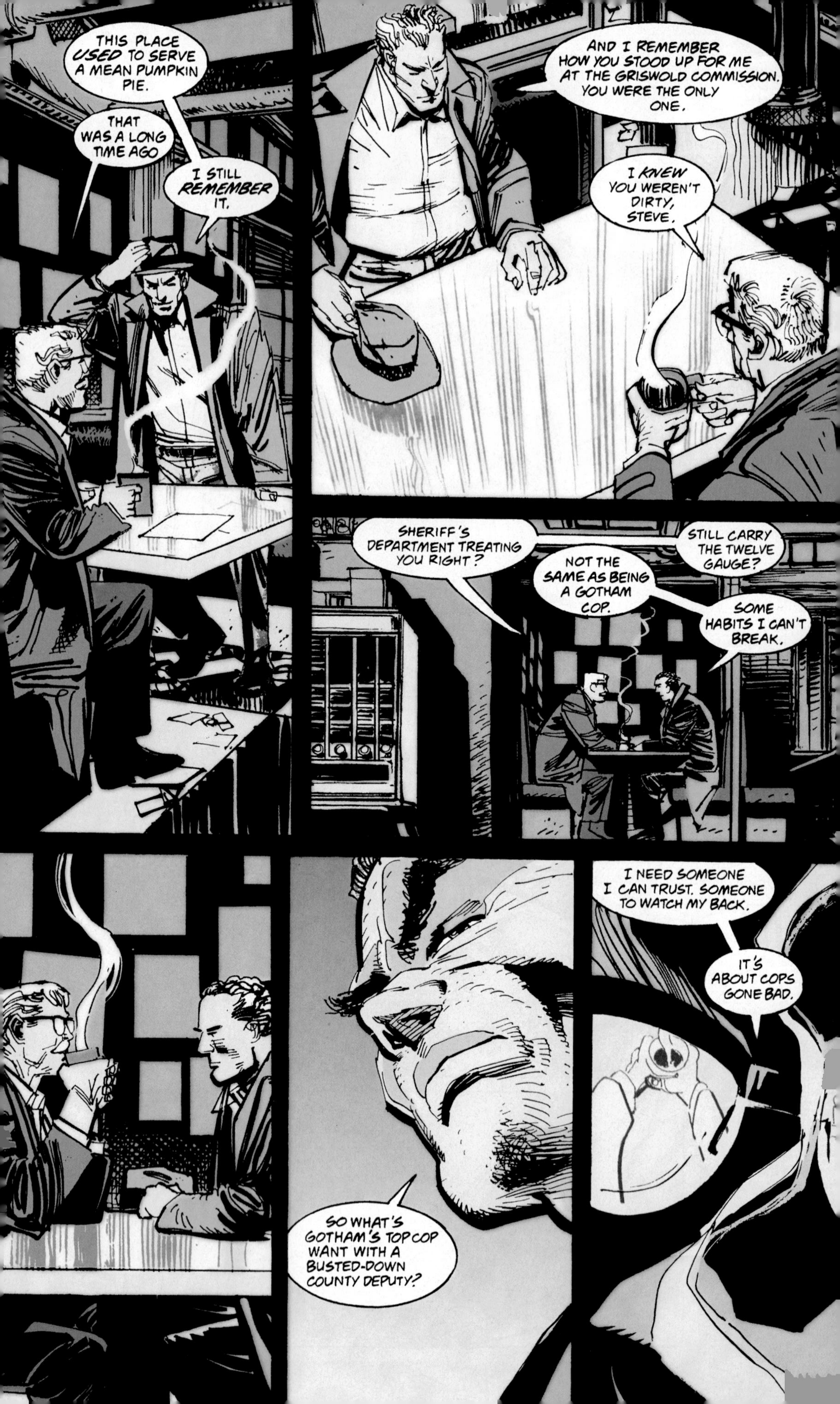

THIS PLACE USED TO SERVE A MEAN PUMPKIN PIE.
THAT WAS A LONG TIME AGO
I STILL REMEMBER IT.
AND I REMEMBER HOW YOU STOOD UP FOR ME AT THE GRISWOLD COMMISSION. YOU WERE THE ONLY ONE.
I KNEW YOU WEREN'T DIRTY, STEVE.
SHERIFF'S DEPARTMENT TREATING YOU RIGHT?
NOT THE SAME AS BEING A GOTHAM COP.
STILL CARRY THE TWELVE GAUGE?
SOME HABITS I CAN'T BREAK.
SO WHAT'S GOTHAM'S TOP COP WANT WITH A BUSTED-DOWN COUNTY DEPUTY?
I NEED SOMEONE I CAN TRUST. SOMEONE TO WATCH MY BACK.
IT'S ABOUT COPS GONE BAD.

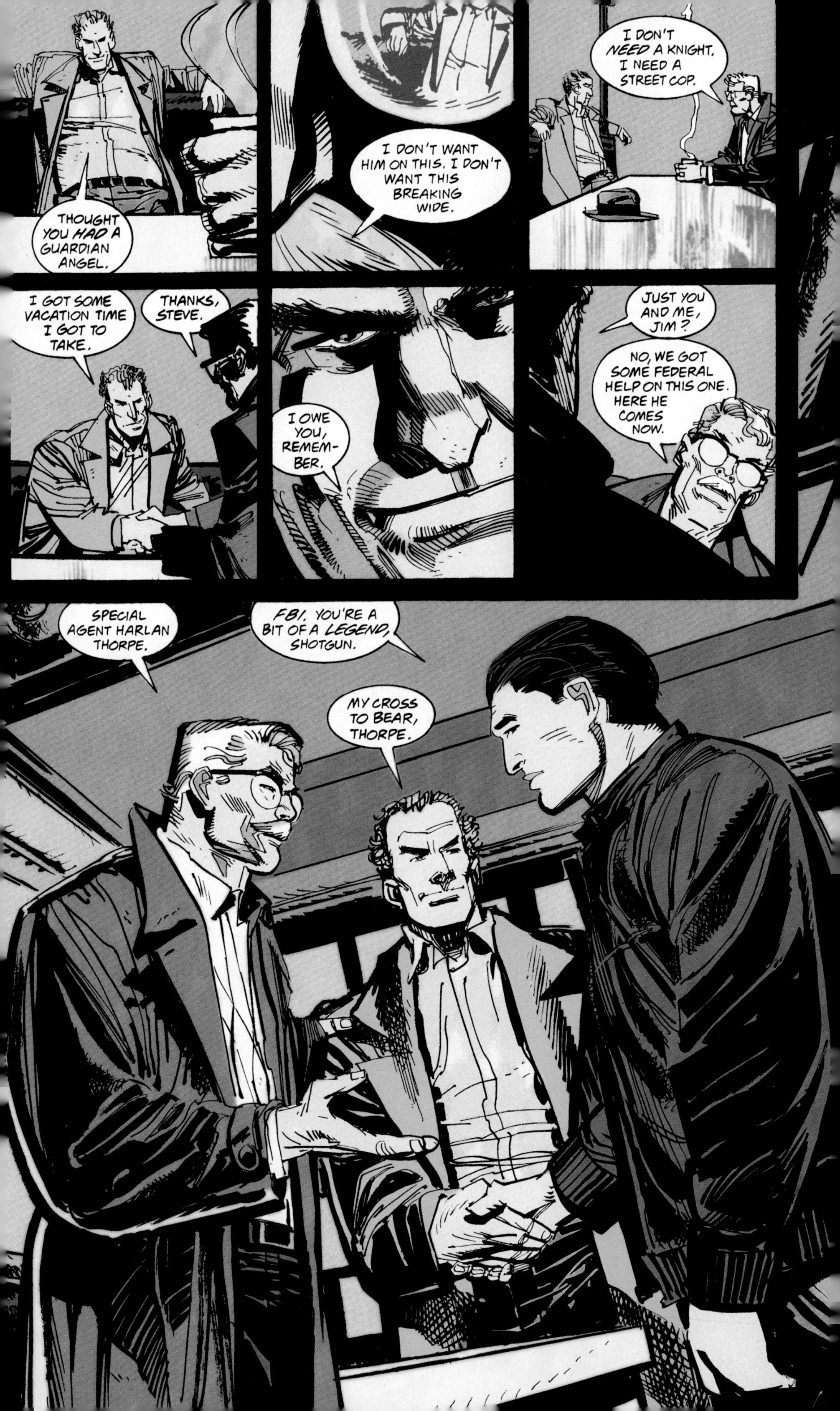
THOUGHT YOU *HAD* A GUARDIAN ANGEL.
I DON'T WANT HIM ON THIS. I DON'T WANT THIS BREAKING WIDE.
I DON'T *NEED* A KNIGHT, I NEED A STREET COP.
I GOT SOME VACATION TIME I GOT TO TAKE.
THANKS, STEVE.
I OWE YOU, REMEMBER.
JUST YOU AND ME, JIM?
NO, WE GOT SOME FEDERAL HELP ON THIS ONE. HERE HE COMES NOW.
SPECIAL AGENT HARLAN THORPE.
FBI. YOU'RE A BIT OF A *LEGEND*, SHOTGUN.
MY CROSS TO BEAR, THORPE.

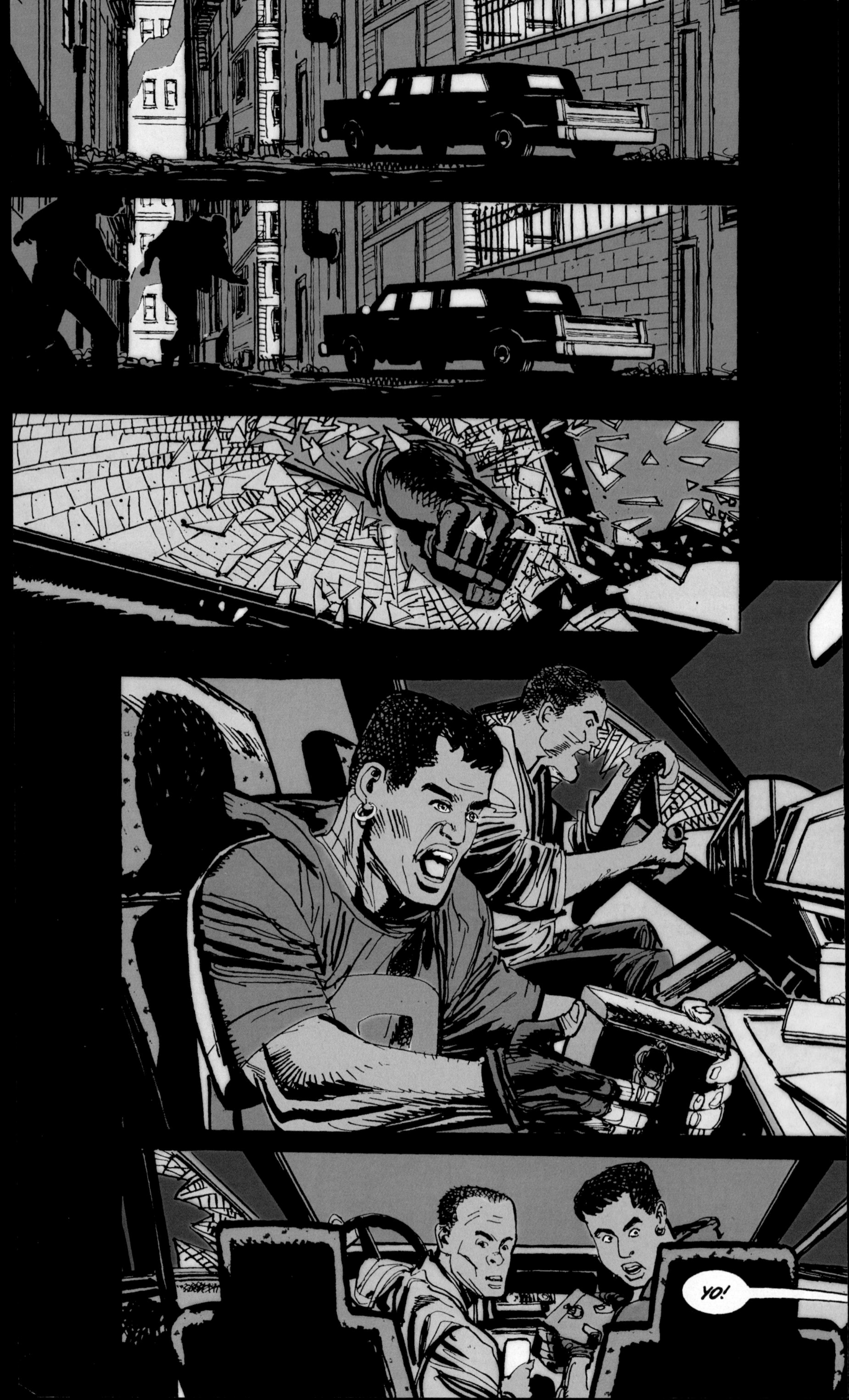
YO!

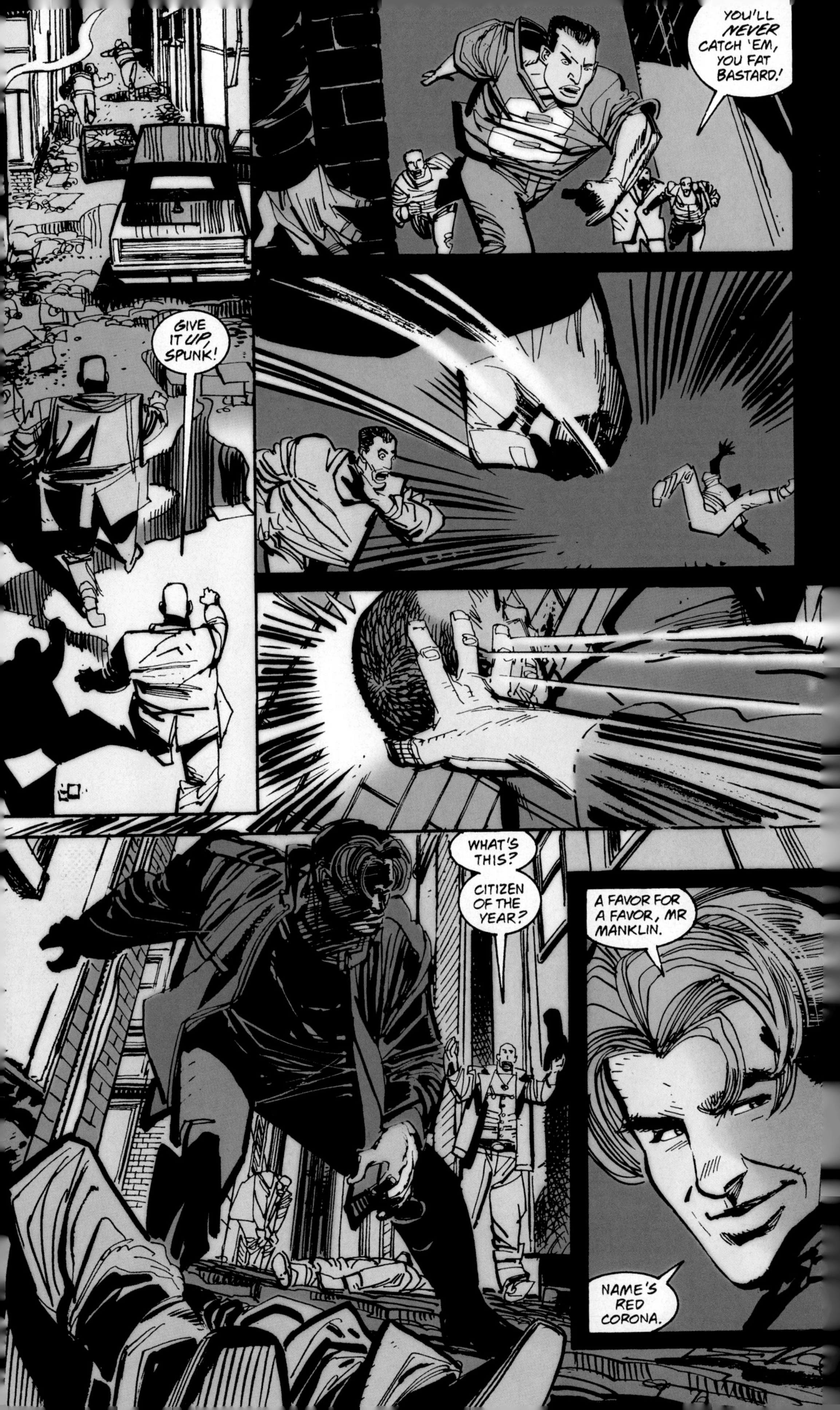

YOU'LL NEVER CATCH 'EM, YOU FAT BASTARD!
GIVE IT UP, SPUNK!
WHAT'S THIS?
CITIZEN OF THE YEAR?
A FAVOR FOR A FAVOR, MR MANKLIN.
NAME'S RED CORONA.

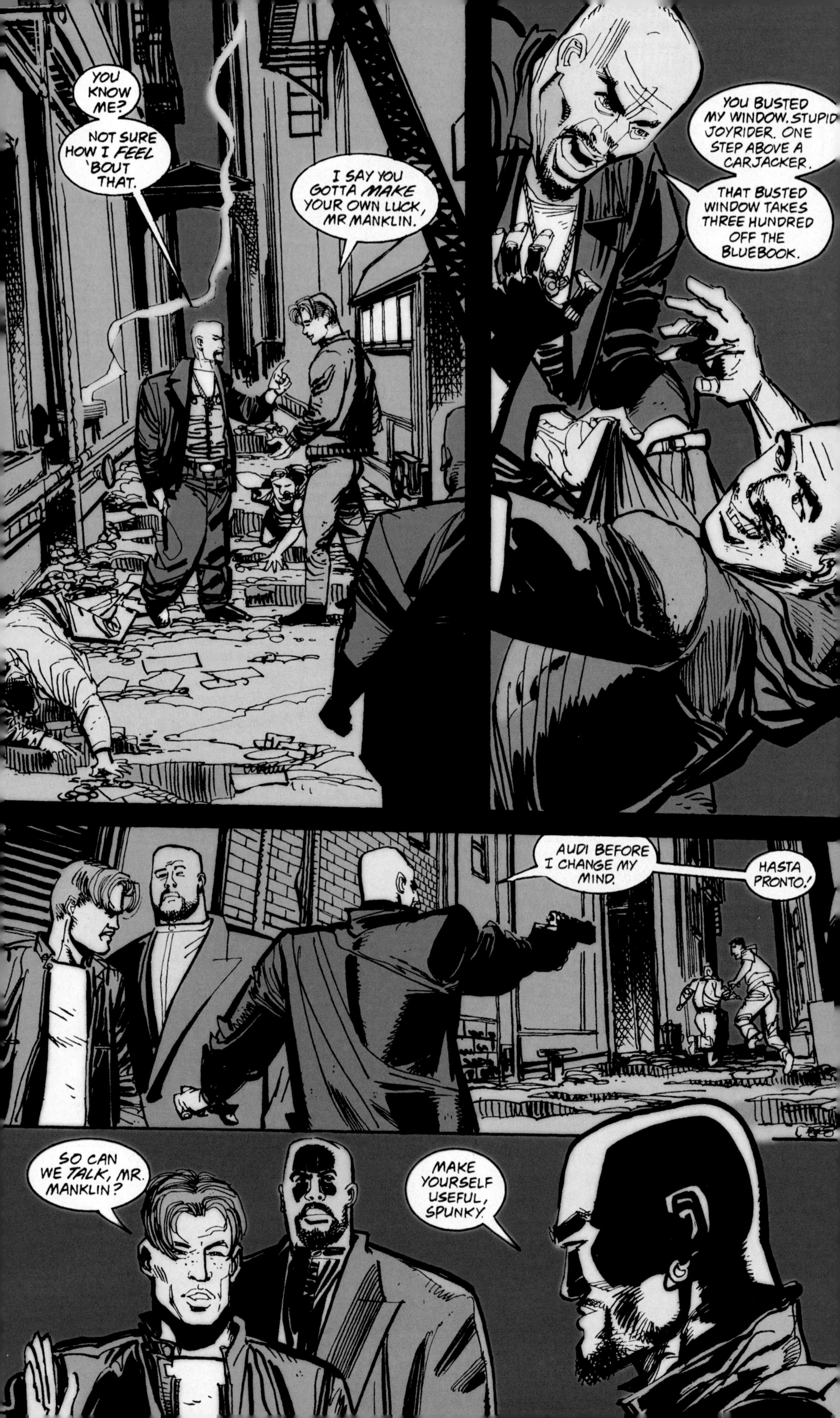
YOU KNOW ME?
NOT SURE HOW I FEEL 'BOUT THAT.
I SAY YOU GOTTA MAKE YOUR OWN LUCK, MR MANKLIN.
YOU BUSTED MY WINDOW. STUPID JOYRIDER. ONE STEP ABOVE A CARJACKER.
THAT BUSTED WINDOW TAKES THREE HUNDRED OFF THE BLUEBOOK.
AUDI BEFORE I CHANGE MY MIND.
HASTA PRONTO!
SO CAN WE TALK, MR. MANKLIN?
MAKE YOURSELF USEFUL, SPUNKY.

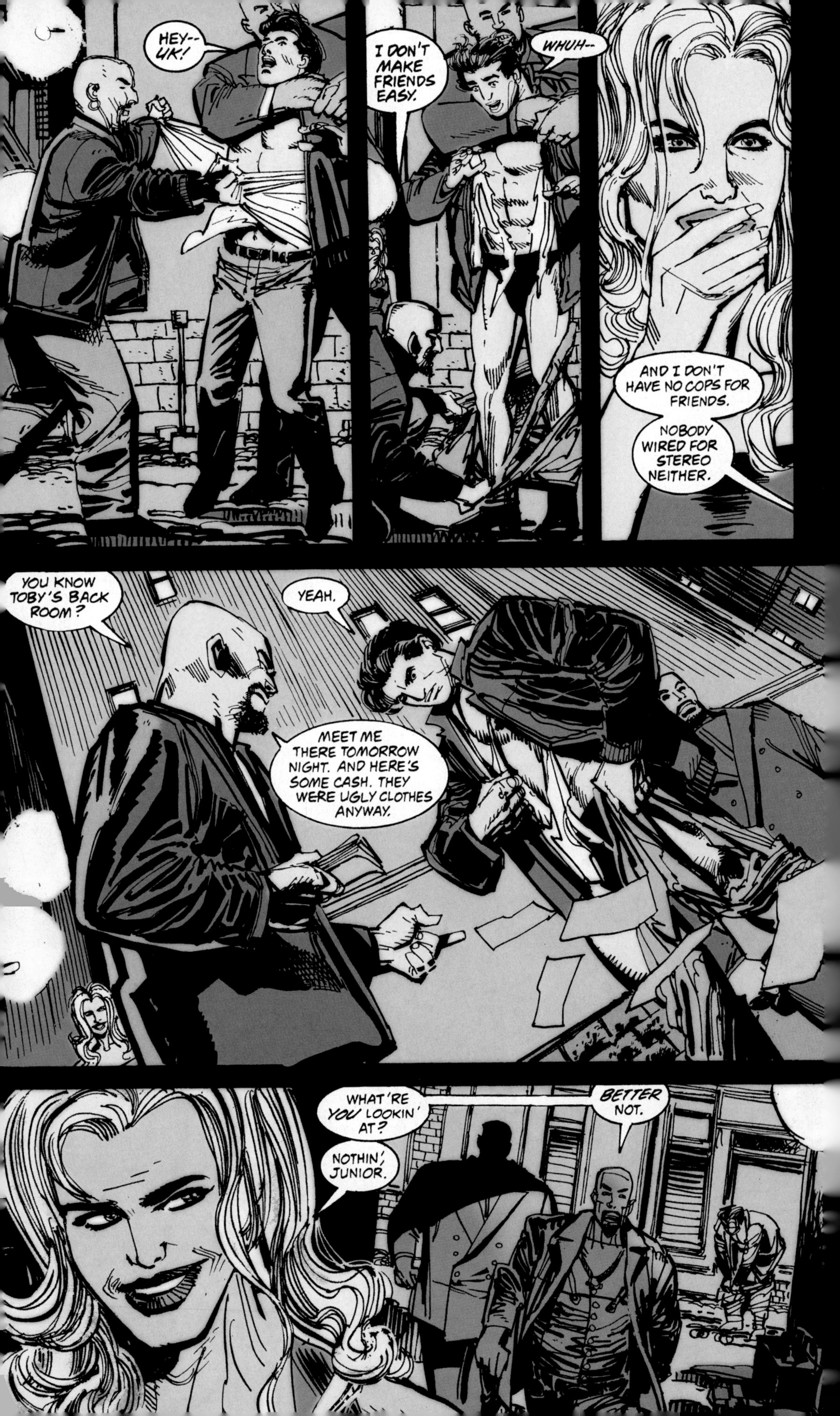
HEY--
UK!
I DON'T MAKE FRIENDS EASY.
WHUH--
AND I DON'T HAVE NO COPS FOR FRIENDS.
NOBODY WIRED FOR STEREO NEITHER.
YOU KNOW TOBY'S BACK ROOM?
YEAH.
MEET ME THERE TOMORROW NIGHT. AND HERE'S SOME CASH. THEY WERE UGLY CLOTHES ANYWAY.
WHAT'RE YOU LOOKIN' AT?
NOTHIN', JUNIOR.
BETTER NOT.

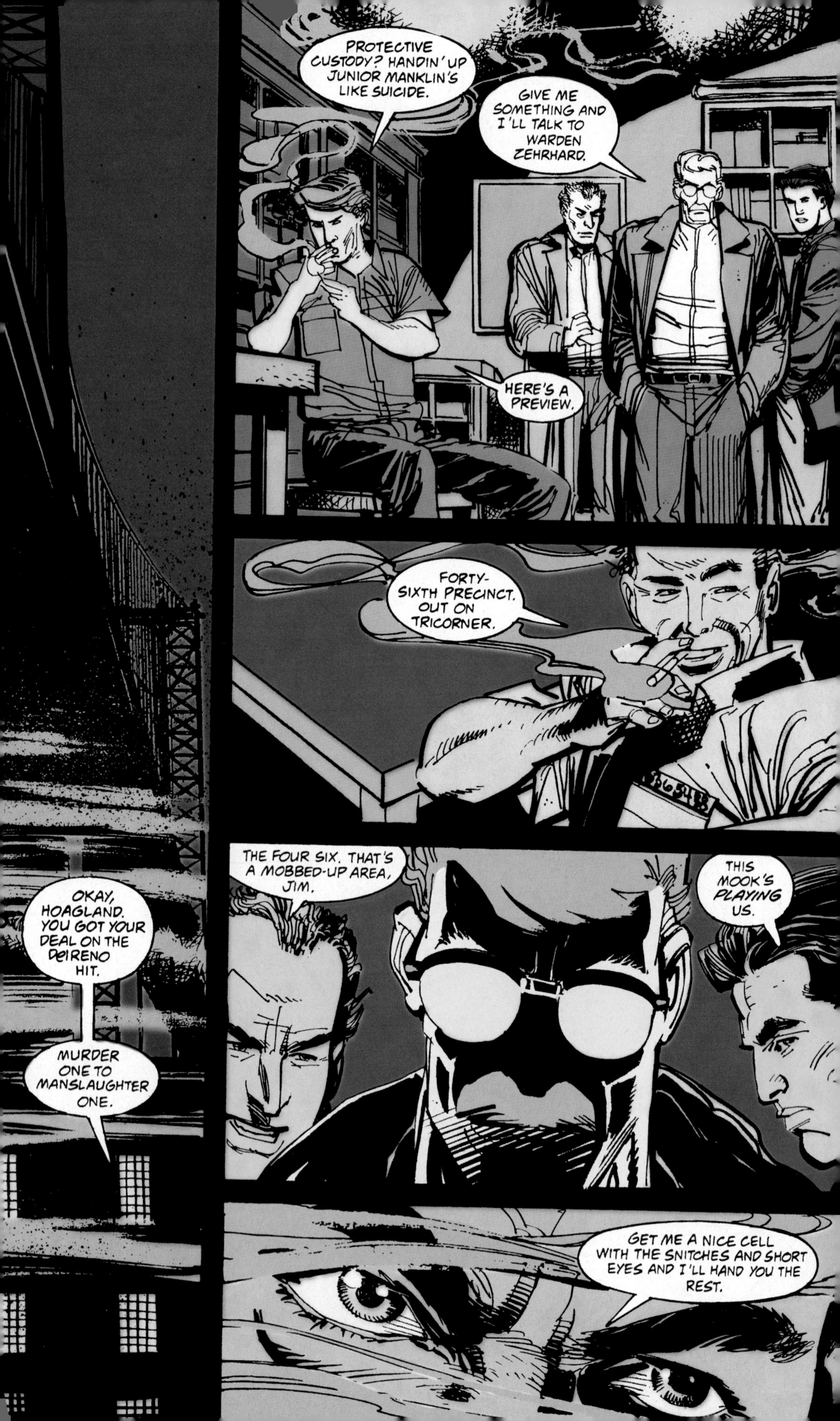
PROTECTIVE CUSTODY? HANDIN' UP JUNIOR MANKLIN'S LIKE SUICIDE.
GIVE ME SOMETHING AND I'LL TALK TO WARDEN ZEHRHARD.
HERE'S A PREVIEW.
FORTY-SIXTH PRECINCT. OUT ON TRICORNER.
OKAY, HOAGLAND. YOU GOT YOUR DEAL ON THE DEIRENO HIT.
MURDER ONE TO MANSLAUGHTER ONE.
THE FOUR SIX. THAT'S A MOBBED-UP AREA, JIM.
THIS MOOK'S PLAYING US.
GET ME A NICE CELL WITH THE SNITCHES AND SHORT EYES AND I'LL HAND YOU THE REST.

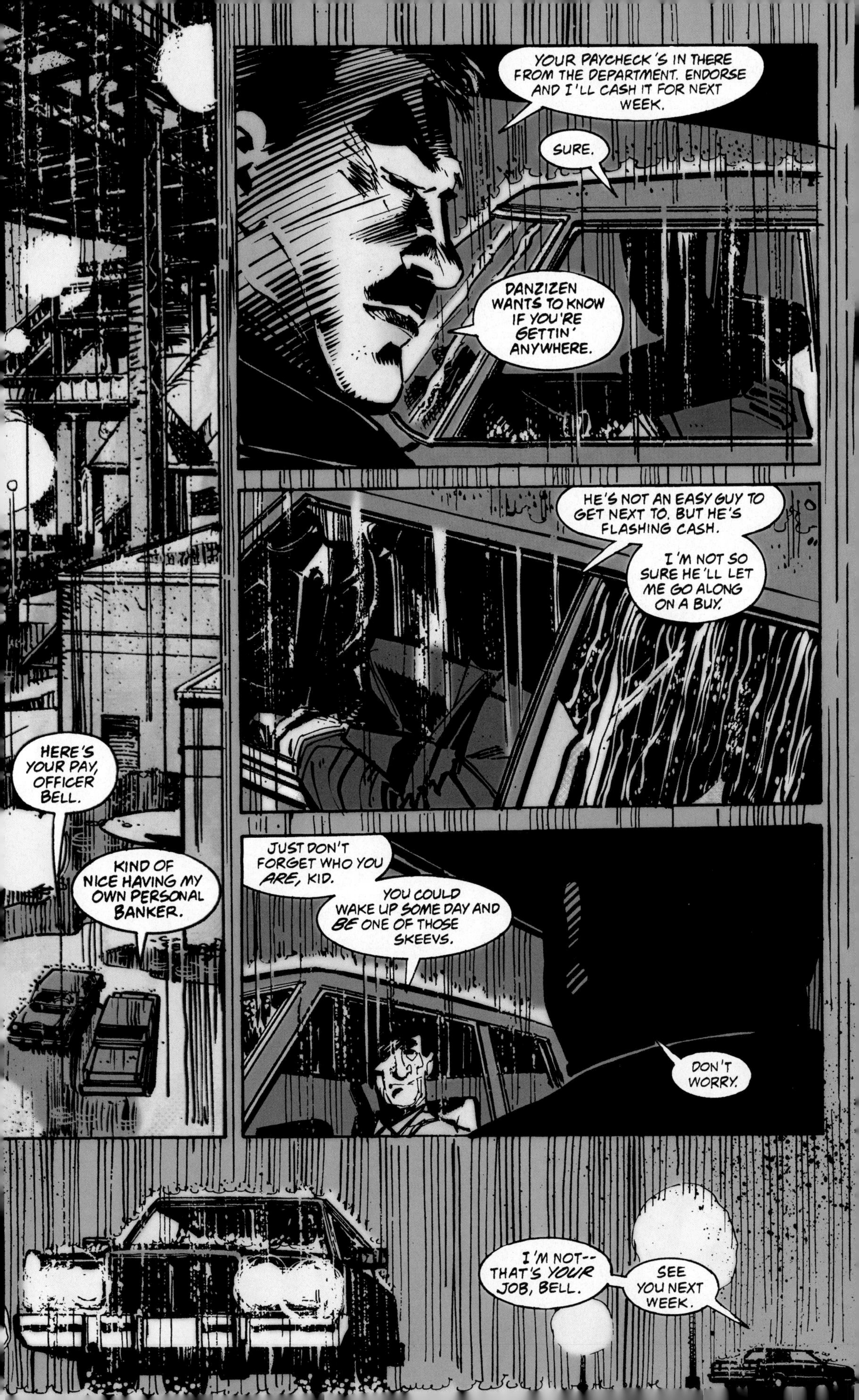
YOUR PAYCHECK'S IN THERE FROM THE DEPARTMENT. ENDORSE AND I'LL CASH IT FOR NEXT WEEK.
SURE.
DANZIZEN WANTS TO KNOW IF YOU'RE GETTIN' ANYWHERE.
HE'S NOT AN EASY GUY TO GET NEXT TO. BUT HE'S FLASHING CASH.
I'M NOT SO SURE HE'LL LET ME GO ALONG ON A BUY.
HERE'S YOUR PAY, OFFICER BELL.
KIND OF NICE HAVING MY OWN PERSONAL BANKER.
JUST DON'T FORGET WHO YOU ARE, KID.
YOU COULD WAKE UP SOME DAY AND BE ONE OF THOSE SKEEVS.
DON'T WORRY.
I'M NOT-- THAT'S YOUR JOB, BELL.
SEE YOU NEXT WEEK.

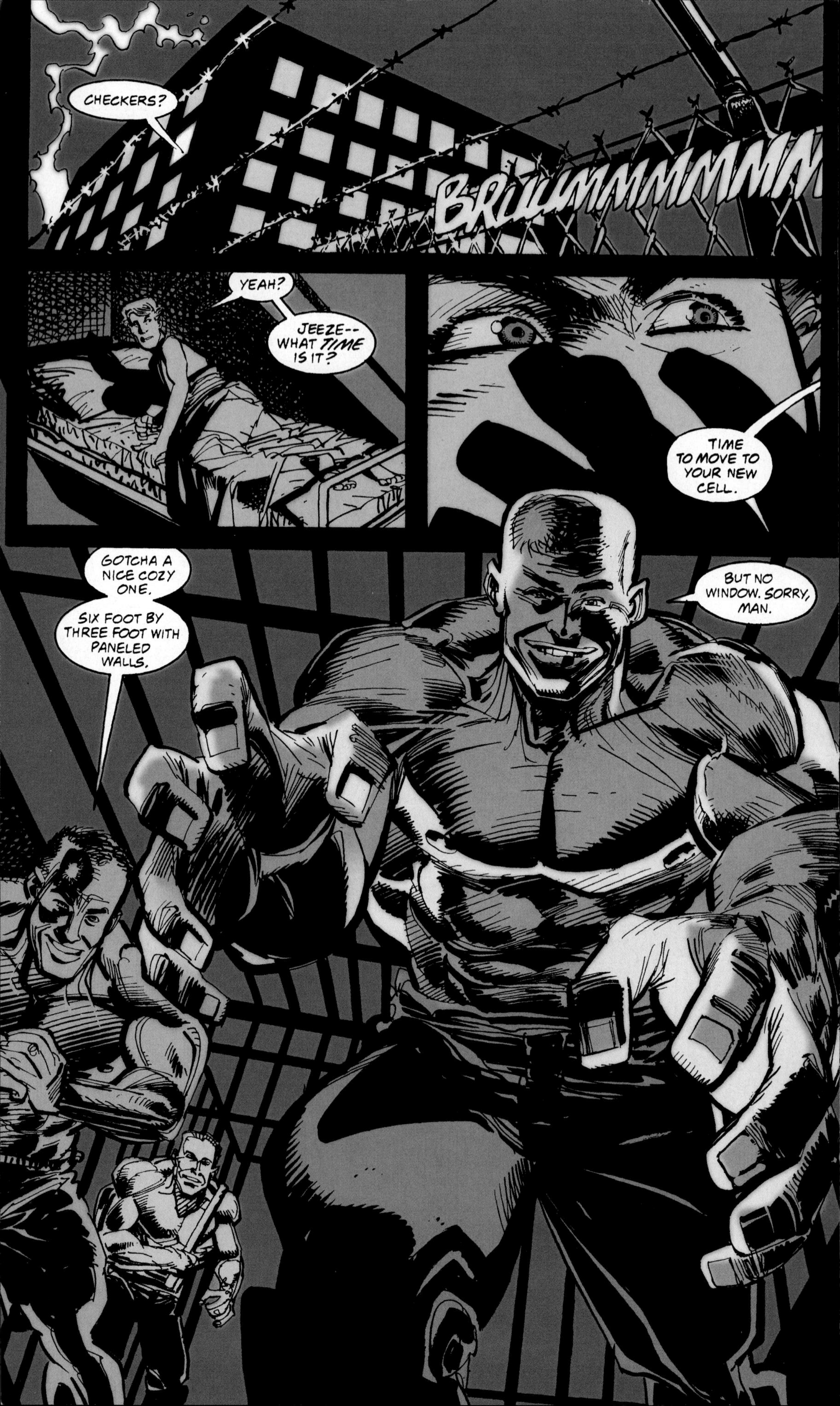
CHECKERS?
BRUUMMMMMMM
YEAH?
JEEZE-- WHAT TIME IS IT?
TIME TO MOVE TO YOUR NEW CELL.
GOTCHA A NICE COZY ONE.
SIX FOOT BY THREE FOOT WITH PANELED WALLS.
BUT NO WINDOW. SORRY, MAN.

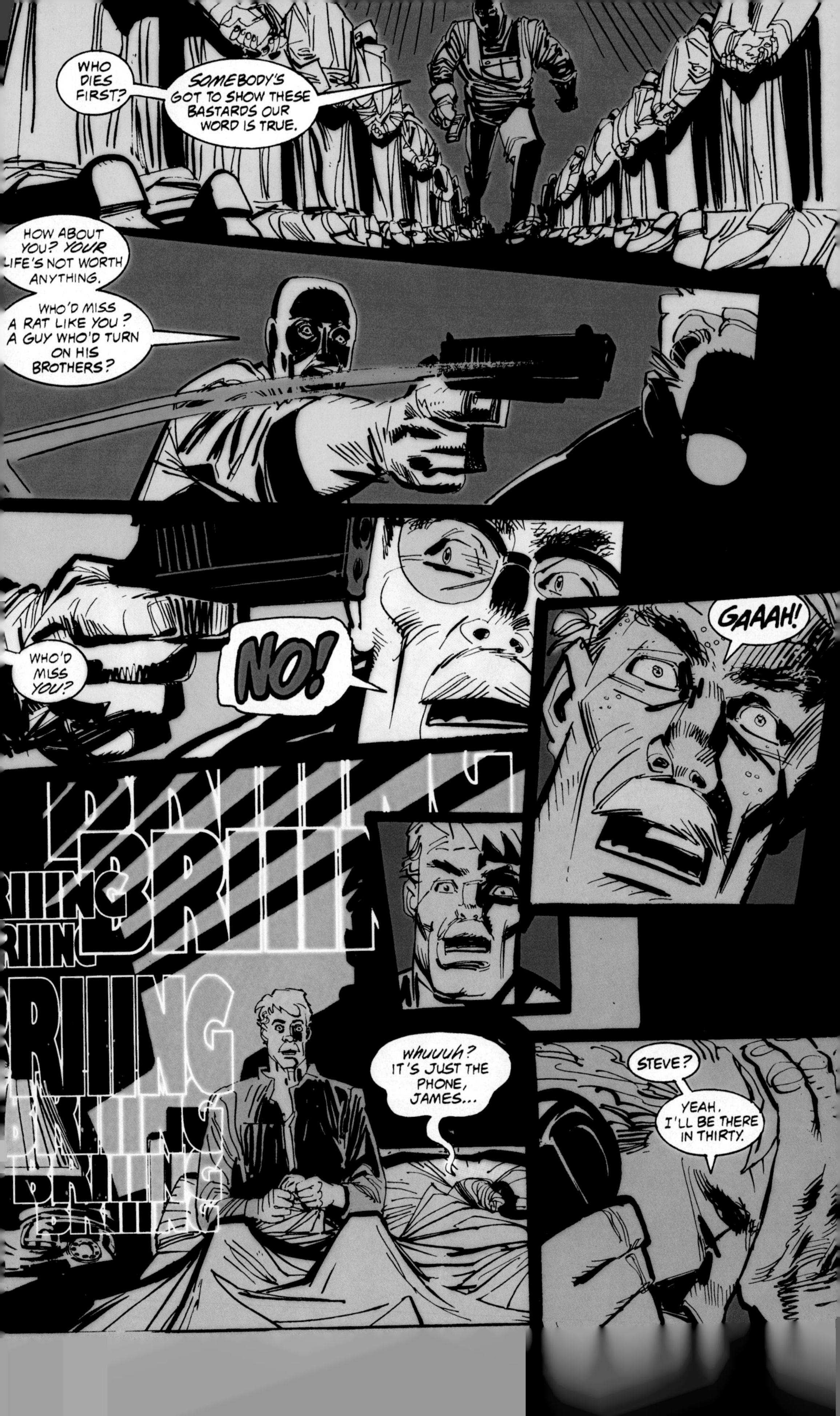

WHO DIES FIRST?
SOMEBODY'S GOT TO SHOW THESE BASTARDS OUR WORD IS TRUE.
HOW ABOUT YOU? YOUR LIFE'S NOT WORTH ANYTHING.
WHO'D MISS A RAT LIKE YOU? A GUY WHO'D TURN ON HIS BROTHERS?
WHO'D MISS YOU?
NO!
GAAAH!
BRIIING
whuuuh? IT'S JUST THE PHONE, JAMES...
STEVE?
YEAH. I'LL BE THERE IN THIRTY.

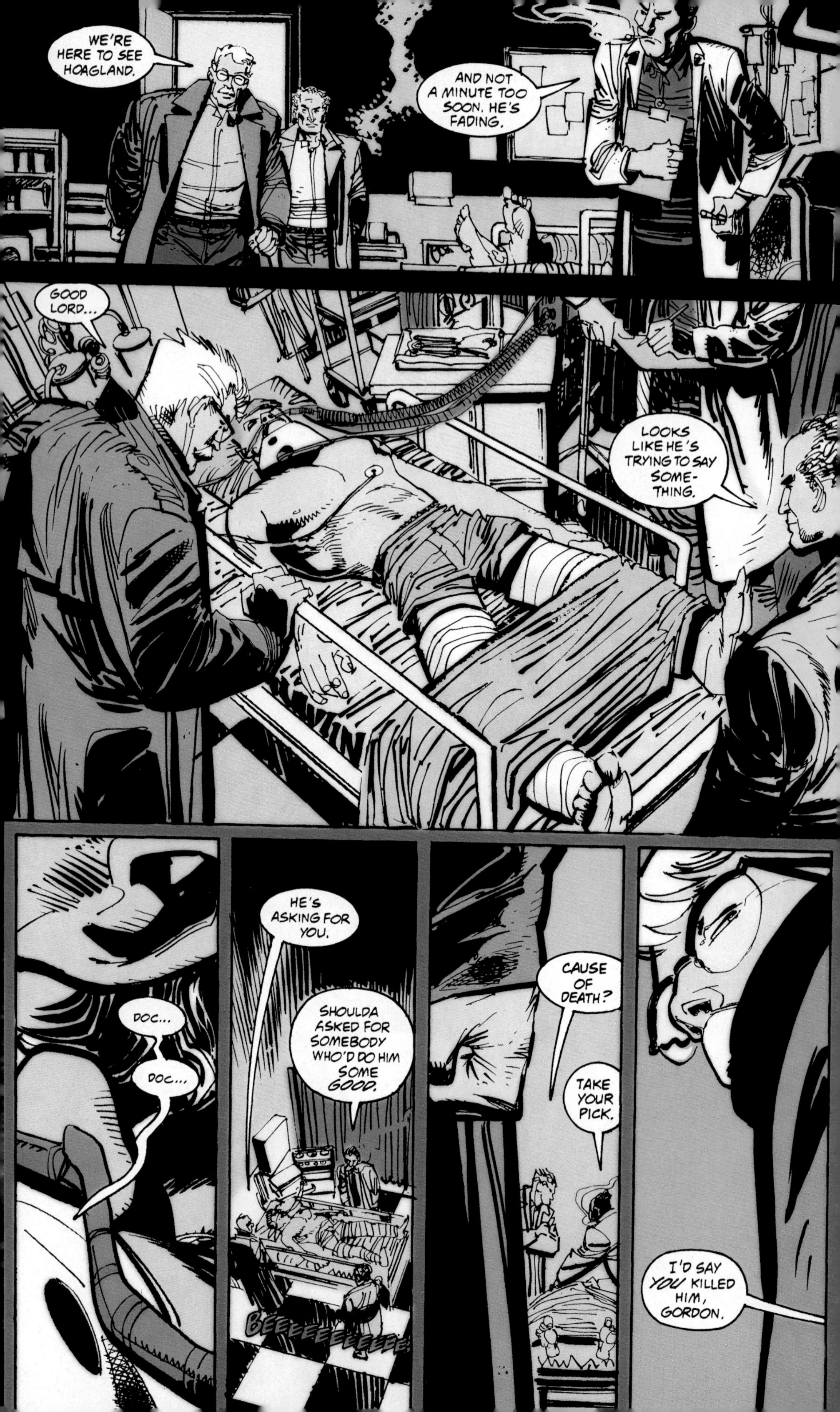
WE'RE HERE TO SEE HOAGLAND.
AND NOT A MINUTE TOO SOON. HE'S FADING.
GOOD LORD...
LOOKS LIKE HE'S TRYING TO SAY SOME-THING.
DOC...
DOC...
HE'S ASKING FOR YOU.
SHOULDA ASKED FOR SOMEBODY WHO'D DO HIM SOME GOOD.
BEEEEEEEEEEEEEE
CAUSE OF DEATH?
TAKE YOUR PICK.
I'D SAY YOU KILLED HIM, GORDON.

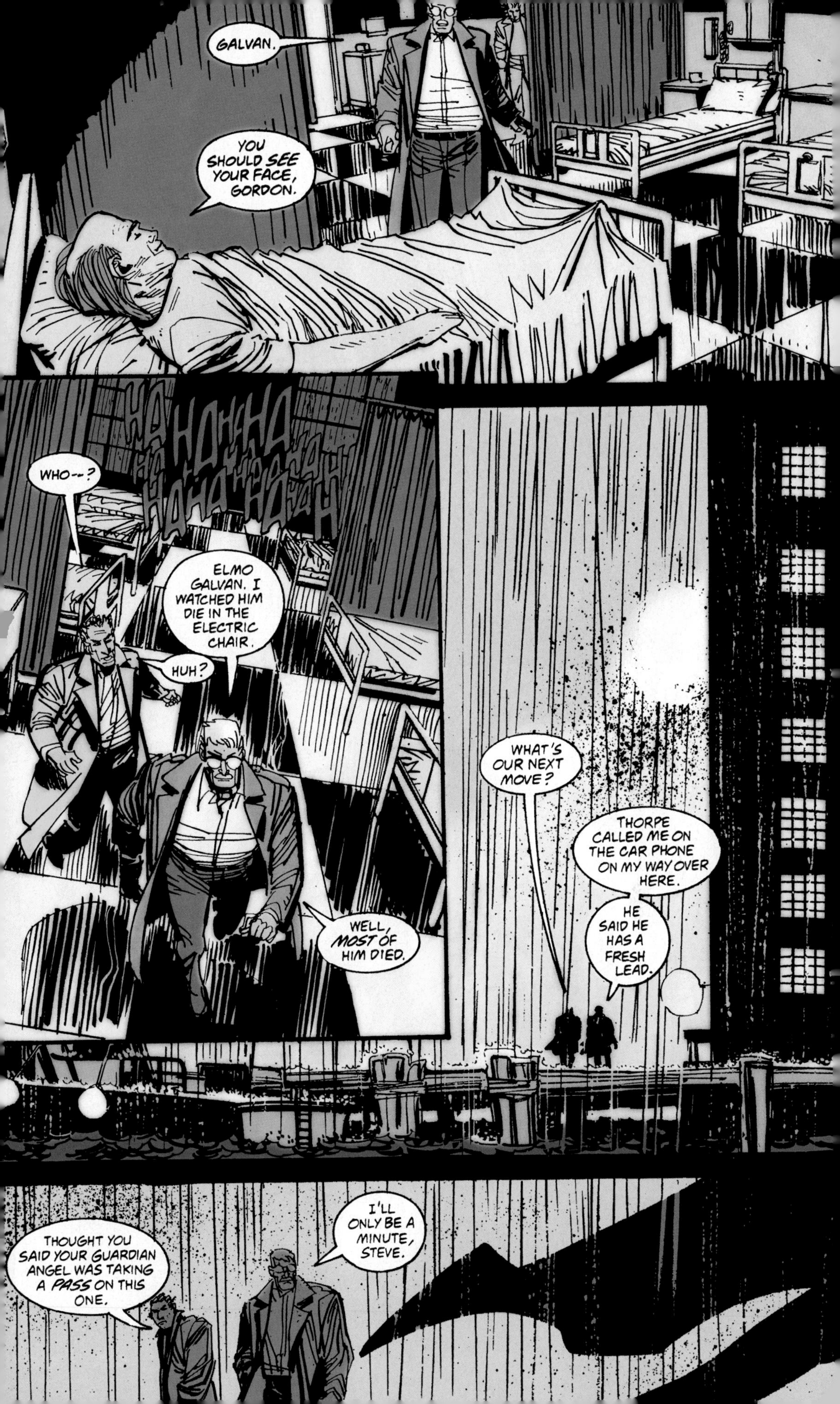
GALVAN.
YOU SHOULD SEE YOUR FACE, GORDON.
HAHAHAHA HAHAHAHAHAH HAHAHAHAHAH
WHO--?
ELMO GALVAN. I WATCHED HIM DIE IN THE ELECTRIC CHAIR.
HUH?
WELL, MOST OF HIM DIED.
WHAT'S OUR NEXT MOVE?
THORPE CALLED ME ON THE CAR PHONE ON MY WAY OVER HERE.
HE SAID HE HAS A FRESH LEAD.
THOUGHT YOU SAID YOUR GUARDIAN ANGEL WAS TAKING A PASS ON THIS ONE.
I'LL ONLY BE A MINUTE, STEVE.

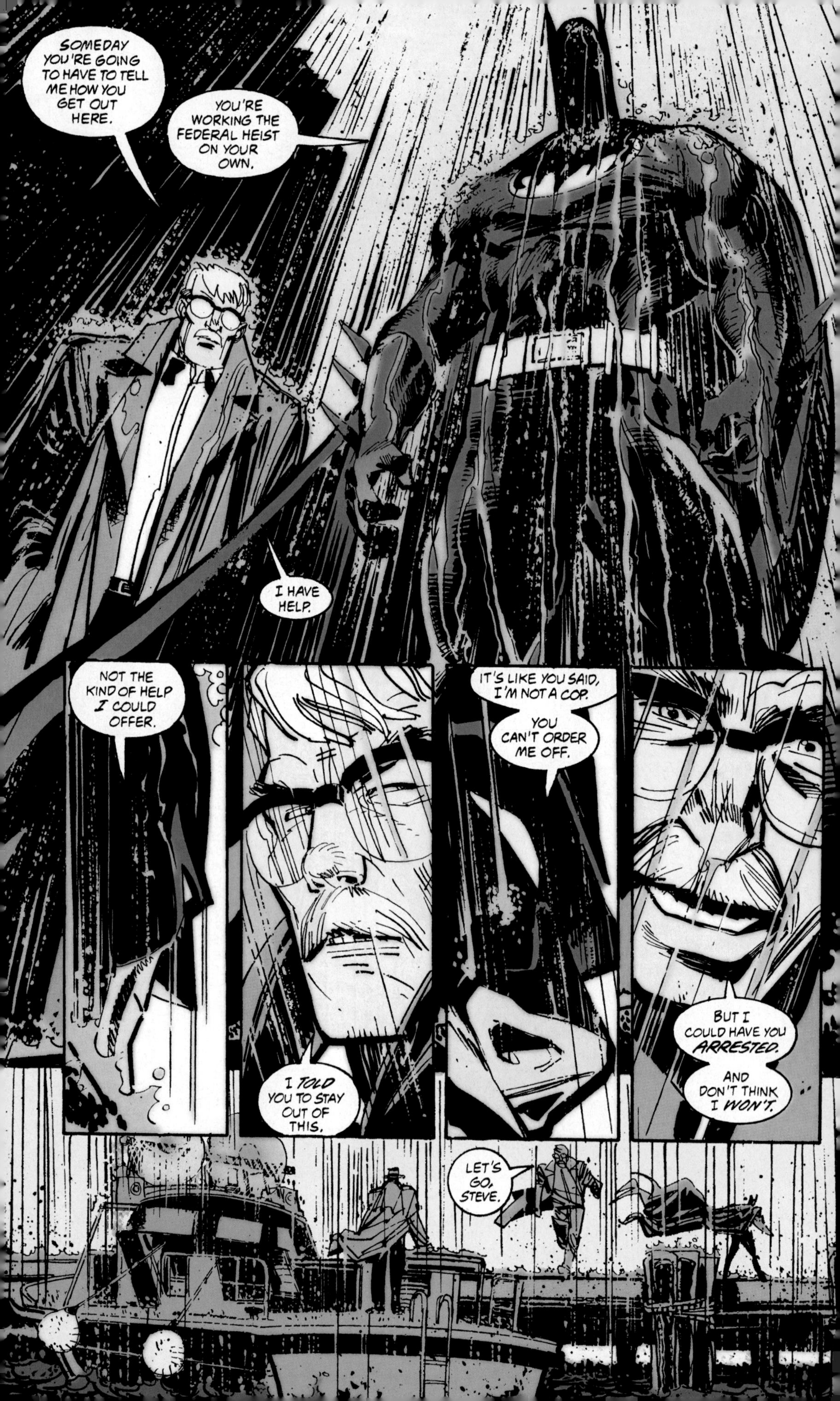
SOMEDAY YOU'RE GOING TO HAVE TO TELL ME HOW YOU GET OUT HERE.
YOU'RE WORKING THE FEDERAL HEIST ON YOUR OWN.
I HAVE HELP.
NOT THE KIND OF HELP I COULD OFFER.
I TOLD YOU TO STAY OUT OF THIS.
IT'S LIKE YOU SAID, I'M NOT A COP.
YOU CAN'T ORDER ME OFF.
BUT I COULD HAVE YOU ARRESTED.
AND DON'T THINK I WON'T.
LET'S GO, STEVE.

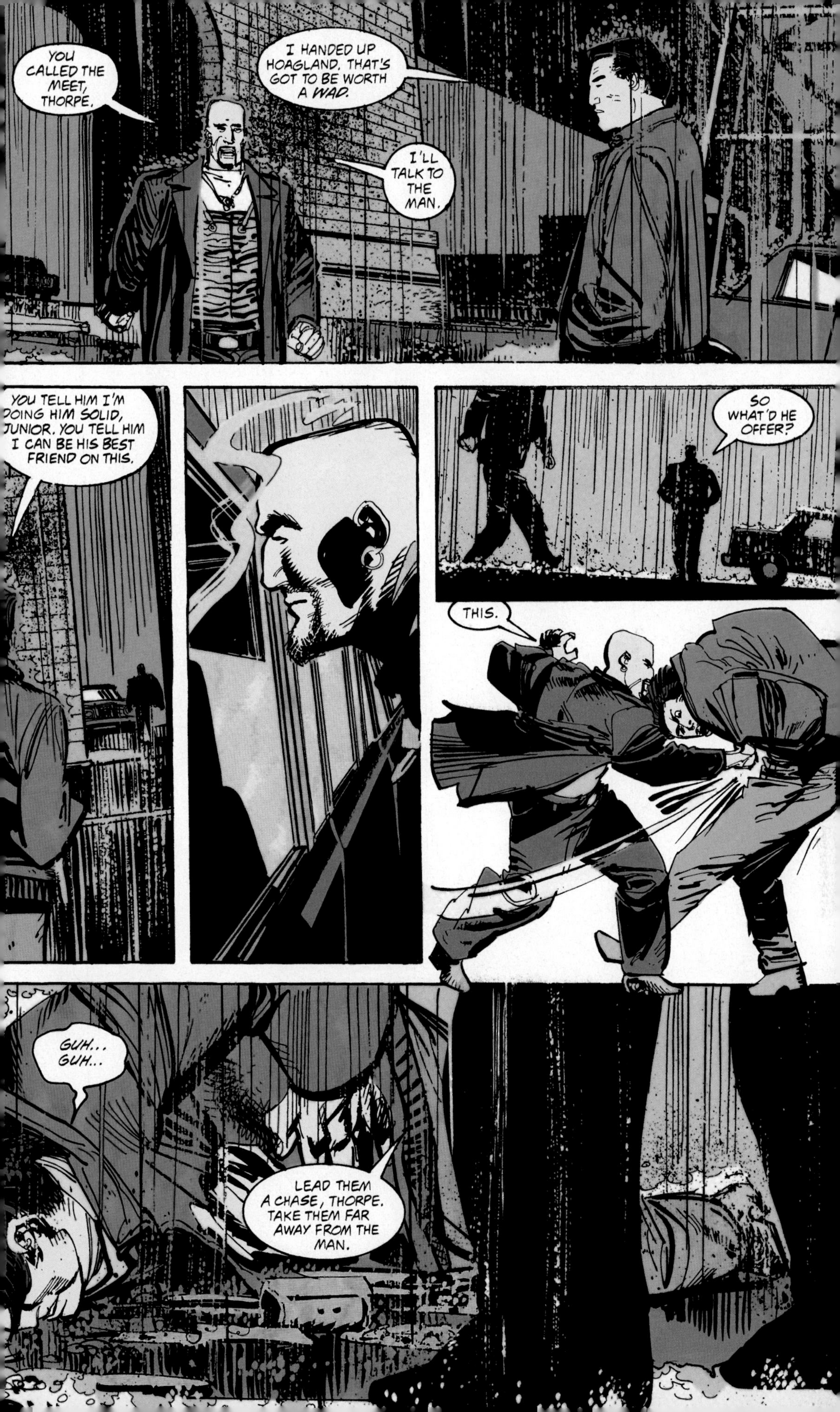
YOU CALLED THE MEET, THORPE.
I HANDED UP HOAGLAND. THAT'S GOT TO BE WORTH A WAD.
I'LL TALK TO THE MAN.
YOU TELL HIM I'M DOING HIM SOLID, JUNIOR. YOU TELL HIM I CAN BE HIS BEST FRIEND ON THIS.
SO WHAT'D HE OFFER?
THIS.
GUH... GUH...
LEAD THEM A CHASE, THORPE. TAKE THEM FAR AWAY FROM THE MAN.

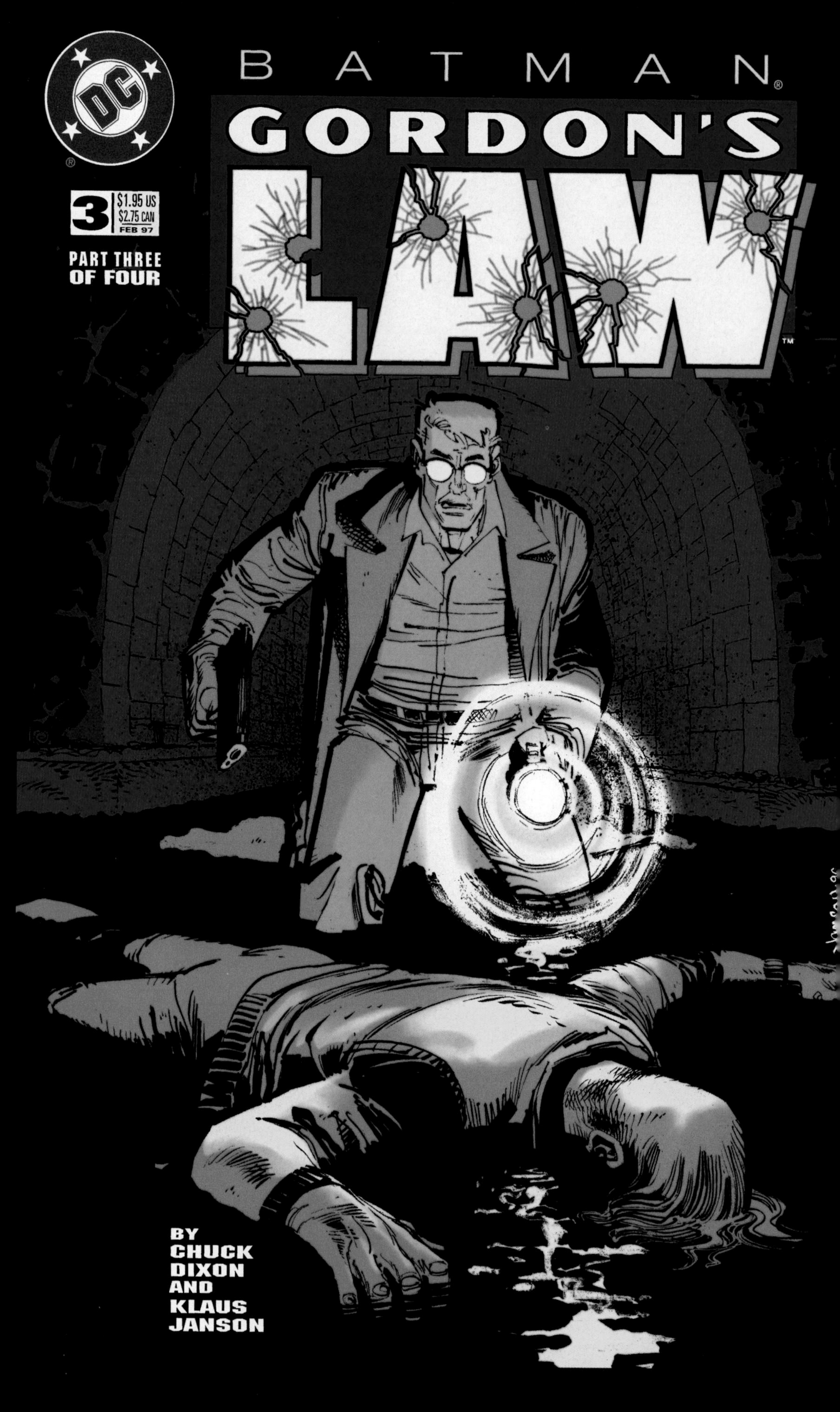
BATMAN®
GORDON'S
LAW™
3
$1.95 US
$2.75 CAN
FEB 97
PART THREE
OF FOUR
BY
CHUCK
DIXON
AND
KLAUS
JANSON

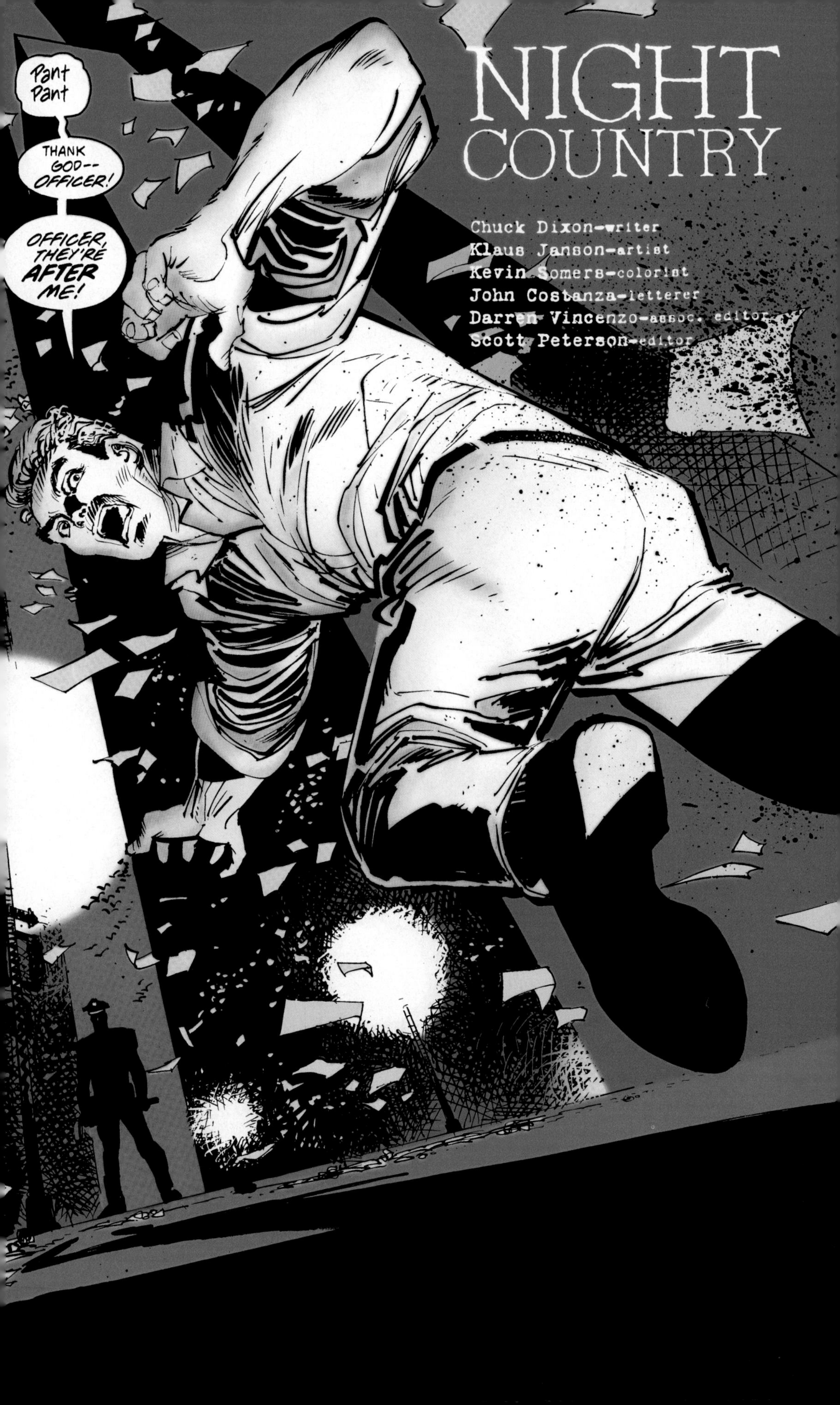
NIGHT COUNTRY
Chuck Dixon-writer
Klaus Janson-artist
Kevin Somers-colorist
John Costanza-letterer
Darren Vincenzo-assoc. editor
Scott Peterson-editor
Pant Pant
THANK GOD-- OFFICER!
OFFICER, THEY'RE AFTER ME!

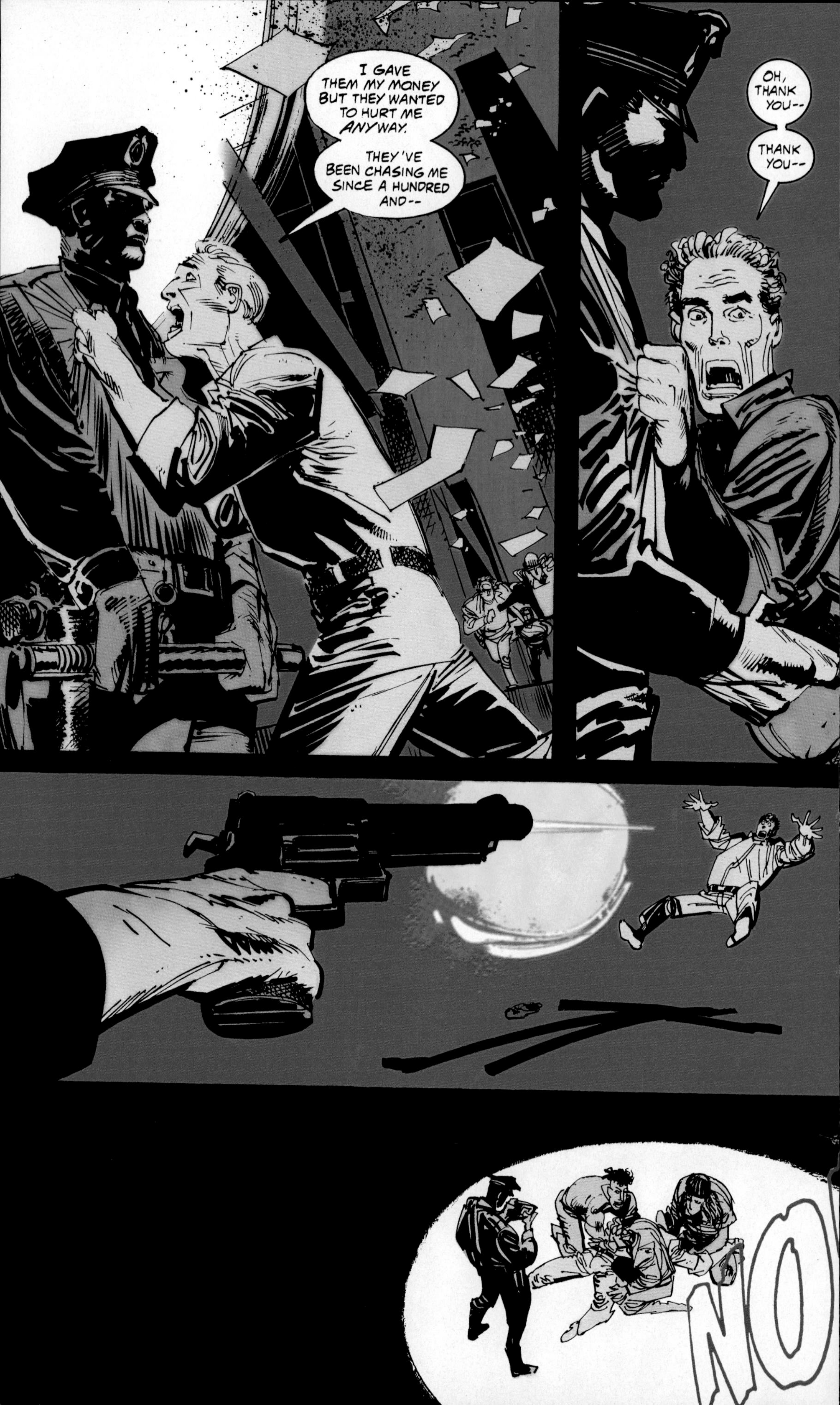
I GAVE THEM MY MONEY BUT THEY WANTED TO HURT ME ANYWAY.
THEY'VE BEEN CHASING ME SINCE A HUNDRED AND--
OH, THANK YOU--
THANK YOU--
NO

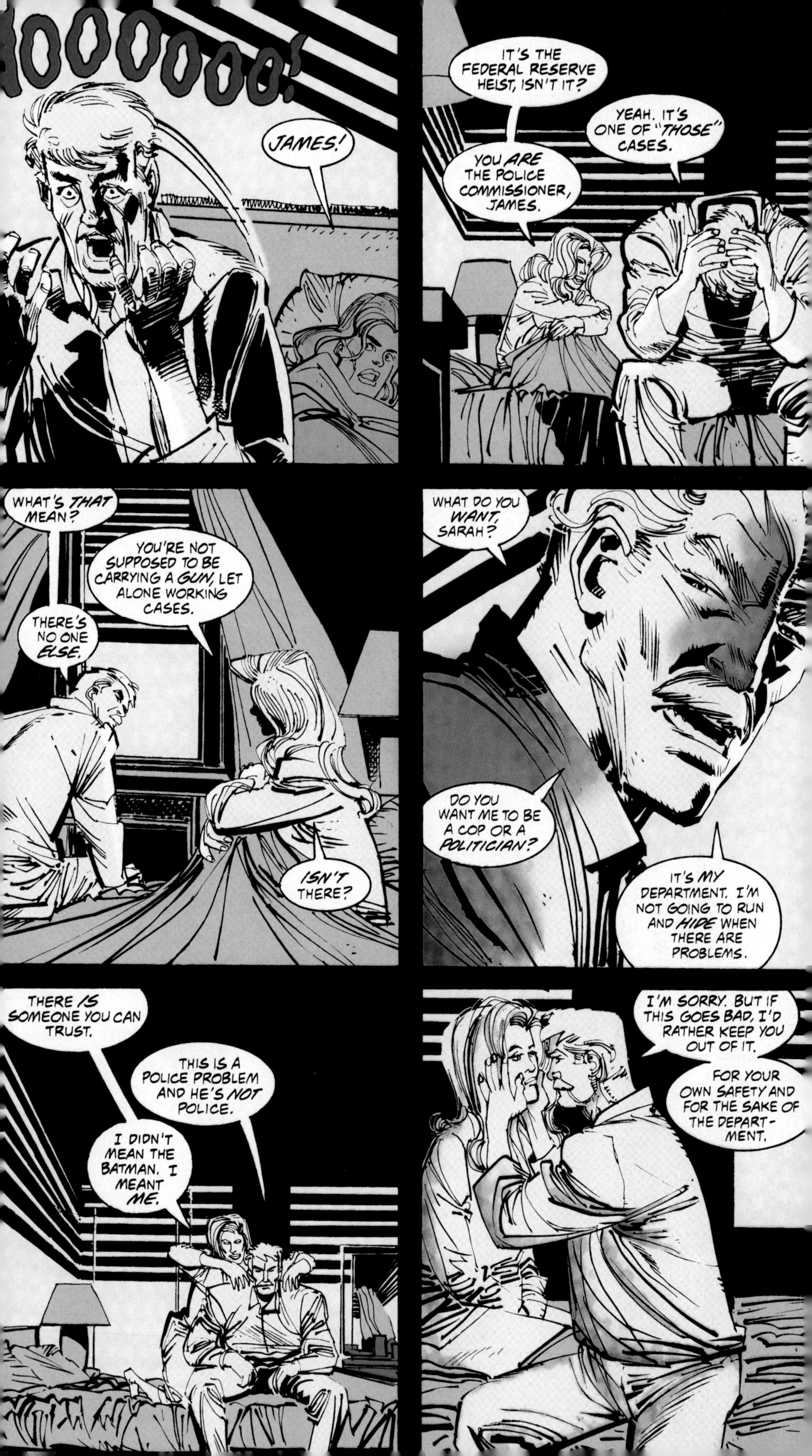
OOOOOOO!
JAMES!
IT'S THE FEDERAL RESERVE HEIST, ISN'T IT?
YOU ARE THE POLICE COMMISSIONER, JAMES.
YEAH. IT'S ONE OF "THOSE" CASES.
WHAT'S THAT MEAN?
YOU'RE NOT SUPPOSED TO BE CARRYING A GUN, LET ALONE WORKING CASES.
THERE'S NO ONE ELSE.
ISN'T THERE?
WHAT DO YOU WANT, SARAH?
DO YOU WANT ME TO BE A COP OR A POLITICIAN?
IT'S MY DEPARTMENT. I'M NOT GOING TO RUN AND HIDE WHEN THERE ARE PROBLEMS.
THERE IS SOMEONE YOU CAN TRUST.
THIS IS A POLICE PROBLEM AND HE'S NOT POLICE.
I DIDN'T MEAN THE BATMAN. I MEANT ME.
I'M SORRY. BUT IF THIS GOES BAD, I'D RATHER KEEP YOU OUT OF IT.
FOR YOUR OWN SAFETY AND FOR THE SAKE OF THE DEPART-MENT.

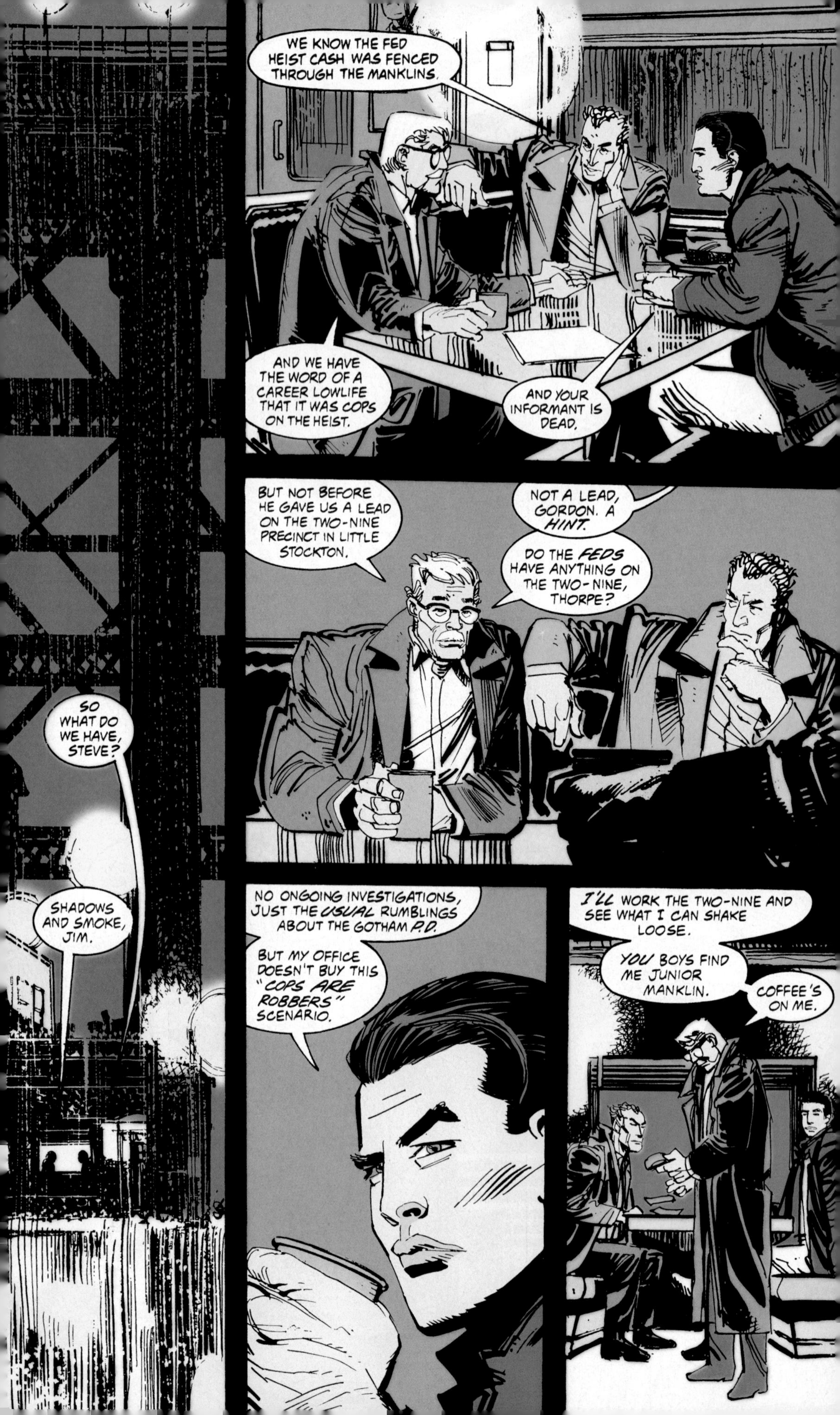
WE KNOW THE FED HEIST CASH WAS FENCED THROUGH THE MANKLINS.
AND WE HAVE THE WORD OF A CAREER LOWLIFE THAT IT WAS COPS ON THE HEIST.
AND YOUR INFORMANT IS DEAD.
BUT NOT BEFORE HE GAVE US A LEAD ON THE TWO-NINE PRECINCT IN LITTLE STOCKTON.
NOT A LEAD, GORDON. A HINT.
DO THE FEDS HAVE ANYTHING ON THE TWO-NINE, THORPE?
SO WHAT DO WE HAVE, STEVE?
SHADOWS AND SMOKE, JIM.
NO ONGOING INVESTIGATIONS, JUST THE USUAL RUMBLINGS ABOUT THE GOTHAM P.D.
BUT MY OFFICE DOESN'T BUY THIS "COPS ARE ROBBERS" SCENARIO.
I'LL WORK THE TWO-NINE AND SEE WHAT I CAN SHAKE LOOSE.
YOU BOYS FIND ME JUNIOR MANKLIN.
COFFEE'S ON ME.

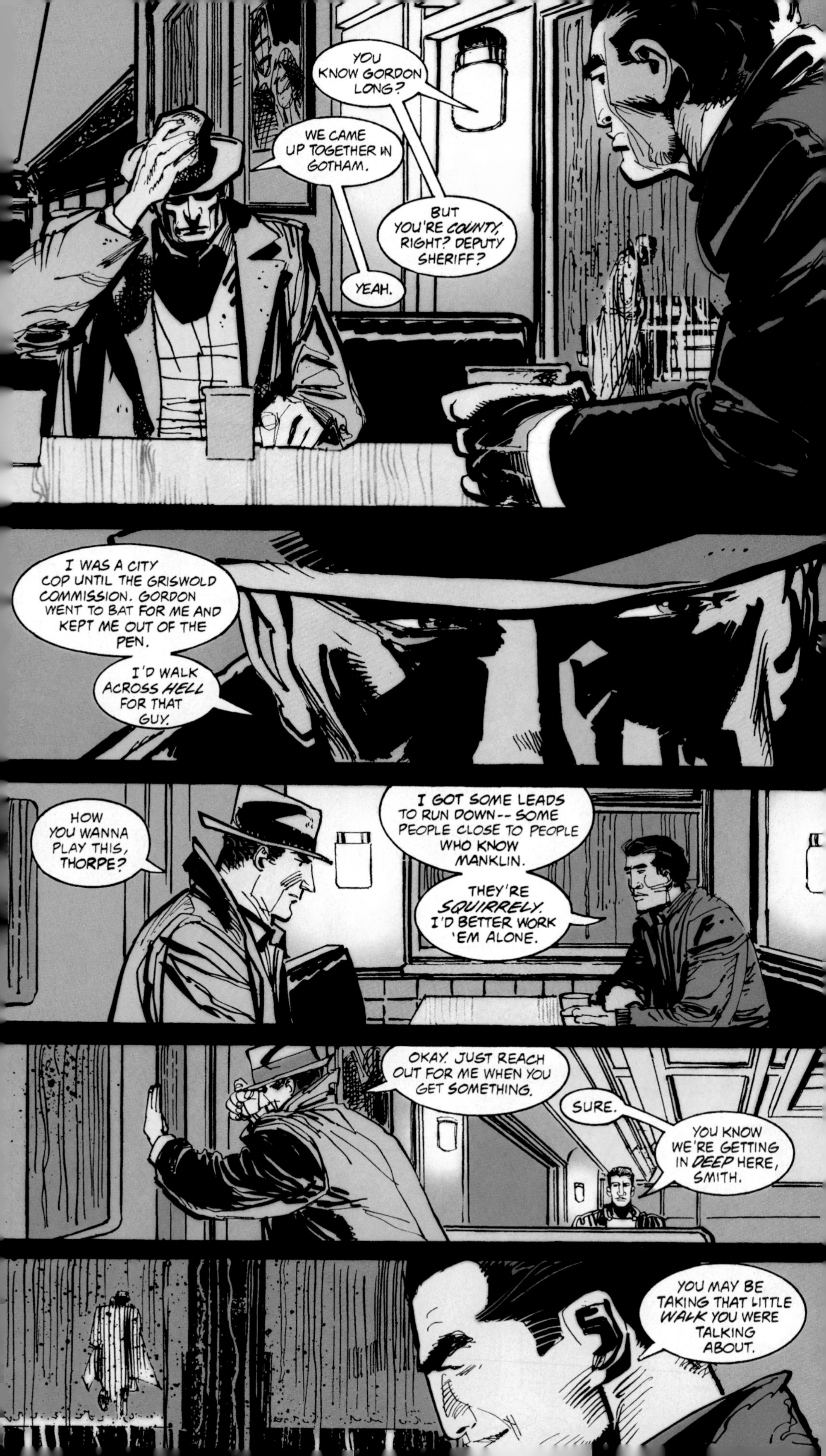
YOU KNOW GORDON LONG?
WE CAME UP TOGETHER IN GOTHAM.
BUT YOU'RE *COUNTY*, RIGHT? DEPUTY SHERIFF?
YEAH.
I WAS A CITY COP UNTIL THE GRISWOLD COMMISSION. GORDON WENT TO BAT FOR ME AND KEPT ME OUT OF THE PEN.
I'D WALK ACROSS *HELL* FOR THAT GUY.
HOW YOU WANNA PLAY THIS, THORPE?
I GOT SOME LEADS TO RUN DOWN-- SOME PEOPLE CLOSE TO PEOPLE WHO KNOW MANKLIN.
THEY'RE *SQUIRRELY*. I'D BETTER WORK 'EM ALONE.
OKAY. JUST REACH OUT FOR ME WHEN YOU GET SOMETHING.
SURE.
YOU KNOW WE'RE GETTING IN *DEEP* HERE, SMITH.
YOU MAY BE TAKING THAT LITTLE *WALK* YOU WERE TALKING ABOUT.

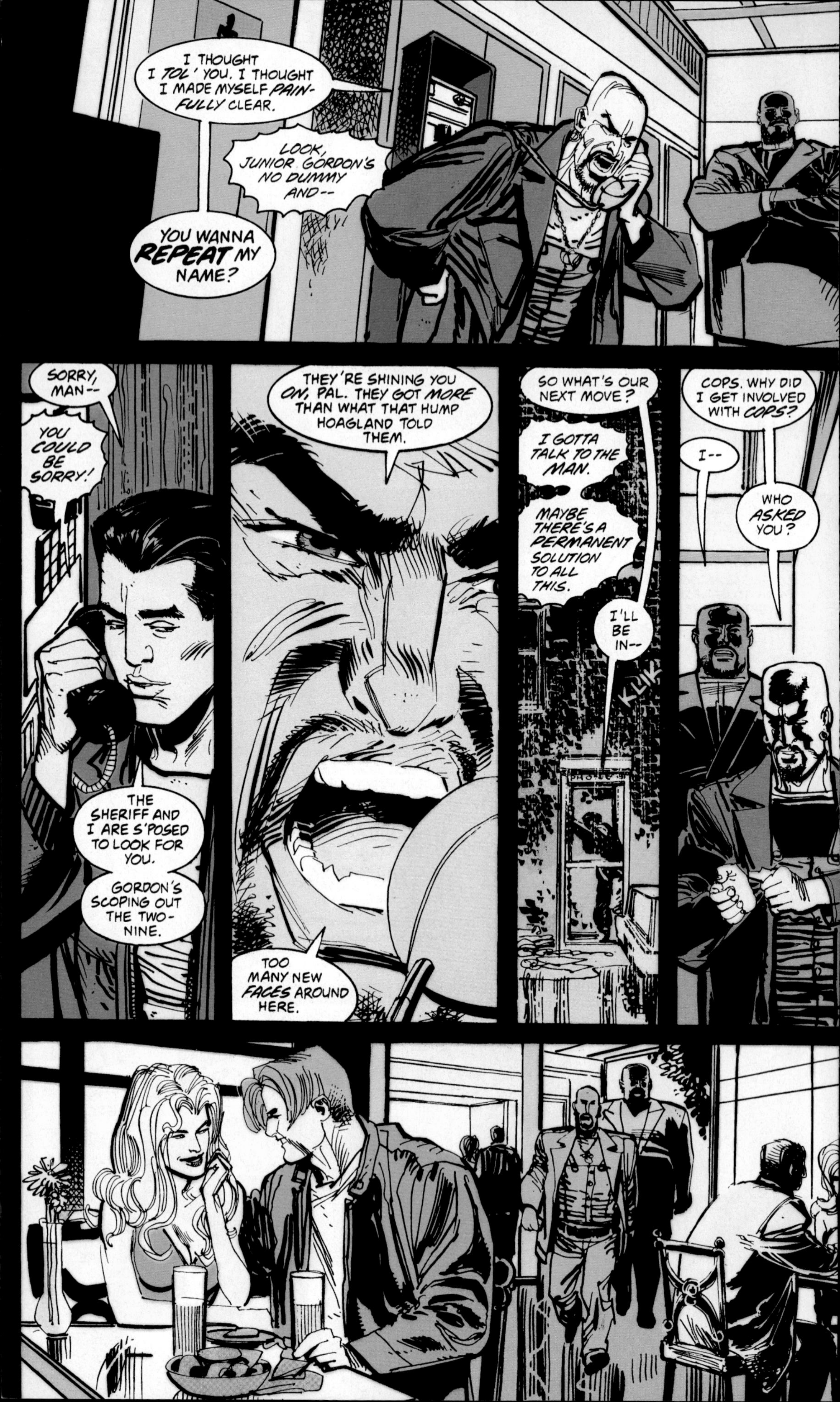
I THOUGHT I TOL' YOU. I THOUGHT I MADE MYSELF PAIN-FULLY CLEAR.
LOOK, JUNIOR GORDON'S NO DUMMY AND--
YOU WANNA REPEAT MY NAME?
SORRY, MAN--
YOU COULD BE SORRY!
THE SHERIFF AND I ARE S'POSED TO LOOK FOR YOU.
GORDON'S SCOPING OUT THE TWO-NINE.
THEY'RE SHINING YOU ON, PAL. THEY GOT MORE THAN WHAT THAT HUMP HOAGLAND TOLD THEM.
TOO MANY NEW FACES AROUND HERE.
SO WHAT'S OUR NEXT MOVE?
I GOTTA TALK TO THE MAN.
MAYBE THERE'S A PERMANENT SOLUTION TO ALL THIS.
I'LL BE IN--
KLIK
COPS. WHY DID I GET INVOLVED WITH COPS?
I--
WHO ASKED YOU?

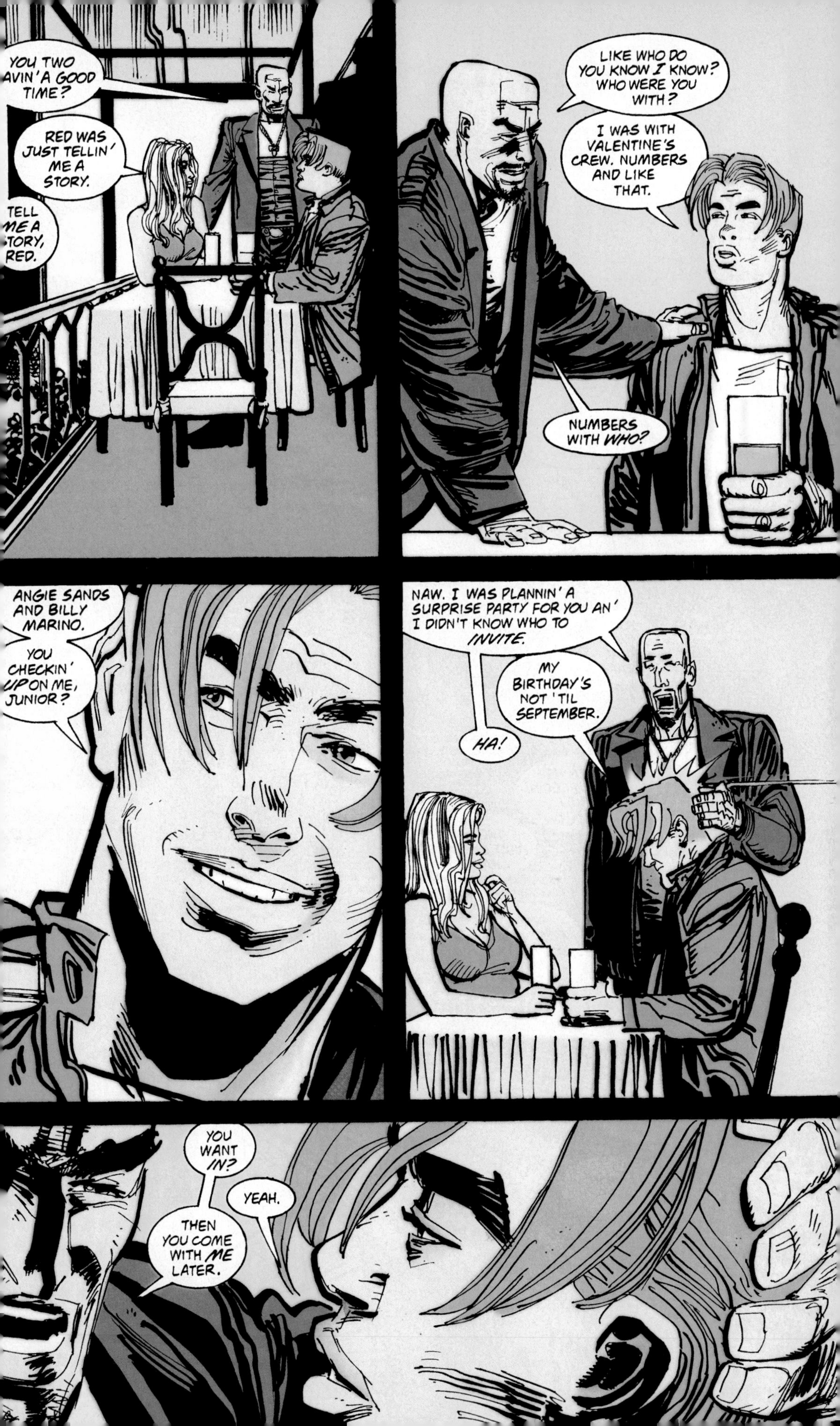
YOU TWO
AVIN' A GOOD TIME?
RED WAS JUST TELLIN' ME A STORY.
TELL ME A
TORY, RED.
LIKE WHO DO YOU KNOW I KNOW? WHO WERE YOU WITH?
I WAS WITH VALENTINE'S CREW. NUMBERS AND LIKE THAT.
NUMBERS WITH WHO?
ANGIE SANDS AND BILLY MARINO.
YOU CHECKIN' UP ON ME, JUNIOR?
NAW. I WAS PLANNIN' A SURPRISE PARTY FOR YOU AN' I DIDN'T KNOW WHO TO INVITE.
MY BIRTHDAY'S NOT 'TIL SEPTEMBER.
HA!
YOU WANT IN?
YEAH.
THEN YOU COME WITH ME LATER.

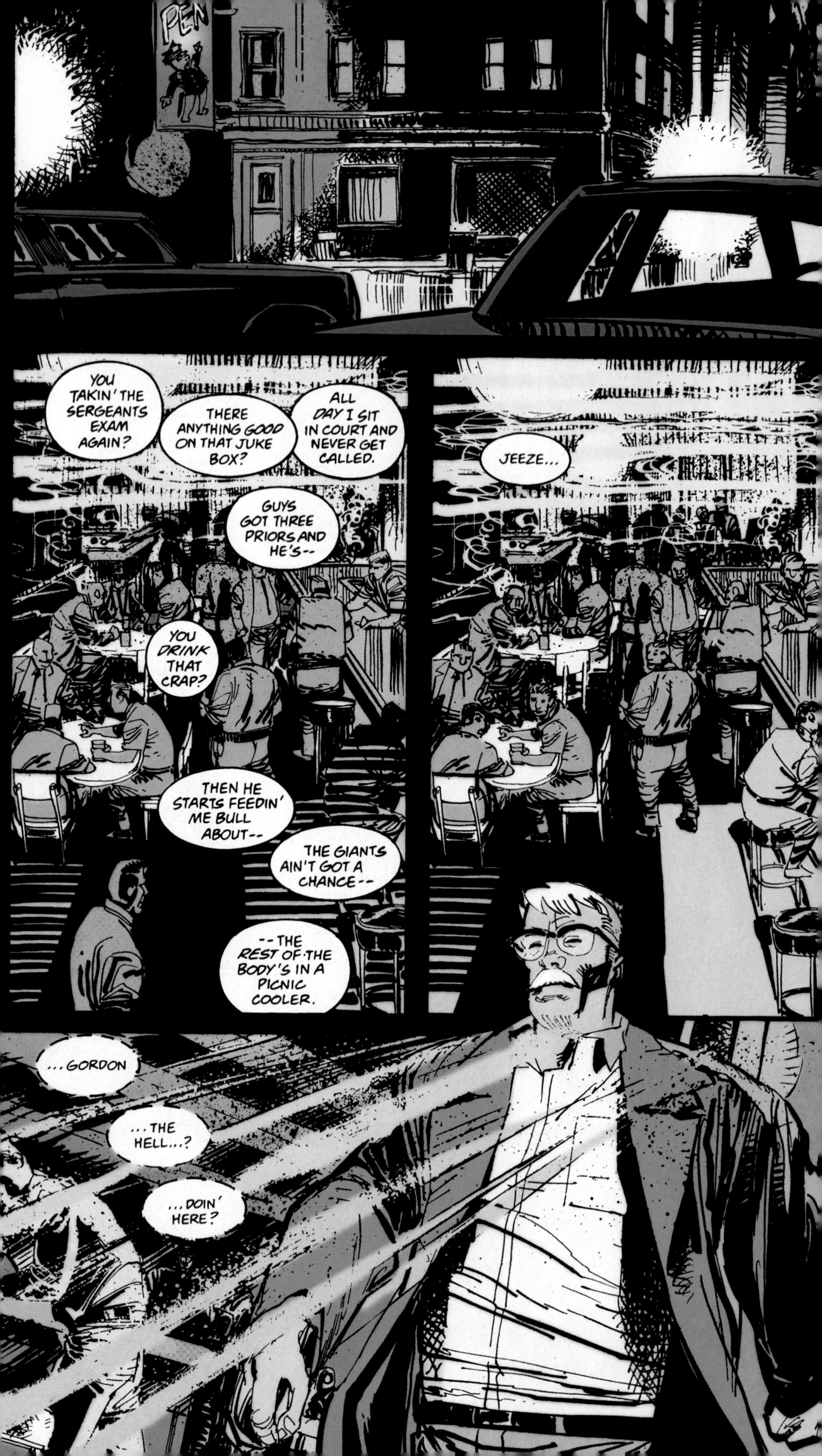
PEN
YOU TAKIN' THE SERGEANTS EXAM AGAIN?
THERE ANYTHING GOOD ON THAT JUKE BOX?
ALL DAY I SIT IN COURT AND NEVER GET CALLED.
GUYS GOT THREE PRIORS AND HE'S--
YOU DRINK THAT CRAP?
THEN HE STARTS FEEDIN' ME BULL ABOUT--
THE GIANTS AIN'T GOT A CHANCE--
--THE REST OF THE BODY'S IN A PICNIC COOLER.
JEEZE...
...GORDON
...THE HELL...?
...DOIN' HERE?

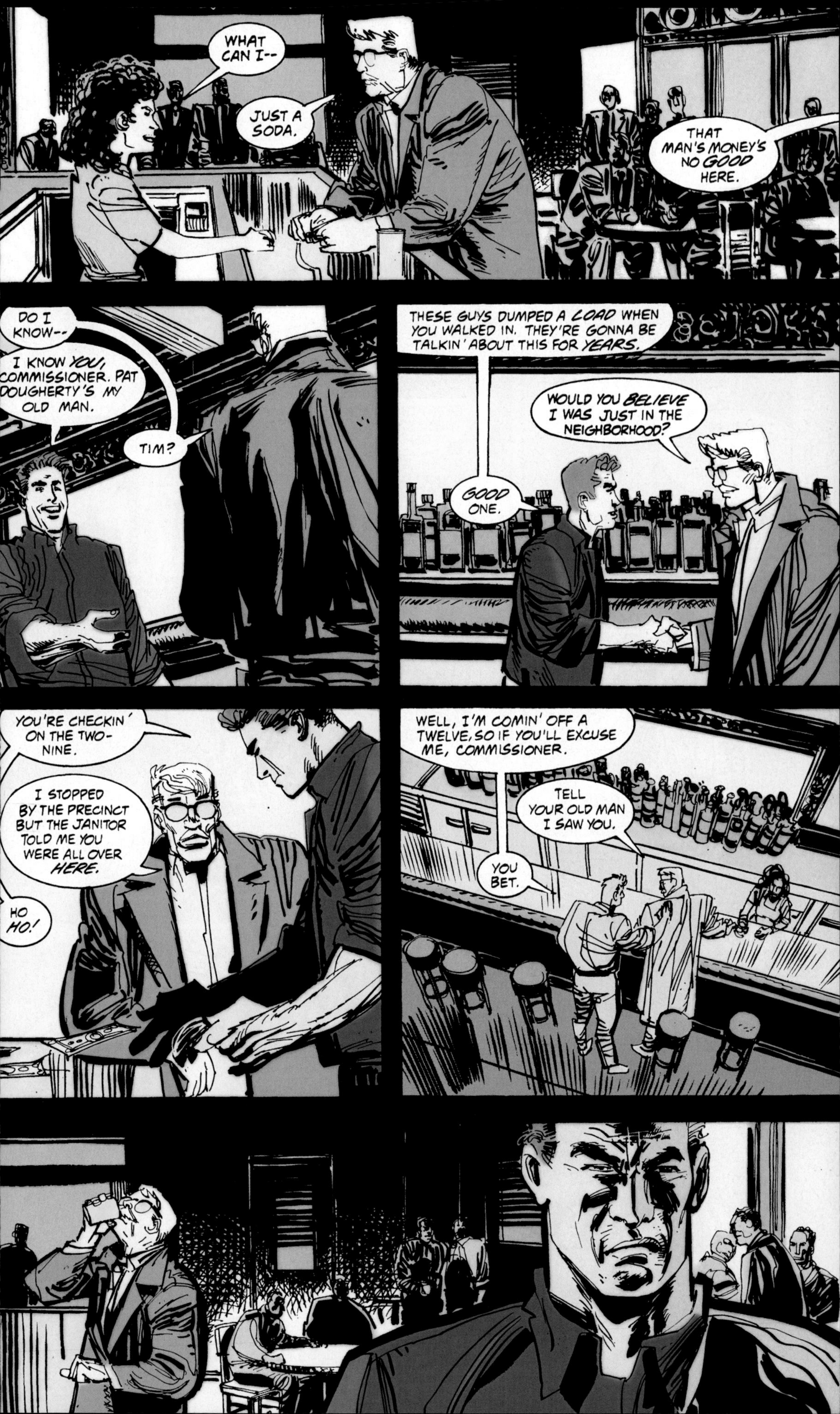
WHAT CAN I--
JUST A SODA.
THAT MAN'S MONEY'S NO GOOD HERE.
DO I KNOW--
I KNOW YOU, COMMISSIONER. PAT DOUGHERTY'S MY OLD MAN.
TIM?
THESE GUYS DUMPED A LOAD WHEN YOU WALKED IN. THEY'RE GONNA BE TALKIN' ABOUT THIS FOR YEARS.
WOULD YOU BELIEVE I WAS JUST IN THE NEIGHBORHOOD?
GOOD ONE.
YOU'RE CHECKIN' ON THE TWO-NINE.
I STOPPED BY THE PRECINCT BUT THE JANITOR TOLD ME YOU WERE ALL OVER HERE.
HO HO!
WELL, I'M COMIN' OFF A TWELVE, SO IF YOU'LL EXCUSE ME, COMMISSIONER.
TELL YOUR OLD MAN I SAW YOU.
YOU BET.

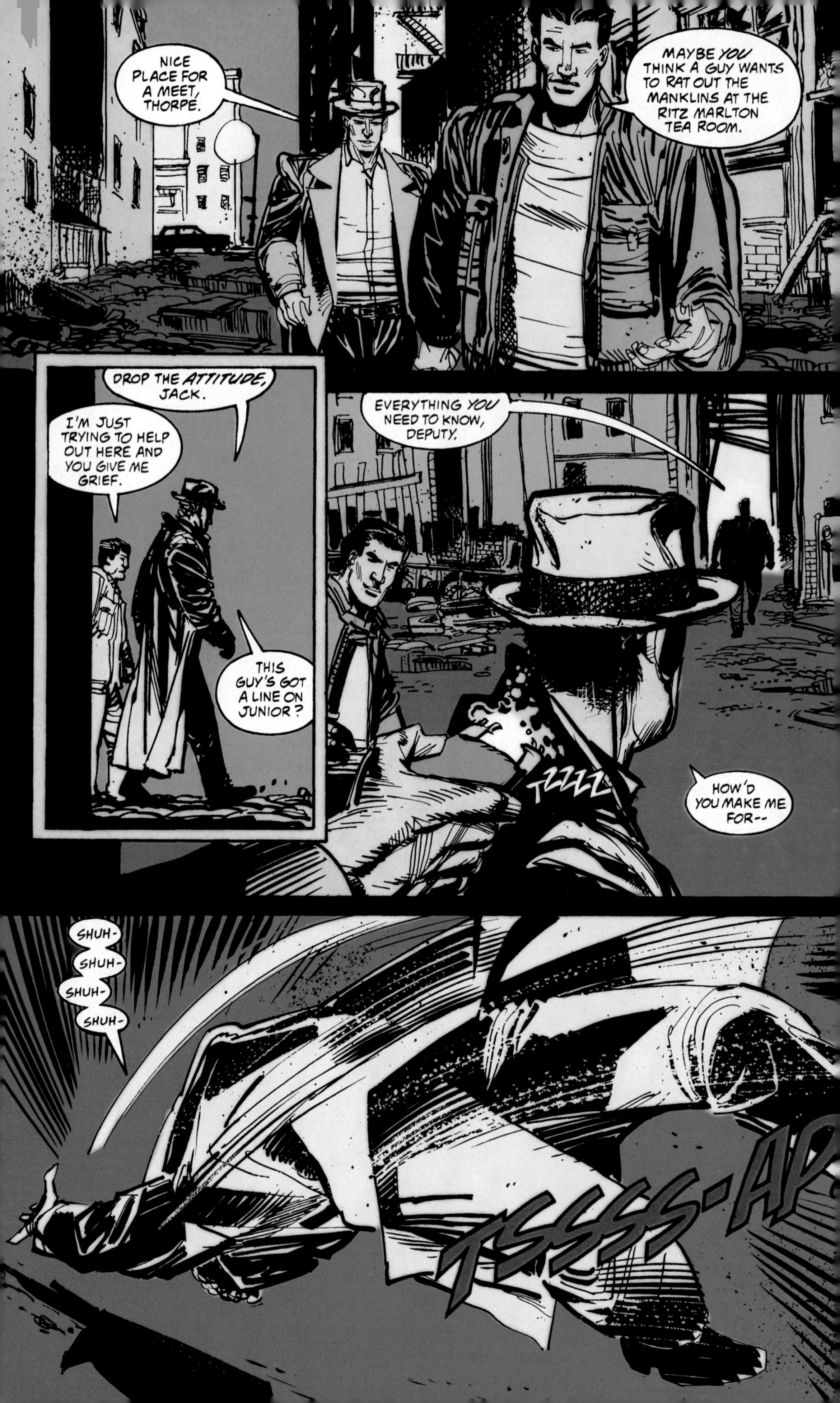
NICE PLACE FOR A MEET, THORPE.
MAYBE YOU THINK A GUY WANTS TO RAT OUT THE MANKLINS AT THE RITZ MARLTON TEA ROOM.
DROP THE ATTITUDE, JACK.
I'M JUST TRYING TO HELP OUT HERE AND YOU GIVE ME GRIEF.
THIS GUY'S GOT A LINE ON JUNIOR?
EVERYTHING YOU NEED TO KNOW, DEPUTY.
TZZZZ
HOW'D YOU MAKE ME FOR--
SHUH-
SHUH-
SHUH-
SHUH-
TSSSS-AP

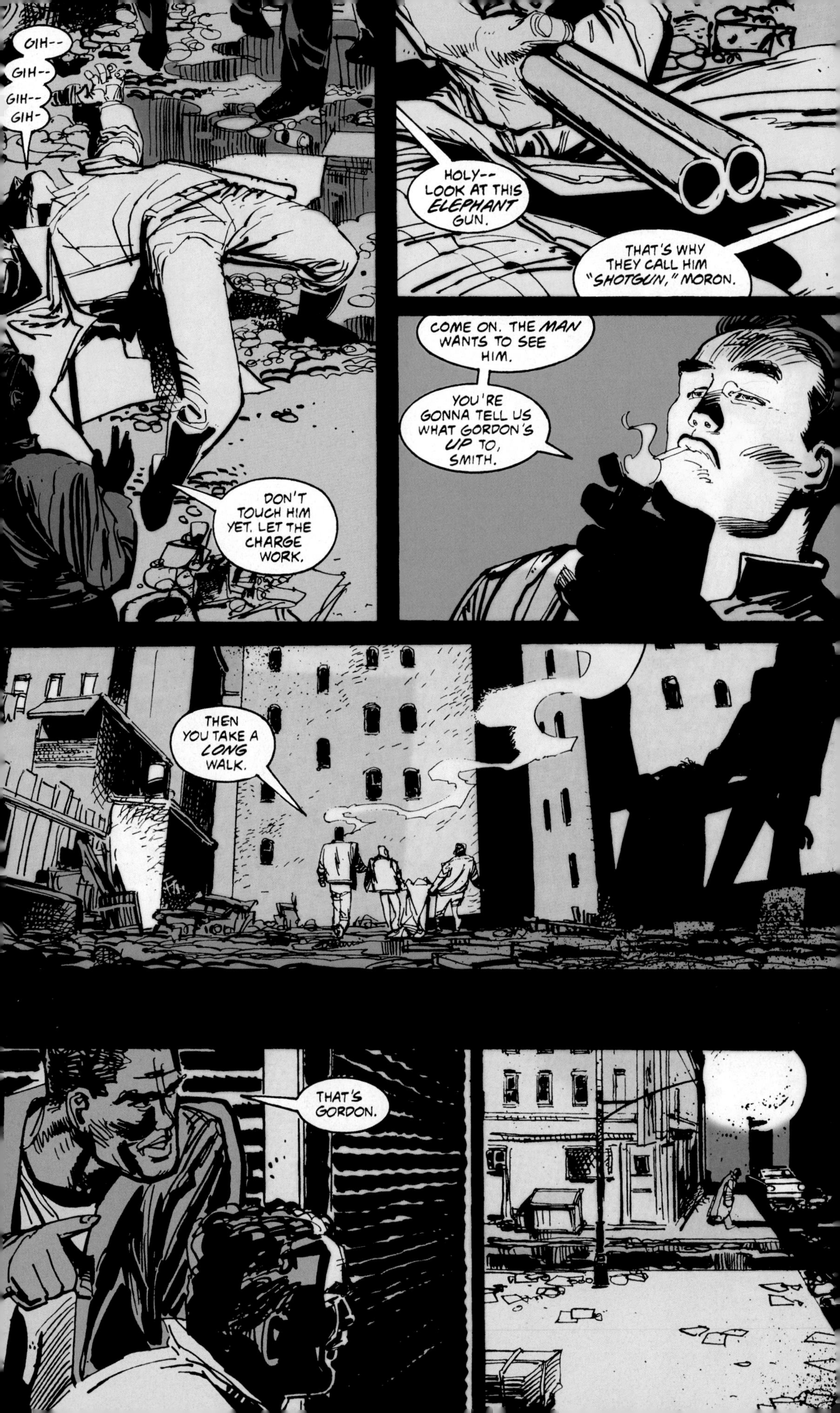
GIH--
GIH--
GIH--
GIH-
DON'T TOUCH HIM YET. LET THE CHARGE WORK.
HOLY-- LOOK AT THIS ELEPHANT GUN.
THAT'S WHY THEY CALL HIM "SHOTGUN," MORON.
COME ON. THE MAN WANTS TO SEE HIM.
YOU'RE GONNA TELL US WHAT GORDON'S UP TO, SMITH.
THEN YOU TAKE A LONG WALK.
THAT'S GORDON.

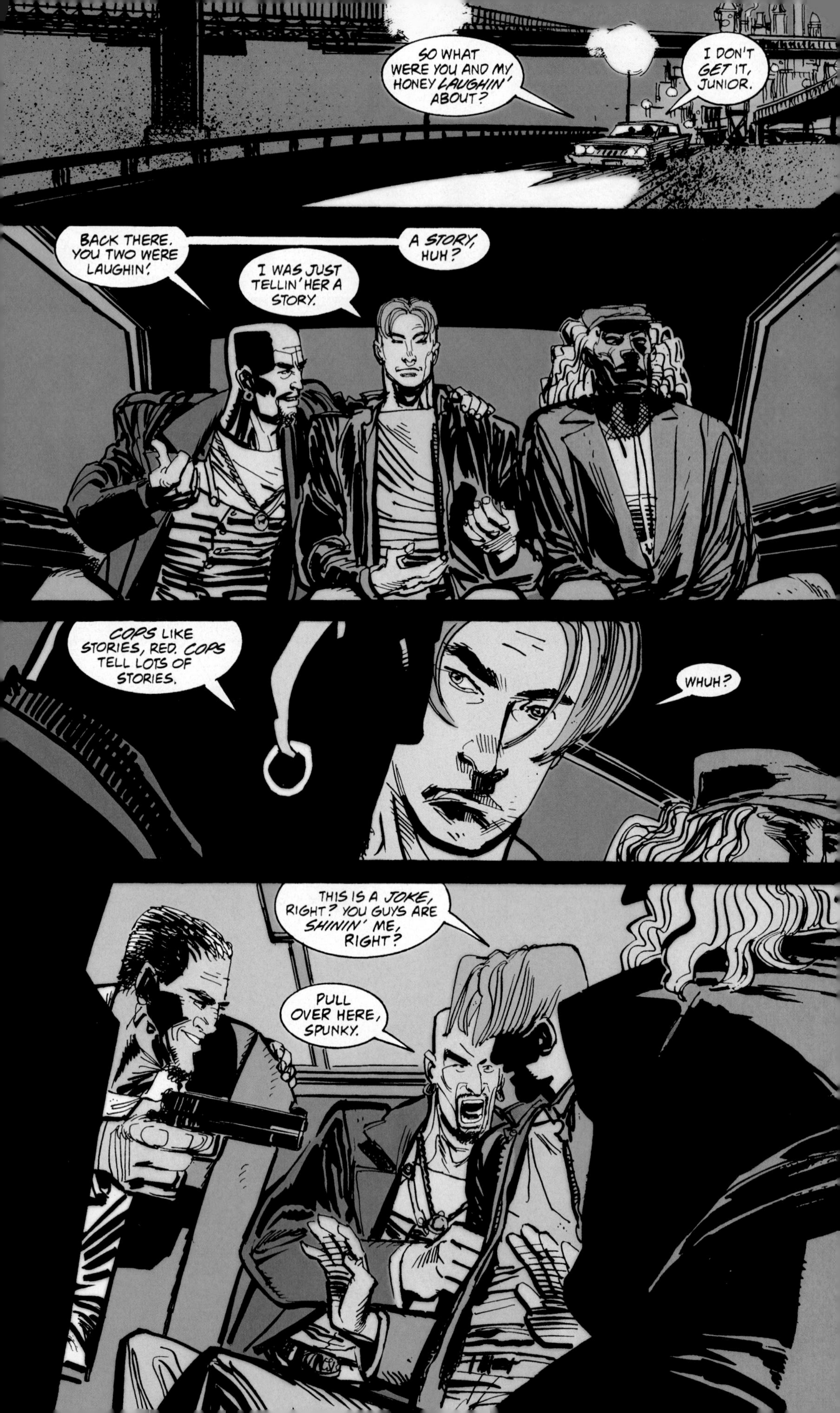

SO WHAT WERE YOU AND MY HONEY LAUGHIN' ABOUT?
I DON'T GET IT, JUNIOR.
BACK THERE. YOU TWO WERE LAUGHIN'.
I WAS JUST TELLIN' HER A STORY.
A STORY, HUH?
COPS LIKE STORIES, RED. COPS TELL LOTS OF STORIES.
WHUH?
THIS IS A JOKE, RIGHT? YOU GUYS ARE SHININ' ME, RIGHT?
PULL OVER HERE, SPUNKY.

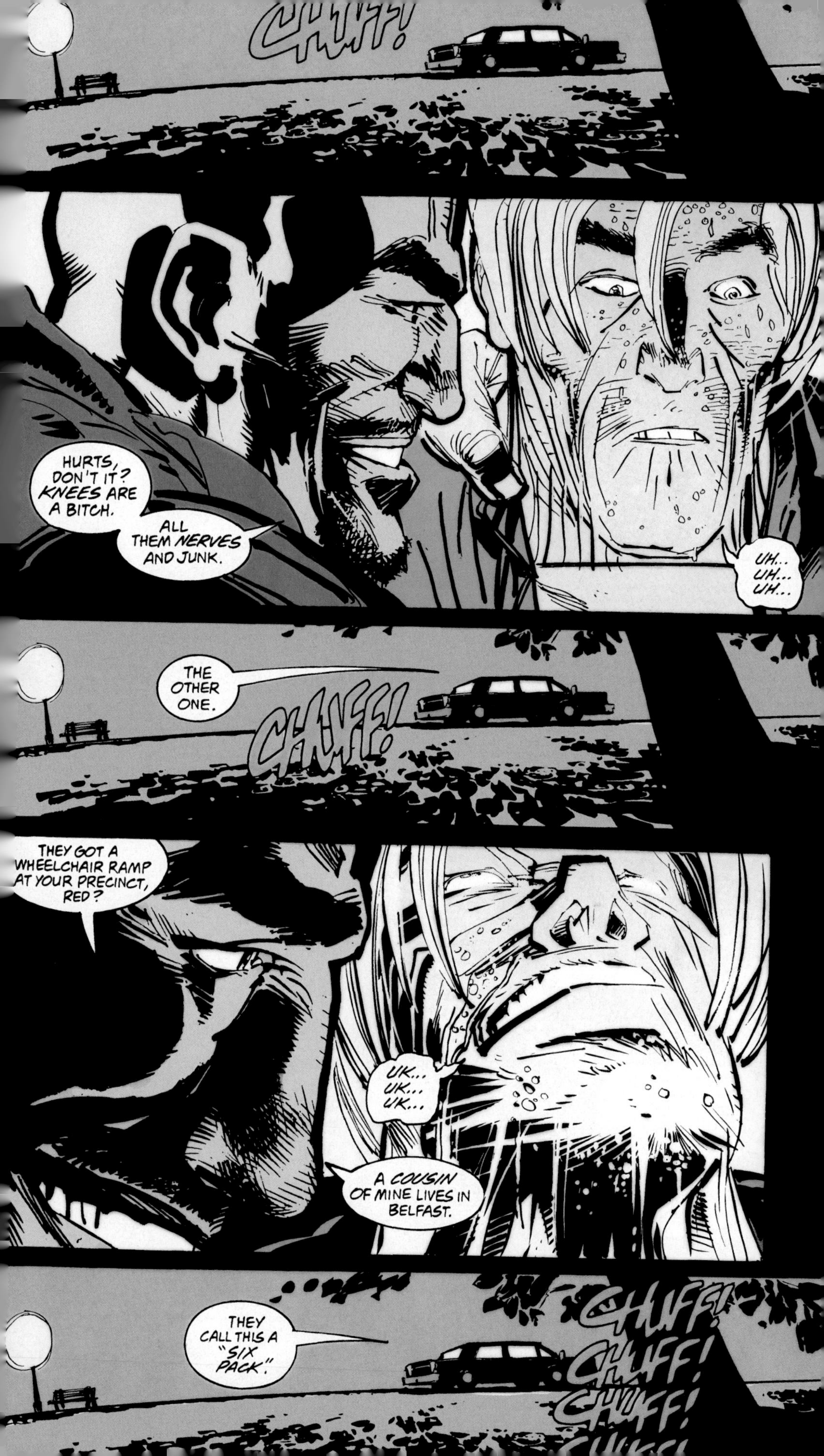
CHUFF!
HURTS, DON'T IT? KNEES ARE A BITCH.
ALL THEM NERVES AND JUNK.
UH... UH... UH...
THE OTHER ONE.
CHUFF!
THEY GOT A WHEELCHAIR RAMP AT YOUR PRECINCT, RED?
UK... UK... UK...
A COUSIN OF MINE LIVES IN BELFAST.
THEY CALL THIS A "SIX PACK."
CHUFF!
CHUFF!
CHUFF!

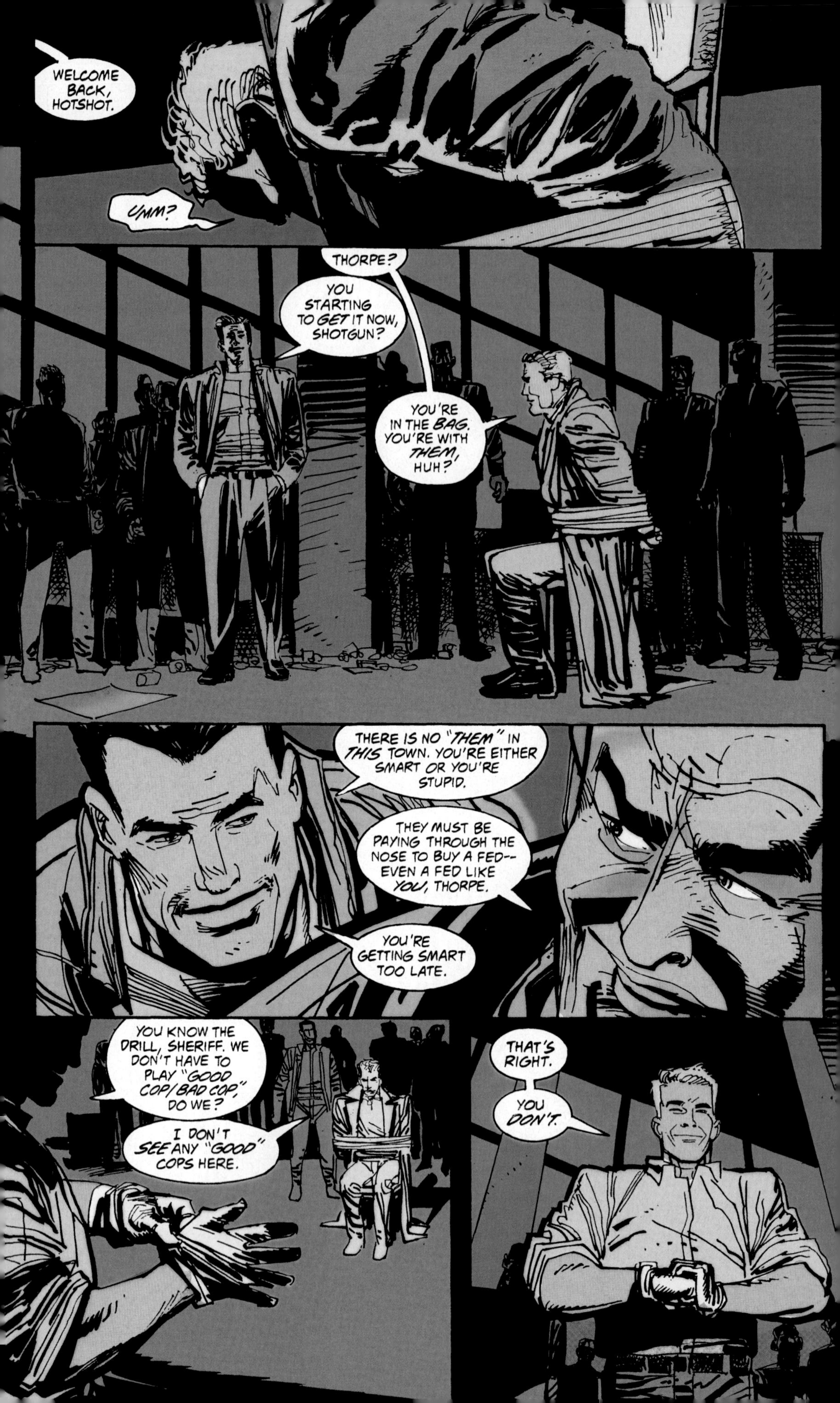
WELCOME BACK, HOTSHOT.
UMM?
THORPE?
YOU STARTING TO GET IT NOW, SHOTGUN?
YOU'RE IN THE BAG. YOU'RE WITH THEM, HUH?
THERE IS NO "THEM" IN THIS TOWN. YOU'RE EITHER SMART OR YOU'RE STUPID.
THEY MUST BE PAYING THROUGH THE NOSE TO BUY A FED-- EVEN A FED LIKE YOU, THORPE.
YOU'RE GETTING SMART TOO LATE.
YOU KNOW THE DRILL, SHERIFF. WE DON'T HAVE TO PLAY "GOOD COP/BAD COP," DO WE?
I DON'T SEE ANY "GOOD" COPS HERE.
THAT'S RIGHT.
YOU DON'T.

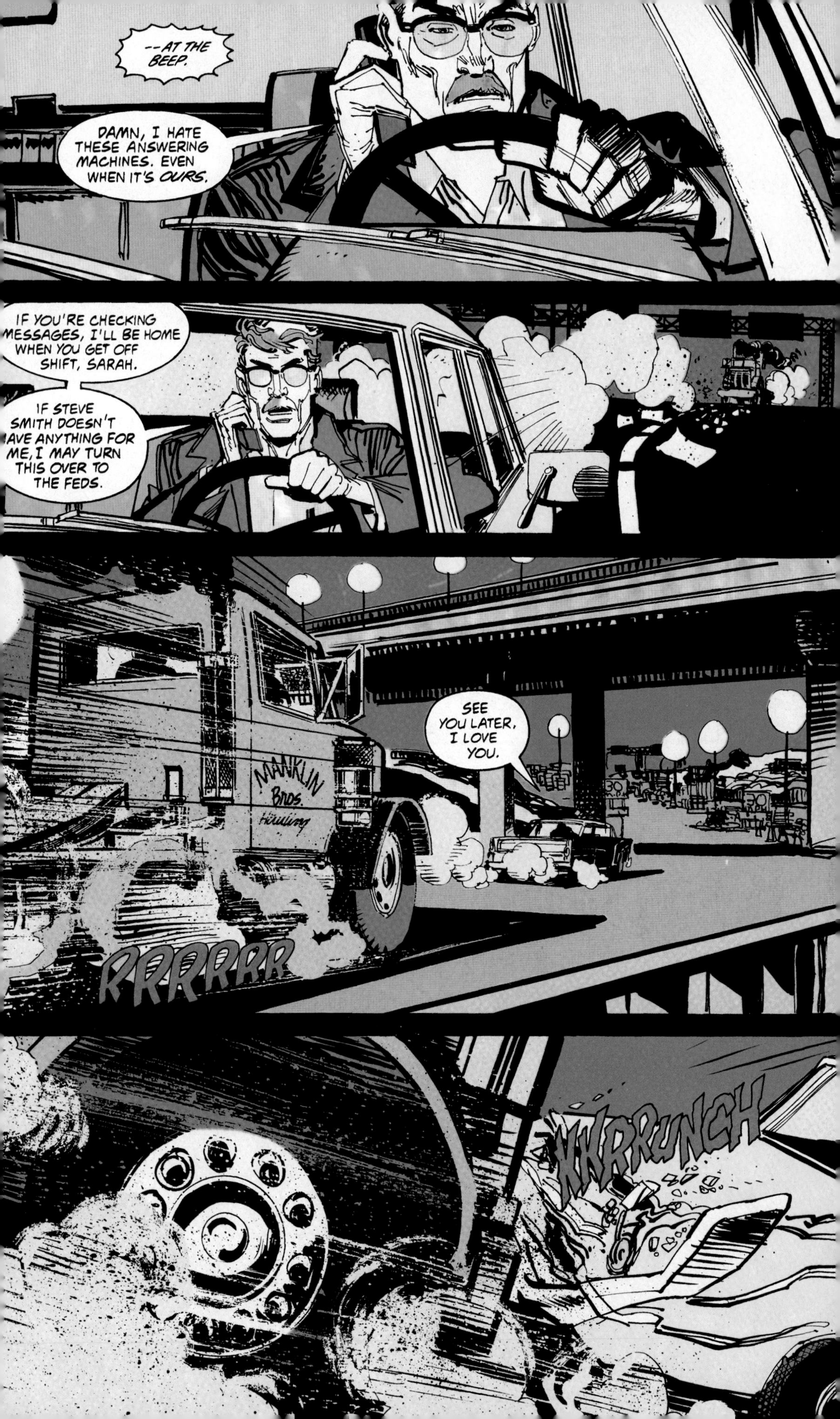
--AT THE BEEP.
DAMN, I HATE THESE ANSWERING MACHINES. EVEN WHEN IT'S OURS.
IF YOU'RE CHECKING MESSAGES, I'LL BE HOME WHEN YOU GET OFF SHIFT, SARAH.
IF STEVE SMITH DOESN'T HAVE ANYTHING FOR ME, I MAY TURN THIS OVER TO THE FEDS.
SEE YOU LATER, I LOVE YOU.
MANKLIN Bros. Hauling
RRRRRR
KKRRUNCH

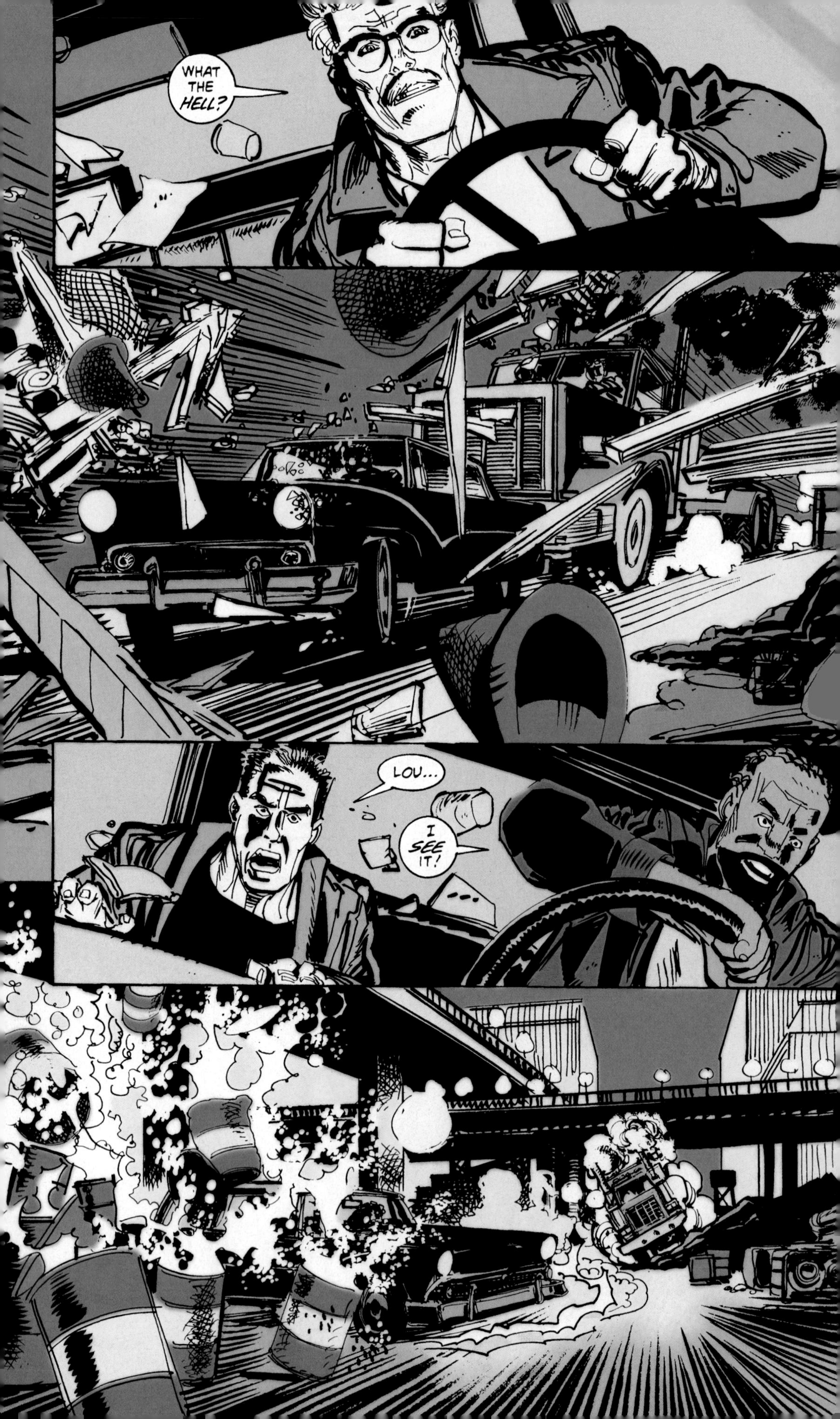
WHAT THE HELL?
LOU...
I SEE IT!

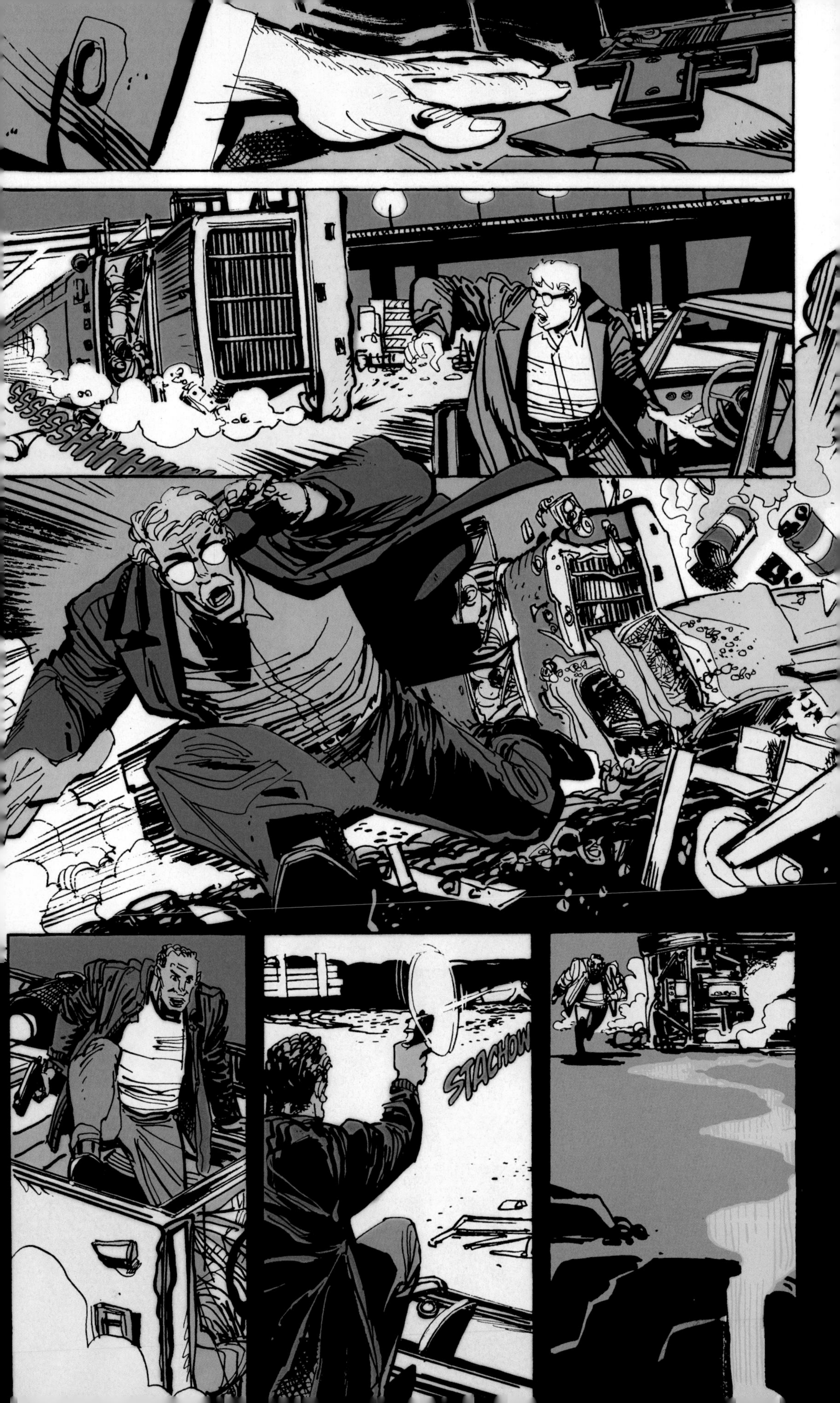
SSSSSSSHHHHHH
STACHOW

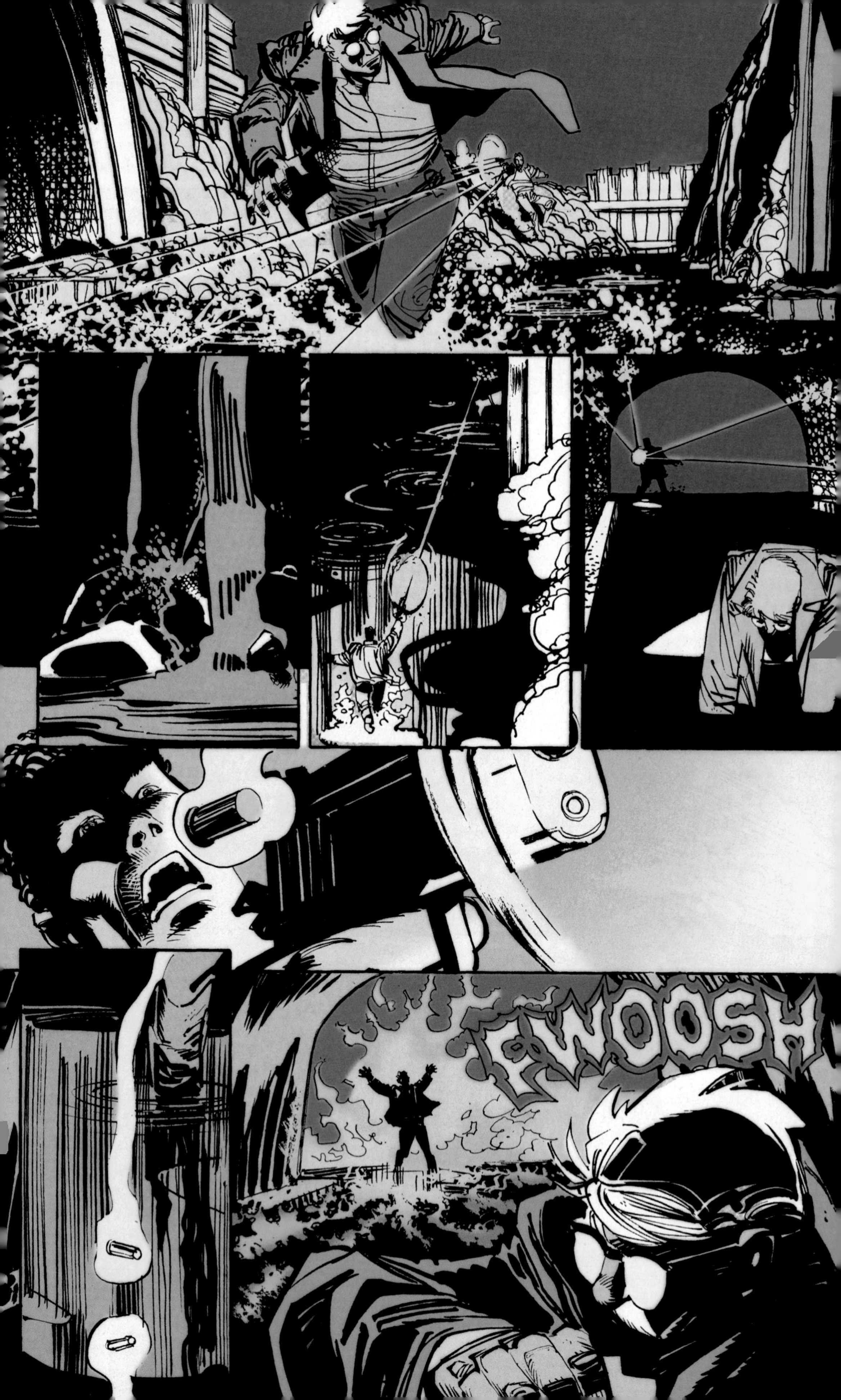
FWOOSH

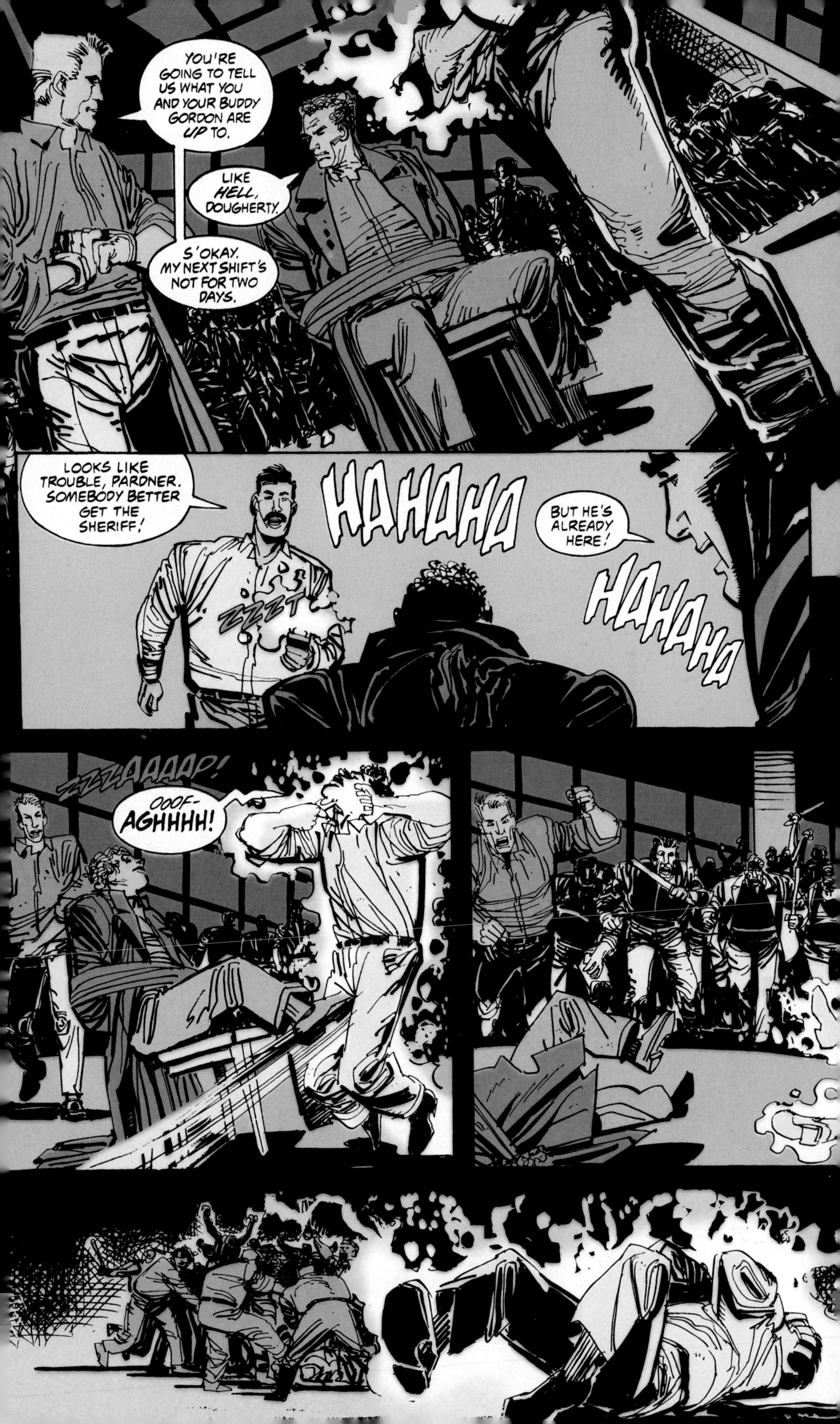
YOU'RE GOING TO TELL US WHAT YOU AND YOUR BUDDY GORDON ARE UP TO.
LIKE HELL, DOUGHERTY.
S'OKAY. MY NEXT SHIFT'S NOT FOR TWO DAYS.
LOOKS LIKE TROUBLE, PARDNER. SOMEBODY BETTER GET THE SHERIFF!
HAHAHA
BUT HE'S ALREADY HERE!
HAHAHA
ZZZT
ZZZZAAAAP!
OOOF-AGHHHH!

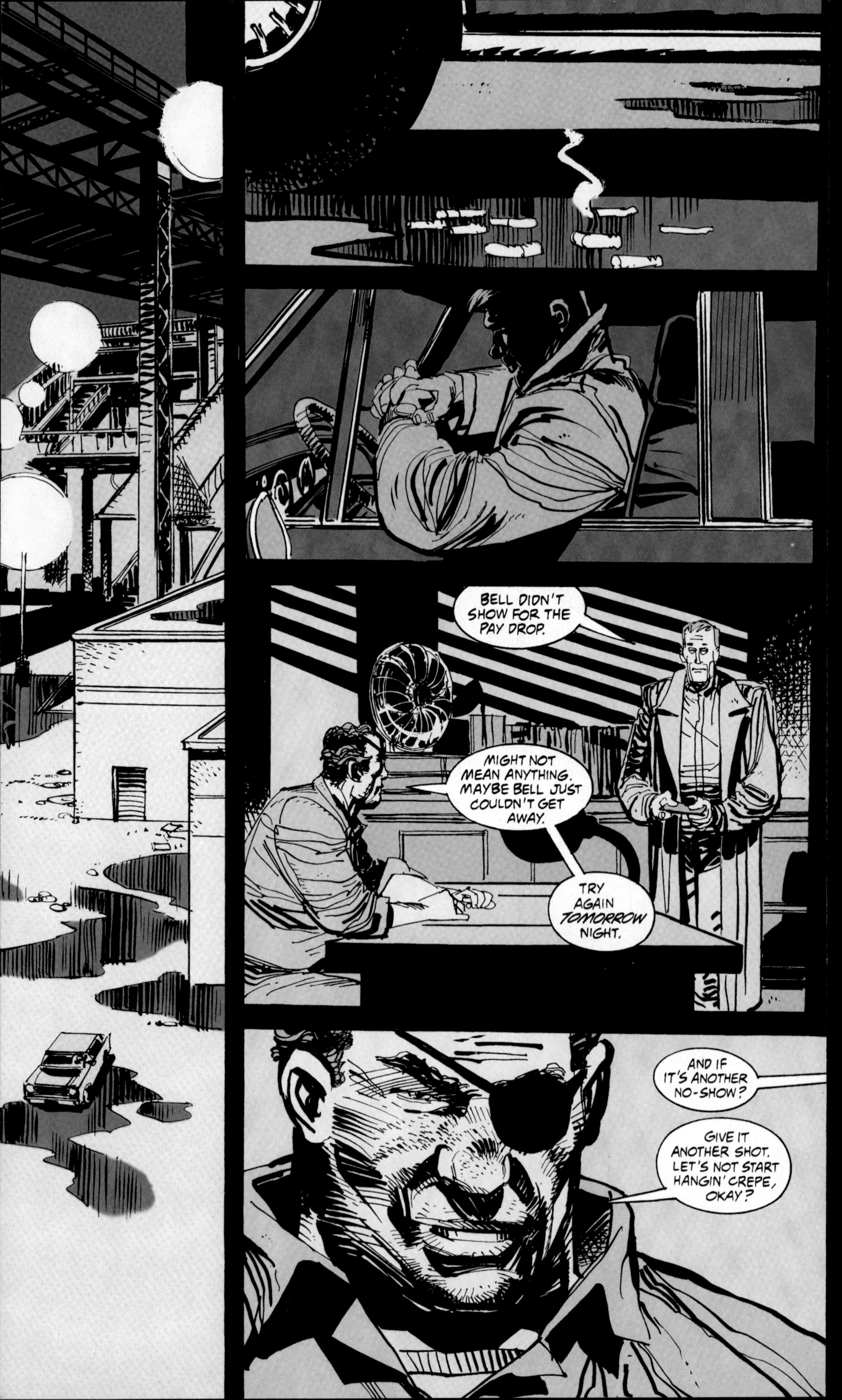

BELL DIDN'T SHOW FOR THE PAY DROP.
MIGHT NOT MEAN ANYTHING. MAYBE BELL JUST COULDN'T GET AWAY.
TRY AGAIN *TOMORROW* NIGHT.
AND IF IT'S ANOTHER NO-SHOW?
GIVE IT ANOTHER SHOT. LET'S NOT START HANGIN' CREPE, OKAY?

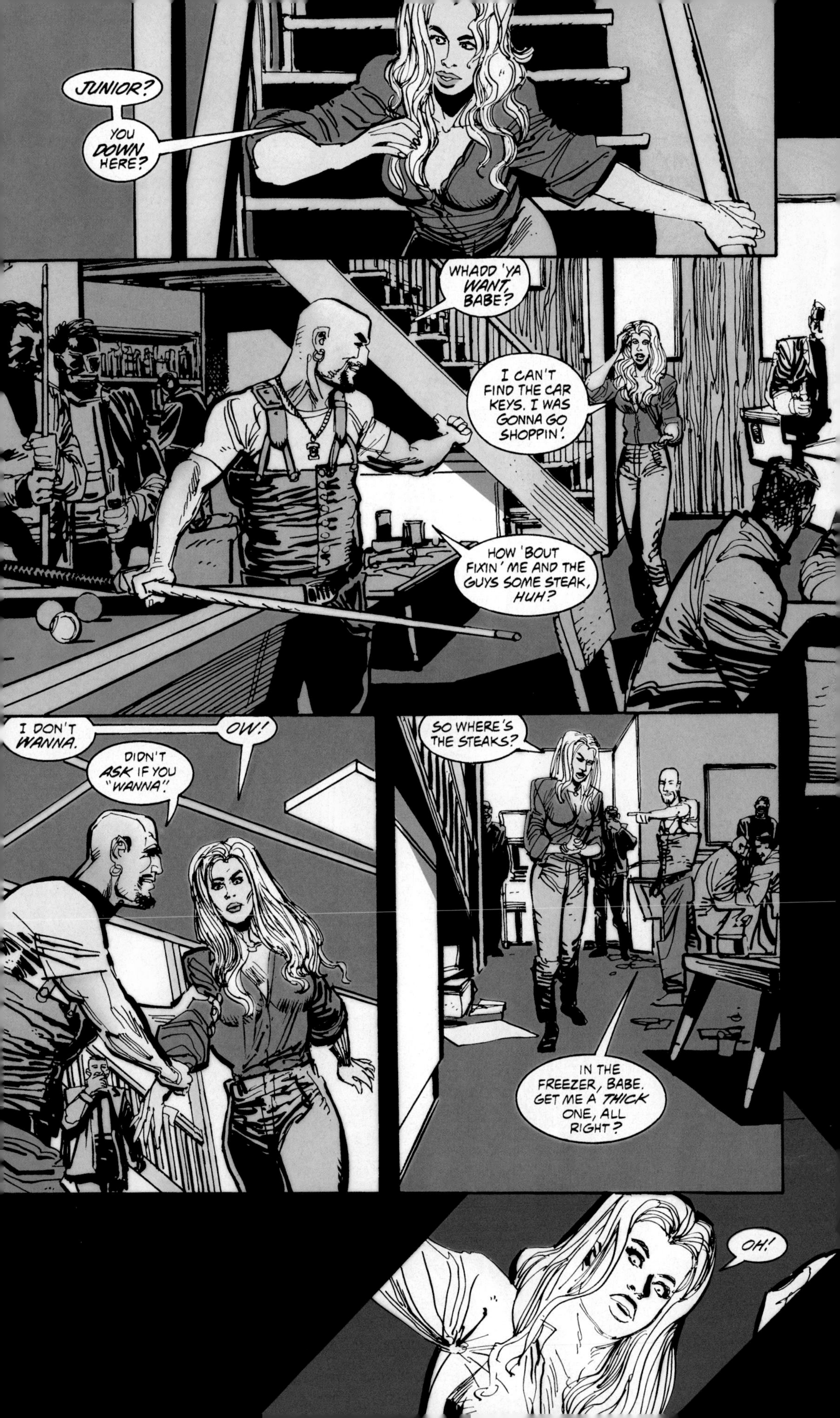
JUNIOR?
YOU DOWN HERE?
WHADD 'YA WANT, BABE?
I CAN'T FIND THE CAR KEYS. I WAS GONNA GO SHOPPIN'.
HOW 'BOUT FIXIN' ME AND THE GUYS SOME STEAK, HUH?
I DON'T WANNA.
OW!
DIDN'T ASK IF YOU "WANNA".
SO WHERE'S THE STEAKS?
IN THE FREEZER, BABE. GET ME A THICK ONE, ALL RIGHT?
OH!

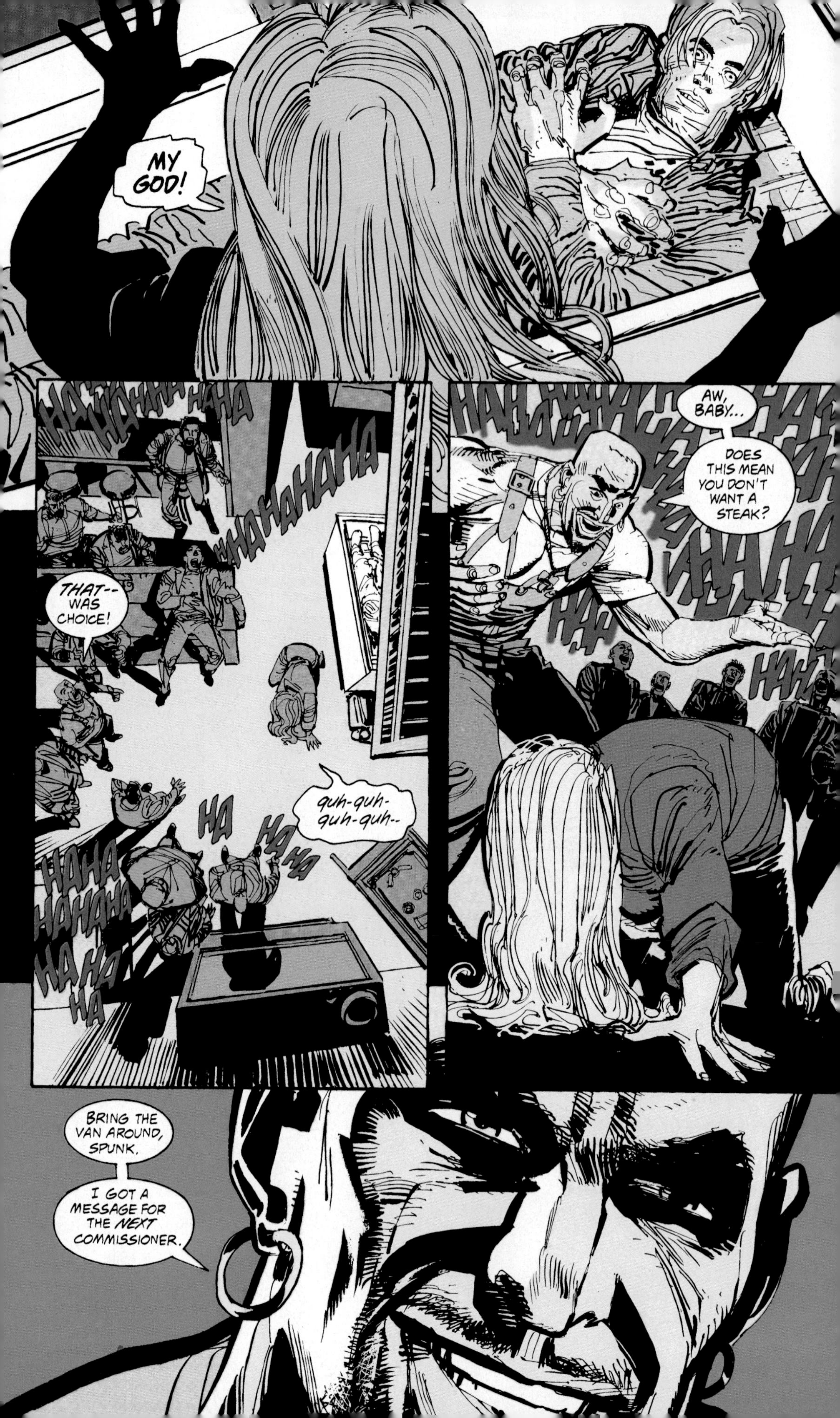
MY GOD!
HAHAHAHAHAHAHA
HAHAHAHAHA
THAT--WAS CHOICE!
quh-quh-quh-quh--
HA HA HA HA
HAHAHAHAHAHAHAHA
AW, BABY...
DOES THIS MEAN YOU DON'T WANT A STEAK?
BRING THE VAN AROUND, SPUNK.
I GOT A MESSAGE FOR THE NEXT COMMISSIONER.

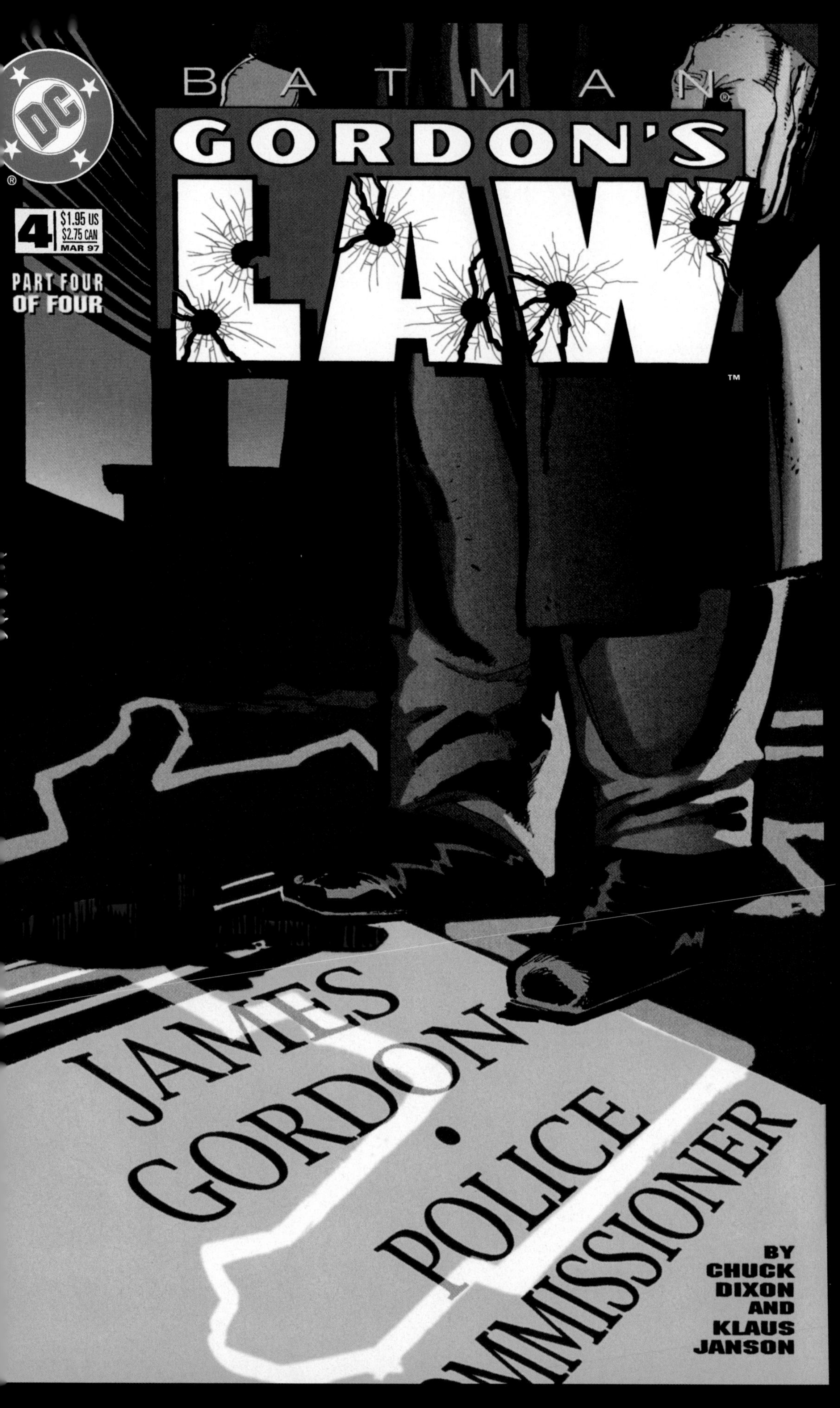

DC
BATMAN
GORDON'S
LAW
4
$1.95 US
$2.75 CAN
MAR 97
PART FOUR
OF FOUR
JAMES
GORDON
POLICE
COMMISSIONER
BY
CHUCK
DIXON
AND
KLAUS
JANSON

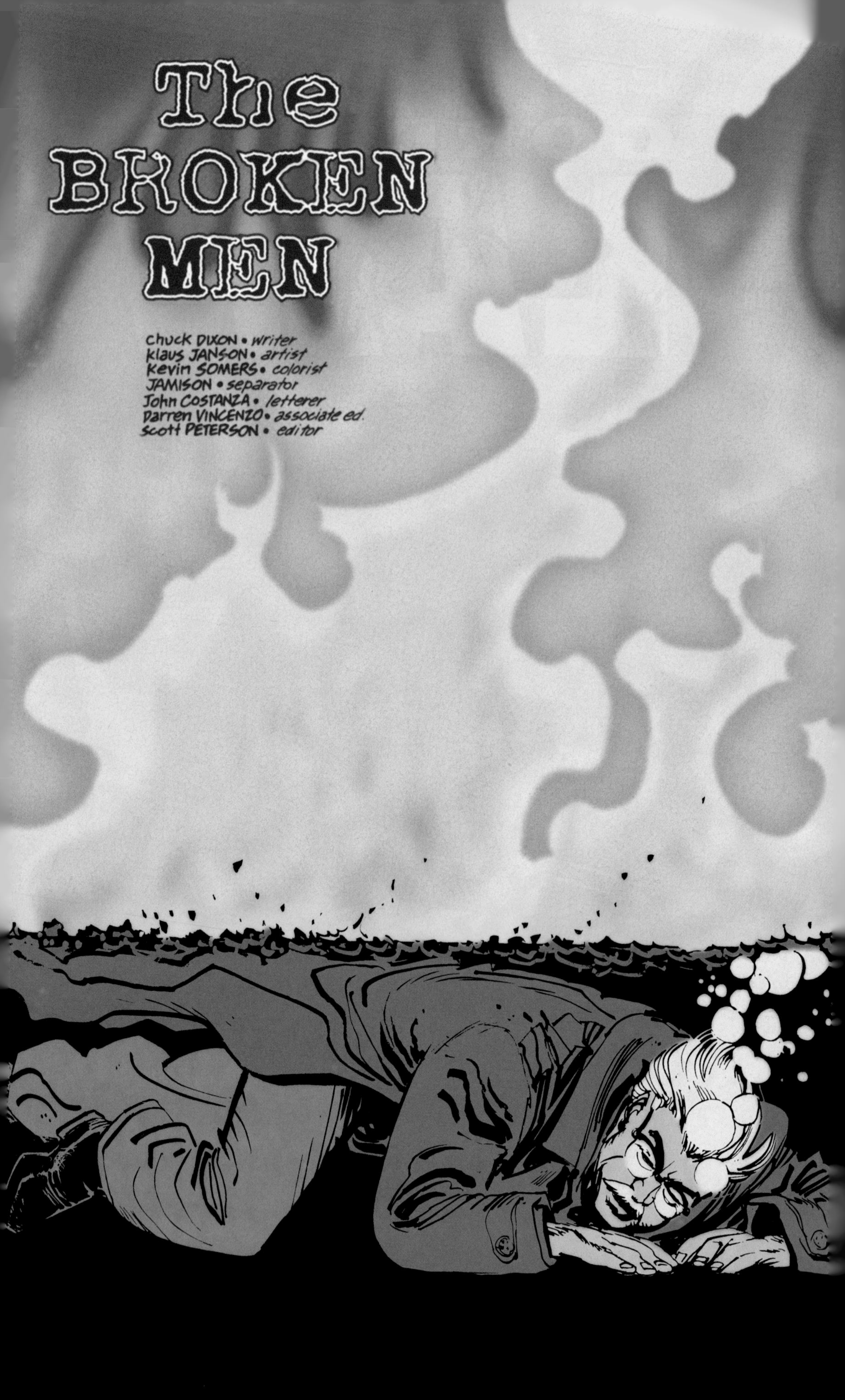
The BROKEN MEN
chuck DIXON • writer
klaus JANSON • artist
kevin SOMERS • colorist
JAMISON • separator
John COSTANZA • letterer
Darren VINCENZO • associate ed.
scott PETERSON • editor

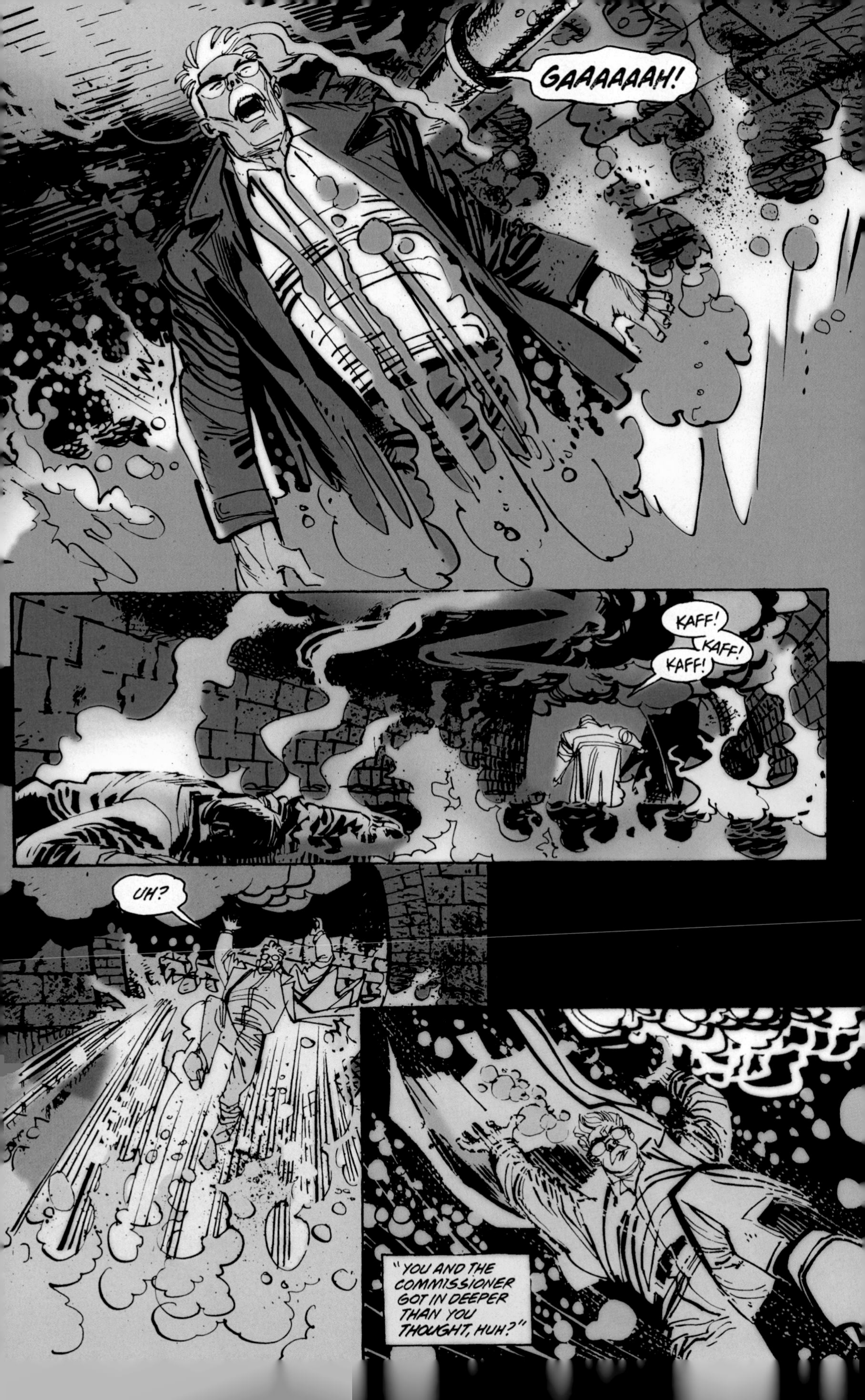
GAAAAAAH!
KAFF!
KAFF!
KAFF!
UH?
"YOU AND THE COMMISSIONER GOT IN DEEPER THAN YOU THOUGHT, HUH?"

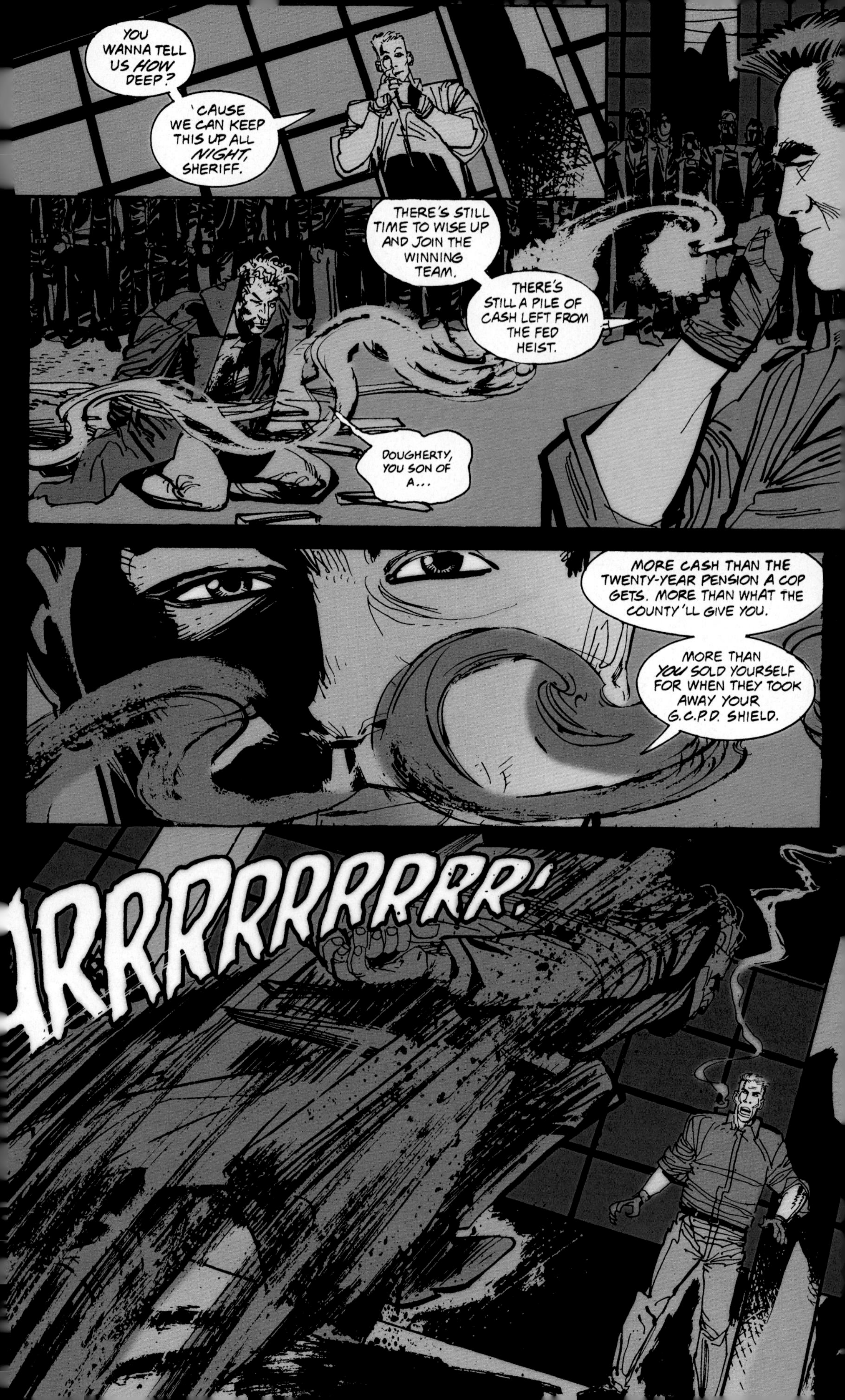
YOU WANNA TELL US HOW DEEP?
'CAUSE WE CAN KEEP THIS UP ALL NIGHT, SHERIFF.
THERE'S STILL TIME TO WISE UP AND JOIN THE WINNING TEAM.
THERE'S STILL A PILE OF CASH LEFT FROM THE FED HEIST.
DOUGHERTY, YOU SON OF A...
MORE CASH THAN THE TWENTY-YEAR PENSION A COP GETS. MORE THAN WHAT THE COUNTY'LL GIVE YOU.
MORE THAN YOU SOLD YOURSELF FOR WHEN THEY TOOK AWAY YOUR G.C.P.D. SHIELD.
RRRRRRRRRR!

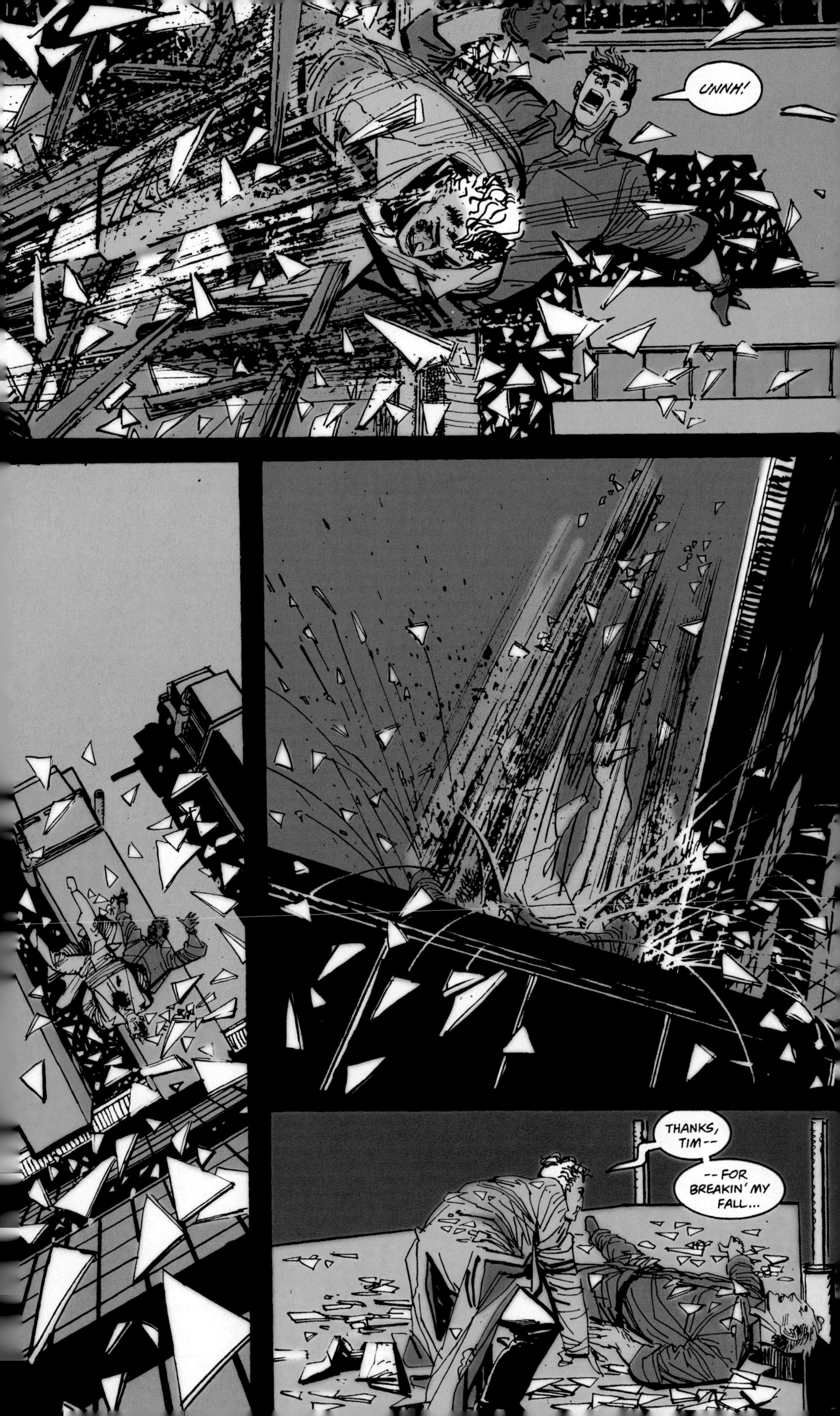
UNNH!
THANKS, TIM--
--FOR BREAKIN' MY FALL...

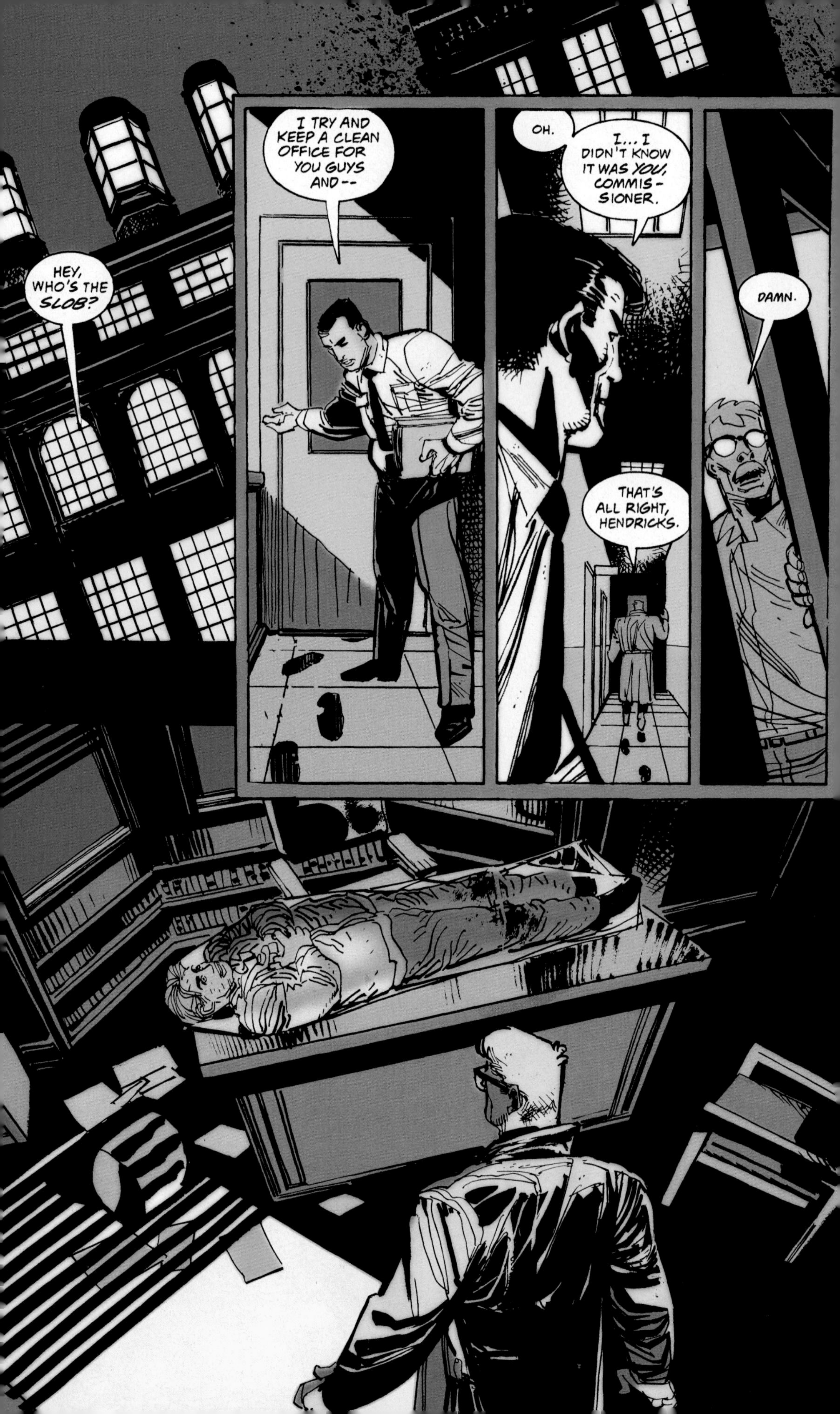
HEY, WHO'S THE *SLOB?*
I TRY AND KEEP A CLEAN OFFICE FOR YOU GUYS AND --
OH.
I... I DIDN'T KNOW IT WAS *YOU,* COMMIS-SIONER.
THAT'S ALL RIGHT, HENDRICKS.
DAMN.

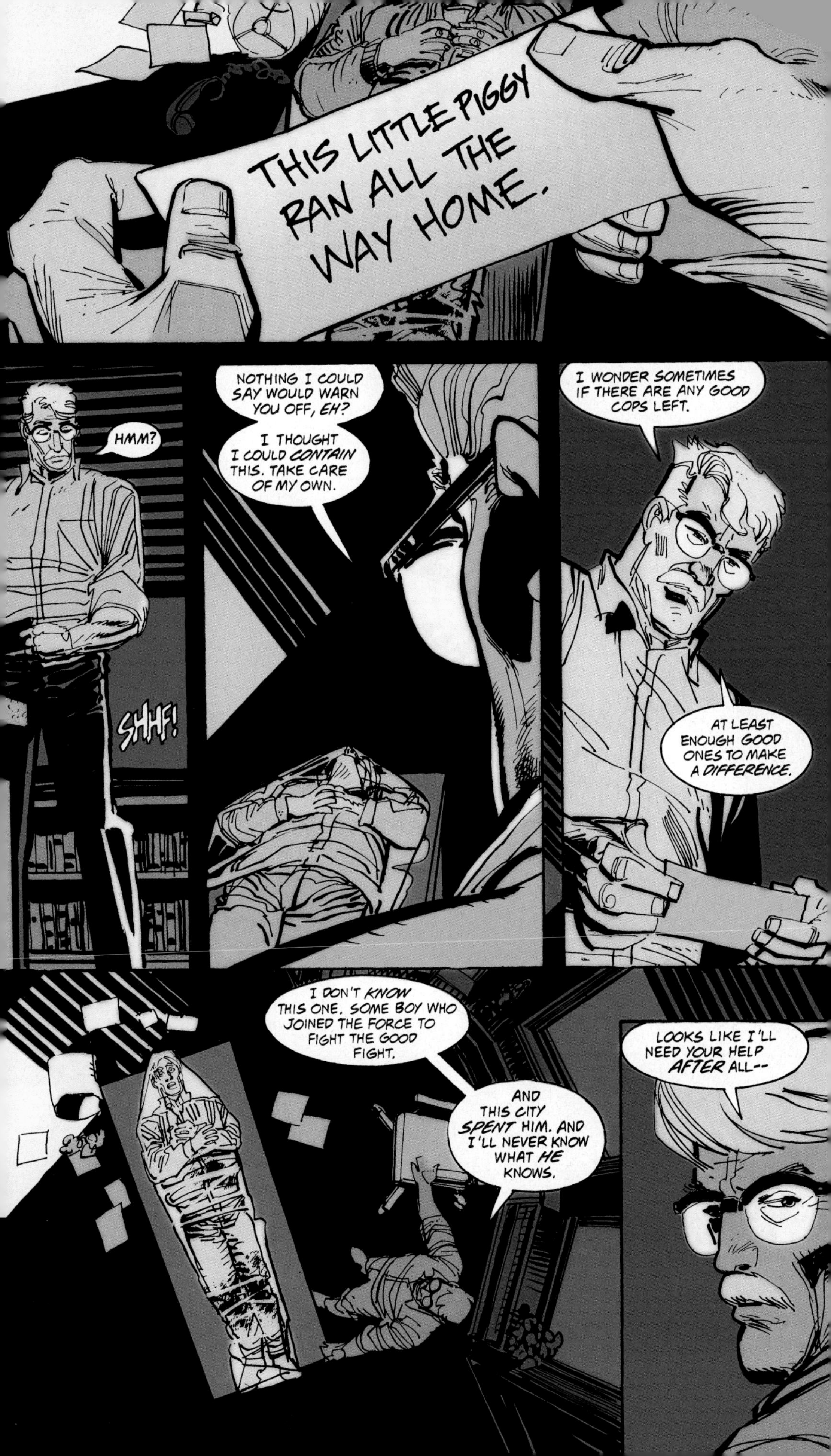
THIS LITTLE PIGGY RAN ALL THE WAY HOME.
HMM?
SHHF!
NOTHING I COULD SAY WOULD WARN YOU OFF, EH?
I THOUGHT I COULD CONTAIN THIS. TAKE CARE OF MY OWN.
I WONDER SOMETIMES IF THERE ARE ANY GOOD COPS LEFT.
AT LEAST ENOUGH GOOD ONES TO MAKE A DIFFERENCE.
I DON'T KNOW THIS ONE. SOME BOY WHO JOINED THE FORCE TO FIGHT THE GOOD FIGHT.
AND THIS CITY SPENT HIM. AND I'LL NEVER KNOW WHAT HE KNOWS.
LOOKS LIKE I'LL NEED YOUR HELP AFTER ALL--

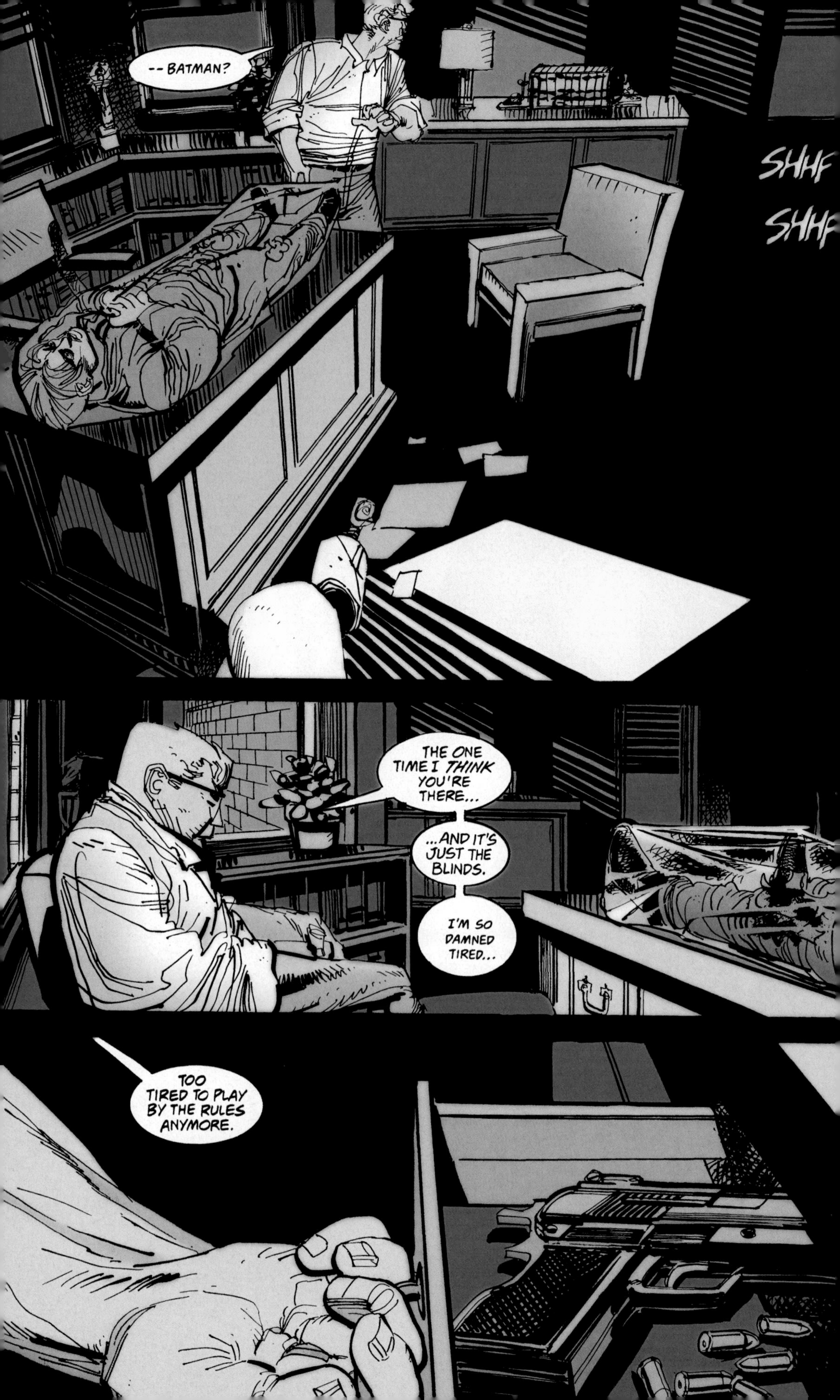
-- BATMAN?
SHHF
SHHF
THE ONE TIME I *THINK* YOU'RE THERE...
...AND IT'S JUST THE BLINDS.
I'M SO DAMNED TIRED...
TOO TIRED TO PLAY BY THE RULES ANYMORE.

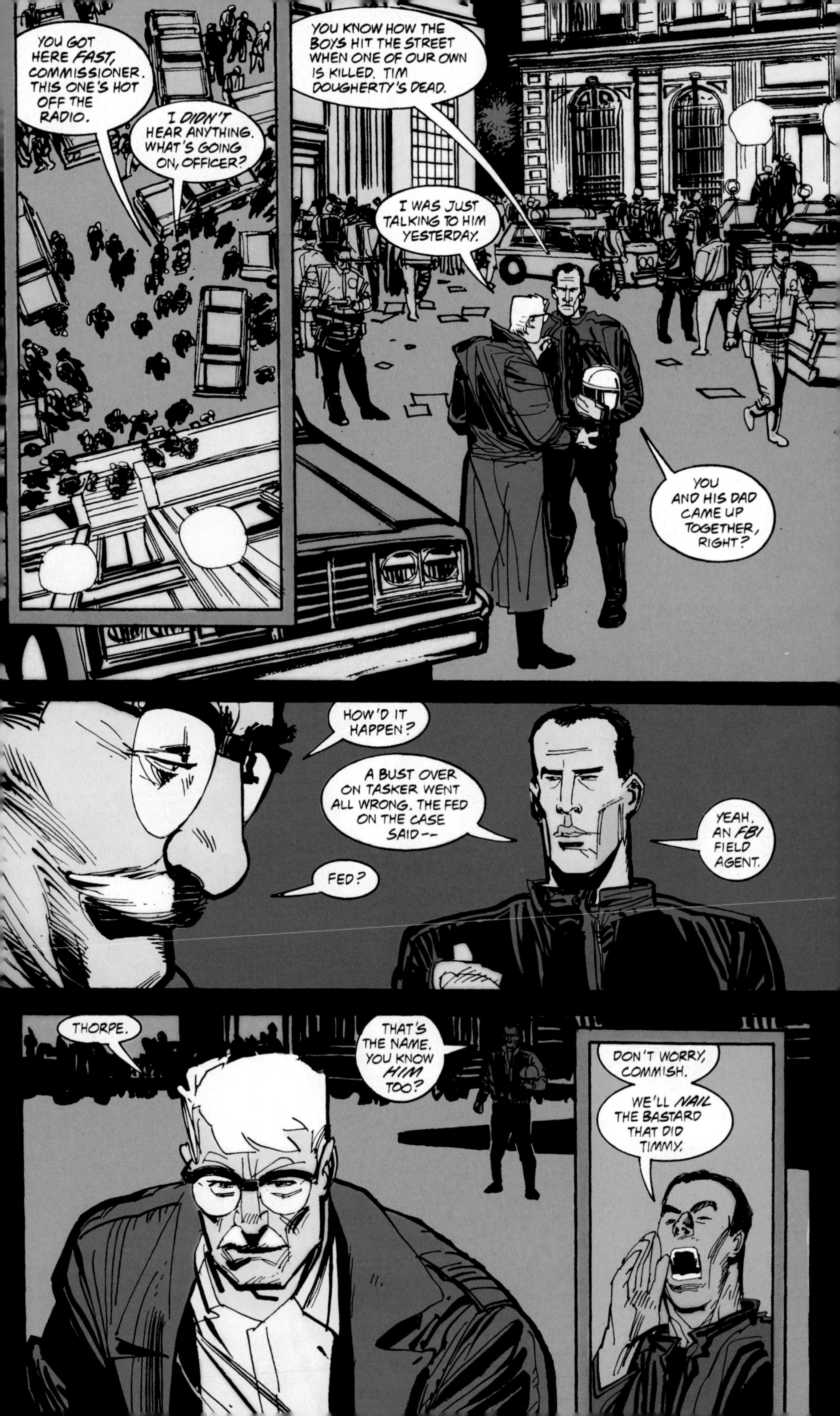
YOU GOT HERE FAST, COMMISSIONER. THIS ONE'S HOT OFF THE RADIO.
I DIDN'T HEAR ANYTHING. WHAT'S GOING ON, OFFICER?
YOU KNOW HOW THE BOYS HIT THE STREET WHEN ONE OF OUR OWN IS KILLED. TIM DOUGHERTY'S DEAD.
I WAS JUST TALKING TO HIM YESTERDAY.
YOU AND HIS DAD CAME UP TOGETHER, RIGHT?
HOW'D IT HAPPEN?
A BUST OVER ON TASKER WENT ALL WRONG. THE FED ON THE CASE SAID--
FED?
YEAH. AN FBI FIELD AGENT.
THORPE.
THAT'S THE NAME. YOU KNOW HIM TOO?
DON'T WORRY, COMMISH.
WE'LL NAIL THE BASTARD THAT DID TIMMY.

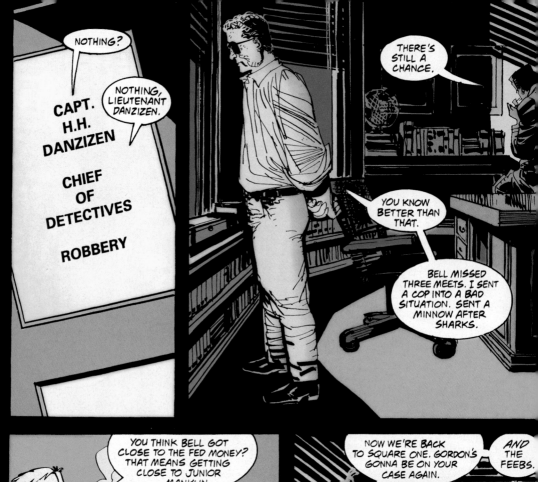

NOTHING?

NOTHING, LIEUTENANT DANZIZEN.

CAPT. H.H. DANZIZEN

CHIEF OF DETECTIVES

ROBBERY

THERE'S STILL A CHANCE.

YOU KNOW BETTER THAN THAT.

BELL MISSED THREE MEETS. I SENT A COP INTO A BAD SITUATION. SENT A MINNOW AFTER SHARKS.

YOU THINK BELL GOT CLOSE TO THE FED MONEY? THAT MEANS GETTING CLOSE TO JUNIOR MANKLIN.

DON'T SOUND GOOD.

NOW WE'RE BACK TO SQUARE ONE. GORDON'S GONNA BE ON YOUR CASE AGAIN.

AND THE FEEBS.

I CAN'T WORRY ABOUT THAT RIGHT NOW.

I'LL PUT AN "ALL POINTS" OUT ON BELL.

AND PUT THAT DAMN THING OUT. I'M TRYING TO QUIT.

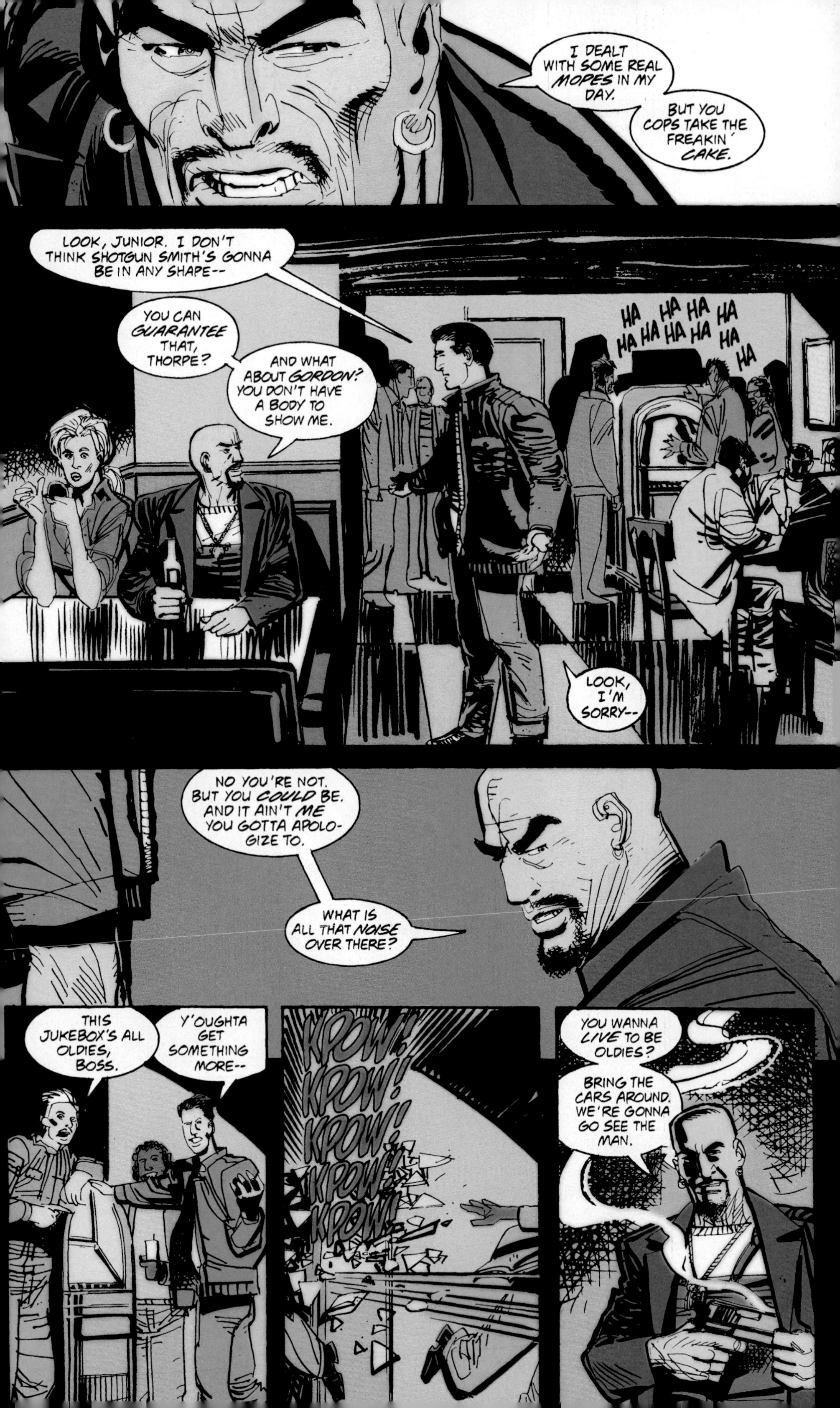

I DEALT WITH SOME REAL MOPES IN MY DAY.
BUT YOU COPS TAKE THE FREAKIN' CAKE.
LOOK, JUNIOR. I DON'T THINK SHOTGUN SMITH'S GONNA BE IN ANY SHAPE--
YOU CAN GUARANTEE THAT, THORPE?
AND WHAT ABOUT GORDON? YOU DON'T HAVE A BODY TO SHOW ME.
HA HA HA HA HA HA HA HA HA HA HA
LOOK, I'M SORRY--
NO YOU'RE NOT. BUT YOU COULD BE. AND IT AIN'T ME YOU GOTTA APOLO-GIZE TO.
WHAT IS ALL THAT NOISE OVER THERE?
THIS JUKEBOX'S ALL OLDIES, BOSS.
Y'OUGHTA GET SOMETHING MORE--
KPOW! KPOW! KPOW! KPOW! KPOW!
YOU WANNA LIVE TO BE OLDIES?
BRING THE CARS AROUND. WE'RE GONNA GO SEE THE MAN.

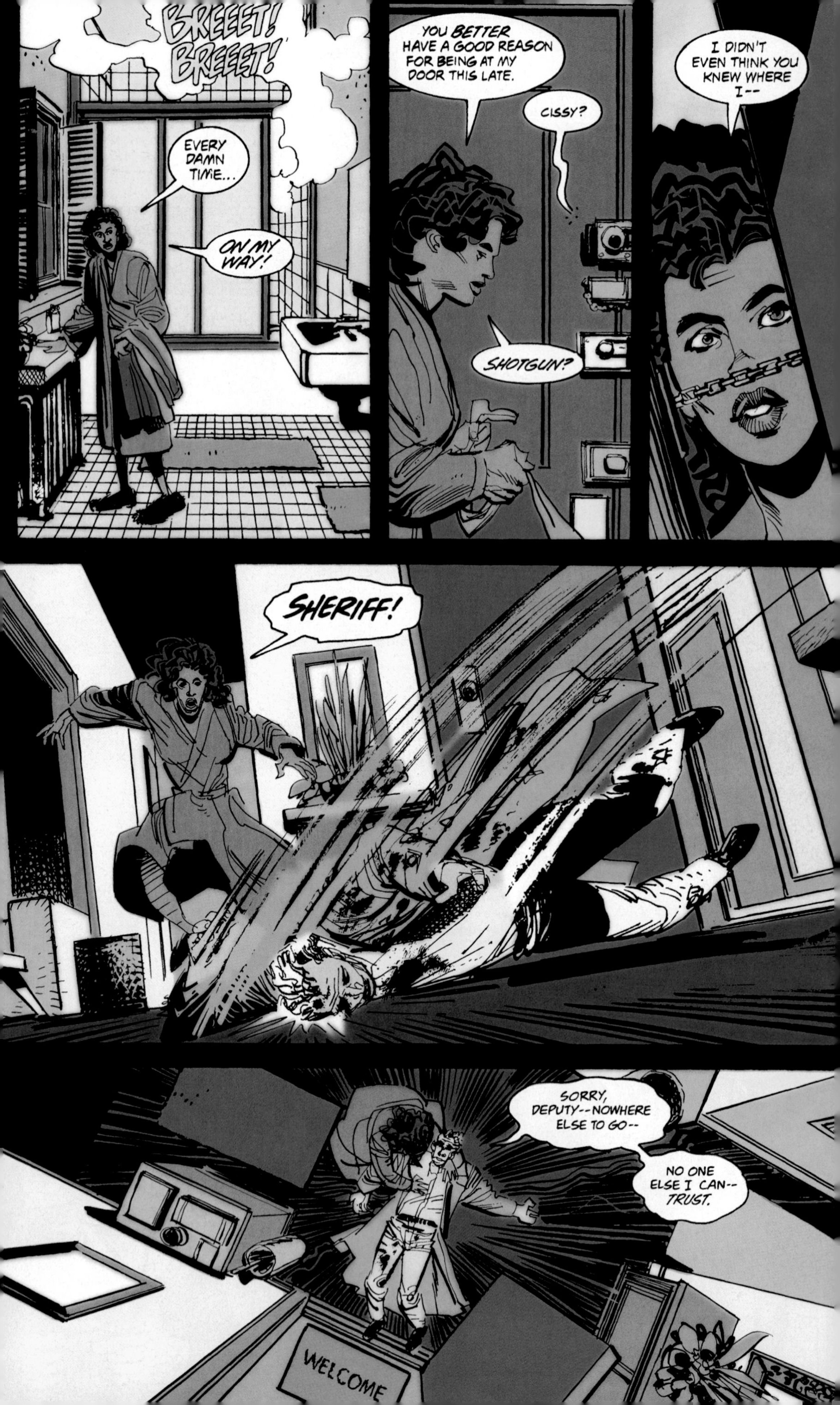
BREEET! BREEET!
EVERY DAMN TIME...
ON MY WAY!
YOU BETTER HAVE A GOOD REASON FOR BEING AT MY DOOR THIS LATE.
CISSY?
SHOTGUN?
I DIDN'T EVEN THINK YOU KNEW WHERE I--
SHERIFF!
SORRY, DEPUTY--NOWHERE ELSE TO GO--
NO ONE ELSE I CAN--TRUST.
WELCOME

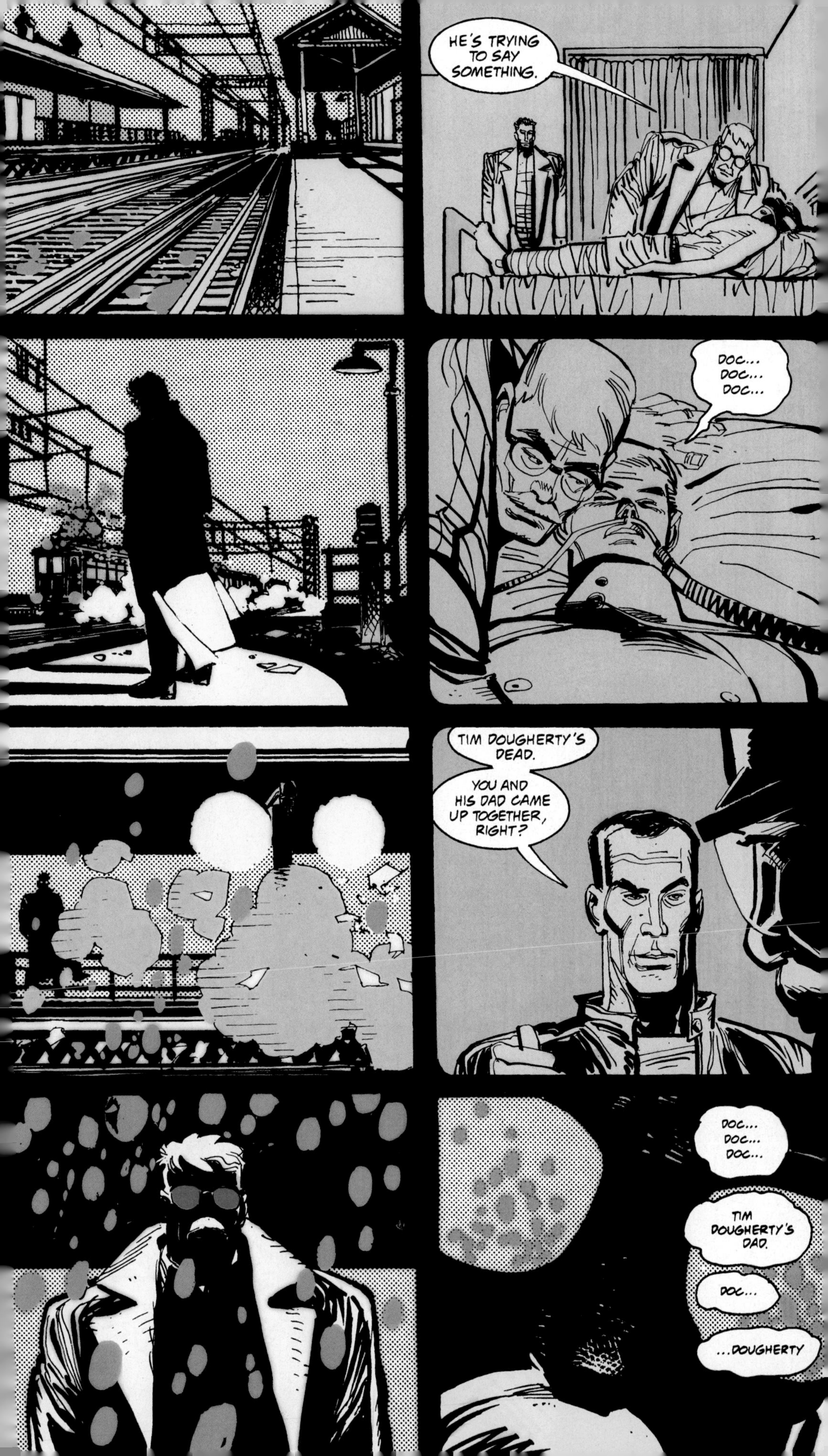
HE'S TRYING TO SAY SOMETHING.
DOC... DOC... DOC...
TIM DOUGHERTY'S DEAD.
YOU AND HIS DAD CAME UP TOGETHER, RIGHT?
DOC... DOC... DOC...
TIM DOUGHERTY'S DAD.
DOC...
...DOUGHERTY

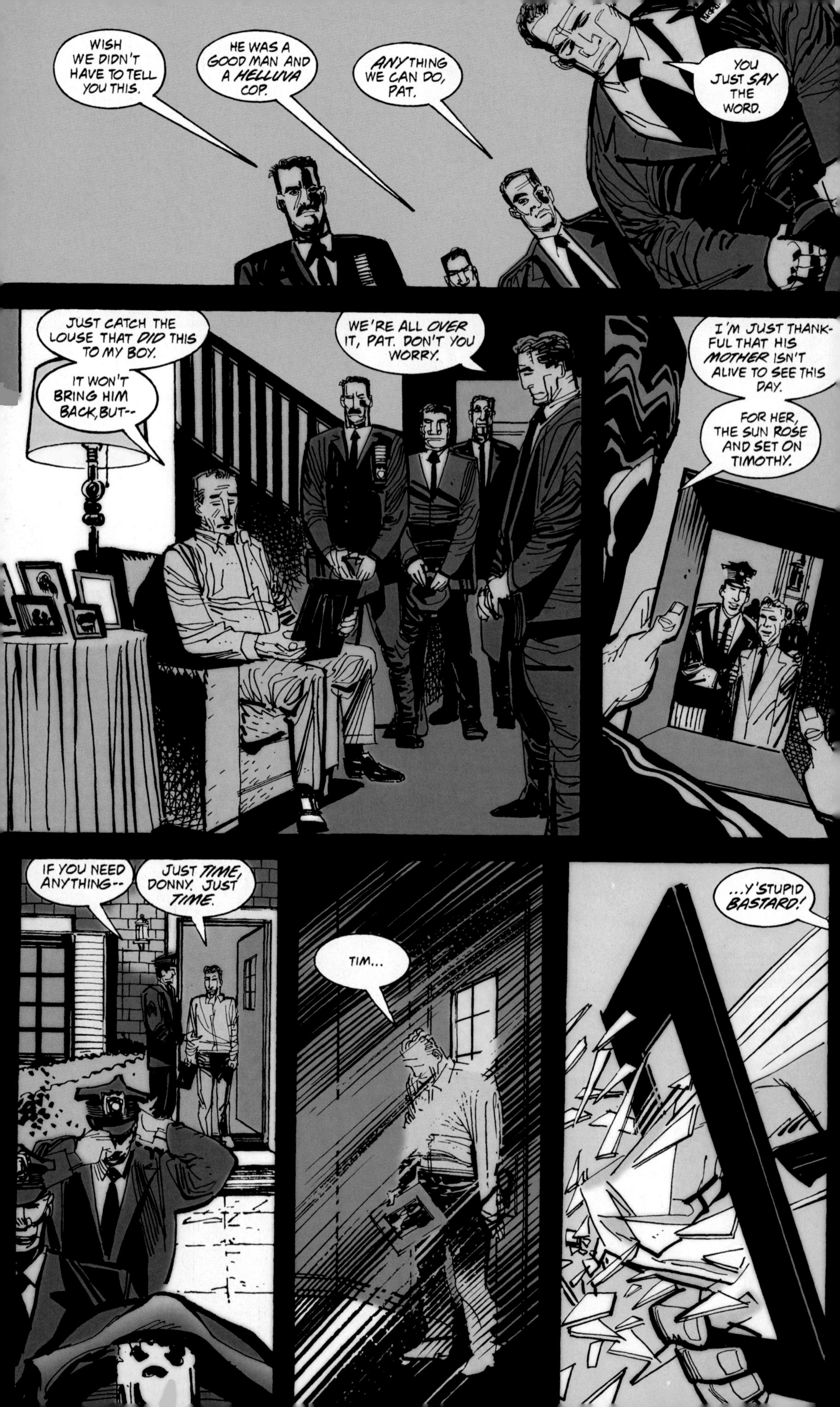
WISH WE DIDN'T HAVE TO TELL YOU THIS.
HE WAS A GOOD MAN AND A HELLUVA COP.
ANYTHING WE CAN DO, PAT.
YOU JUST SAY THE WORD.
JUST CATCH THE LOUSE THAT DID THIS TO MY BOY.
IT WON'T BRING HIM BACK, BUT--
WE'RE ALL OVER IT, PAT. DON'T YOU WORRY.
I'M JUST THANKFUL THAT HIS MOTHER ISN'T ALIVE TO SEE THIS DAY.
FOR HER, THE SUN ROSE AND SET ON TIMOTHY.
IF YOU NEED ANYTHING--
JUST TIME, DONNY. JUST TIME.
TIM...
...Y'STUPID BASTARD!

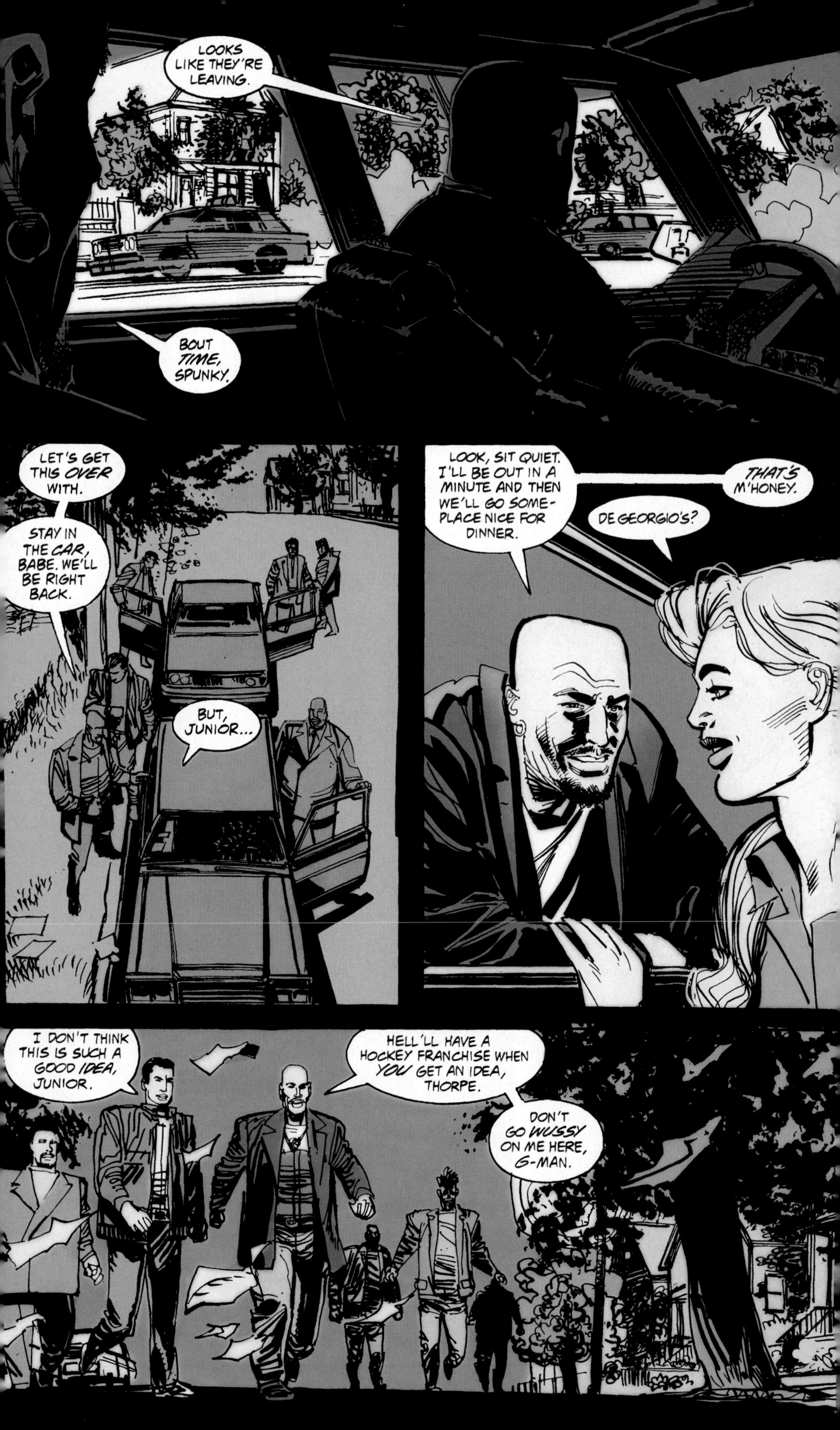
LOOKS LIKE THEY'RE LEAVING.
BOUT TIME, SPUNKY.
LET'S GET THIS OVER WITH.
STAY IN THE CAR, BABE. WE'LL BE RIGHT BACK.
BUT, JUNIOR...
LOOK, SIT QUIET. I'LL BE OUT IN A MINUTE AND THEN WE'LL GO SOME-PLACE NICE FOR DINNER.
DE GEORGIO'S?
THAT'S M'HONEY.
I DON'T THINK THIS IS SUCH A GOOD IDEA, JUNIOR.
HELL'LL HAVE A HOCKEY FRANCHISE WHEN YOU GET AN IDEA, THORPE.
DON'T GO WUSSY ON ME HERE, G-MAN.

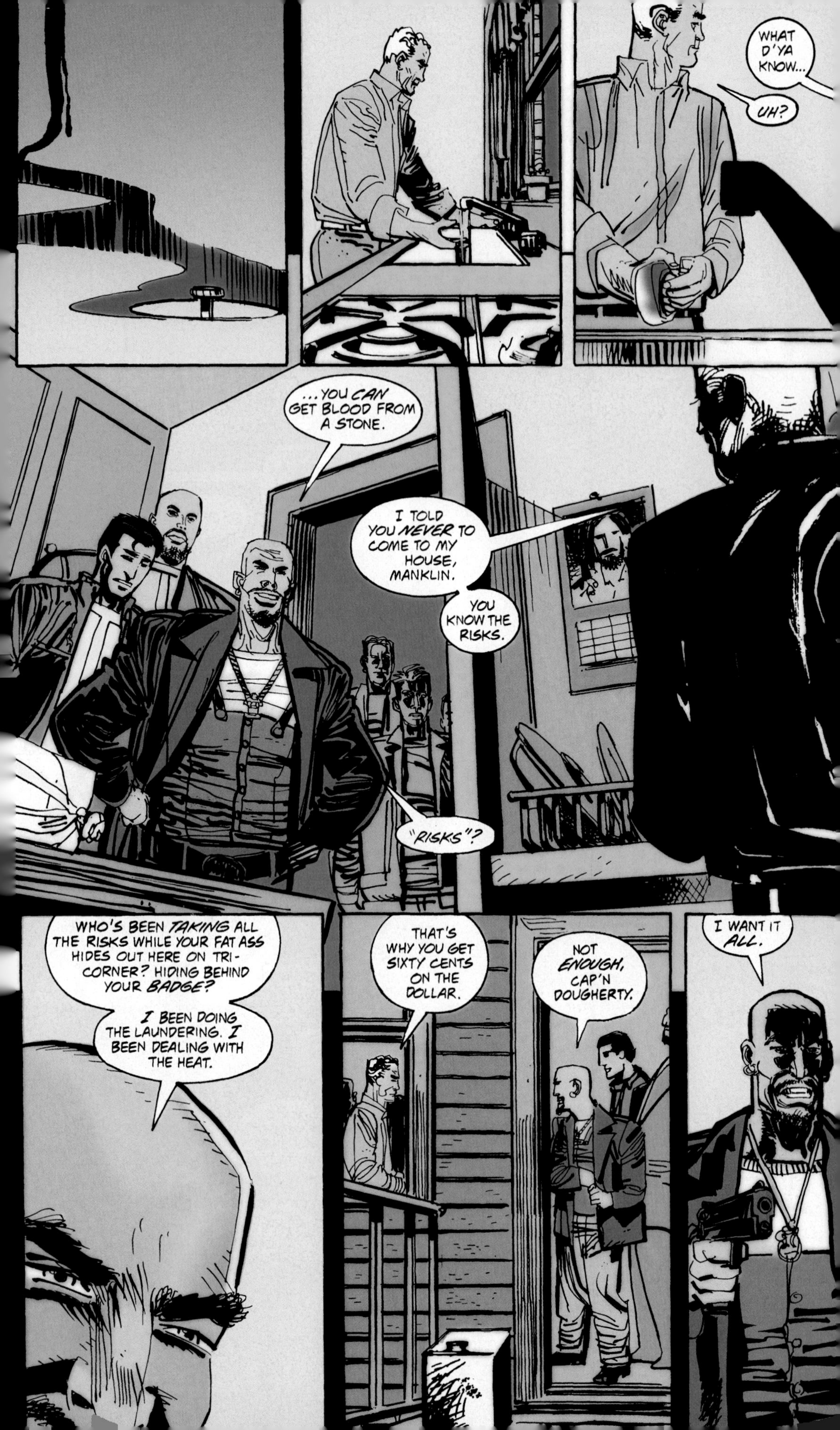
WHAT D'YA KNOW...
UH?
...YOU CAN GET BLOOD FROM A STONE.
I TOLD YOU NEVER TO COME TO MY HOUSE, MANKLIN.
YOU KNOW THE RISKS.
"RISKS"?
WHO'S BEEN TAKING ALL THE RISKS WHILE YOUR FAT ASS HIDES OUT HERE ON TRI-CORNER? HIDING BEHIND YOUR BADGE?
I BEEN DOING THE LAUNDERING. I BEEN DEALING WITH THE HEAT.
THAT'S WHY YOU GET SIXTY CENTS ON THE DOLLAR.
NOT ENOUGH, CAP'N DOUGHERTY.
I WANT IT ALL.

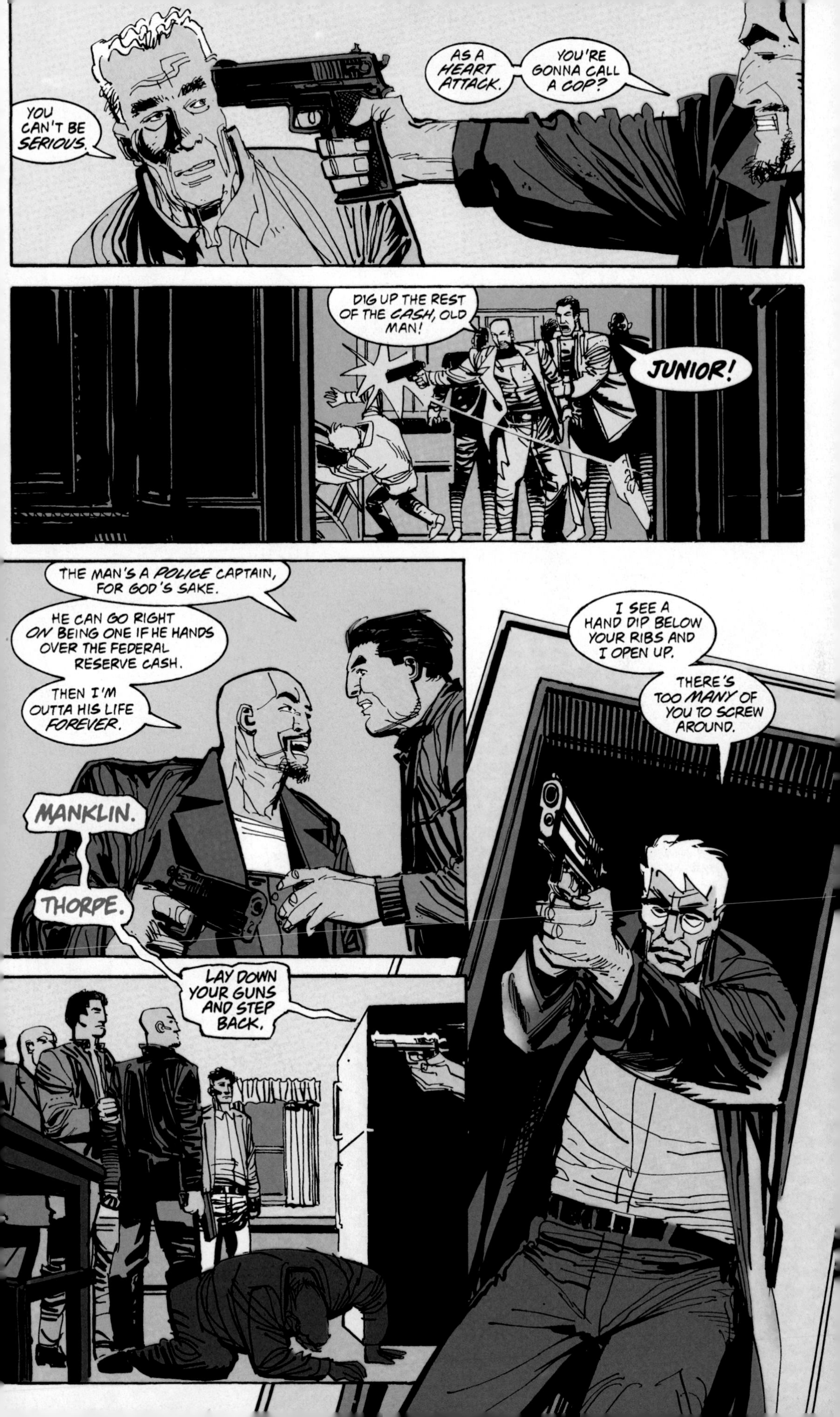
YOU CAN'T BE SERIOUS.
YOU'RE GONNA CALL A COP?
AS A HEART ATTACK.
DIG UP THE REST OF THE CASH, OLD MAN!
JUNIOR!
THE MAN'S A POLICE CAPTAIN, FOR GOD'S SAKE.
HE CAN GO RIGHT ON BEING ONE IF HE HANDS OVER THE FEDERAL RESERVE CASH.
THEN I'M OUTTA HIS LIFE FOREVER.
MANKLIN.
THORPE.
LAY DOWN YOUR GUNS AND STEP BACK.
I SEE A HAND DIP BELOW YOUR RIBS AND I OPEN UP.
THERE'S TOO MANY OF YOU TO SCREW AROUND.

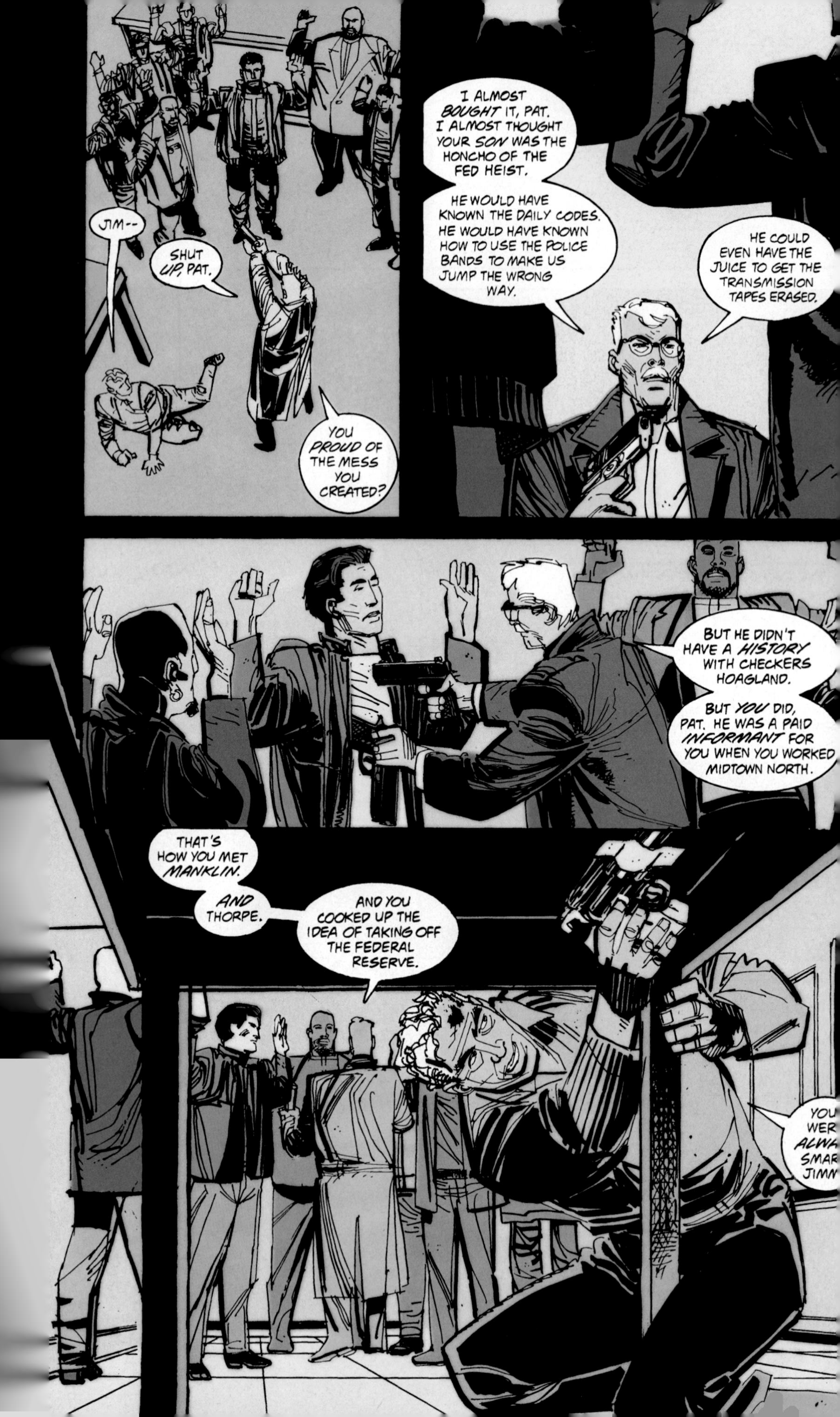
JIM--
SHUT UP, PAT.
YOU PROUD OF THE MESS YOU CREATED?
I ALMOST BOUGHT IT, PAT. I ALMOST THOUGHT YOUR SON WAS THE HONCHO OF THE FED HEIST.
HE WOULD HAVE KNOWN THE DAILY CODES. HE WOULD HAVE KNOWN HOW TO USE THE POLICE BANDS TO MAKE US JUMP THE WRONG WAY.
HE COULD EVEN HAVE THE JUICE TO GET THE TRANSMISSION TAPES ERASED.
BUT HE DIDN'T HAVE A HISTORY WITH CHECKERS HOAGLAND.
BUT YOU DID, PAT. HE WAS A PAID INFORMANT FOR YOU WHEN YOU WORKED MIDTOWN NORTH.
THAT'S HOW YOU MET MANKLIN.
AND THORPE.
AND YOU COOKED UP THE IDEA OF TAKING OFF THE FEDERAL RESERVE.

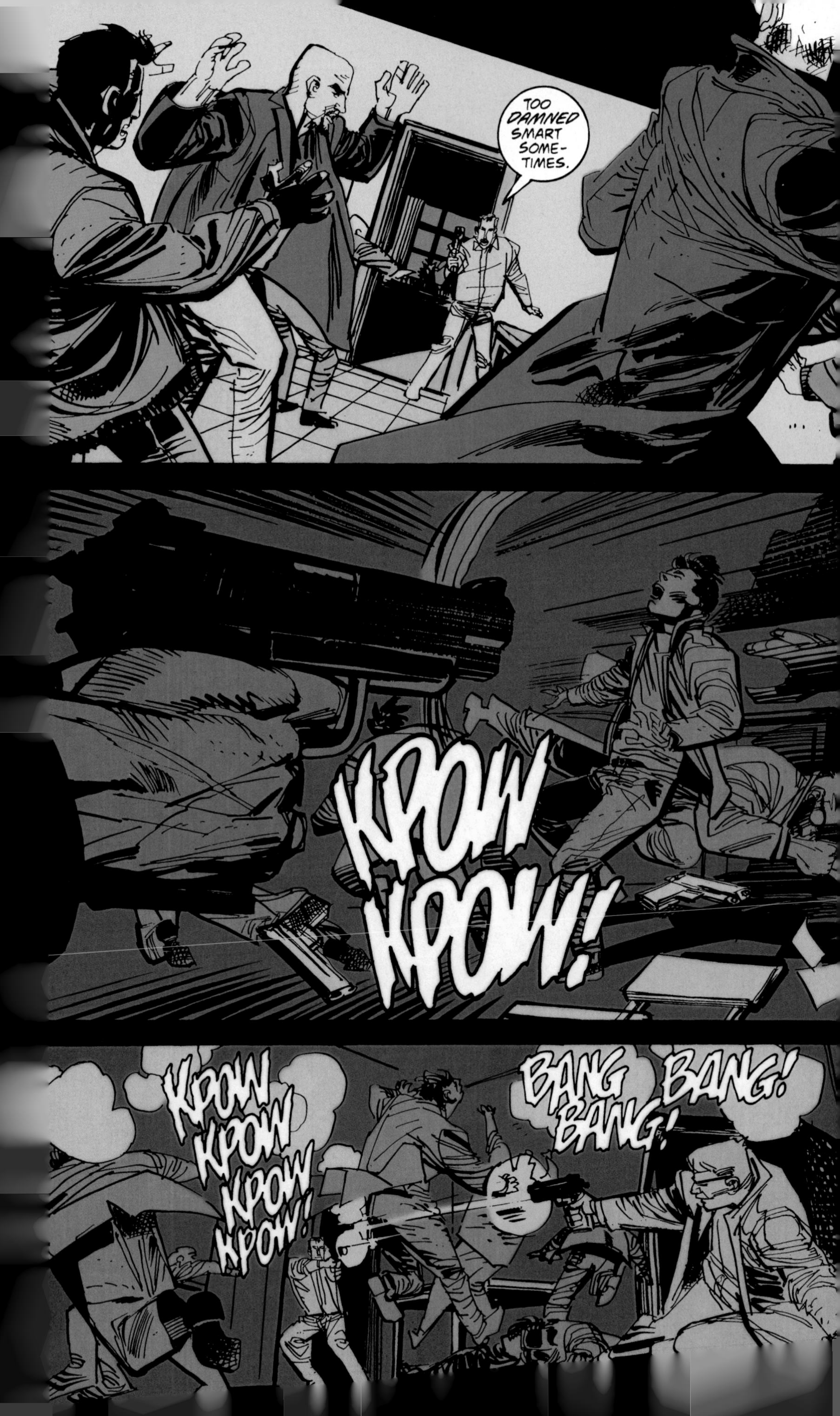
TOO DAMNED SMART SOME-TIMES.
KPOW KPOW!
KPOW KPOW KPOW KPOW!
BANG BANG! BANG!

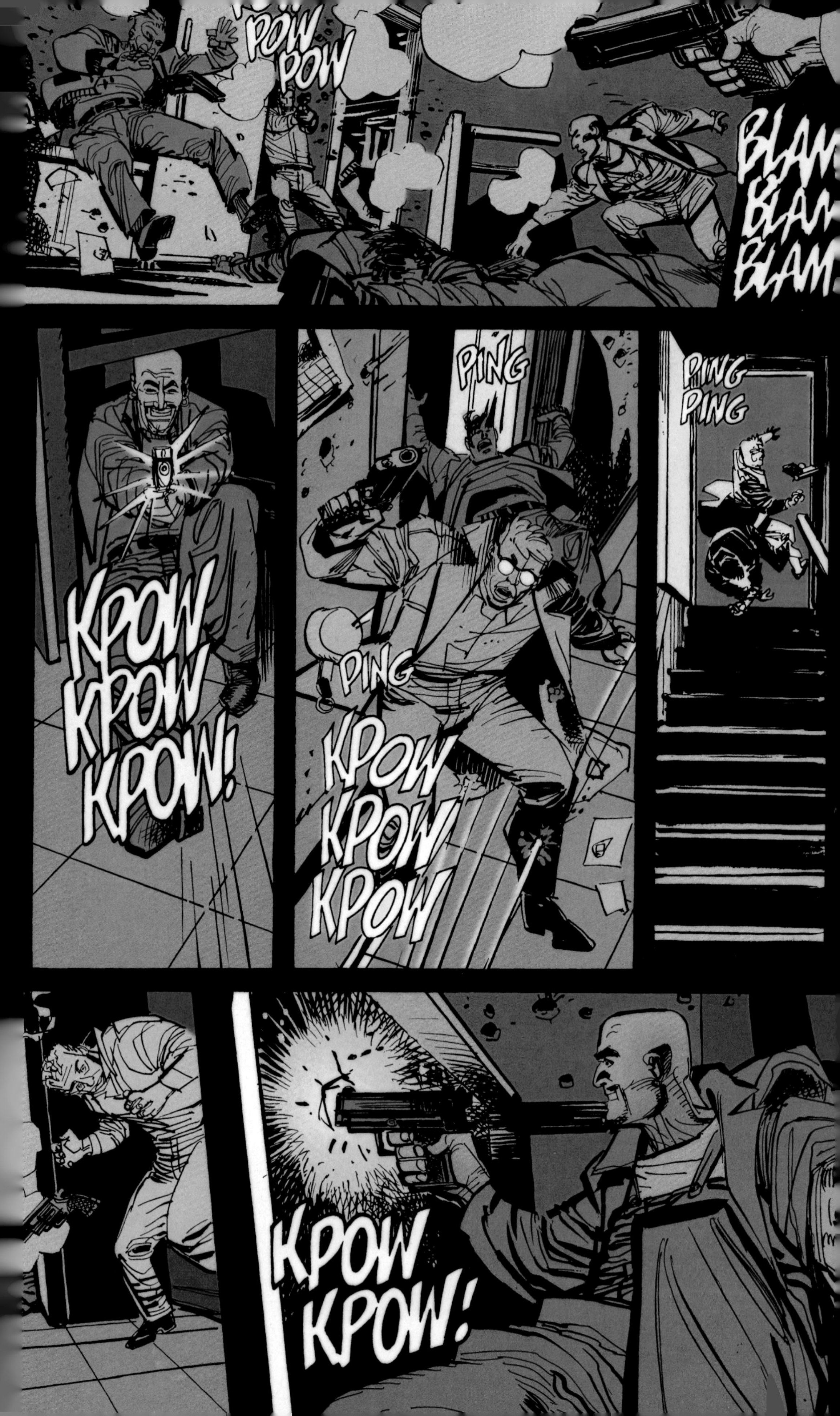
POW POW
BLAM BLAM BLAM
KPOW KPOW KPOW!
PING
PING
KPOW KPOW KPOW
PING PING
KPOW KPOW!

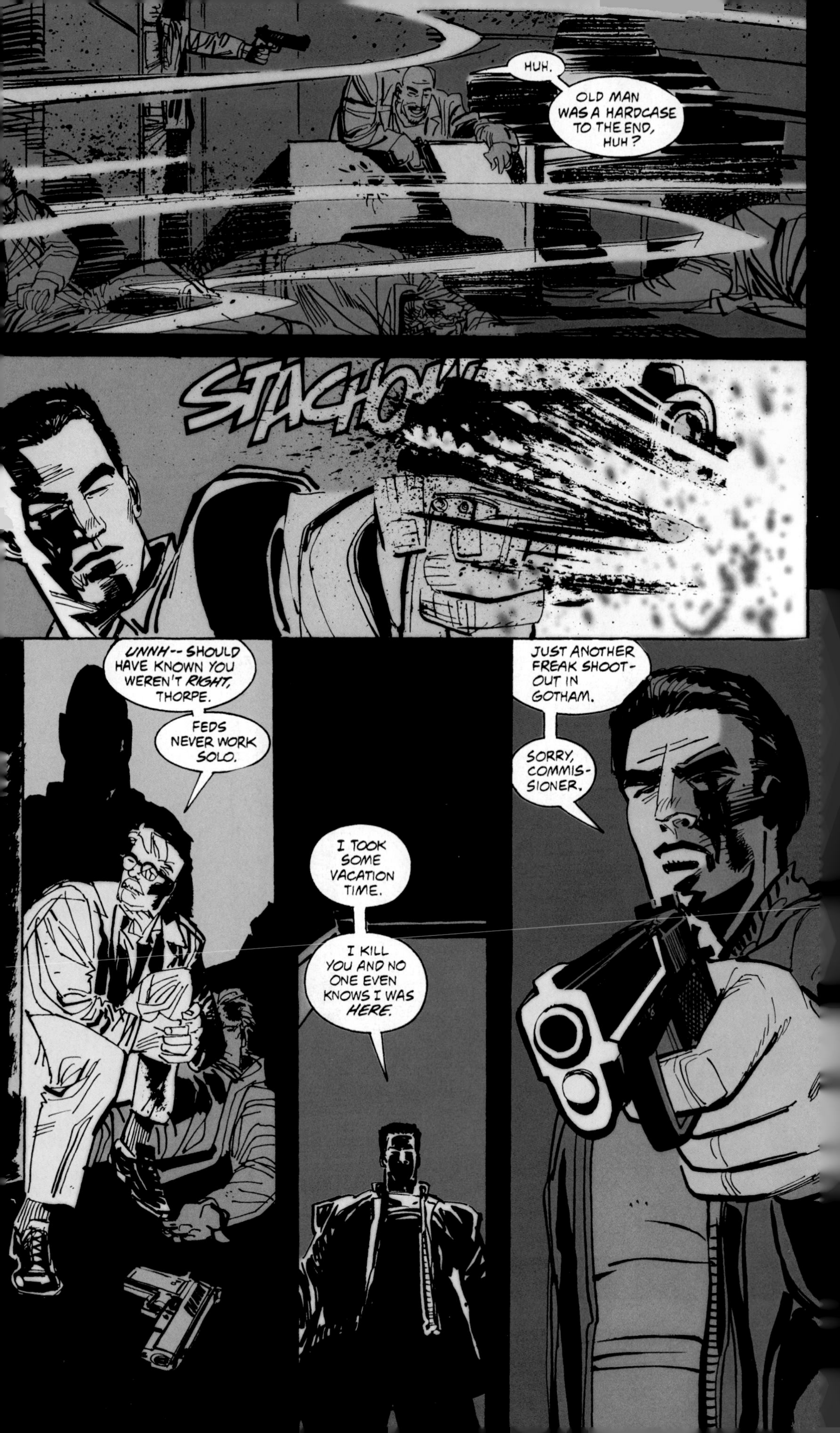
HUH.
OLD MAN WAS A HARDCASE TO THE END, HUH?
STACHOW
UNNH-- SHOULD HAVE KNOWN YOU WEREN'T RIGHT, THORPE.
FEDS NEVER WORK SOLO.
I TOOK SOME VACATION TIME.
I KILL YOU AND NO ONE EVEN KNOWS I WAS HERE.
JUST ANOTHER FREAK SHOOT-OUT IN GOTHAM.
SORRY, COMMIS-SIONER.

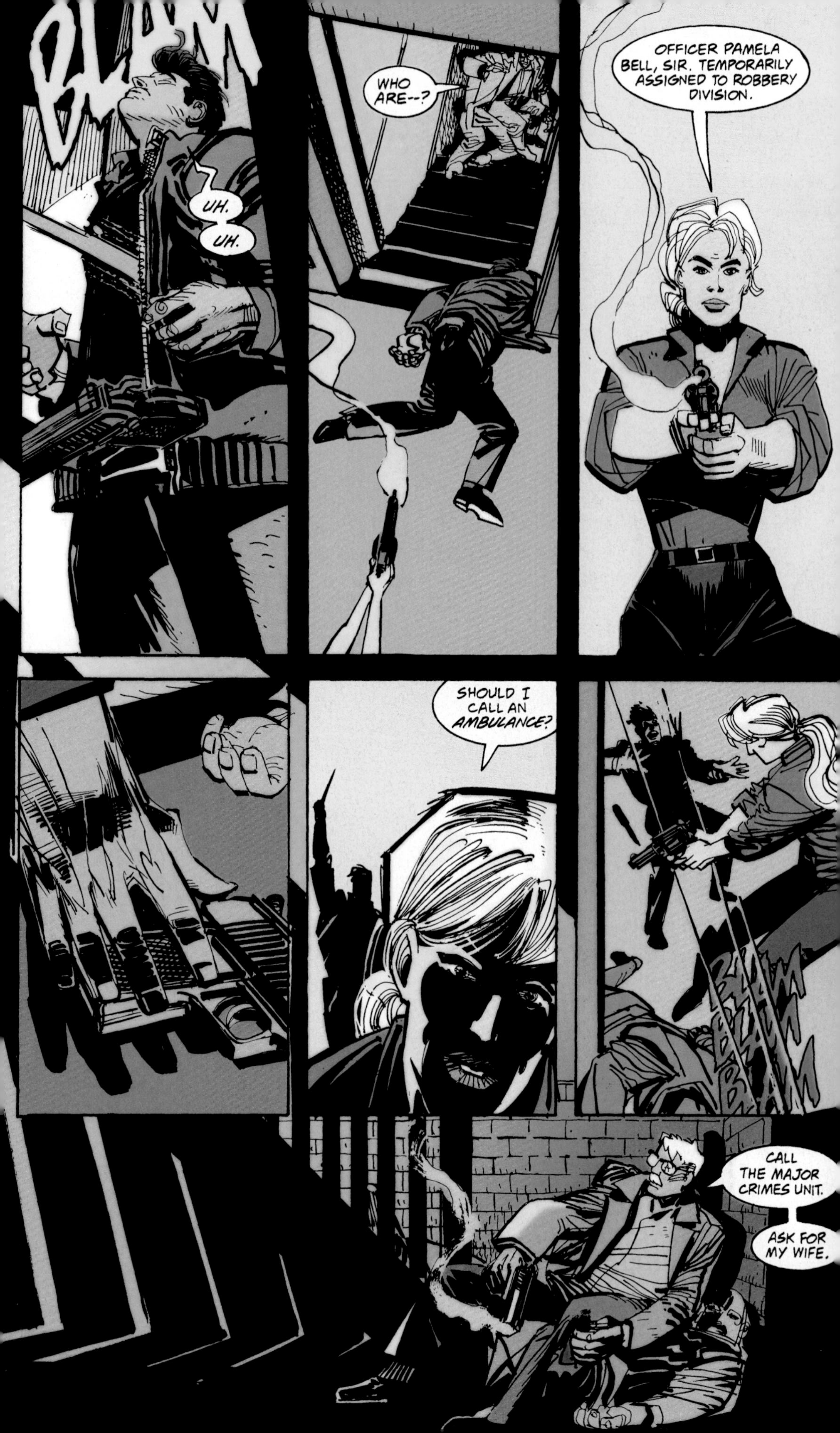

BLAM
UH.
UH.
WHO ARE--?
OFFICER PAMELA BELL, SIR. TEMPORARILY ASSIGNED TO ROBBERY DIVISION.
SHOULD I CALL AN AMBULANCE?
BLAM BLAM BLAM BLAM
CALL THE MAJOR CRIMES UNIT.
ASK FOR MY WIFE.

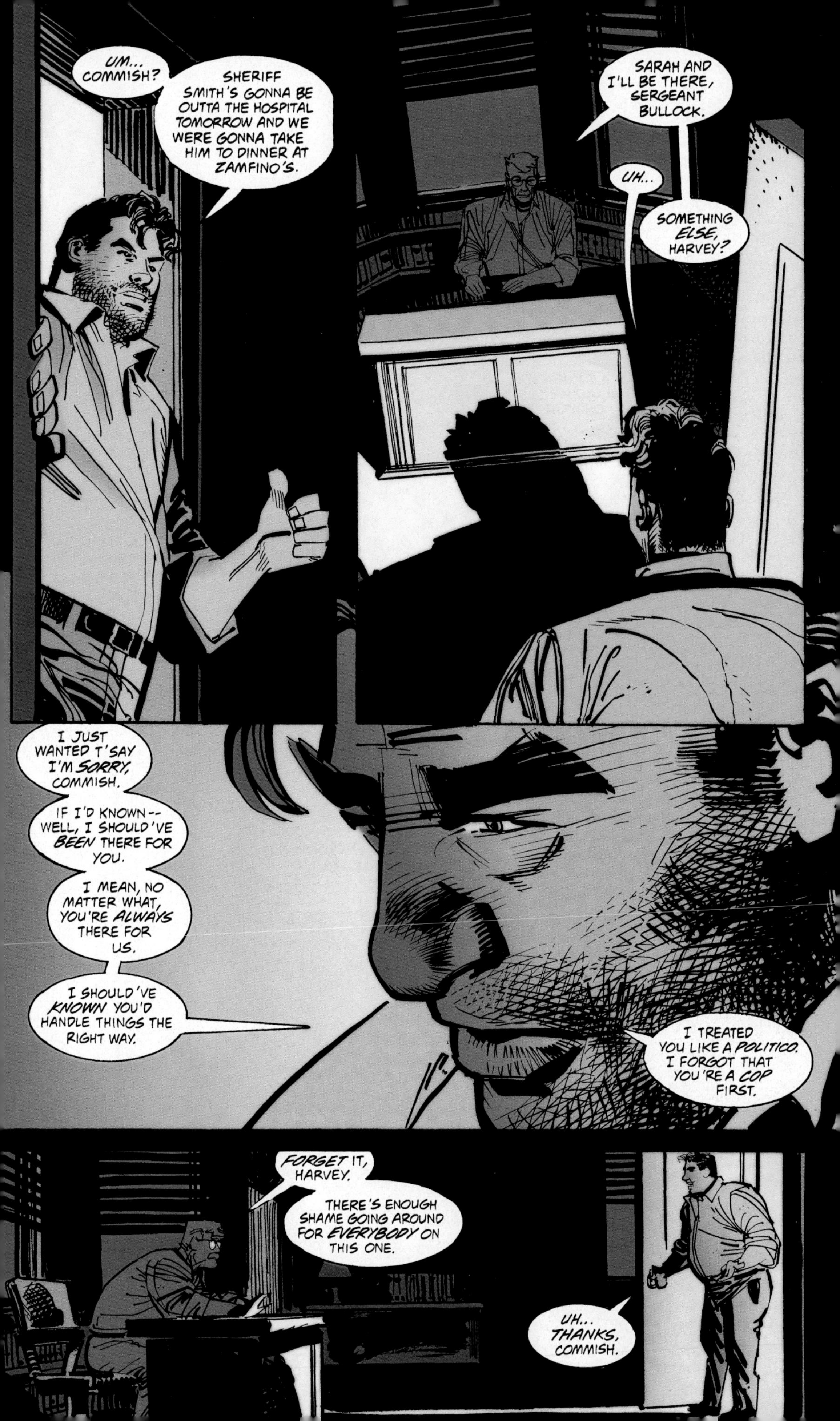
UM... COMMISH?
SHERIFF SMITH'S GONNA BE OUTTA THE HOSPITAL TOMORROW AND WE WERE GONNA TAKE HIM TO DINNER AT ZAMFINO'S.
SARAH AND I'LL BE THERE, SERGEANT BULLOCK.
UH...
SOMETHING ELSE, HARVEY?
I JUST WANTED T'SAY I'M SORRY, COMMISH.
IF I'D KNOWN -- WELL, I SHOULD'VE BEEN THERE FOR YOU.
I MEAN, NO MATTER WHAT, YOU'RE ALWAYS THERE FOR US.
I SHOULD'VE KNOWN YOU'D HANDLE THINGS THE RIGHT WAY.
I TREATED YOU LIKE A POLITICO. I FORGOT THAT YOU'RE A COP FIRST.
FORGET IT, HARVEY.
THERE'S ENOUGH SHAME GOING AROUND FOR EVERYBODY ON THIS ONE.
UH... THANKS, COMMISH.

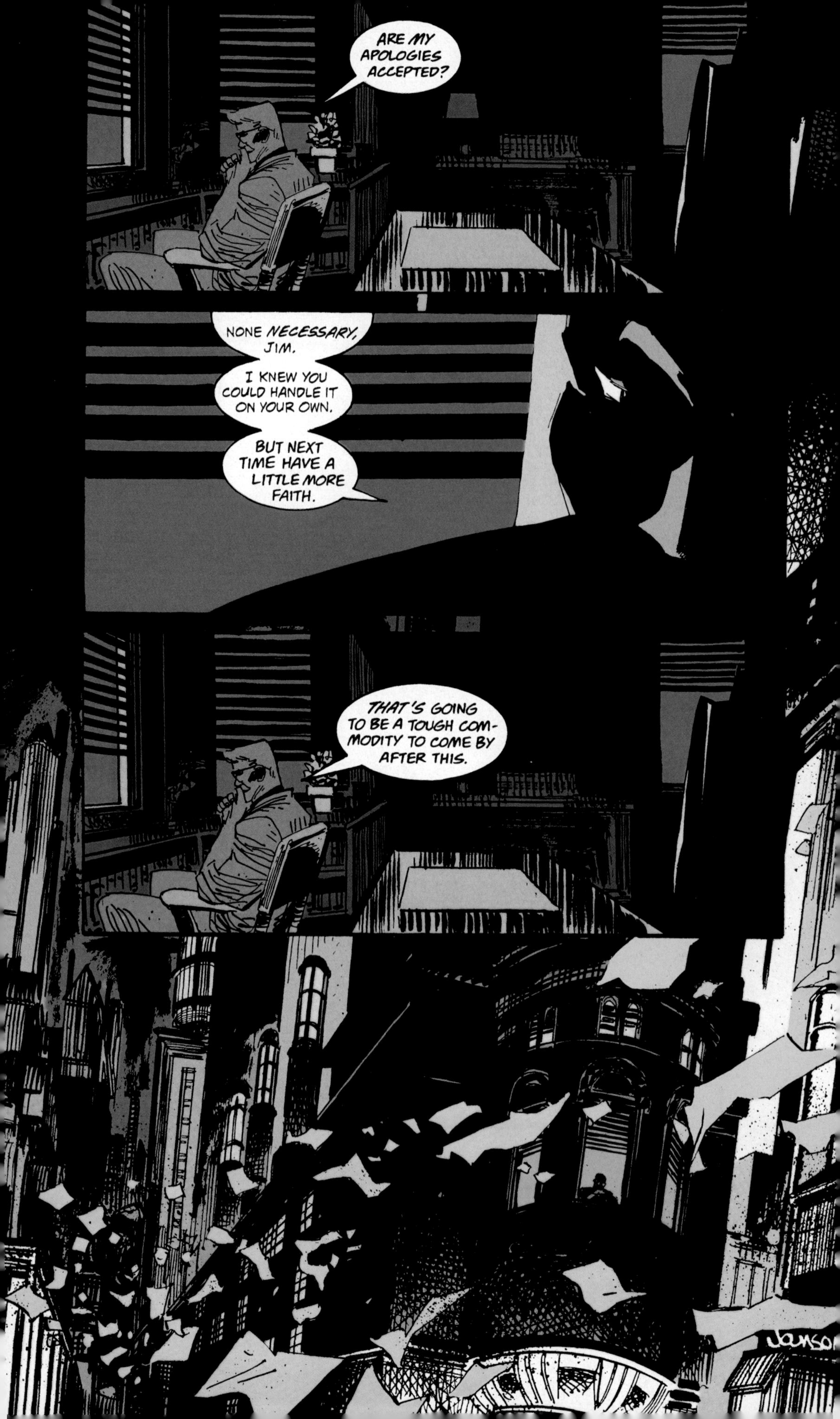
ARE MY APOLOGIES ACCEPTED?
NONE NECESSARY, JIM.
I KNEW YOU COULD HANDLE IT ON YOUR OWN.
BUT NEXT TIME HAVE A LITTLE MORE FAITH.
THAT'S GOING TO BE A TOUGH COMMODITY TO COME BY AFTER THIS.

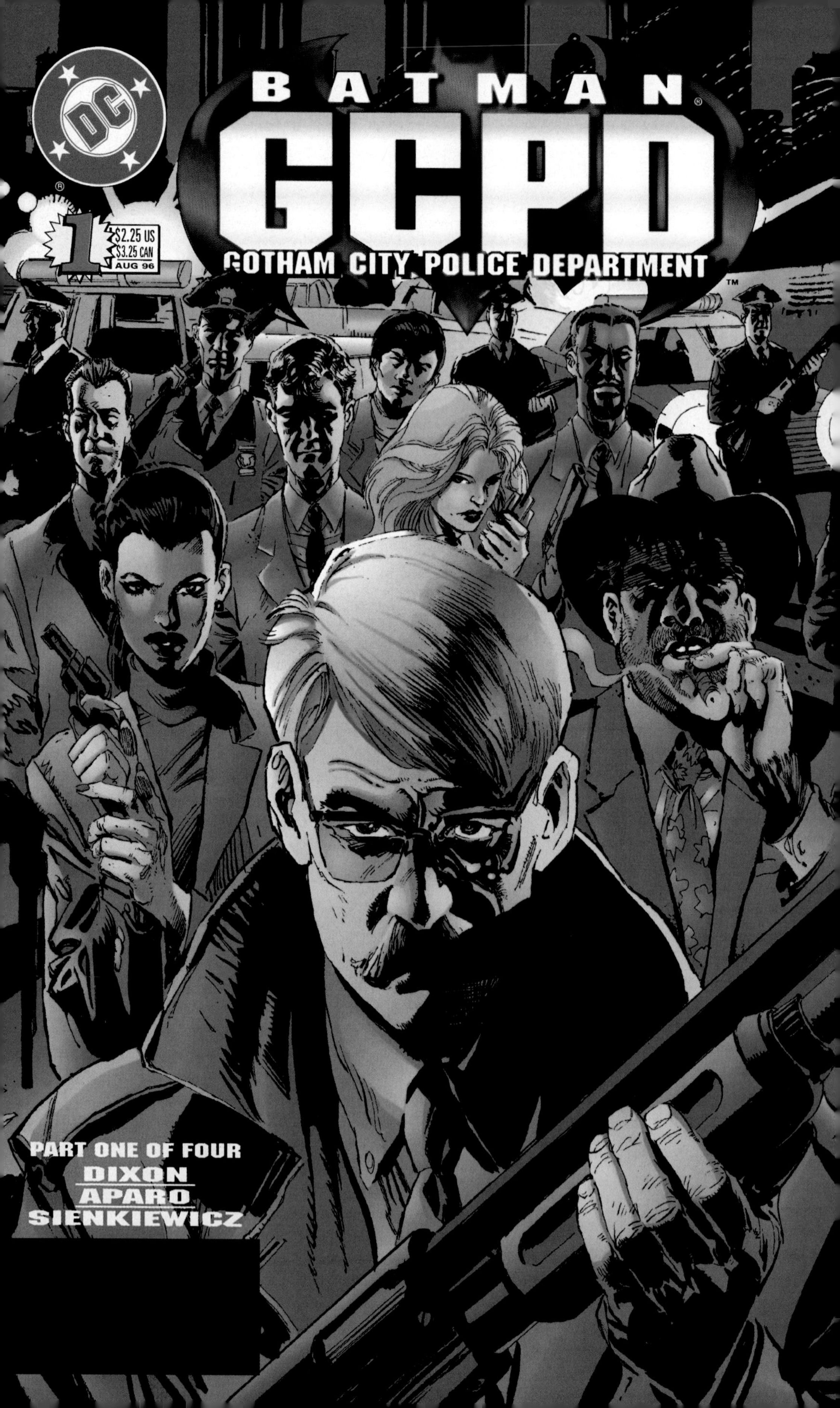

DC
BATMAN
GCPD
GOTHAM CITY POLICE DEPARTMENT
1
$2.25 US
$3.25 CAN
AUG 96
PART ONE OF FOUR
DIXON
APARO
SIENKIEWICZ

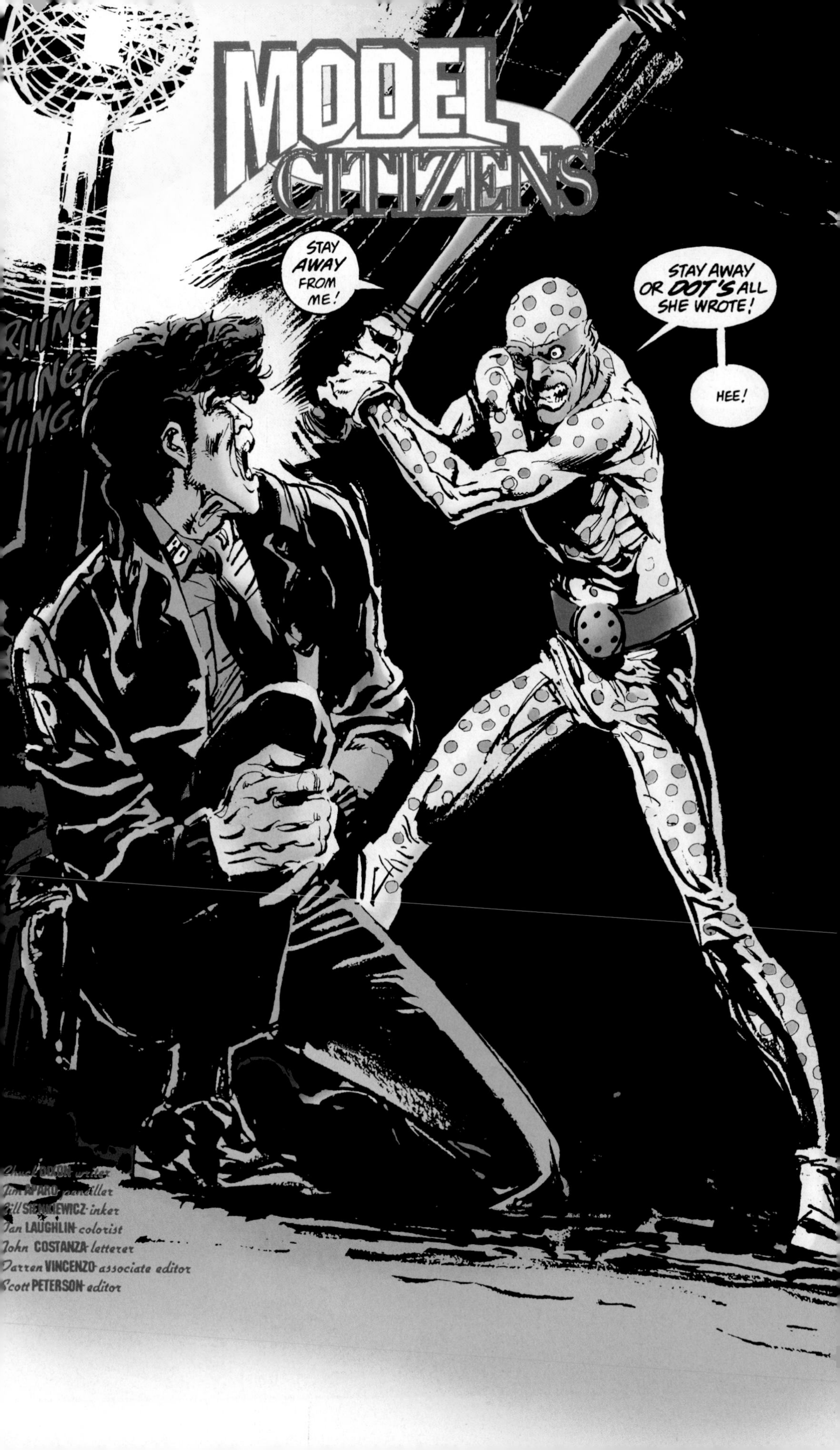
MODEL CITIZENS
STAY AWAY FROM ME!
STAY AWAY OR DOT'S ALL SHE WROTE!
HEE!
Chuck DIXON writer
Jim APARO penciller
Bill SIENKIEWICZ inker
Jan LAUGHLIN colorist
John COSTANZA letterer
Darren VINCENZO associate editor
Scott PETERSON editor

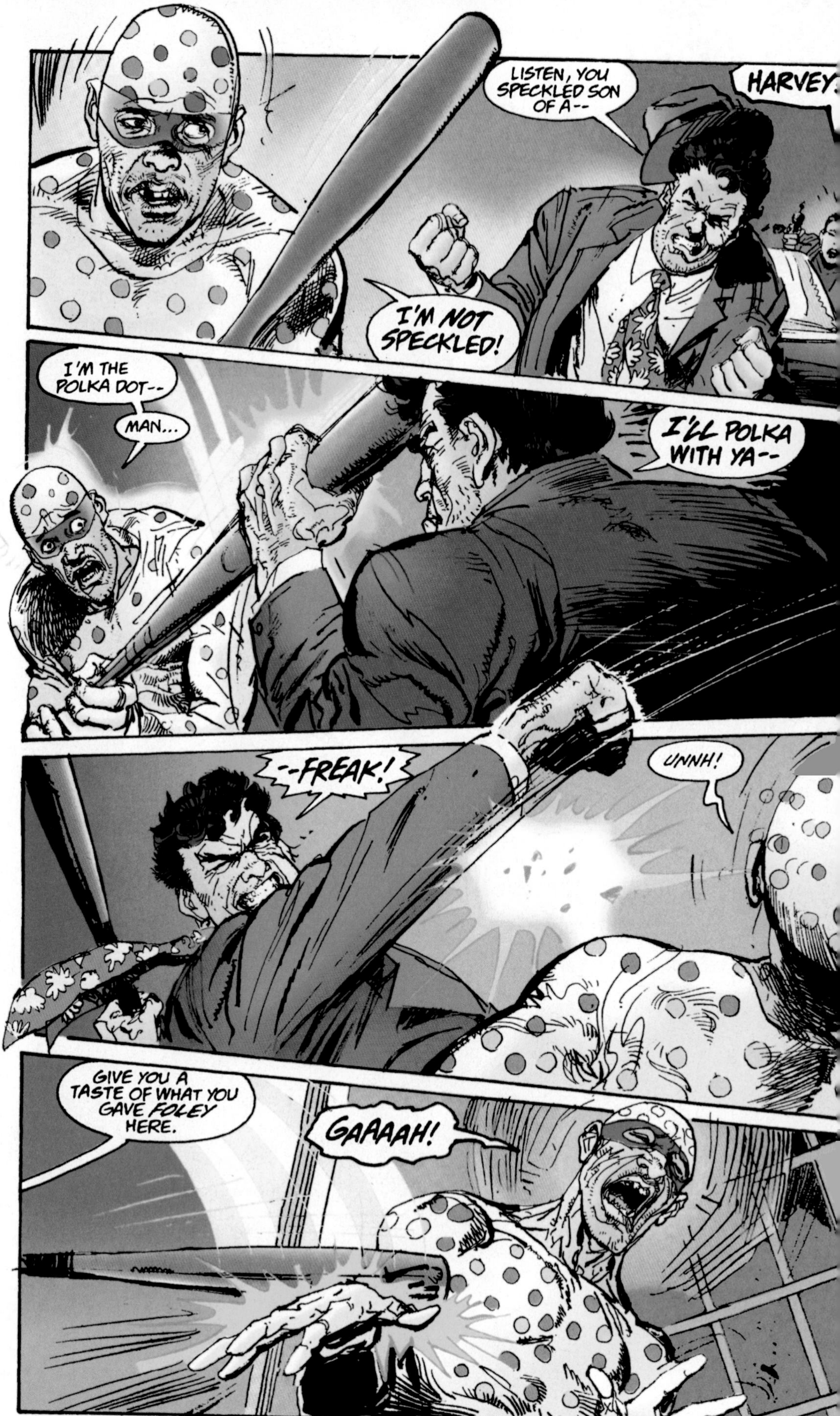
LISTEN, YOU SPECKLED SON OF A--
HARVEY!
I'M NOT SPECKLED!
I'M THE POLKA DOT--
MAN...
I'LL POLKA WITH YA--
--FREAK!
UNNH!
GIVE YOU A TASTE OF WHAT YOU GAVE FOLEY HERE.
GAAAAH!

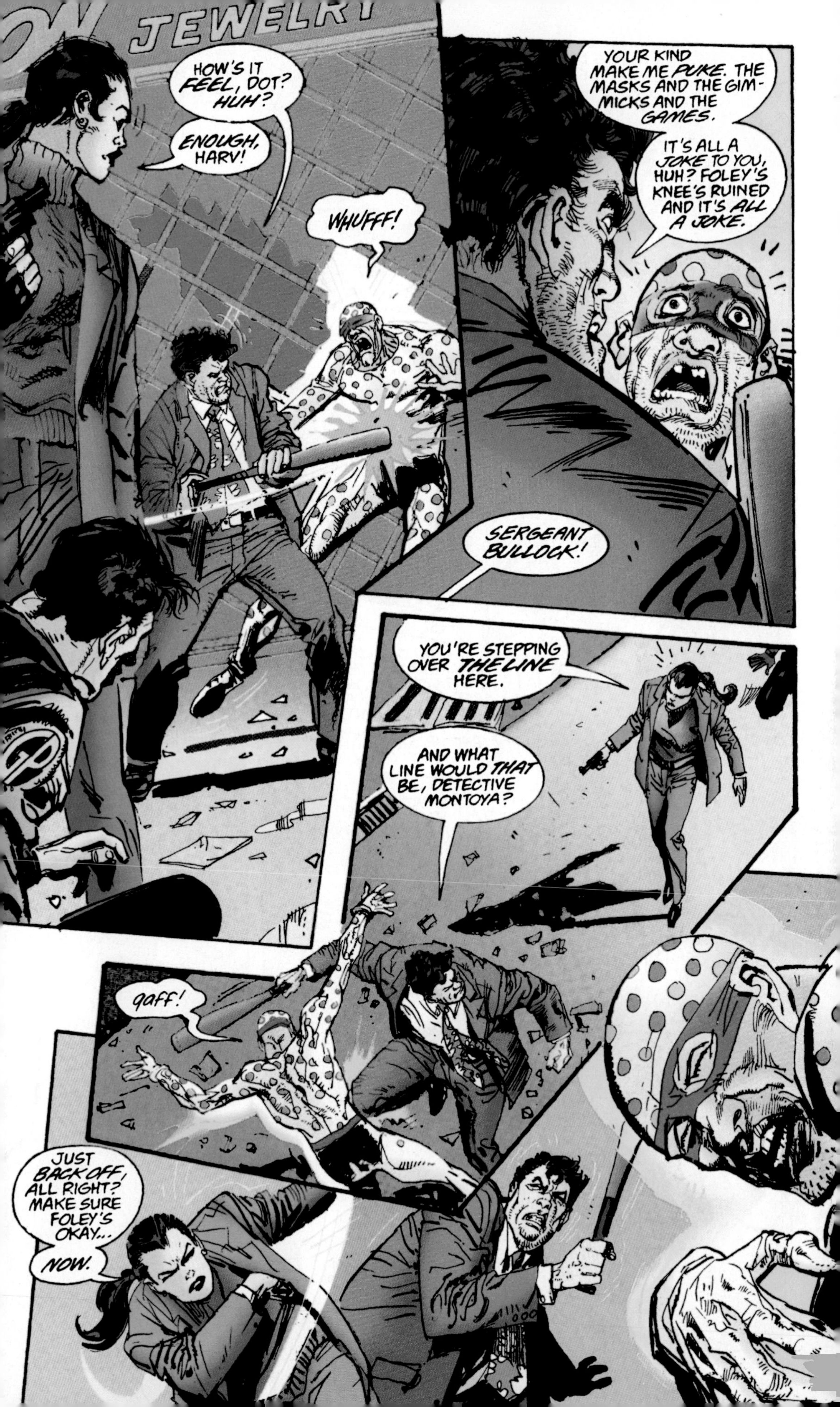
JEWELRY
HOW'S IT FEEL, DOT? HUH?
ENOUGH, HARV!
WHUFFF!
YOUR KIND MAKE ME PUKE. THE MASKS AND THE GIMMICKS AND THE GAMES.
IT'S ALL A JOKE TO YOU, HUH? FOLEY'S KNEE'S RUINED AND IT'S ALL A JOKE.
SERGEANT BULLOCK!
YOU'RE STEPPING OVER THE LINE HERE.
AND WHAT LINE WOULD THAT BE, DETECTIVE MONTOYA?
gaff!
JUST BACK OFF, ALL RIGHT? MAKE SURE FOLEY'S OKAY...
NOW.

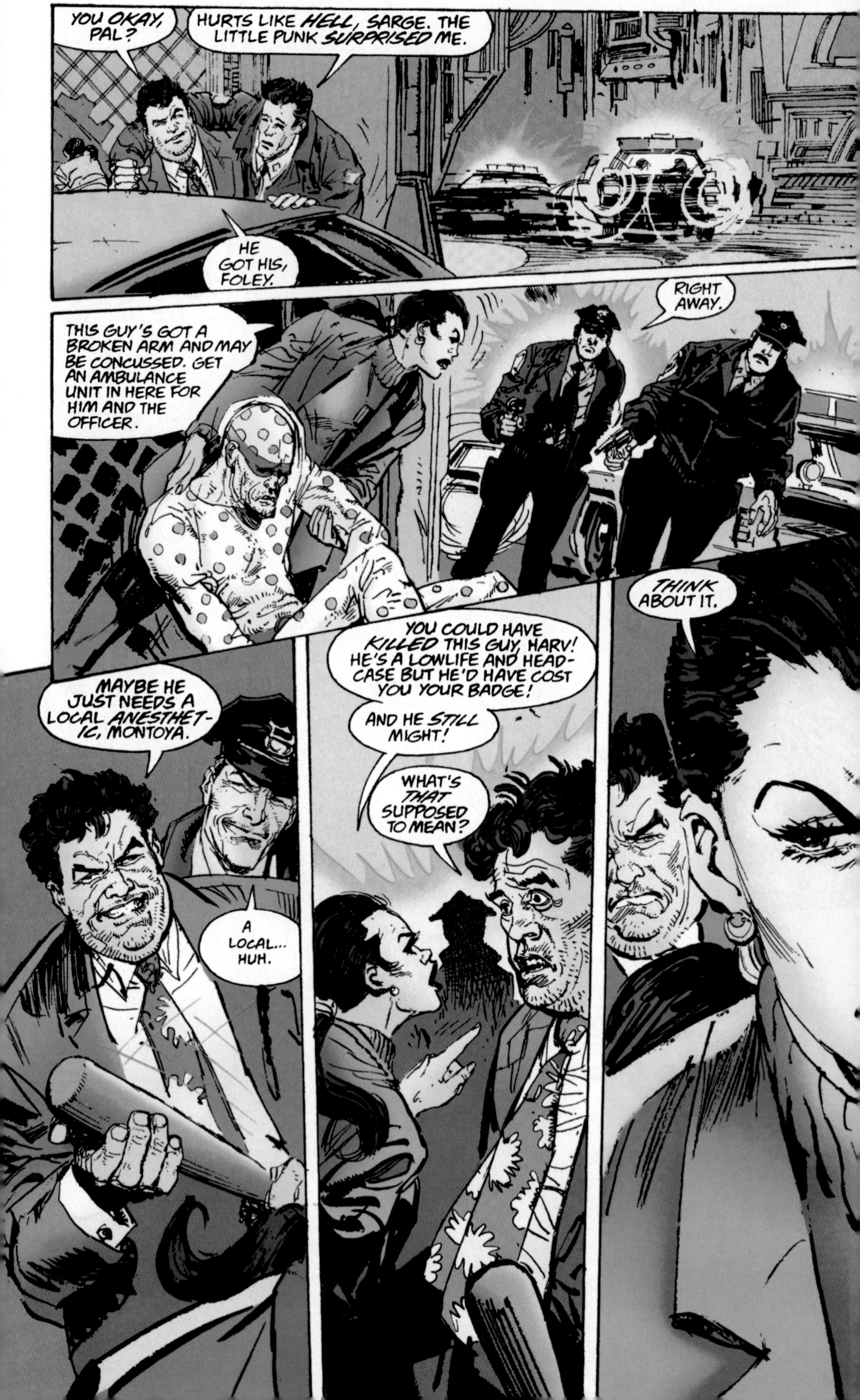

YOU OKAY, PAL?
HURTS LIKE HELL, SARGE. THE LITTLE PUNK SURPRISED ME.
HE GOT HIS, FOLEY.
THIS GUY'S GOT A BROKEN ARM AND MAY BE CONCUSSED. GET AN AMBULANCE UNIT IN HERE FOR HIM AND THE OFFICER.
RIGHT AWAY.
MAYBE HE JUST NEEDS A LOCAL ANESTHETIC, MONTOYA.
A LOCAL... HUH.
YOU COULD HAVE KILLED THIS GUY, HARV! HE'S A LOWLIFE AND HEAD-CASE BUT HE'D HAVE COST YOU YOUR BADGE!
AND HE STILL MIGHT!
WHAT'S THAT SUPPOSED TO MEAN?
THINK ABOUT IT.

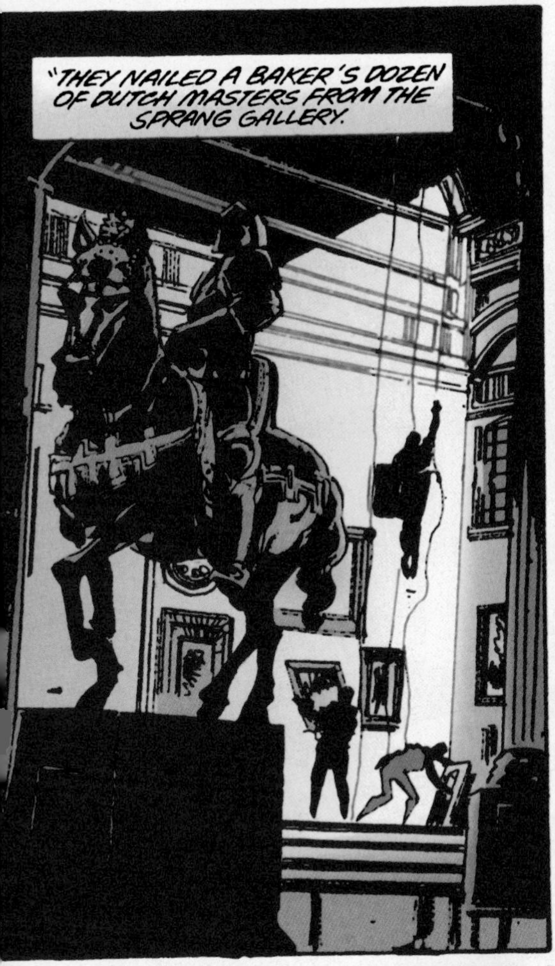
"THEY NAILED A BAKER'S DOZEN OF DUTCH MASTERS FROM THE SPRANG GALLERY.

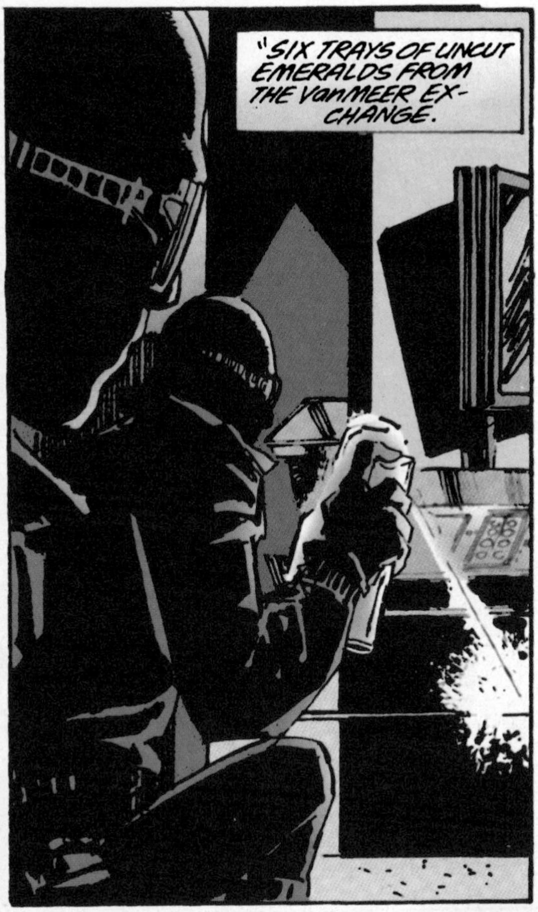
"SIX TRAYS OF UNCUT EMERALDS FROM THE VanMEER EX-CHANGE.

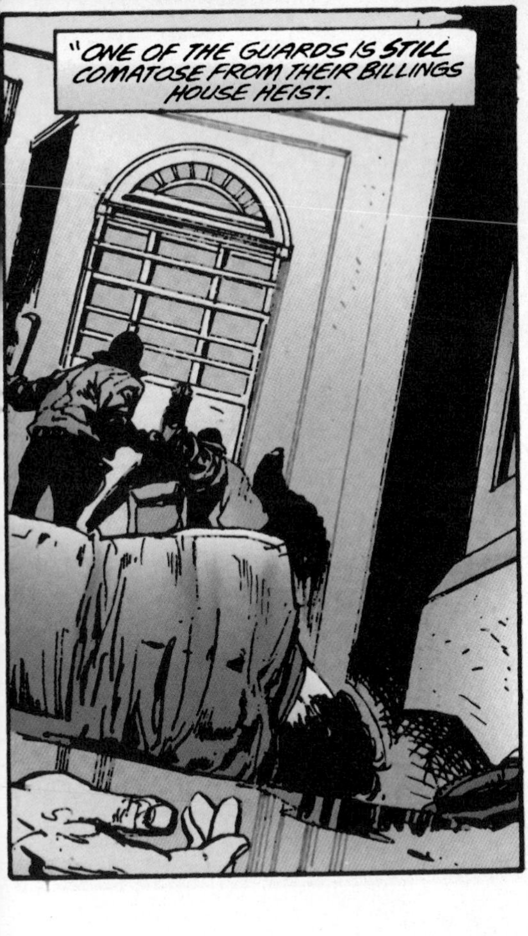
"ONE OF THE GUARDS IS STILL COMATOSE FROM THEIR BILLINGS HOUSE HEIST.

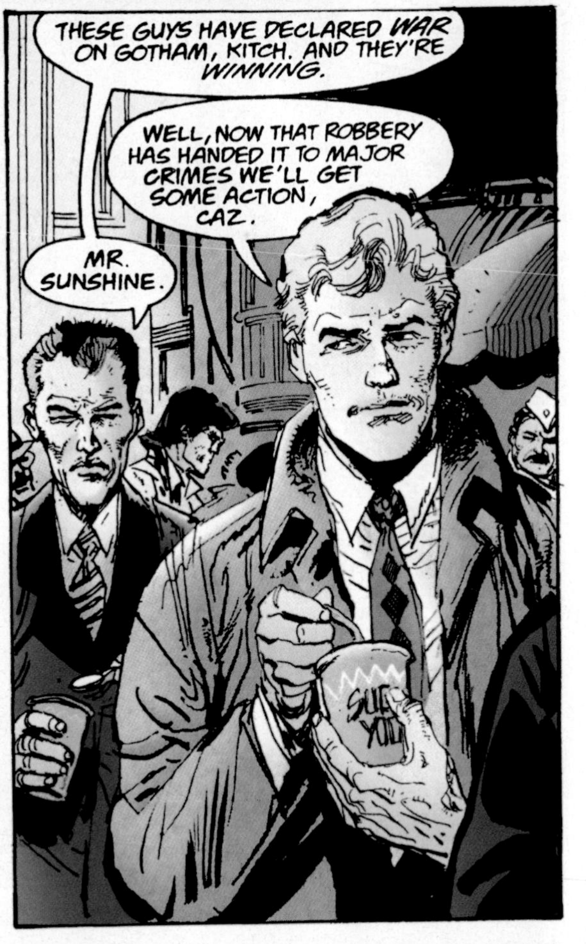
THESE GUYS HAVE DECLARED WAR ON GOTHAM, KITCH. AND THEY'RE WINNING.
WELL, NOW THAT ROBBERY HAS HANDED IT TO MAJOR CRIMES WE'LL GET SOME ACTION, CAZ.
MR. SUNSHINE.

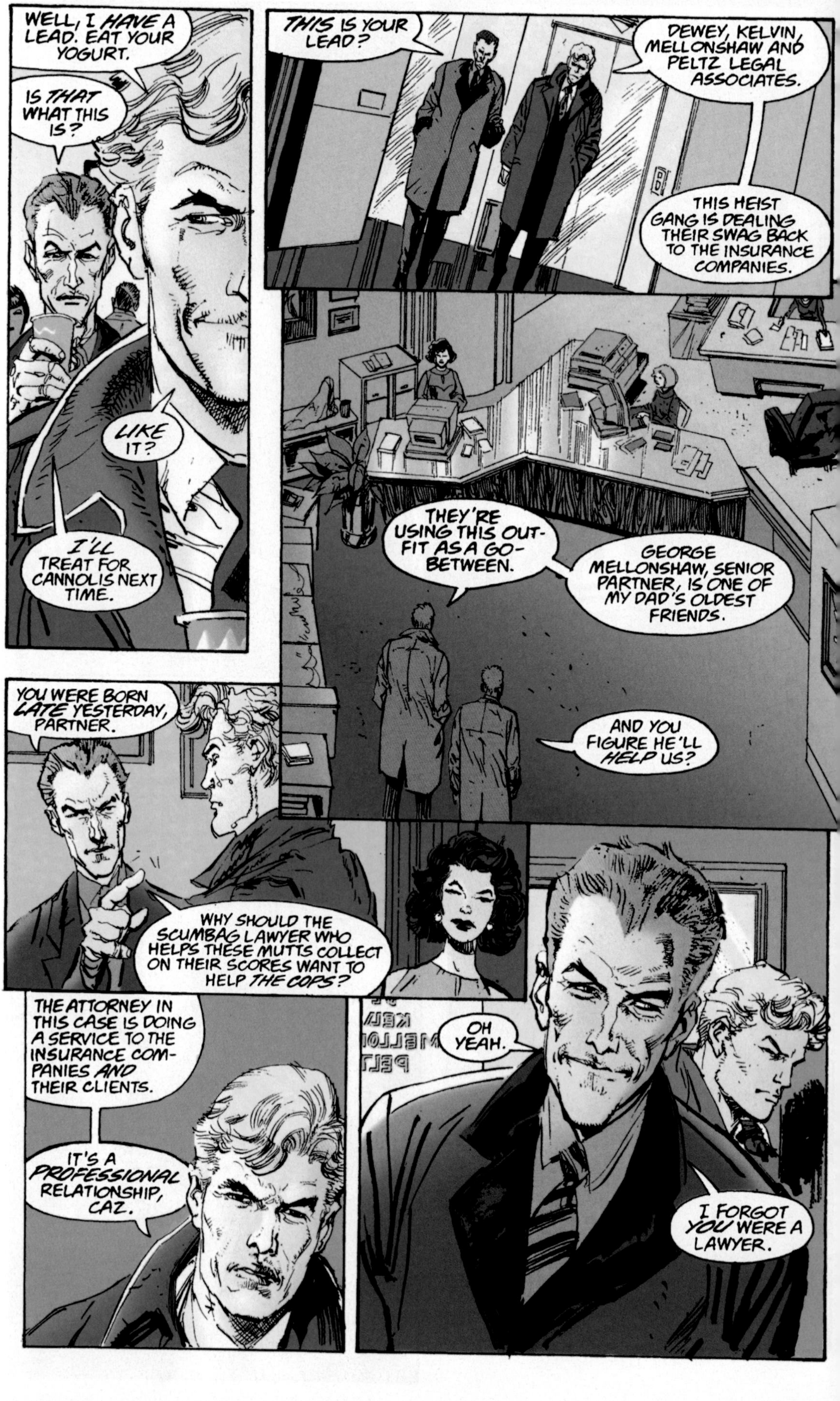

WELL, I HAVE A LEAD. EAT YOUR YOGURT.
IS THAT WHAT THIS IS?
LIKE IT?
I'LL TREAT FOR CANNOLIS NEXT TIME.
THIS IS YOUR LEAD?
DEWEY, KELVIN, MELLONSHAW AND PELTZ LEGAL ASSOCIATES.
THIS HEIST GANG IS DEALING THEIR SWAG BACK TO THE INSURANCE COMPANIES.
THEY'RE USING THIS OUT-FIT AS A GO-BETWEEN.
GEORGE MELLONSHAW, SENIOR PARTNER, IS ONE OF MY DAD'S OLDEST FRIENDS.
AND YOU FIGURE HE'LL HELP US?
YOU WERE BORN LATE YESTERDAY, PARTNER.
WHY SHOULD THE SCUMBAG LAWYER WHO HELPS THESE MUTTS COLLECT ON THEIR SCORES WANT TO HELP THE COPS?
THE ATTORNEY IN THIS CASE IS DOING A SERVICE TO THE INSURANCE COM-PANIES AND THEIR CLIENTS.
IT'S A PROFESSIONAL RELATIONSHIP, CAZ.
OH YEAH.
I FORGOT YOU WERE A LAWYER.

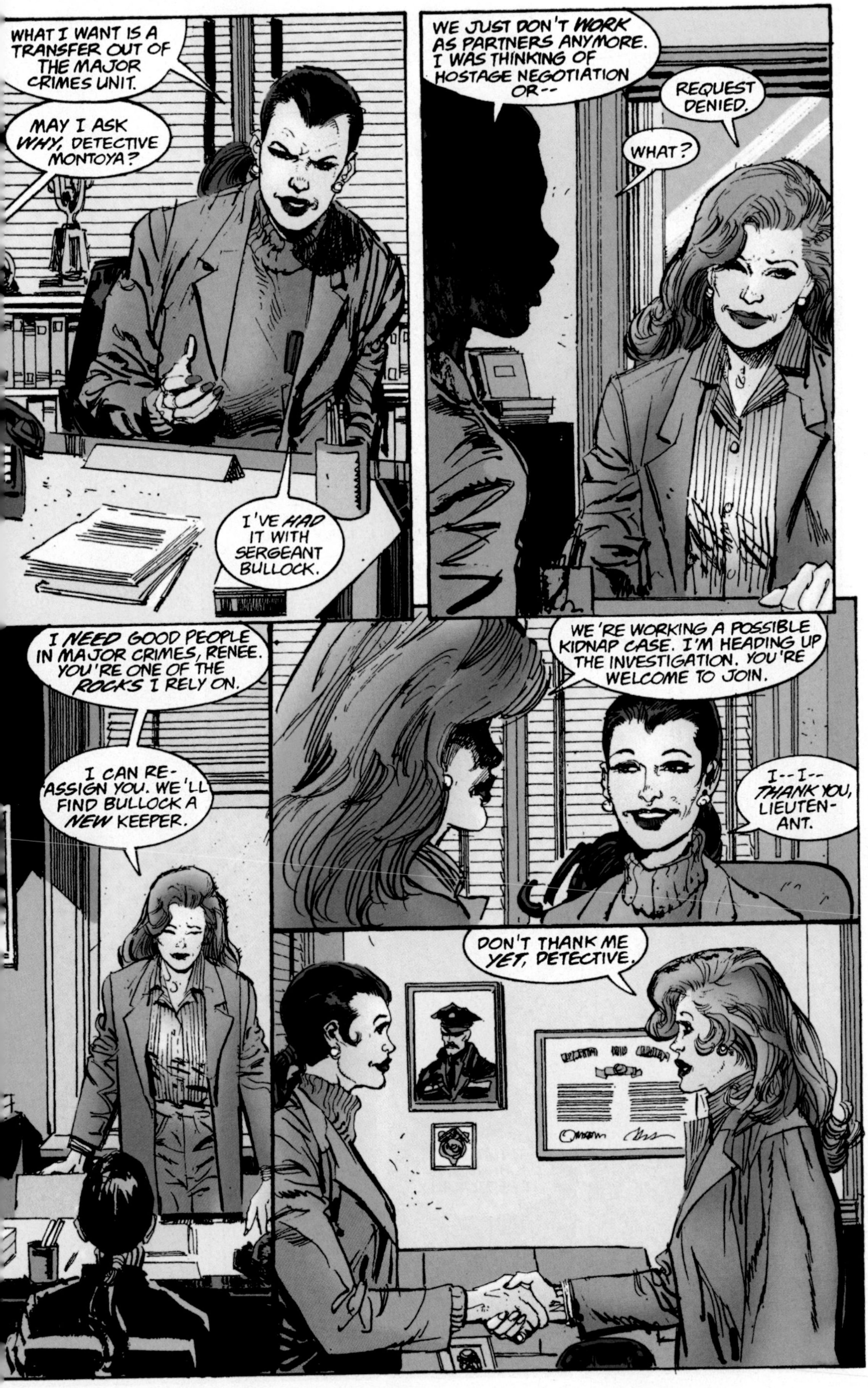
WHAT I WANT IS A TRANSFER OUT OF THE MAJOR CRIMES UNIT.
MAY I ASK WHY, DETECTIVE MONTOYA?
I'VE HAD IT WITH SERGEANT BULLOCK.
WE JUST DON'T WORK AS PARTNERS ANYMORE. I WAS THINKING OF HOSTAGE NEGOTIATION OR--
REQUEST DENIED.
WHAT?
I NEED GOOD PEOPLE IN MAJOR CRIMES, RENEE. YOU'RE ONE OF THE ROCKS I RELY ON.
I CAN RE-ASSIGN YOU. WE'LL FIND BULLOCK A NEW KEEPER.
WE'RE WORKING A POSSIBLE KIDNAP CASE. I'M HEADING UP THE INVESTIGATION. YOU'RE WELCOME TO JOIN.
I--I--THANK YOU, LIEUTEN-ANT.
DON'T THANK ME YET, DETECTIVE.

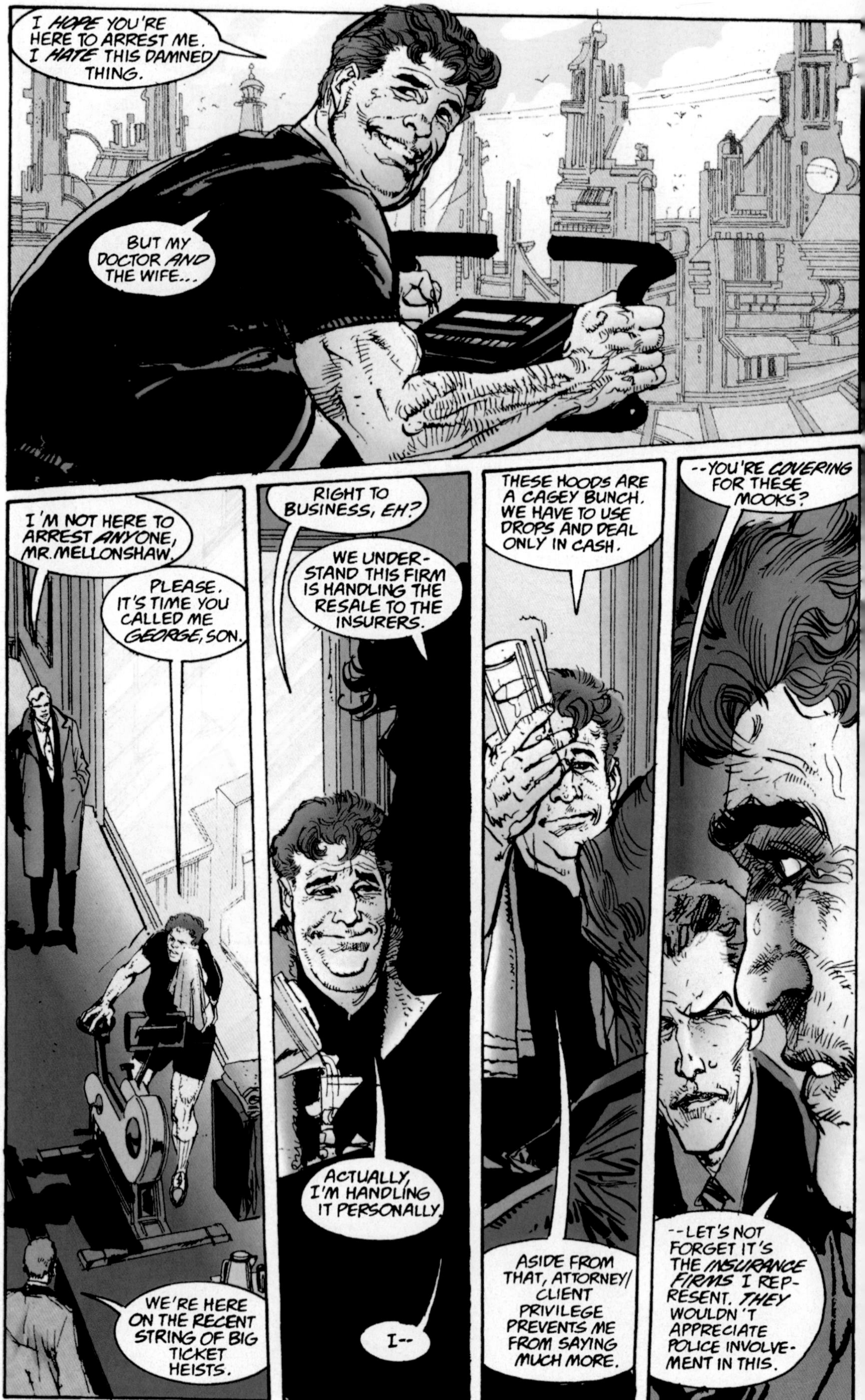

I HOPE YOU'RE HERE TO ARREST ME. I HATE THIS DAMNED THING.
BUT MY DOCTOR AND THE WIFE...
I'M NOT HERE TO ARREST ANYONE, MR. MELLONSHAW.
PLEASE. IT'S TIME YOU CALLED ME GEORGE, SON.
WE'RE HERE ON THE RECENT STRING OF BIG TICKET HEISTS.
RIGHT TO BUSINESS, EH?
WE UNDERSTAND THIS FIRM IS HANDLING THE RESALE TO THE INSURERS.
ACTUALLY, I'M HANDLING IT PERSONALLY.
I--
THESE HOODS ARE A CASEY BUNCH. WE HAVE TO USE DROPS AND DEAL ONLY IN CASH.
ASIDE FROM THAT, ATTORNEY/CLIENT PRIVILEGE PREVENTS ME FROM SAYING MUCH MORE.
--YOU'RE COVERING FOR THESE MOOKS?
--LET'S NOT FORGET IT'S THE INSURANCE FIRMS I REPRESENT. THEY WOULDN'T APPRECIATE POLICE INVOLVEMENT IN THIS.

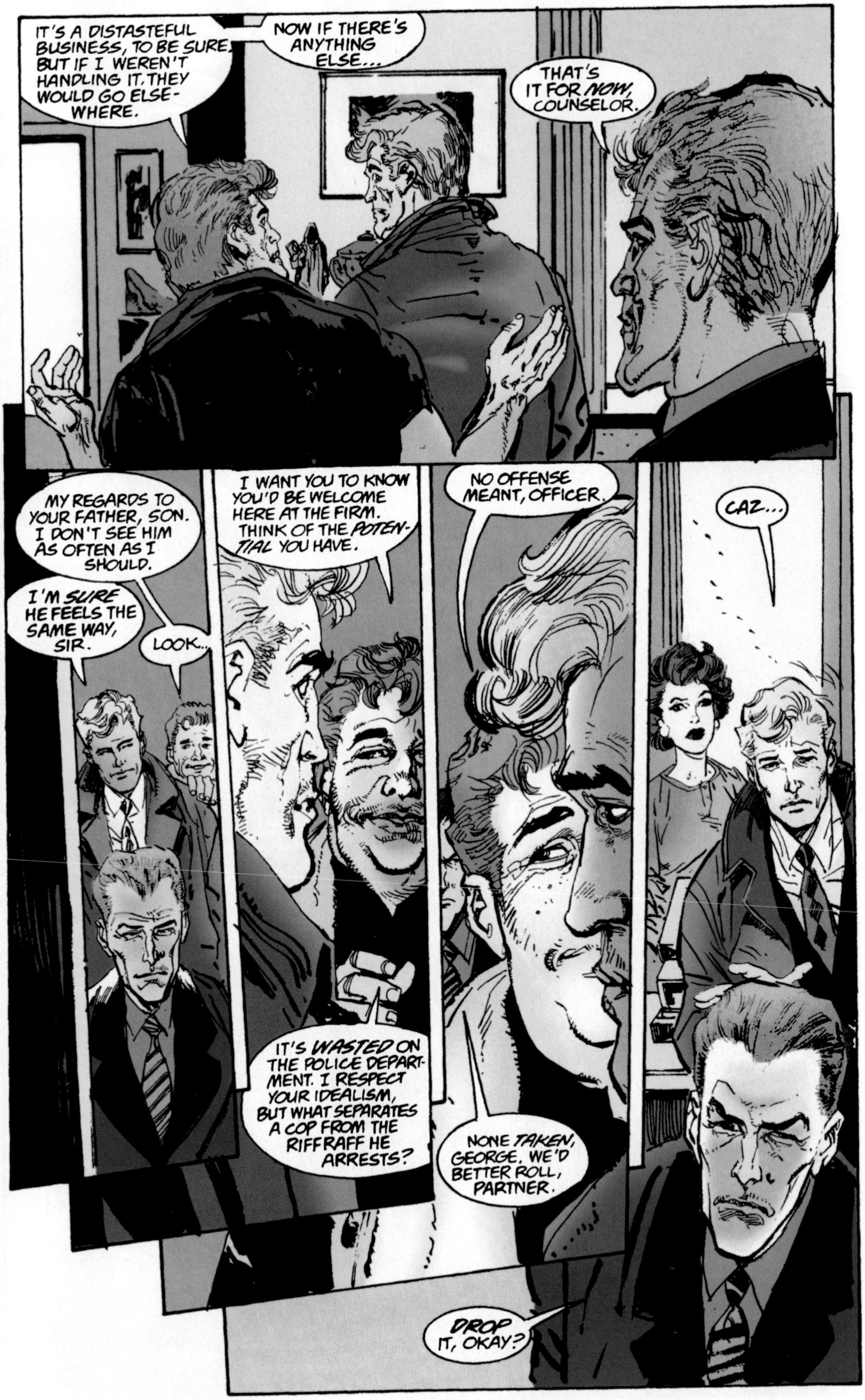

IT'S A DISTASTEFUL BUSINESS, TO BE SURE, BUT IF I WEREN'T HANDLING IT, THEY WOULD GO ELSE-WHERE.
NOW IF THERE'S ANYTHING ELSE...
THAT'S IT FOR *NOW*, COUNSELOR.
MY REGARDS TO YOUR FATHER, SON. I DON'T SEE HIM AS OFTEN AS I SHOULD.
I'M *SURE* HE FEELS THE SAME WAY, SIR.
LOOK...
I WANT YOU TO KNOW YOU'D BE WELCOME HERE AT THE FIRM. THINK OF THE *POTEN-TIAL* YOU HAVE.
IT'S *WASTED* ON THE POLICE DEPART-MENT. I RESPECT YOUR IDEALISM, BUT WHAT SEPARATES A COP FROM THE RIFFRAFF HE ARRESTS?
NO OFFENSE MEANT, OFFICER.
NONE *TAKEN*, GEORGE. WE'D BETTER ROLL, PARTNER.
CAZ...
DROP IT, OKAY?

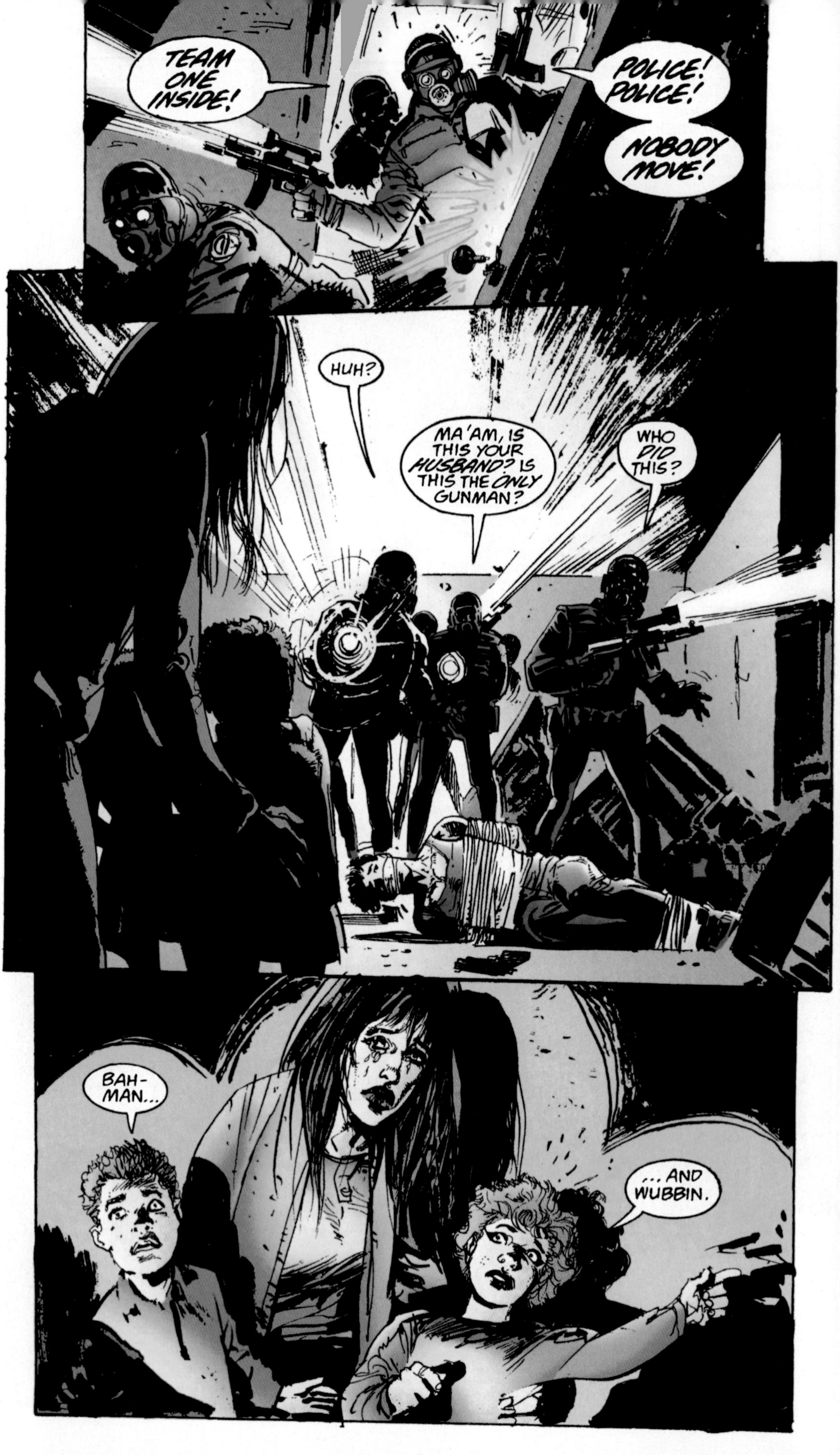
TEAM ONE INSIDE!
POLICE! POLICE!
NOBODY MOVE!
HUH?
MA'AM, IS THIS YOUR HUSBAND? IS THIS THE ONLY GUNMAN?
WHO DID THIS?
BAH-MAN...
...AND WUBBIN.

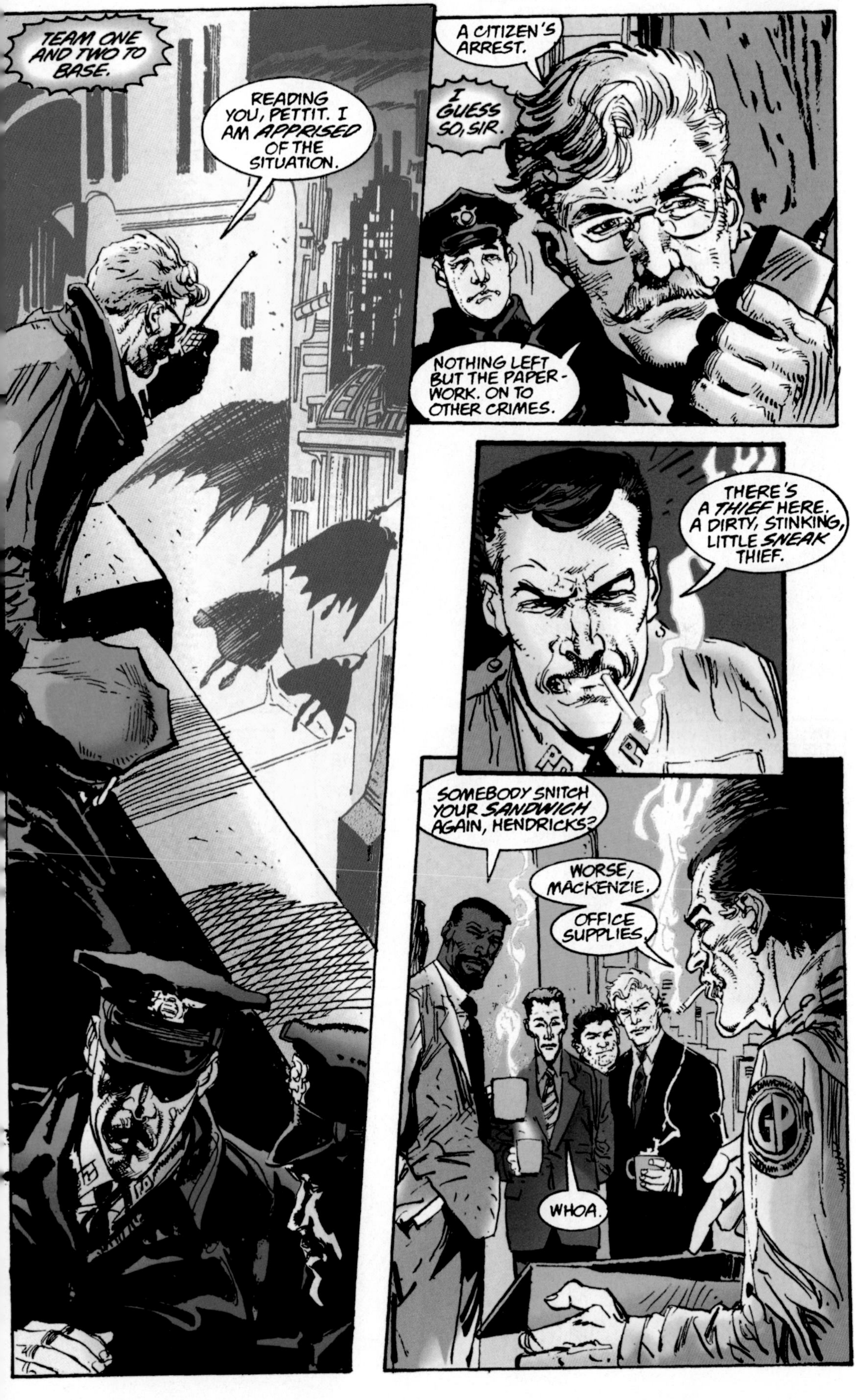
TEAM ONE AND TWO TO BASE.
READING YOU, PETTIT. I AM APPRISED OF THE SITUATION.
A CITIZEN'S ARREST.
I GUESS SO, SIR.
NOTHING LEFT BUT THE PAPER-WORK. ON TO OTHER CRIMES.
THERE'S A THIEF HERE. A DIRTY, STINKING, LITTLE SNEAK THIEF.
SOMEBODY SNITCH YOUR SANDWICH AGAIN, HENDRICKS?
WORSE, MACKENZIE.
OFFICE SUPPLIES.
WHOA.

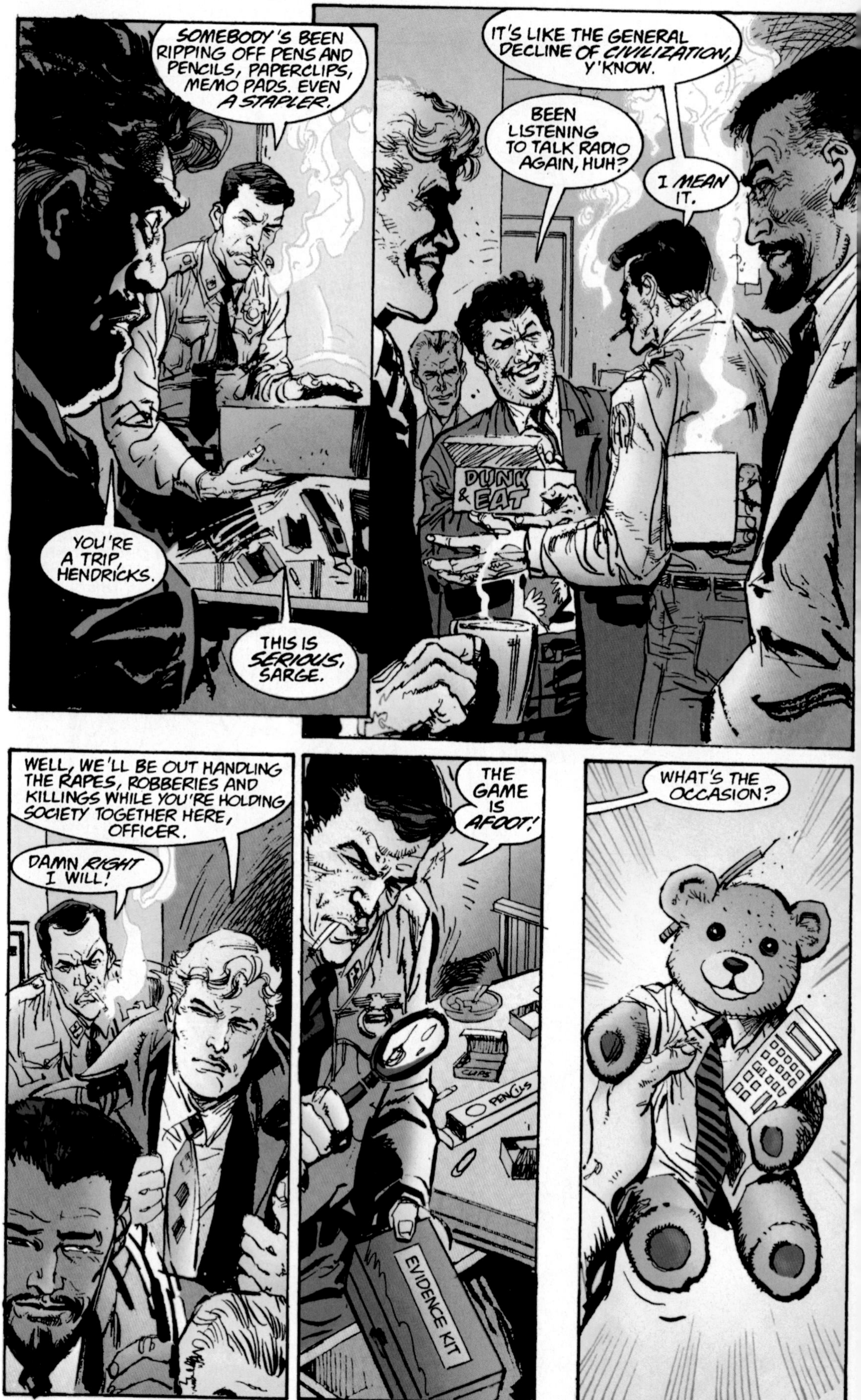

SOMEBODY'S BEEN RIPPING OFF PENS AND PENCILS, PAPERCLIPS, MEMO PADS. EVEN A STAPLER.
YOU'RE A TRIP, HENDRICKS.
THIS IS SERIOUS, SARGE.
IT'S LIKE THE GENERAL DECLINE OF CIVILIZATION, Y'KNOW.
BEEN LISTENING TO TALK RADIO AGAIN, HUH?
I MEAN IT.
DUNK & EAT
WELL, WE'LL BE OUT HANDLING THE RAPES, ROBBERIES AND KILLINGS WHILE YOU'RE HOLDING SOCIETY TOGETHER HERE, OFFICER.
DAMN RIGHT I WILL!
THE GAME IS AFOOT!
CLIPS
PENCILS
EVIDENCE KIT
WHAT'S THE OCCASION?

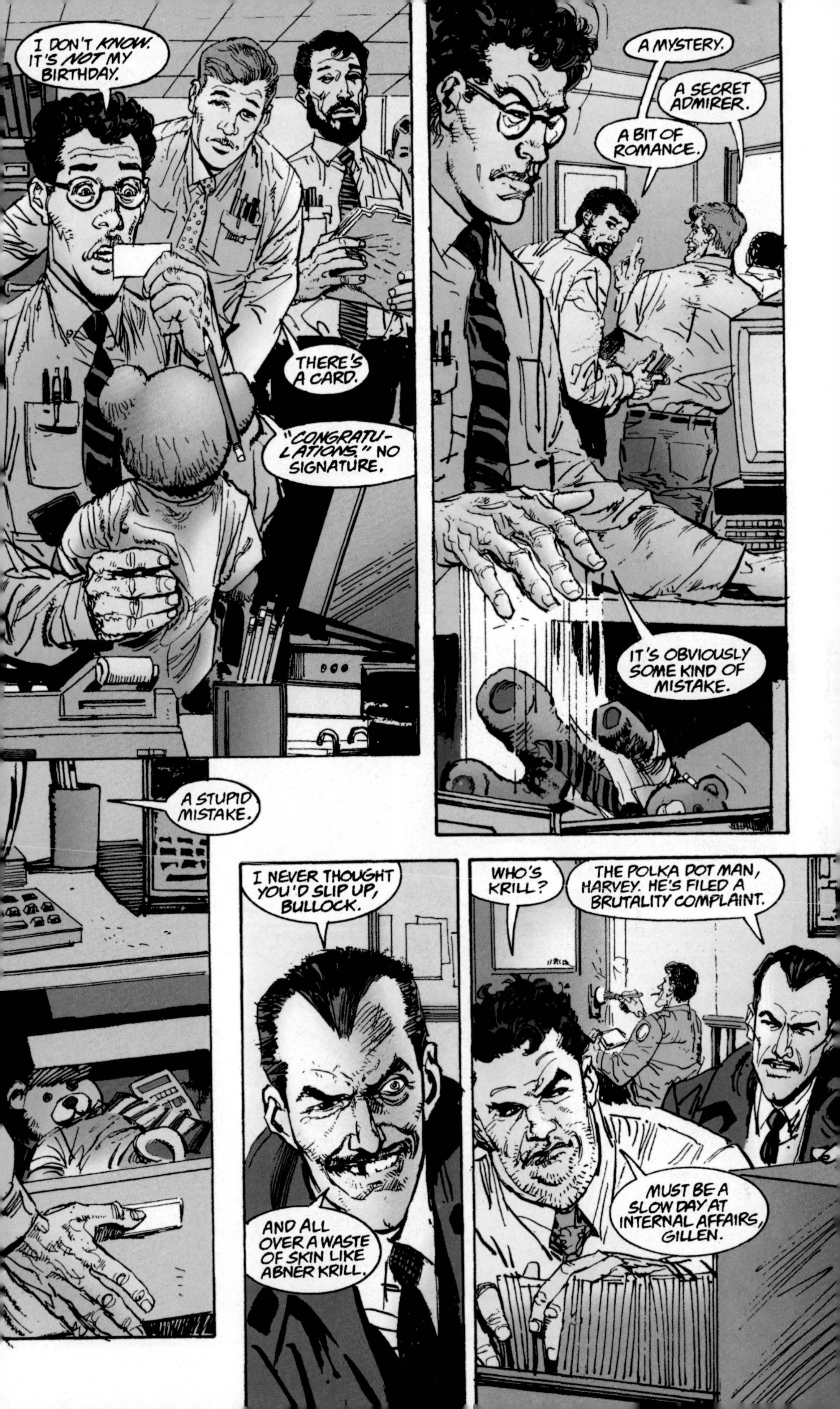

I DON'T KNOW. IT'S NOT MY BIRTHDAY.
THERE'S A CARD.
"CONGRATULATIONS." NO SIGNATURE.
A MYSTERY.
A SECRET ADMIRER.
A BIT OF ROMANCE.
IT'S OBVIOUSLY SOME KIND OF MISTAKE.
A STUPID MISTAKE.
I NEVER THOUGHT YOU'D SLIP UP, BULLOCK.
AND ALL OVER A WASTE OF SKIN LIKE ABNER KRILL.
WHO'S KRILL?
THE POLKA DOT MAN, HARVEY. HE'S FILED A BRUTALITY COMPLAINT.
MUST BE A SLOW DAY AT INTERNAL AFFAIRS, GILLEN.

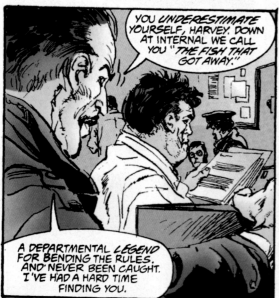

YOU *UNDERESTIMATE* YOURSELF, HARVEY. DOWN AT INTERNAL WE CALL YOU "*THE FISH THAT GOT AWAY.*"

A DEPARTMENTAL *LEGEND* FOR BENDING THE RULES. AND NEVER BEEN CAUGHT. I'VE HAD A HARD TIME FINDING YOU.

KRILL'S GOT A *GOOD CASE.* YOU PUT HIM IN *TRACTION.*

HELL, EVEN YOUR *PARTNER* GAVE YOU UP.

GILLEN...

EITHER YA *GOT SOMETHING* OR YA *DON'T.* I DON'T *GIVE* A RAT'S BEHIND EITHER WAY.

JUST. GET. OUT. OF. MY. *FACE.*

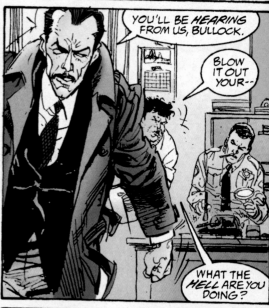

YOU'LL BE *HEARING* FROM US, BULLOCK.

BLOW IT OUT YOUR--

WHAT THE *HELL* ARE YOU DOING?

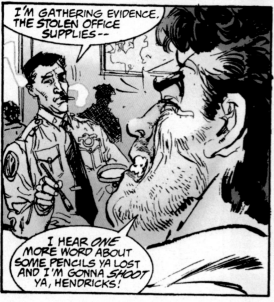

I'M GATHERING EVIDENCE. THE STOLEN OFFICE SUPPLIES--

I HEAR *ONE* MORE WORD ABOUT SOME PENCILS YA LOST AND I'M GONNA *SHOOT* YA, HENDRICKS!

SERGEANT BULLOCK?

WHAT D' *YOU* WANT?

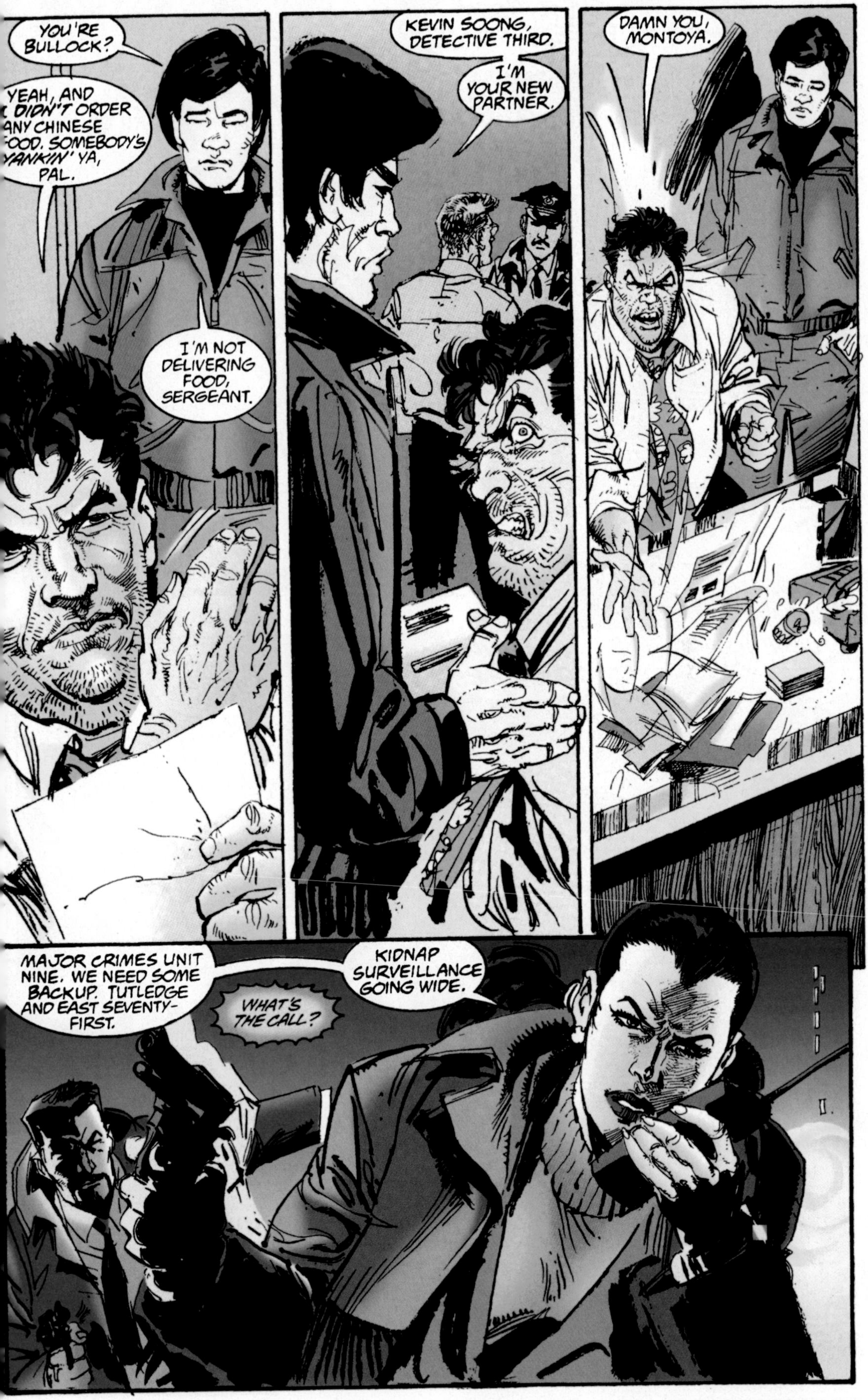

YOU'RE BULLOCK?
YEAH, AND I DIDN'T ORDER ANY CHINESE FOOD. SOMEBODY'S YANKIN' YA, PAL.
I'M NOT DELIVERING FOOD, SERGEANT.
KEVIN SOONG, DETECTIVE THIRD.
I'M YOUR NEW PARTNER.
DAMN YOU, MONTOYA.
MAJOR CRIMES UNIT NINE. WE NEED SOME BACKUP. TUTLEDGE AND EAST SEVENTY-FIRST.
WHAT'S THE CALL?
KIDNAP SURVEILLANCE GOING WIDE.

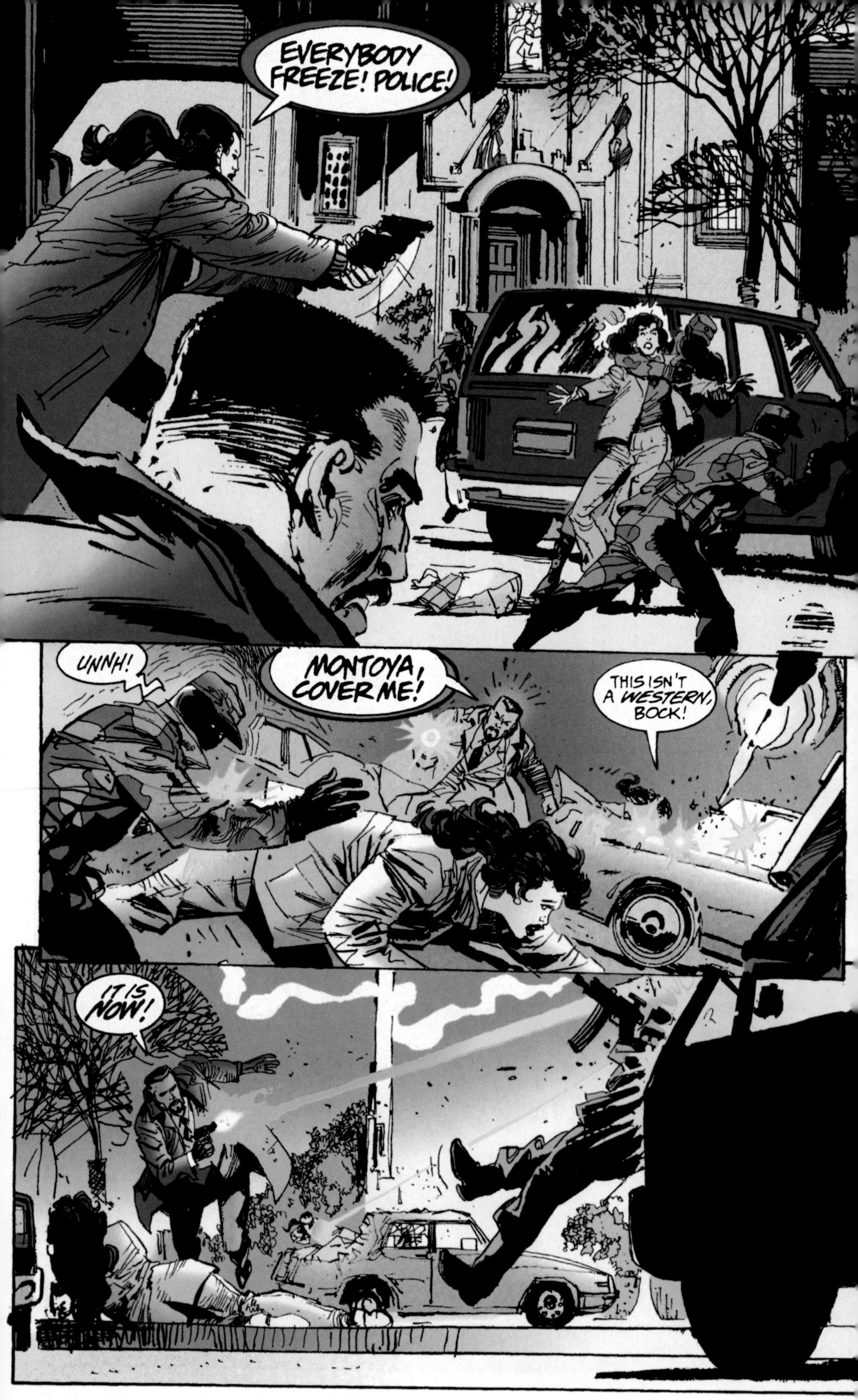
EVERYBODY FREEZE! POLICE!
UNNH!
MONTOYA, COVER ME!
THIS ISN'T A WESTERN, BOCK!
IT IS NOW!

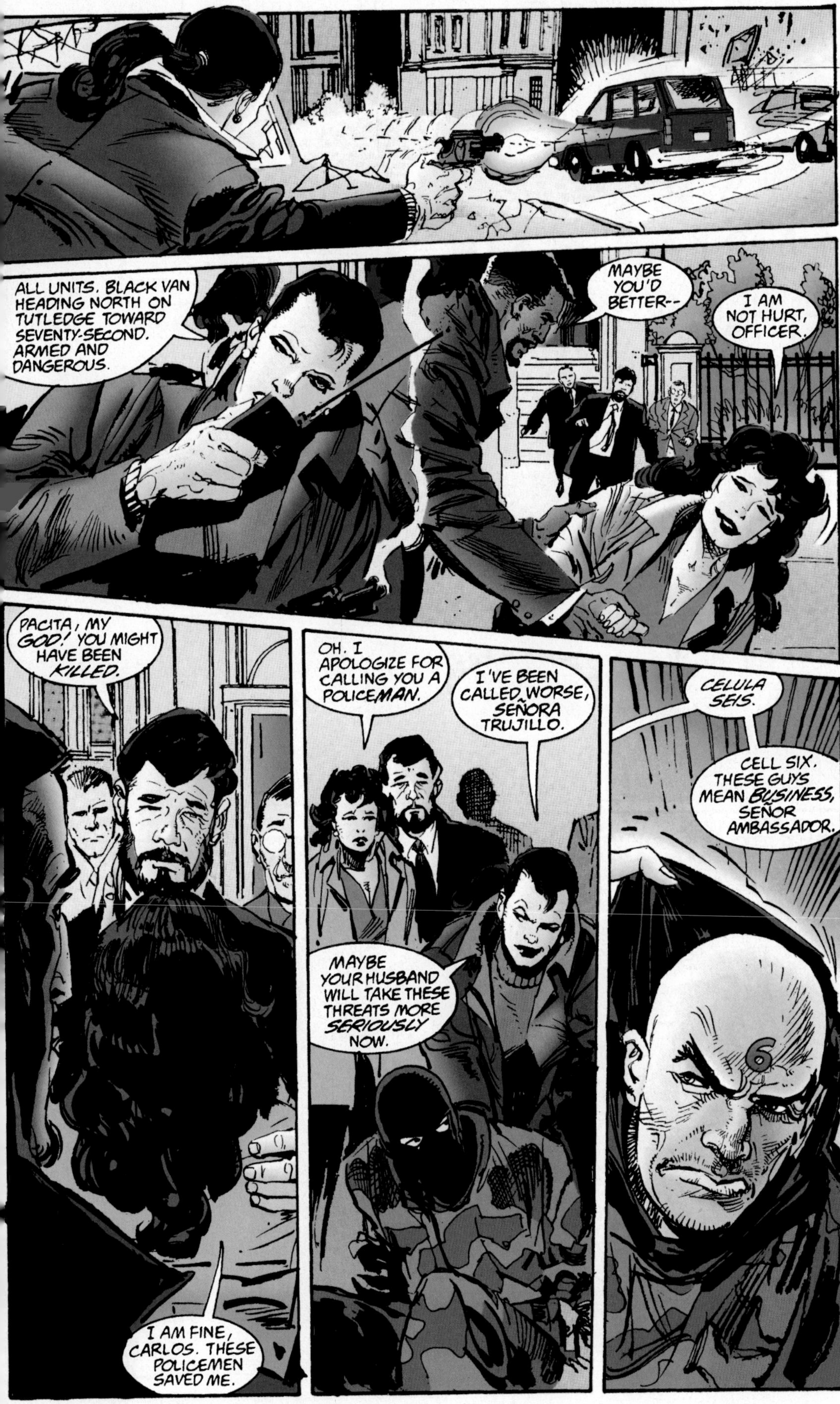
ALL UNITS. BLACK VAN HEADING NORTH ON TUTLEDGE TOWARD SEVENTY-SECOND. ARMED AND DANGEROUS.
MAYBE YOU'D BETTER--
I AM NOT HURT, OFFICER.
PACITA, MY GOD! YOU MIGHT HAVE BEEN KILLED.
I AM FINE, CARLOS. THESE POLICEMEN SAVED ME.
OH. I APOLOGIZE FOR CALLING YOU A POLICEMAN.
I'VE BEEN CALLED WORSE, SEÑORA TRUJILLO.
MAYBE YOUR HUSBAND WILL TAKE THESE THREATS MORE SERIOUSLY NOW.
CELULA SEIS.
CELL SIX. THESE GUYS MEAN BUSINESS, SEÑOR AMBASSADOR.
6

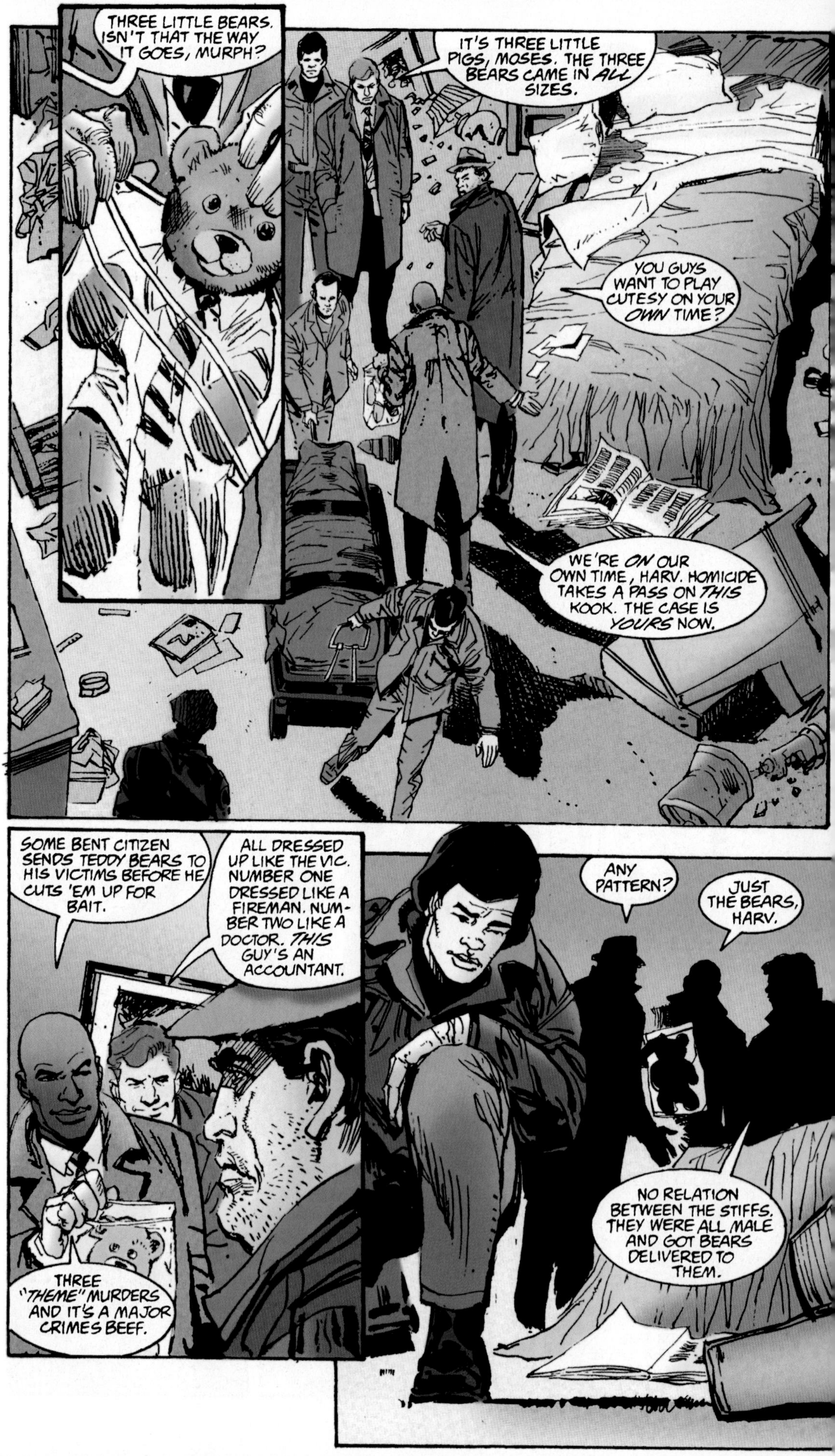
THREE LITTLE BEARS. ISN'T THAT THE WAY IT GOES, MURPH?
IT'S THREE LITTLE PIGS, MOSES. THE THREE BEARS CAME IN ALL SIZES.
YOU GUYS WANT TO PLAY CUTESY ON YOUR OWN TIME?
WE'RE ON OUR OWN TIME, HARV. HOMICIDE TAKES A PASS ON THIS KOOK. THE CASE IS YOURS NOW.
SOME BENT CITIZEN SENDS TEDDY BEARS TO HIS VICTIMS BEFORE HE CUTS 'EM UP FOR BAIT.
ALL DRESSED UP LIKE THE VIC. NUMBER ONE DRESSED LIKE A FIREMAN. NUMBER TWO LIKE A DOCTOR. THIS GUY'S AN ACCOUNTANT.
THREE "THEME" MURDERS AND IT'S A MAJOR CRIMES BEEF.
ANY PATTERN?
JUST THE BEARS, HARV.
NO RELATION BETWEEN THE STIFFS. THEY WERE ALL MALE AND GOT BEARS DELIVERED TO THEM.

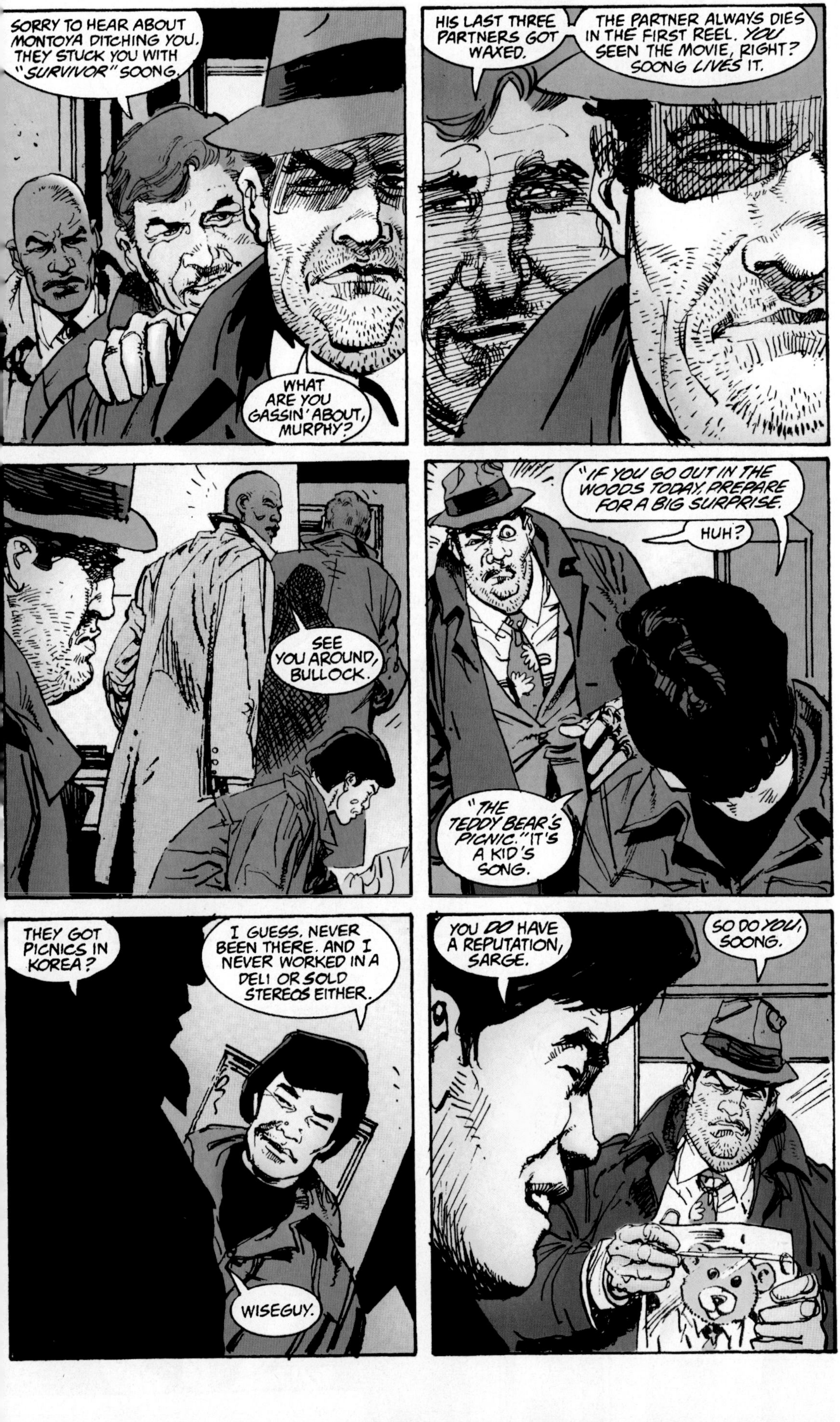

SORRY TO HEAR ABOUT MONTOYA DITCHING YOU. THEY STUCK YOU WITH "SURVIVOR" SOONG.
WHAT ARE YOU GASSIN' ABOUT, MURPHY?
HIS LAST THREE PARTNERS GOT WAXED.
THE PARTNER ALWAYS DIES IN THE FIRST REEL. YOU SEEN THE MOVIE, RIGHT? SOONG LIVES IT.
SEE YOU AROUND, BULLOCK.
"IF YOU GO OUT IN THE WOODS TODAY, PREPARE FOR A BIG SURPRISE."
HUH?
"THE TEDDY BEAR'S PICNIC." IT'S A KID'S SONG.
THEY GOT PICNICS IN KOREA?
I GUESS. NEVER BEEN THERE. AND I NEVER WORKED IN A DELI OR SOLD STEREOS EITHER.
WISEGUY.
YOU DO HAVE A REPUTATION, SARGE.
SO DO YOU, SOONG.

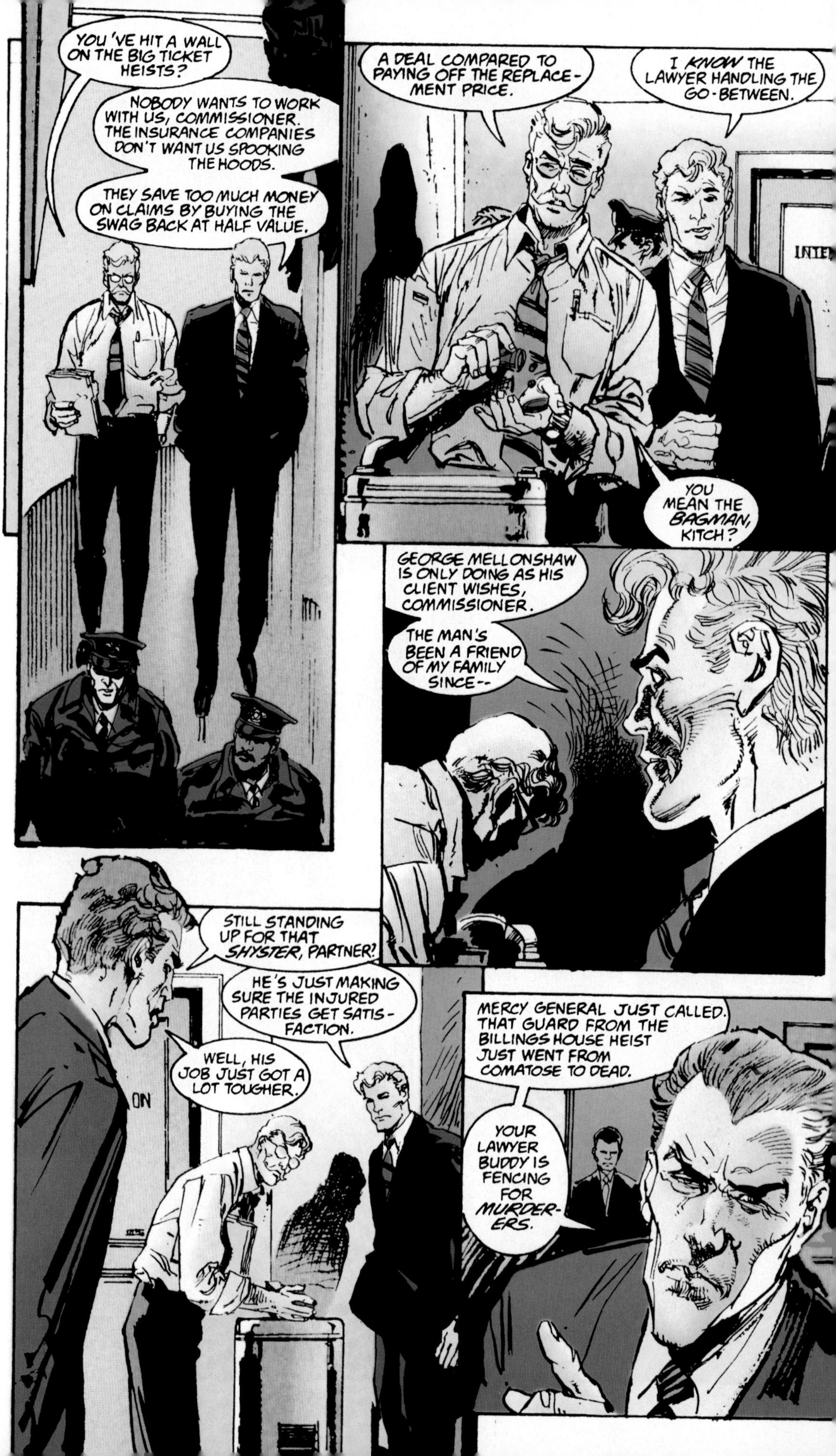
YOU'VE HIT A WALL ON THE BIG TICKET HEISTS?
NOBODY WANTS TO WORK WITH US, COMMISSIONER. THE INSURANCE COMPANIES DON'T WANT US SPOOKING THE HOODS.
THEY SAVE TOO MUCH MONEY ON CLAIMS BY BUYING THE SWAG BACK AT HALF VALUE.
A DEAL COMPARED TO PAYING OFF THE REPLACEMENT PRICE.
I KNOW THE LAWYER HANDLING THE GO-BETWEEN.
YOU MEAN THE BAGMAN, KITCH?
GEORGE MELLONSHAW IS ONLY DOING AS HIS CLIENT WISHES, COMMISSIONER.
THE MAN'S BEEN A FRIEND OF MY FAMILY SINCE--
STILL STANDING UP FOR THAT SHYSTER, PARTNER?
HE'S JUST MAKING SURE THE INJURED PARTIES GET SATISFACTION.
WELL, HIS JOB JUST GOT A LOT TOUGHER.
MERCY GENERAL JUST CALLED. THAT GUARD FROM THE BILLINGS HOUSE HEIST JUST WENT FROM COMATOSE TO DEAD.
YOUR LAWYER BUDDY IS FENCING FOR MURDERERS.

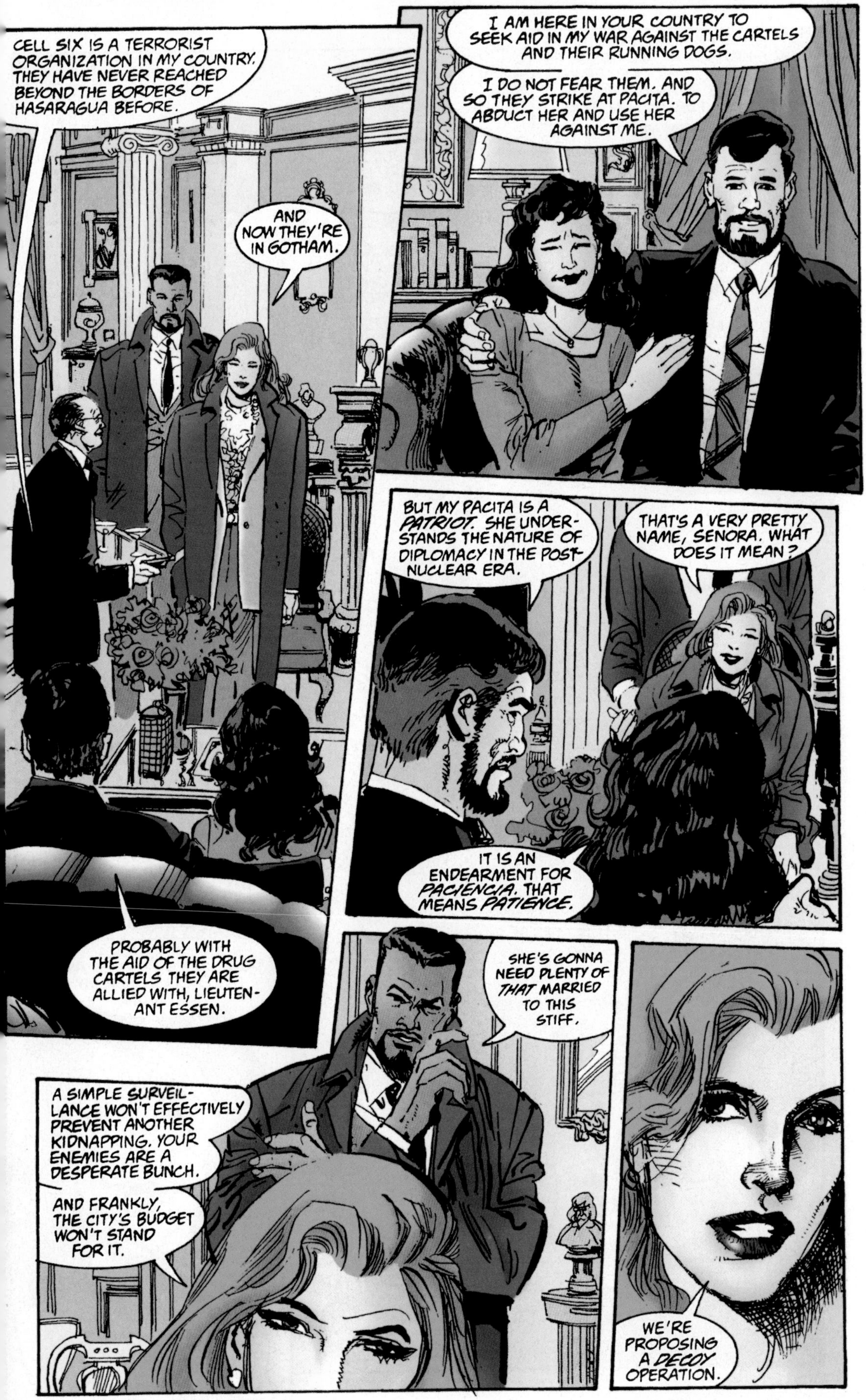
CELL SIX IS A TERRORIST ORGANIZATION IN MY COUNTRY. THEY HAVE NEVER REACHED BEYOND THE BORDERS OF HASARAGUA BEFORE.
AND NOW THEY'RE IN GOTHAM.
PROBABLY WITH THE AID OF THE DRUG CARTELS THEY ARE ALLIED WITH, LIEUTENANT ESSEN.
I AM HERE IN YOUR COUNTRY TO SEEK AID IN MY WAR AGAINST THE CARTELS AND THEIR RUNNING DOGS.
I DO NOT FEAR THEM. AND SO THEY STRIKE AT PACITA. TO ABDUCT HER AND USE HER AGAINST ME.
BUT MY PACITA IS A PATRIOT. SHE UNDERSTANDS THE NATURE OF DIPLOMACY IN THE POST-NUCLEAR ERA.
THAT'S A VERY PRETTY NAME, SENORA. WHAT DOES IT MEAN?
IT IS AN ENDEARMENT FOR PACIENCIA. THAT MEANS PATIENCE.
SHE'S GONNA NEED PLENTY OF THAT MARRIED TO THIS STIFF.
A SIMPLE SURVEILLANCE WON'T EFFECTIVELY PREVENT ANOTHER KIDNAPPING. YOUR ENEMIES ARE A DESPERATE BUNCH.
AND FRANKLY, THE CITY'S BUDGET WON'T STAND FOR IT.
WE'RE PROPOSING A DECOY OPERATION.

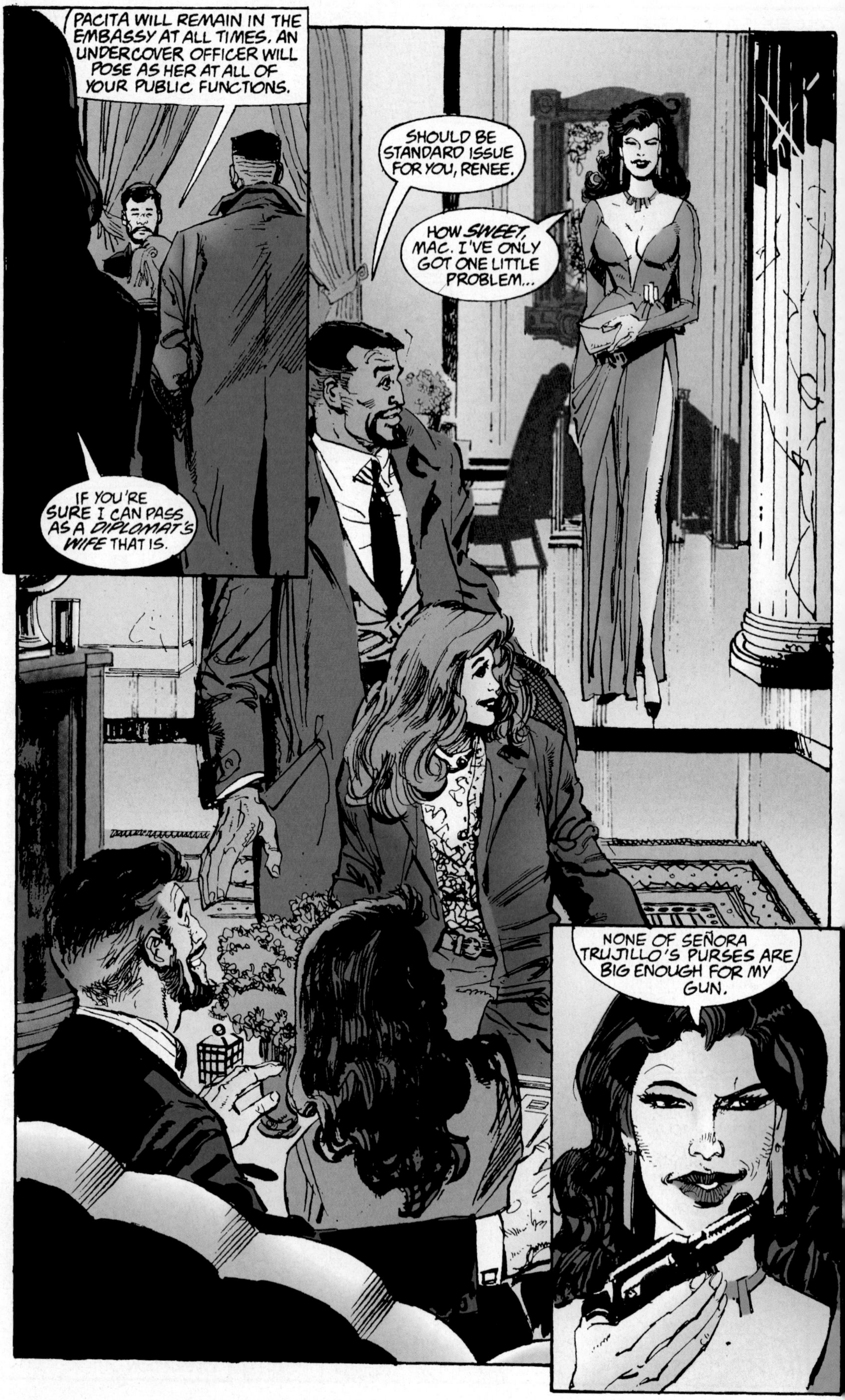
PACITA WILL REMAIN IN THE EMBASSY AT ALL TIMES. AN UNDERCOVER OFFICER WILL POSE AS HER AT ALL OF YOUR PUBLIC FUNCTIONS.
IF YOU'RE SURE I CAN PASS AS A *DIPLOMAT'S WIFE* THAT IS.
SHOULD BE STANDARD ISSUE FOR YOU, RENEE.
HOW *SWEET*, MAC. I'VE ONLY GOT ONE LITTLE PROBLEM...
NONE OF SEÑORA TRUJILLO'S PURSES ARE BIG ENOUGH FOR MY GUN.

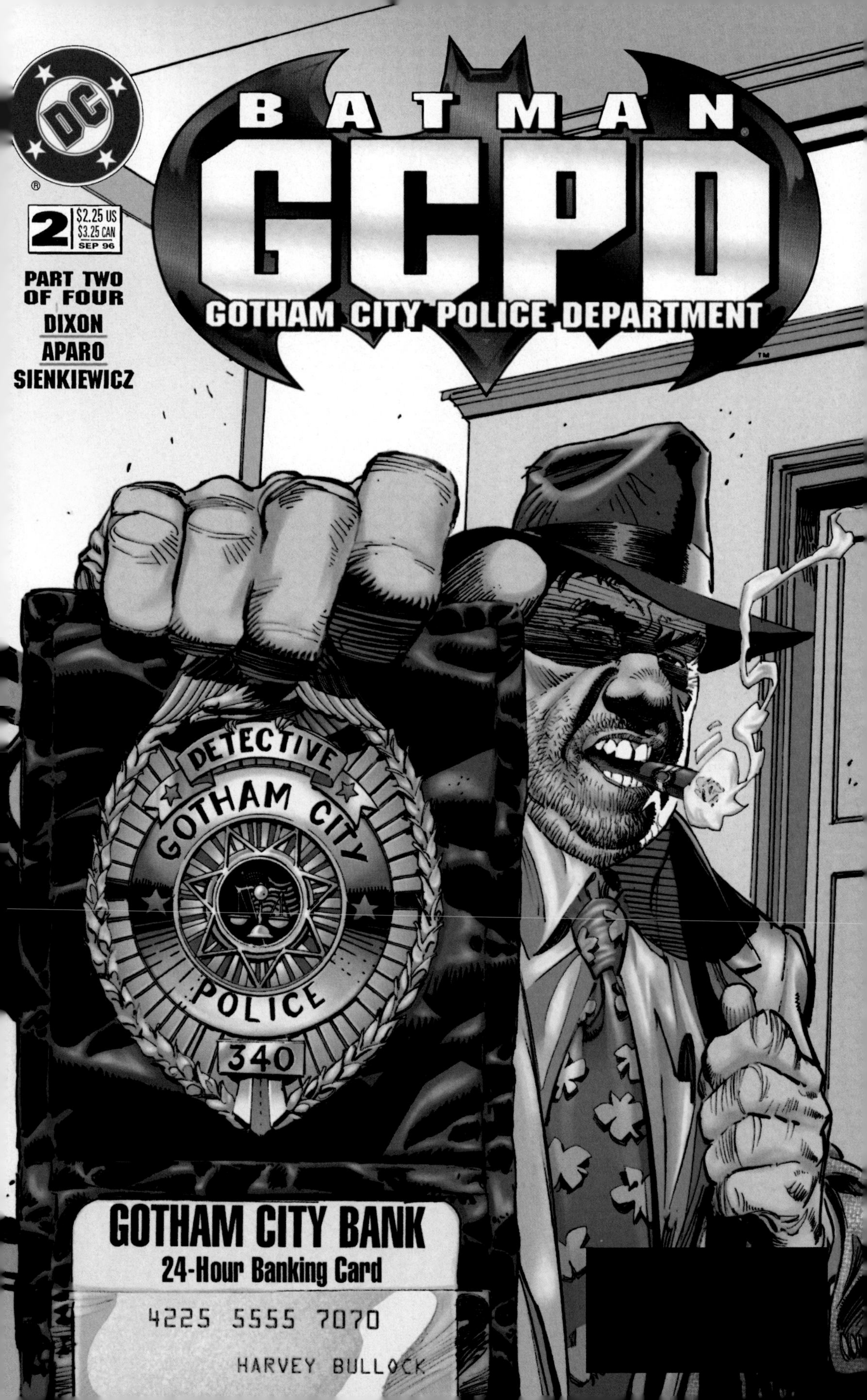
DC
BATMAN
GCPD
GOTHAM CITY POLICE DEPARTMENT
2
$2.25 US
$3.25 CAN
SEP 96
PART TWO OF FOUR
DIXON
APARO
SIENKIEWICZ
DETECTIVE
GOTHAM CITY
POLICE
340
GOTHAM CITY BANK
24-Hour Banking Card
4225 5555 7070
HARVEY BULLOCK

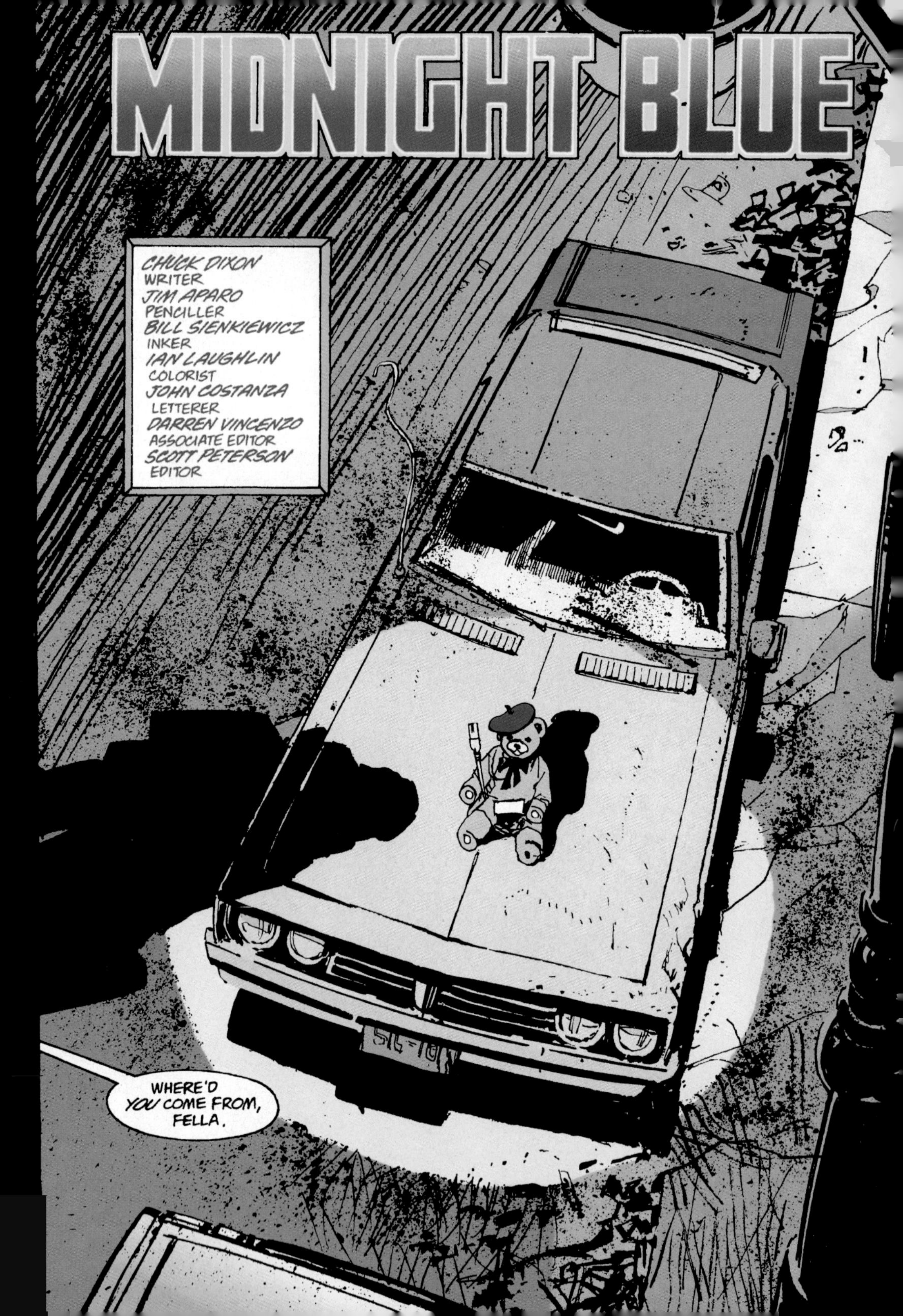
MIDNIGHT BLUE
CHUCK DIXON WRITER
JIM APARO PENCILLER
BILL SIENKIEWICZ INKER
IAN LAUGHLIN COLORIST
JOHN COSTANZA LETTERER
DARREN VINCENZO ASSOCIATE EDITOR
SCOTT PETERSON EDITOR
WHERE'D YOU COME FROM, FELLA.

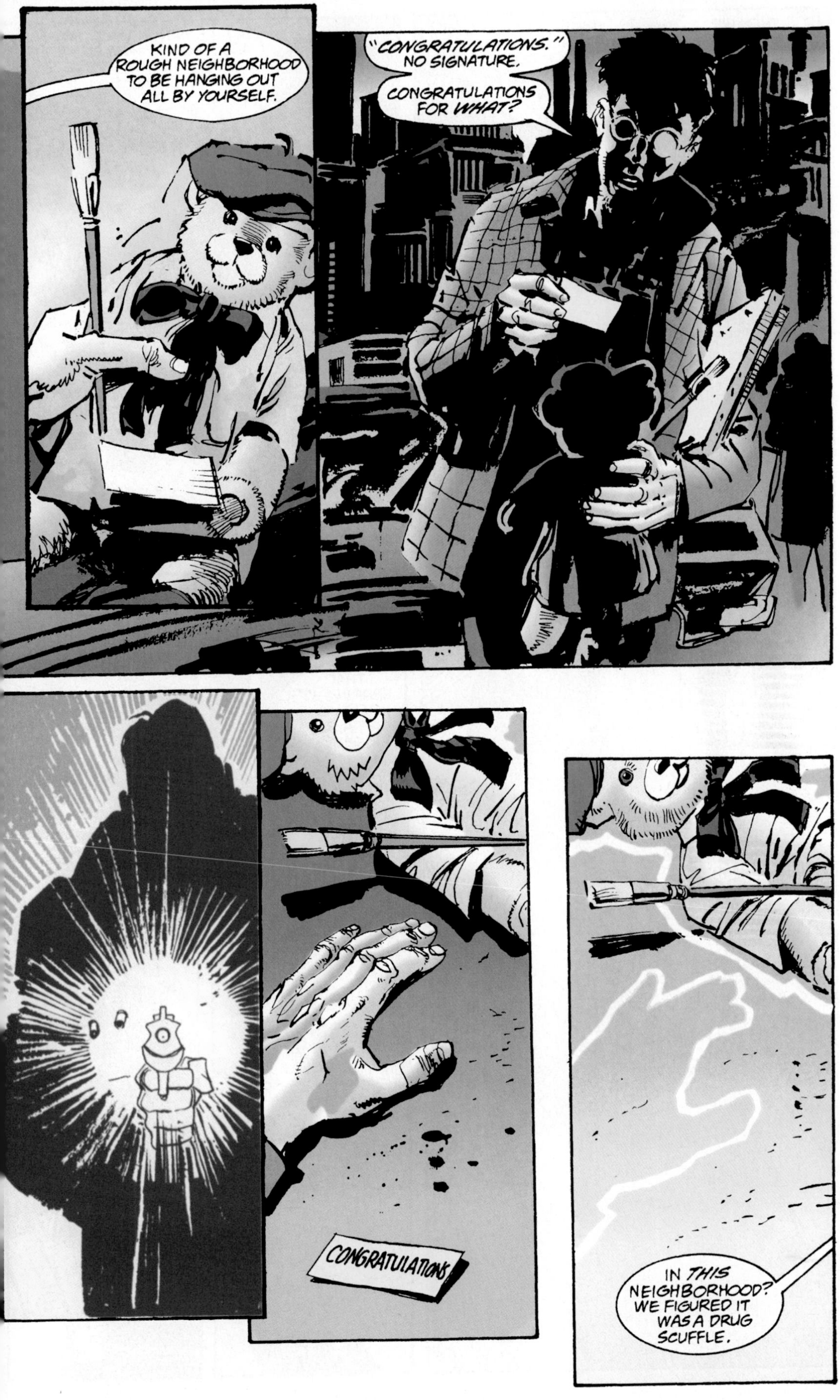
KIND OF A ROUGH NEIGHBORHOOD TO BE HANGING OUT ALL BY YOURSELF.
"CONGRATULATIONS." NO SIGNATURE.
CONGRATULATIONS FOR WHAT?
CONGRATULATIONS
IN THIS NEIGHBORHOOD? WE FIGURED IT WAS A DRUG SCUFFLE.

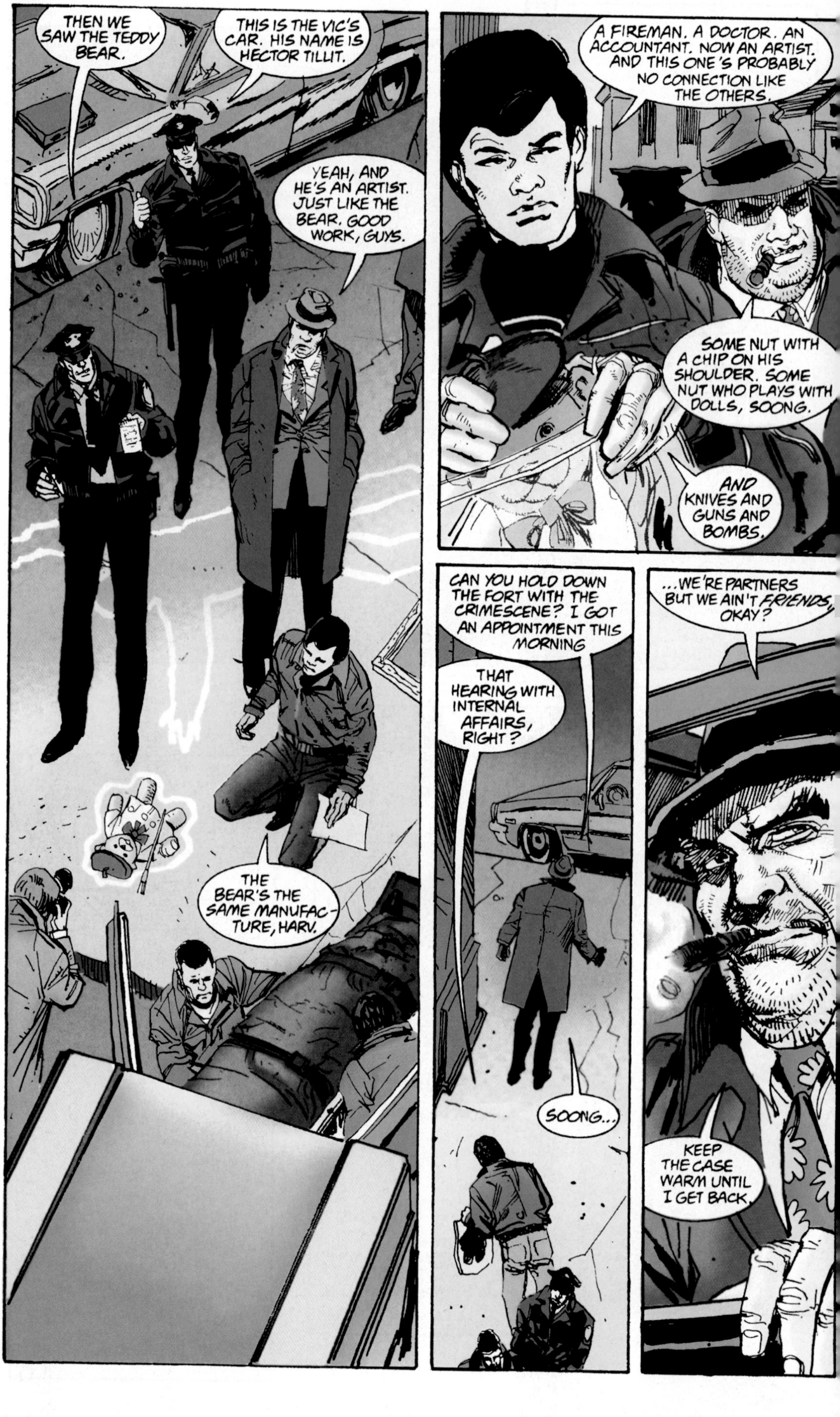
THEN WE SAW THE TEDDY BEAR.
THIS IS THE VIC'S CAR. HIS NAME IS HECTOR TILLIT.
YEAH, AND HE'S AN ARTIST. JUST LIKE THE BEAR. GOOD WORK, GUYS.
THE BEAR'S THE SAME MANUFAC-TURE, HARV.
A FIREMAN. A DOCTOR. AN ACCOUNTANT. NOW AN ARTIST. AND THIS ONE'S PROBABLY NO CONNECTION LIKE THE OTHERS.
SOME NUT WITH A CHIP ON HIS SHOULDER. SOME NUT WHO PLAYS WITH DOLLS, SOONG.
AND KNIVES AND GUNS AND BOMBS.
CAN YOU HOLD DOWN THE FORT WITH THE CRIMESCENE? I GOT AN APPOINTMENT THIS MORNING
THAT HEARING WITH INTERNAL AFFAIRS, RIGHT?
SOONG...
...WE'RE PARTNERS BUT WE AIN'T FRIENDS, OKAY?
KEEP THE CASE WARM UNTIL I GET BACK.

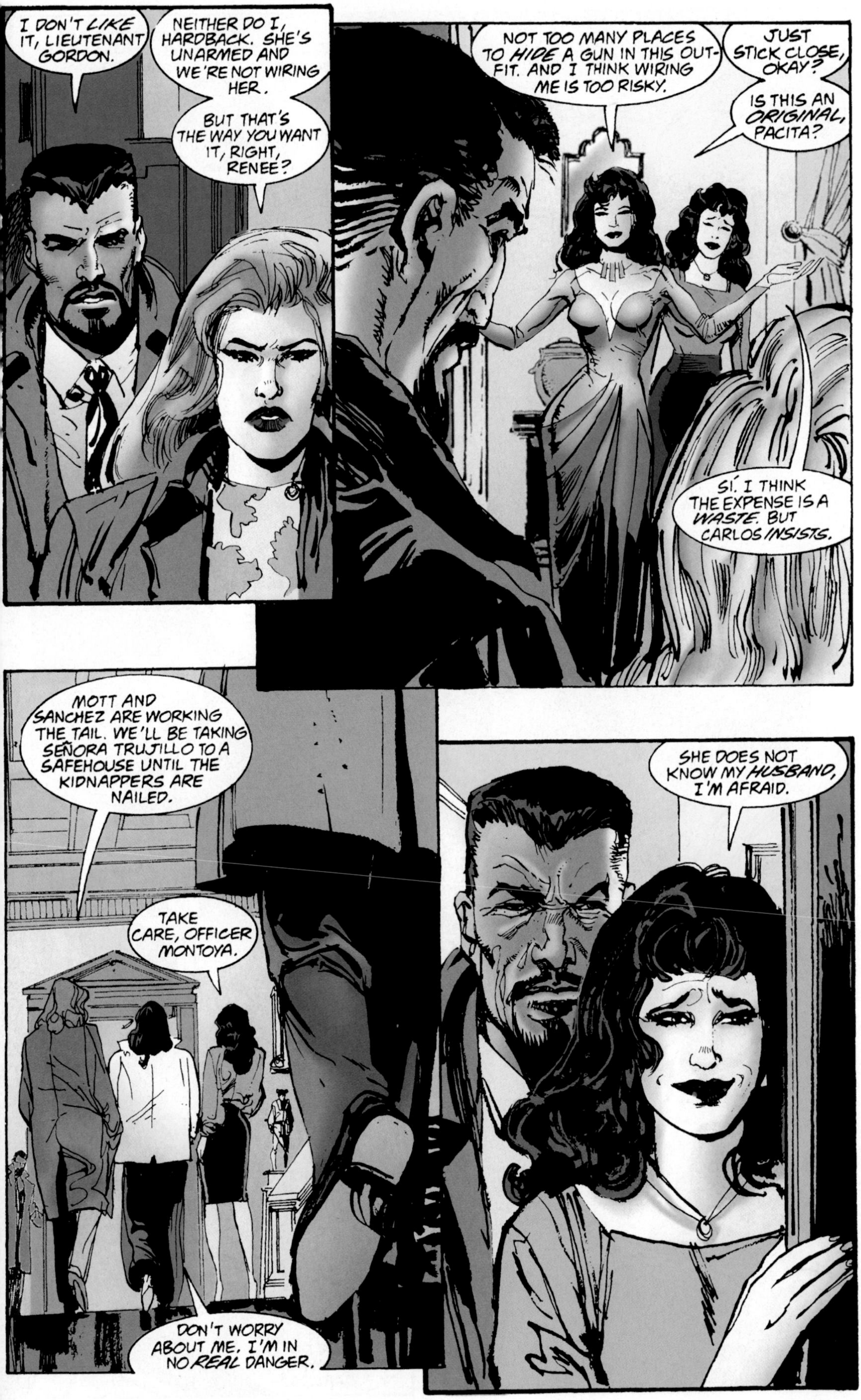

I DON'T LIKE IT, LIEUTENANT GORDON.
NEITHER DO I, HARDBACK. SHE'S UNARMED AND WE'RE NOT WIRING HER.
BUT THAT'S THE WAY YOU WANT IT, RIGHT, RENEE?
NOT TOO MANY PLACES TO HIDE A GUN IN THIS OUTFIT. AND I THINK WIRING ME IS TOO RISKY.
JUST STICK CLOSE, OKAY?
IS THIS AN ORIGINAL, PACITA?
SÍ. I THINK THE EXPENSE IS A WASTE. BUT CARLOS INSISTS.
MOTT AND SANCHEZ ARE WORKING THE TAIL. WE'LL BE TAKING SEÑORA TRUJILLO TO A SAFEHOUSE UNTIL THE KIDNAPPERS ARE NAILED.
TAKE CARE, OFFICER MONTOYA.
DON'T WORRY ABOUT ME. I'M IN NO REAL DANGER.
SHE DOES NOT KNOW MY HUSBAND, I'M AFRAID.

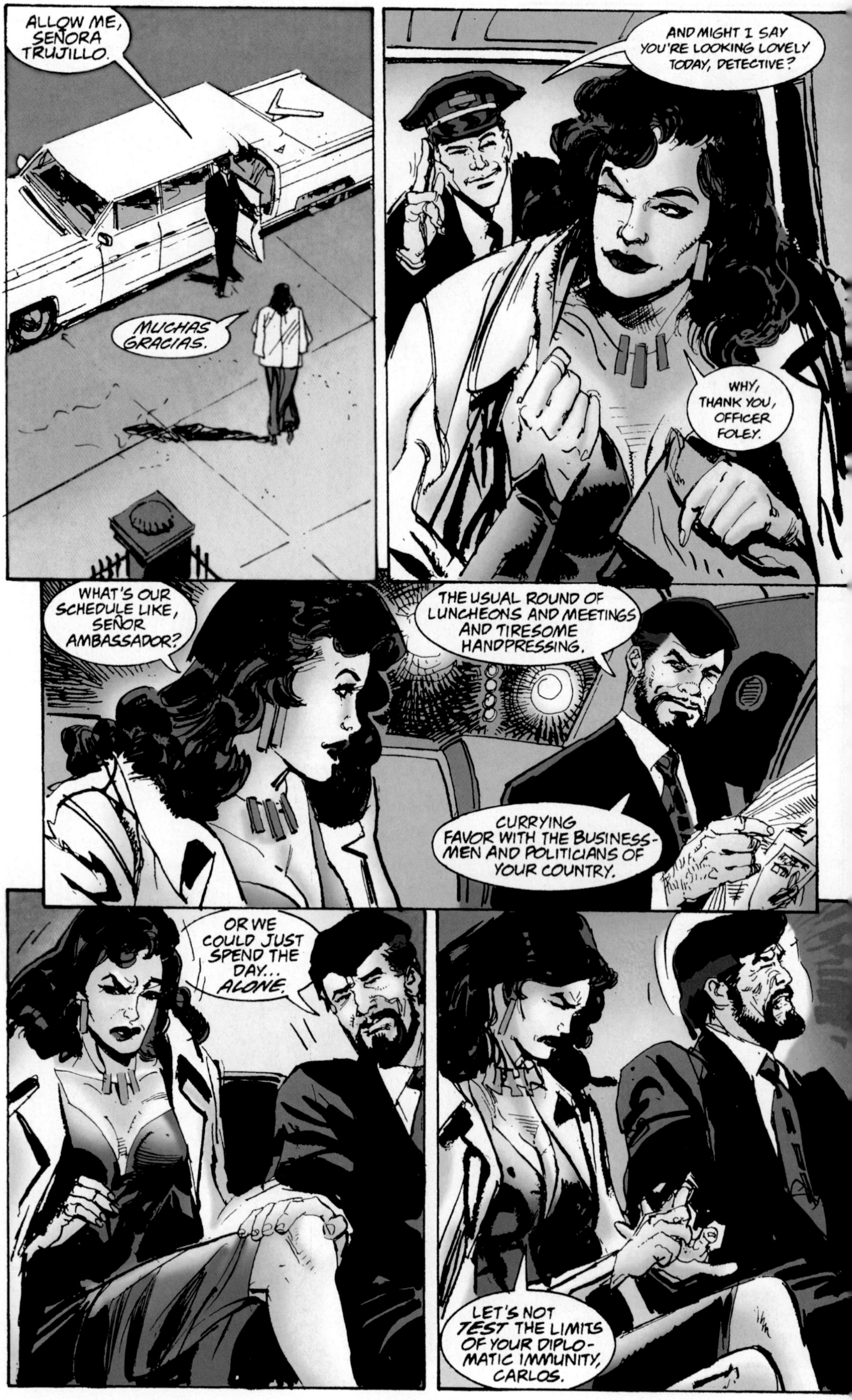
ALLOW ME, SEÑORA TRUJILLO.
MUCHAS GRACIAS.
AND MIGHT I SAY YOU'RE LOOKING LOVELY TODAY, DETECTIVE?
WHY, THANK YOU, OFFICER FOLEY.
WHAT'S OUR SCHEDULE LIKE, SEÑOR AMBASSADOR?
THE USUAL ROUND OF LUNCHEONS AND MEETINGS AND TIRESOME HANDPRESSING.
CURRYING FAVOR WITH THE BUSINESSMEN AND POLITICIANS OF YOUR COUNTRY.
OR WE COULD JUST SPEND THE DAY... ALONE.
LET'S NOT TEST THE LIMITS OF YOUR DIPLOMATIC IMMUNITY, CARLOS.

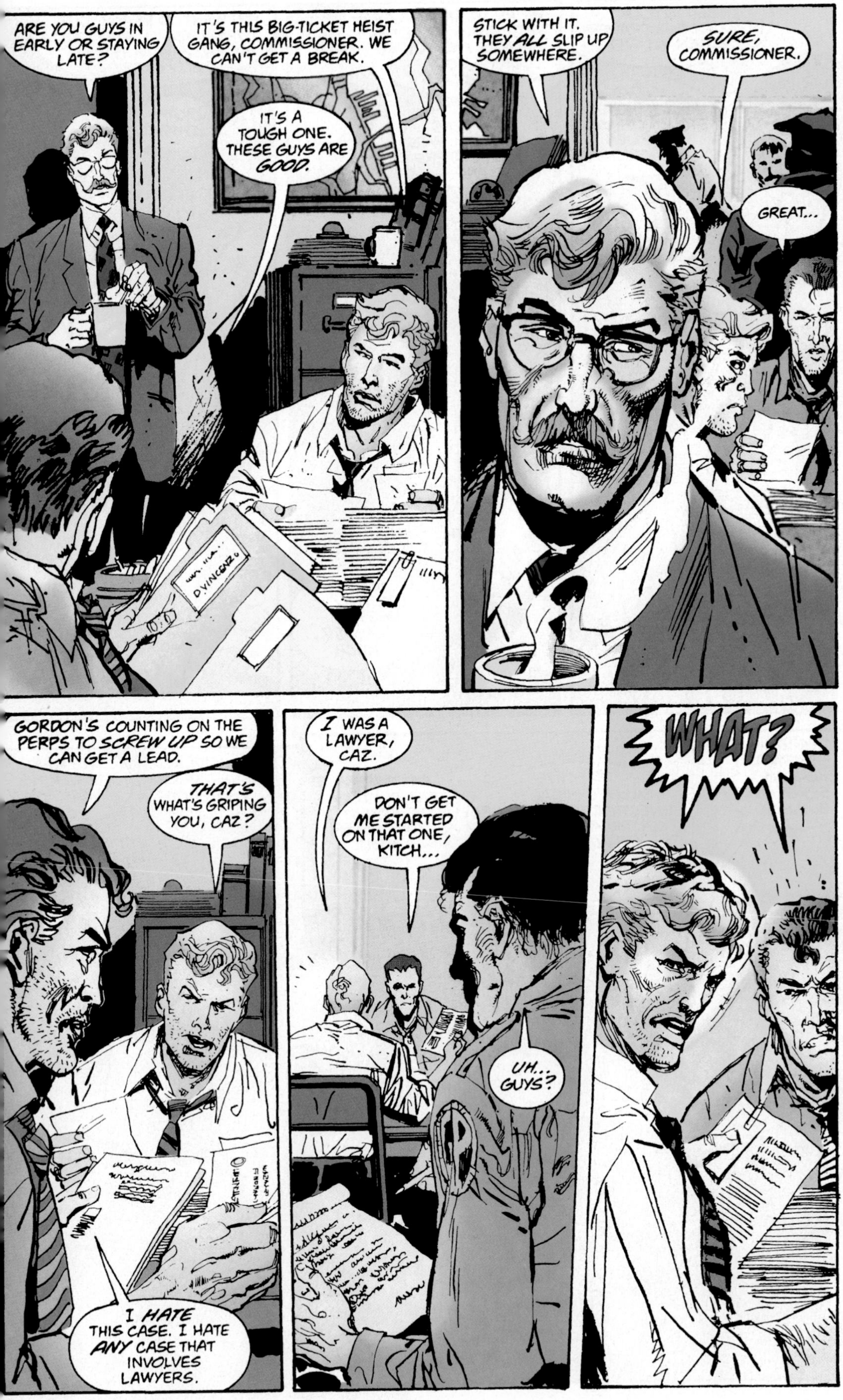
ARE YOU GUYS IN EARLY OR STAYING LATE?
IT'S THIS BIG-TICKET HEIST GANG, COMMISSIONER. WE CAN'T GET A BREAK.
IT'S A TOUGH ONE. THESE GUYS ARE GOOD.
D.VINCENZO
STICK WITH IT. THEY ALL SLIP UP SOMEWHERE.
SURE, COMMISSIONER.
GREAT...
GORDON'S COUNTING ON THE PERPS TO SCREW UP SO WE CAN GET A LEAD.
THAT'S WHAT'S GRIPING YOU, CAZ?
I HATE THIS CASE. I HATE ANY CASE THAT INVOLVES LAWYERS.
I WAS A LAWYER, CAZ.
DON'T GET ME STARTED ON THAT ONE, KITCH...
UH... GUYS?
WHAT?

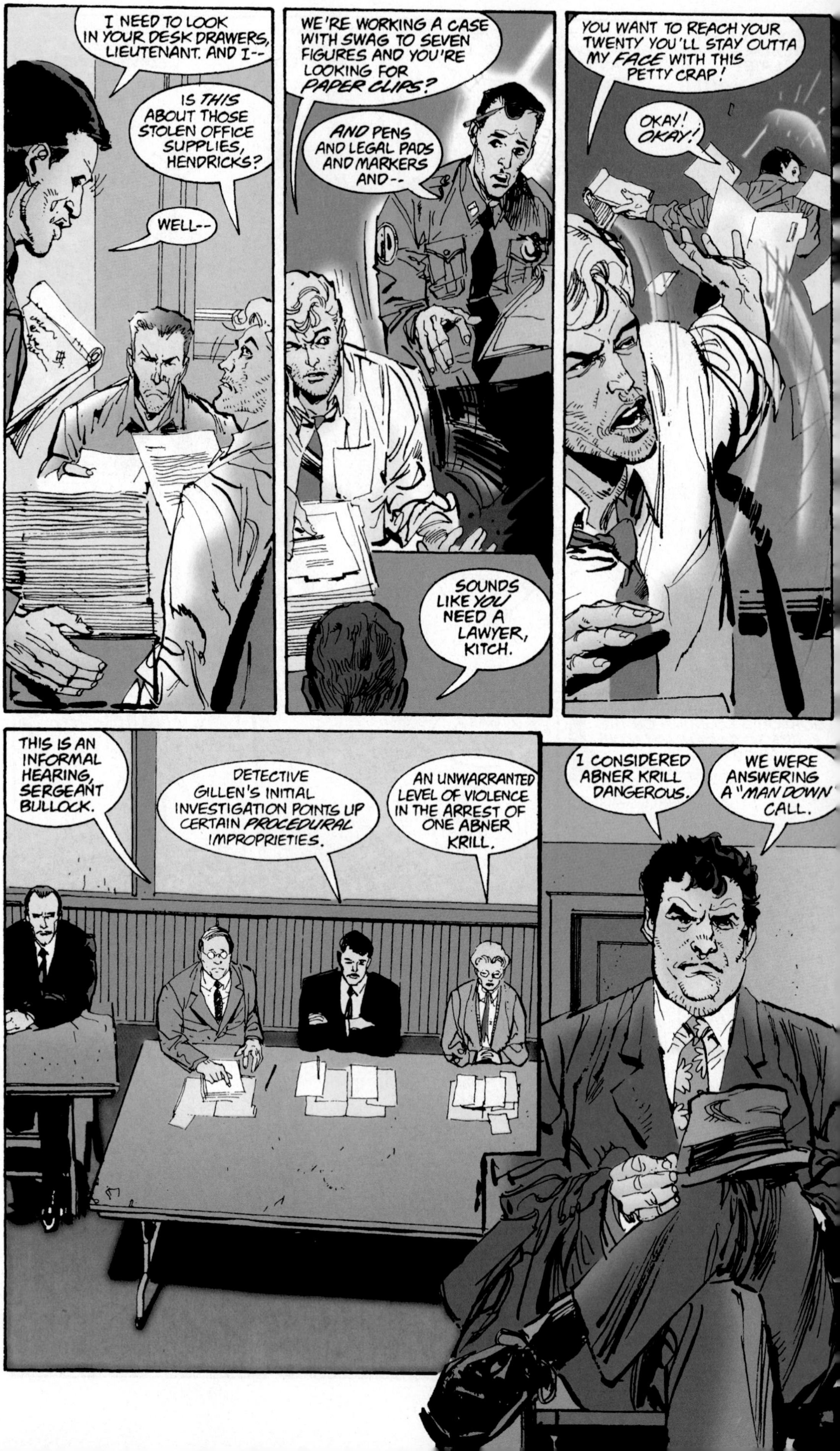
I NEED TO LOOK IN YOUR DESK DRAWERS, LIEUTENANT. AND I--
IS THIS ABOUT THOSE STOLEN OFFICE SUPPLIES, HENDRICKS?
WELL--
WE'RE WORKING A CASE WITH SWAG TO SEVEN FIGURES AND YOU'RE LOOKING FOR PAPER CLIPS?
AND PENS AND LEGAL PADS AND MARKERS AND--
SOUNDS LIKE YOU NEED A LAWYER, KITCH.
YOU WANT TO REACH YOUR TWENTY YOU'LL STAY OUTTA MY FACE WITH THIS PETTY CRAP!
OKAY! OKAY!
THIS IS AN INFORMAL HEARING, SERGEANT BULLOCK.
DETECTIVE GILLEN'S INITIAL INVESTIGATION POINTS UP CERTAIN PROCEDURAL IMPROPRIETIES.
AN UNWARRANTED LEVEL OF VIOLENCE IN THE ARREST OF ONE ABNER KRILL.
I CONSIDERED ABNER KRILL DANGEROUS.
WE WERE ANSWERING A "MAN DOWN" CALL.

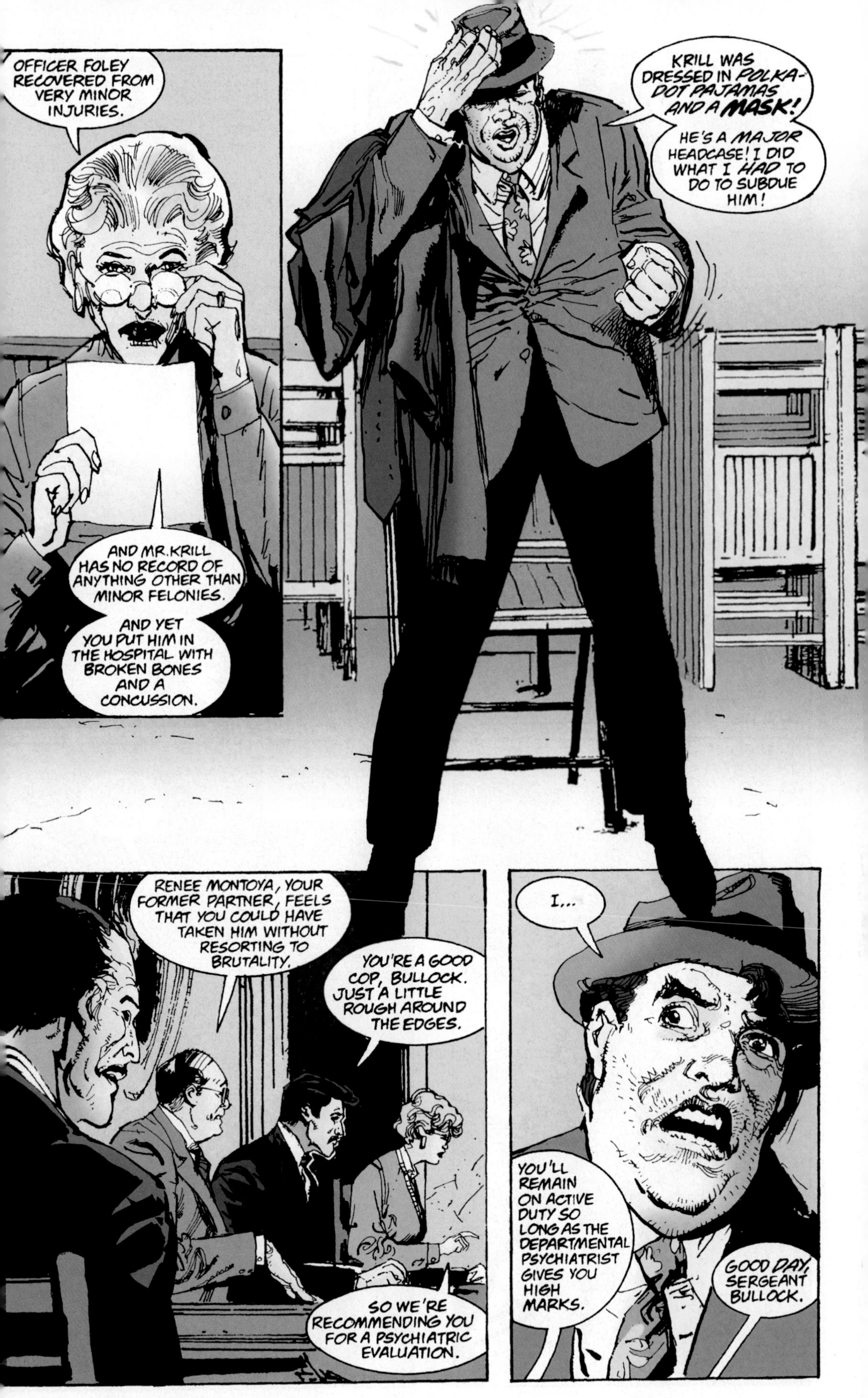
OFFICER FOLEY RECOVERED FROM VERY MINOR INJURIES.
AND MR. KRILL HAS NO RECORD OF ANYTHING OTHER THAN MINOR FELONIES.
AND YET YOU PUT HIM IN THE HOSPITAL WITH BROKEN BONES AND A CONCUSSION.
KRILL WAS DRESSED IN POLKA-DOT PAJAMAS AND A MASK!
HE'S A MAJOR HEADCASE! I DID WHAT I HAD TO DO TO SUBDUE HIM!
RENEE MONTOYA, YOUR FORMER PARTNER, FEELS THAT YOU COULD HAVE TAKEN HIM WITHOUT RESORTING TO BRUTALITY.
YOU'RE A GOOD COP, BULLOCK. JUST A LITTLE ROUGH AROUND THE EDGES.
SO WE'RE RECOMMENDING YOU FOR A PSYCHIATRIC EVALUATION.
I...
YOU'LL REMAIN ON ACTIVE DUTY SO LONG AS THE DEPARTMENTAL PSYCHIATRIST GIVES YOU HIGH MARKS.
GOOD DAY, SERGEANT BULLOCK.

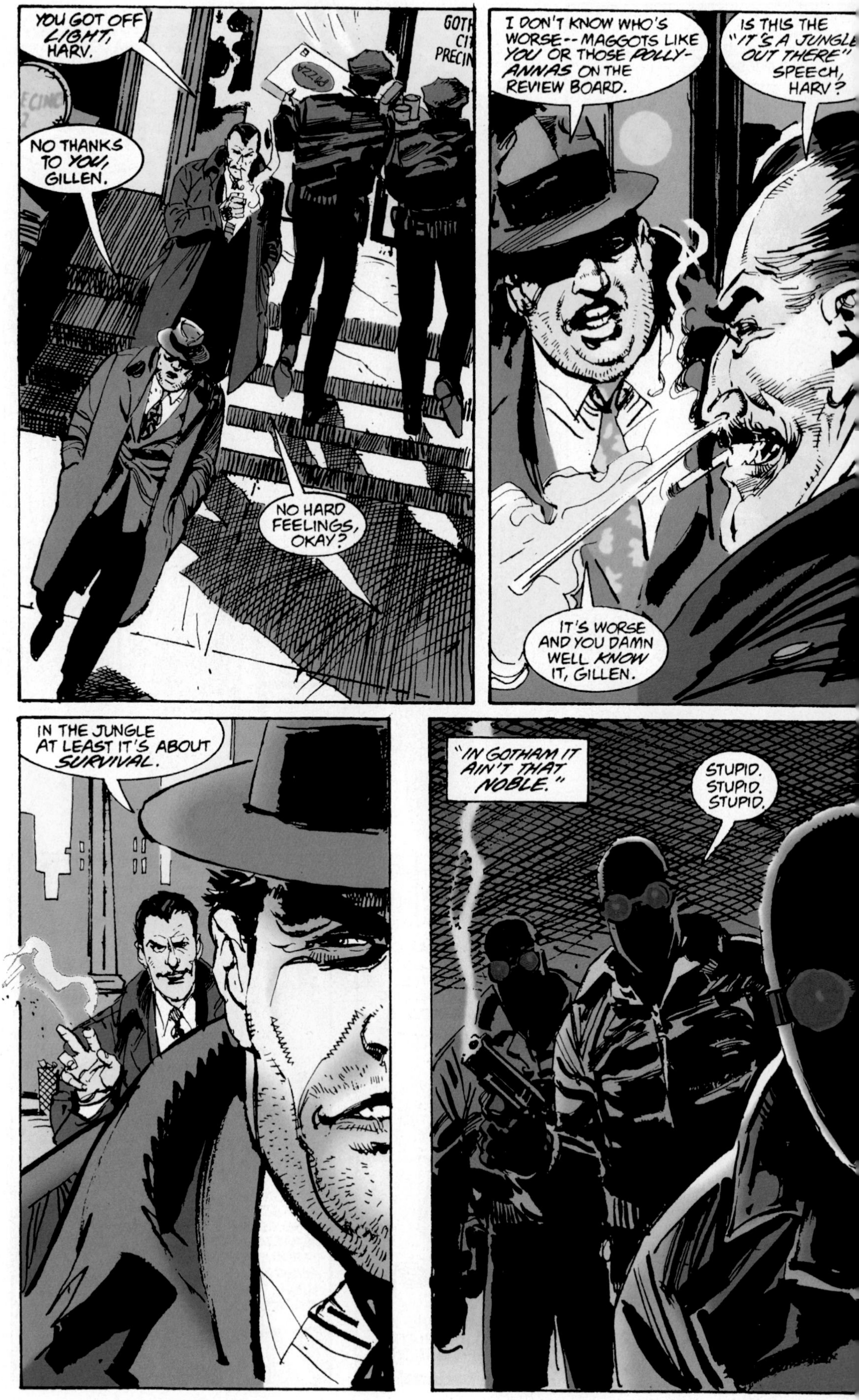
YOU GOT OFF *LIGHT*, HARV.
NO THANKS TO *YOU*, GILLEN.
NO HARD FEELINGS, OKAY?
I DON'T KNOW WHO'S WORSE-- MAGGOTS LIKE *YOU* OR THOSE *POLLY-ANNAS* ON THE REVIEW BOARD.
IS THIS THE "*IT'S A JUNGLE OUT THERE*" SPEECH, HARV?
IT'S WORSE AND YOU DAMN WELL *KNOW* IT, GILLEN.
IN THE JUNGLE AT LEAST IT'S ABOUT *SURVIVAL*.
"*IN GOTHAM IT AIN'T THAT NOBLE*."
STUPID. STUPID. STUPID.

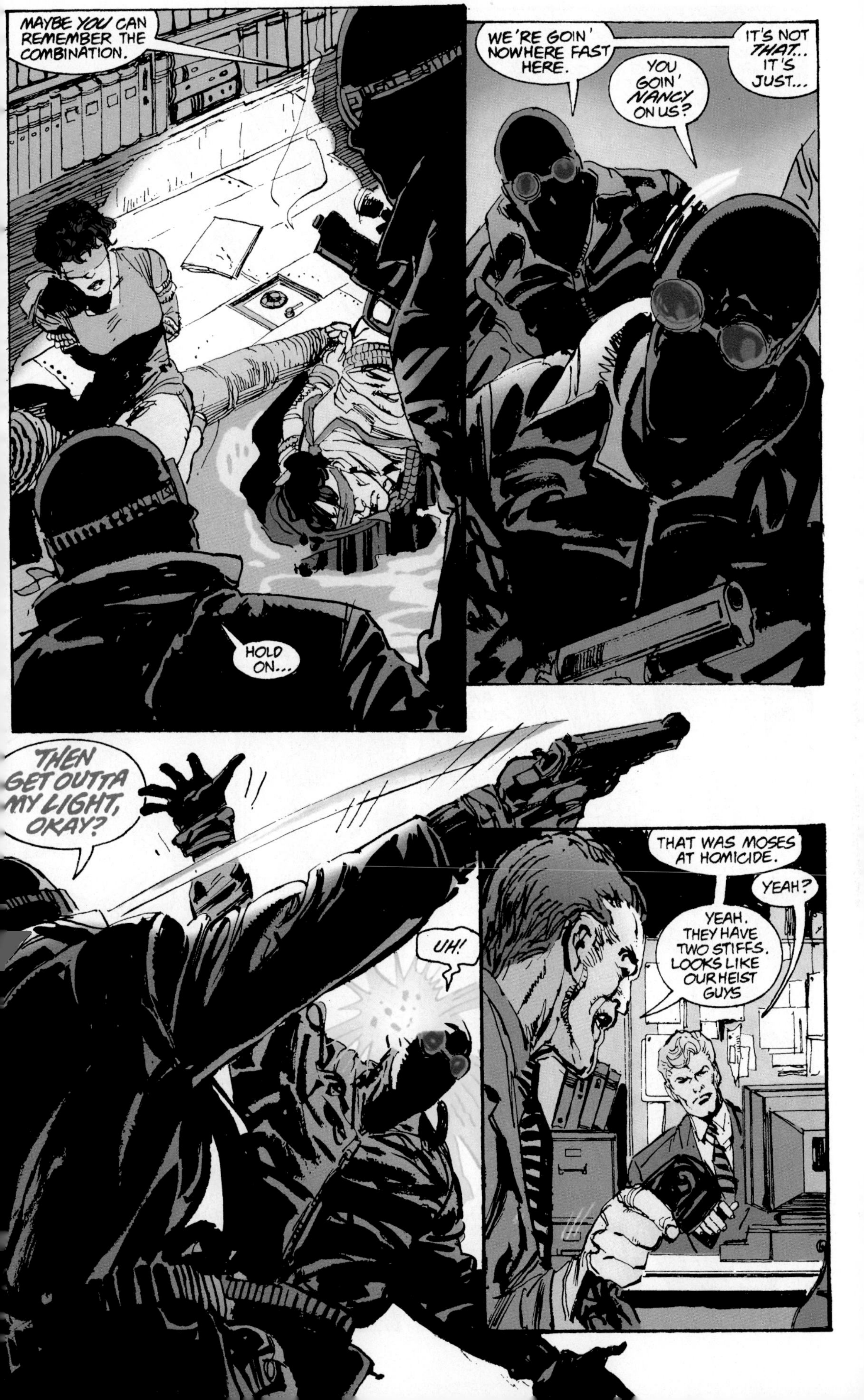

MAYBE YOU CAN REMEMBER THE COMBINATION.
HOLD ON...
WE'RE GOIN' NOWHERE FAST HERE.
IT'S NOT THAT... IT'S JUST...
YOU GOIN' NANCY ON US?
THEN GET OUTTA MY LIGHT, OKAY?
UH!
THAT WAS MOSES AT HOMICIDE.
YEAH?
YEAH. THEY HAVE TWO STIFFS. LOOKS LIKE OUR HEIST GUYS

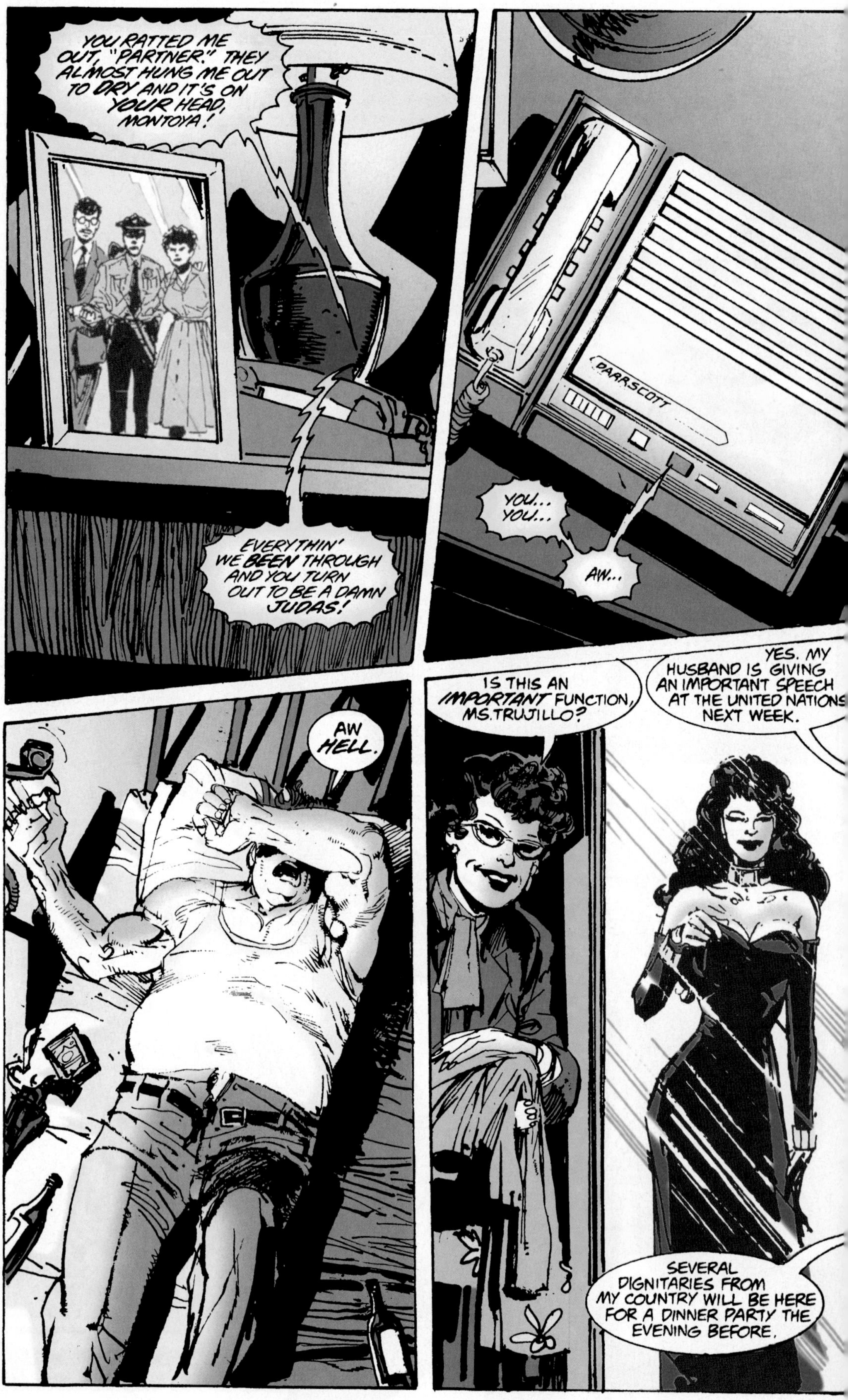
YOU RATTED ME OUT, "PARTNER." THEY ALMOST HUNG ME OUT TO DRY AND IT'S ON YOUR HEAD, MONTOYA!
EVERYTHIN' WE BEEN THROUGH AND YOU TURN OUT TO BE A DAMN JUDAS!
DARRSCOTT
YOU... YOU...
AW...
AW HELL.
IS THIS AN IMPORTANT FUNCTION, MS. TRUJILLO?
YES. MY HUSBAND IS GIVING AN IMPORTANT SPEECH AT THE UNITED NATIONS NEXT WEEK.
SEVERAL DIGNITARIES FROM MY COUNTRY WILL BE HERE FOR A DINNER PARTY THE EVENING BEFORE.

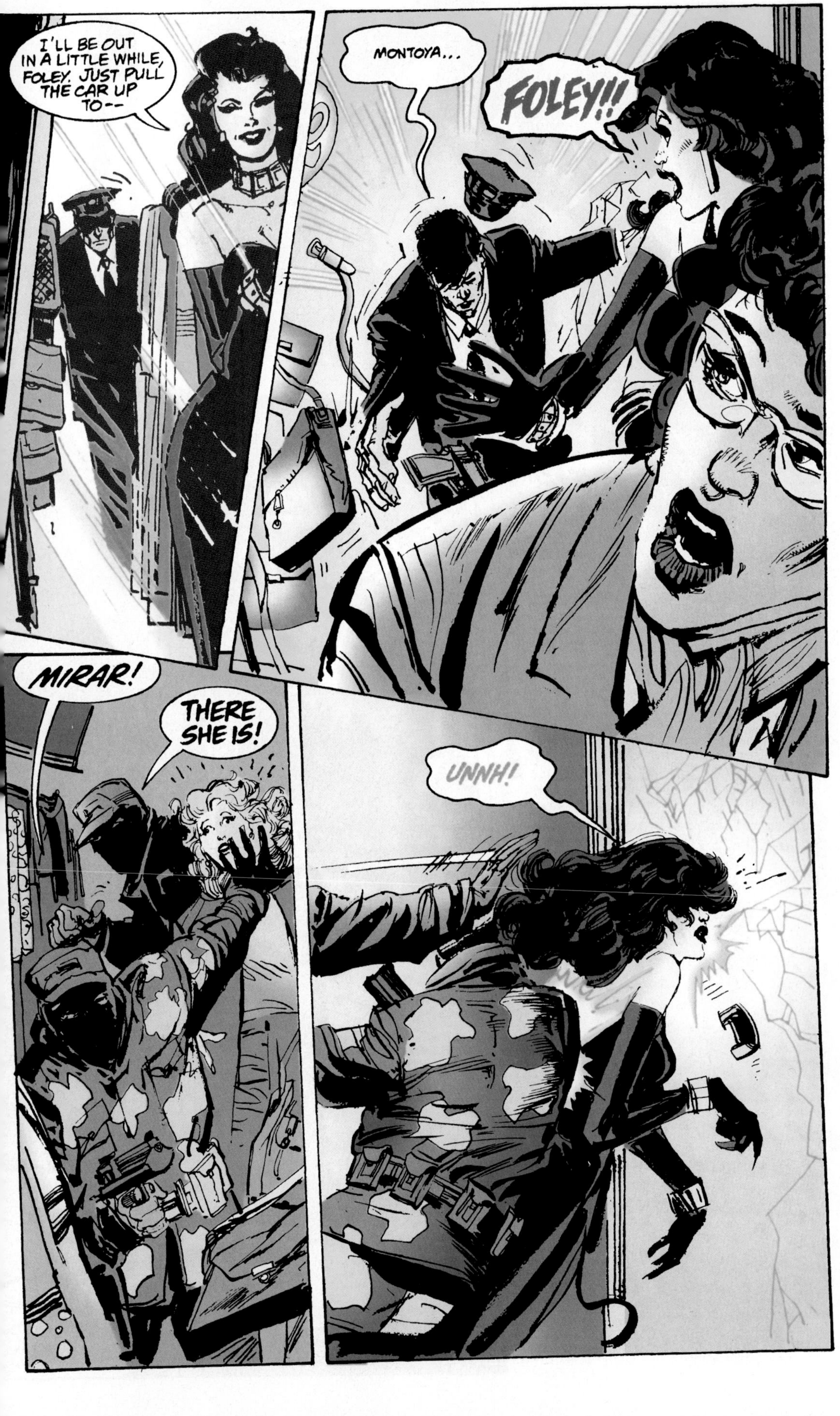
I'LL BE OUT IN A LITTLE WHILE, FOLEY. JUST PULL THE CAR UP TO--
MONTOYA...
FOLEY!!
MIRAR!
THERE SHE IS!
UNNH!

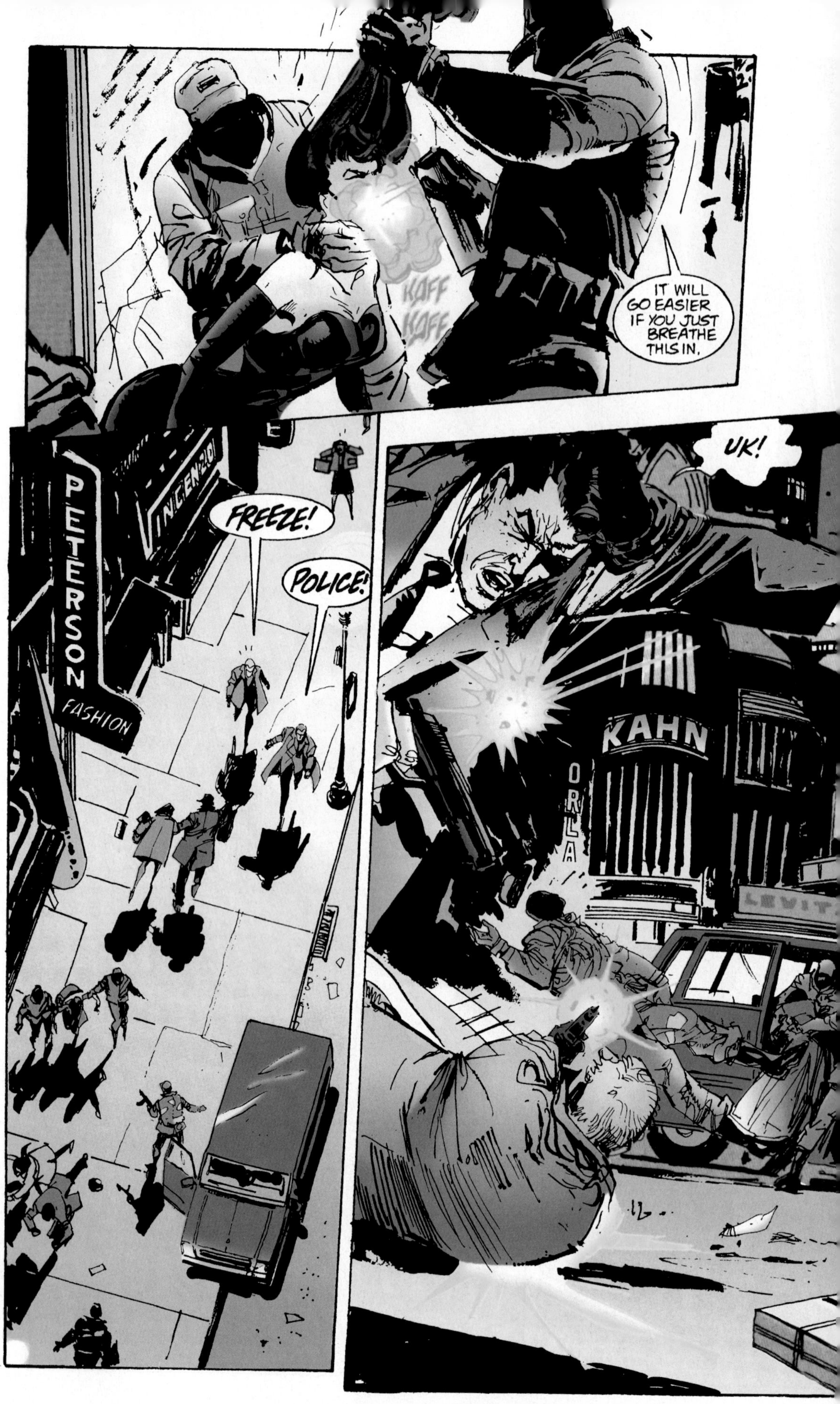
KOFF
KOFF
IT WILL GO EASIER IF YOU JUST BREATHE THIS IN.
PETERSON FASHION
FREEZE!
POLICE!
UK!
KAHN
ORLA

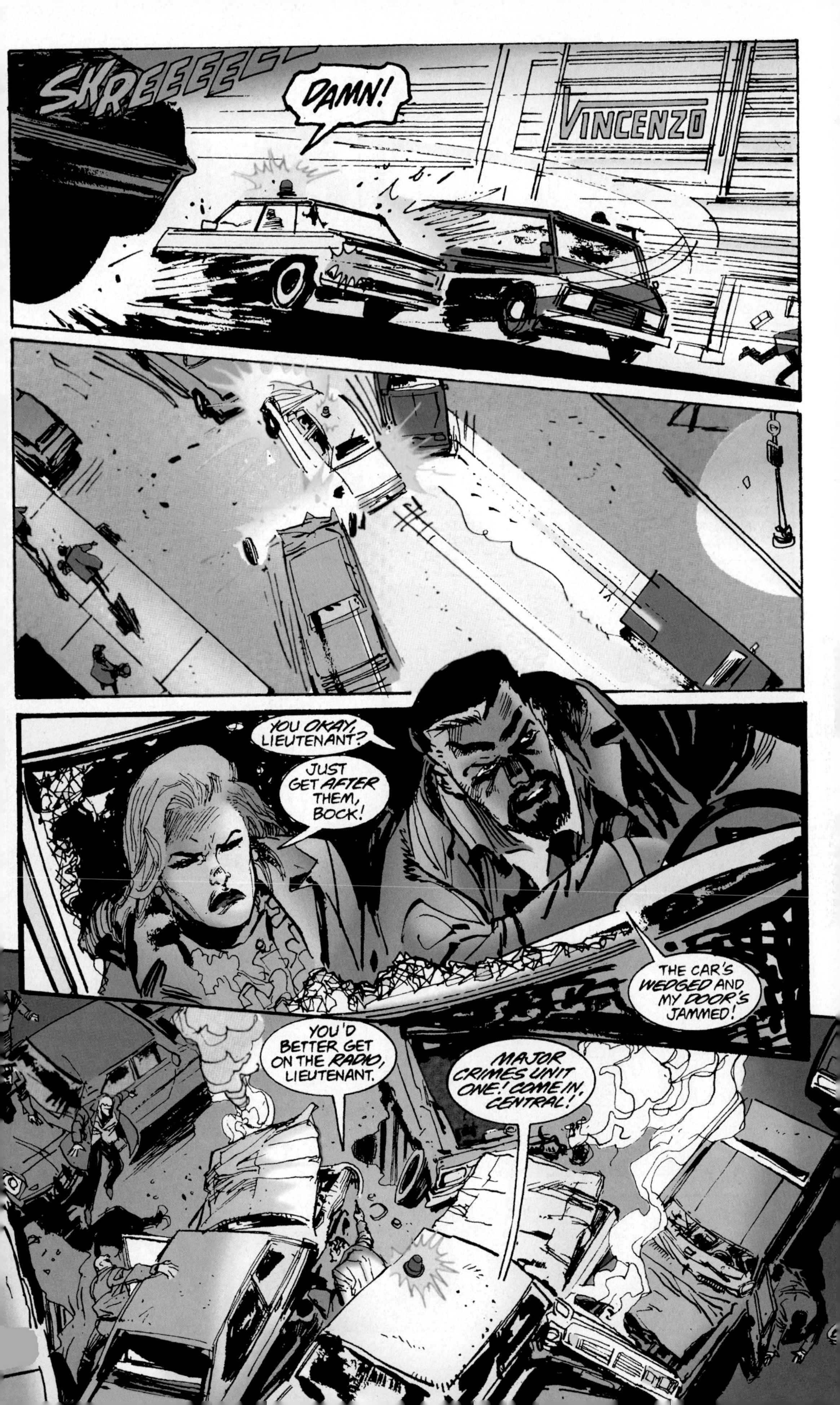
SKREEEEEE
DAMN!
VINCENZO
YOU OKAY, LIEUTENANT?
JUST GET AFTER THEM, BOCK!
THE CAR'S WEDGED AND MY DOOR'S JAMMED!
YOU'D BETTER GET ON THE RADIO, LIEUTENANT.
MAJOR CRIMES UNIT ONE! COME IN, CENTRAL!

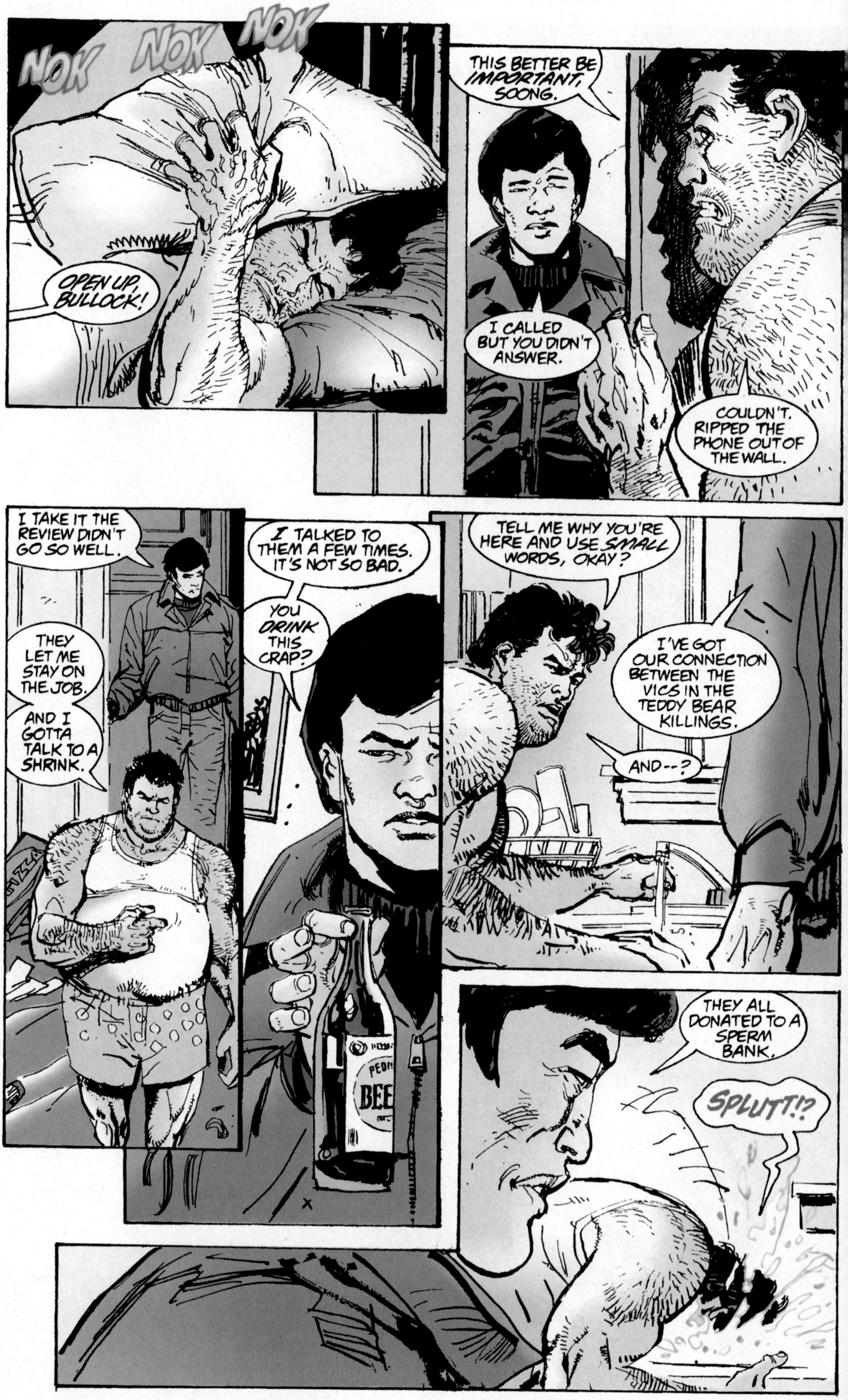
NOK NOK NOK
OPEN UP, BULLOCK!
THIS BETTER BE IMPORTANT, SOONG.
I CALLED BUT YOU DIDN'T ANSWER.
COULDN'T. RIPPED THE PHONE OUT OF THE WALL.
I TAKE IT THE REVIEW DIDN'T GO SO WELL.
THEY LET ME STAY ON THE JOB.
AND I GOTTA TALK TO A SHRINK.
I TALKED TO THEM A FEW TIMES. IT'S NOT SO BAD.
YOU DRINK THIS CRAP?
TELL ME WHY YOU'RE HERE AND USE SMALL WORDS, OKAY?
I'VE GOT OUR CONNECTION BETWEEN THE VICS IN THE TEDDY BEAR KILLINGS.
AND--?
THEY ALL DONATED TO A SPERM BANK.
SPLUTT!?

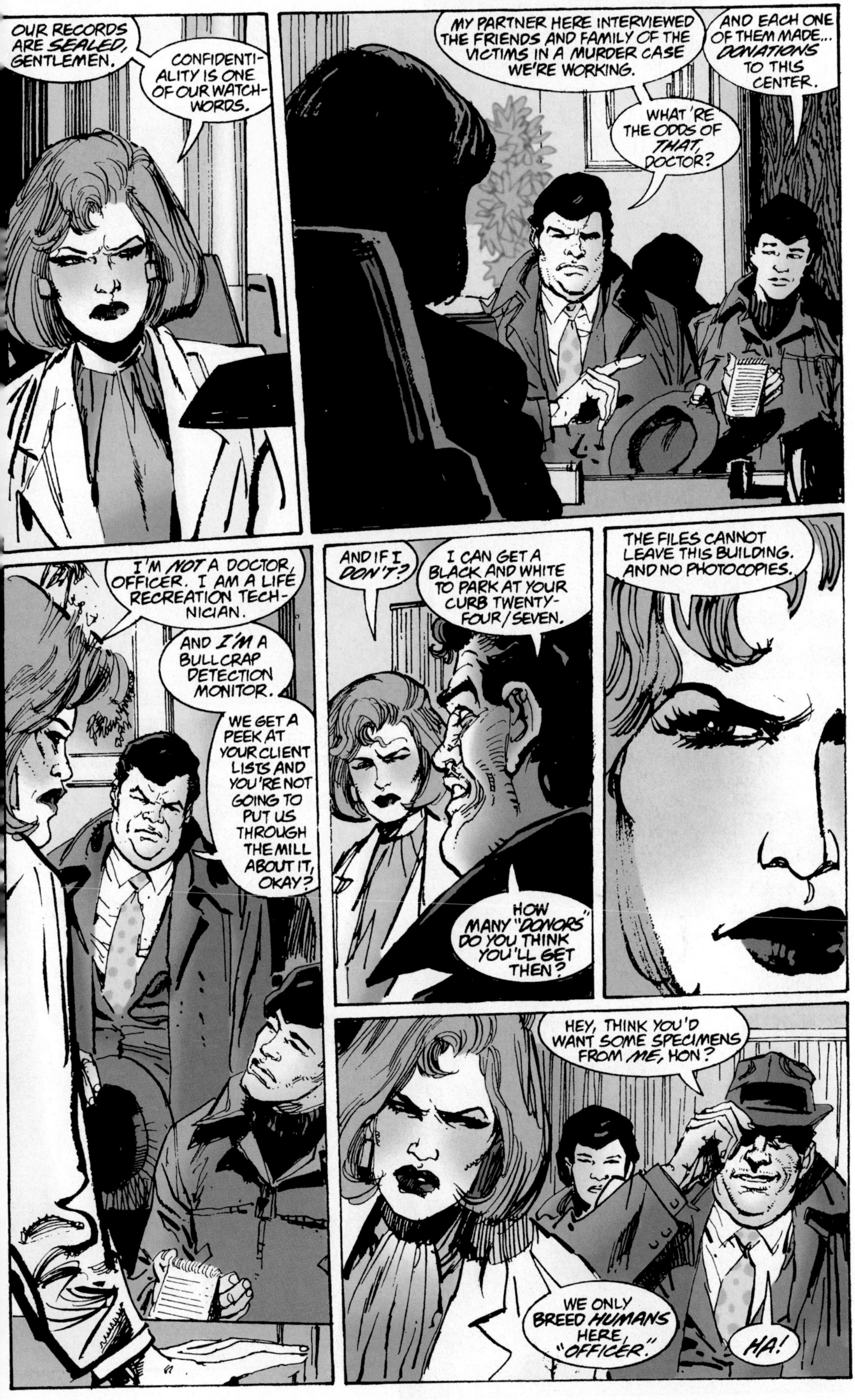

OUR RECORDS ARE SEALED, GENTLEMEN.
CONFIDENTIALITY IS ONE OF OUR WATCHWORDS.
MY PARTNER HERE INTERVIEWED THE FRIENDS AND FAMILY OF THE VICTIMS IN A MURDER CASE WE'RE WORKING.
AND EACH ONE OF THEM MADE... DONATIONS TO THIS CENTER.
WHAT'RE THE ODDS OF THAT, DOCTOR?
I'M NOT A DOCTOR, OFFICER. I AM A LIFE RECREATION TECHNICIAN.
AND I'M A BULLCRAP DETECTION MONITOR.
WE GET A PEEK AT YOUR CLIENT LISTS AND YOU'RE NOT GOING TO PUT US THROUGH THE MILL ABOUT IT, OKAY?
AND IF I DON'T?
I CAN GET A BLACK AND WHITE TO PARK AT YOUR CURB TWENTY-FOUR/SEVEN.
HOW MANY "DONORS" DO YOU THINK YOU'LL GET THEN?
THE FILES CANNOT LEAVE THIS BUILDING. AND NO PHOTOCOPIES.
HEY, THINK YOU'D WANT SOME SPECIMENS FROM ME, HON?
WE ONLY BREED HUMANS HERE, "OFFICER."
HA!

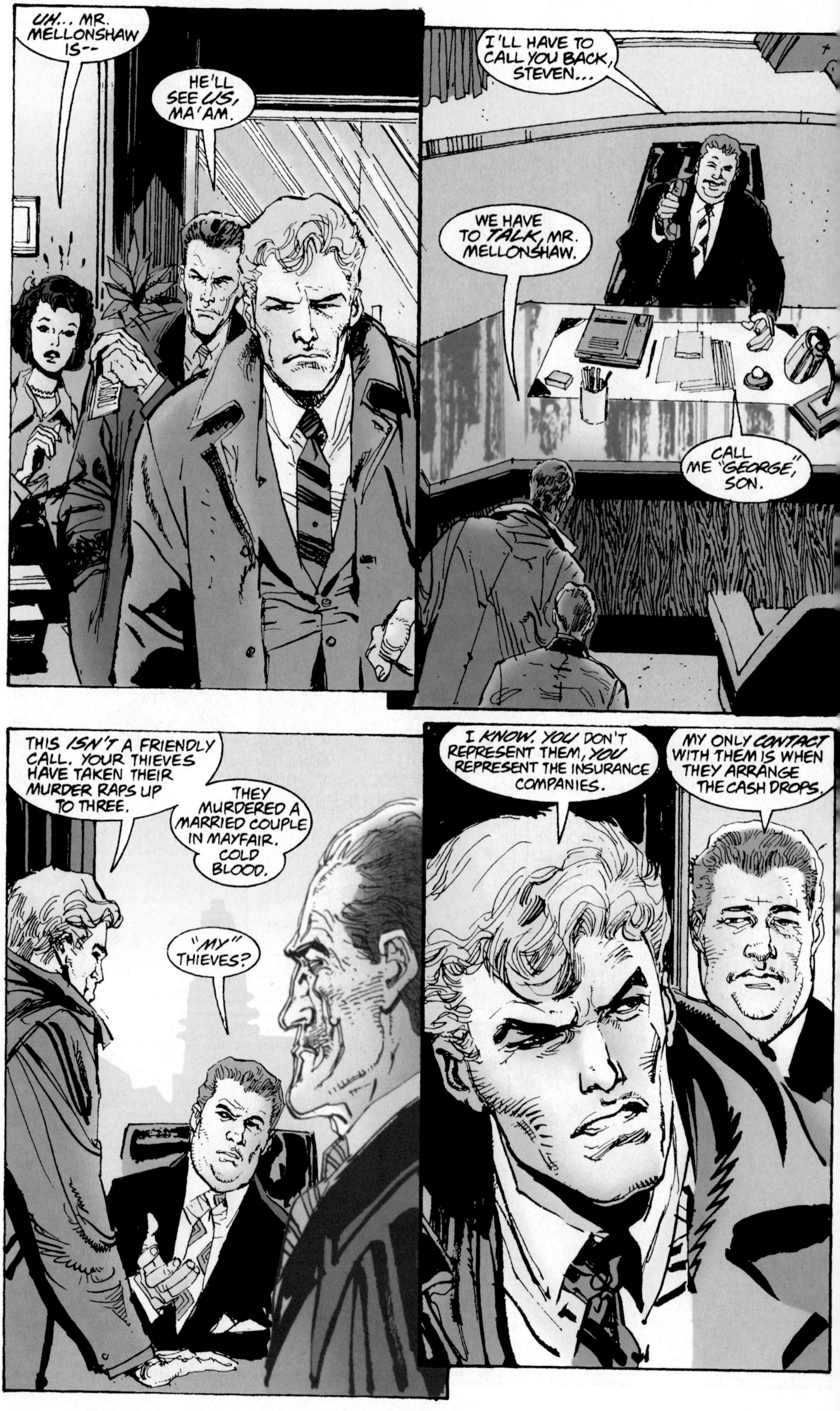
UH... MR. MELLONSHAW IS--
HE'LL SEE US, MA'AM.
I'LL HAVE TO CALL YOU BACK, STEVEN...
WE HAVE TO TALK, MR. MELLONSHAW.
CALL ME "GEORGE," SON.
THIS ISN'T A FRIENDLY CALL. YOUR THIEVES HAVE TAKEN THEIR MURDER RAPS UP TO THREE.
THEY MURDERED A MARRIED COUPLE IN MAYFAIR. COLD BLOOD.
"MY" THIEVES?
I KNOW. YOU DON'T REPRESENT THEM, YOU REPRESENT THE INSURANCE COMPANIES.
MY ONLY CONTACT WITH THEM IS WHEN THEY ARRANGE THE CASH DROPS.

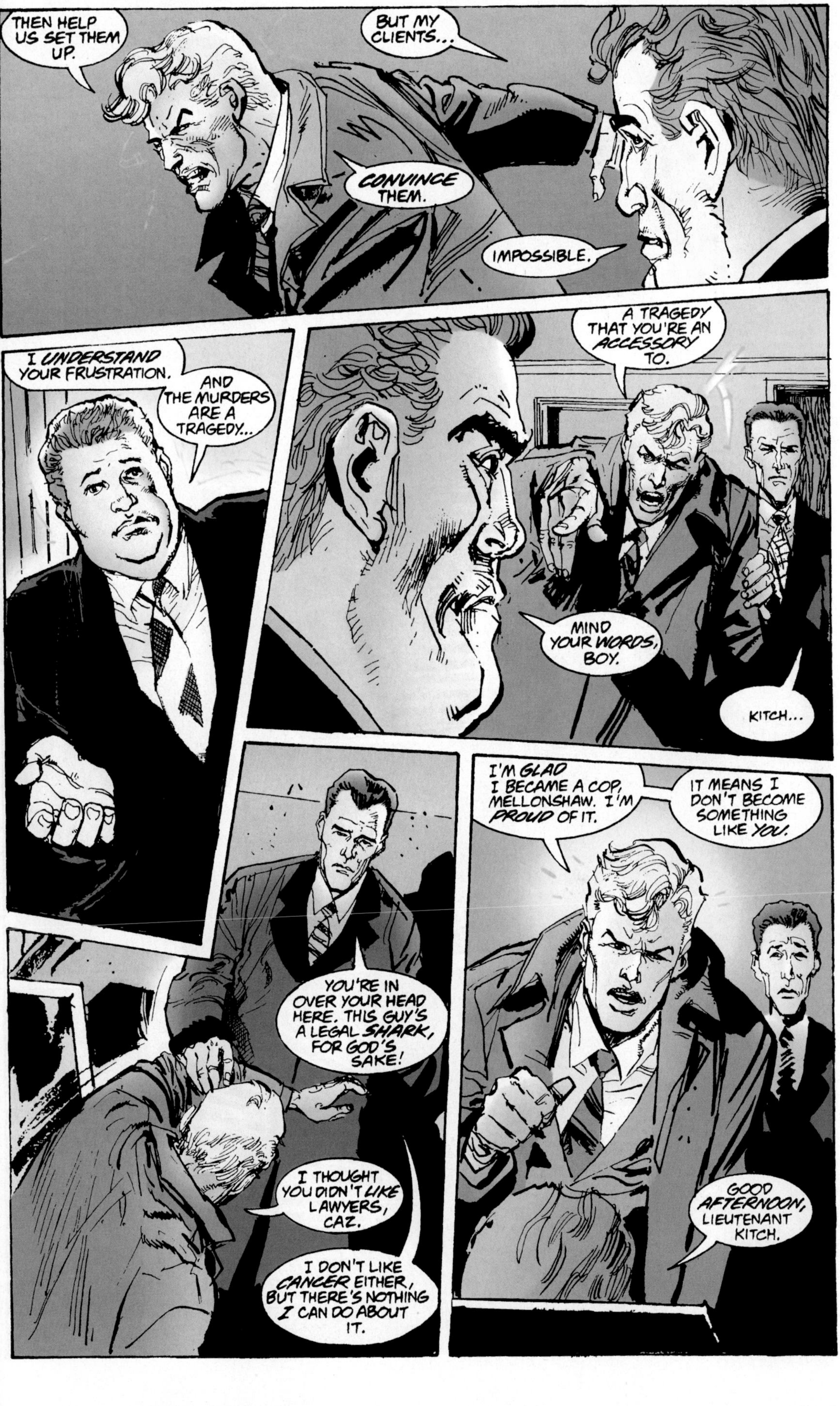
THEN HELP US SET THEM UP.
BUT MY CLIENTS...
CONVINCE THEM.
IMPOSSIBLE.
I UNDERSTAND YOUR FRUSTRATION.
AND THE MURDERS ARE A TRAGEDY...
A TRAGEDY THAT YOU'RE AN ACCESSORY TO.
MIND YOUR WORDS, BOY.
KITCH...
YOU'RE IN OVER YOUR HEAD HERE. THIS GUY'S A LEGAL SHARK, FOR GOD'S SAKE!
I THOUGHT YOU DIDN'T LIKE LAWYERS, CAZ.
I DON'T LIKE CANCER EITHER, BUT THERE'S NOTHING I CAN DO ABOUT IT.
I'M GLAD I BECAME A COP, MELLONSHAW. I'M PROUD OF IT.
IT MEANS I DON'T BECOME SOMETHING LIKE YOU.
GOOD AFTERNOON, LIEUTENANT KITCH.

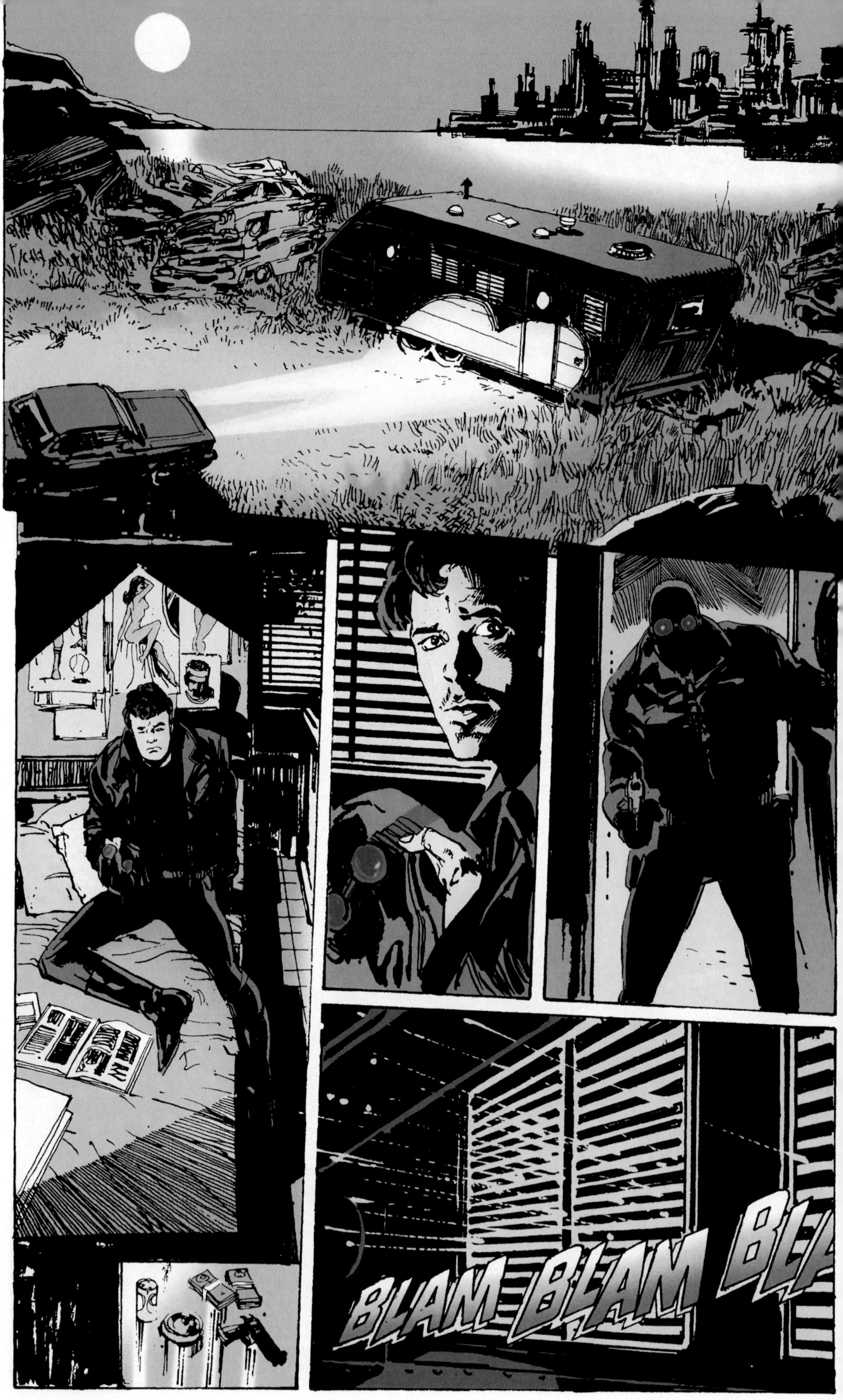
BLAM BLAM BLA

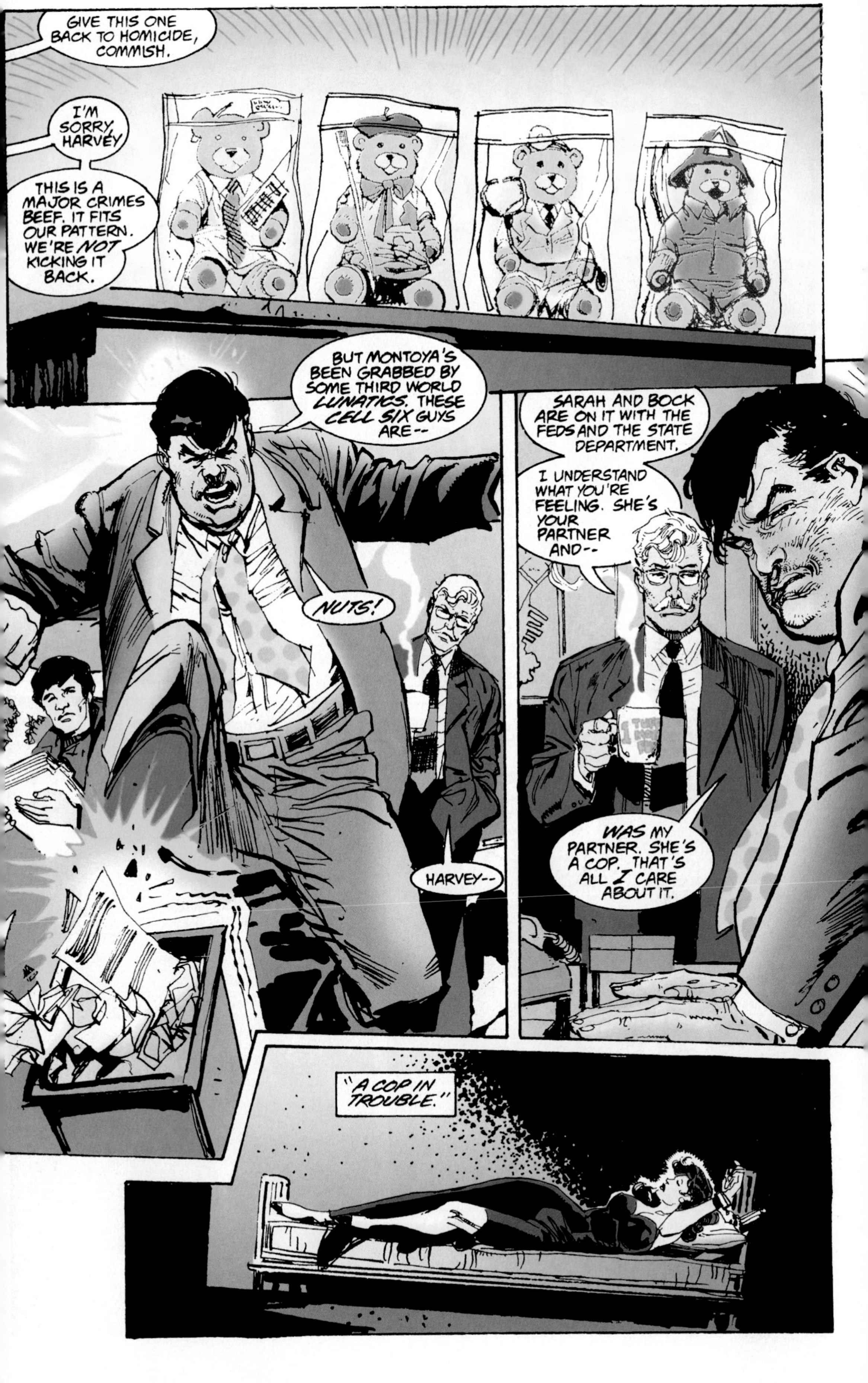
GIVE THIS ONE BACK TO HOMICIDE, COMMISH.
I'M SORRY, HARVEY.
THIS IS A MAJOR CRIMES BEEF. IT FITS OUR PATTERN. WE'RE NOT KICKING IT BACK.
BUT MONTOYA'S BEEN GRABBED BY SOME THIRD WORLD LUNATICS. THESE CELL SIX GUYS ARE--
NUTS!
HARVEY--
SARAH AND BOCK ARE ON IT WITH THE FEDS AND THE STATE DEPARTMENT.
I UNDERSTAND WHAT YOU'RE FEELING. SHE'S YOUR PARTNER AND--
WAS MY PARTNER. SHE'S A COP. THAT'S ALL I CARE ABOUT IT.
"A COP IN TROUBLE."

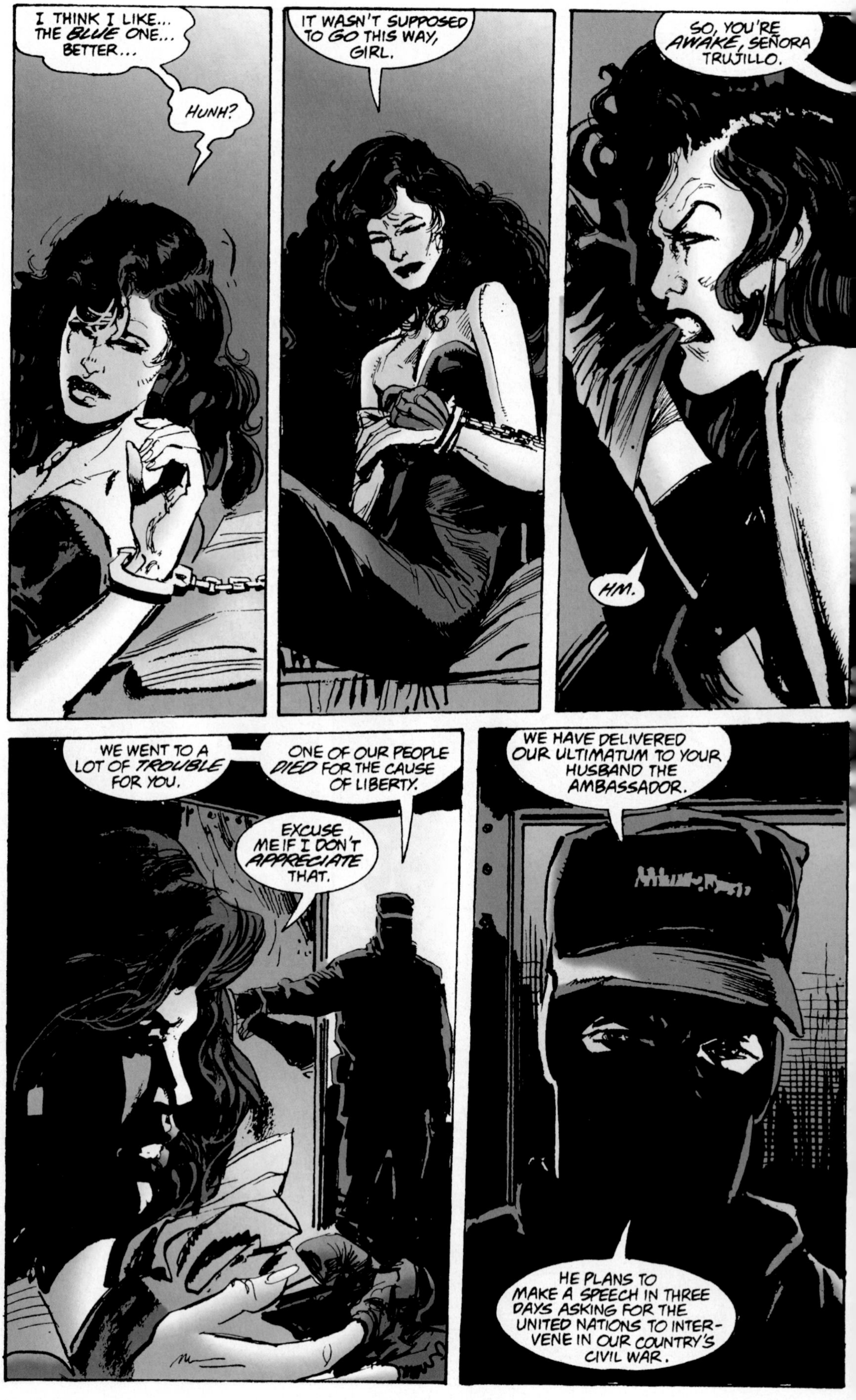

I THINK I LIKE... THE BLUE ONE... BETTER...
HUNH?
IT WASN'T SUPPOSED TO GO THIS WAY, GIRL.
SO, YOU'RE AWAKE, SEÑORA TRUJILLO.
HM.
WE WENT TO A LOT OF TROUBLE FOR YOU.
ONE OF OUR PEOPLE DIED FOR THE CAUSE OF LIBERTY.
EXCUSE ME IF I DON'T APPRECIATE THAT.
WE HAVE DELIVERED OUR ULTIMATUM TO YOUR HUSBAND THE AMBASSADOR.
HE PLANS TO MAKE A SPEECH IN THREE DAYS ASKING FOR THE UNITED NATIONS TO INTER-VENE IN OUR COUNTRY'S CIVIL WAR.

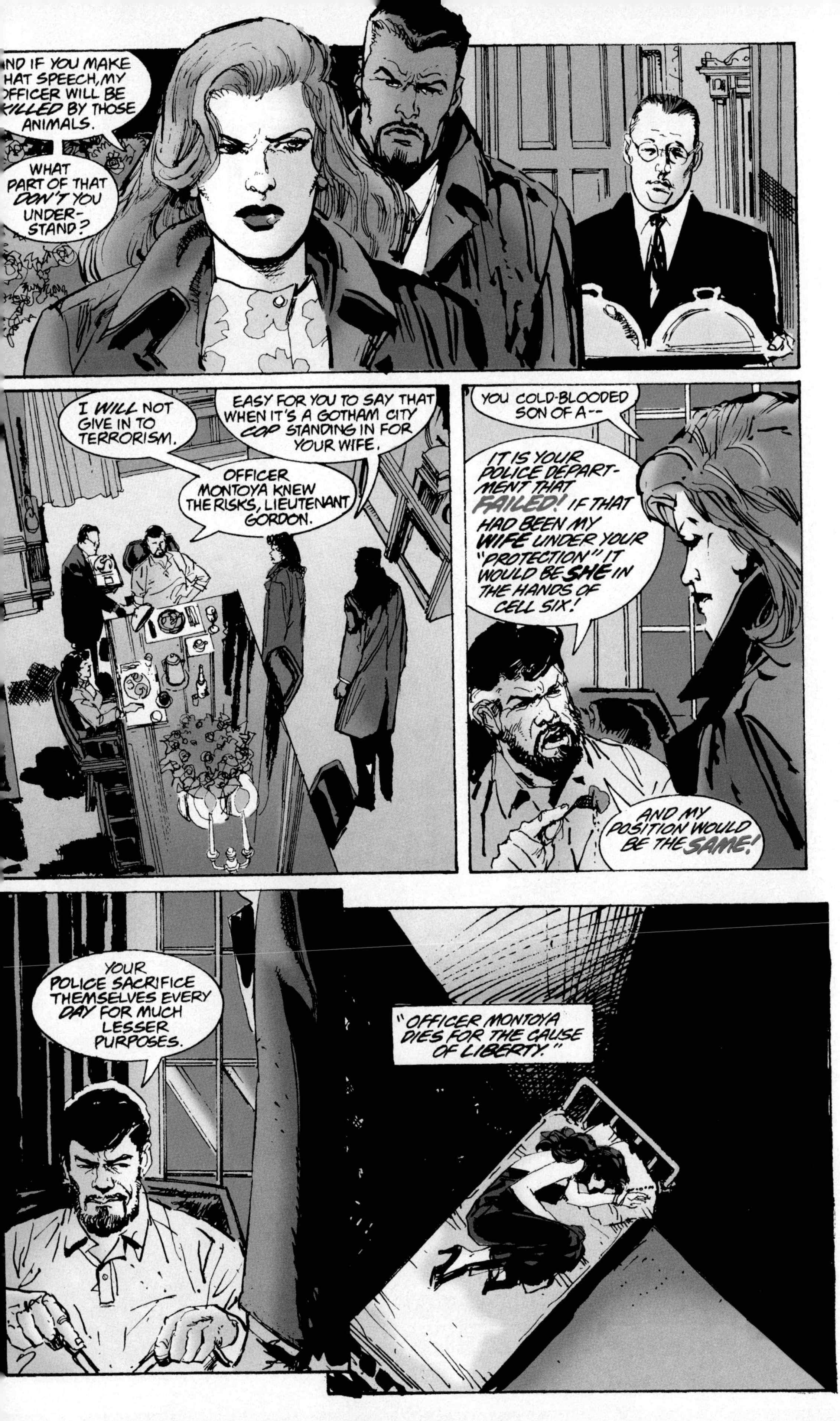
ND IF YOU MAKE HAT SPEECH, MY OFFICER WILL BE KILLED BY THOSE ANIMALS.
WHAT PART OF THAT DON'T YOU UNDERSTAND?
I WILL NOT GIVE IN TO TERRORISM.
EASY FOR YOU TO SAY THAT WHEN IT'S A GOTHAM CITY COP STANDING IN FOR YOUR WIFE.
OFFICER MONTOYA KNEW THE RISKS, LIEUTENANT GORDON.
YOU COLD-BLOODED SON OF A--
IT IS YOUR POLICE DEPARTMENT THAT FAILED! IF THAT HAD BEEN MY WIFE UNDER YOUR "PROTECTION" IT WOULD BE SHE IN THE HANDS OF CELL SIX!
AND MY POSITION WOULD BE THE SAME!
YOUR POLICE SACRIFICE THEMSELVES EVERY DAY FOR MUCH LESSER PURPOSES.
"OFFICER MONTOYA DIES FOR THE CAUSE OF LIBERTY."

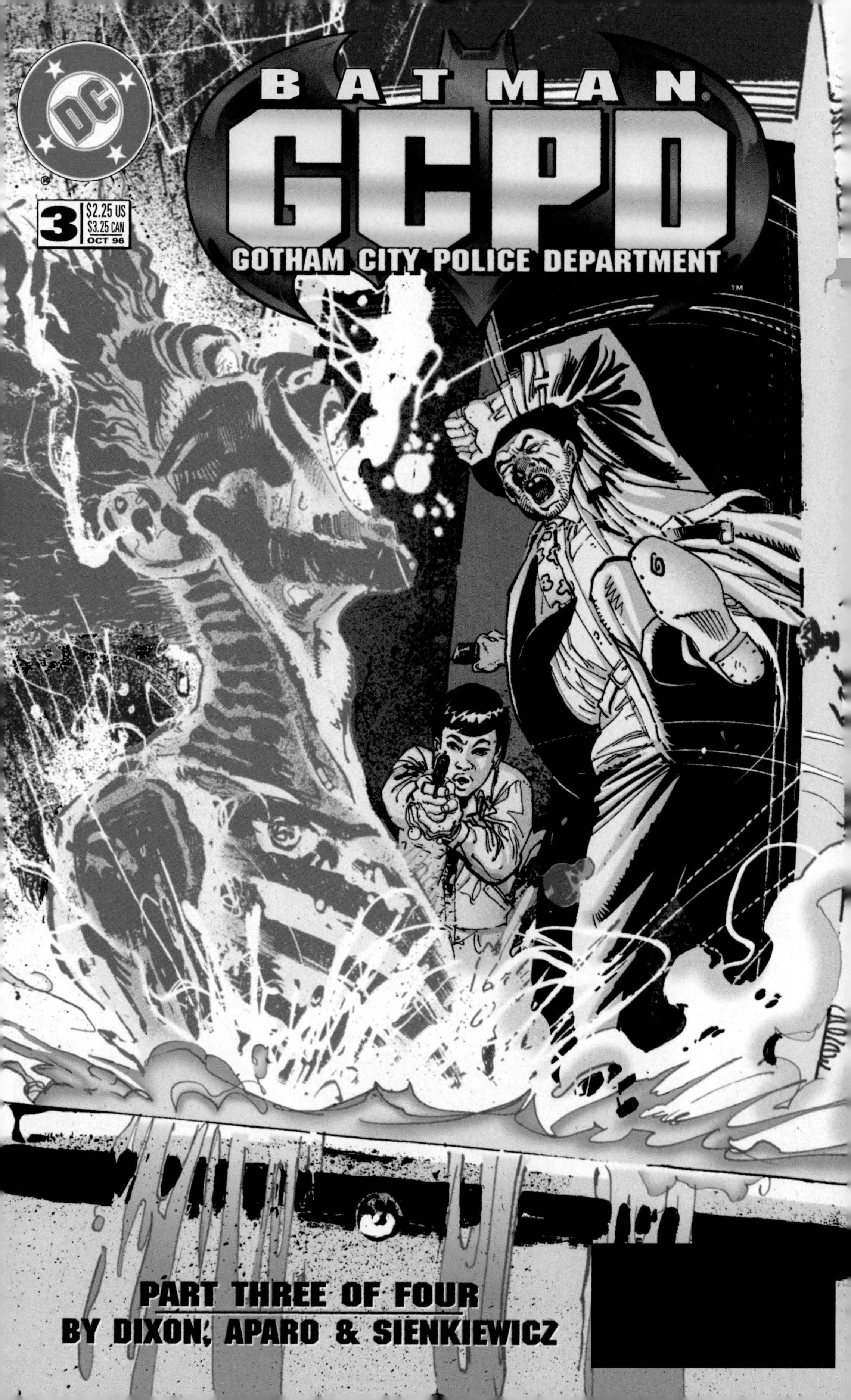
DC
BATMAN
GCPD
GOTHAM CITY POLICE DEPARTMENT
3
$2.25 US
$3.25 CAN
OCT 96
PART THREE OF FOUR
BY DIXON, APARO & SIENKIEWICZ

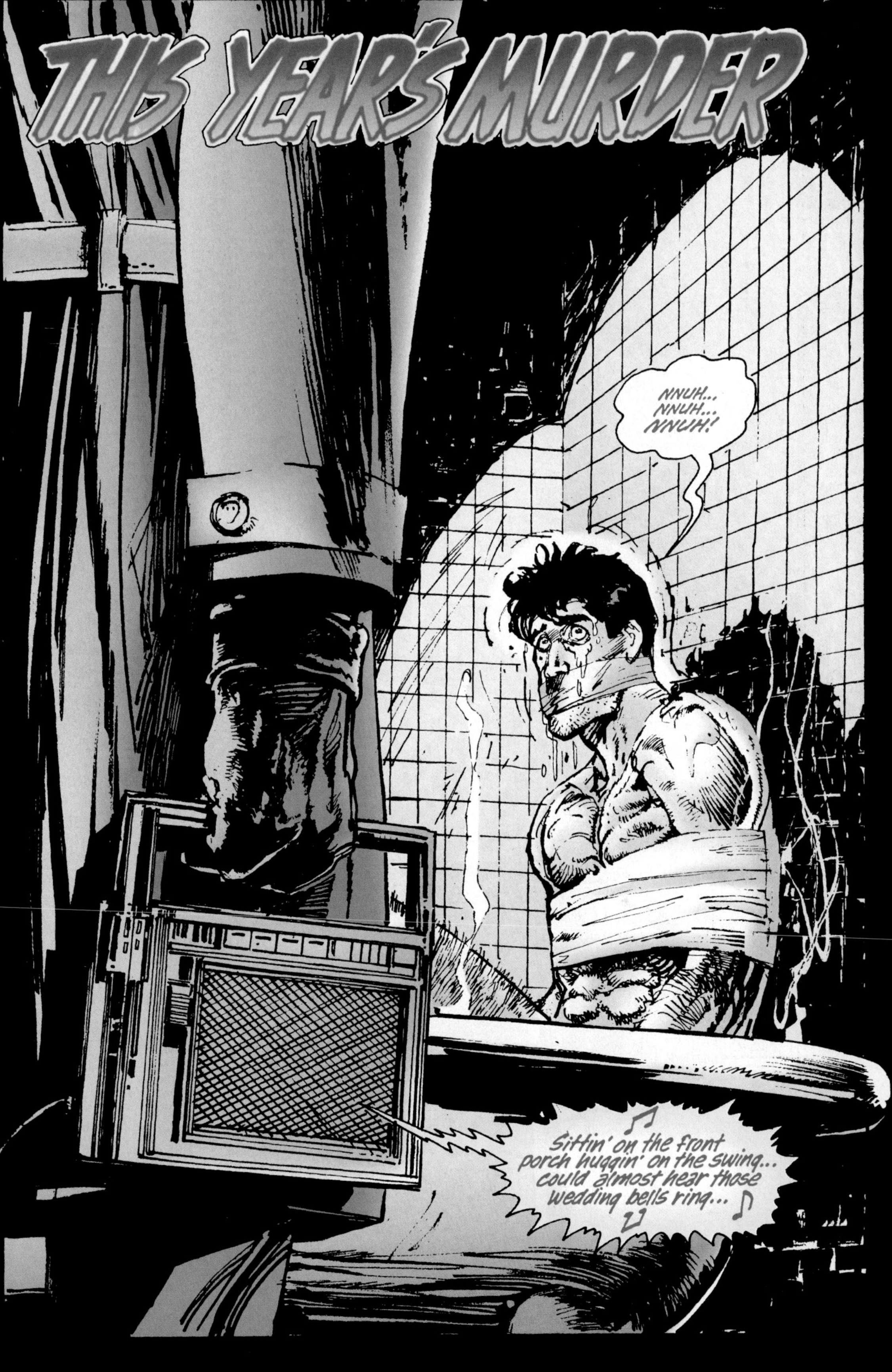
THIS YEAR'S MURDER
NNUH... NNUH... NNUH!
Sittin' on the front porch huggin' on the swing... could almost hear those wedding bells ring...

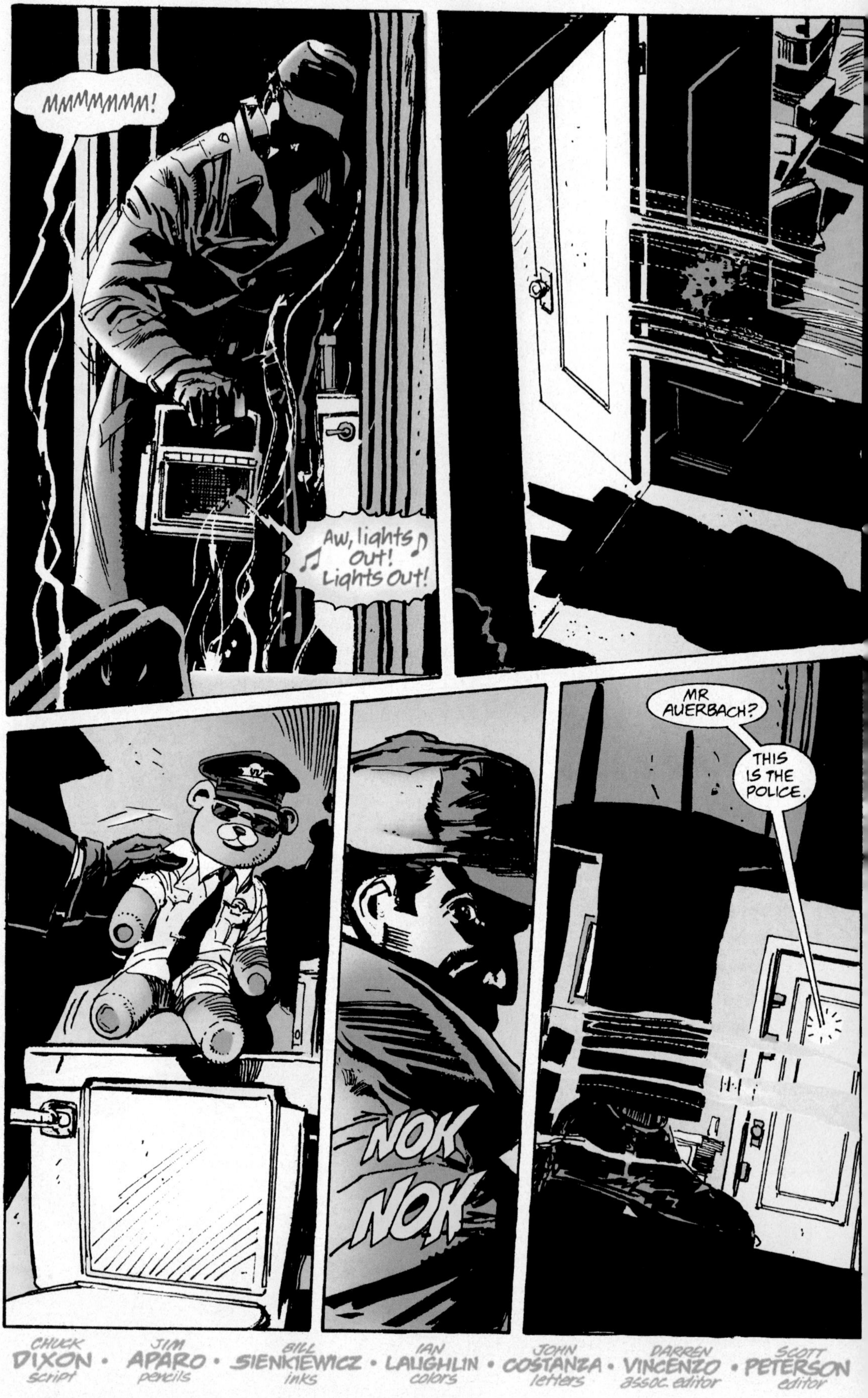
MMMMMMM!
Aw, lights out! Lights Out!
MR AUERBACH?
THIS IS THE POLICE.
NOK NOK

CHUCK DIXON • script · JIM APARO • pencils · BILL SIENKIEWICZ • inks · IAN LAUGHLIN • colors · JOHN COSTANZA • letters · DARREN VINCENZO • assoc. editor · SCOTT PETERSON • editor

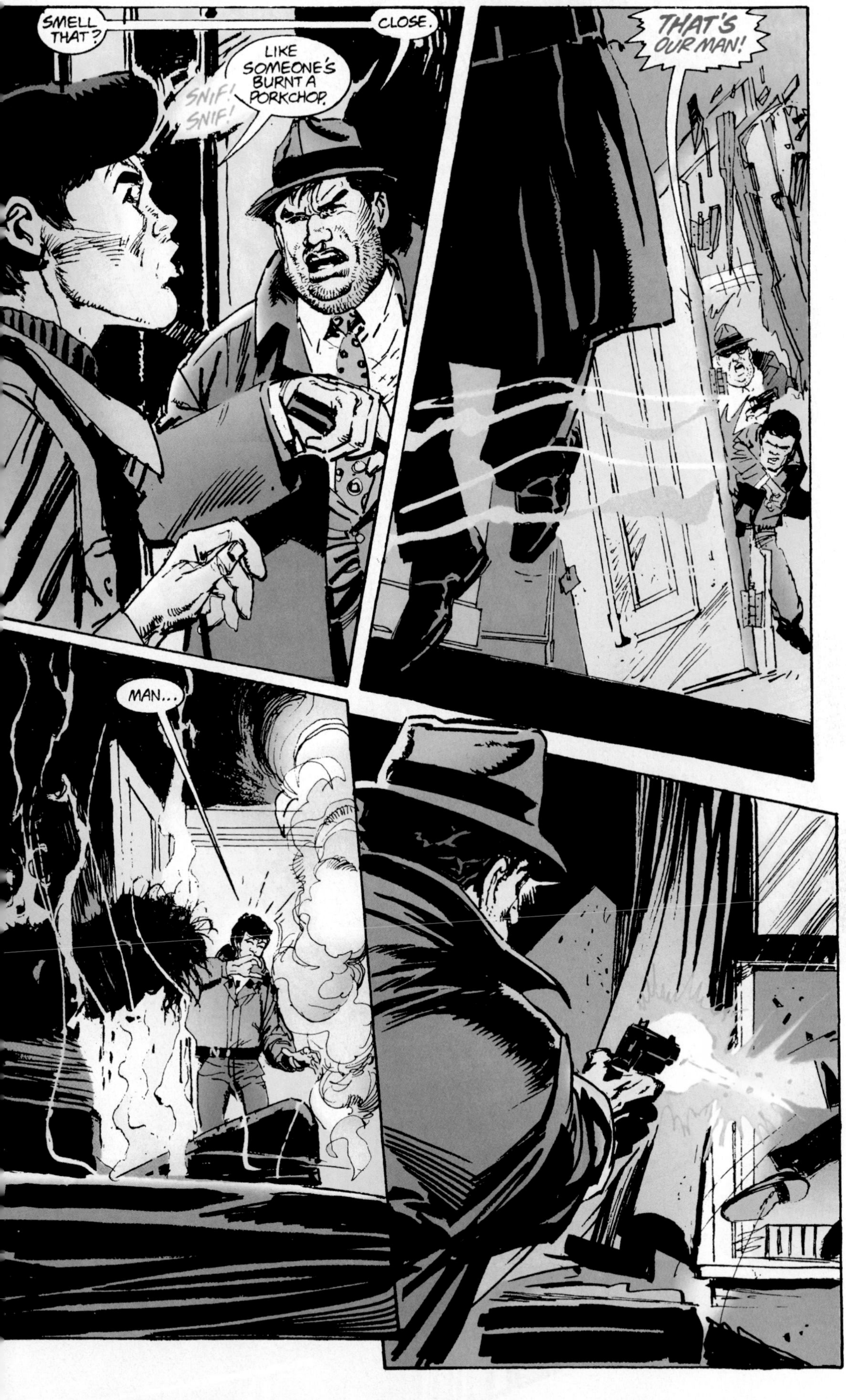
SMELL THAT?
CLOSE.
SNIF! SNIF!
LIKE SOMEONE'S BURNT A PORKCHOP.
THAT'S OUR MAN!
MAN...

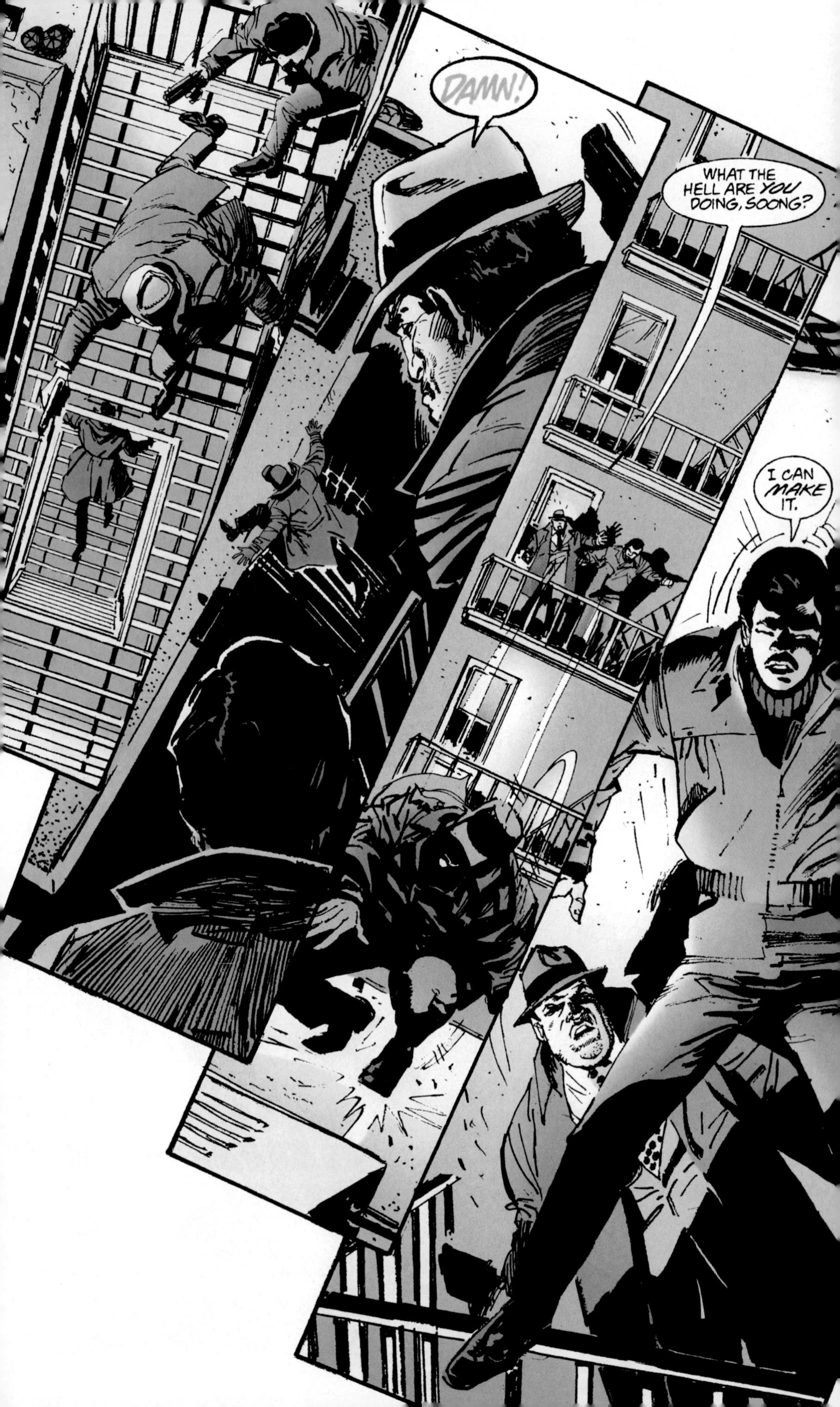
DAMN!
WHAT THE HELL ARE YOU DOING, SOONG?
I CAN MAKE IT.

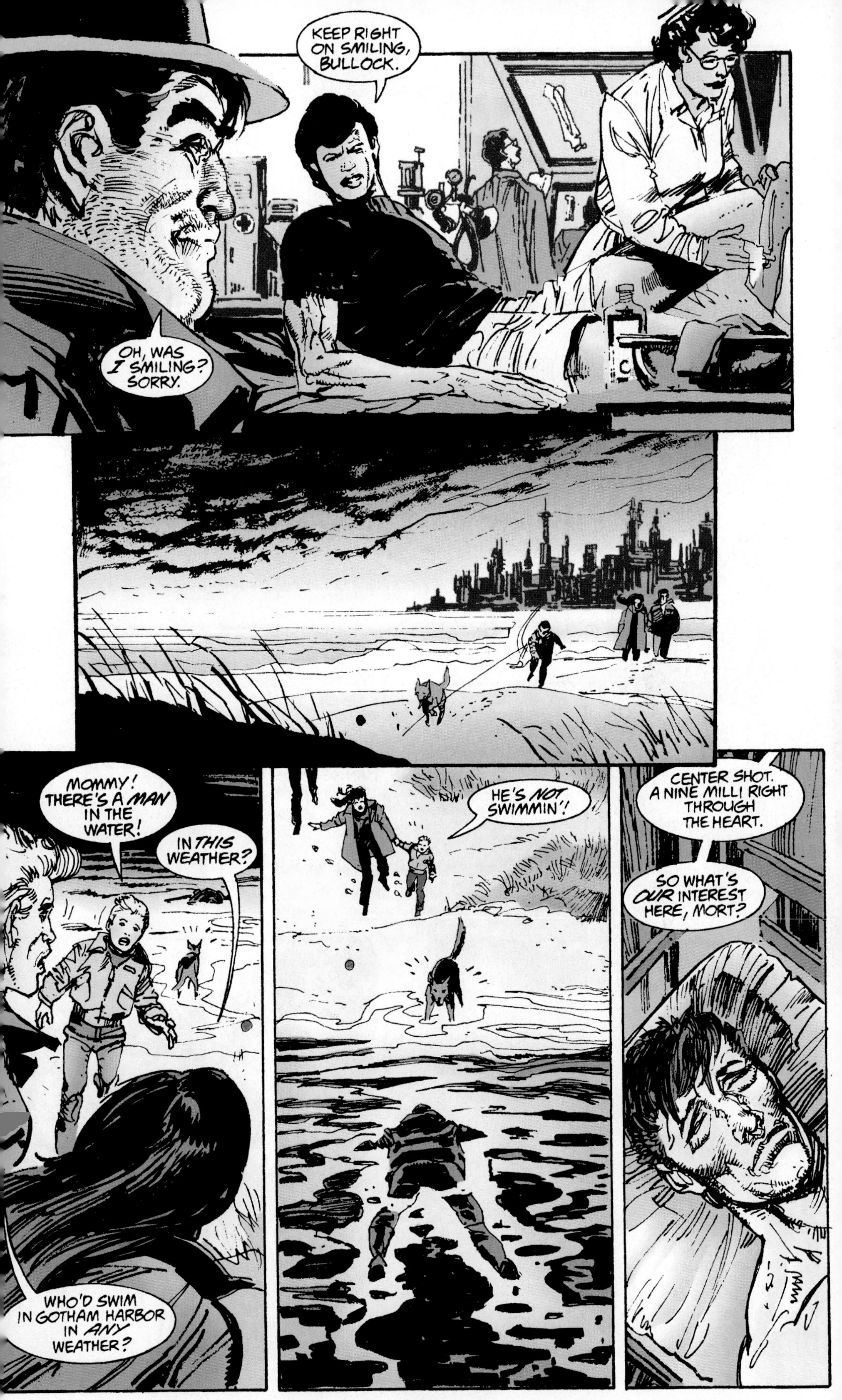

KEEP RIGHT ON SMILING, BULLOCK.
OH, WAS I SMILING? SORRY.
MOMMY! THERE'S A MAN IN THE WATER!
IN THIS WEATHER?
WHO'D SWIM IN GOTHAM HARBOR IN ANY WEATHER?
HE'S NOT SWIMMIN'!
CENTER SHOT. A NINE MILLI RIGHT THROUGH THE HEART.
SO WHAT'S OUR INTEREST HERE, MORT?

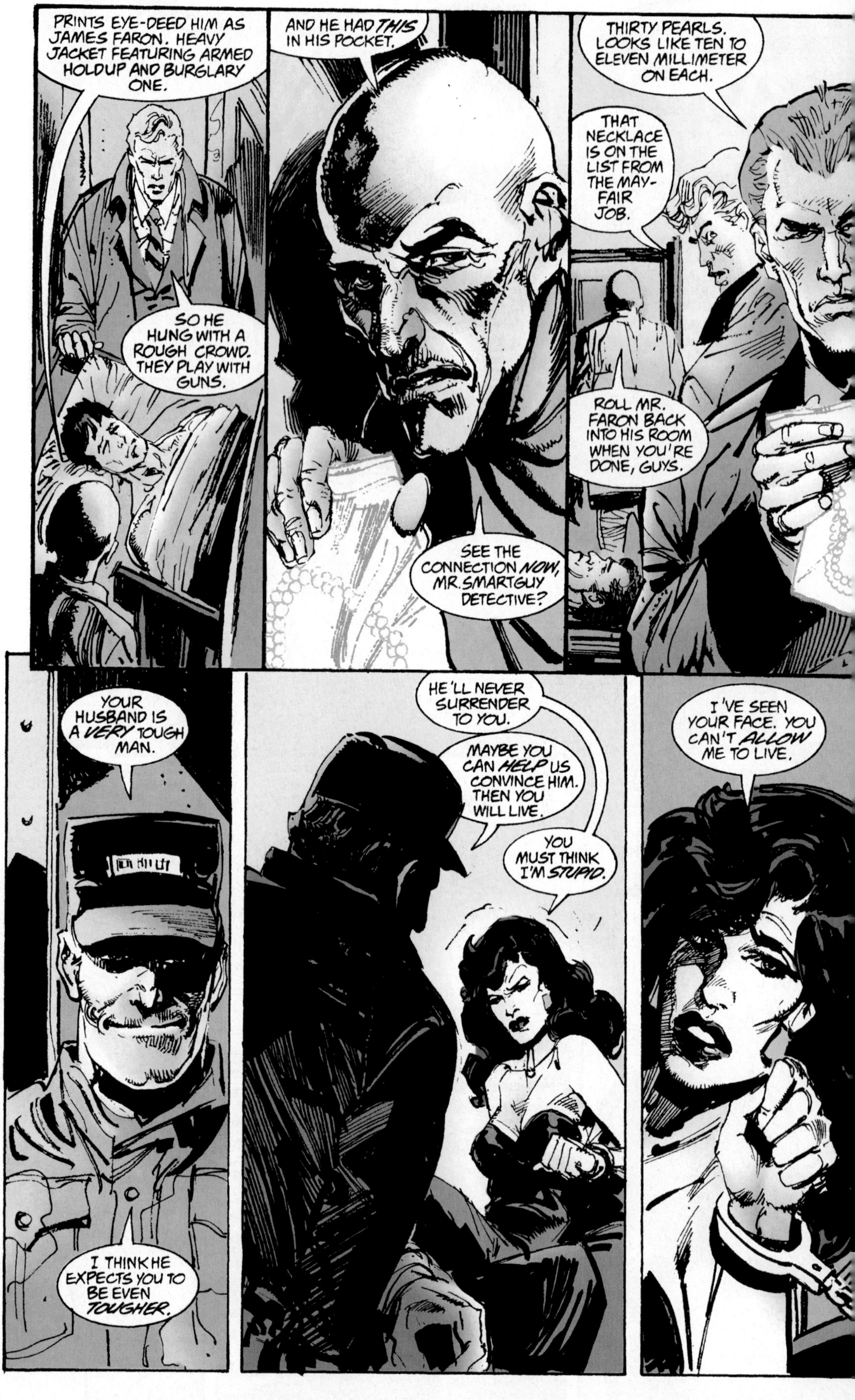
PRINTS EYE-DEED HIM AS JAMES FARON. HEAVY JACKET FEATURING ARMED HOLDUP AND BURGLARY ONE.
SO HE HUNG WITH A ROUGH CROWD. THEY PLAY WITH GUNS.
AND HE HAD THIS IN HIS POCKET.
SEE THE CONNECTION NOW, MR. SMARTGUY DETECTIVE?
THIRTY PEARLS. LOOKS LIKE TEN TO ELEVEN MILLIMETER ON EACH.
THAT NECKLACE IS ON THE LIST FROM THE MAY-FAIR JOB.
ROLL MR. FARON BACK INTO HIS ROOM WHEN YOU'RE DONE, GUYS.
YOUR HUSBAND IS A VERY TOUGH MAN.
I THINK HE EXPECTS YOU TO BE EVEN TOUGHER.
HE'LL NEVER SURRENDER TO YOU.
MAYBE YOU CAN HELP US CONVINCE HIM. THEN YOU WILL LIVE.
YOU MUST THINK I'M STUPID.
I'VE SEEN YOUR FACE. YOU CAN'T ALLOW ME TO LIVE.

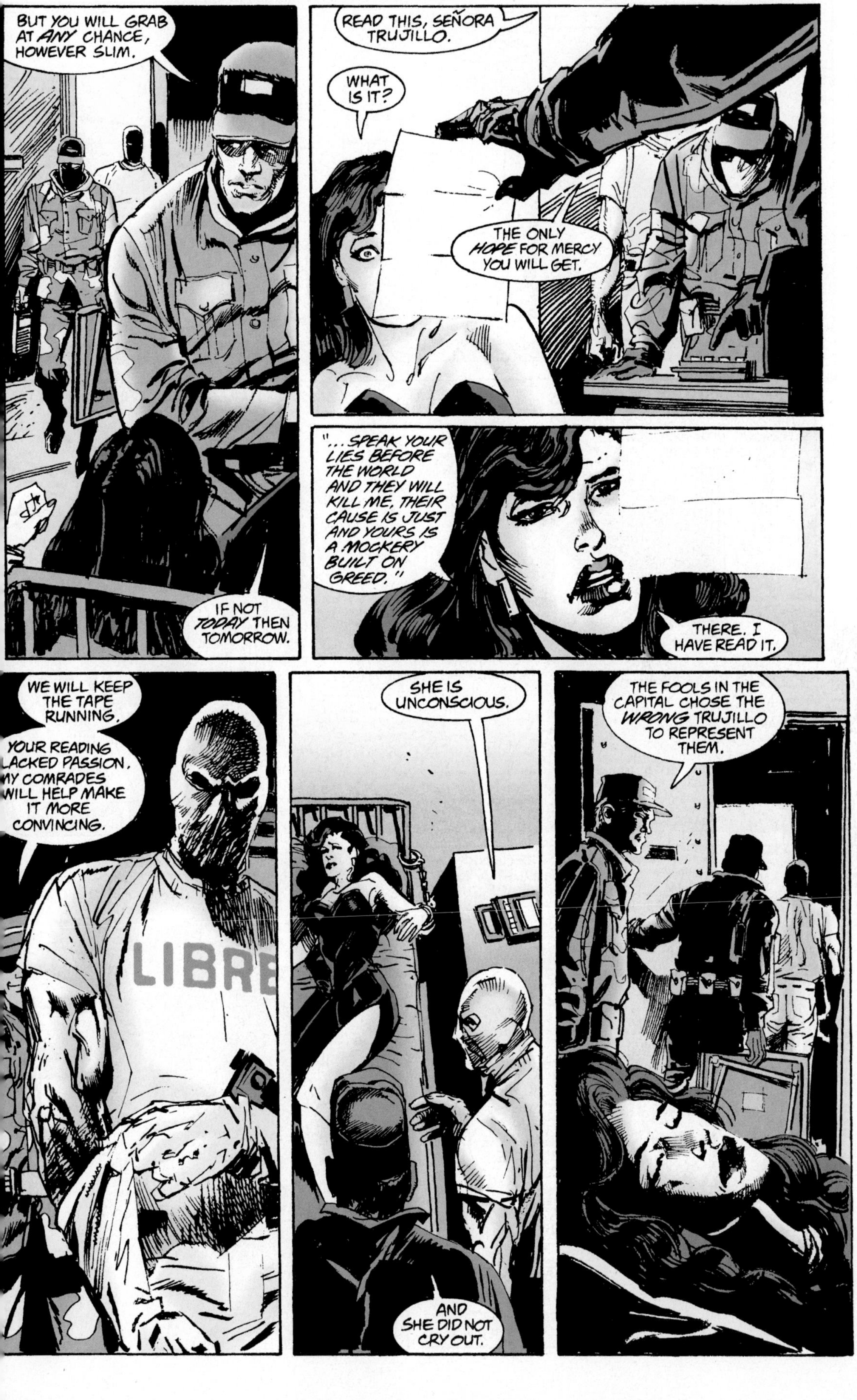
BUT YOU WILL GRAB AT *ANY* CHANCE, HOWEVER SLIM.
IF NOT *TODAY* THEN TOMORROW.
READ THIS, SEÑORA TRUJILLO.
WHAT IS IT?
THE ONLY *HOPE* FOR MERCY YOU WILL GET.
"...SPEAK YOUR LIES BEFORE THE WORLD AND THEY WILL KILL ME. THEIR CAUSE IS JUST AND YOURS IS A MOCKERY BUILT ON GREED."
THERE. I HAVE READ IT.
WE WILL KEEP THE TAPE RUNNING.
YOUR READING LACKED PASSION. MY COMRADES WILL HELP MAKE IT MORE CONVINCING.
LIBRE
SHE IS UNCONSCIOUS.
AND SHE DID NOT CRY OUT.
THE FOOLS IN THE CAPITAL CHOSE THE *WRONG* TRUJILLO TO REPRESENT THEM.

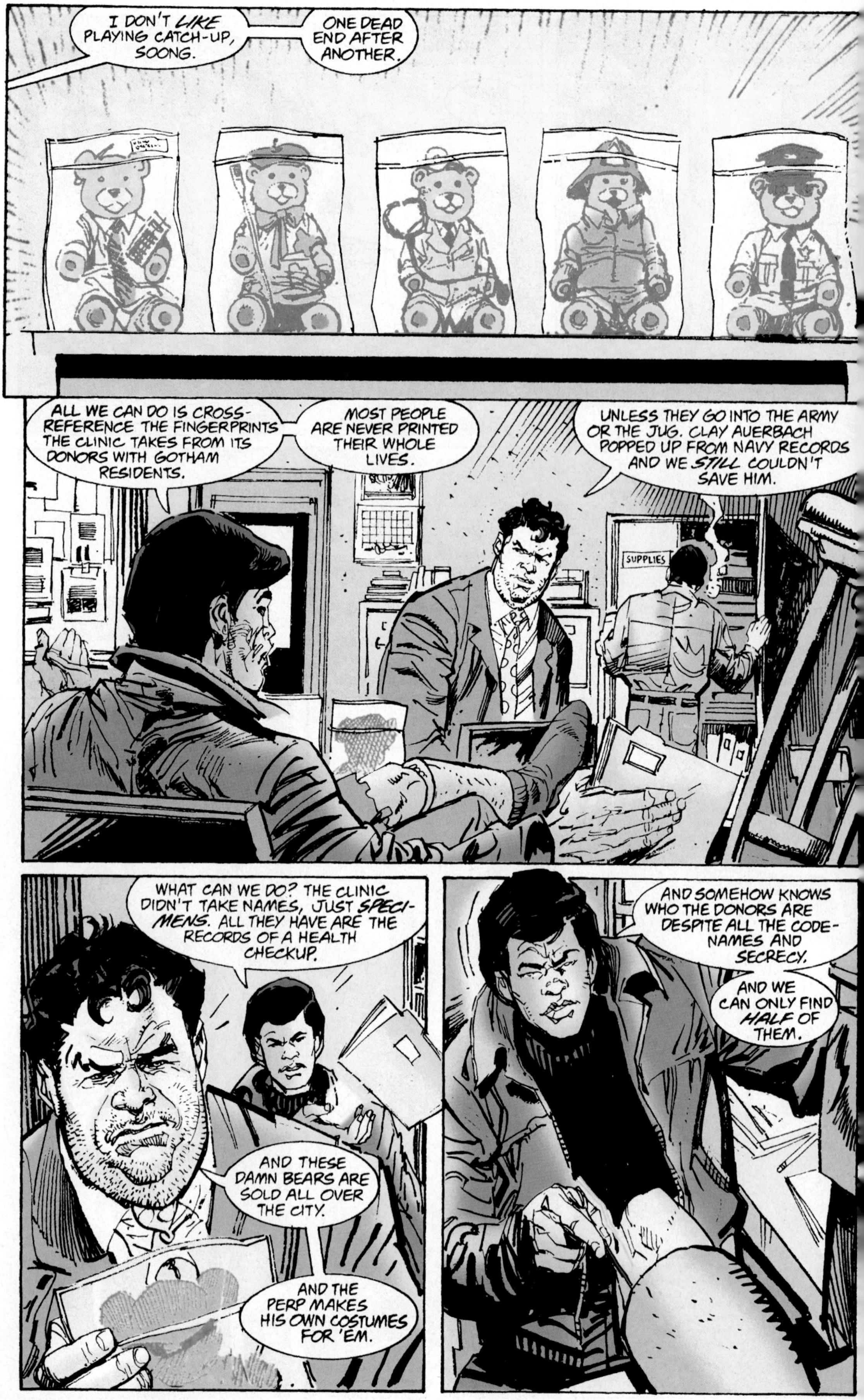
I DON'T LIKE PLAYING CATCH-UP, SOONG.
ONE DEAD END AFTER ANOTHER.
ALL WE CAN DO IS CROSS-REFERENCE THE FINGERPRINTS THE CLINIC TAKES FROM ITS DONORS WITH GOTHAM RESIDENTS.
MOST PEOPLE ARE NEVER PRINTED THEIR WHOLE LIVES.
UNLESS THEY GO INTO THE ARMY OR THE JUG. CLAY AUERBACH POPPED UP FROM NAVY RECORDS AND WE STILL COULDN'T SAVE HIM.
SUPPLIES
WHAT CAN WE DO? THE CLINIC DIDN'T TAKE NAMES, JUST SPECIMENS. ALL THEY HAVE ARE THE RECORDS OF A HEALTH CHECKUP.
AND THESE DAMN BEARS ARE SOLD ALL OVER THE CITY.
AND THE PERP MAKES HIS OWN COSTUMES FOR 'EM.
AND SOMEHOW KNOWS WHO THE DONORS ARE DESPITE ALL THE CODE-NAMES AND SECRECY.
AND WE CAN ONLY FIND HALF OF THEM.

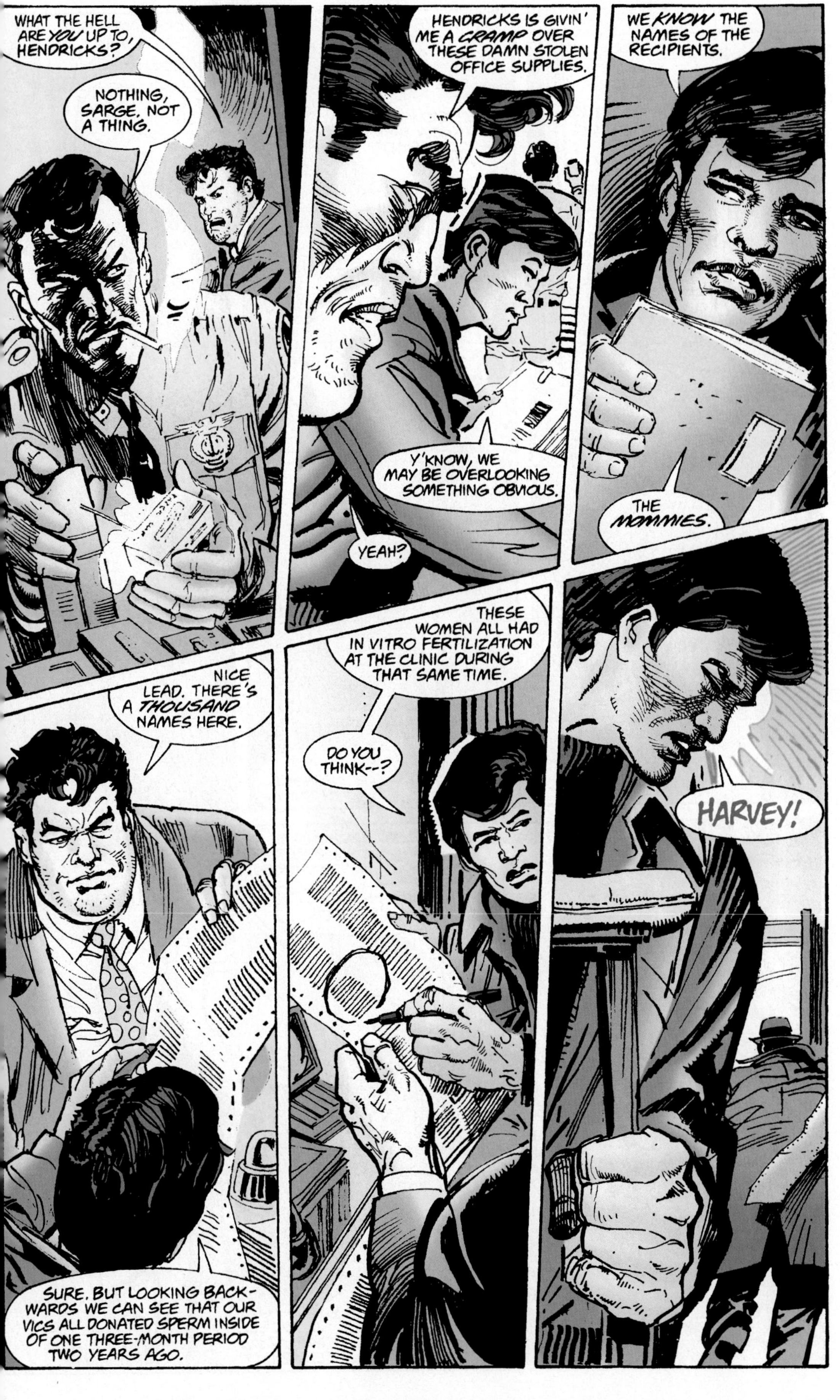
WHAT THE HELL ARE YOU UP TO, HENDRICKS?
NOTHING, SARGE. NOT A THING.
HENDRICKS IS GIVIN' ME A CRAMP OVER THESE DAMN STOLEN OFFICE SUPPLIES.
Y'KNOW, WE MAY BE OVERLOOKING SOMETHING OBVIOUS.
YEAH?
WE KNOW THE NAMES OF THE RECIPIENTS.
THE MOMMIES.
NICE LEAD. THERE'S A THOUSAND NAMES HERE.
SURE. BUT LOOKING BACKWARDS WE CAN SEE THAT OUR VICS ALL DONATED SPERM INSIDE OF ONE THREE-MONTH PERIOD TWO YEARS AGO.
THESE WOMEN ALL HAD IN VITRO FERTILIZATION AT THE CLINIC DURING THAT SAME TIME.
DO YOU THINK--?
HARVEY!

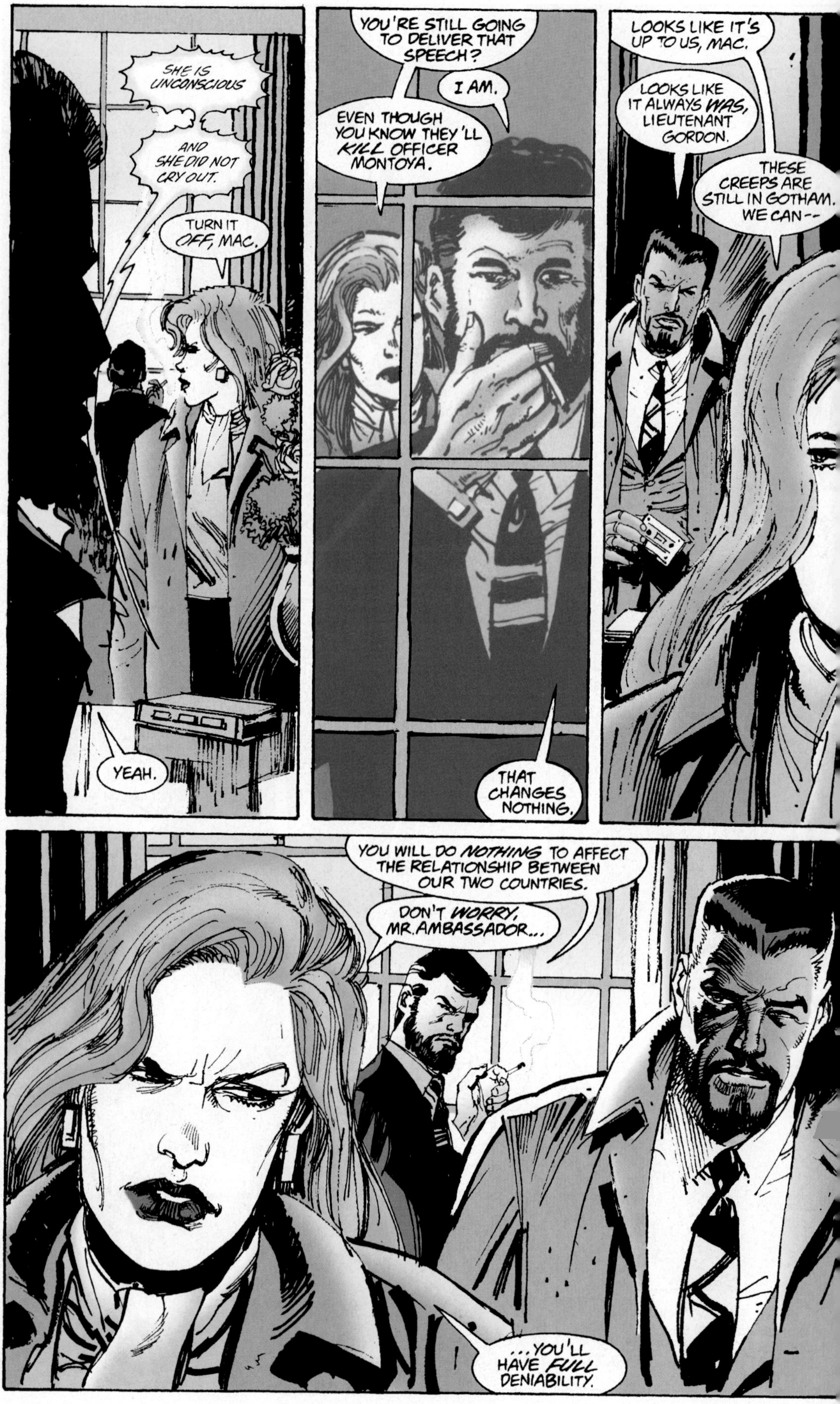
SHE IS UNCONSCIOUS
AND SHE DID NOT CRY OUT.
TURN IT OFF, MAC.
YEAH.
YOU'RE STILL GOING TO DELIVER THAT SPEECH?
I AM.
EVEN THOUGH YOU KNOW THEY'LL KILL OFFICER MONTOYA.
THAT CHANGES NOTHING.
LOOKS LIKE IT'S UP TO US, MAC.
LOOKS LIKE IT ALWAYS WAS, LIEUTENANT GORDON.
THESE CREEPS ARE STILL IN GOTHAM. WE CAN--
YOU WILL DO NOTHING TO AFFECT THE RELATIONSHIP BETWEEN OUR TWO COUNTRIES.
DON'T WORRY, MR. AMBASSADOR...
...YOU'LL HAVE FULL DENIABILITY.

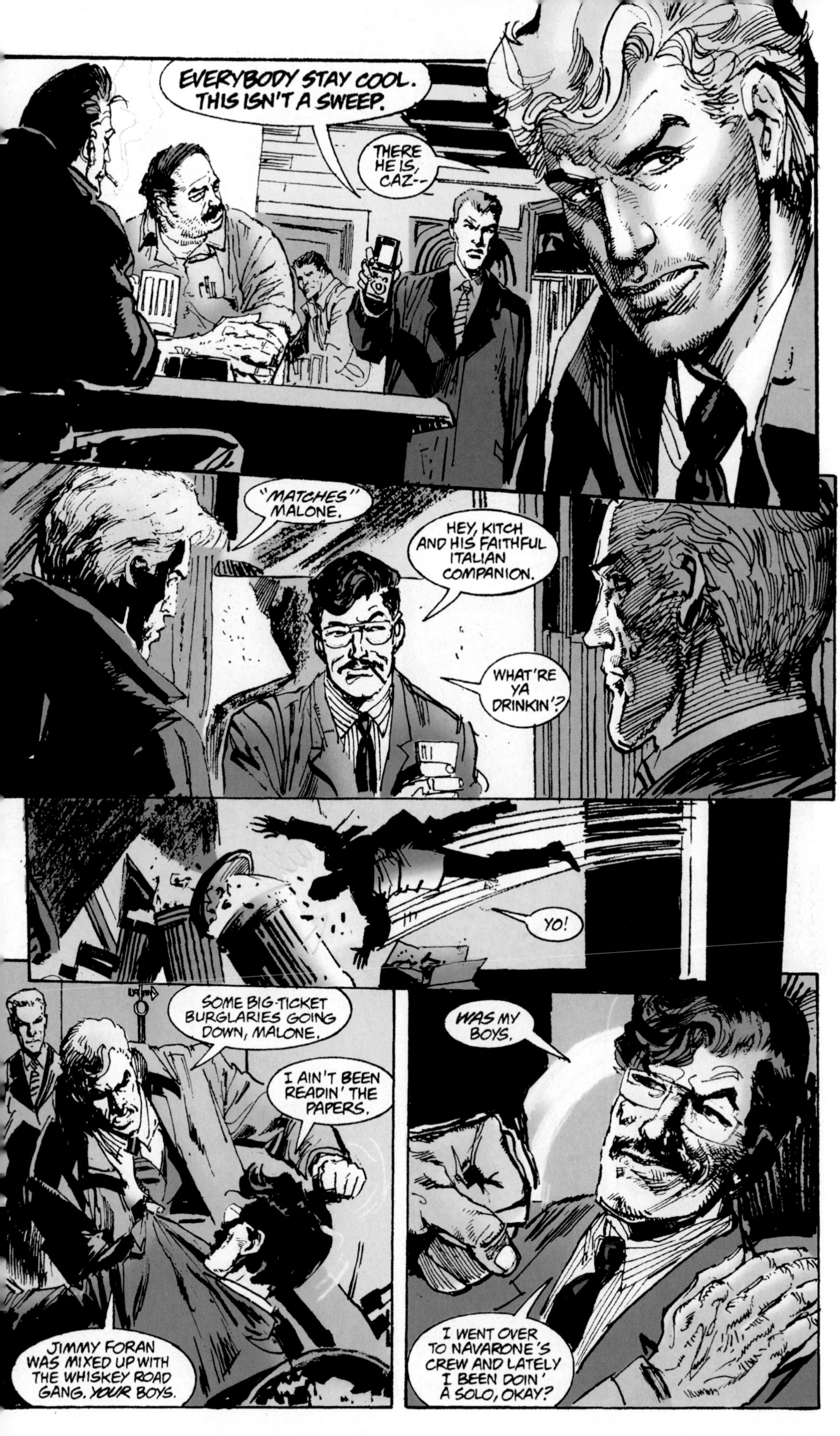
EVERYBODY STAY COOL. THIS ISN'T A SWEEP.
THERE HE IS, CAZ--
"MATCHES" MALONE.
HEY, KITCH AND HIS FAITHFUL ITALIAN COMPANION.
WHAT'RE YA DRINKIN'?
YO!
SOME BIG-TICKET BURGLARIES GOING DOWN, MALONE.
I AIN'T BEEN READIN' THE PAPERS.
JIMMY FORAN WAS MIXED UP WITH THE WHISKEY ROAD GANG. *YOUR* BOYS.
WAS MY BOYS.
I WENT OVER TO NAVARONE'S CREW AND LATELY I BEEN DOIN' A SOLO, OKAY?

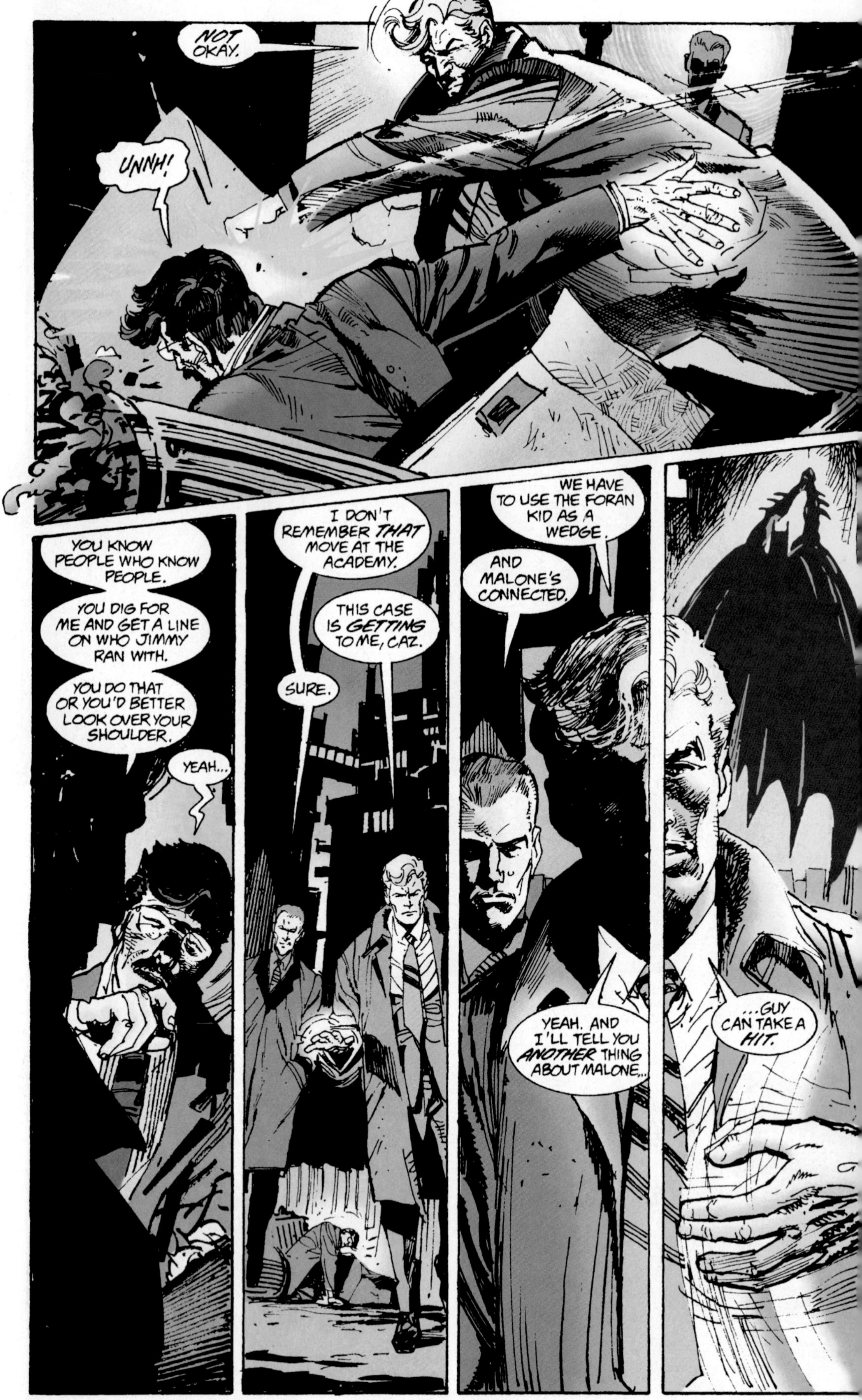
NOT OKAY.
UNNH!
YOU KNOW PEOPLE WHO KNOW PEOPLE.
YOU DIG FOR ME AND GET A LINE ON WHO JIMMY RAN WITH.
YOU DO THAT OR YOU'D BETTER LOOK OVER YOUR SHOULDER.
YEAH...
I DON'T REMEMBER THAT MOVE AT THE ACADEMY.
SURE.
THIS CASE IS GETTING TO ME, CAZ.
WE HAVE TO USE THE FORAN KID AS A WEDGE.
AND MALONE'S CONNECTED.
YEAH. AND I'LL TELL YOU ANOTHER THING ABOUT MALONE...
...GUY CAN TAKE A HIT.

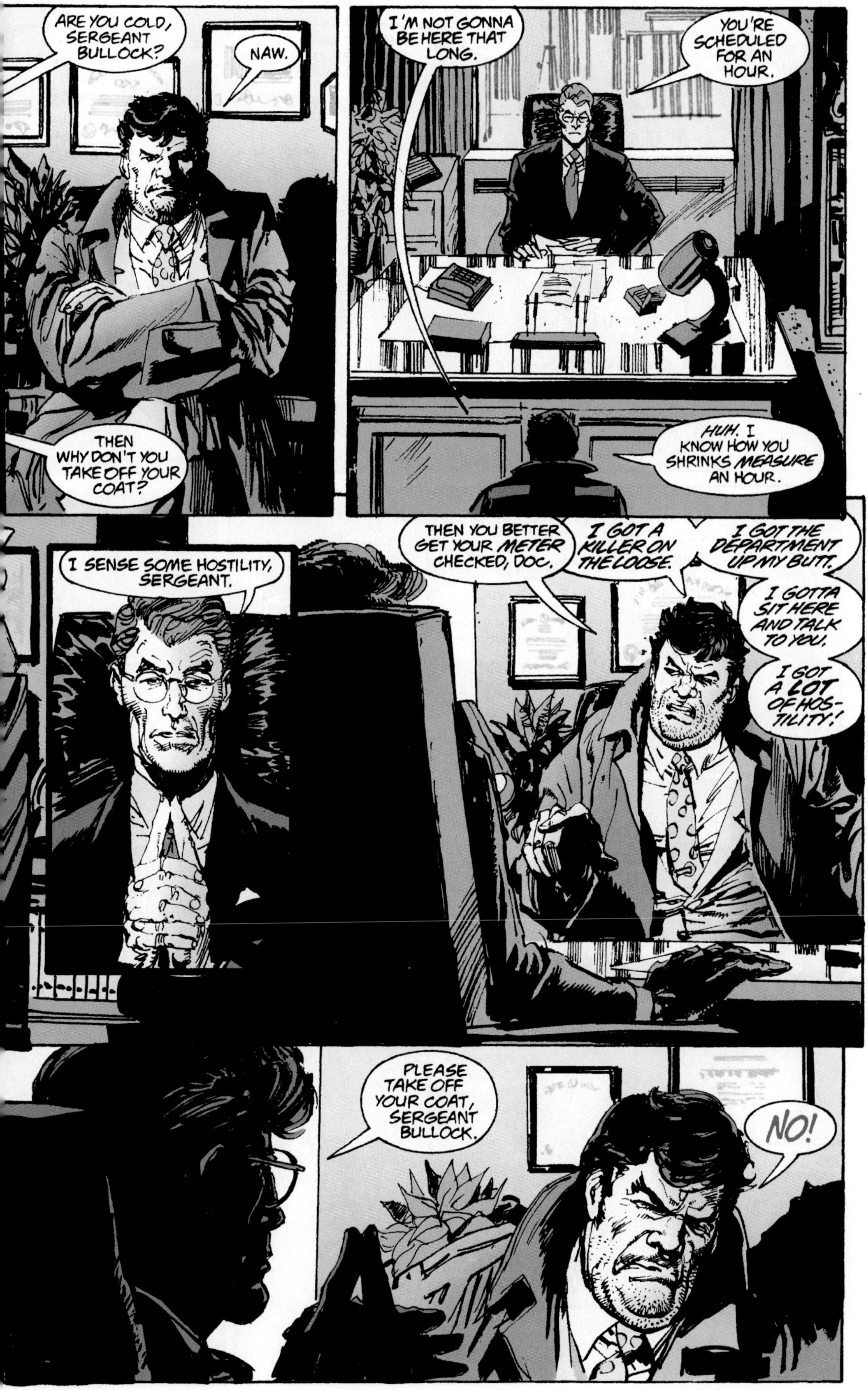

ARE YOU COLD, SERGEANT BULLOCK?
NAW.
THEN WHY DON'T YOU TAKE OFF YOUR COAT?
I'M NOT GONNA BE HERE THAT LONG.
YOU'RE SCHEDULED FOR AN HOUR.
HUH. I KNOW HOW YOU SHRINKS MEASURE AN HOUR.
I SENSE SOME HOSTILITY, SERGEANT.
THEN YOU BETTER GET YOUR METER CHECKED, DOC.
I GOT A KILLER ON THE LOOSE.
I GOT THE DEPARTMENT UP MY BUTT.
I GOTTA SIT HERE AND TALK TO YOU.
I GOT A LOT OF HOS-TILITY!
PLEASE TAKE OFF YOUR COAT, SERGEANT BULLOCK.
NO!

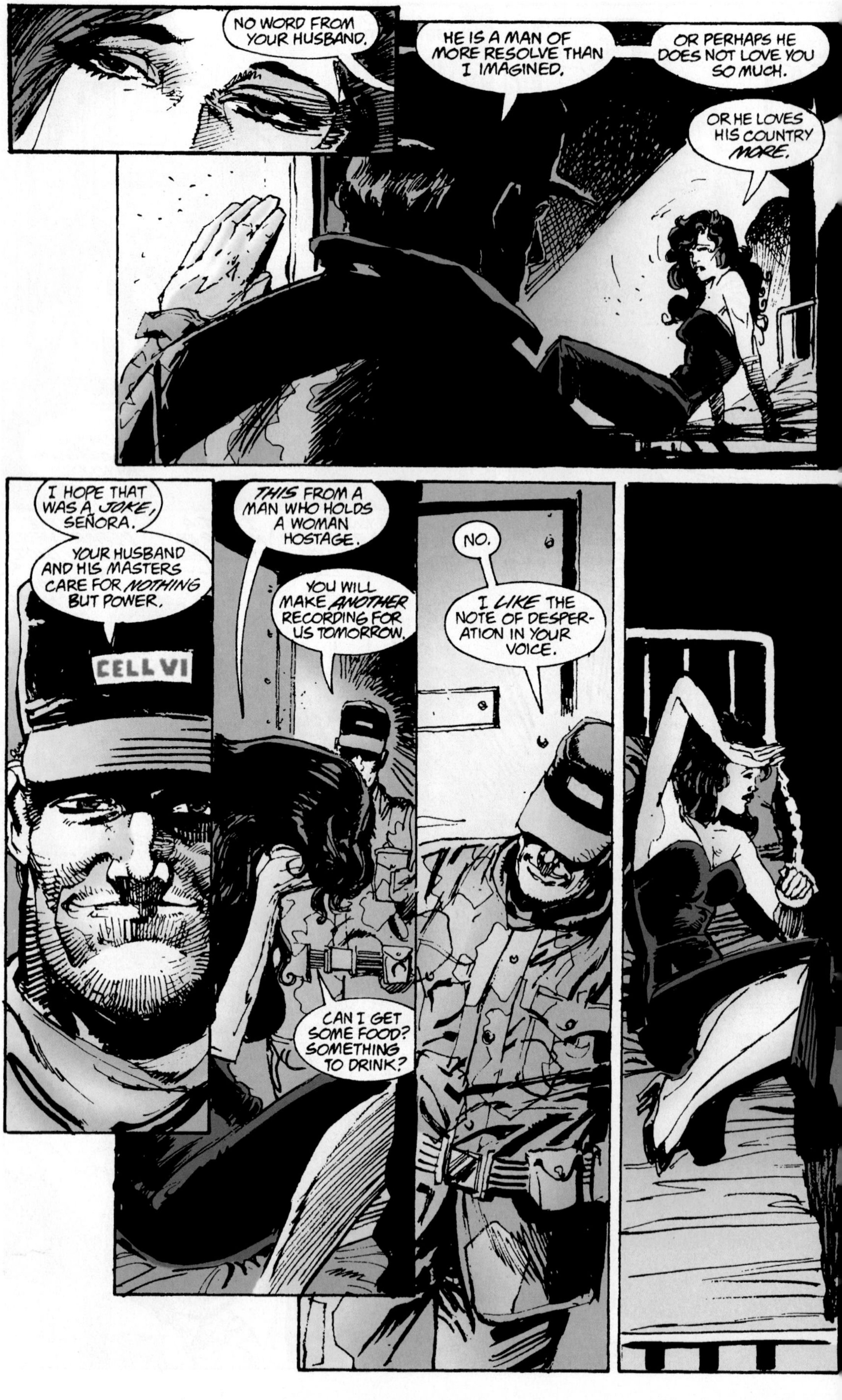
NO WORD FROM YOUR HUSBAND.
HE IS A MAN OF MORE RESOLVE THAN I IMAGINED.
OR PERHAPS HE DOES NOT LOVE YOU SO MUCH.
OR HE LOVES HIS COUNTRY *MORE.*
I HOPE THAT WAS A *JOKE,* SEÑORA.
YOUR HUSBAND AND HIS MASTERS CARE FOR *NOTHING* BUT POWER.
CELL VI
THIS FROM A MAN WHO HOLDS A WOMAN HOSTAGE.
YOU WILL MAKE *ANOTHER* RECORDING FOR US TOMORROW.
CAN I GET SOME FOOD? SOMETHING TO DRINK?
NO.
I *LIKE* THE NOTE OF DESPERATION IN YOUR VOICE.

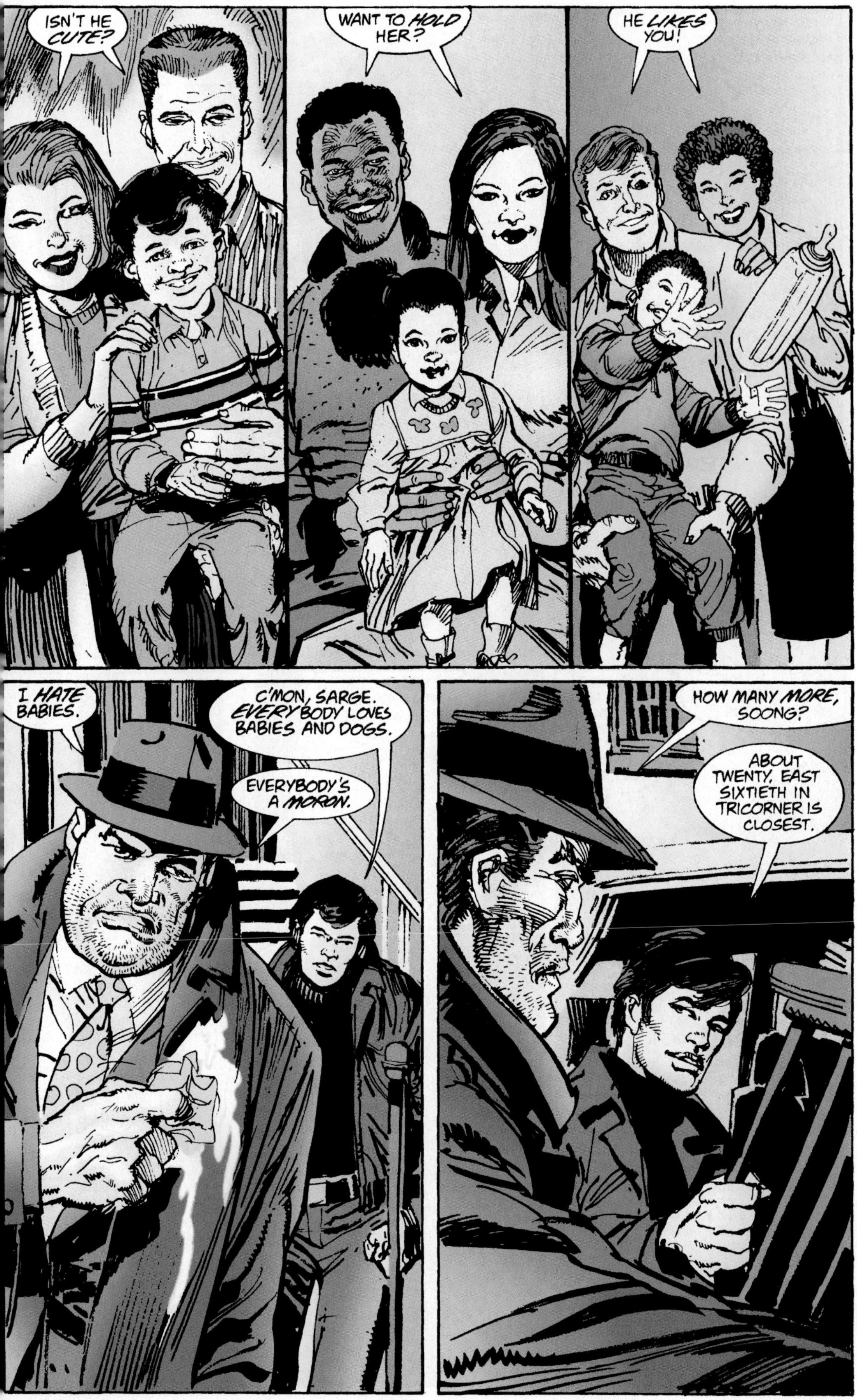
ISN'T HE CUTE?
WANT TO HOLD HER?
HE LIKES YOU!
I HATE BABIES.
C'MON, SARGE. EVERYBODY LOVES BABIES AND DOGS.
EVERYBODY'S A MORON.
HOW MANY MORE, SOONG?
ABOUT TWENTY. EAST SIXTIETH IN TRICORNER IS CLOSEST.

I'M AFRAID YOU WASTED A TRIP, OFFICERS.

MY SESSION AT THE CLINIC NEVER *TOOK*.

SAY AGAIN?

I DIDN'T GET PREGNANT.

THEY GOT A *MONEY-BACK* ON THAT?

NO, MY HUSBAND AND I HAD TO PAY ANYWAY.

COULD I USE YOUR BATHROOM, MRS. WILKINS?

TAKE YOUR TIME, I'LL RUN DOWN THE SAME OLD QUESTIONS, SOONG.

DO YOU OWN A SEWING MACHINE, MRS. WILKINS?

THAT'S A FUNNY QUESTION.

I GOT A *MILLION* OF 'EM.

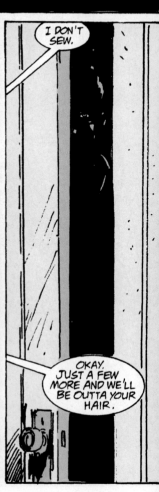

I DON'T SEW.

OKAY. JUST A FEW MORE AND WE'LL BE OUTTA YOUR HAIR.

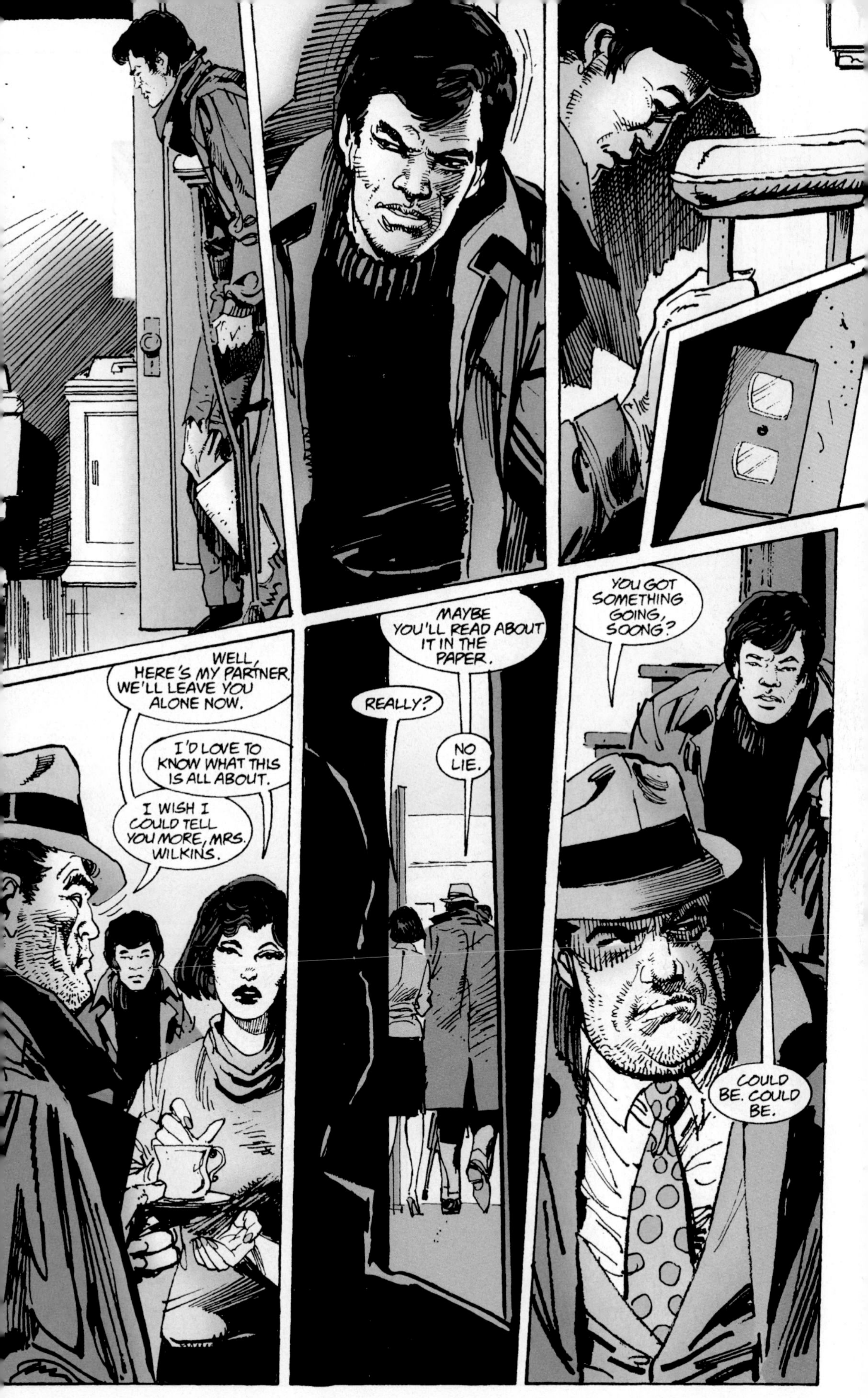
WELL, HERE'S MY PARTNER. WE'LL LEAVE YOU ALONE NOW.
I'D LOVE TO KNOW WHAT THIS IS ALL ABOUT.
I WISH I COULD TELL YOU MORE, MRS. WILKINS.
REALLY?
MAYBE YOU'LL READ ABOUT IT IN THE PAPER.
NO LIE.
YOU GOT SOMETHING GOING, SOONG?
COULD BE. COULD BE.

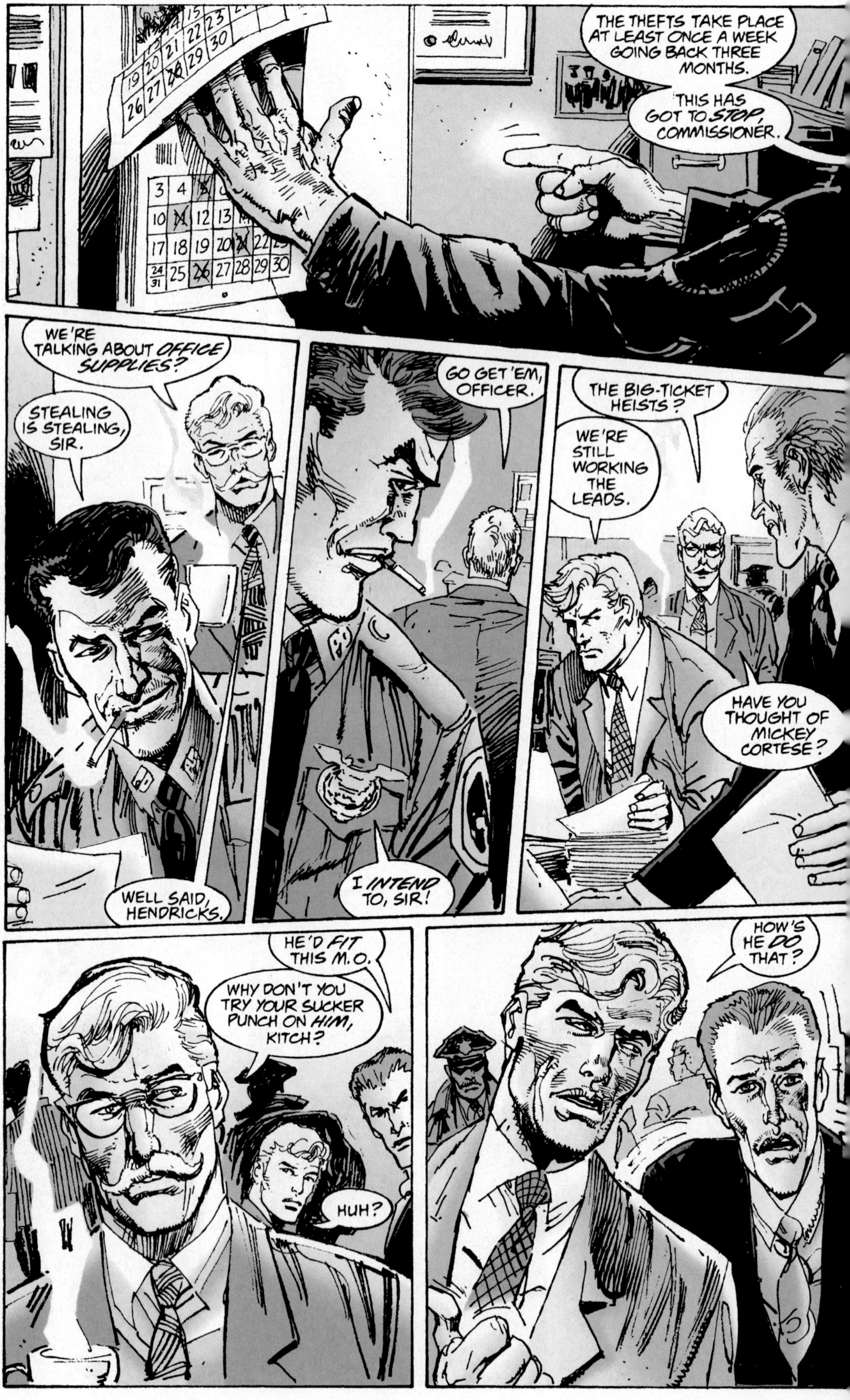
THE THEFTS TAKE PLACE AT LEAST ONCE A WEEK GOING BACK THREE MONTHS.
THIS HAS GOT TO STOP, COMMISSIONER.
WE'RE TALKING ABOUT OFFICE SUPPLIES?
STEALING IS STEALING, SIR.
WELL SAID, HENDRICKS.
GO GET 'EM, OFFICER.
I INTEND TO, SIR!
THE BIG-TICKET HEISTS?
WE'RE STILL WORKING THE LEADS.
HAVE YOU THOUGHT OF MICKEY CORTESE?
HE'D FIT THIS M.O.
WHY DON'T YOU TRY YOUR SUCKER PUNCH ON HIM, KITCH?
HUH?
HOW'S HE DO THAT?

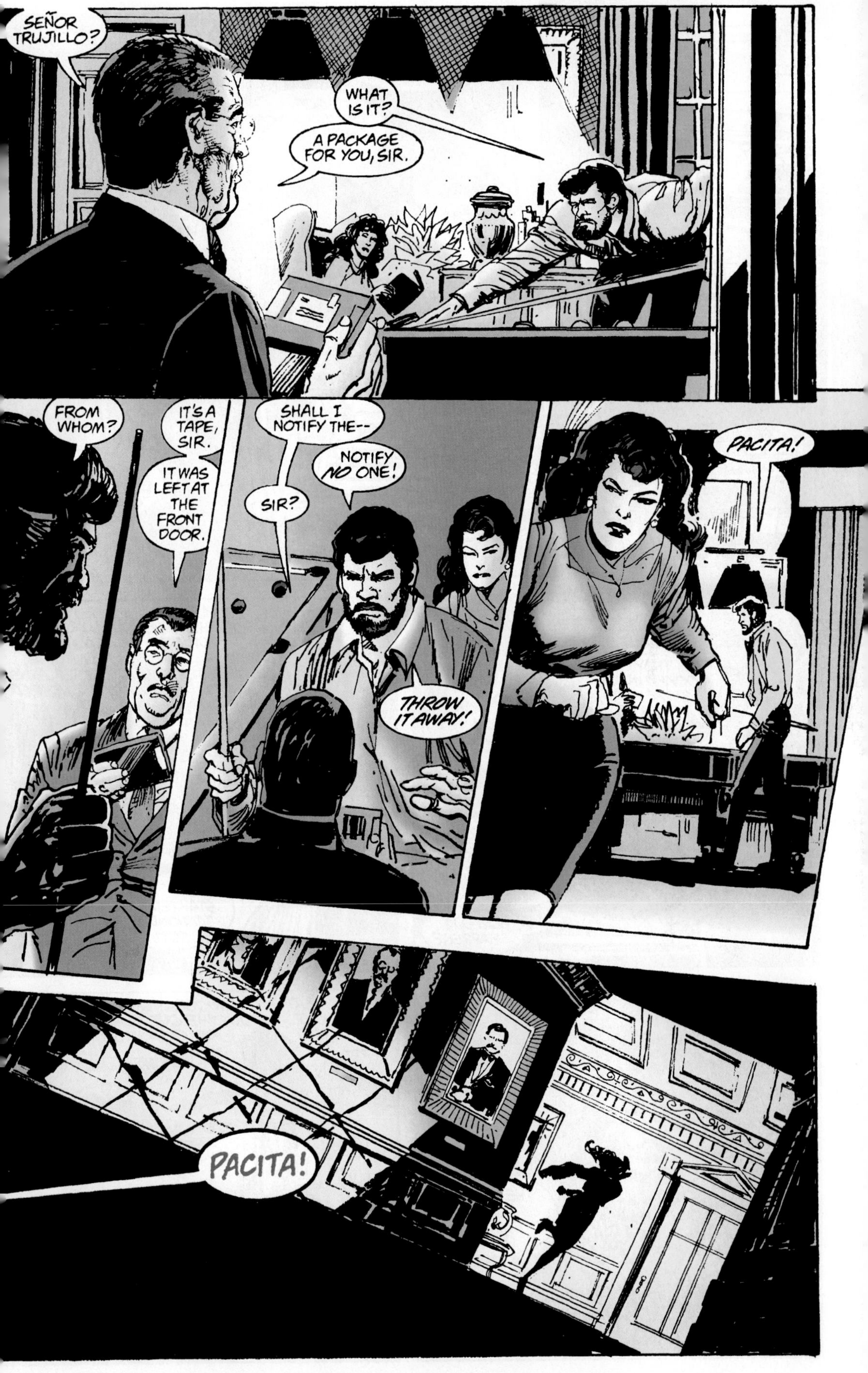
SEÑOR TRUJILLO?
WHAT IS IT?
A PACKAGE FOR YOU, SIR.
FROM WHOM?
IT'S A TAPE, SIR.
IT WAS LEFT AT THE FRONT DOOR.
SHALL I NOTIFY THE--
NOTIFY NO ONE!
SIR?
THROW IT AWAY!
PACITA!
PACITA!

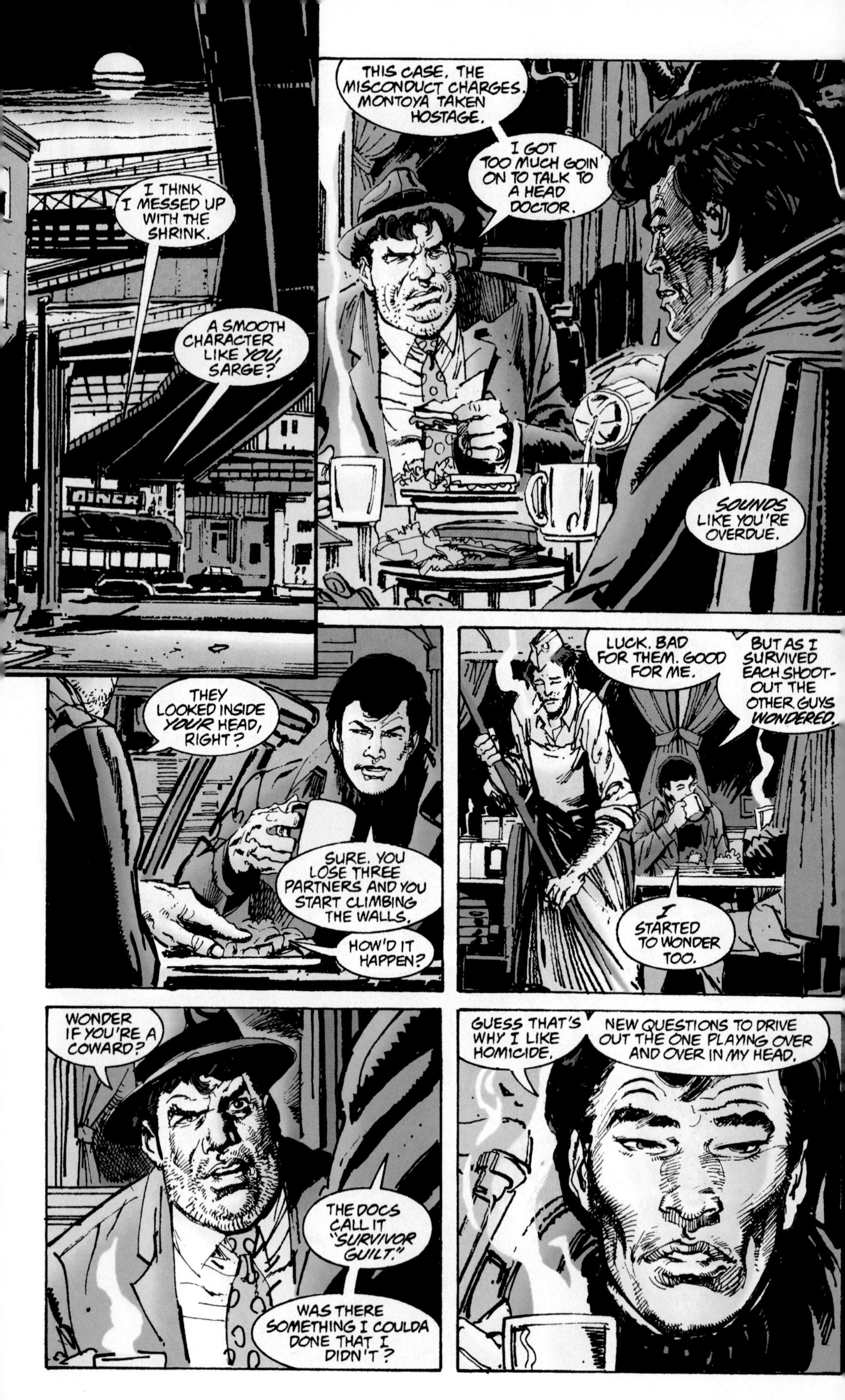
I THINK I MESSED UP WITH THE SHRINK.
A SMOOTH CHARACTER LIKE YOU, SARGE?
DINER
THIS CASE. THE MISCONDUCT CHARGES. MONTOYA TAKEN HOSTAGE.
I GOT TOO MUCH GOIN' ON TO TALK TO A HEAD DOCTOR.
SOUNDS LIKE YOU'RE OVERDUE.
THEY LOOKED INSIDE YOUR HEAD, RIGHT?
SURE. YOU LOSE THREE PARTNERS AND YOU START CLIMBING THE WALLS.
HOW'D IT HAPPEN?
LUCK. BAD FOR THEM. GOOD FOR ME.
BUT AS I SURVIVED EACH SHOOT-OUT THE OTHER GUYS WONDERED.
I STARTED TO WONDER TOO.
WONDER IF YOU'RE A COWARD?
THE DOCS CALL IT "SURVIVOR GUILT."
WAS THERE SOMETHING I COULDA DONE THAT I DIDN'T?
GUESS THAT'S WHY I LIKE HOMICIDE.
NEW QUESTIONS TO DRIVE OUT THE ONE PLAYING OVER AND OVER IN MY HEAD.

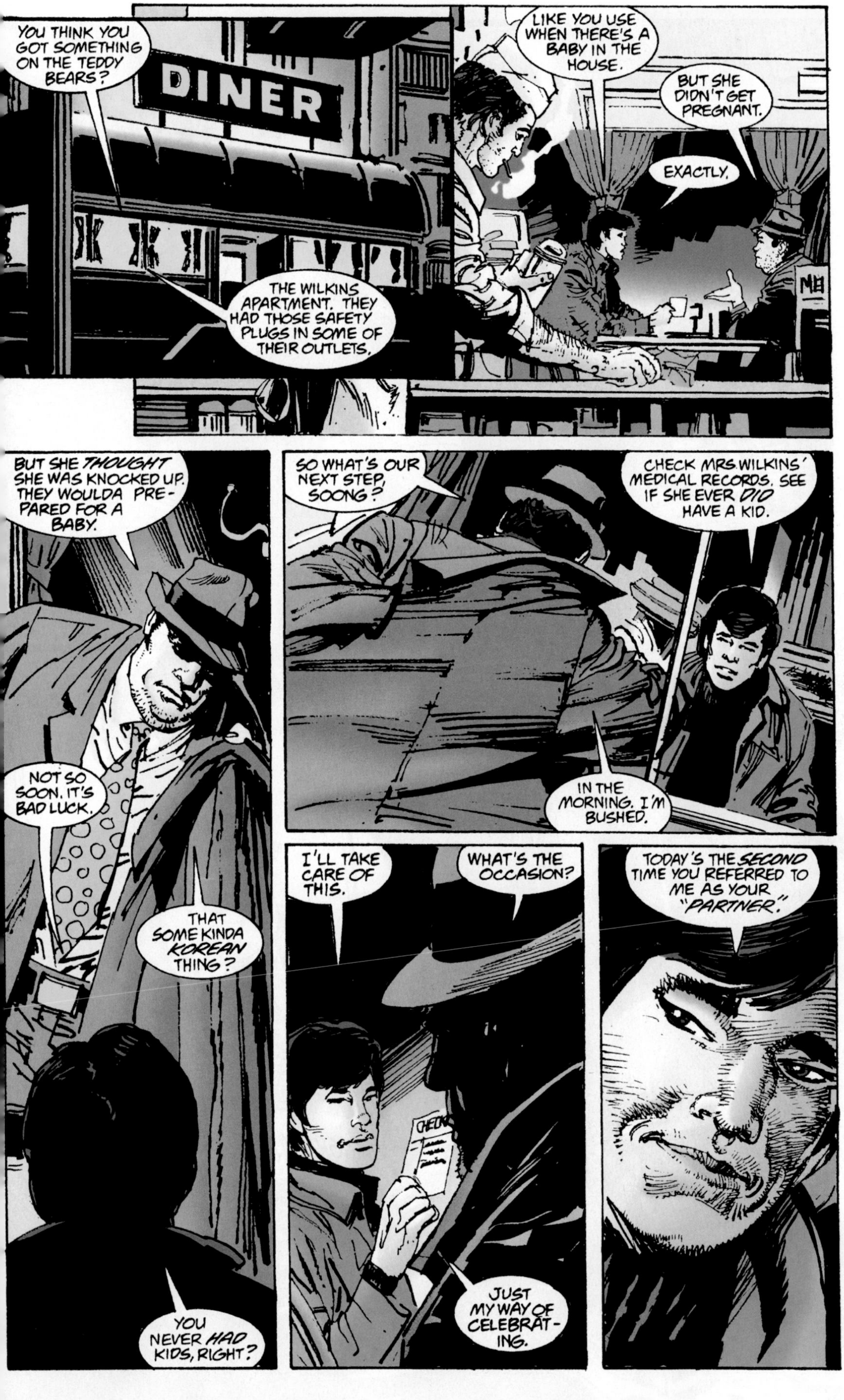

YOU THINK YOU GOT SOMETHING ON THE TEDDY BEARS?
DINER
THE WILKINS APARTMENT. THEY HAD THOSE SAFETY PLUGS IN SOME OF THEIR OUTLETS.
LIKE YOU USE WHEN THERE'S A BABY IN THE HOUSE.
BUT SHE DIDN'T GET PREGNANT.
EXACTLY.
BUT SHE *THOUGHT* SHE WAS KNOCKED UP. THEY WOULDA PRE-PARED FOR A BABY.
NOT SO SOON. IT'S BAD LUCK.
THAT SOME KINDA *KOREAN* THING?
YOU NEVER *HAD* KIDS, RIGHT?
SO WHAT'S OUR NEXT STEP, SOONG?
CHECK MRS. WILKINS' MEDICAL RECORDS. SEE IF SHE EVER *DID* HAVE A KID.
IN THE MORNING. I'M BUSHED.
I'LL TAKE CARE OF THIS.
WHAT'S THE OCCASION?
JUST MY WAY OF CELEBRAT-ING.
TODAY'S THE *SECOND* TIME YOU REFERRED TO ME AS YOUR "*PARTNER*."

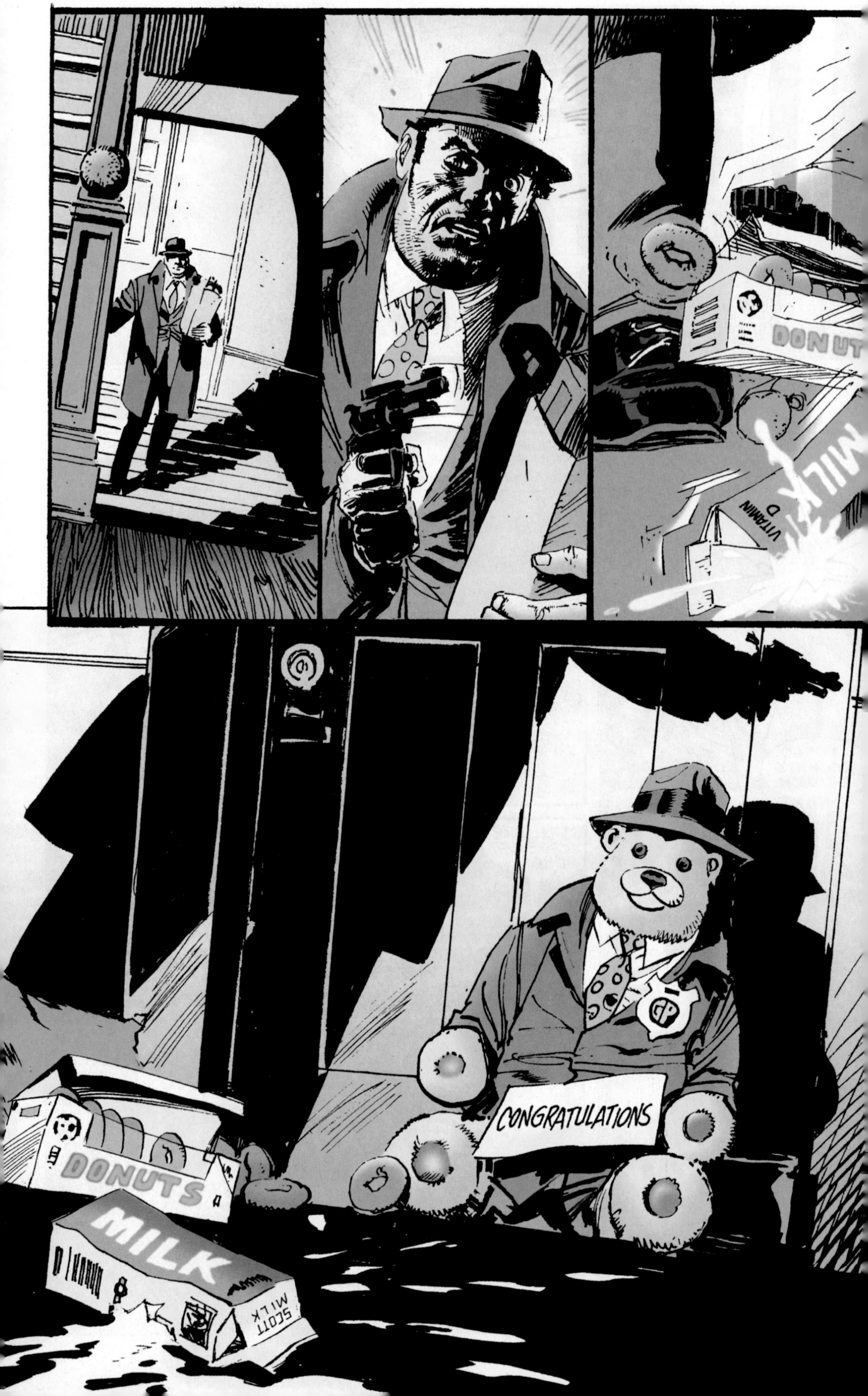

DON UT
MILK
VITAMIN D
CONGRATULATIONS
DONUTS
MILK
SCOTT MILK

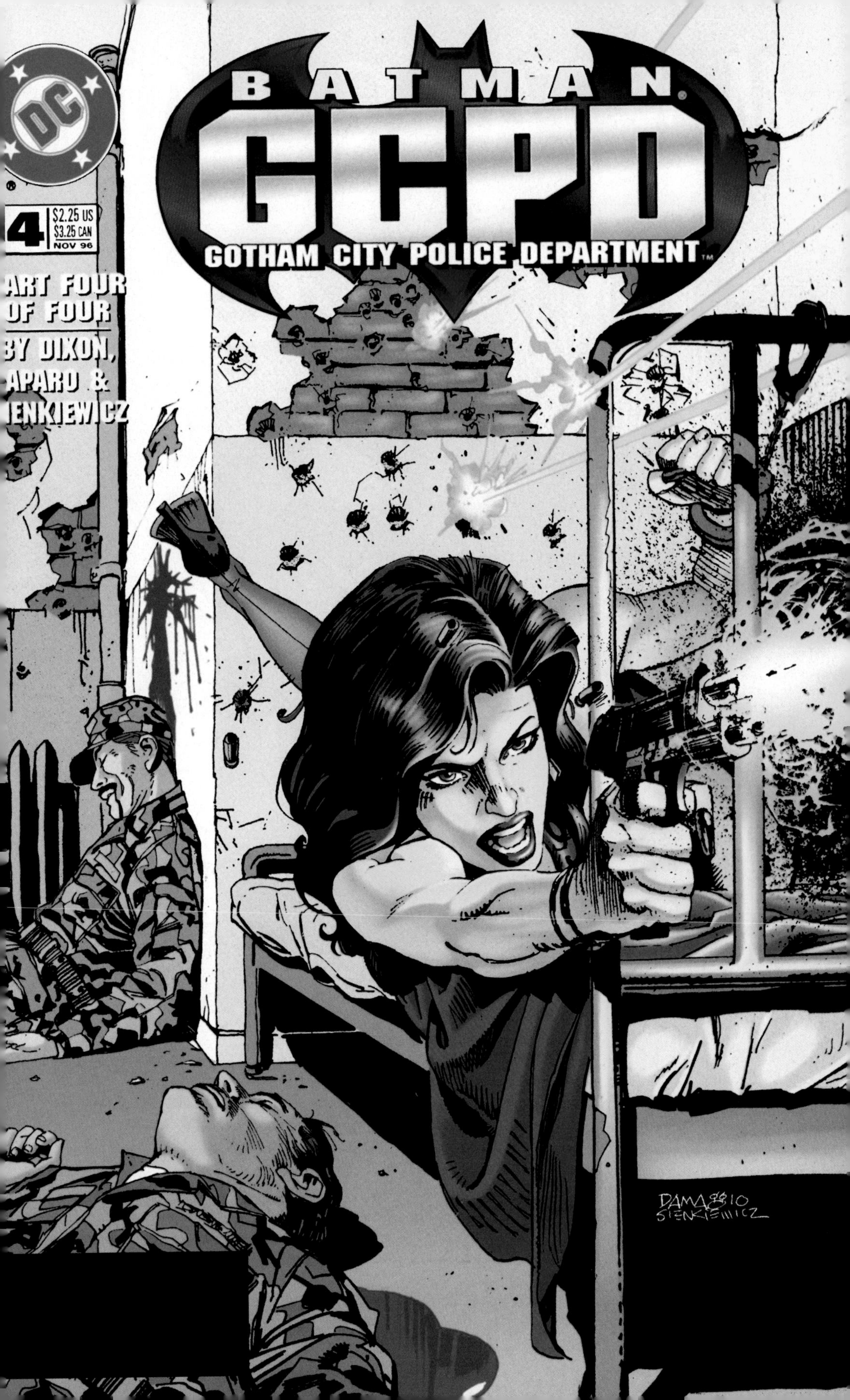

DC
4
$2.25 US
$3.25 CAN
NOV 96
BATMAN
GCPD
GOTHAM CITY POLICE DEPARTMENT
ART FOUR
OF FOUR
BY DIXON,
APARO &
IENKIEWICZ
DAMAGGIO
SIENKIEWICZ

MORTAL REMAINS

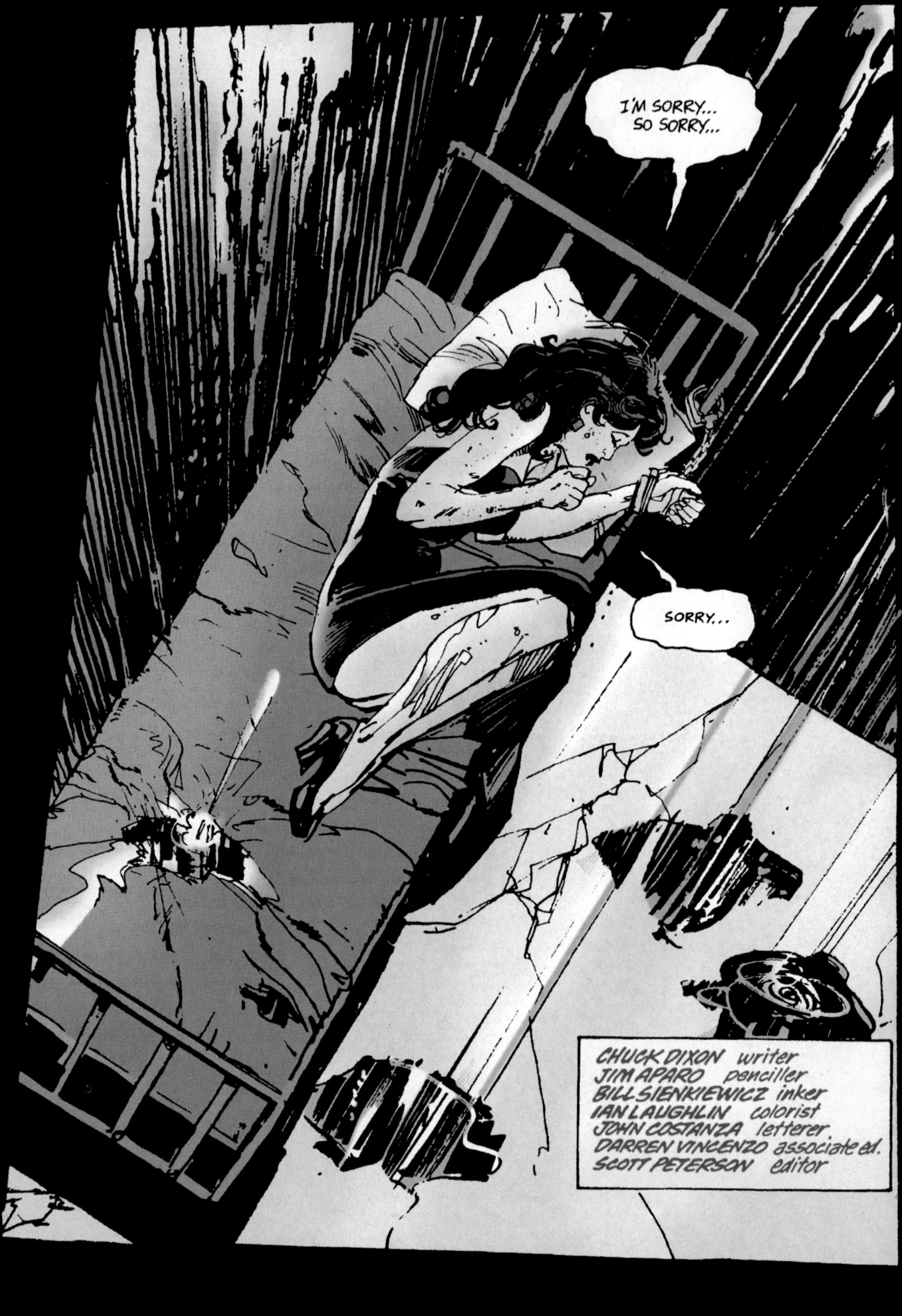

I'M SORRY... SO SORRY...
SORRY...
CHUCK DIXON writer
JIM APARO penciller
BILL SIENKIEWICZ inker
IAN LAUGHLIN colorist
JOHN COSTANZA letterer
DARREN VINCENZO associate ed.
SCOTT PETERSON editor

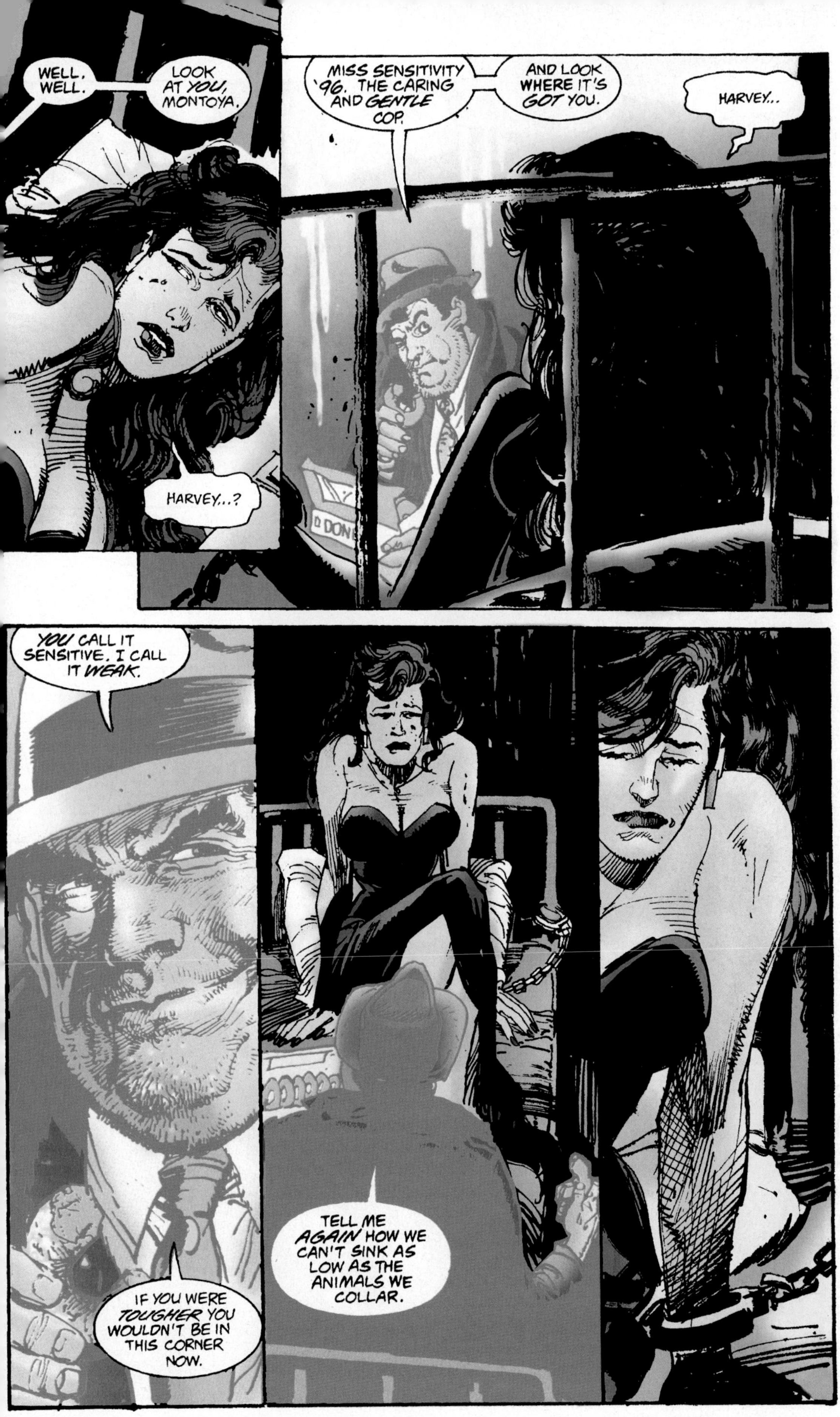

WELL, WELL.
LOOK AT YOU, MONTOYA.
HARVEY...?
MISS SENSITIVITY '96. THE CARING AND GENTLE COP.
AND LOOK WHERE IT'S GOT YOU.
HARVEY...
YOU CALL IT SENSITIVE. I CALL IT WEAK.
IF YOU WERE TOUGHER YOU WOULDN'T BE IN THIS CORNER NOW.
TELL ME AGAIN HOW WE CAN'T SINK AS LOW AS THE ANIMALS WE COLLAR.

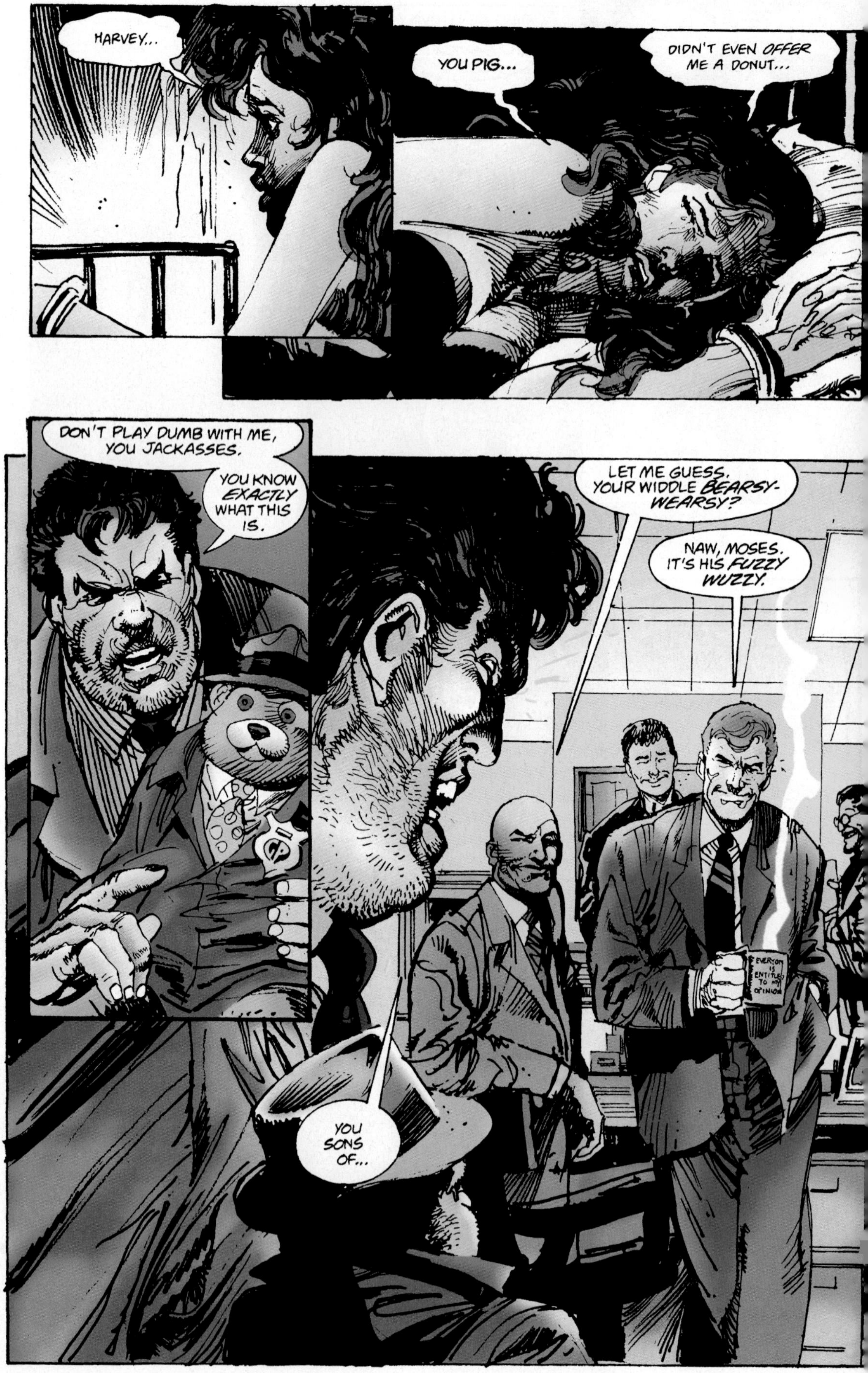
HARVEY...
YOU PIG...
DIDN'T EVEN OFFER ME A DONUT...
DON'T PLAY DUMB WITH ME, YOU JACKASSES.
YOU KNOW EXACTLY WHAT THIS IS.
LET ME GUESS. YOUR WIDDLE BEARSY-WEARSY?
NAW, MOSES. IT'S HIS FUZZY WUZZY.
YOU SONS OF...

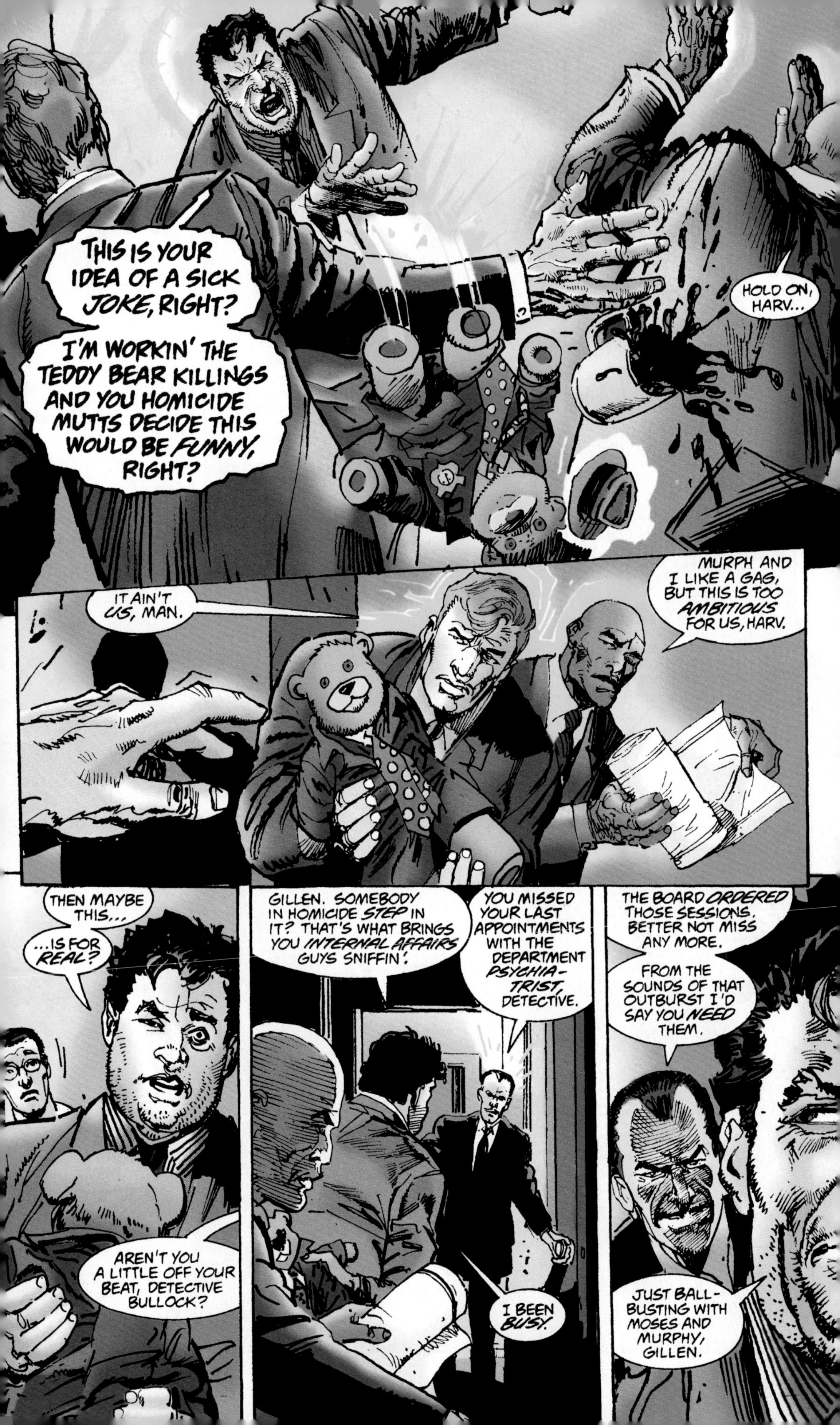
THIS IS YOUR IDEA OF A SICK JOKE, RIGHT?
I'M WORKIN' THE TEDDY BEAR KILLINGS AND YOU HOMICIDE MUTTS DECIDE THIS WOULD BE FUNNY, RIGHT?
HOLD ON, HARV...
IT AIN'T US, MAN.
MURPH AND I LIKE A GAG, BUT THIS IS TOO AMBITIOUS FOR US, HARV.
THEN MAYBE THIS...
...IS FOR REAL?
AREN'T YOU A LITTLE OFF YOUR BEAT, DETECTIVE BULLOCK?
GILLEN. SOMEBODY IN HOMICIDE STEP IN IT? THAT'S WHAT BRINGS YOU INTERNAL AFFAIRS GUYS SNIFFIN'.
YOU MISSED YOUR LAST APPOINTMENTS WITH THE DEPARTMENT PSYCHIA-TRIST, DETECTIVE.
I BEEN BUSY.
THE BOARD ORDERED THOSE SESSIONS. BETTER NOT MISS ANY MORE.
FROM THE SOUNDS OF THAT OUTBURST I'D SAY YOU NEED THEM.
JUST BALL-BUSTING WITH MOSES AND MURPHY, GILLEN.

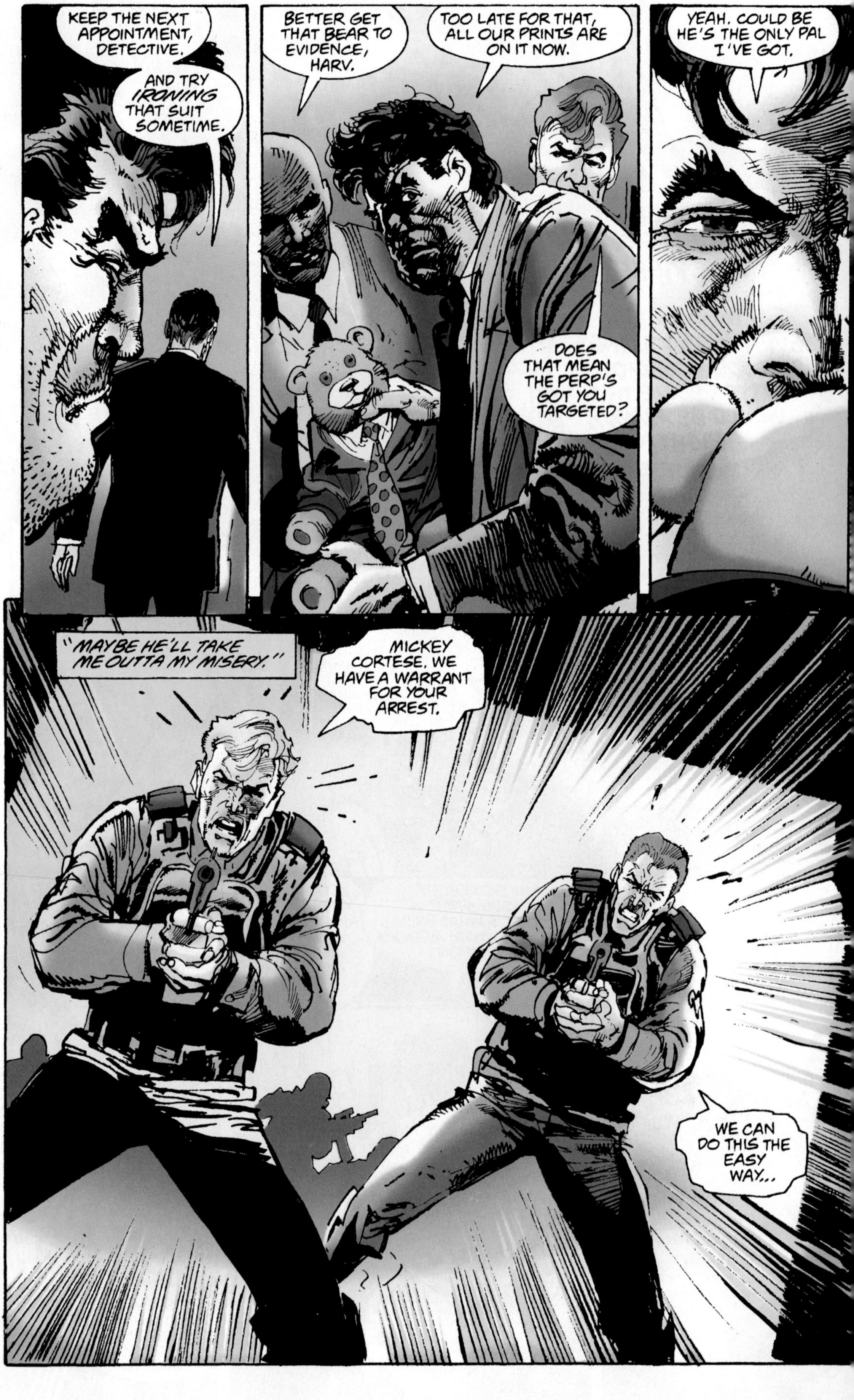
KEEP THE NEXT APPOINTMENT, DETECTIVE.
AND TRY IRONING THAT SUIT SOMETIME.
BETTER GET THAT BEAR TO EVIDENCE, HARV.
TOO LATE FOR THAT, ALL OUR PRINTS ARE ON IT NOW.
DOES THAT MEAN THE PERP'S GOT YOU TARGETED?
YEAH. COULD BE HE'S THE ONLY PAL I'VE GOT.
"MAYBE HE'LL TAKE ME OUTTA MY MISERY."
MICKEY CORTESE. WE HAVE A WARRANT FOR YOUR ARREST.
WE CAN DO THIS THE EASY WAY...

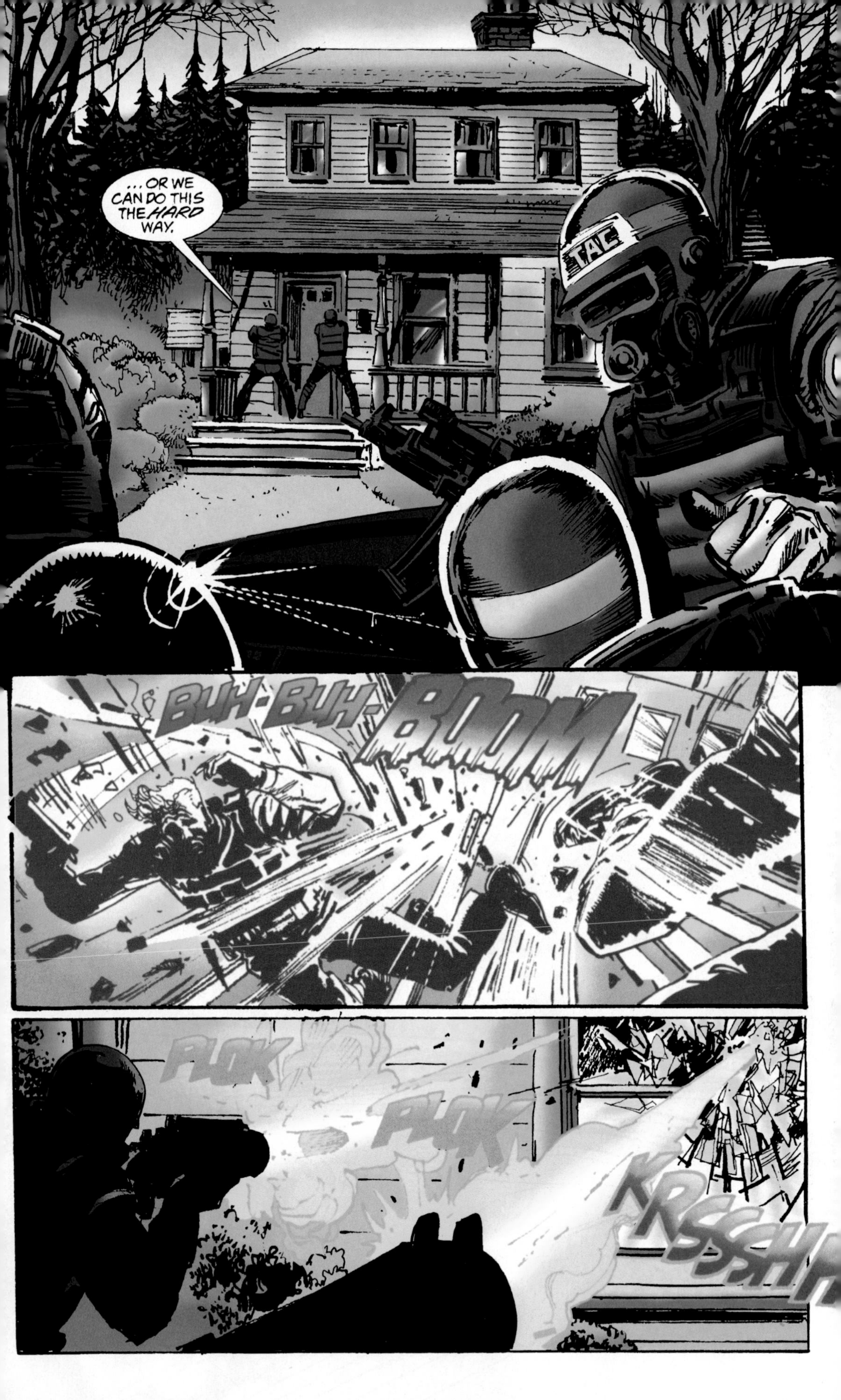
...OR WE CAN DO THIS THE HARD WAY.
BUH-BUH-BOOM
PLOK
PLOK
KRSSHH

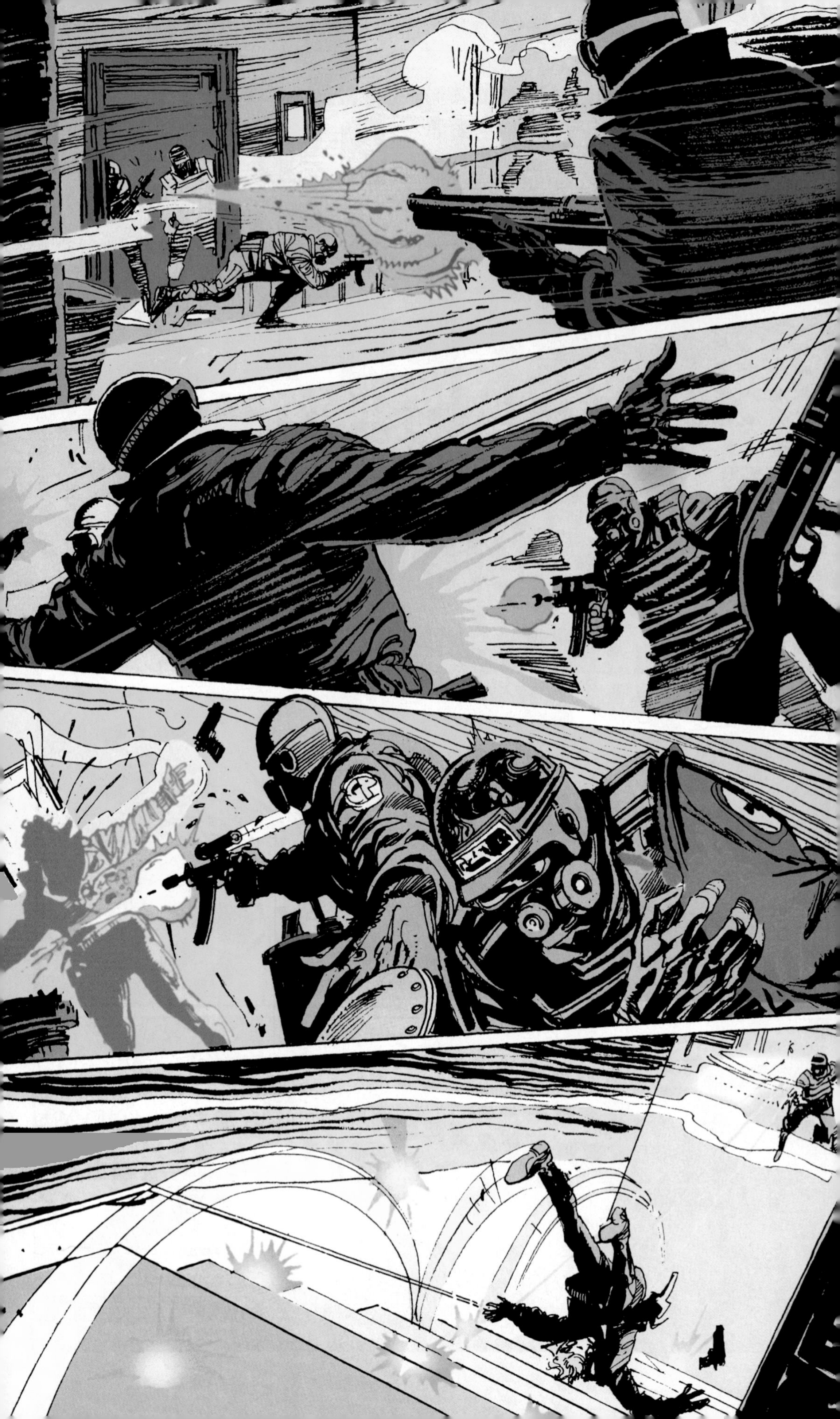

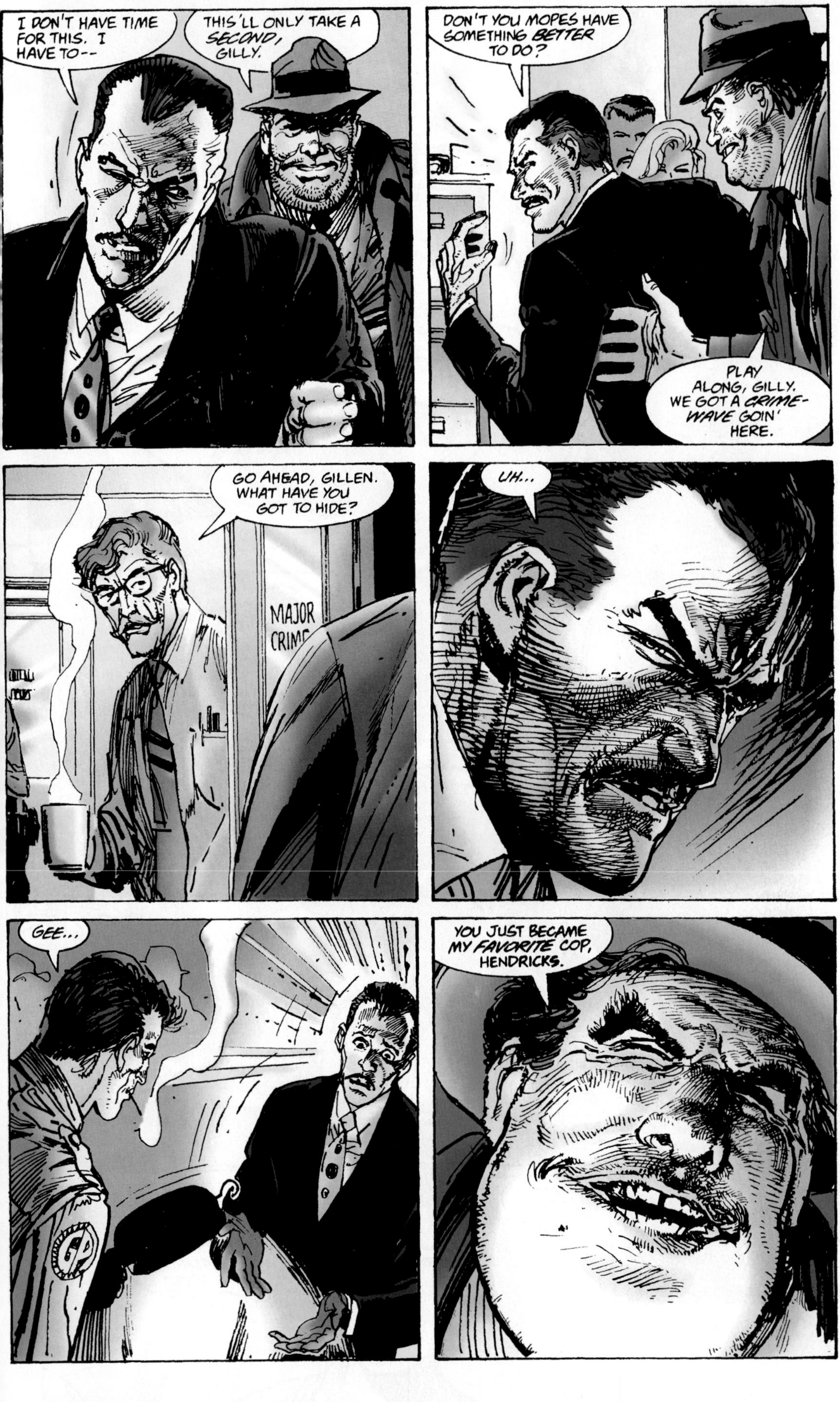
I DON'T HAVE TIME FOR THIS. I HAVE TO--
THIS'LL ONLY TAKE A SECOND, GILLY.
DON'T YOU MOPES HAVE SOMETHING BETTER TO DO?
PLAY ALONG, GILLY. WE GOT A CRIME-WAVE GOIN' HERE.
GO AHEAD, GILLEN. WHAT HAVE YOU GOT TO HIDE?
MAJOR CRIME
UH...
GEE...
YOU JUST BECAME MY FAVORITE COP, HENDRICKS.

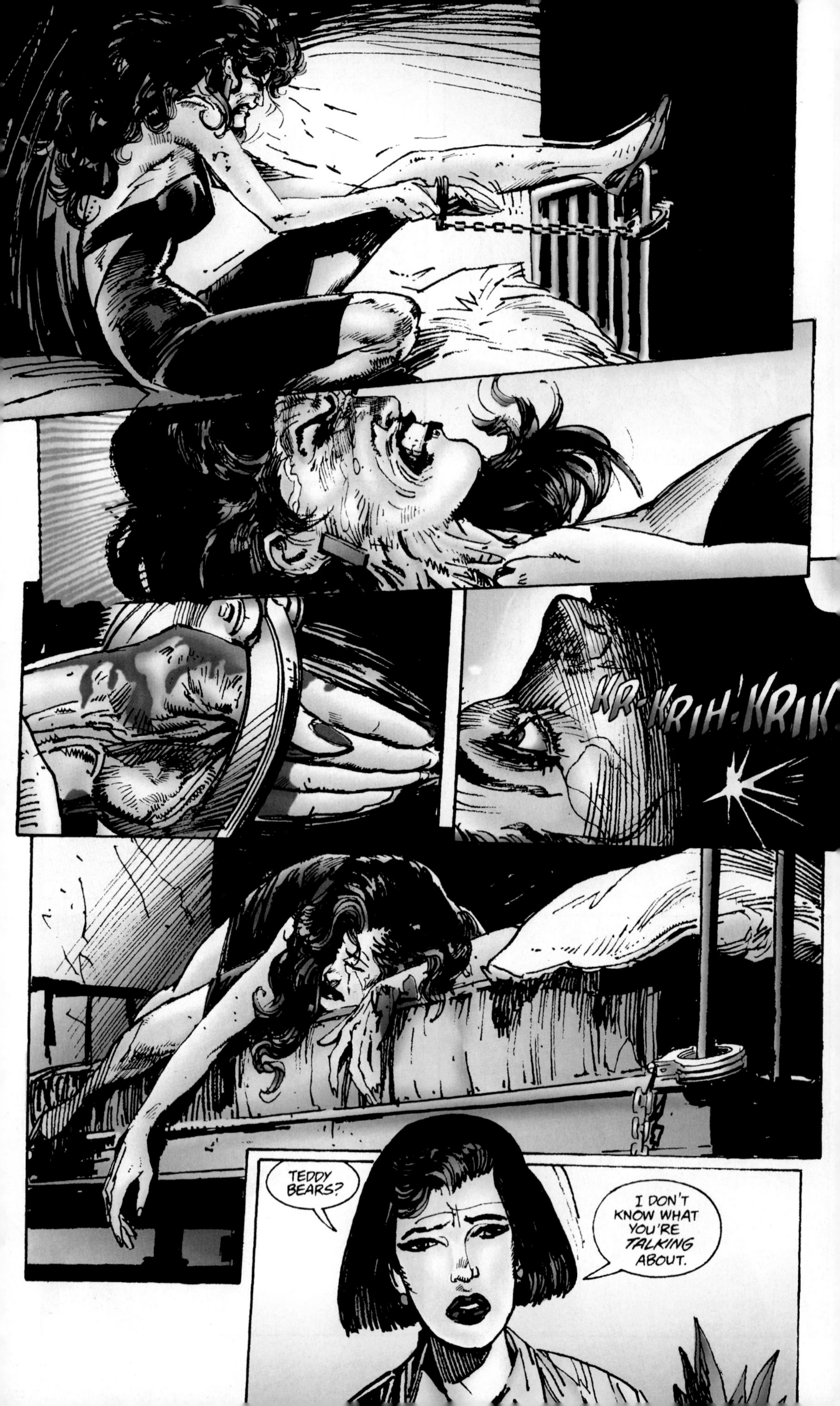
KR-KRIH-KRIK
TEDDY BEARS?
I DON'T KNOW WHAT YOU'RE *TALKING* ABOUT.

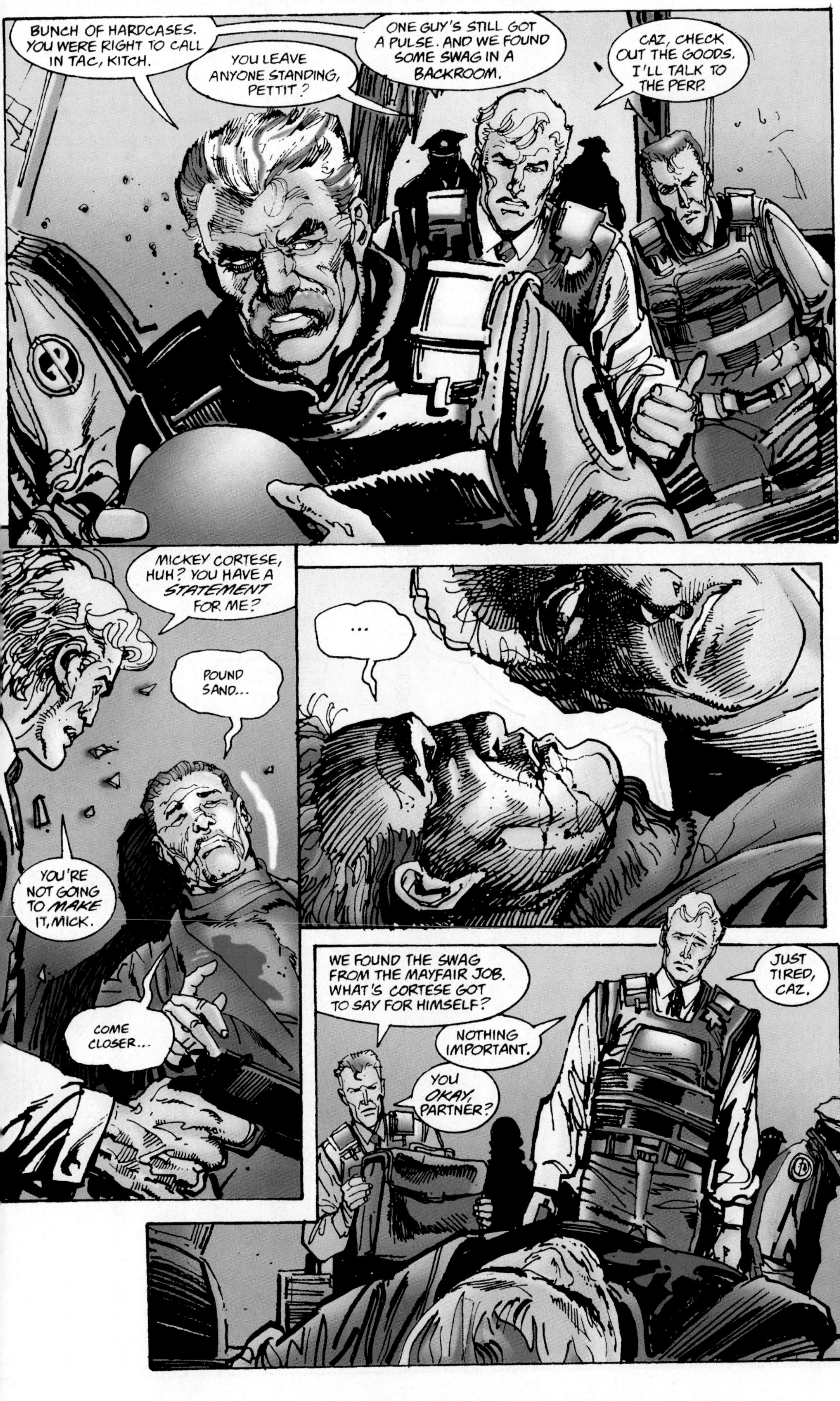
BUNCH OF HARDCASES. YOU WERE RIGHT TO CALL IN TAC, KITCH.
YOU LEAVE ANYONE STANDING, PETTIT?
ONE GUY'S STILL GOT A PULSE. AND WE FOUND SOME SWAG IN A BACKROOM.
CAZ, CHECK OUT THE GOODS. I'LL TALK TO THE PERP.
MICKEY CORTESE, HUH? YOU HAVE A STATEMENT FOR ME?
POUND SAND...
YOU'RE NOT GOING TO MAKE IT, MICK.
COME CLOSER...
...
WE FOUND THE SWAG FROM THE MAYFAIR JOB. WHAT'S CORTESE GOT TO SAY FOR HIMSELF?
NOTHING IMPORTANT.
YOU OKAY, PARTNER?
JUST TIRED, CAZ.

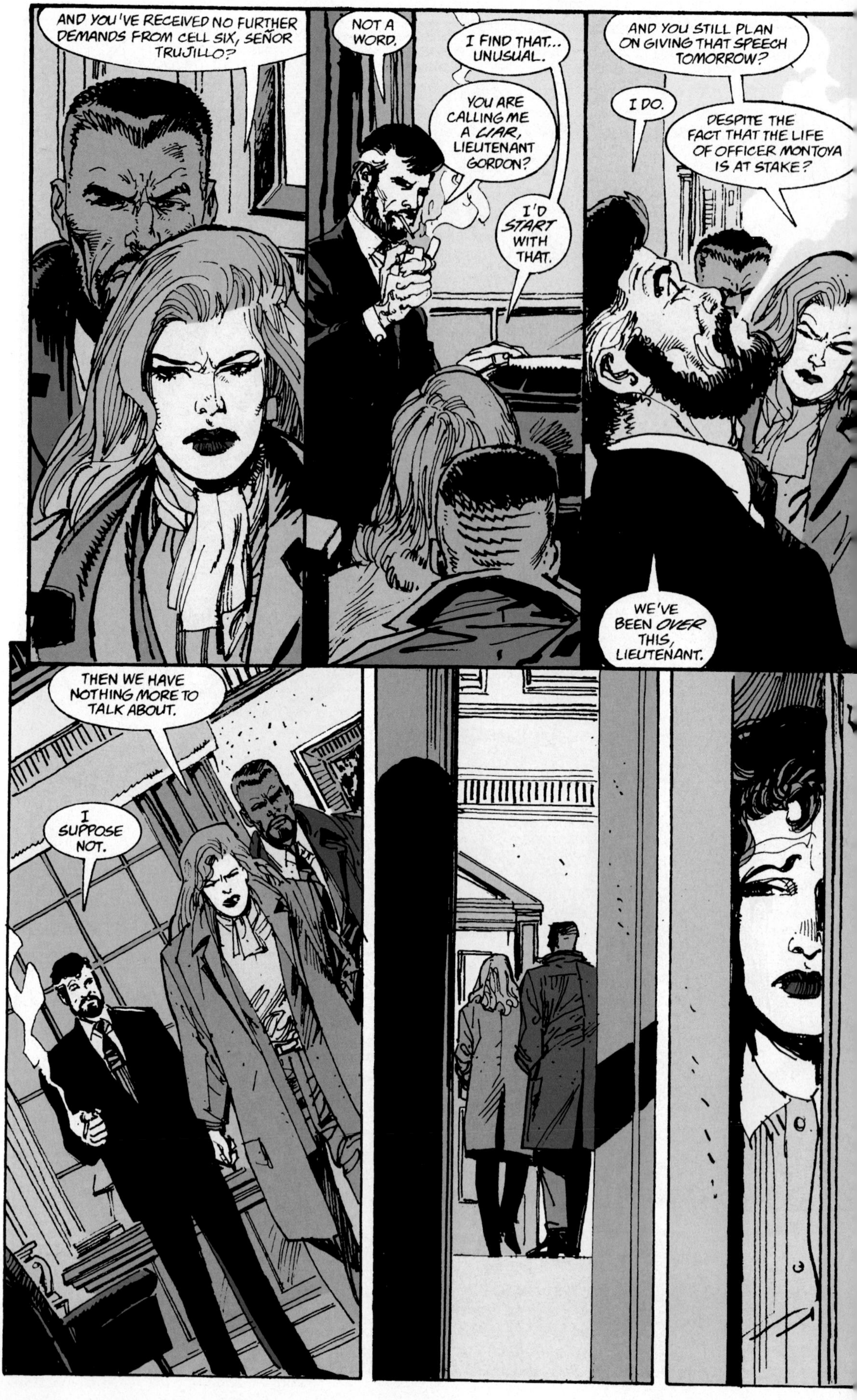
AND YOU'VE RECEIVED NO FURTHER DEMANDS FROM CELL SIX, SEÑOR TRUJILLO?
NOT A WORD.
I FIND THAT... UNUSUAL.
YOU ARE CALLING ME A *LIAR*, LIEUTENANT GORDON?
I'D *START* WITH THAT.
AND YOU STILL PLAN ON GIVING THAT SPEECH TOMORROW?
I DO.
DESPITE THE FACT THAT THE LIFE OF OFFICER MONTOYA IS AT STAKE?
WE'VE BEEN *OVER* THIS, LIEUTENANT.
THEN WE HAVE NOTHING MORE TO TALK ABOUT.
I SUPPOSE NOT.

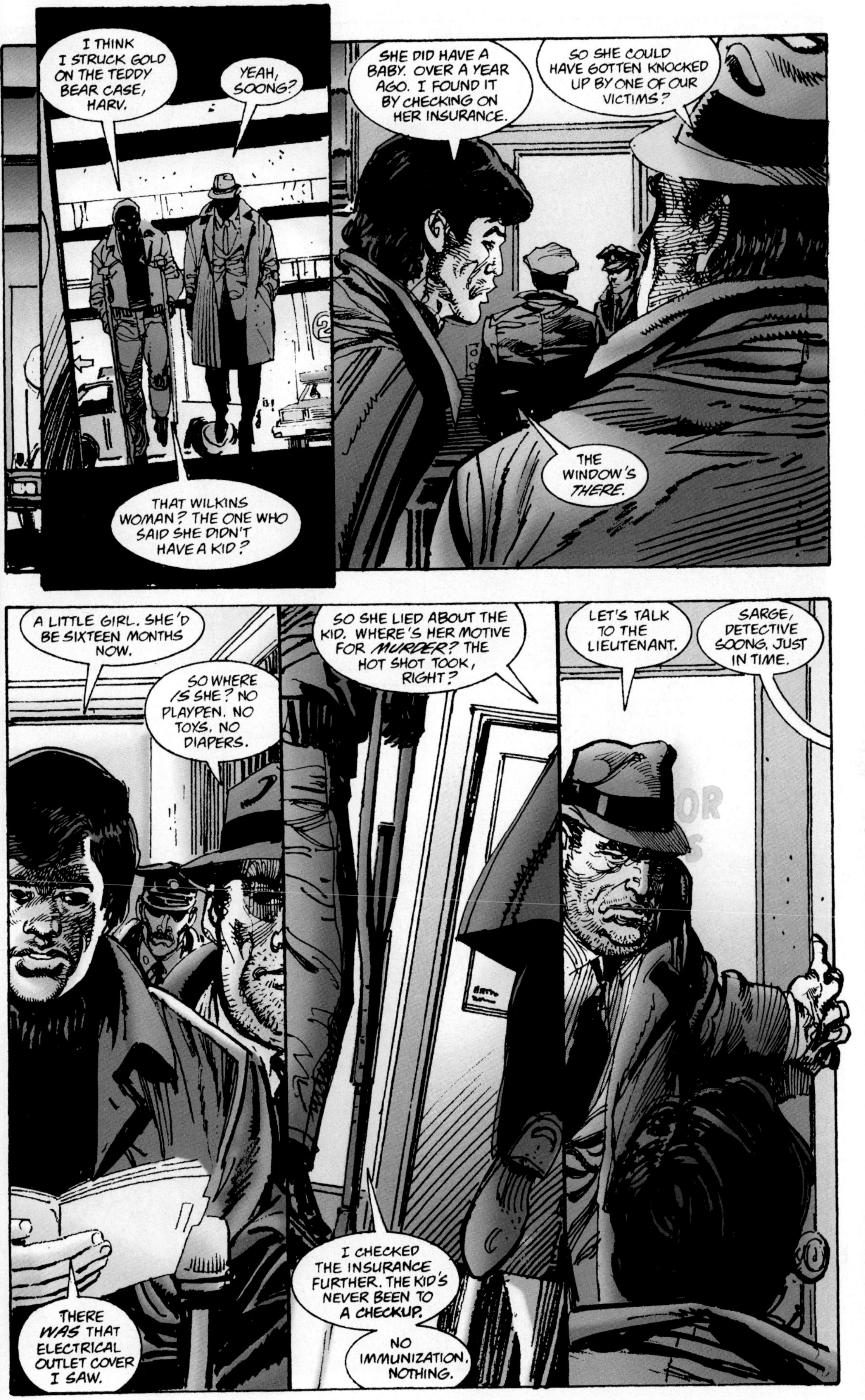

I THINK I STRUCK GOLD ON THE TEDDY BEAR CASE, HARV.
YEAH, SOONG?
THAT WILKINS WOMAN? THE ONE WHO SAID SHE DIDN'T HAVE A KID?
SHE DID HAVE A BABY. OVER A YEAR AGO. I FOUND IT BY CHECKING ON HER INSURANCE.
SO SHE COULD HAVE GOTTEN KNOCKED UP BY ONE OF OUR VICTIMS?
THE WINDOW'S THERE.
A LITTLE GIRL. SHE'D BE SIXTEEN MONTHS NOW.
SO WHERE IS SHE? NO PLAYPEN. NO TOYS. NO DIAPERS.
THERE WAS THAT ELECTRICAL OUTLET COVER I SAW.
SO SHE LIED ABOUT THE KID. WHERE'S HER MOTIVE FOR MURDER? THE HOT SHOT TOOK, RIGHT?
I CHECKED THE INSURANCE FURTHER. THE KID'S NEVER BEEN TO A CHECKUP.
NO IMMUNIZATION. NOTHING.
LET'S TALK TO THE LIEUTENANT.
SARGE, DETECTIVE SOONG. JUST IN TIME.

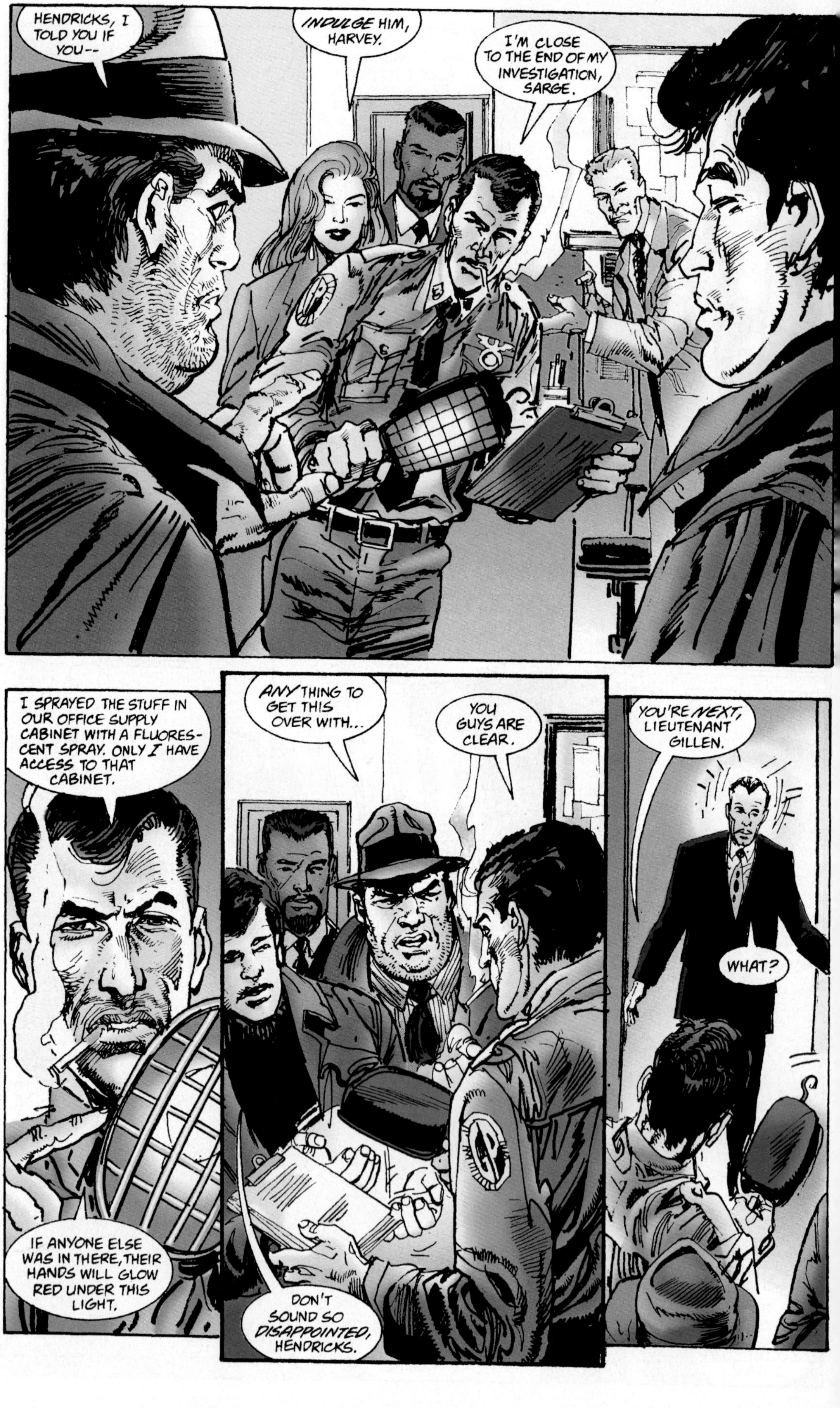
HENDRICKS, I TOLD YOU IF YOU--
INDULGE HIM, HARVEY.
I'M CLOSE TO THE END OF MY INVESTIGATION, SARGE.
I SPRAYED THE STUFF IN OUR OFFICE SUPPLY CABINET WITH A FLUORESCENT SPRAY. ONLY I HAVE ACCESS TO THAT CABINET.
IF ANYONE ELSE WAS IN THERE, THEIR HANDS WILL GLOW RED UNDER THIS LIGHT.
ANYTHING TO GET THIS OVER WITH...
YOU GUYS ARE CLEAR.
DON'T SOUND SO DISAPPOINTED, HENDRICKS.
YOU'RE NEXT, LIEUTENANT GILLEN.
WHAT?

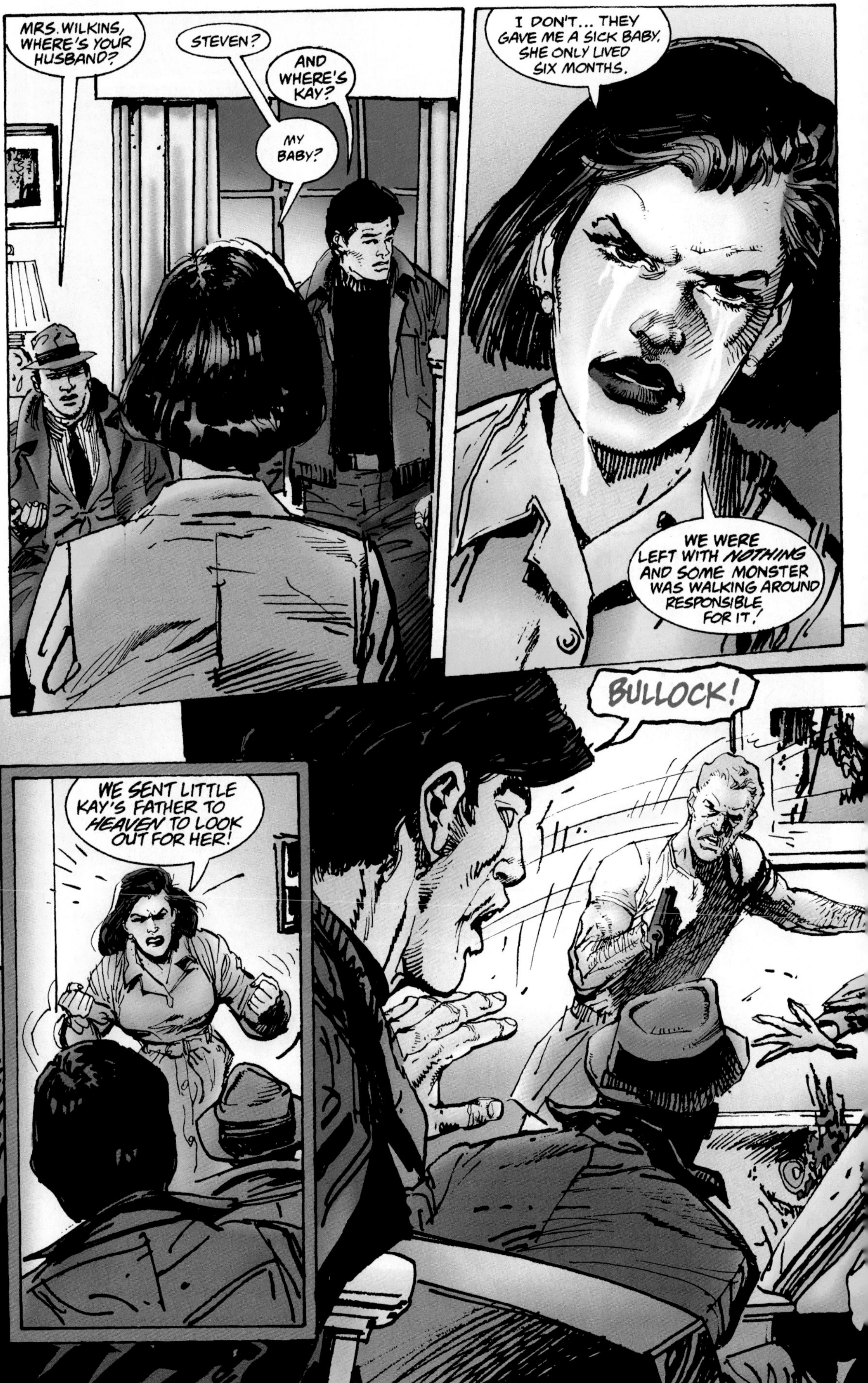
MRS. WILKINS, WHERE'S YOUR HUSBAND?
STEVEN?
AND WHERE'S KAY?
MY BABY?
I DON'T... THEY GAVE ME A SICK BABY. SHE ONLY LIVED SIX MONTHS.
WE WERE LEFT WITH NOTHING AND SOME MONSTER WAS WALKING AROUND RESPONSIBLE FOR IT!
WE SENT LITTLE KAY'S FATHER TO HEAVEN TO LOOK OUT FOR HER!
BULLOCK!

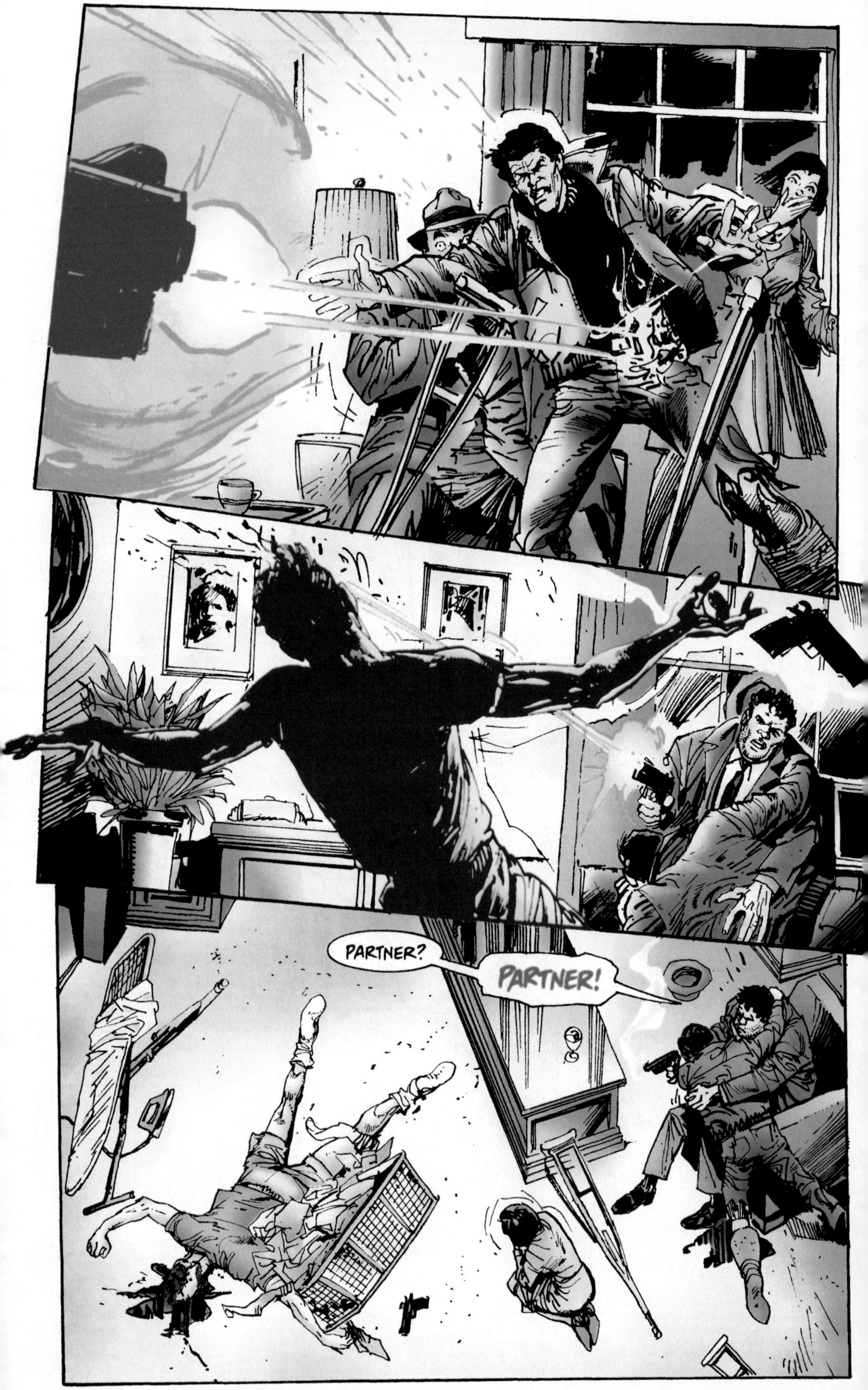
PARTNER?
PARTNER!

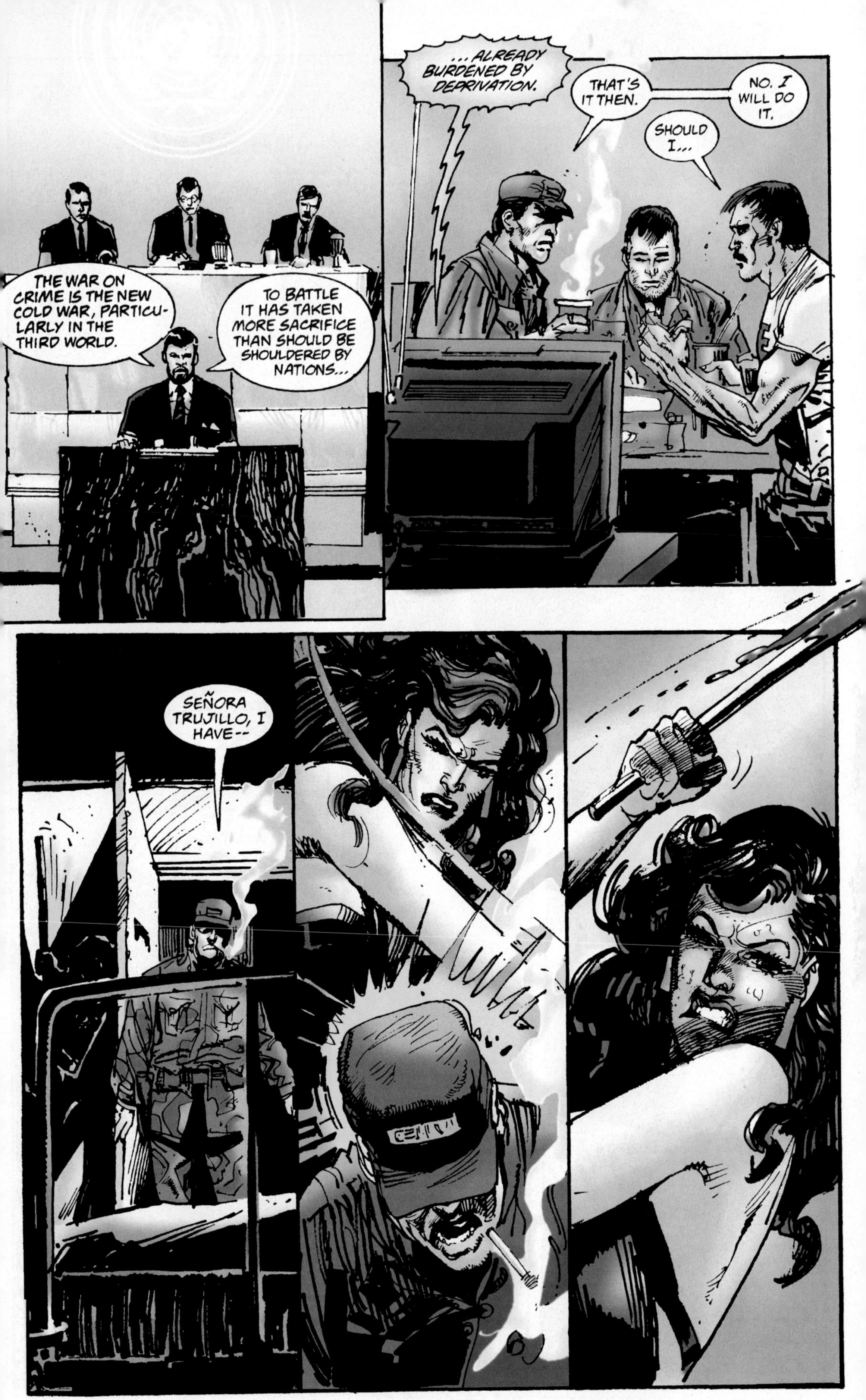
THE WAR ON CRIME IS THE NEW COLD WAR, PARTICULARLY IN THE THIRD WORLD.
TO BATTLE IT HAS TAKEN MORE SACRIFICE THAN SHOULD BE SHOULDERED BY NATIONS...
...ALREADY BURDENED BY DEPRIVATION.
THAT'S IT THEN.
SHOULD I...
NO. I WILL DO IT.
SEÑORA TRUJILLO, I HAVE--

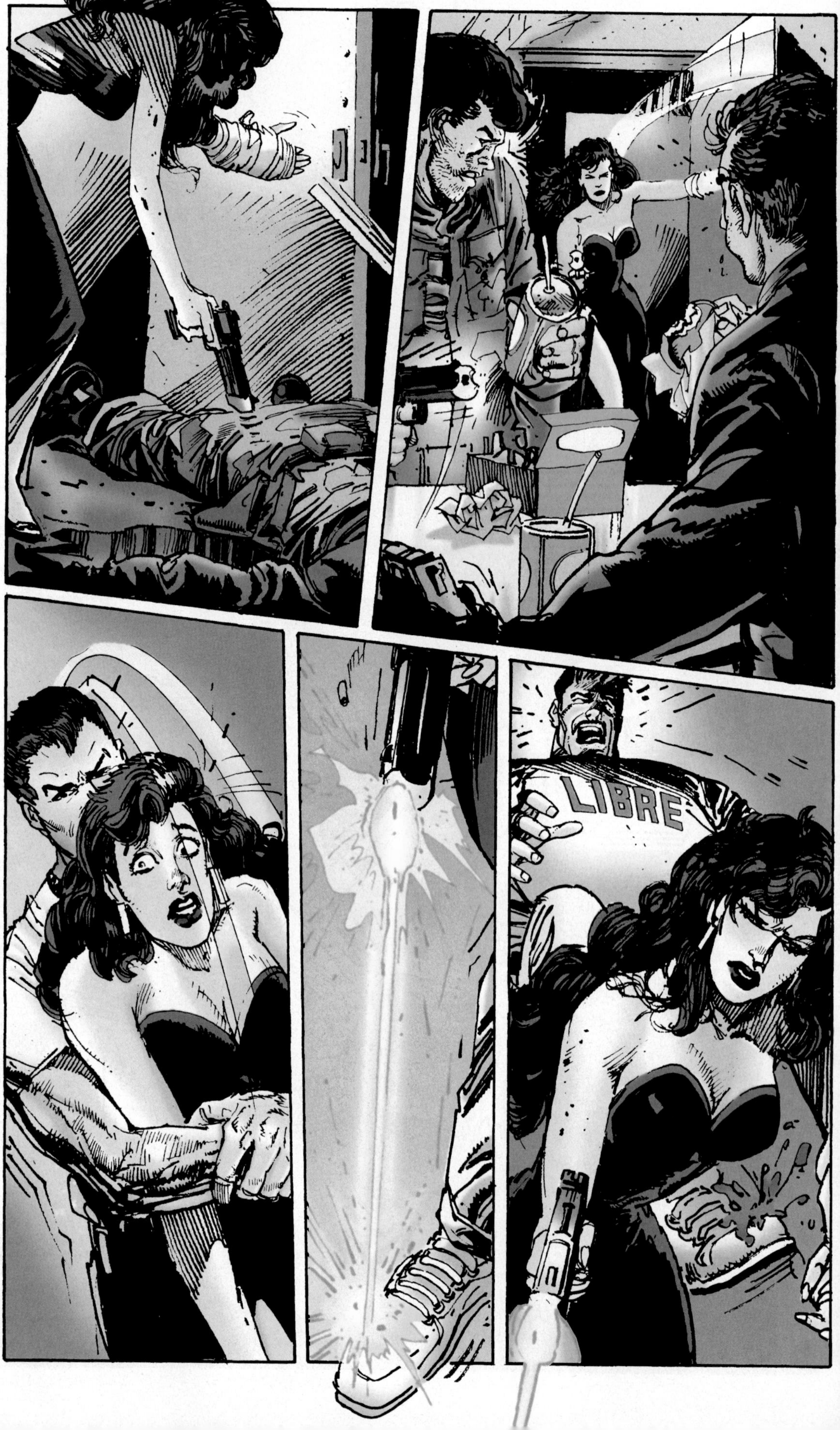
LIBRE

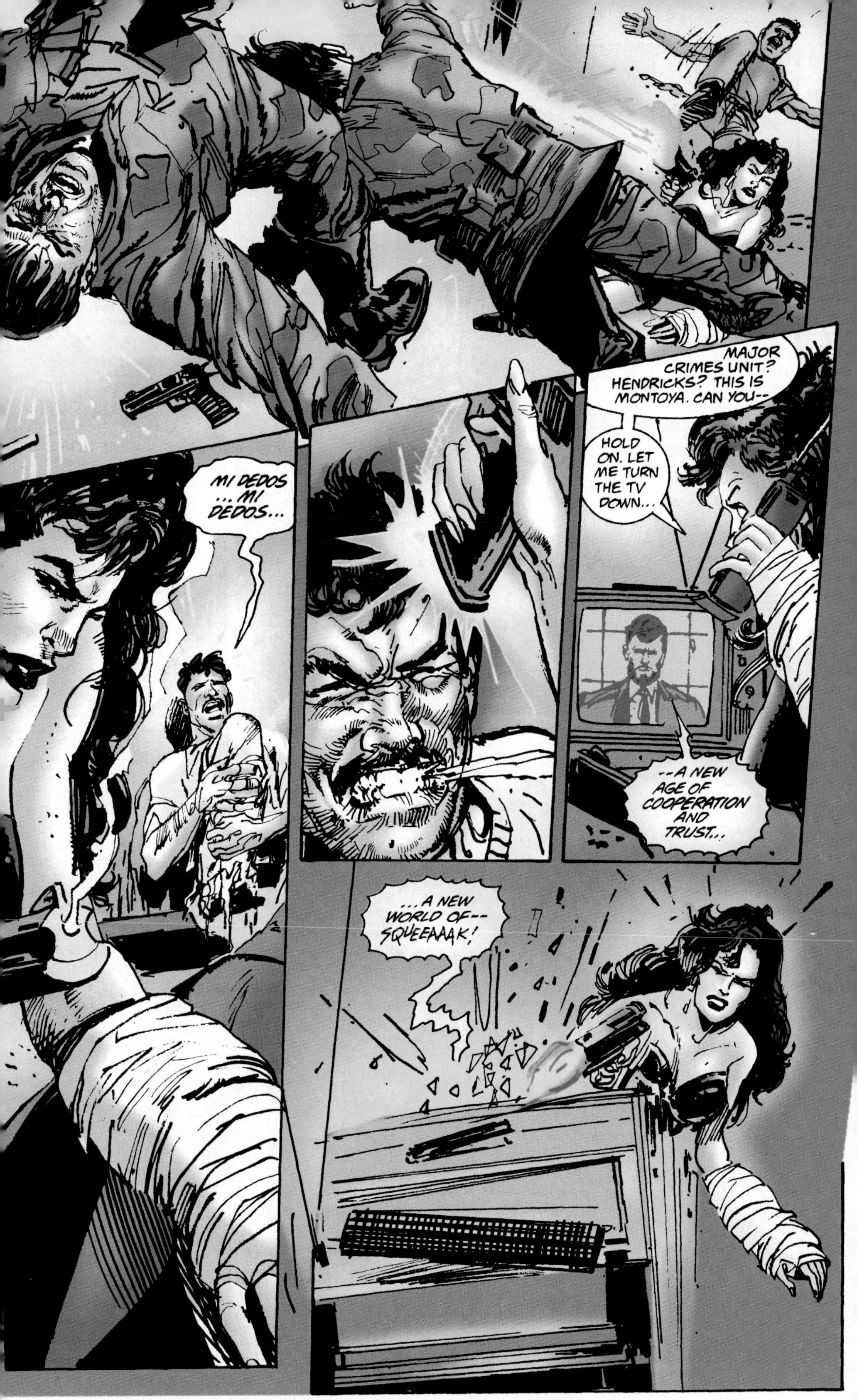
MAJOR CRIMES UNIT? HENDRICKS? THIS IS MONTOYA. CAN YOU--
MI DEDOS ...MI DEDOS...
HOLD ON. LET ME TURN THE TV DOWN...
--A NEW AGE OF COOPERATION AND TRUST...
...A NEW WORLD OF-- SQUEEAAAK!

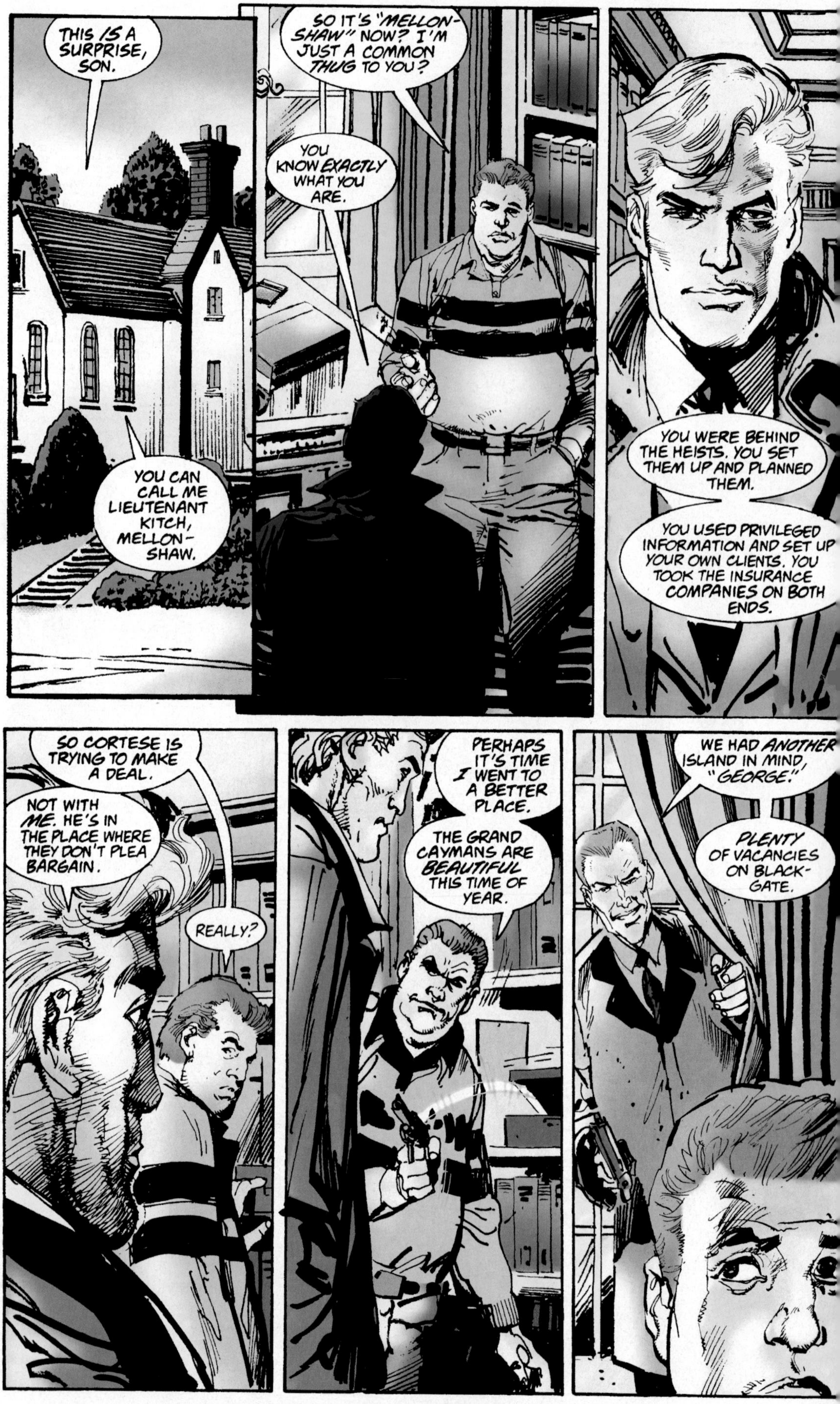

THIS *IS* A SURPRISE, SON.
YOU CAN CALL ME LIEUTENANT KITCH, MELLON-SHAW.
SO IT'S "*MELLON-SHAW*" NOW? I'M JUST A COMMON *THUG* TO YOU?
YOU KNOW *EXACTLY* WHAT YOU ARE.
YOU WERE BEHIND THE HEISTS. YOU SET THEM UP AND PLANNED THEM.
YOU USED PRIVILEGED INFORMATION AND SET UP YOUR OWN CLIENTS. YOU TOOK THE INSURANCE COMPANIES ON BOTH ENDS.
SO CORTESE IS TRYING TO MAKE A DEAL.
NOT WITH *ME*. HE'S IN THE PLACE WHERE THEY DON'T PLEA BARGAIN.
REALLY?
PERHAPS IT'S TIME *I* WENT TO A BETTER PLACE.
THE GRAND CAYMANS ARE *BEAUTIFUL* THIS TIME OF YEAR.
WE HAD *ANOTHER* ISLAND IN MIND, "*GEORGE*."
PLENTY OF VACANCIES ON BLACKGATE.

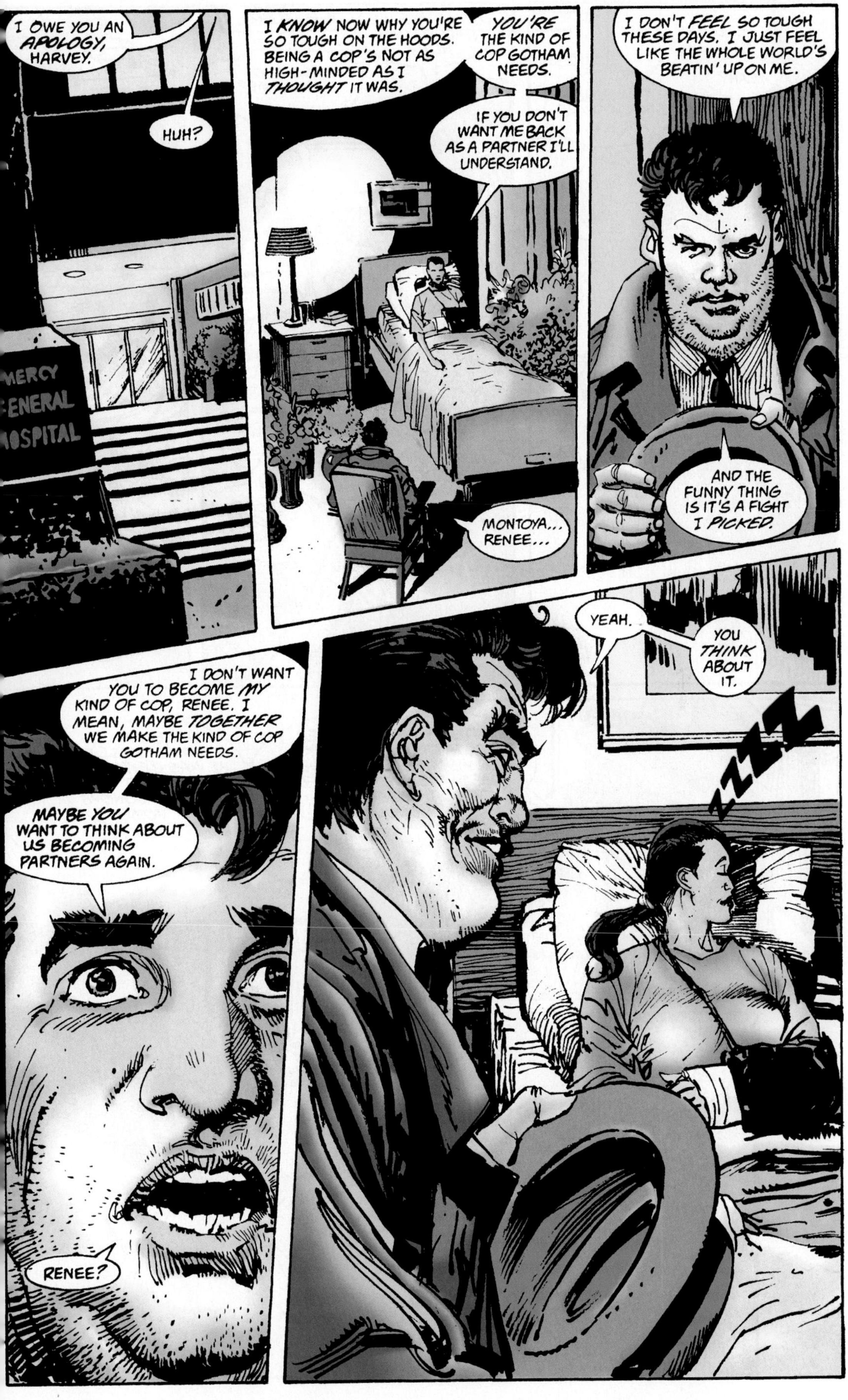

I OWE YOU AN APOLOGY, HARVEY.
HUH?
MERCY GENERAL HOSPITAL
I KNOW NOW WHY YOU'RE SO TOUGH ON THE HOODS. BEING A COP'S NOT AS HIGH-MINDED AS I THOUGHT IT WAS.
YOU'RE THE KIND OF COP GOTHAM NEEDS.
IF YOU DON'T WANT ME BACK AS A PARTNER I'LL UNDERSTAND.
MONTOYA... RENEE...
I DON'T FEEL SO TOUGH THESE DAYS. I JUST FEEL LIKE THE WHOLE WORLD'S BEATIN' UP ON ME.
AND THE FUNNY THING IS IT'S A FIGHT I PICKED.
I DON'T WANT YOU TO BECOME MY KIND OF COP, RENEE. I MEAN, MAYBE TOGETHER WE MAKE THE KIND OF COP GOTHAM NEEDS.
MAYBE YOU WANT TO THINK ABOUT US BECOMING PARTNERS AGAIN.
RENEE?
YEAH.
YOU THINK ABOUT IT.
ZZZZ

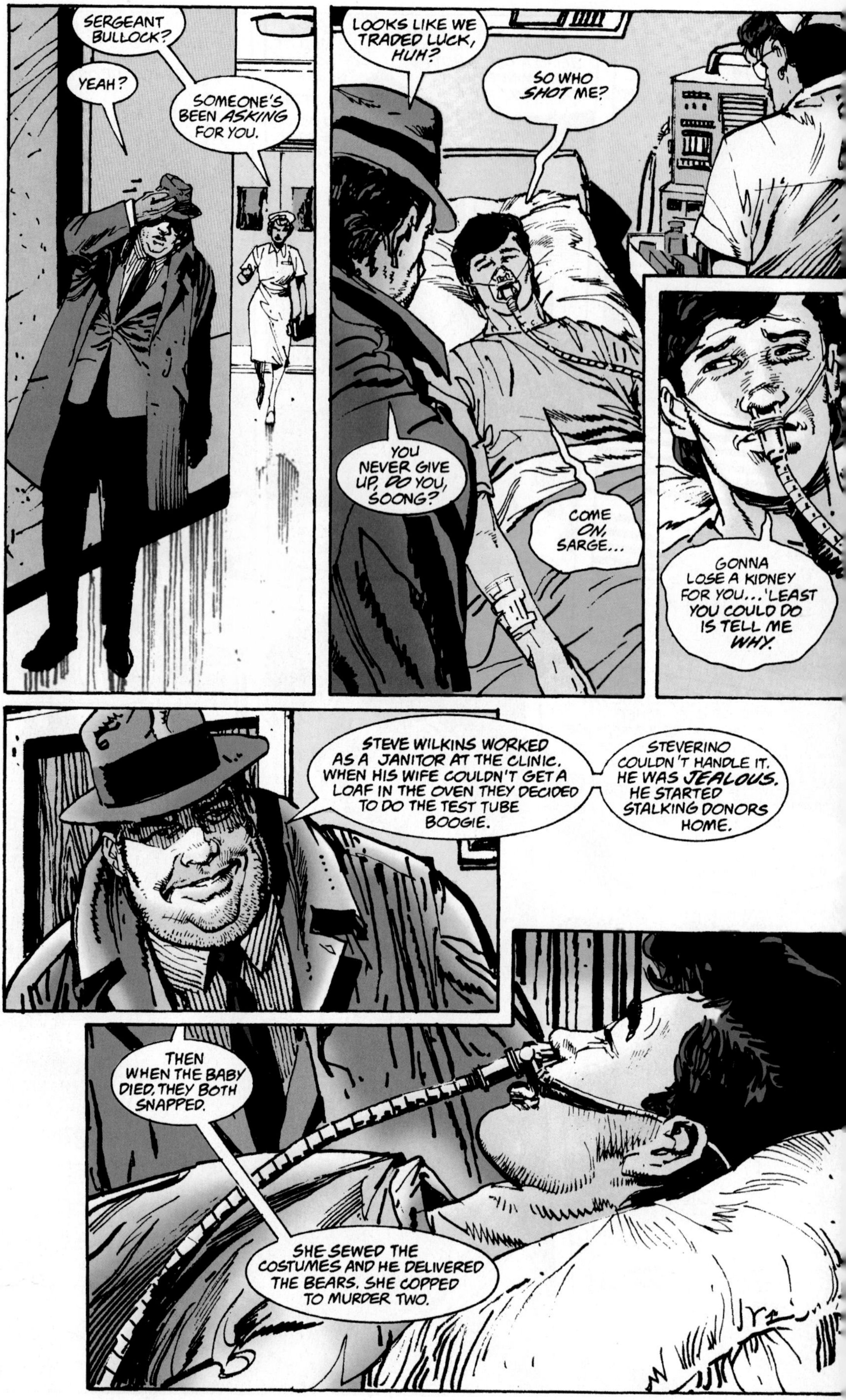
SERGEANT BULLOCK?
YEAH?
SOMEONE'S BEEN ASKING FOR YOU.
LOOKS LIKE WE TRADED LUCK, HUH?
SO WHO SHOT ME?
YOU NEVER GIVE UP, DO YOU, SOONG?
COME ON, SARGE...
GONNA LOSE A KIDNEY FOR YOU... 'LEAST YOU COULD DO IS TELL ME WHY.
STEVE WILKINS WORKED AS A JANITOR AT THE CLINIC. WHEN HIS WIFE COULDN'T GET A LOAF IN THE OVEN THEY DECIDED TO DO THE TEST TUBE BOOGIE.
STEVERINO COULDN'T HANDLE IT. HE WAS JEALOUS. HE STARTED STALKING DONORS HOME.
THEN WHEN THE BABY DIED, THEY BOTH SNAPPED.
SHE SEWED THE COSTUMES AND HE DELIVERED THE BEARS. SHE COPPED TO MURDER TWO.

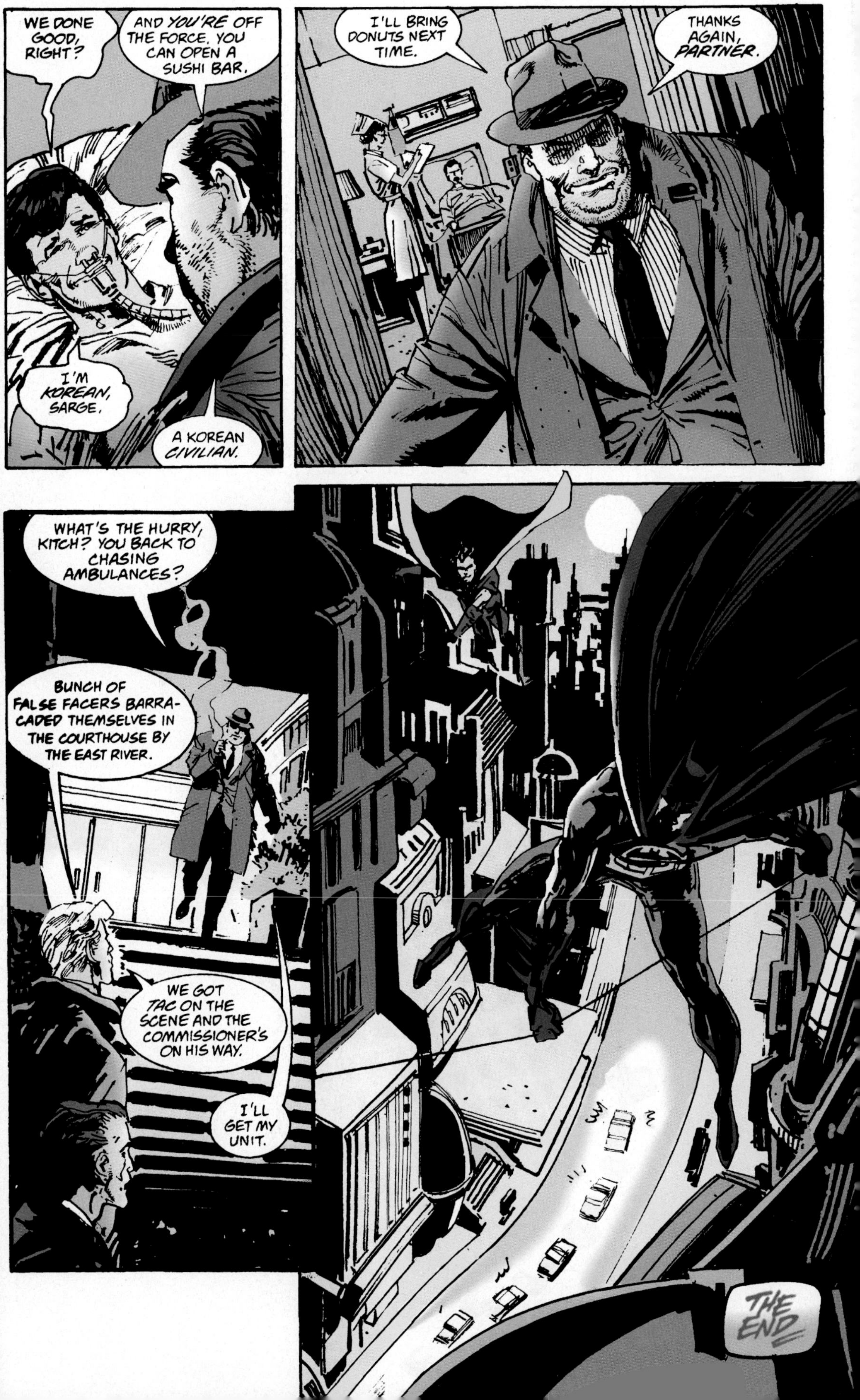
WE DONE GOOD, RIGHT?
AND YOU'RE OFF THE FORCE. YOU CAN OPEN A SUSHI BAR.
I'M KOREAN, SARGE.
A KOREAN CIVILIAN.
I'LL BRING DONUTS NEXT TIME.
THANKS AGAIN, PARTNER.
WHAT'S THE HURRY, KITCH? YOU BACK TO CHASING AMBULANCES?
BUNCH OF FALSE FACERS BARRACADED THEMSELVES IN THE COURTHOUSE BY THE EAST RIVER.
WE GOT TAC ON THE SCENE AND THE COMMISSIONER'S ON HIS WAY.
I'LL GET MY UNIT.
THE END

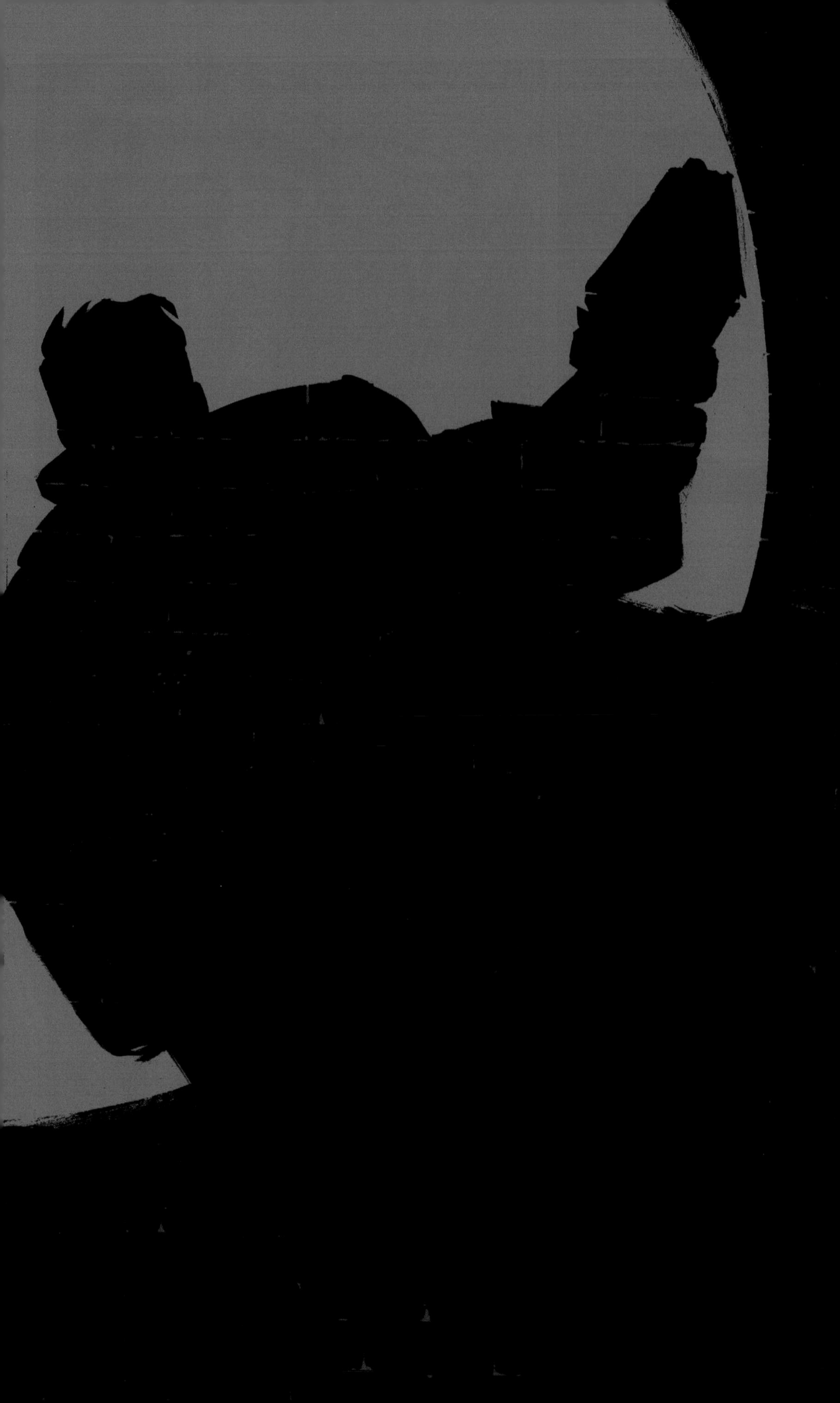

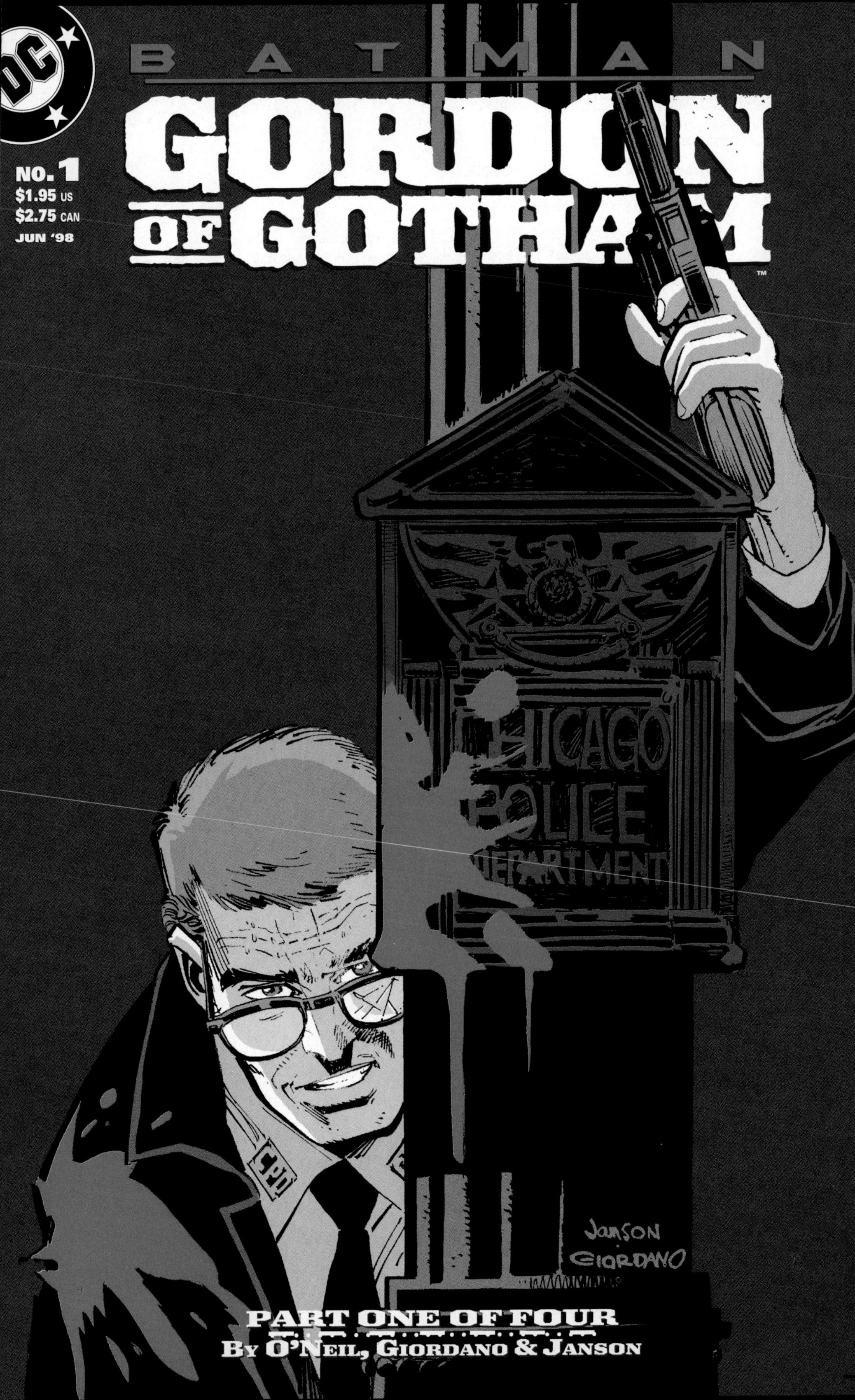
BATMAN
GORDON OF GOTHAM
NO. 1
$1.95 US
$2.75 CAN
JUN '98
JANSON
GIORDANO
PART ONE OF FOUR
By O'Neil, Giordano & Janson

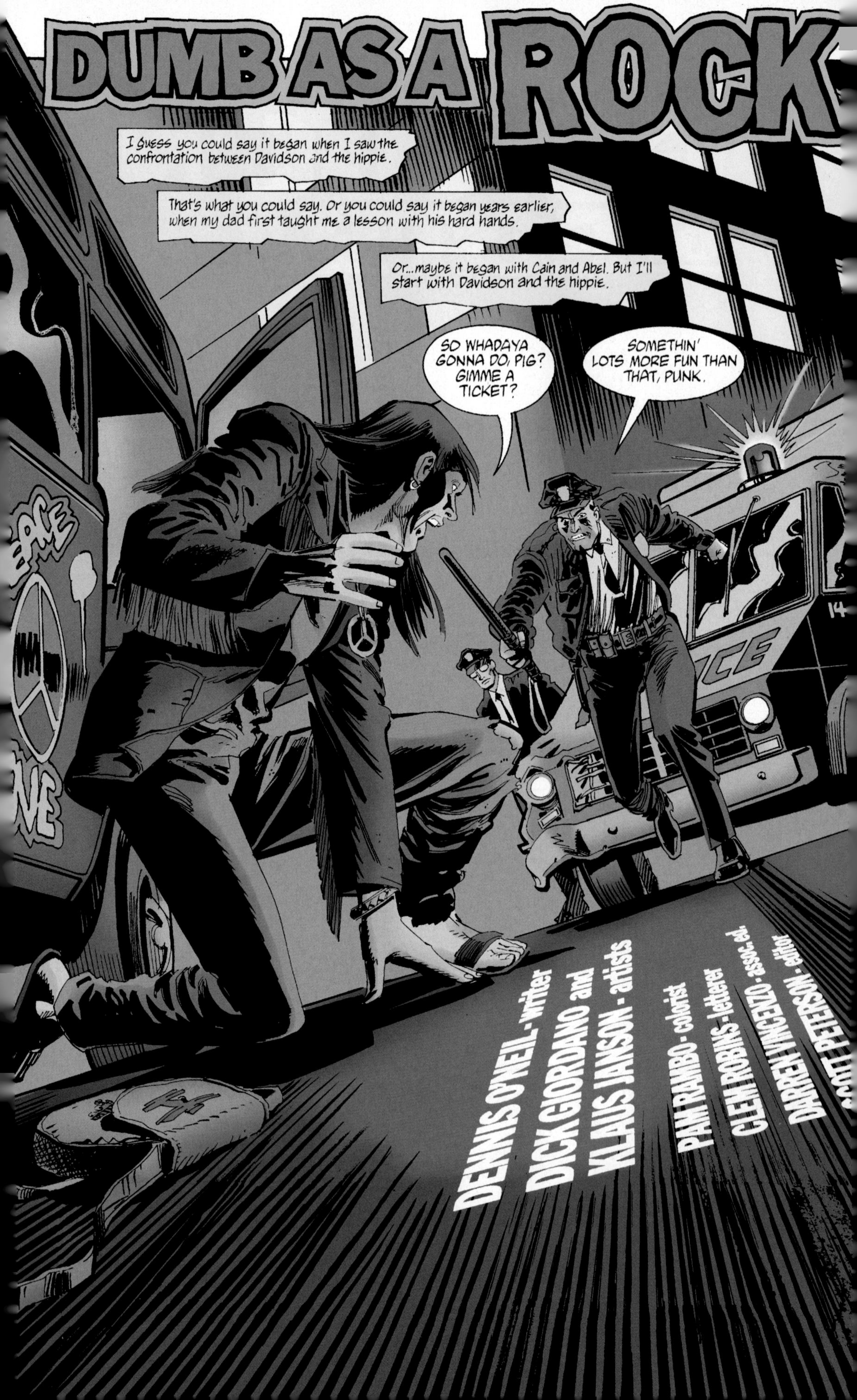
DUMB AS A ROCK
I guess you could say it began when I saw the confrontation between Davidson and the hippie.
That's what you could say. Or you could say it began years earlier, when my dad first taught me a lesson with his hard hands.
Or...maybe it began with Cain and Abel. But I'll start with Davidson and the hippie.
SO WHADAYA GONNA DO, PIG? GIMME A TICKET?
SOMETHIN' LOTS MORE FUN THAN THAT, PUNK.
DENNIS O'NEIL - writer
DICK GIORDANO and
KLAUS JANSON - artists
PAM RAMBO - colorist
CLEM ROBINS - letterer
DARREN VINCENZO - assoc. ed.
PETERSON - editor

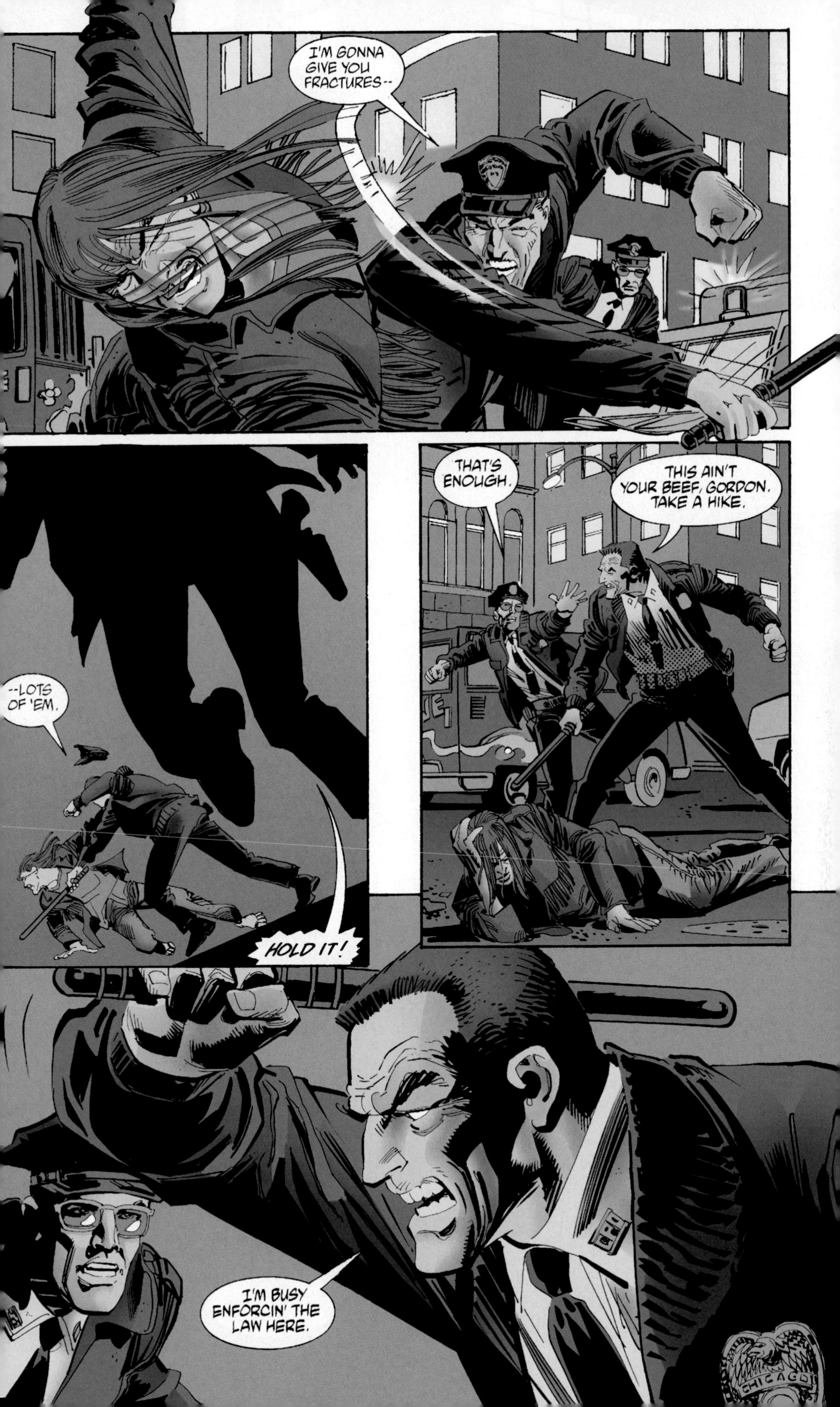

I'M GONNA GIVE YOU FRACTURES--
--LOTS OF 'EM.
HOLD IT!
THAT'S ENOUGH.
THIS AIN'T YOUR BEEF, GORDON. TAKE A HIKE.
I'M BUSY ENFORCIN' THE LAW HERE.
CHICAGO

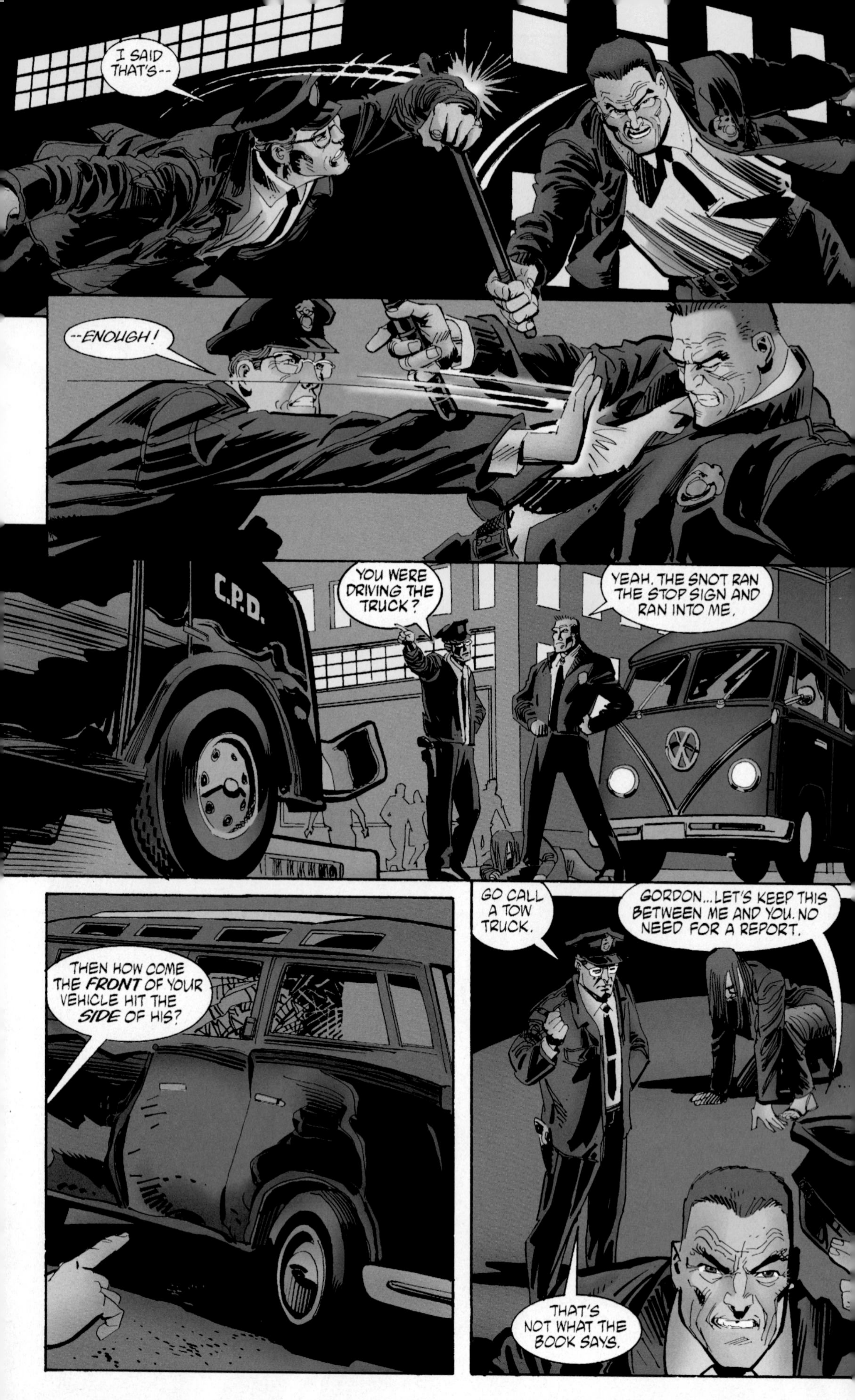
I SAID THAT'S--
--ENOUGH!
YOU WERE DRIVING THE TRUCK?
YEAH. THE SNOT RAN THE STOP SIGN AND RAN INTO ME.
THEN HOW COME THE FRONT OF YOUR VEHICLE HIT THE SIDE OF HIS?
GO CALL A TOW TRUCK.
GORDON...LET'S KEEP THIS BETWEEN ME AND YOU. NO NEED FOR A REPORT.
THAT'S NOT WHAT THE BOOK SAYS.
C.P.D.

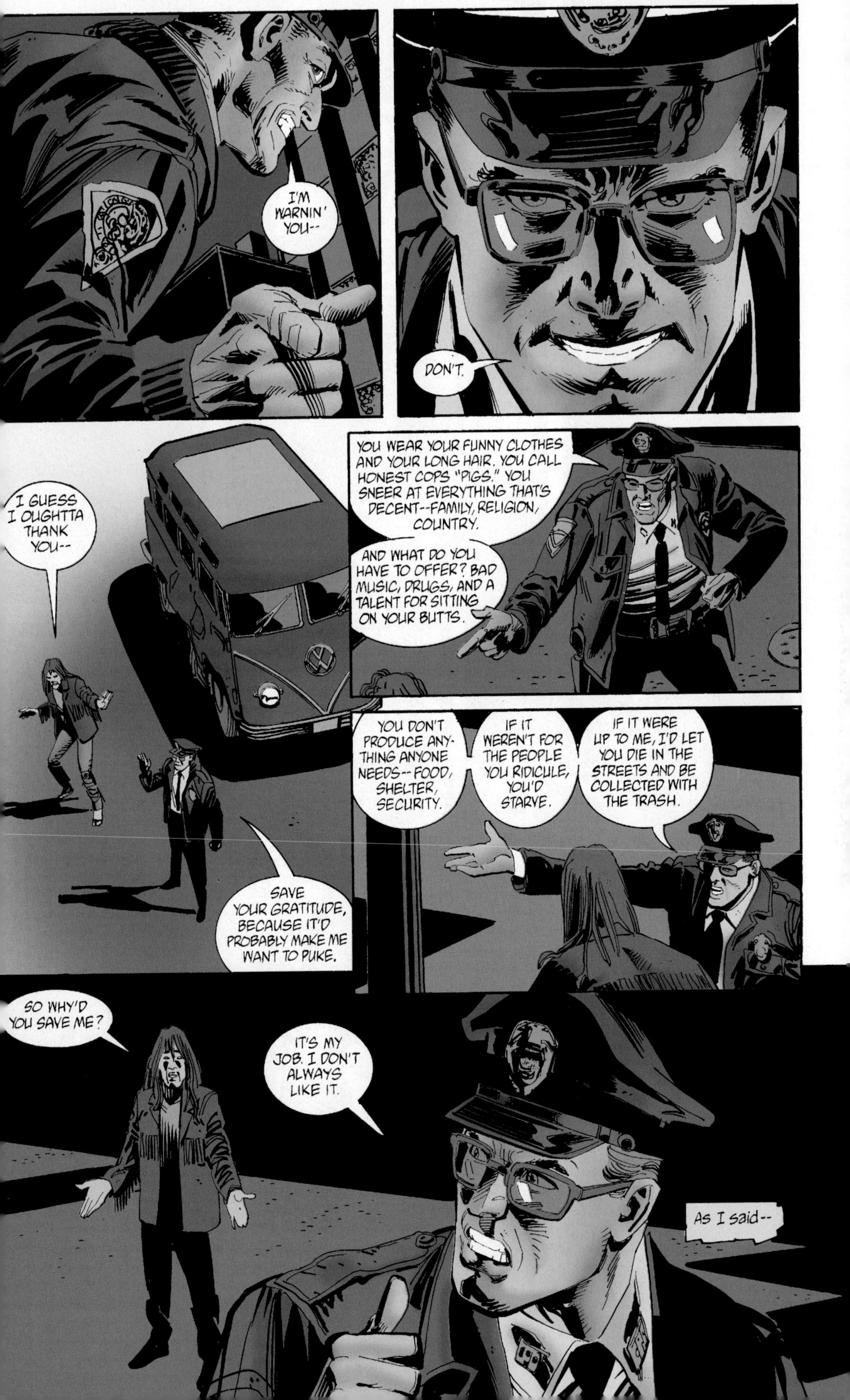
I'M WARNIN' YOU--
DON'T.
YOU WEAR YOUR FUNNY CLOTHES AND YOUR LONG HAIR. YOU CALL HONEST COPS "PIGS." YOU SNEER AT EVERYTHING THAT'S DECENT--FAMILY, RELIGION, COUNTRY.
AND WHAT DO YOU HAVE TO OFFER? BAD MUSIC, DRUGS, AND A TALENT FOR SITTING ON YOUR BUTTS.
I GUESS I OUGHTTA THANK YOU--
SAVE YOUR GRATITUDE, BECAUSE IT'D PROBABLY MAKE ME WANT TO PUKE.
YOU DON'T PRODUCE ANYTHING ANYONE NEEDS-- FOOD, SHELTER, SECURITY.
IF IT WEREN'T FOR THE PEOPLE YOU RIDICULE, YOU'D STARVE.
IF IT WERE UP TO ME, I'D LET YOU DIE IN THE STREETS AND BE COLLECTED WITH THE TRASH.
SO WHY'D YOU SAVE ME?
IT'S MY JOB. I DON'T ALWAYS LIKE IT.
As I said--

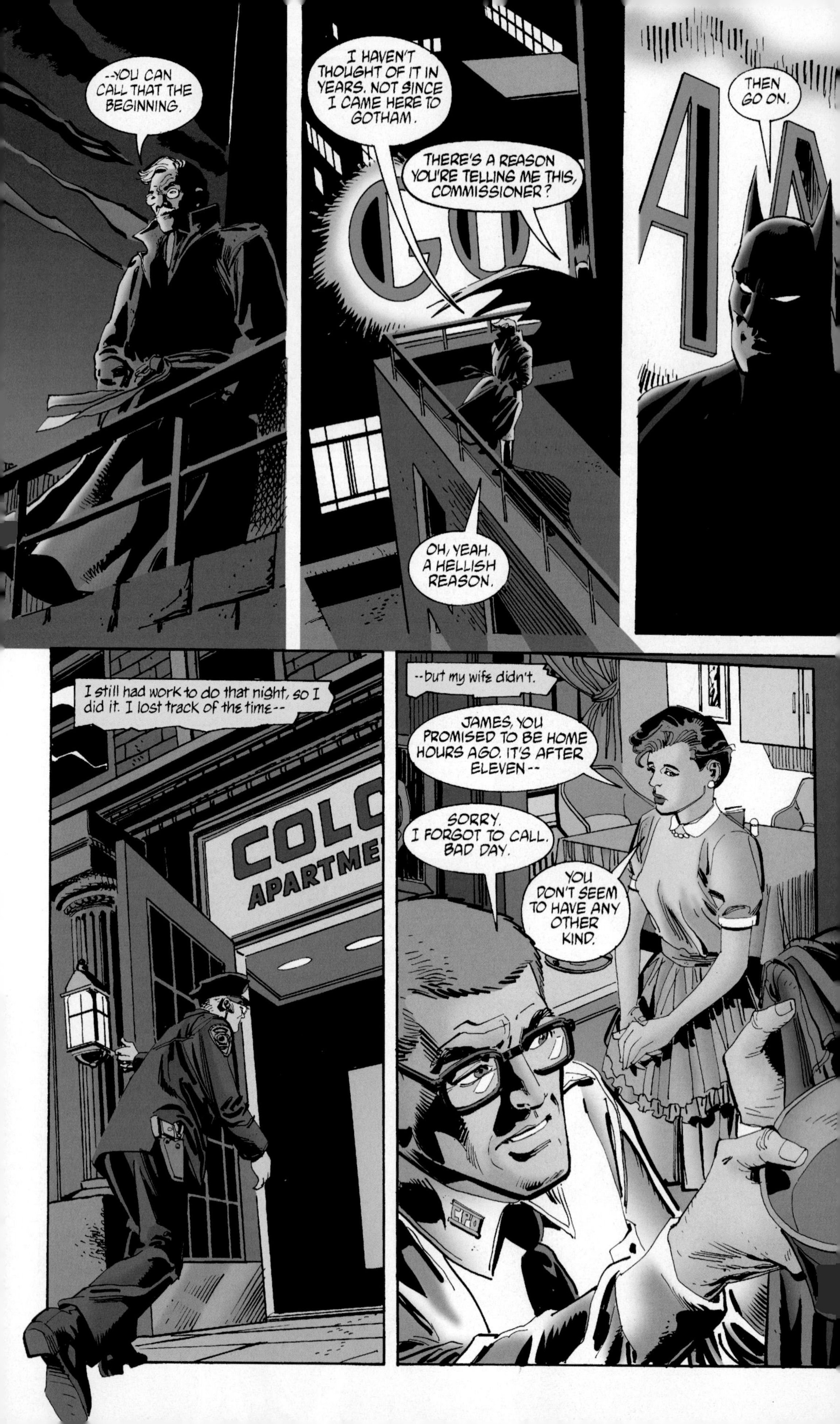
--YOU CAN CALL THAT THE BEGINNING.
I HAVEN'T THOUGHT OF IT IN YEARS. NOT SINCE I CAME HERE TO GOTHAM.
THERE'S A REASON YOU'RE TELLING ME THIS, COMMISSIONER?
OH, YEAH. A HELLISH REASON.
THEN GO ON.
I still had work to do that night, so I did it. I lost track of the time--
COLO
APARTME
--but my wife didn't.
JAMES, YOU PROMISED TO BE HOME HOURS AGO. IT'S AFTER ELEVEN--
SORRY. I FORGOT TO CALL. BAD DAY.
YOU DON'T SEEM TO HAVE ANY OTHER KIND.
GPD

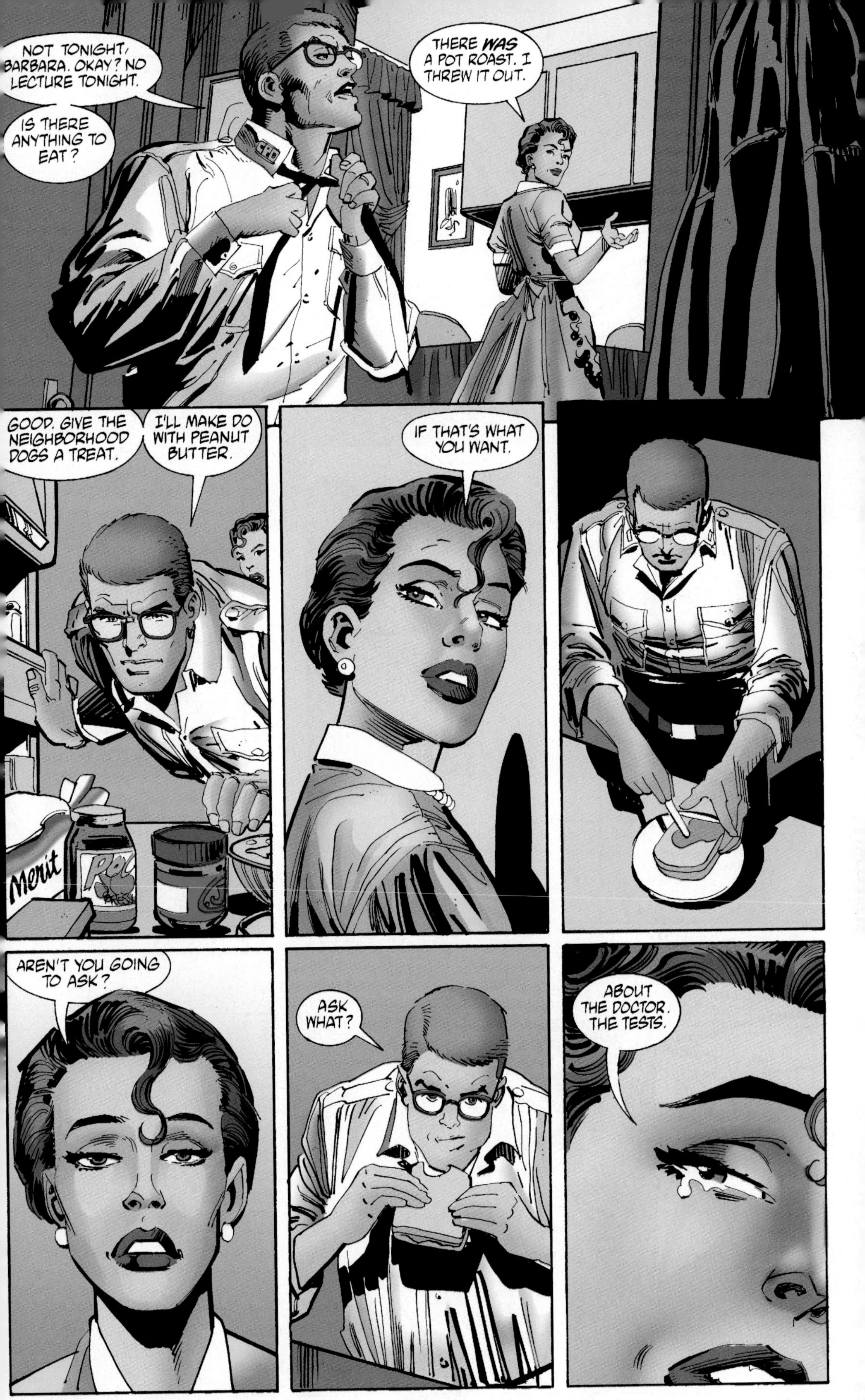

NOT TONIGHT, BARBARA. OKAY? NO LECTURE TONIGHT.
IS THERE ANYTHING TO EAT?
THERE WAS A POT ROAST. I THREW IT OUT.
GOOD. GIVE THE NEIGHBORHOOD DOGS A TREAT.
I'LL MAKE DO WITH PEANUT BUTTER.
Merit
IF THAT'S WHAT YOU WANT.
AREN'T YOU GOING TO ASK?
ASK WHAT?
ABOUT THE DOCTOR. THE TESTS.

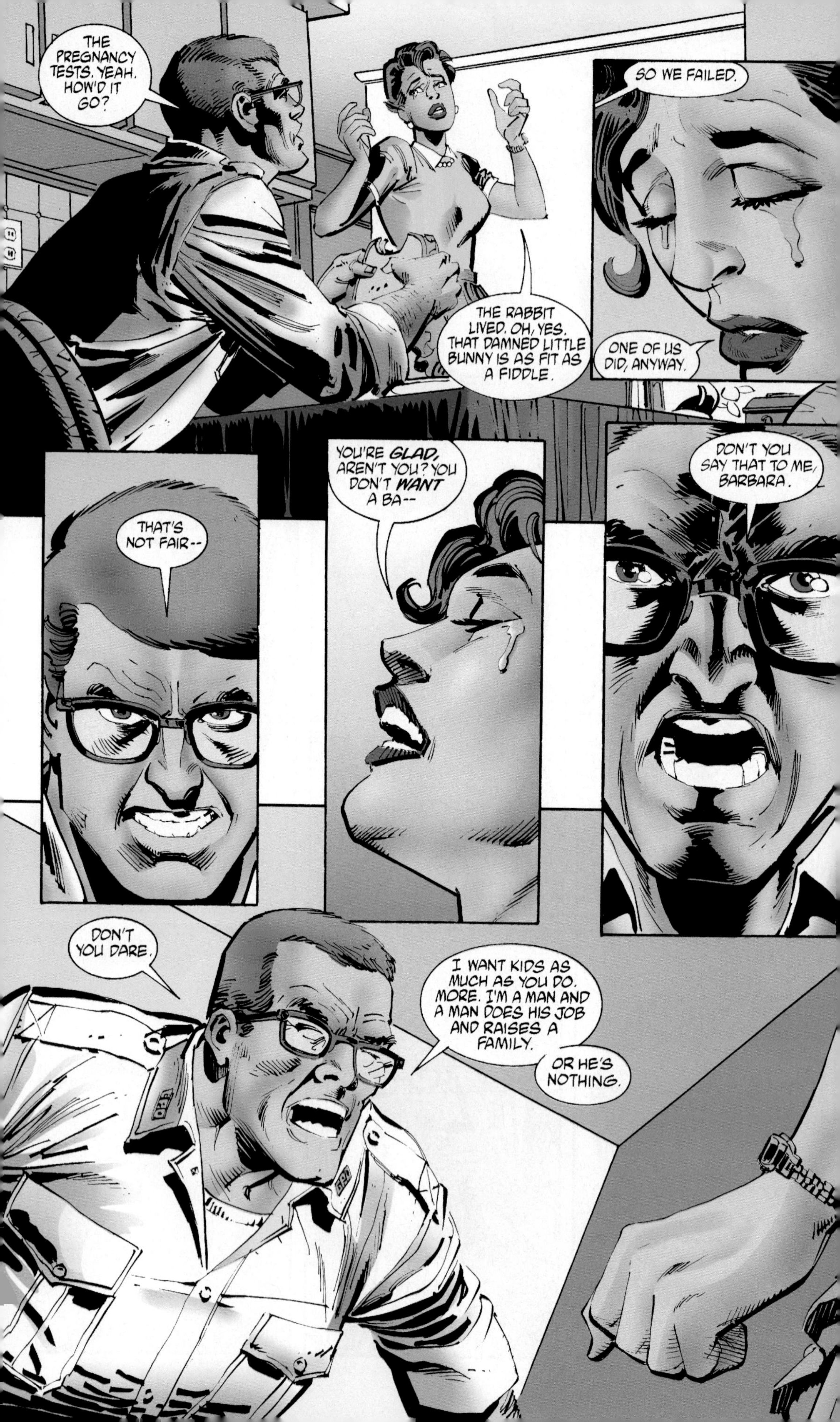
THE PREGNANCY TESTS. YEAH. HOW'D IT GO?
THE RABBIT LIVED. OH, YES. THAT DAMNED LITTLE BUNNY IS AS FIT AS A FIDDLE.
SO WE FAILED.
ONE OF US DID, ANYWAY.
THAT'S NOT FAIR--
YOU'RE GLAD, AREN'T YOU? YOU DON'T WANT A BA--
DON'T YOU SAY THAT TO ME, BARBARA.
DON'T YOU DARE.
I WANT KIDS AS MUCH AS YOU DO. MORE. I'M A MAN AND A MAN DOES HIS JOB AND RAISES A FAMILY.
OR HE'S NOTHING.

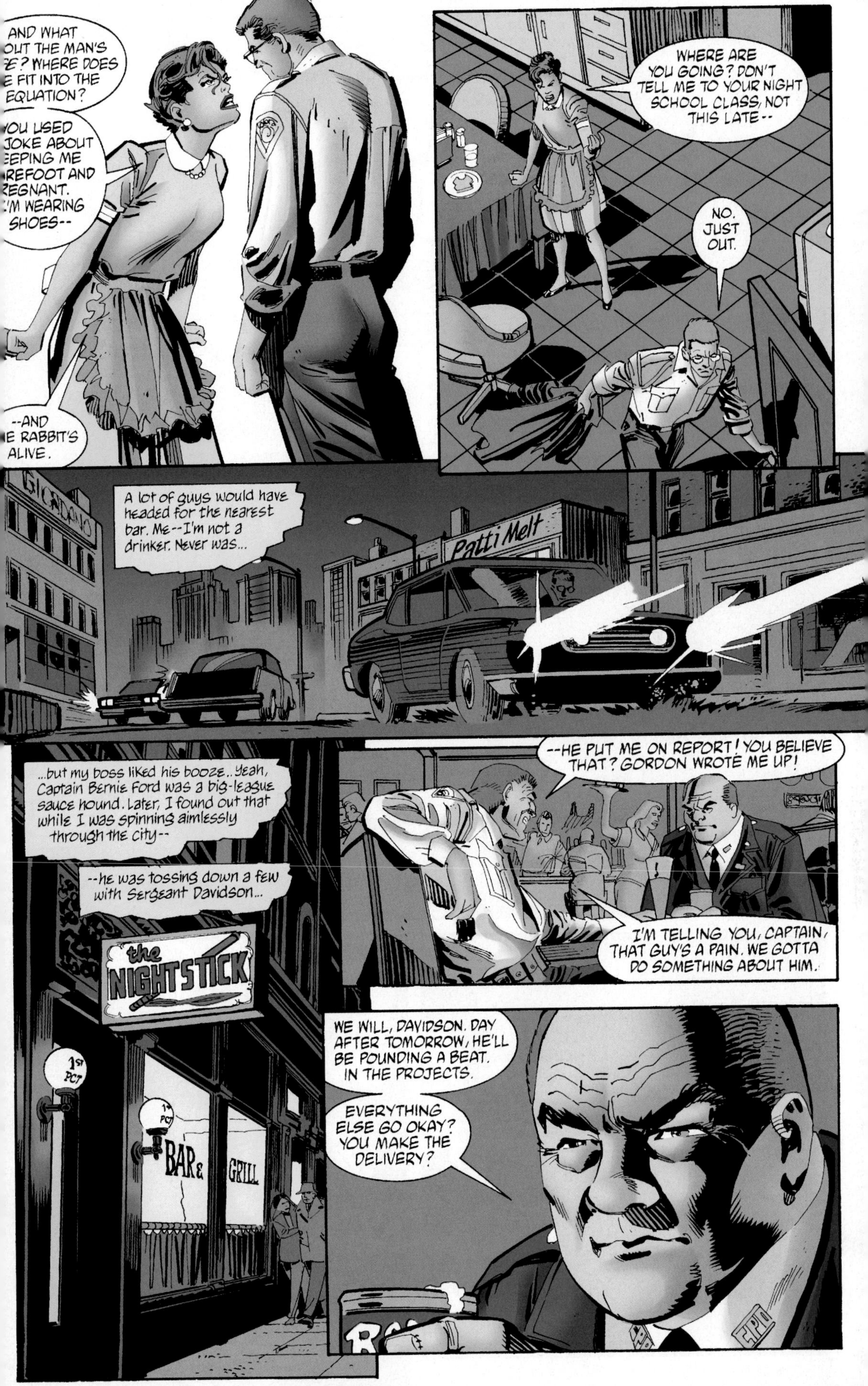
AND WHAT
OUT THE MAN'S
E? WHERE DOES
E FIT INTO THE
EQUATION?
YOU USED
JOKE ABOUT
EEPING ME
REFOOT AND
REGNANT.
I'M WEARING
SHOES--
--AND
E RABBIT'S
ALIVE.
WHERE ARE YOU GOING? DON'T TELL ME TO YOUR NIGHT SCHOOL CLASS, NOT THIS LATE--
NO. JUST OUT.
A lot of guys would have headed for the nearest bar. Me--I'm not a drinker. Never was...
Patti Melt
...but my boss liked his booze. Yeah, Captain Bernie Ford was a big-league sauce hound. Later, I found out that while I was spinning aimlessly through the city--
--he was tossing down a few with Sergeant Davidson...
the NIGHTSTICK
1st PCT
BAR & GRILL
--HE PUT ME ON REPORT! YOU BELIEVE THAT? GORDON WROTE ME UP!
I'M TELLING YOU, CAPTAIN, THAT GUY'S A PAIN. WE GOTTA DO SOMETHING ABOUT HIM.
WE WILL, DAVIDSON. DAY AFTER TOMORROW, HE'LL BE POUNDING A BEAT. IN THE PROJECTS.
EVERYTHING ELSE GO OKAY? YOU MAKE THE DELIVERY?

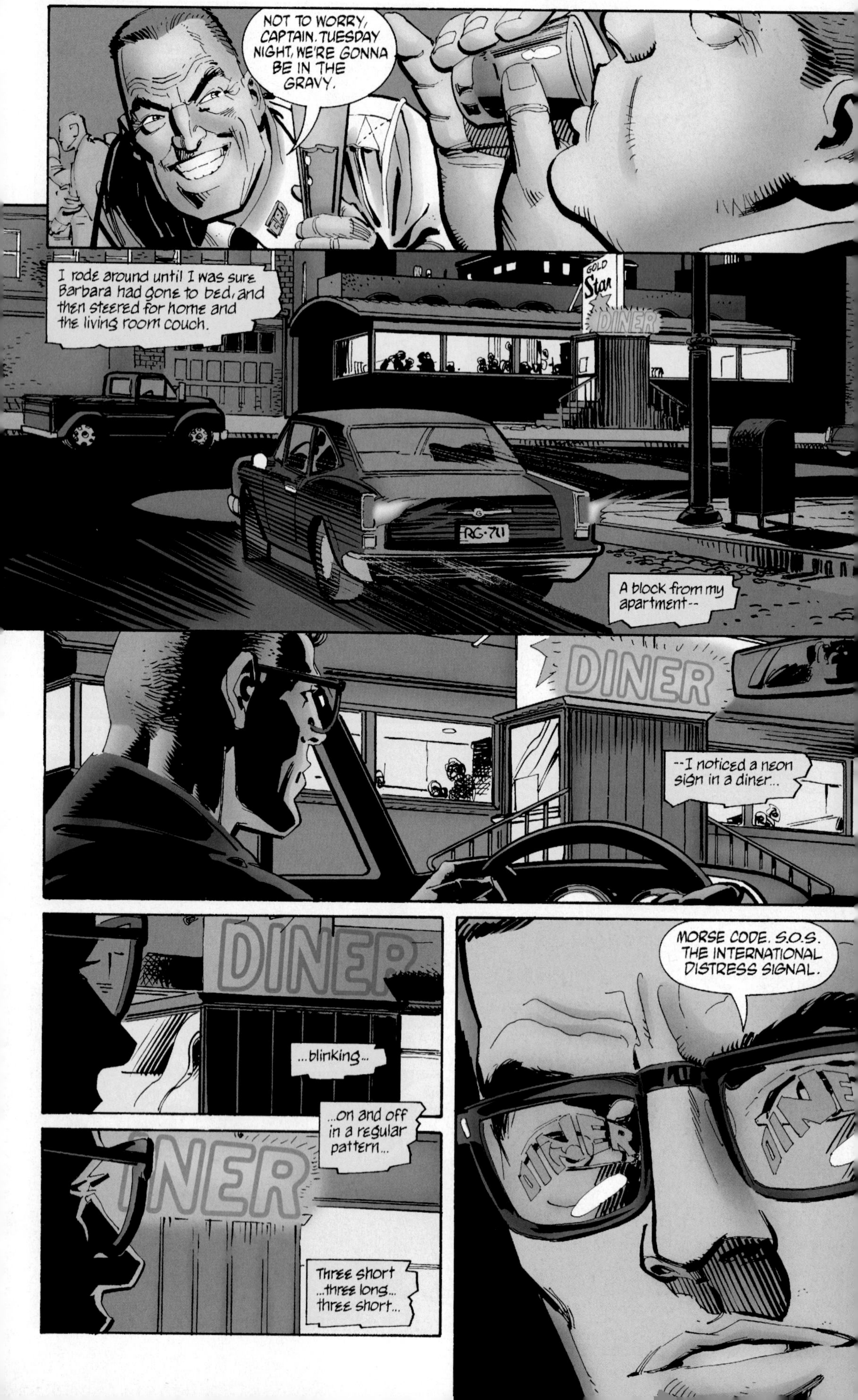
NOT TO WORRY, CAPTAIN. TUESDAY NIGHT, WE'RE GONNA BE IN THE GRAVY.
I rode around until I was sure Barbara had gone to bed, and then steered for home and the living room couch.
GOLD Star DINER
RG-711
A block from my apartment--
DINER
--I noticed a neon sign in a diner...
DINER
...blinking...
...on and off in a regular pattern...
NER
Three short ...three long... three short...
MORSE CODE. S.O.S. THE INTERNATIONAL DISTRESS SIGNAL.

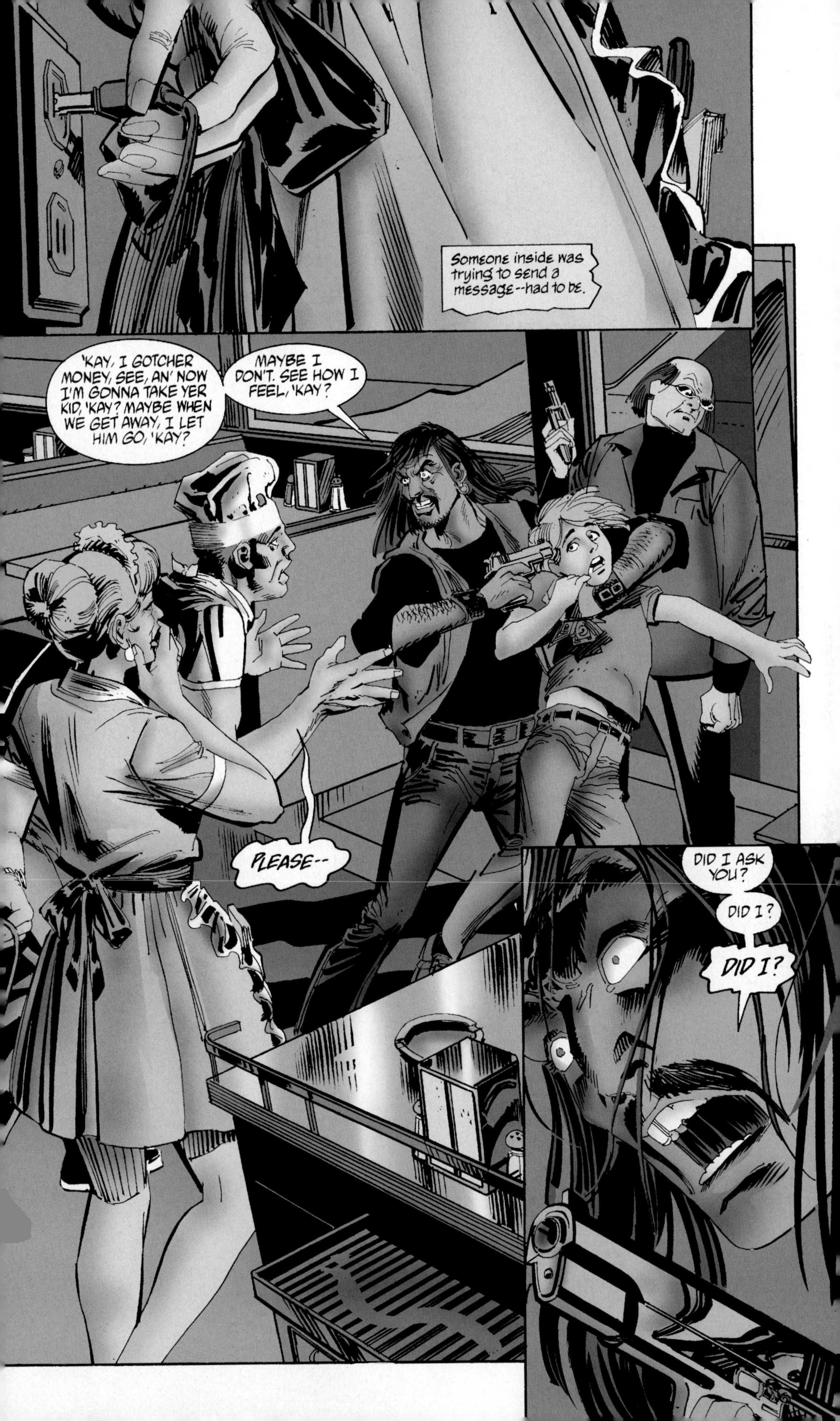
Someone inside was trying to send a message--had to be.
'KAY, I GOTCHER MONEY, SEE, AN' NOW I'M GONNA TAKE YER KID, 'KAY? MAYBE WHEN WE GET AWAY, I LET HIM GO, 'KAY?
MAYBE I DON'T. SEE HOW I FEEL, 'KAY?
PLEASE--
DID I ASK YOU?
DID I?
DID I?

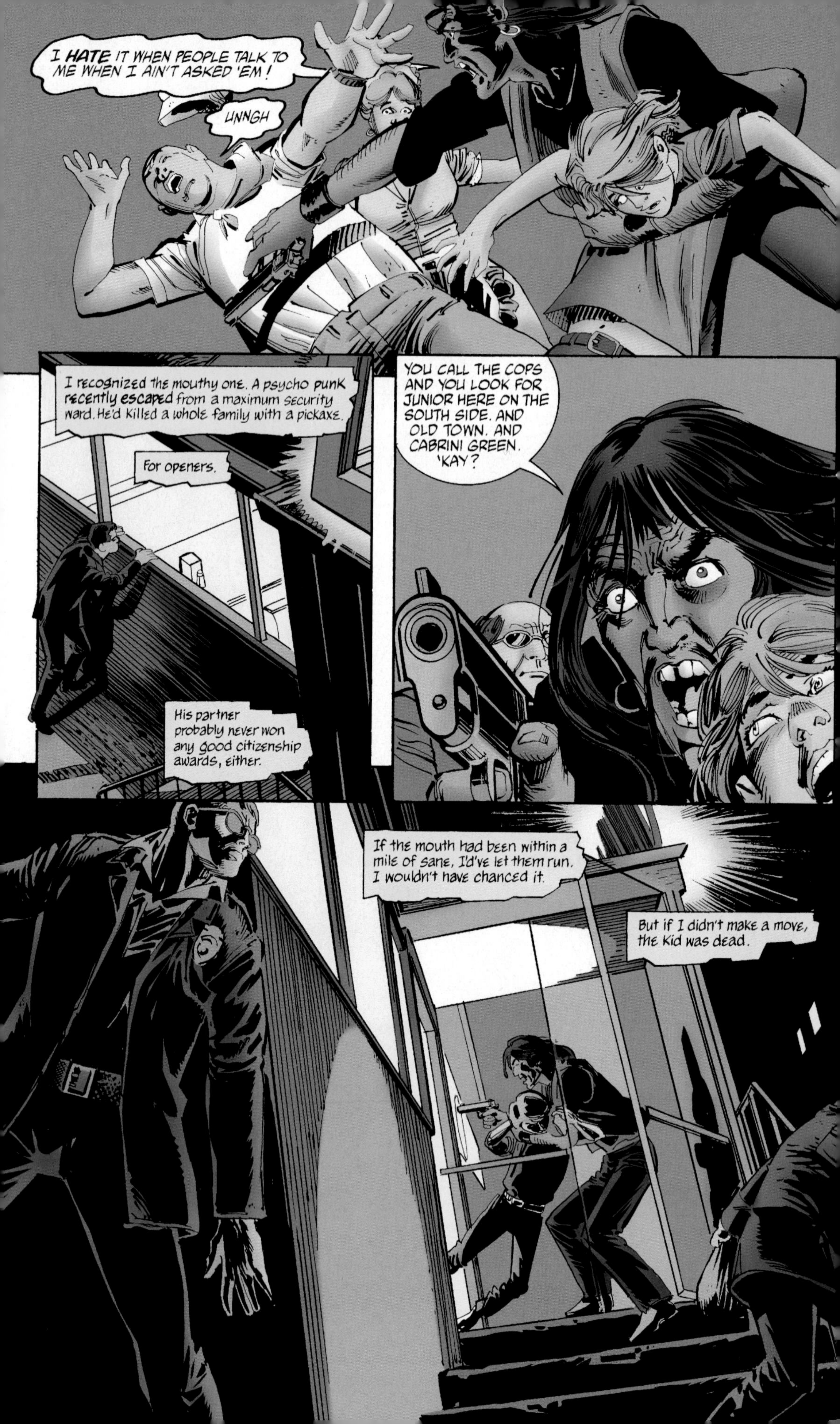
I HATE IT WHEN PEOPLE TALK TO ME WHEN I AIN'T ASKED 'EM!
UNNGH
I recognized the mouthy one. A psycho punk recently escaped from a maximum security ward. He'd killed a whole family with a pickaxe.
For openers.
His partner probably never won any good citizenship awards, either.
YOU CALL THE COPS AND YOU LOOK FOR JUNIOR HERE ON THE SOUTH SIDE. AND OLD TOWN. AND CABRINI GREEN. 'KAY?
If the mouth had been within a mile of sane, I'd've let them run. I wouldn't have chanced it.
But if I didn't make a move, the kid was dead.

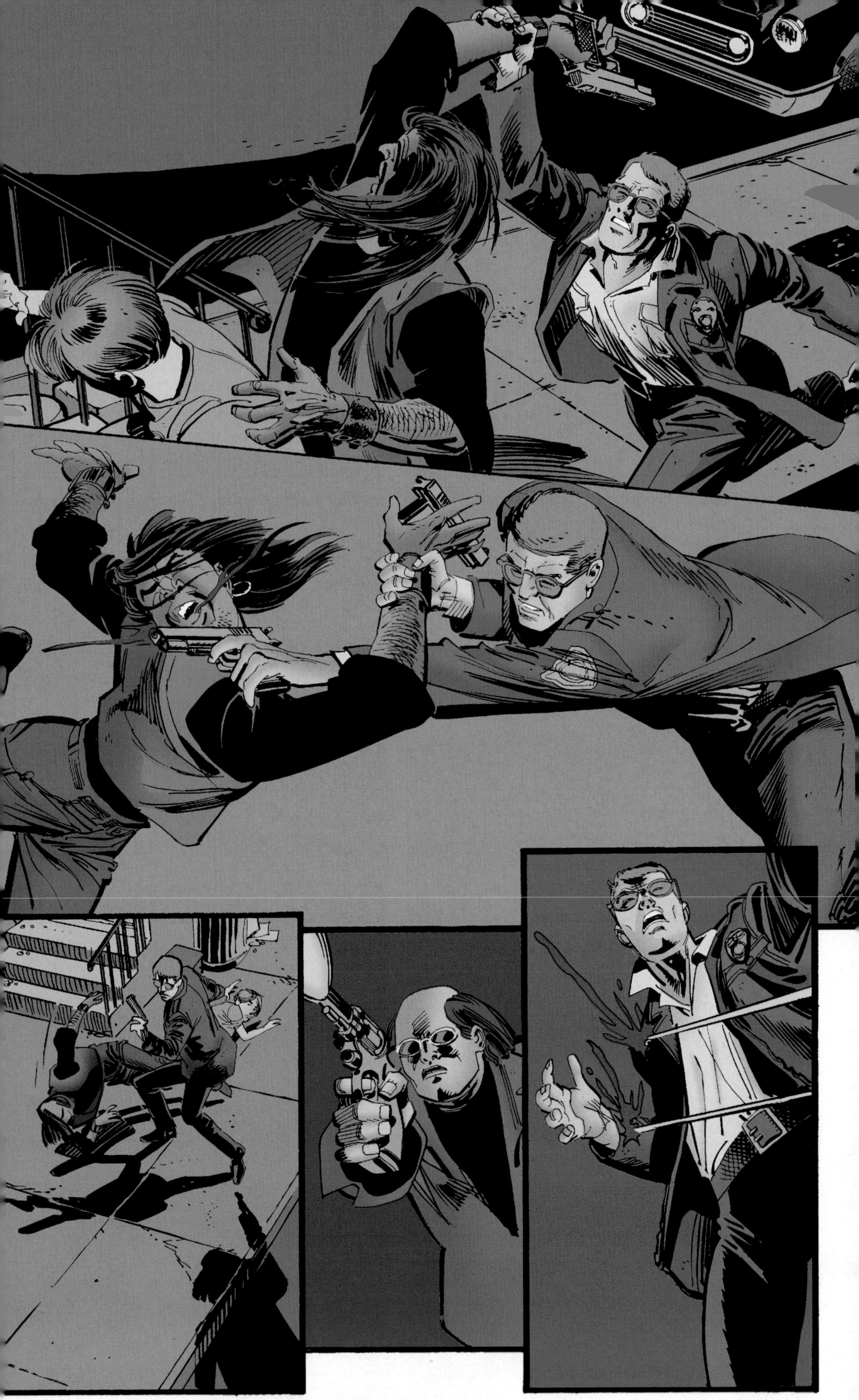

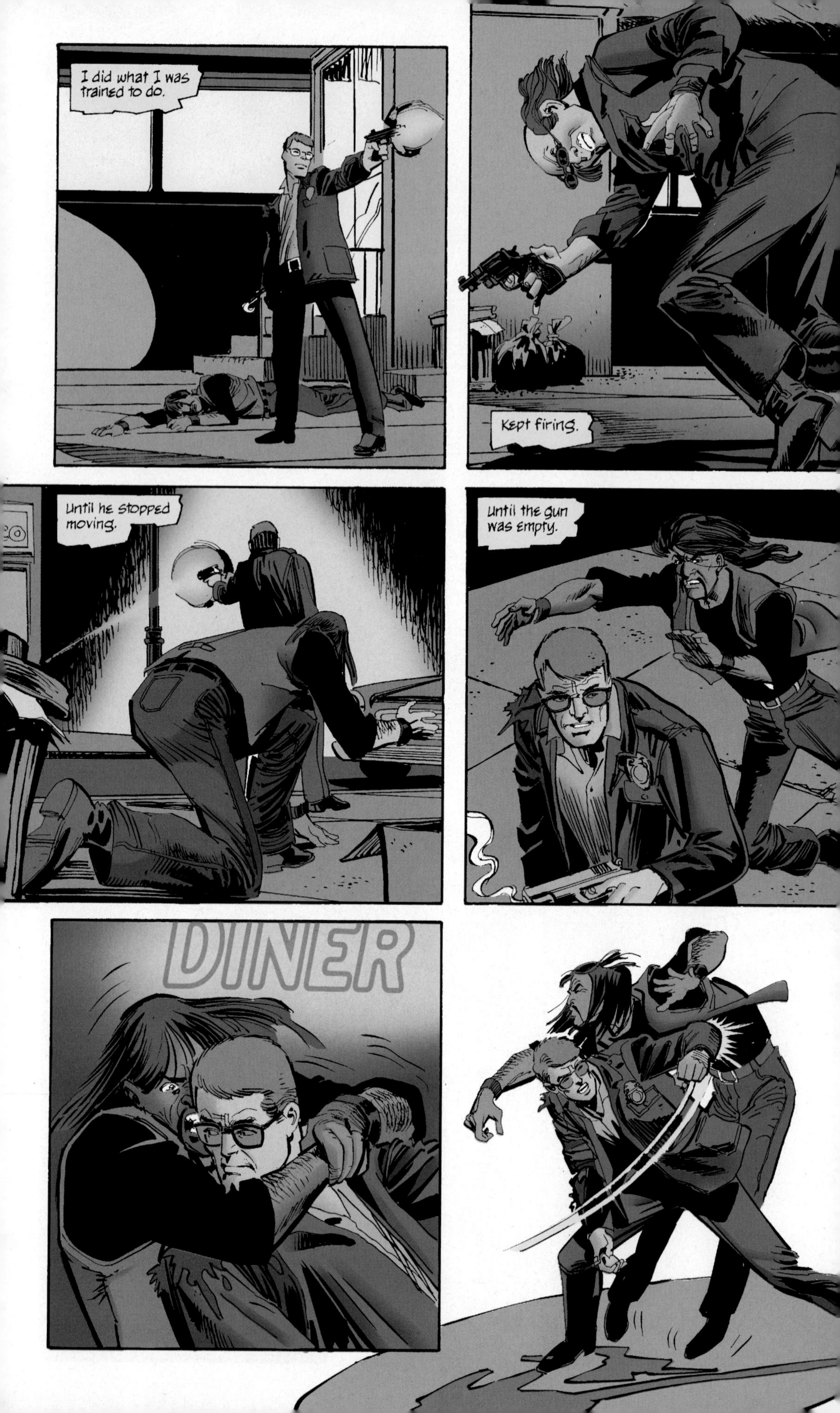
I did what I was trained to do.
Kept firing.
Until he stopped moving.
Until the gun was empty.
DINER

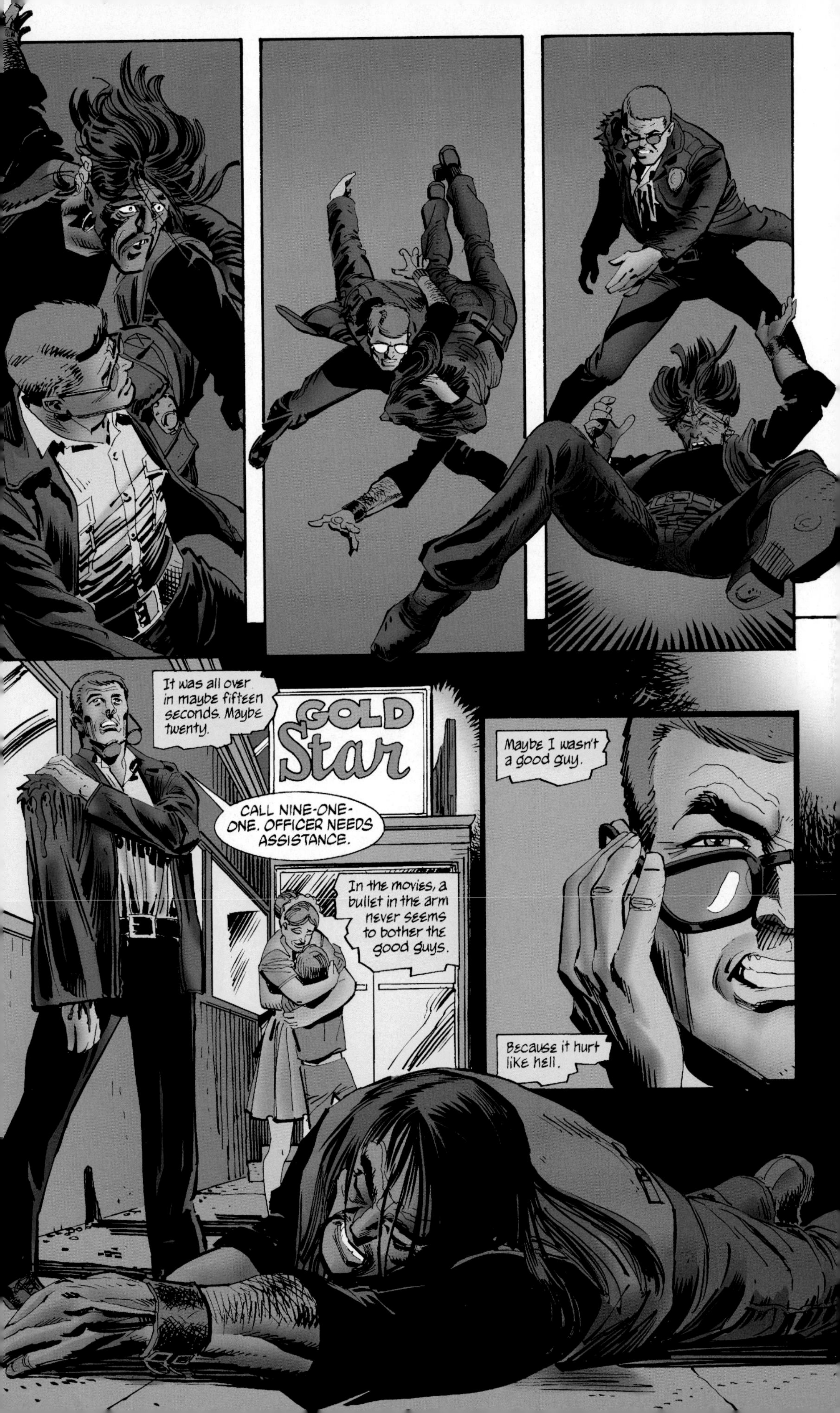

It was all over in maybe fifteen seconds. Maybe twenty.
GOLD Star
CALL NINE-ONE-ONE. OFFICER NEEDS ASSISTANCE.
In the movies, a bullet in the arm never seems to bother the good guys.
Maybe I wasn't a good guy.
Because it hurt like hell.

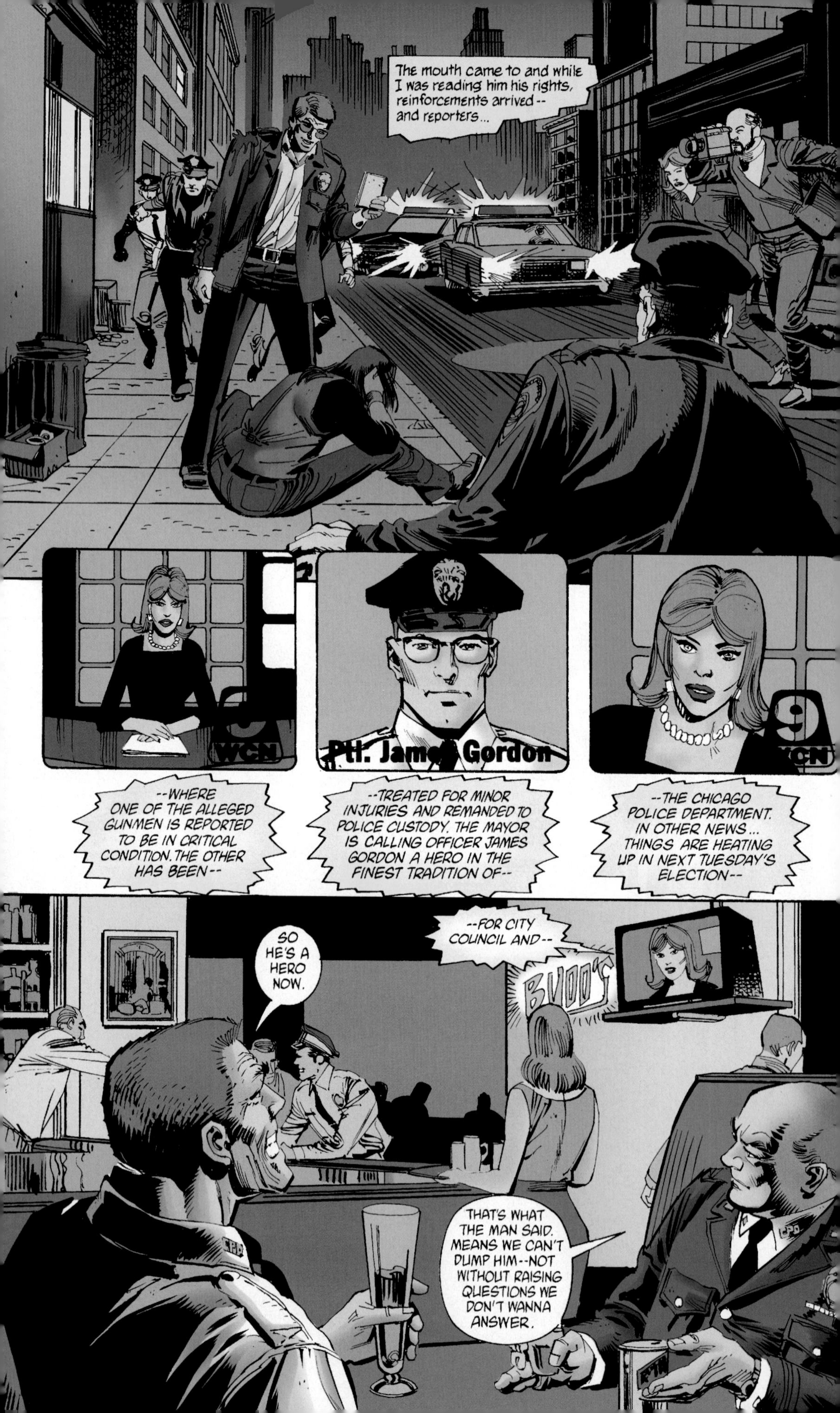

The mouth came to and while I was reading him his rights, reinforcements arrived -- and reporters...
Ptl. James Gordon
WCN
--WHERE ONE OF THE ALLEGED GUNMEN IS REPORTED TO BE IN CRITICAL CONDITION. THE OTHER HAS BEEN--
--TREATED FOR MINOR INJURIES AND REMANDED TO POLICE CUSTODY. THE MAYOR IS CALLING OFFICER JAMES GORDON A HERO IN THE FINEST TRADITION OF--
9
WCN
--THE CHICAGO POLICE DEPARTMENT. IN OTHER NEWS... THINGS ARE HEATING UP IN NEXT TUESDAY'S ELECTION--
SO HE'S A HERO NOW.
--FOR CITY COUNCIL AND--
THAT'S WHAT THE MAN SAID. MEANS WE CAN'T DUMP HIM--NOT WITHOUT RAISING QUESTIONS WE DON'T WANNA ANSWER.

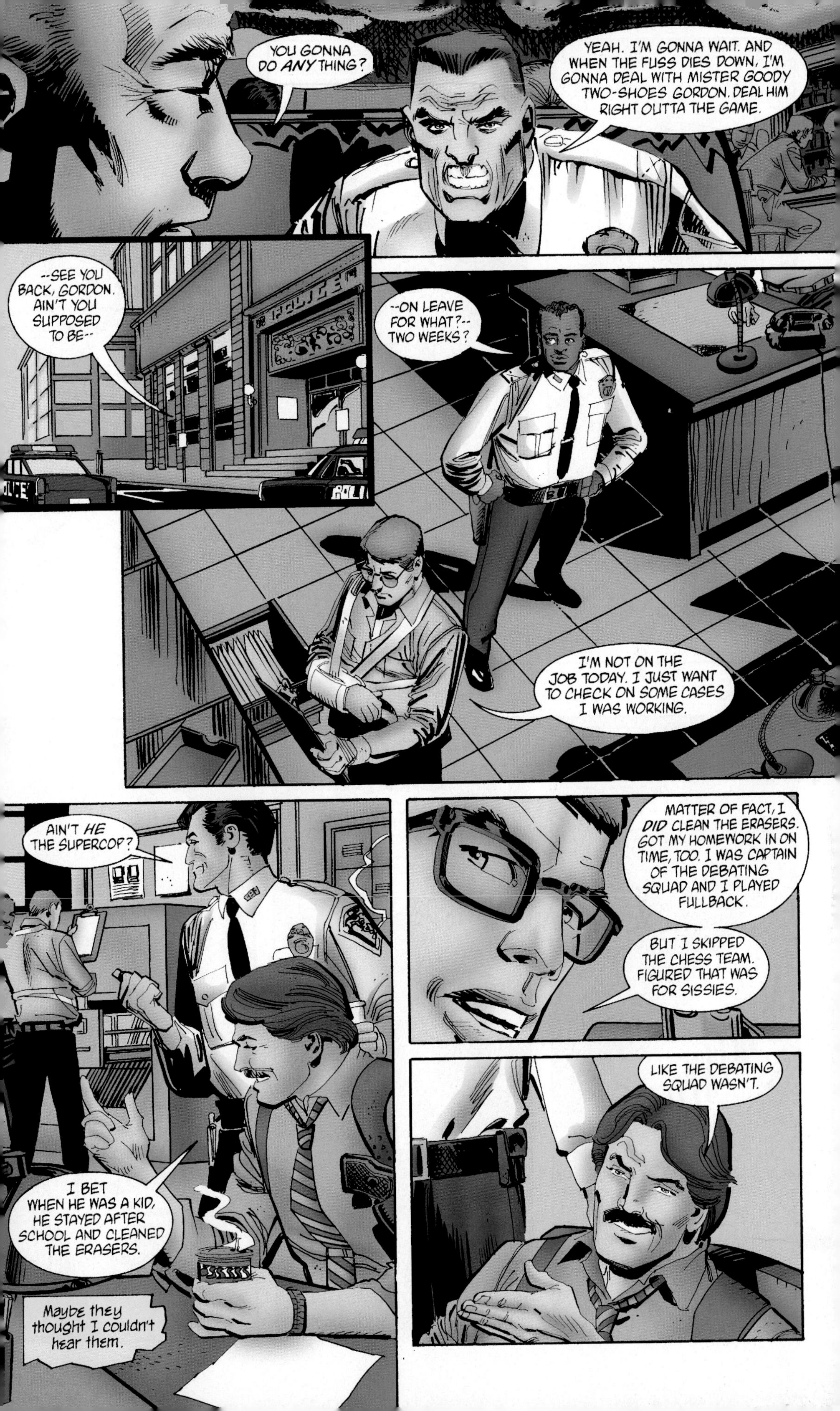
YOU GONNA DO ANY THING?
YEAH. I'M GONNA WAIT. AND WHEN THE FUSS DIES DOWN, I'M GONNA DEAL WITH MISTER GOODY TWO-SHOES GORDON. DEAL HIM RIGHT OUTTA THE GAME.
--SEE YOU BACK, GORDON. AIN'T YOU SUPPOSED TO BE--
--ON LEAVE FOR WHAT?-- TWO WEEKS?
I'M NOT ON THE JOB TODAY. I JUST WANT TO CHECK ON SOME CASES I WAS WORKING.
AIN'T HE THE SUPERCOP?
I BET WHEN HE WAS A KID, HE STAYED AFTER SCHOOL AND CLEANED THE ERASERS.
Maybe they thought I couldn't hear them.
MATTER OF FACT, I DID CLEAN THE ERASERS. GOT MY HOMEWORK IN ON TIME, TOO. I WAS CAPTAIN OF THE DEBATING SQUAD AND I PLAYED FULLBACK.
BUT I SKIPPED THE CHESS TEAM. FIGURED THAT WAS FOR SISSIES.
LIKE THE DEBATING SQUAD WASN'T.

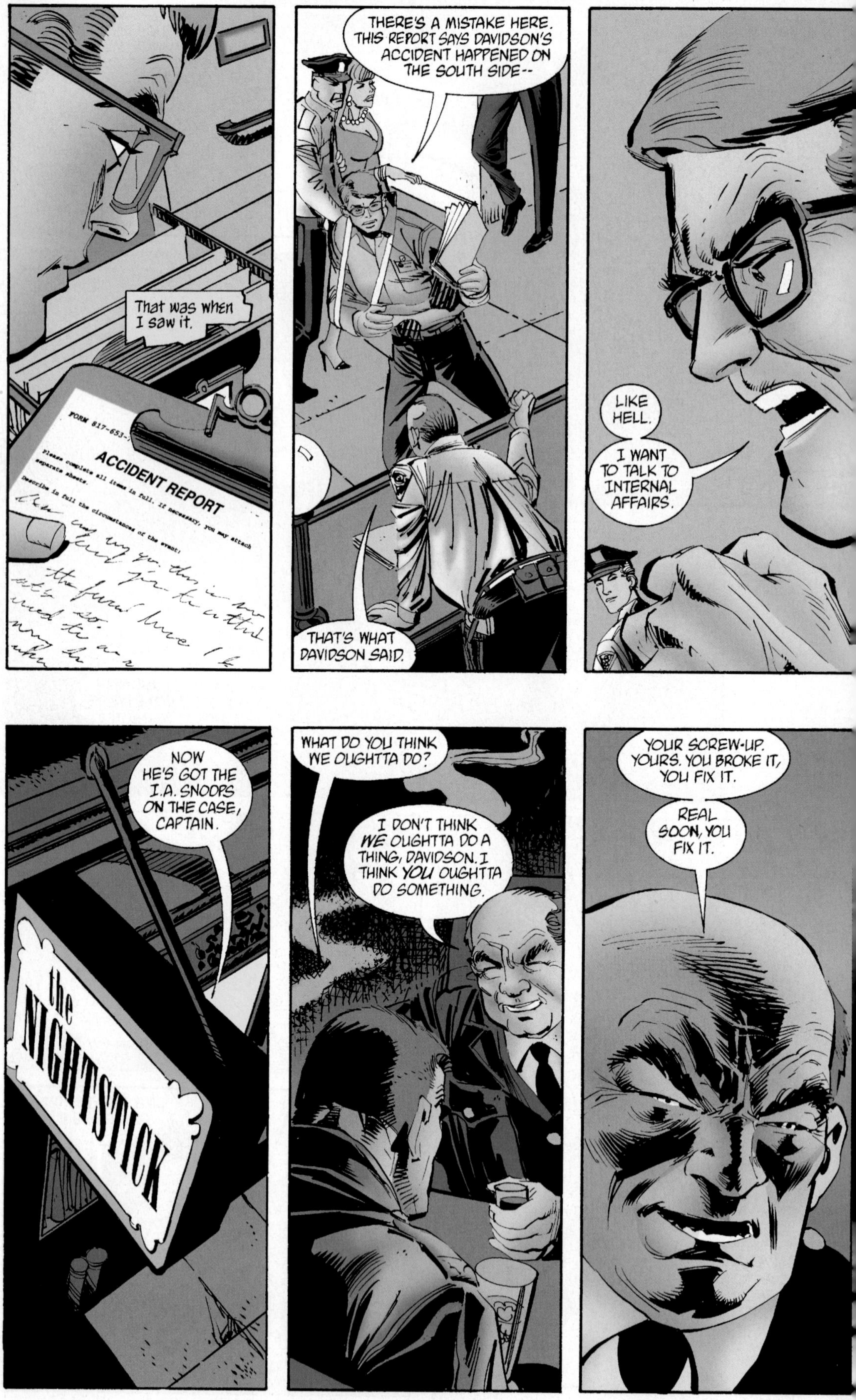
That was when I saw it.
ACCIDENT REPORT
THERE'S A MISTAKE HERE. THIS REPORT SAYS DAVIDSON'S ACCIDENT HAPPENED ON THE SOUTH SIDE--
THAT'S WHAT DAVIDSON SAID.
LIKE HELL.
I WANT TO TALK TO INTERNAL AFFAIRS.
NOW HE'S GOT THE I.A. SNOOPS ON THE CASE, CAPTAIN.
the NIGHTSTICK
WHAT DO YOU THINK WE OUGHTTA DO?
I DON'T THINK WE OUGHTTA DO A THING, DAVIDSON. I THINK YOU OUGHTTA DO SOMETHING.
YOUR SCREW-UP. YOURS. YOU BROKE IT, YOU FIX IT.
REAL SOON, YOU FIX IT.

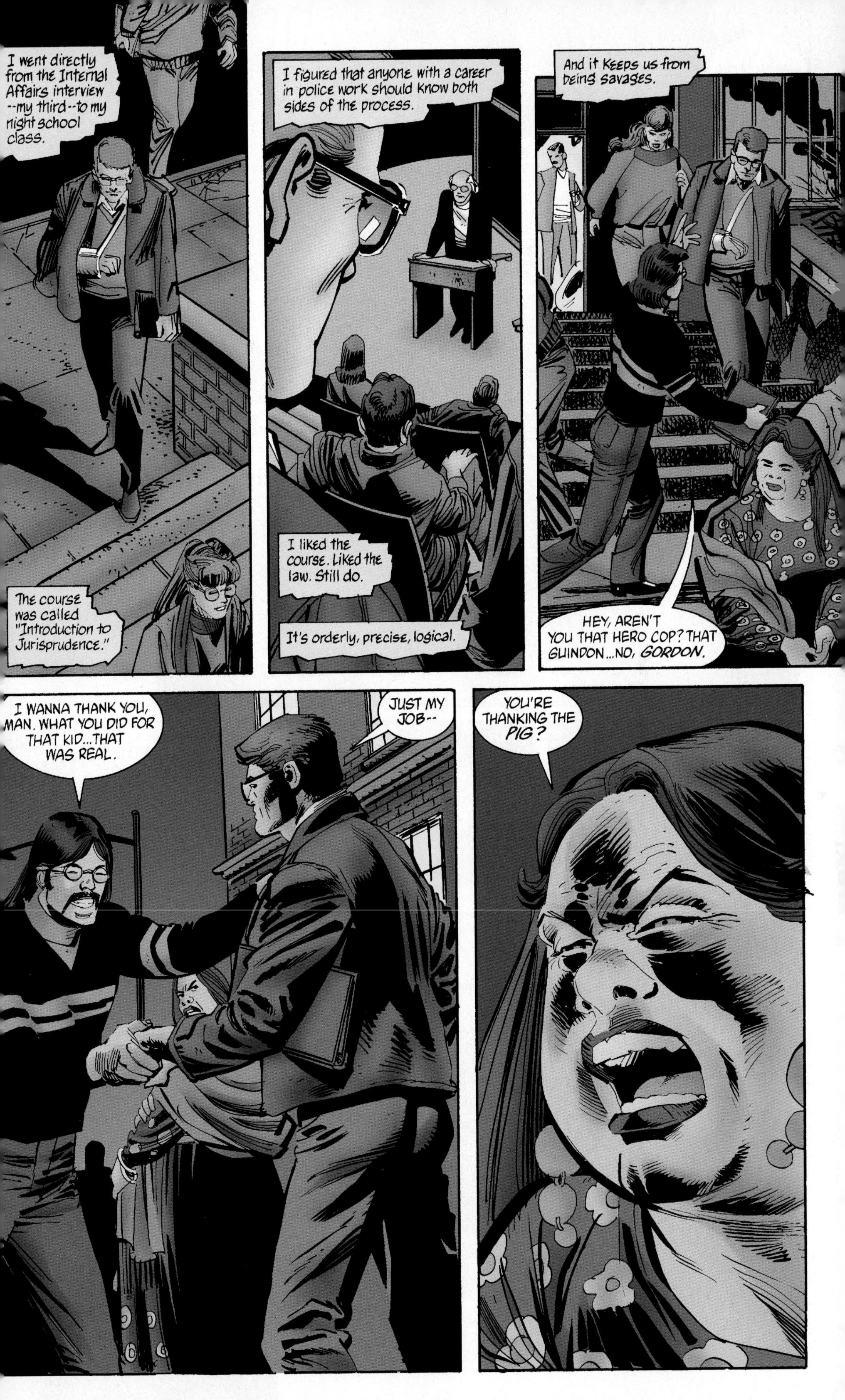

I went directly from the Internal Affairs interview --my third--to my night school class.
The course was called "Introduction to Jurisprudence."
I figured that anyone with a career in police work should know both sides of the process.
I liked the course. Liked the law. Still do.
It's orderly, precise, logical.
And it keeps us from being savages.
HEY, AREN'T YOU THAT HERO COP? THAT GUINDON...NO, GORDON.
I WANNA THANK YOU, MAN. WHAT YOU DID FOR THAT KID...THAT WAS REAL.
JUST MY JOB--
YOU'RE THANKING THE PIG?

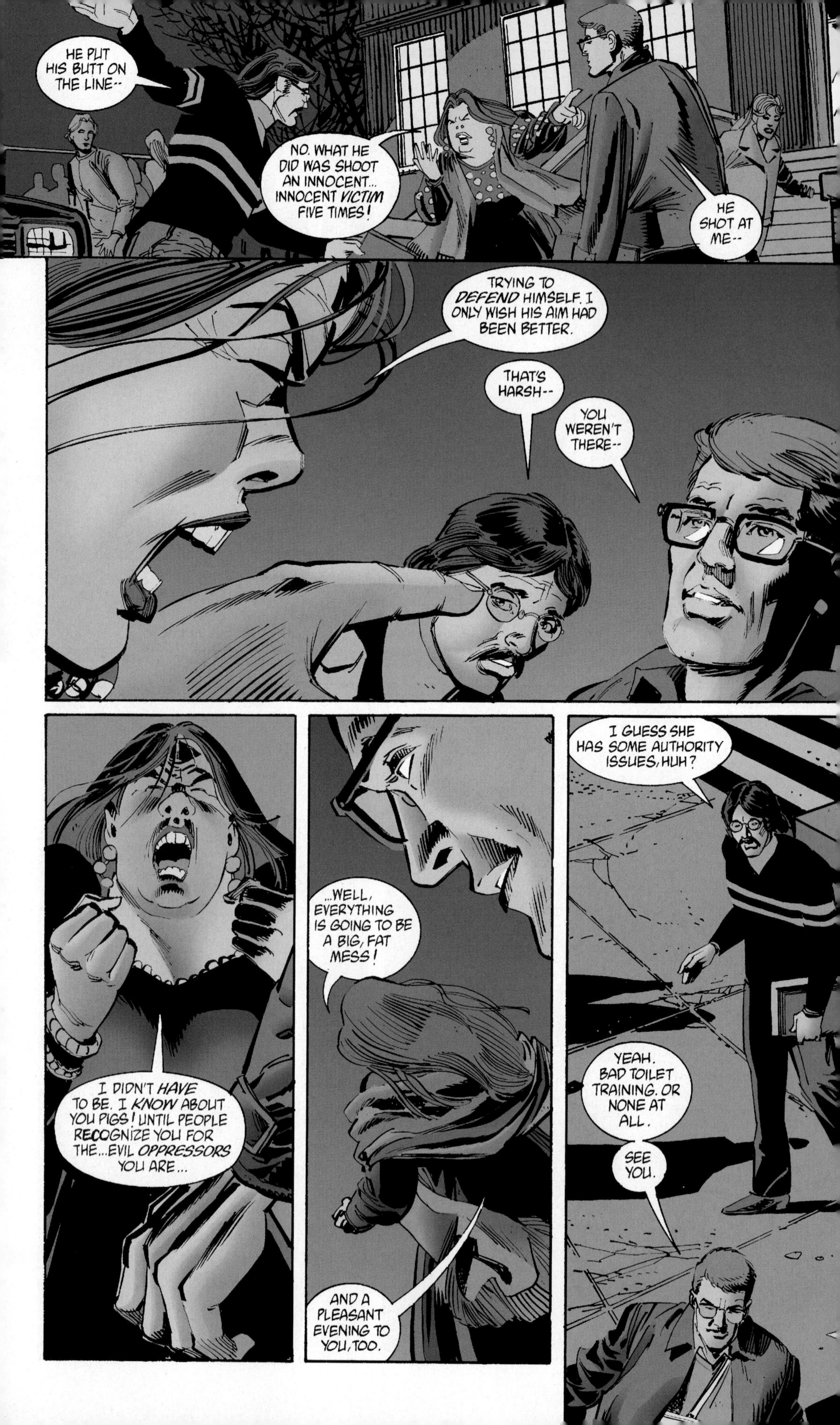
HE PUT HIS BUTT ON THE LINE--
NO. WHAT HE DID WAS SHOOT AN INNOCENT... INNOCENT *VICTIM* FIVE TIMES!
HE SHOT AT ME--
TRYING TO *DEFEND* HIMSELF. I ONLY WISH HIS AIM HAD BEEN BETTER.
THAT'S HARSH--
YOU WEREN'T THERE--
I DIDN'T *HAVE* TO BE. I *KNOW* ABOUT YOU PIGS! UNTIL PEOPLE RECOGNIZE YOU FOR THE...EVIL *OPPRESSORS* YOU ARE...
...WELL, EVERYTHING IS GOING TO BE A BIG, FAT MESS!
AND A PLEASANT EVENING TO YOU, TOO.
I GUESS SHE HAS SOME AUTHORITY ISSUES, HUH?
YEAH. BAD TOILET TRAINING. OR NONE AT ALL.
SEE YOU.

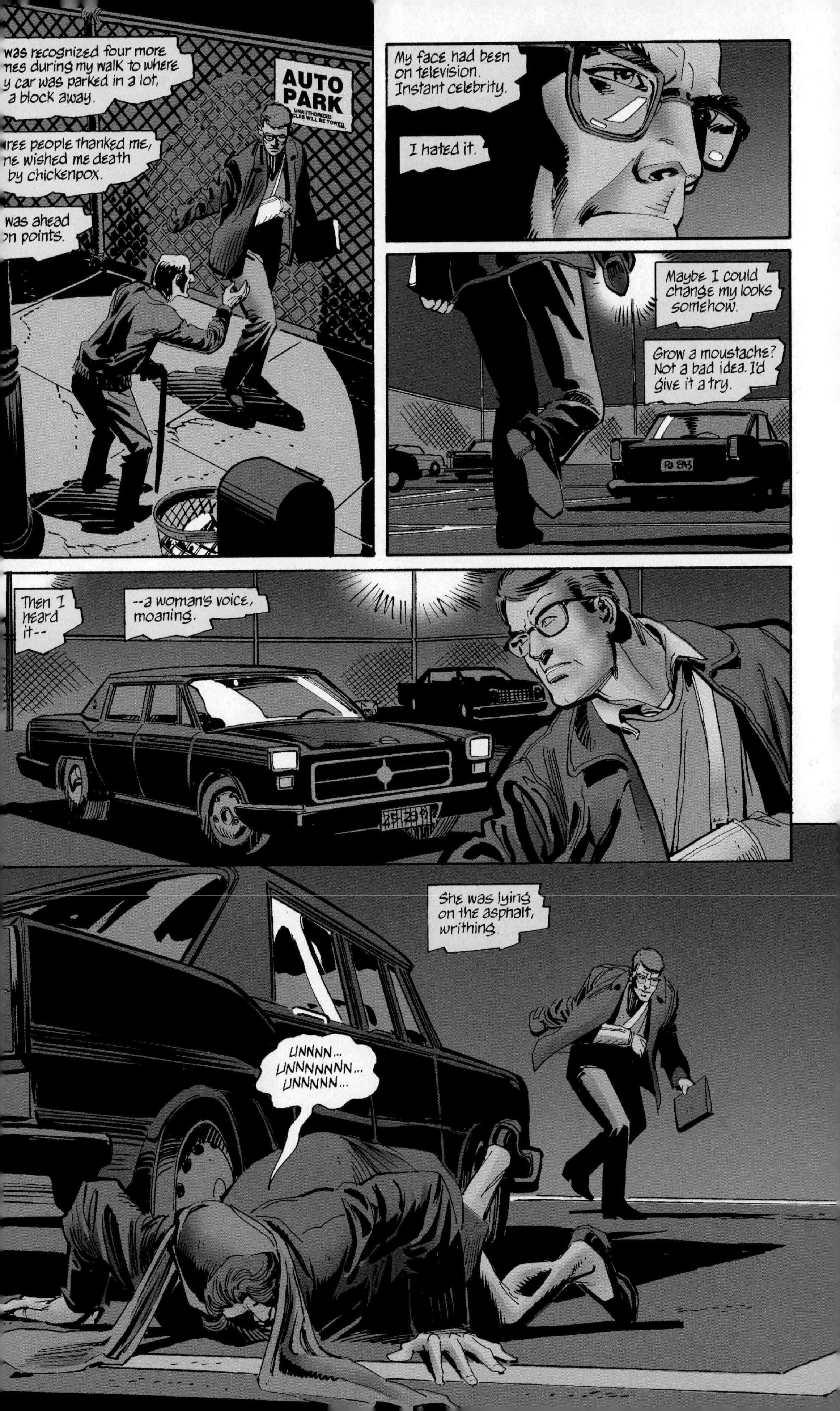
was recognized four more
nes during my walk to where
y car was parked in a lot,
a block away.
AUTO
PARK
UNAUTHORIZED
CLES WILL BE TOWED
ree people thanked me,
ne wished me death
by chickenpox.
was ahead
on points.
My face had been
on television.
Instant celebrity.
I hated it.
Maybe I could
change my looks
somehow.
Grow a moustache?
Not a bad idea. I'd
give it a try.
Then I
heard
it--
--a woman's voice,
moaning.
She was lying
on the asphalt,
writhing.
UNNNN...
UNNNNNNN...
UNNNNN...

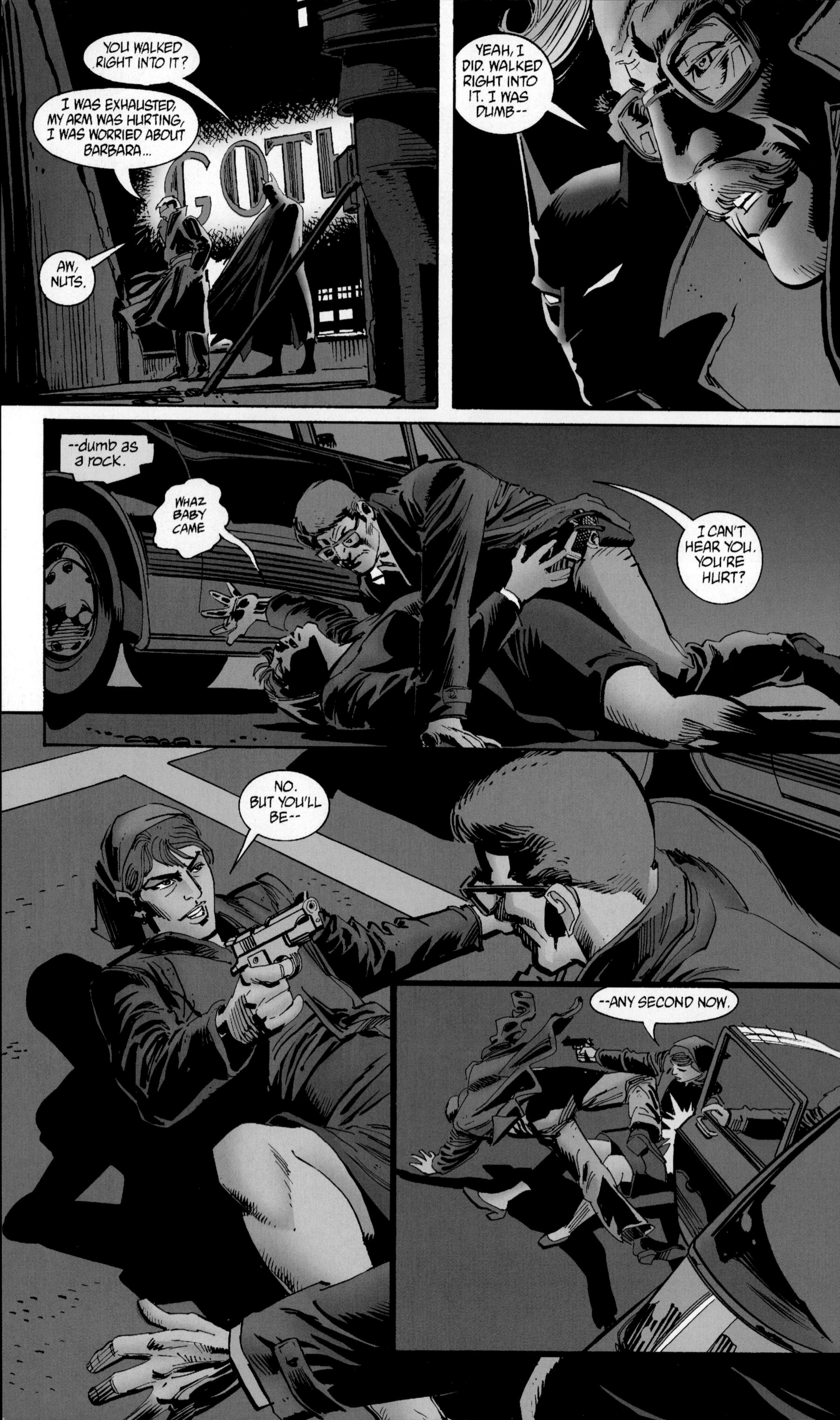
YOU WALKED RIGHT INTO IT?
I WAS EXHAUSTED, MY ARM WAS HURTING, I WAS WORRIED ABOUT BARBARA...
AW, NUTS.
GOTH
YEAH, I DID. WALKED RIGHT INTO IT. I WAS DUMB--
--dumb as a rock.
WHAZ BABY CAME
I CAN'T HEAR YOU. YOU'RE HURT?
NO. BUT YOU'LL BE--
--ANY SECOND NOW.

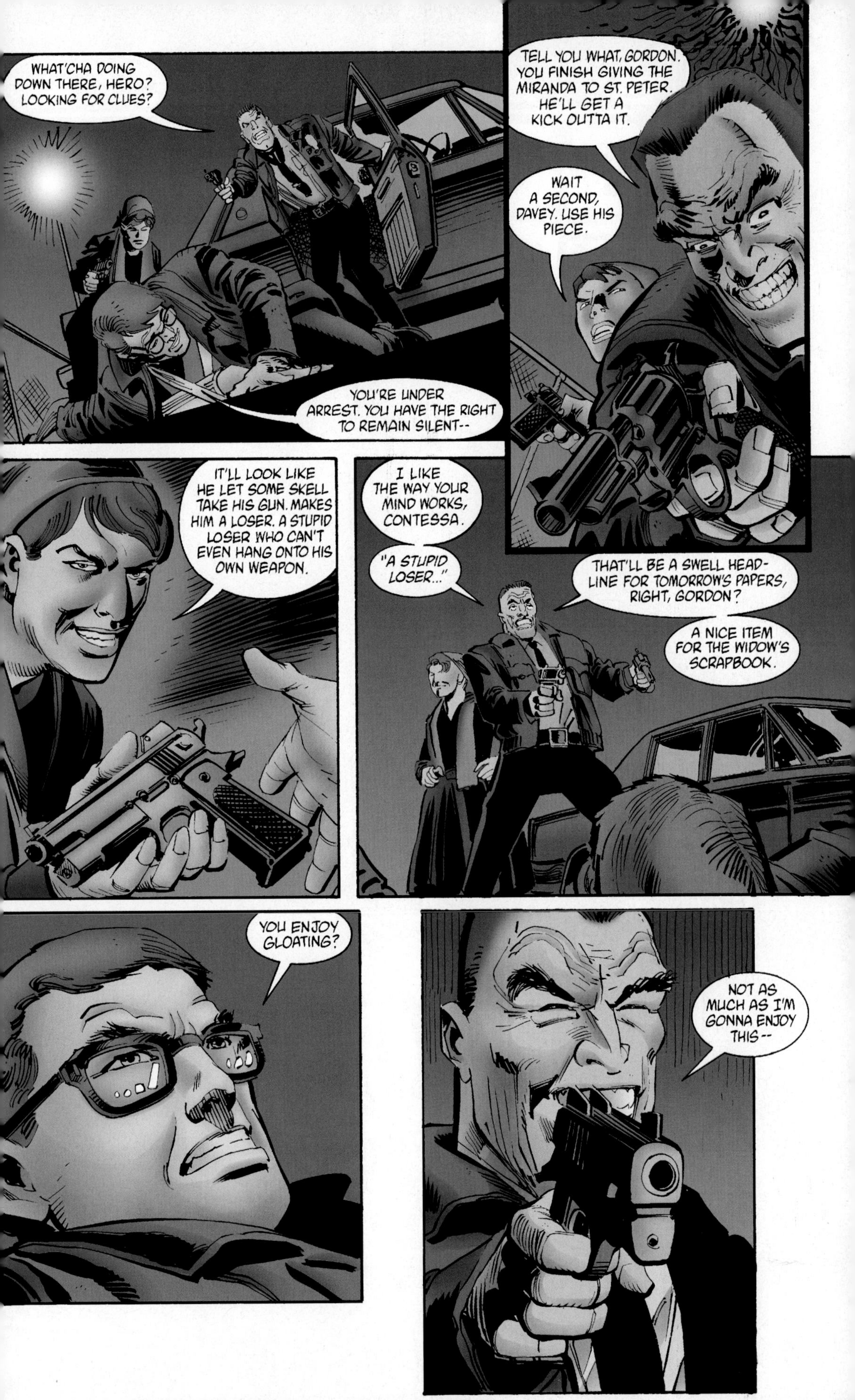
WHAT'CHA DOING DOWN THERE, HERO? LOOKING FOR CLUES?
YOU'RE UNDER ARREST. YOU HAVE THE RIGHT TO REMAIN SILENT--
TELL YOU WHAT, GORDON. YOU FINISH GIVING THE MIRANDA TO ST. PETER. HE'LL GET A KICK OUTTA IT.
WAIT A SECOND, DAVEY. USE HIS PIECE.
IT'LL LOOK LIKE HE LET SOME SKELL TAKE HIS GUN. MAKES HIM A LOSER. A STUPID LOSER WHO CAN'T EVEN HANG ONTO HIS OWN WEAPON.
I LIKE THE WAY YOUR MIND WORKS, CONTESSA.
"A STUPID LOSER..."
THAT'LL BE A SWELL HEAD-LINE FOR TOMORROW'S PAPERS, RIGHT, GORDON?
A NICE ITEM FOR THE WIDOW'S SCRAPBOOK.
YOU ENJOY GLOATING?
NOT AS MUCH AS I'M GONNA ENJOY THIS--

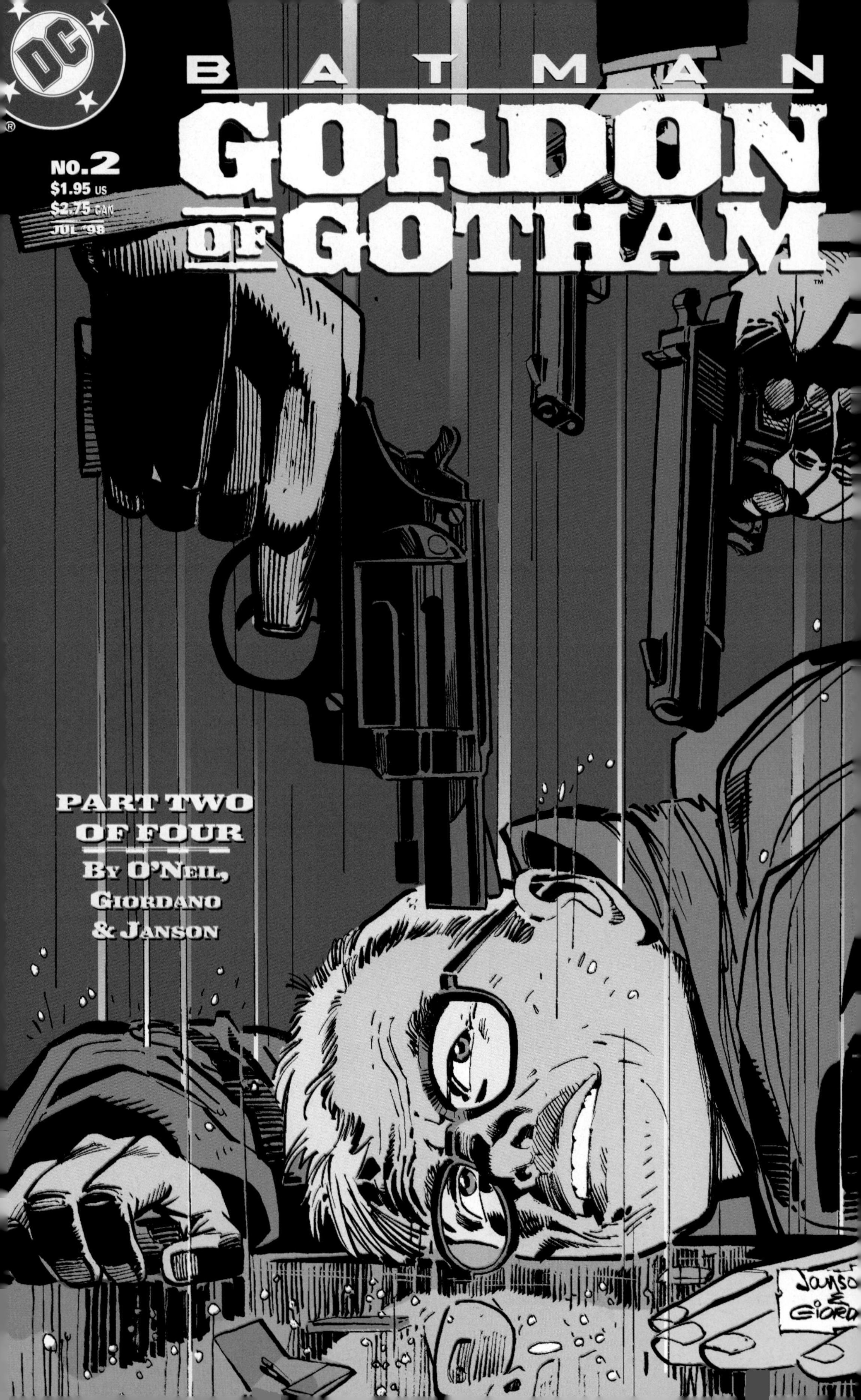
BATMAN
GORDON OF GOTHAM
NO.2
$1.95 US
$2.75 CAN
JUL '98
PART TWO OF FOUR
BY O'NEIL, GIORDANO & JANSON

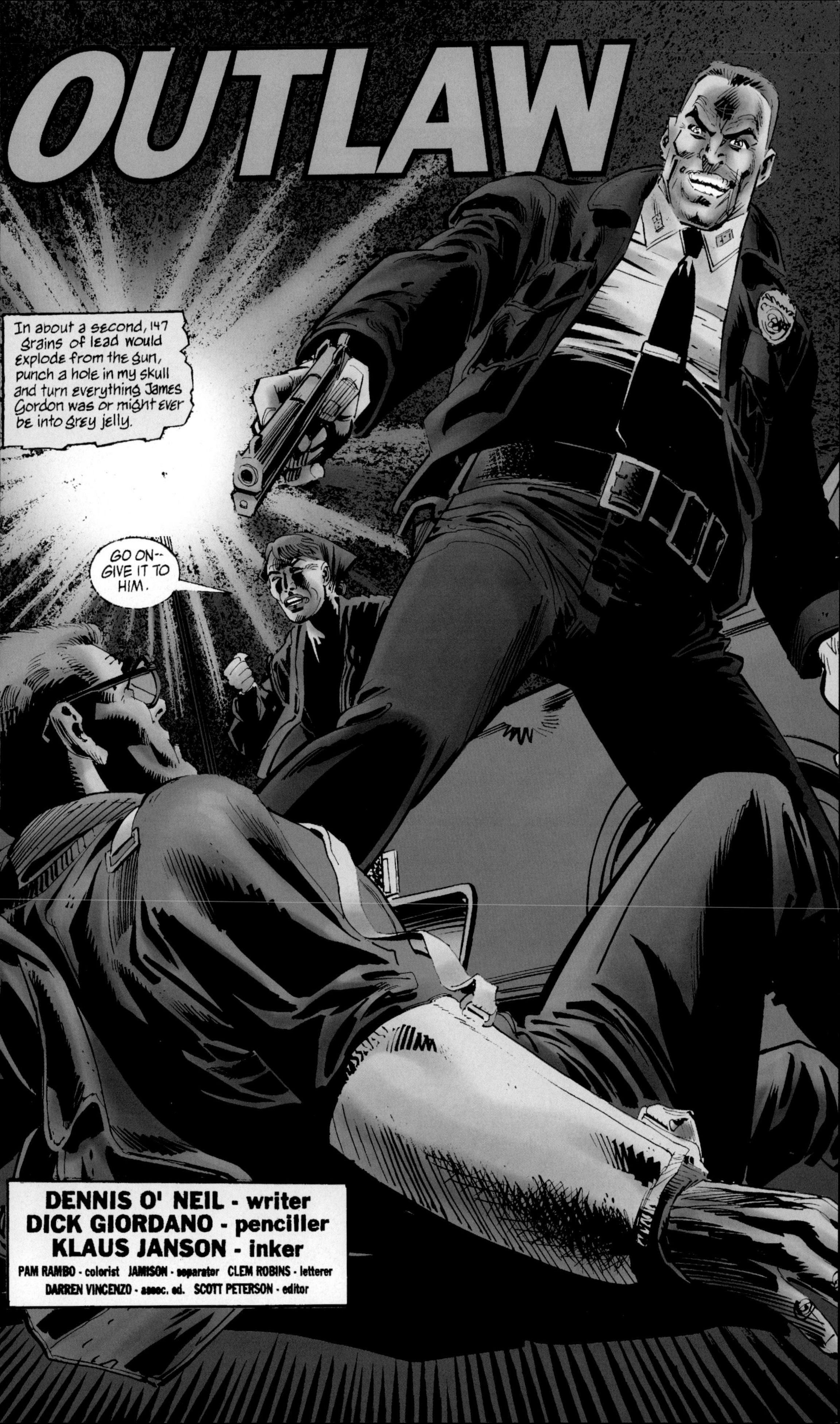

OUTLAW
In about a second, 147 grains of lead would explode from the gun, punch a hole in my skull and turn everything James Gordon was or might ever be into grey jelly.
GO ON-- GIVE IT TO HIM.
DENNIS O' NEIL - writer
DICK GIORDANO - penciller
KLAUS JANSON - inker
PAM RAMBO - colorist JAMISON - separator CLEM ROBINS - letterer
DARREN VINCENZO - assoc. ed. SCOTT PETERSON - editor

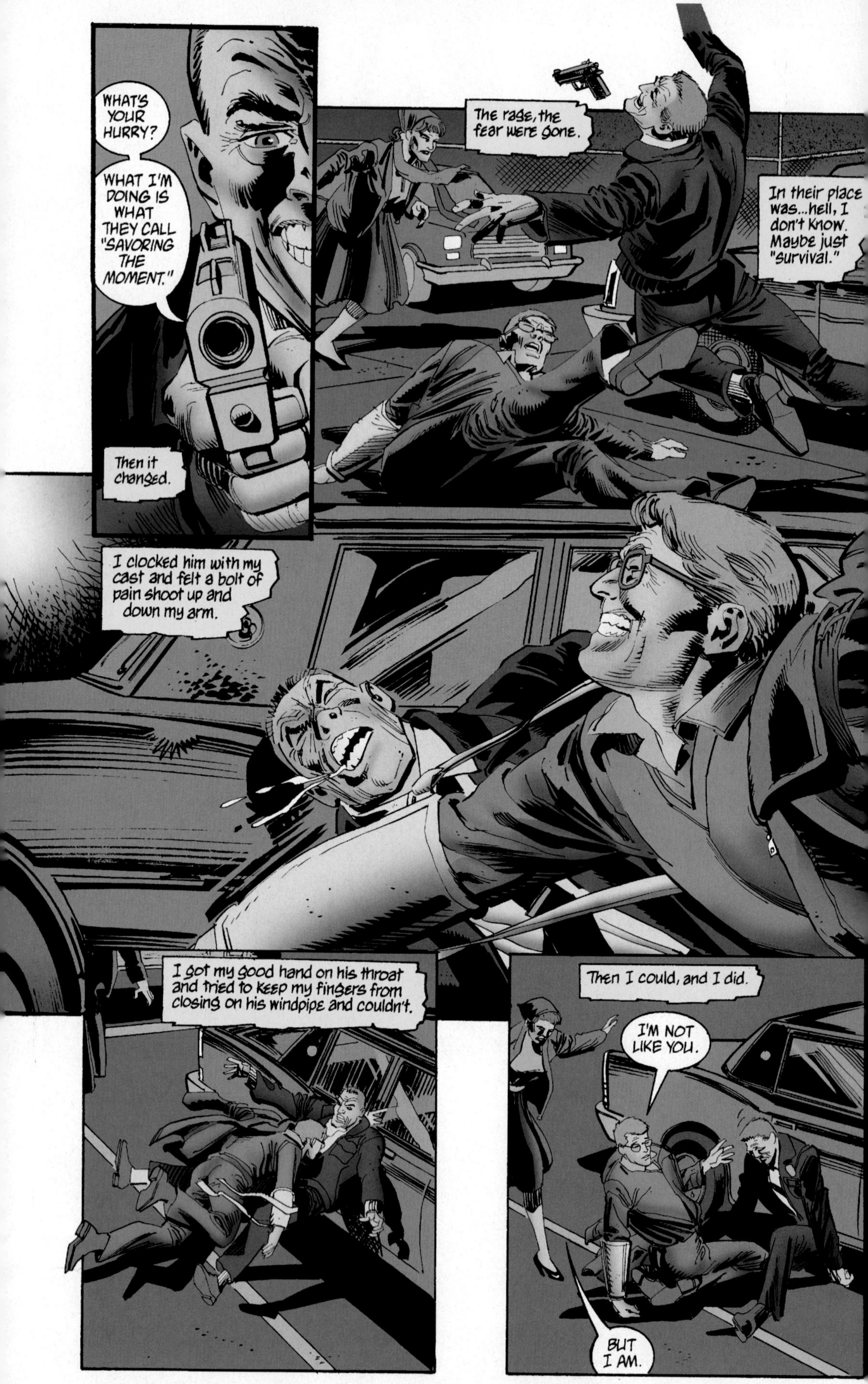
WHAT'S YOUR HURRY?
WHAT I'M DOING IS WHAT THEY CALL "SAVORING THE MOMENT."
Then it changed.
The rage, the fear were gone.
In their place was...hell, I don't know. Maybe just "survival."
I clocked him with my cast and felt a bolt of pain shoot up and down my arm.
I got my good hand on his throat and tried to keep my fingers from closing on his windpipe and couldn't.
Then I could, and I did.
I'M NOT LIKE YOU.
BUT I AM.

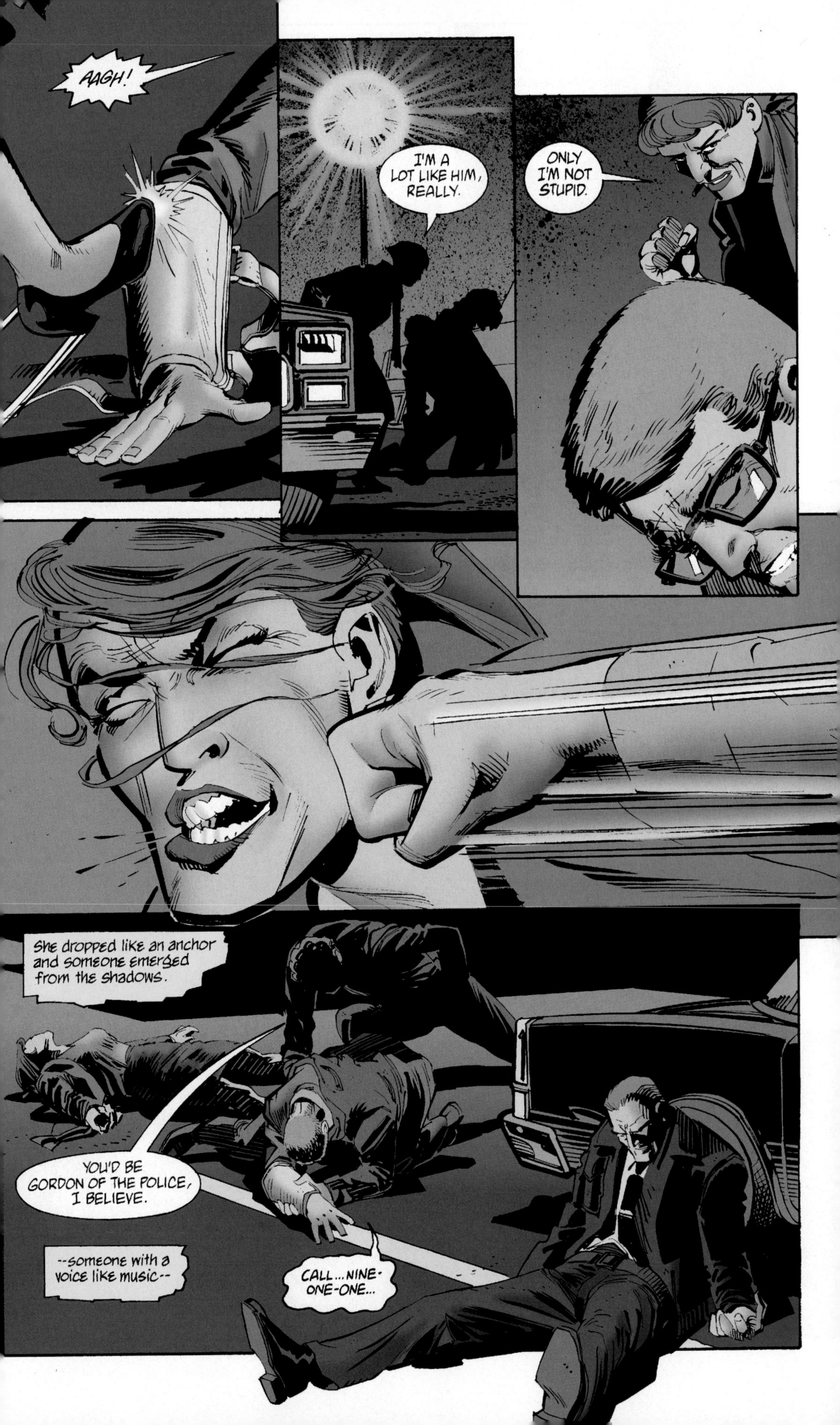
AAGH!
I'M A LOT LIKE HIM, REALLY.
ONLY I'M NOT STUPID.
She dropped like an anchor and someone emerged from the shadows.
YOU'D BE GORDON OF THE POLICE, I BELIEVE.
--someone with a voice like music--
CALL... NINE-ONE-ONE...

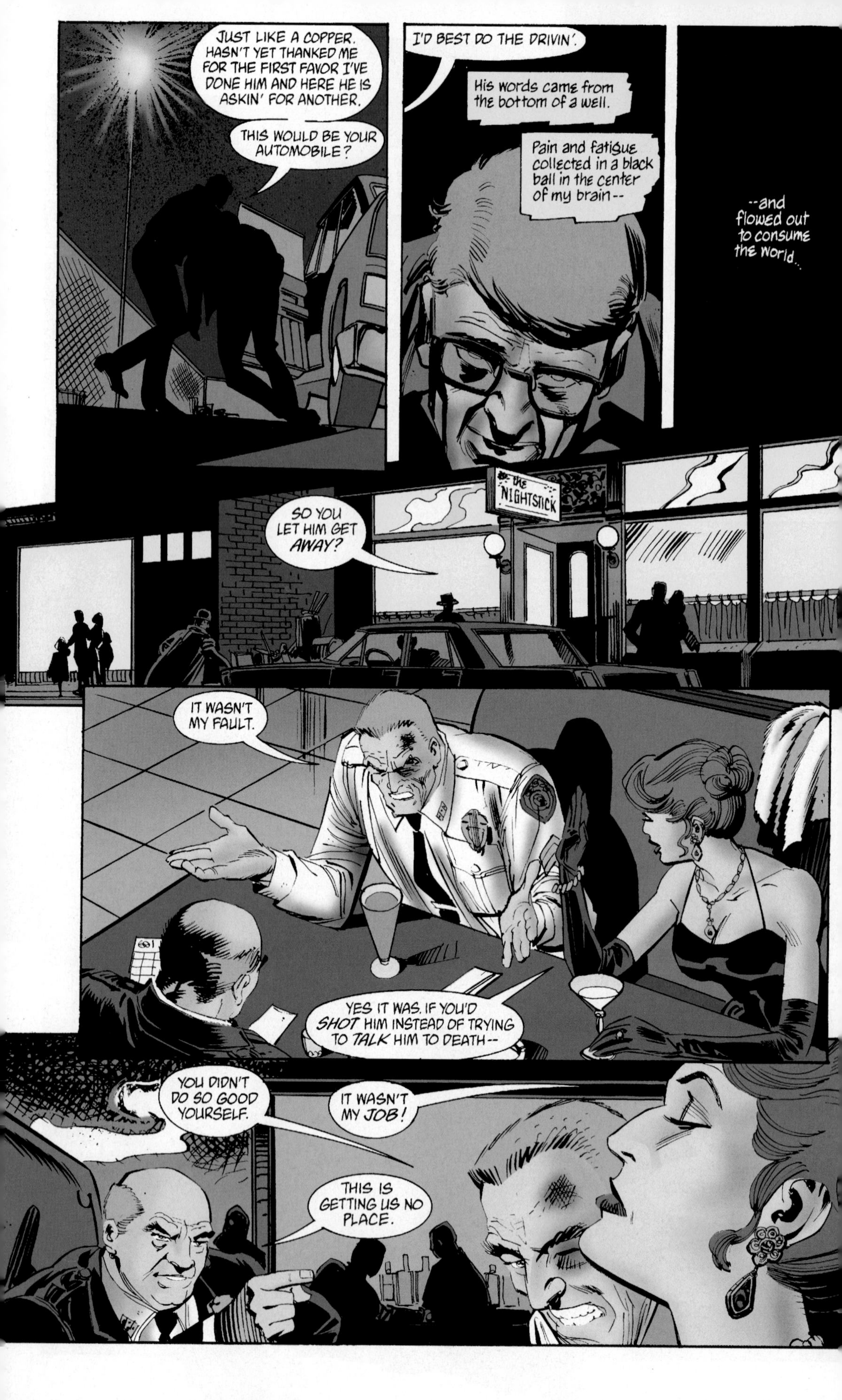
JUST LIKE A COPPER. HASN'T YET THANKED ME FOR THE FIRST FAVOR I'VE DONE HIM AND HERE HE IS ASKIN' FOR ANOTHER.
THIS WOULD BE YOUR AUTOMOBILE?
I'D BEST DO THE DRIVIN'.
His words came from the bottom of a well.
Pain and fatigue collected in a black ball in the center of my brain--
--and flowed out to consume the world...
the NIGHTSTICK
SO YOU LET HIM GET AWAY?
IT WASN'T MY FAULT.
YES IT WAS. IF YOU'D SHOT HIM INSTEAD OF TRYING TO TALK HIM TO DEATH--
YOU DIDN'T DO SO GOOD YOURSELF.
IT WASN'T MY JOB!
THIS IS GETTING US NO PLACE.

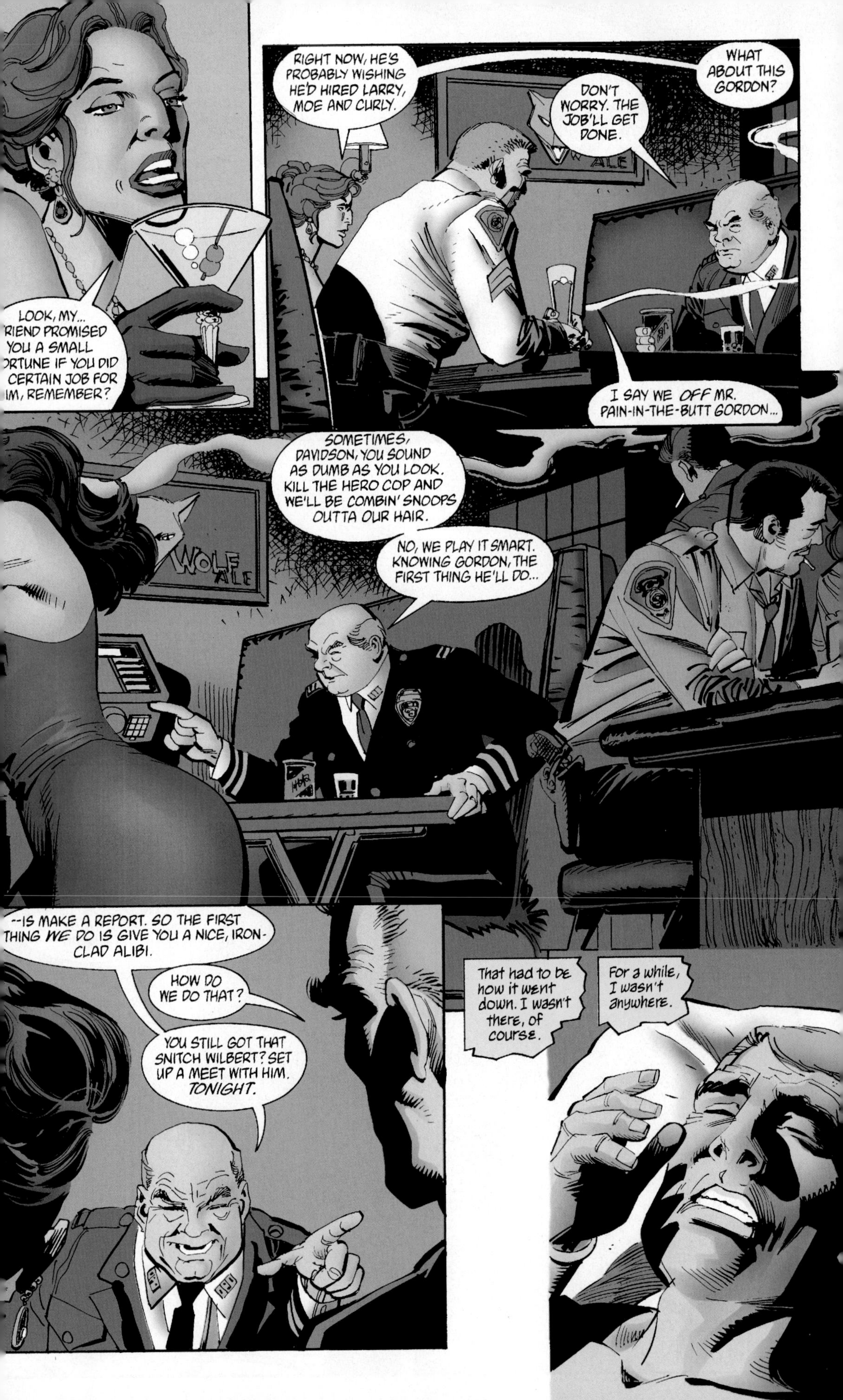
LOOK, MY... RIEND PROMISED YOU A SMALL ORTUNE IF YOU DID CERTAIN JOB FOR IM, REMEMBER?
RIGHT NOW, HE'S PROBABLY WISHING HE'D HIRED LARRY, MOE AND CURLY.
WHAT ABOUT THIS GORDON?
DON'T WORRY. THE JOB'LL GET DONE.
I SAY WE OFF MR. PAIN-IN-THE-BUTT GORDON...
SOMETIMES, DAVIDSON, YOU SOUND AS DUMB AS YOU LOOK. KILL THE HERO COP AND WE'LL BE COMBIN' SNOOPS OUTTA OUR HAIR.
NO, WE PLAY IT SMART. KNOWING GORDON, THE FIRST THING HE'LL DO...
WOLF ALE
--IS MAKE A REPORT. SO THE FIRST THING WE DO IS GIVE YOU A NICE, IRON-CLAD ALIBI.
HOW DO WE DO THAT?
YOU STILL GOT THAT SNITCH WILBERT? SET UP A MEET WITH HIM. TONIGHT.
That had to be how it went down. I wasn't there, of course.
For a while, I wasn't anywhere.

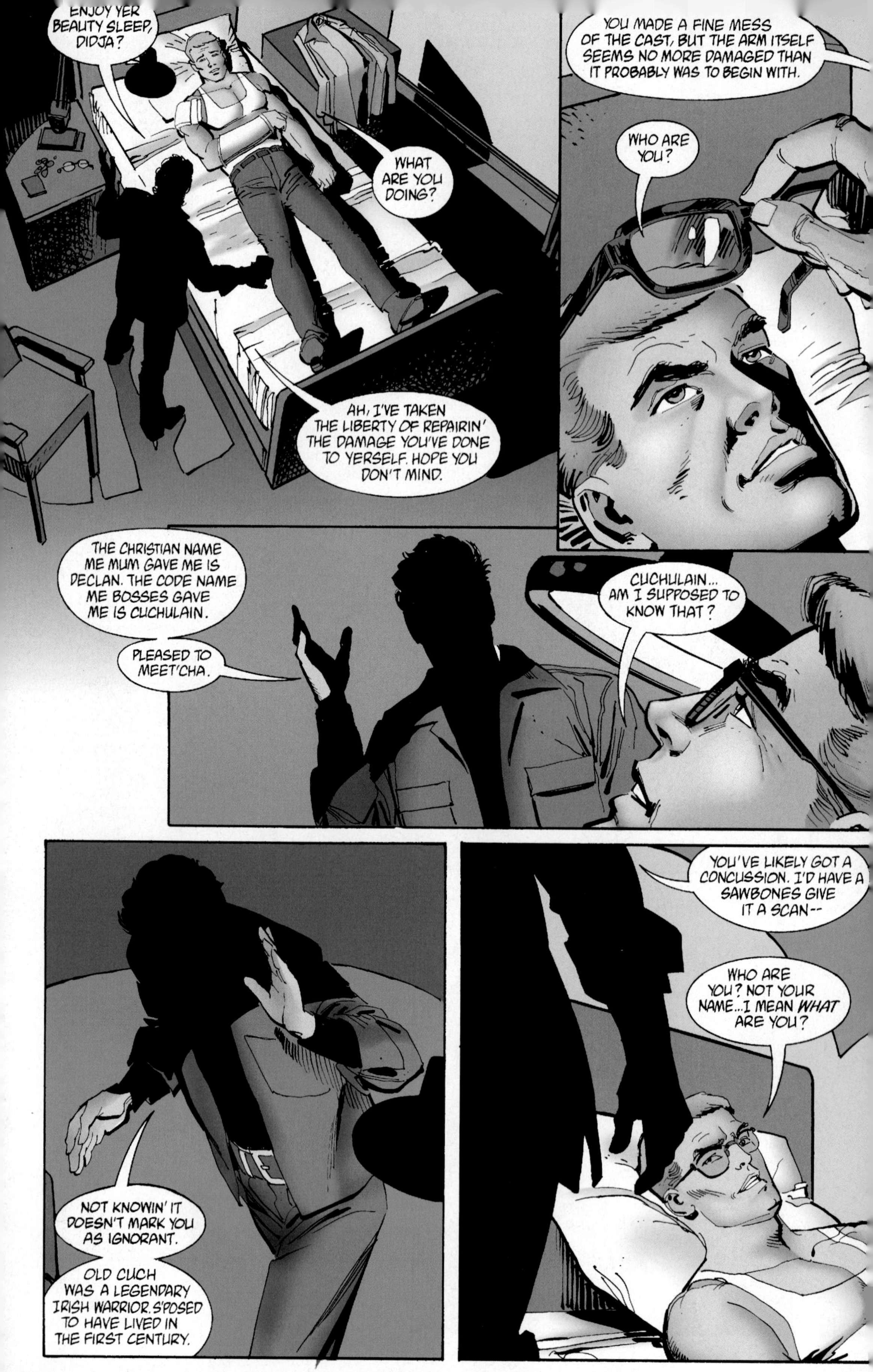
ENJOY YER BEAUTY SLEEP, DIDJA?
WHAT ARE YOU DOING?
AH, I'VE TAKEN THE LIBERTY OF REPAIRIN' THE DAMAGE YOU'VE DONE TO YERSELF. HOPE YOU DON'T MIND.
YOU MADE A FINE MESS OF THE CAST, BUT THE ARM ITSELF SEEMS NO MORE DAMAGED THAN IT PROBABLY WAS TO BEGIN WITH.
WHO ARE YOU?
THE CHRISTIAN NAME ME MUM GAVE ME IS DECLAN. THE CODE NAME ME BOSSES GAVE ME IS CUCHULAIN.
PLEASED TO MEET'CHA.
CUCHULAIN... AM I SUPPOSED TO KNOW THAT?
NOT KNOWIN' IT DOESN'T MARK YOU AS IGNORANT.
OLD CUCH WAS A LEGENDARY IRISH WARRIOR. S'POSED TO HAVE LIVED IN THE FIRST CENTURY.
YOU'VE LIKELY GOT A CONCUSSION. I'D HAVE A SAWBONES GIVE IT A SCAN--
WHO ARE YOU? NOT YOUR NAME...I MEAN *WHAT* ARE YOU?

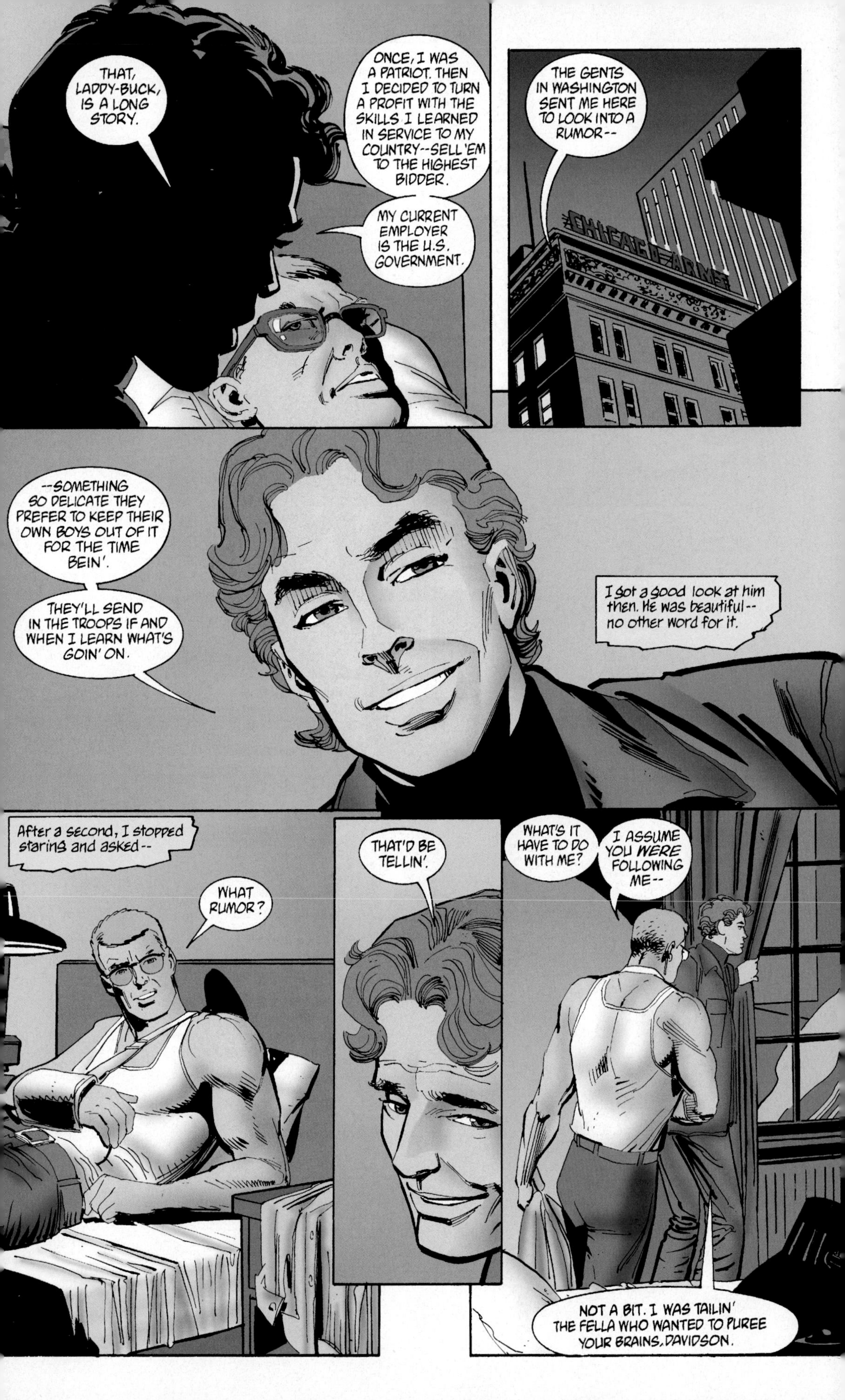
THAT, LADDY-BUCK, IS A LONG STORY.
ONCE, I WAS A PATRIOT. THEN I DECIDED TO TURN A PROFIT WITH THE SKILLS I LEARNED IN SERVICE TO MY COUNTRY--SELL 'EM TO THE HIGHEST BIDDER.
MY CURRENT EMPLOYER IS THE U.S. GOVERNMENT.
THE GENTS IN WASHINGTON SENT ME HERE TO LOOK INTO A RUMOR--
--SOMETHING SO DELICATE THEY PREFER TO KEEP THEIR OWN BOYS OUT OF IT FOR THE TIME BEIN'.
THEY'LL SEND IN THE TROOPS IF AND WHEN I LEARN WHAT'S GOIN' ON.
I got a good look at him then. He was beautiful--no other word for it.
After a second, I stopped staring and asked--
WHAT RUMOR?
THAT'D BE TELLIN'.
WHAT'S IT HAVE TO DO WITH ME?
I ASSUME YOU *WERE* FOLLOWING ME--
NOT A BIT. I WAS TAILIN' THE FELLA WHO WANTED TO PUREE YOUR BRAINS, DAVIDSON.

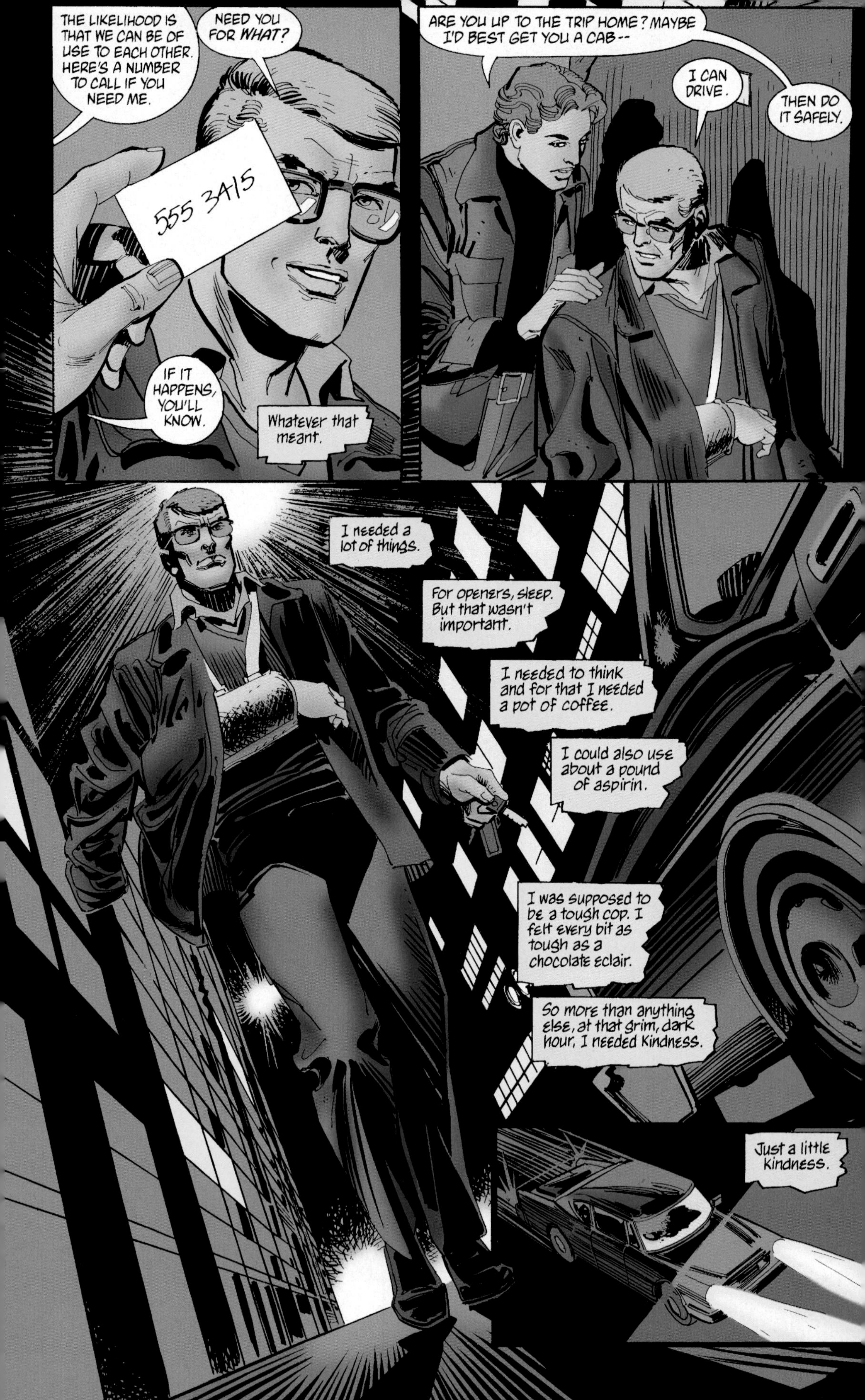
THE LIKELIHOOD IS THAT WE CAN BE OF USE TO EACH OTHER. HERE'S A NUMBER TO CALL IF YOU NEED ME.
NEED YOU FOR *WHAT?*
555 3415
IF IT HAPPENS, YOU'LL KNOW.
Whatever that meant.
ARE YOU UP TO THE TRIP HOME? MAYBE I'D BEST GET YOU A CAB--
I CAN DRIVE.
THEN DO IT SAFELY.
I needed a lot of things.
For openers, sleep. But that wasn't important.
I needed to think and for that I needed a pot of coffee.
I could also use about a pound of aspirin.
I was supposed to be a tough cop. I felt every bit as tough as a chocolate eclair.
So more than anything else, at that grim, dark hour, I needed Kindness.
Just a little Kindness.

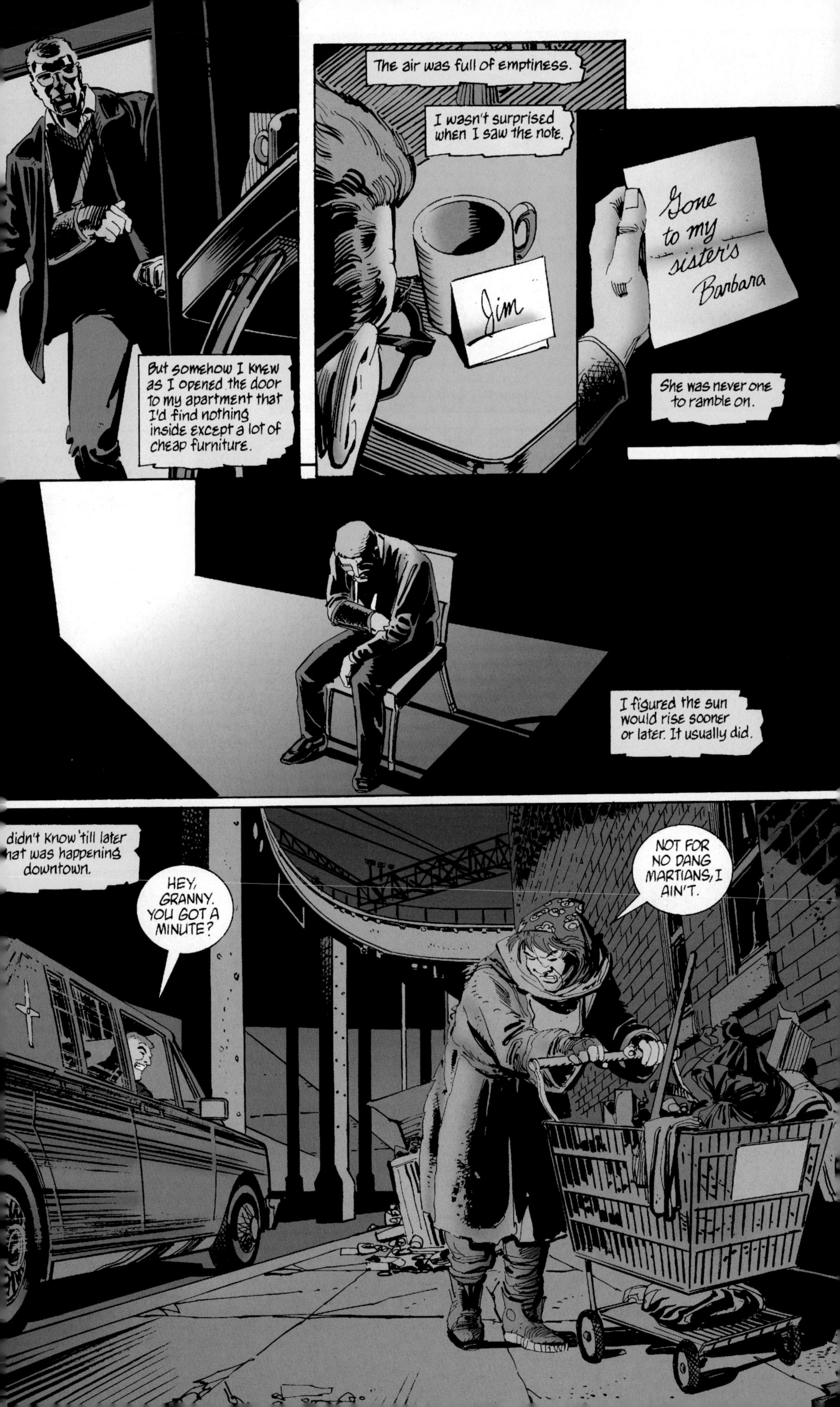

But somehow I knew as I opened the door to my apartment that I'd find nothing inside except a lot of cheap furniture.
The air was full of emptiness.
I wasn't surprised when I saw the note.
Jim
Gone to my sister's Barbara
She was never one to ramble on.
I figured the sun would rise sooner or later. It usually did.
didn't know 'till later
hat was happening
downtown.
HEY, GRANNY. YOU GOT A MINUTE?
NOT FOR NO DANG MARTIANS, I AIN'T.

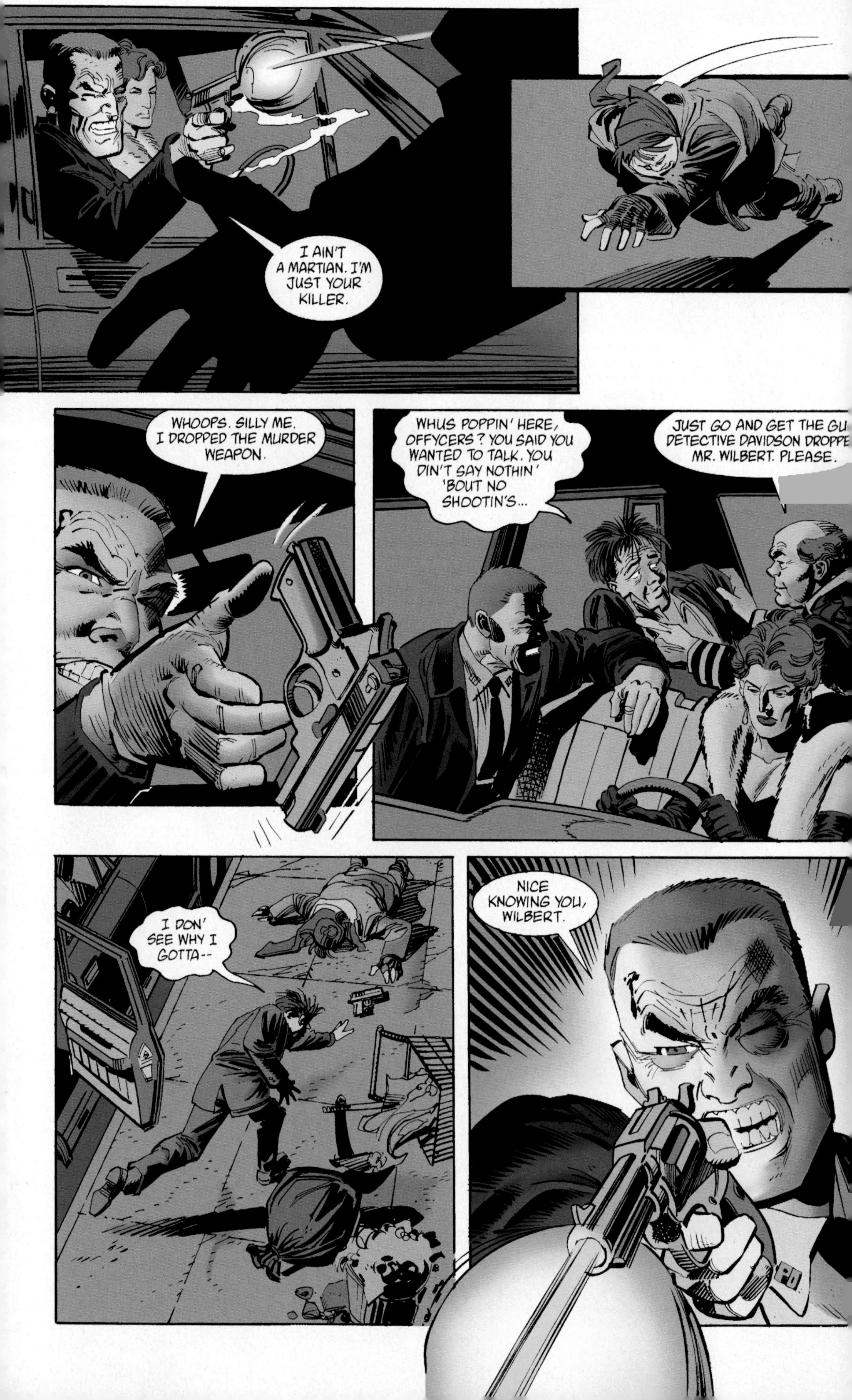

I AIN'T A MARTIAN. I'M JUST YOUR KILLER.
WHOOPS. SILLY ME. I DROPPED THE MURDER WEAPON.
WHUS POPPIN' HERE, OFFYCERS? YOU SAID YOU WANTED TO TALK. YOU DIN'T SAY NOTHIN' 'BOUT NO SHOOTIN'S...
JUST GO AND GET THE GU
DETECTIVE DAVIDSON DROPPE
MR. WILBERT. PLEASE.
I DON' SEE WHY I GOTTA--
NICE KNOWING YOU, WILBERT.

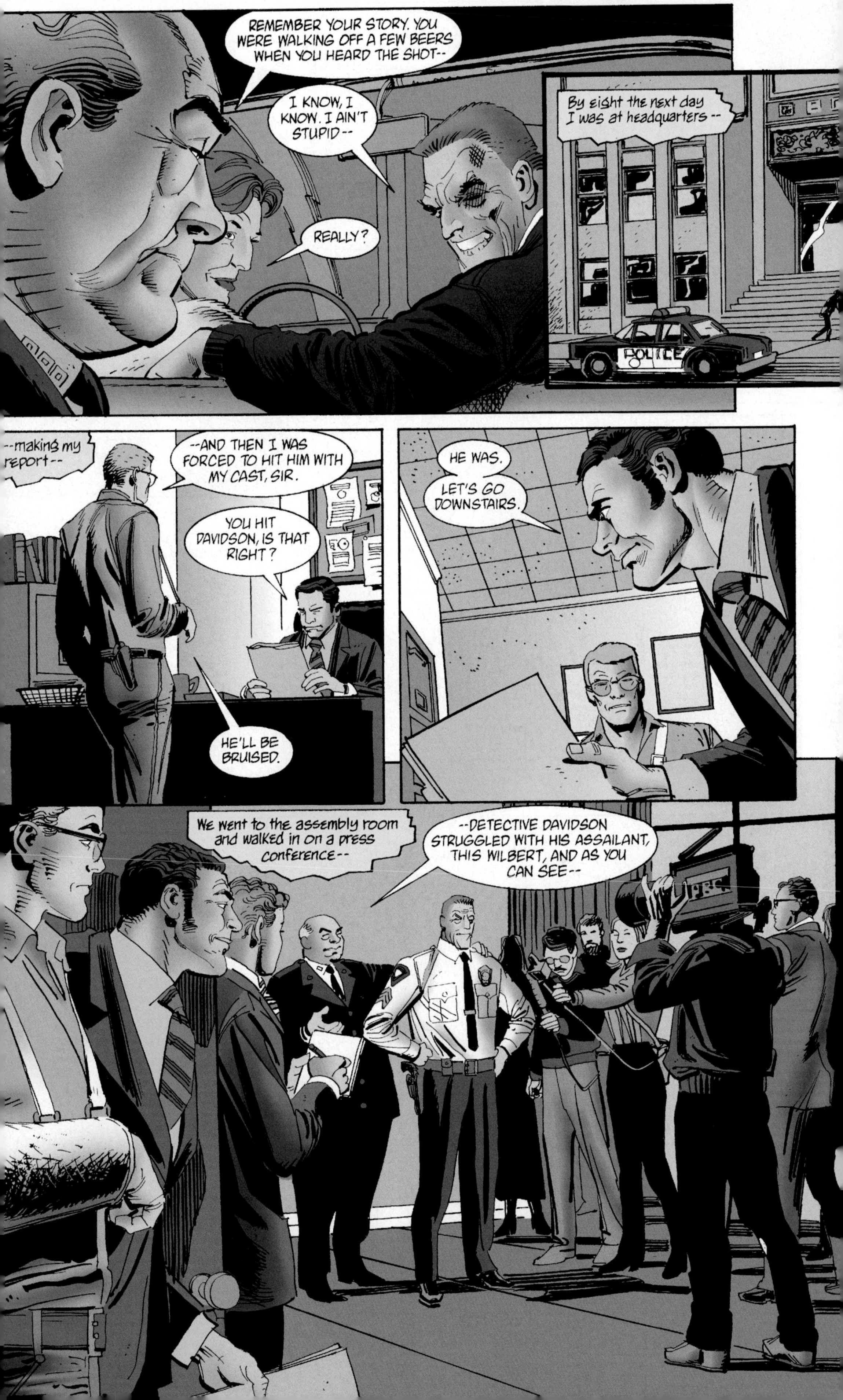
REMEMBER YOUR STORY. YOU WERE WALKING OFF A FEW BEERS WHEN YOU HEARD THE SHOT--
I KNOW, I KNOW. I AIN'T STUPID--
REALLY?
By eight the next day I was at headquarters--
POLICE
--making my report--
--AND THEN I WAS FORCED TO HIT HIM WITH MY CAST, SIR.
YOU HIT DAVIDSON, IS THAT RIGHT?
HE'LL BE BRUISED.
HE WAS.
LET'S GO DOWNSTAIRS.
We went to the assembly room and walked in on a press conference--
--DETECTIVE DAVIDSON STRUGGLED WITH HIS ASSAILANT, THIS WILBERT, AND AS YOU CAN SEE--

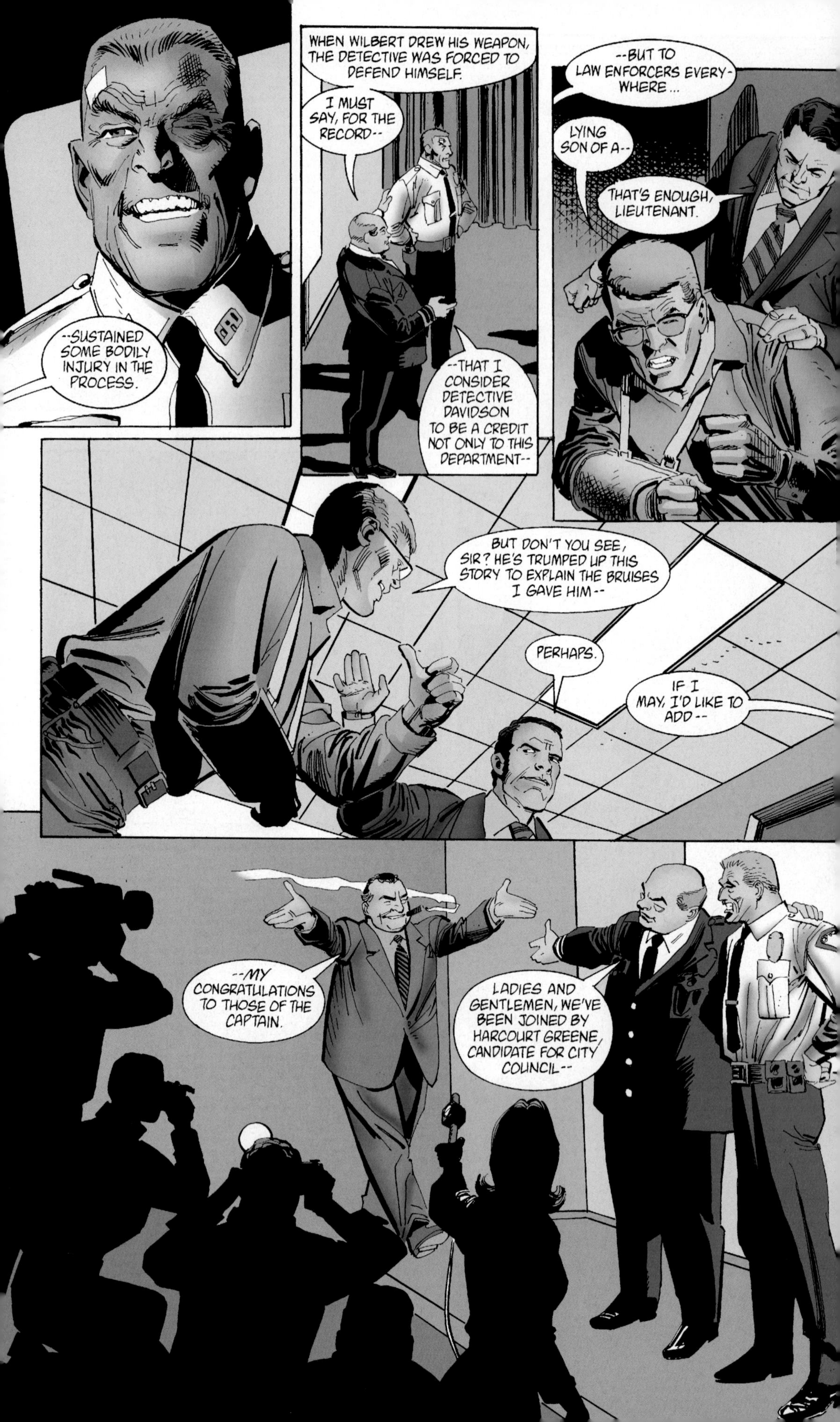
--SUSTAINED SOME BODILY INJURY IN THE PROCESS.
WHEN WILBERT DREW HIS WEAPON, THE DETECTIVE WAS FORCED TO DEFEND HIMSELF.
I MUST SAY, FOR THE RECORD--
--THAT I CONSIDER DETECTIVE DAVIDSON TO BE A CREDIT NOT ONLY TO THIS DEPARTMENT--
--BUT TO LAW ENFORCERS EVERYWHERE...
LYING SON OF A--
THAT'S ENOUGH, LIEUTENANT.
BUT DON'T YOU SEE, SIR? HE'S TRUMPED UP THIS STORY TO EXPLAIN THE BRUISES I GAVE HIM--
PERHAPS.
IF I MAY, I'D LIKE TO ADD--
LADIES AND GENTLEMEN, WE'VE BEEN JOINED BY HARCOURT GREENE, CANDIDATE FOR CITY COUNCIL--
--MY CONGRATULATIONS TO THOSE OF THE CAPTAIN.

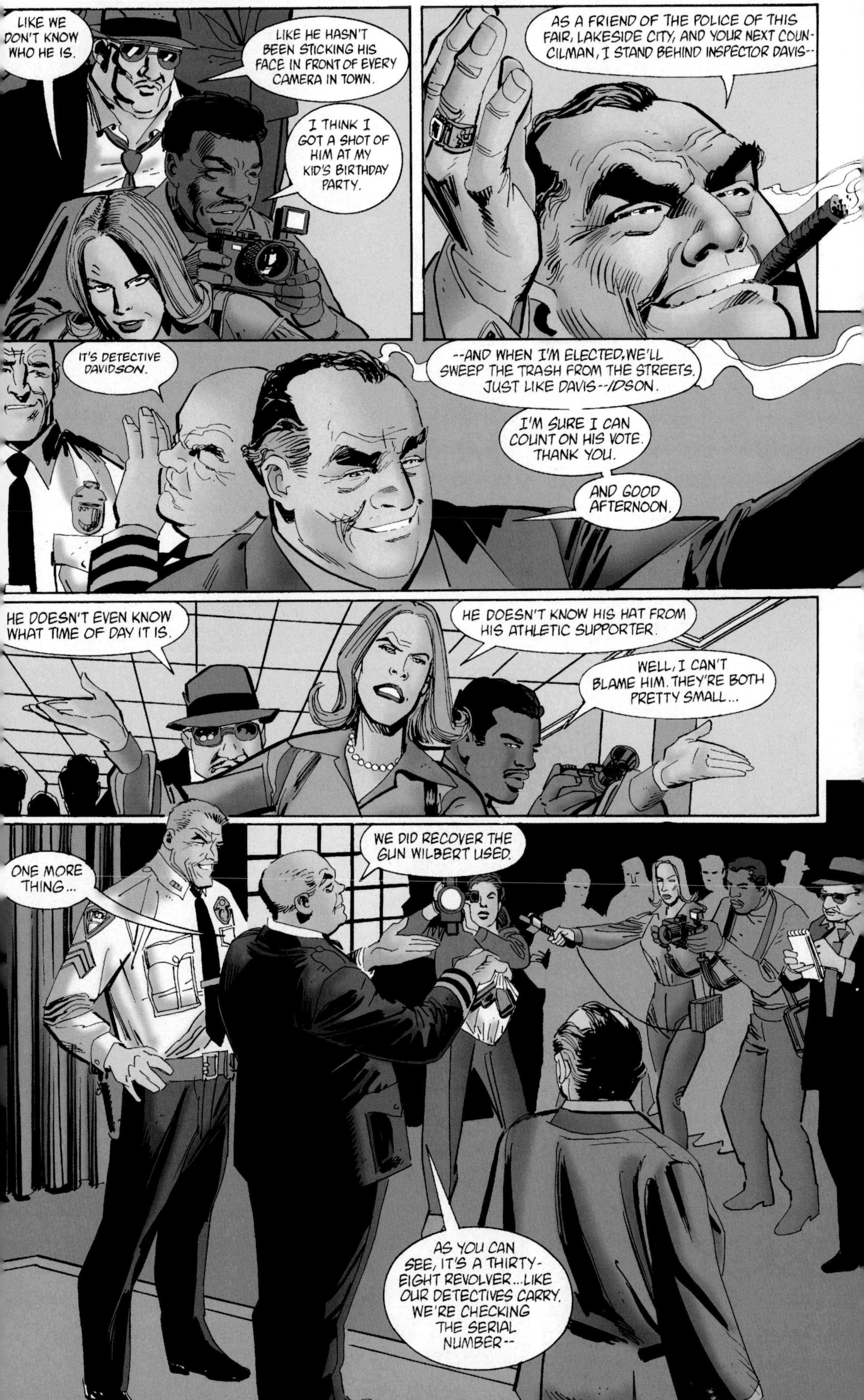

LIKE WE DON'T KNOW WHO HE IS.
LIKE HE HASN'T BEEN STICKING HIS FACE IN FRONT OF EVERY CAMERA IN TOWN.
I THINK I GOT A SHOT OF HIM AT MY KID'S BIRTHDAY PARTY.
AS A FRIEND OF THE POLICE OF THIS FAIR, LAKESIDE CITY, AND YOUR NEXT COUNCILMAN, I STAND BEHIND INSPECTOR DAVIS--
IT'S DETECTIVE DAVIDSON.
--AND WHEN I'M ELECTED, WE'LL SWEEP THE TRASH FROM THE STREETS. JUST LIKE DAVIS--IDSON.
I'M SURE I CAN COUNT ON HIS VOTE. THANK YOU.
AND GOOD AFTERNOON.
HE DOESN'T EVEN KNOW WHAT TIME OF DAY IT IS.
HE DOESN'T KNOW HIS HAT FROM HIS ATHLETIC SUPPORTER.
WELL, I CAN'T BLAME HIM. THEY'RE BOTH PRETTY SMALL...
ONE MORE THING...
WE DID RECOVER THE GUN WILBERT USED.
AS YOU CAN SEE, IT'S A THIRTY-EIGHT REVOLVER...LIKE OUR DETECTIVES CARRY. WE'RE CHECKING THE SERIAL NUMBER--

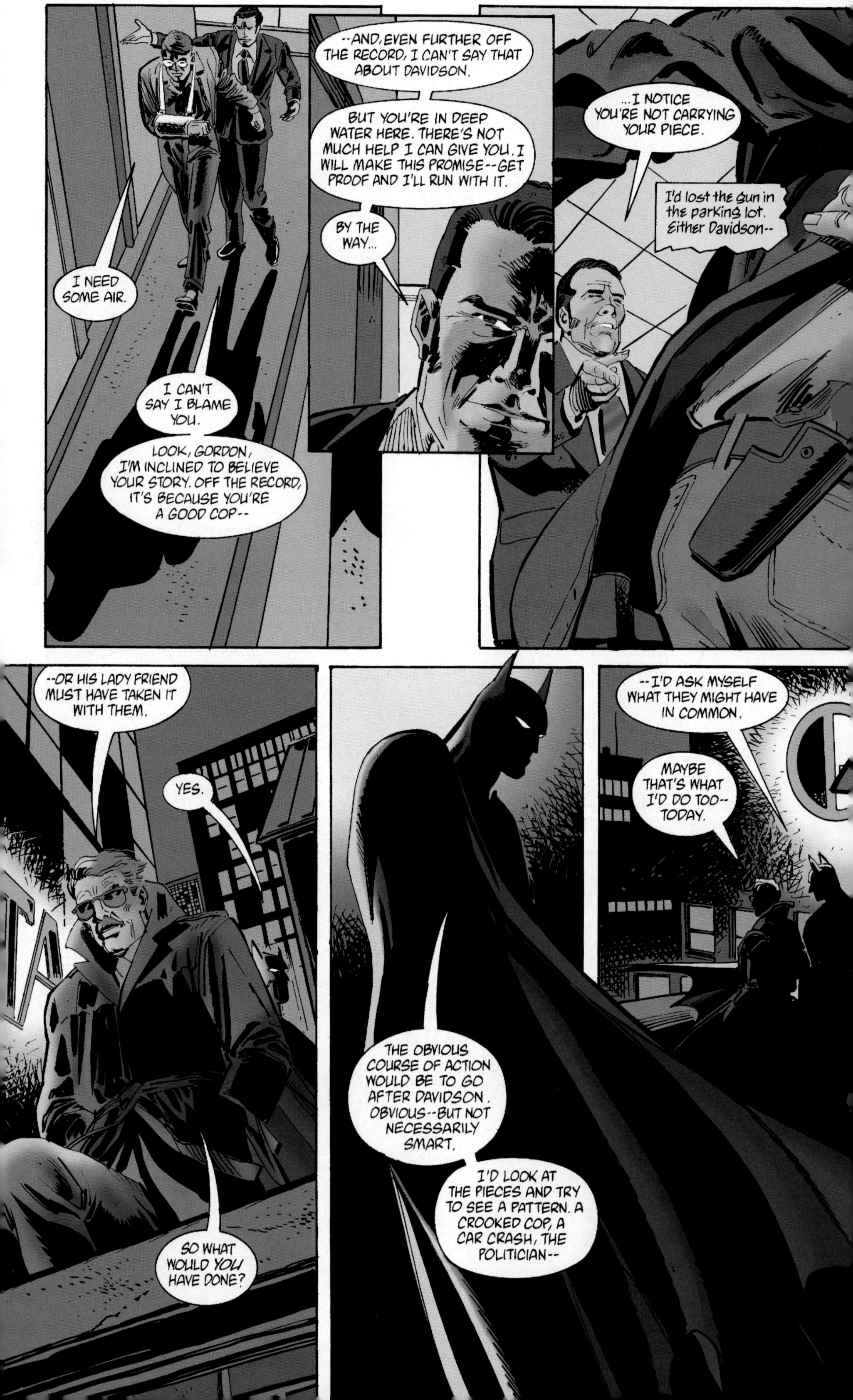
I NEED SOME AIR.
I CAN'T SAY I BLAME YOU.
LOOK, GORDON, I'M INCLINED TO BELIEVE YOUR STORY. OFF THE RECORD, IT'S BECAUSE YOU'RE A GOOD COP--
--AND, EVEN FURTHER OFF THE RECORD, I CAN'T SAY THAT ABOUT DAVIDSON.
BUT YOU'RE IN DEEP WATER HERE. THERE'S NOT MUCH HELP I CAN GIVE YOU. I WILL MAKE THIS PROMISE--GET PROOF AND I'LL RUN WITH IT.
BY THE WAY...
...I NOTICE YOU'RE NOT CARRYING YOUR PIECE.
I'd lost the gun in the parking lot. Either Davidson--
--OR HIS LADY FRIEND MUST HAVE TAKEN IT WITH THEM.
YES.
SO WHAT WOULD YOU HAVE DONE?
THE OBVIOUS COURSE OF ACTION WOULD BE TO GO AFTER DAVIDSON. OBVIOUS--BUT NOT NECESSARILY SMART.
I'D LOOK AT THE PIECES AND TRY TO SEE A PATTERN. A CROOKED COP, A CAR CRASH, THE POLITICIAN--
--I'D ASK MYSELF WHAT THEY MIGHT HAVE IN COMMON.
MAYBE THAT'S WHAT I'D DO TOO--TODAY.

BUT BACK THEN, I WAS YOUNG, INEXPERIENCED. I DIDN'T THINK IN TERMS OF PATTERNS. I WAS LIKE A BULL--WAVE A RED FLAG AT ME AND I'D CHARGE IT.

DAVIDSON IS THE RED FLAG.

MY FIRST MOVE--

--was to ask for a search warrant for Davidson's apartment. The judge made me wait six hours.

Then he laughed at me.

HEY, GORDON!

YEAH?

I JUST WANT YOU TO KNOW--

--THAT SOME OF US THINK YOU'RE GETTING A RAW DEAL--

WHAT ARE YOU TALKING ABOUT?

YOU AIN'T HEARD?

THAT GUN DAVIDSON FOUND LAST NIGHT... THEY MADE A MATCH ON THE SERIAL NUMBER.

IT'S YOURS.

INTERNAL AFFAIRS WANTS TO SEE YOU IN THE MORNING.

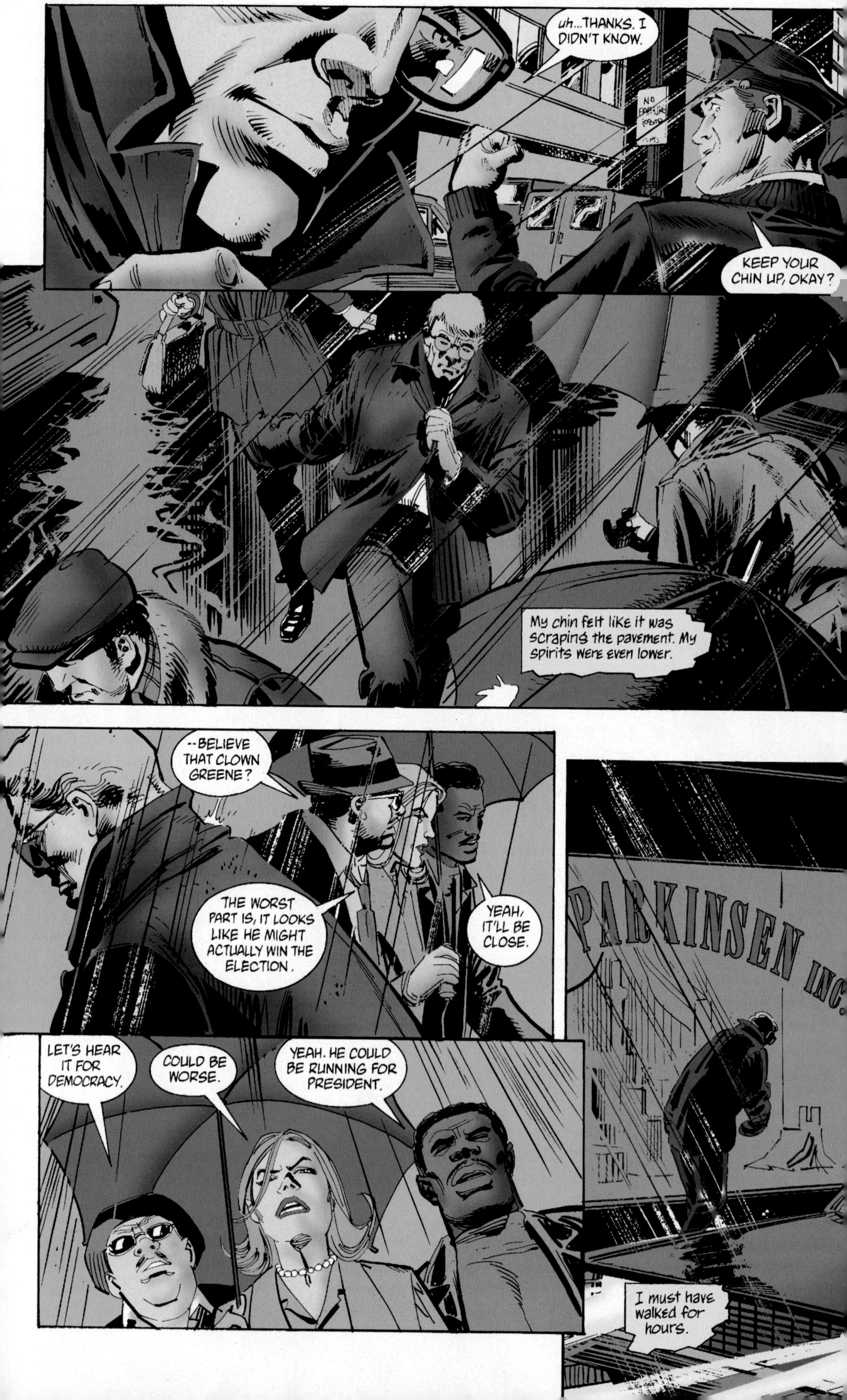
uh...THANKS. I DIDN'T KNOW.
NO PARKING
KEEP YOUR CHIN UP, OKAY?
My chin felt like it was scraping the pavement. My spirits were even lower.
--BELIEVE THAT CLOWN GREENE?
THE WORST PART IS, IT LOOKS LIKE HE MIGHT ACTUALLY WIN THE ELECTION.
YEAH, IT'LL BE CLOSE.
PARKINSEN INC.
LET'S HEAR IT FOR DEMOCRACY.
COULD BE WORSE.
YEAH. HE COULD BE RUNNING FOR PRESIDENT.
I must have walked for hours.

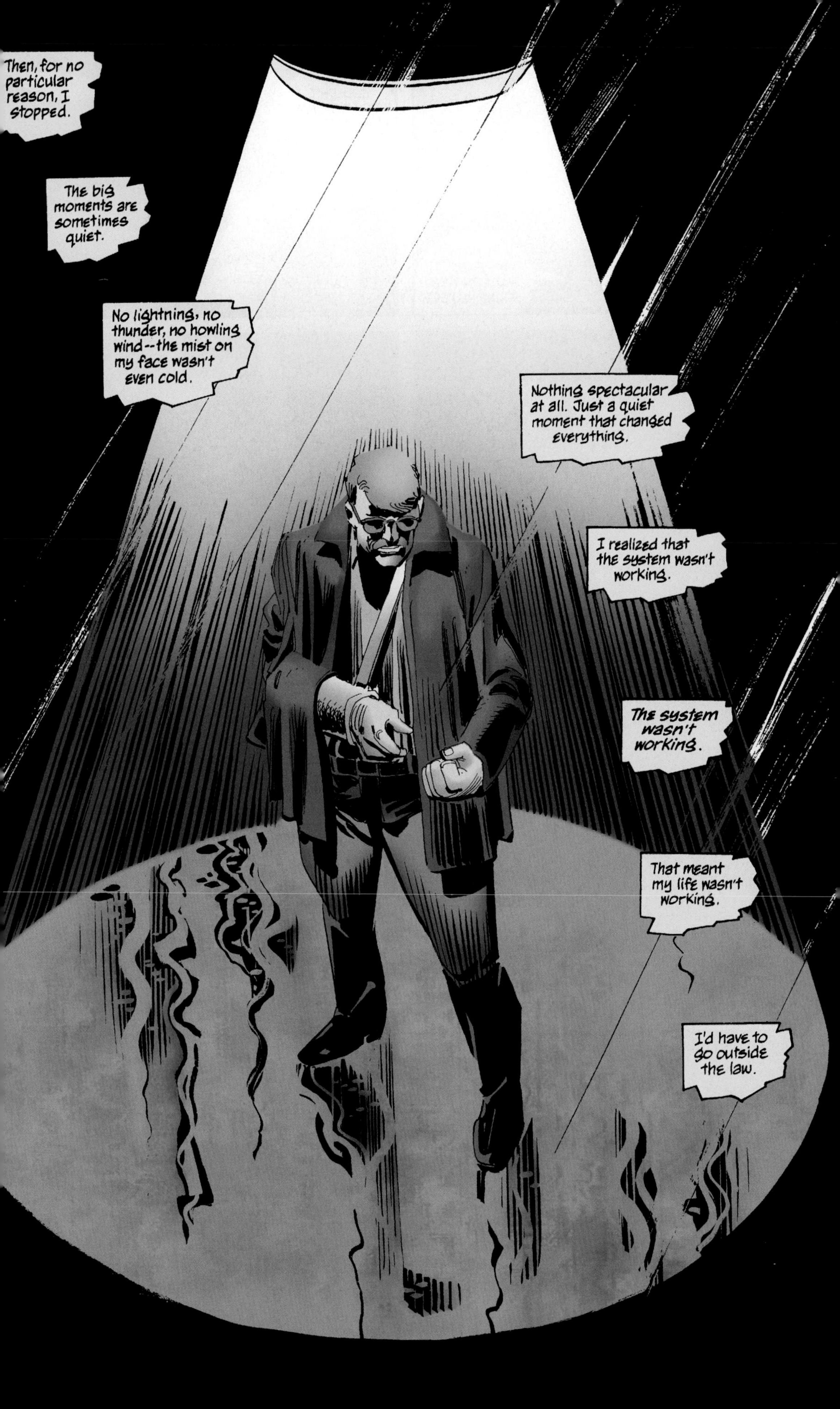

Then, for no particular reason, I stopped.
The big moments are sometimes quiet.
No lightning, no thunder, no howling wind--the mist on my face wasn't even cold.
Nothing spectacular at all. Just a quiet moment that changed everything.
I realized that the system wasn't working.
The system wasn't working.
That meant my life wasn't working.
I'd have to go outside the law.

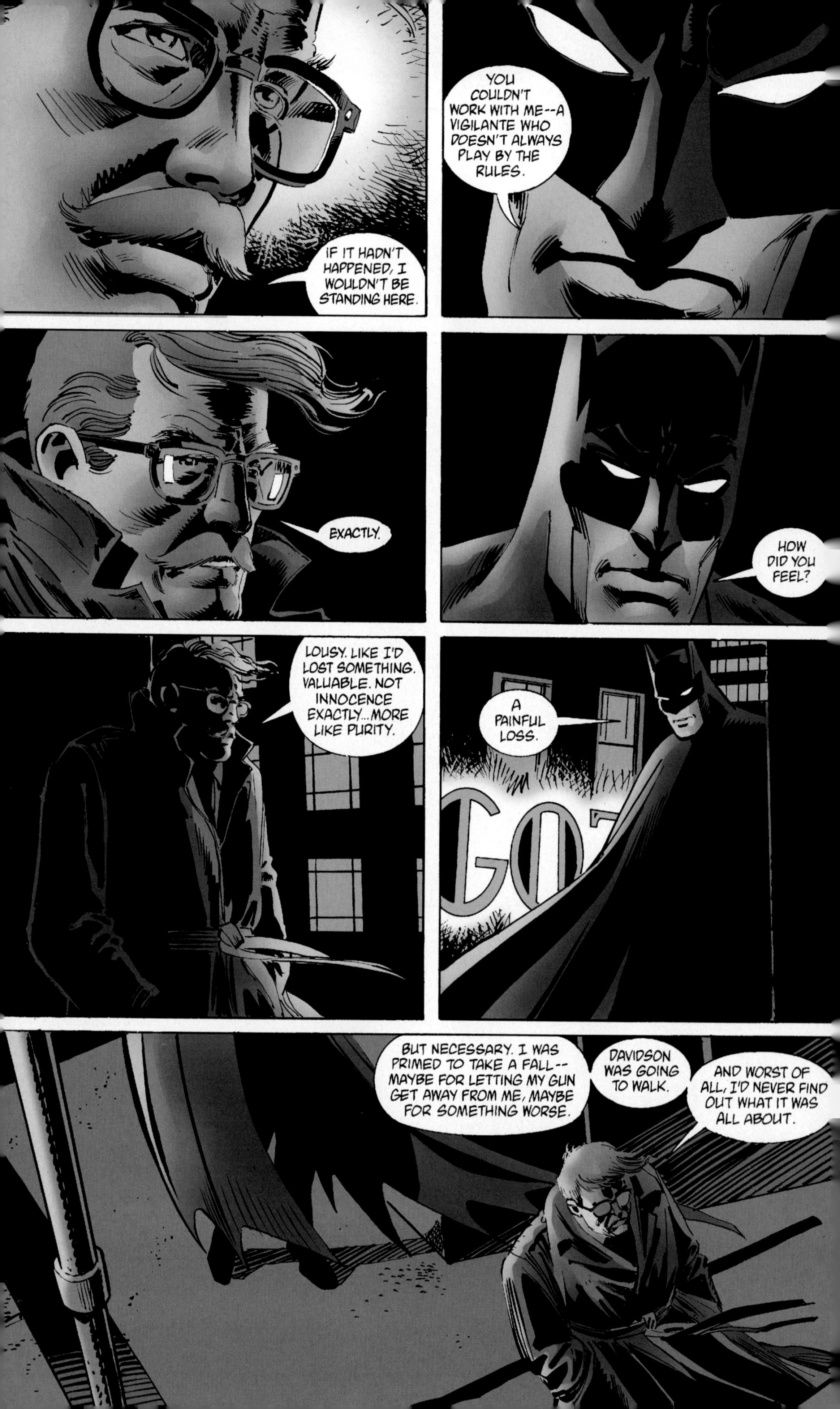
YOU COULDN'T WORK WITH ME--A VIGILANTE WHO DOESN'T ALWAYS PLAY BY THE RULES.
IF IT HADN'T HAPPENED, I WOULDN'T BE STANDING HERE.
EXACTLY.
HOW DID YOU FEEL?
LOUSY. LIKE I'D LOST SOMETHING. VALUABLE. NOT INNOCENCE EXACTLY...MORE LIKE PURITY.
A PAINFUL LOSS.
BUT NECESSARY. I WAS PRIMED TO TAKE A FALL--MAYBE FOR LETTING MY GUN GET AWAY FROM ME, MAYBE FOR SOMETHING WORSE.
DAVIDSON WAS GOING TO WALK.
AND WORST OF ALL, I'D NEVER FIND OUT WHAT IT WAS ALL ABOUT.

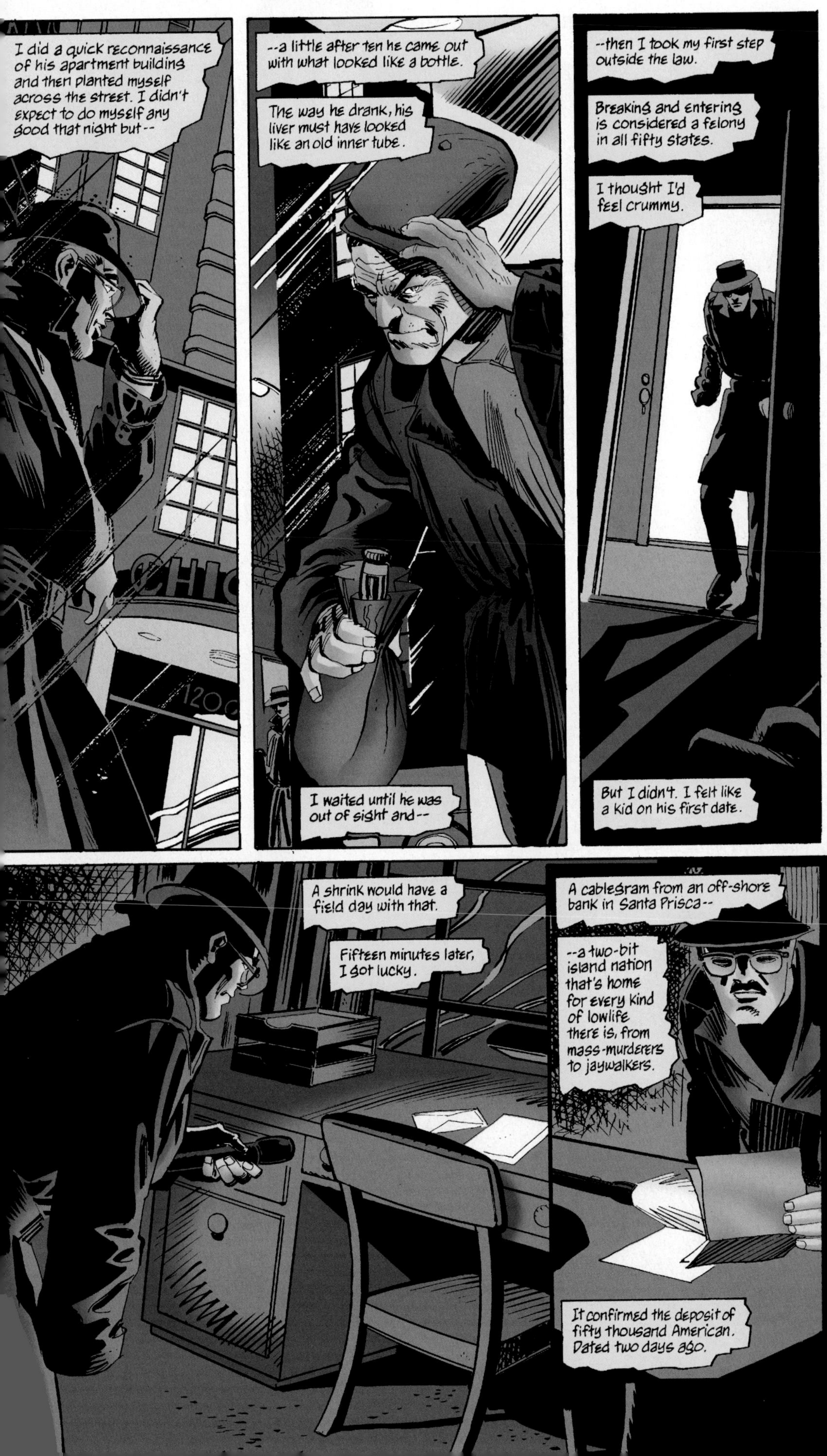
I did a quick reconnaissance of his apartment building and then planted myself across the street. I didn't expect to do myself any good that night but--
CHIC
1200
--a little after ten he came out with what looked like a bottle.
The way he drank, his liver must have looked like an old inner tube.
I waited until he was out of sight and--
--then I took my first step outside the law.
Breaking and entering is considered a felony in all fifty states.
I thought I'd feel crummy.
But I didn't. I felt like a kid on his first date.
A shrink would have a field day with that.
Fifteen minutes later, I got lucky.
A cablegram from an off-shore bank in Santa Prisca--
--a two-bit island nation that's home for every kind of lowlife there is, from mass-murderers to jaywalkers.
It confirmed the deposit of fifty thousand American. Dated two days ago.

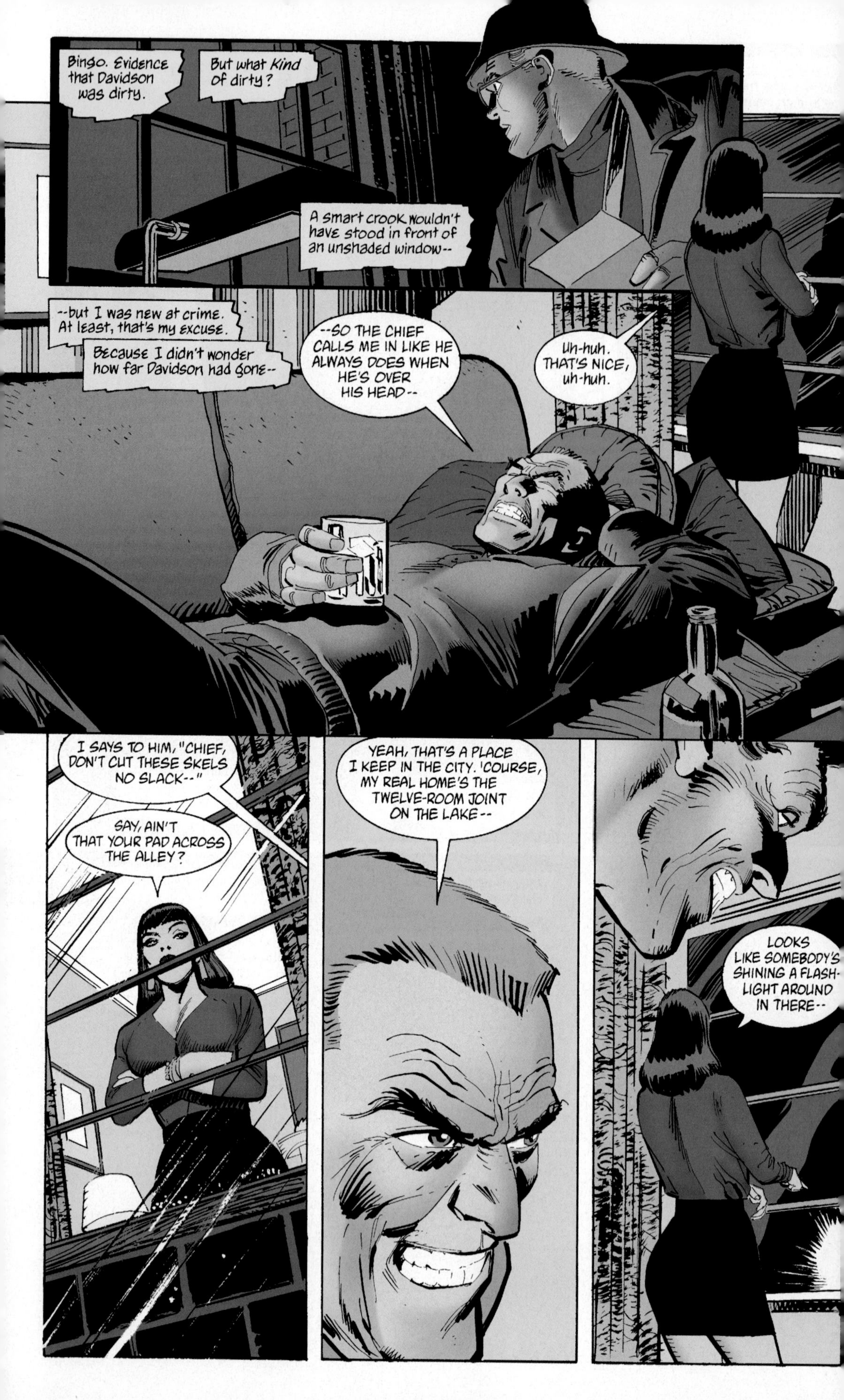
Bingo. Evidence that Davidson was dirty.
But what *kind* of dirty?
A smart crook wouldn't have stood in front of an unshaded window--
--but I was new at crime. At least, that's my excuse.
Because I didn't wonder how far Davidson had gone--
--SO THE CHIEF CALLS ME IN LIKE HE ALWAYS DOES WHEN HE'S OVER HIS HEAD--
Uh-huh. THAT'S NICE, uh-huh.
I SAYS TO HIM, "CHIEF, DON'T CUT THESE SKELS NO SLACK--"
SAY, AIN'T THAT YOUR PAD ACROSS THE ALLEY?
YEAH, THAT'S A PLACE I KEEP IN THE CITY. 'COURSE, MY REAL HOME'S THE TWELVE-ROOM JOINT ON THE LAKE--
LOOKS LIKE SOMEBODY'S SHINING A FLASH-LIGHT AROUND IN THERE--

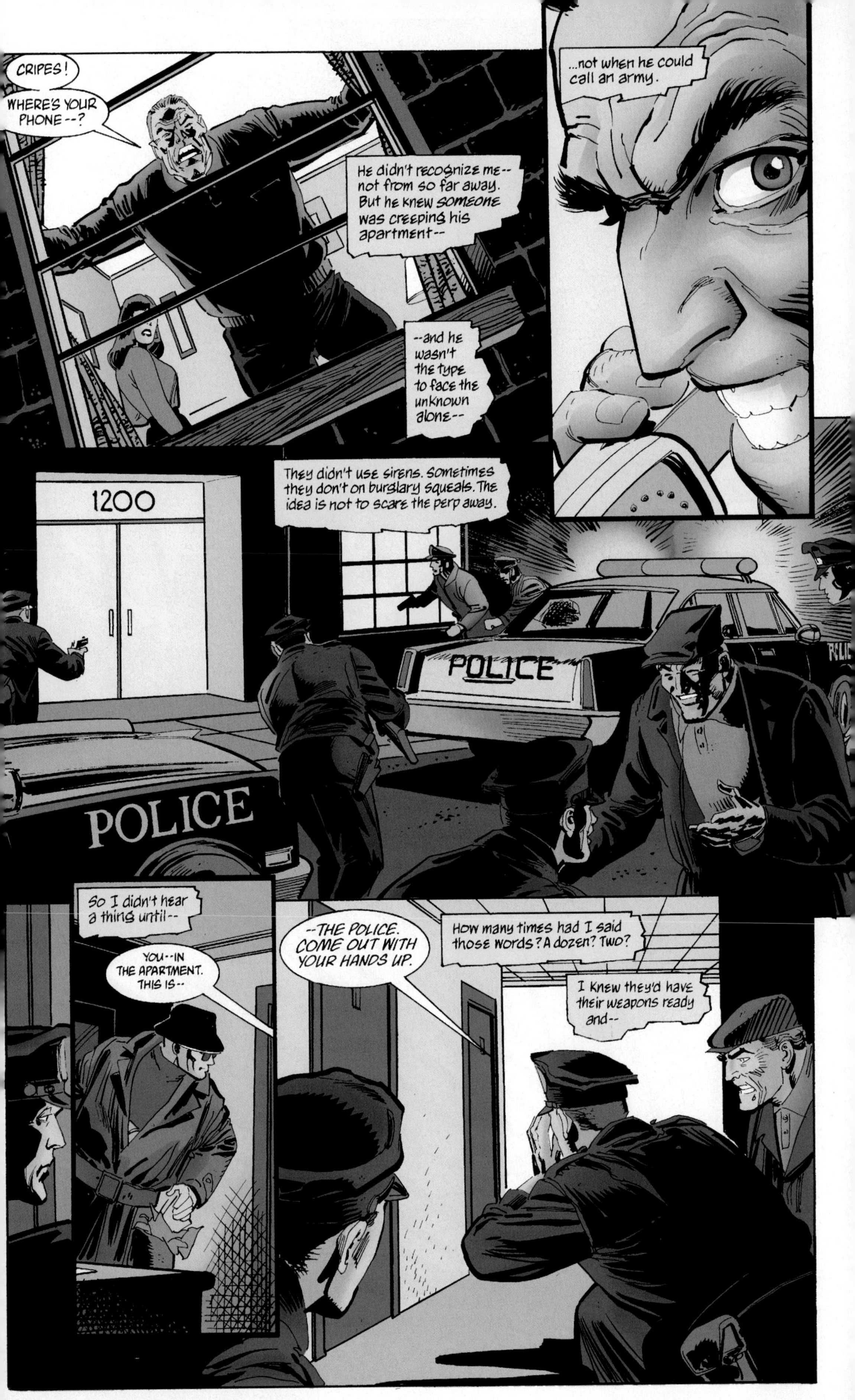
CRIPES!
WHERE'S YOUR PHONE--?
He didn't recognize me--not from so far away. But he knew SOMEONE was creeping his apartment--
--and he wasn't the type to face the unknown alone--
...not when he could call an army.
They didn't use sirens. Sometimes they don't on burglary squeals. The idea is not to scare the perp away.
1200
POLICE
POLICE
So I didn't hear a thing until--
YOU--IN THE APARTMENT. THIS IS--
--THE POLICE. COME OUT WITH YOUR HANDS UP.
How many times had I said those words? A dozen? Two?
I knew they'd have their weapons ready and--

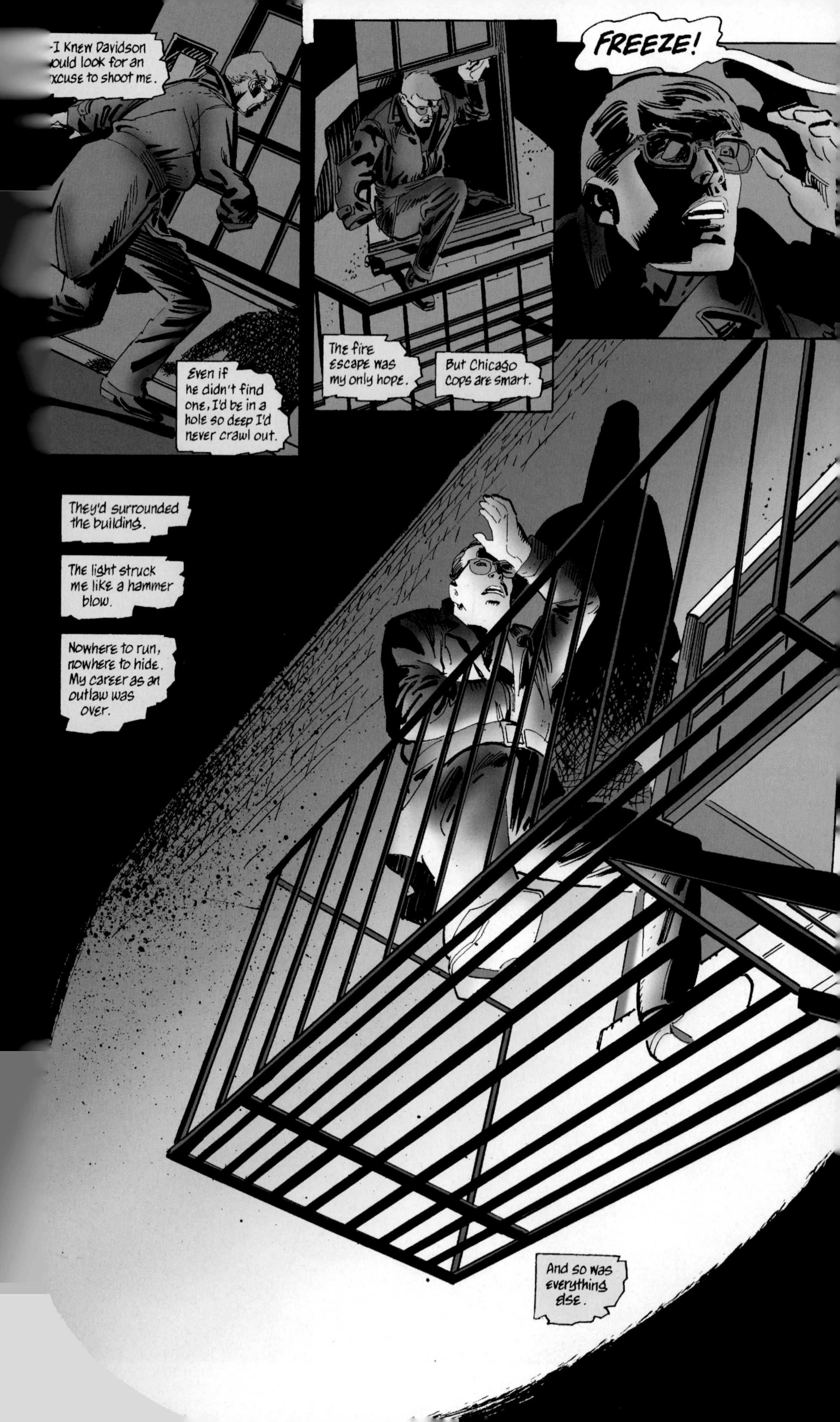
-I Knew Davidson
would look for an
excuse to shoot me.
Even if he didn't find one, I'd be in a hole so deep I'd never crawl out.
The fire escape was my only hope.
But Chicago cops are smart.
FREEZE!
They'd surrounded the building.
The light struck me like a hammer blow.
Nowhere to run, nowhere to hide. My career as an outlaw was over.
And so was everything else.

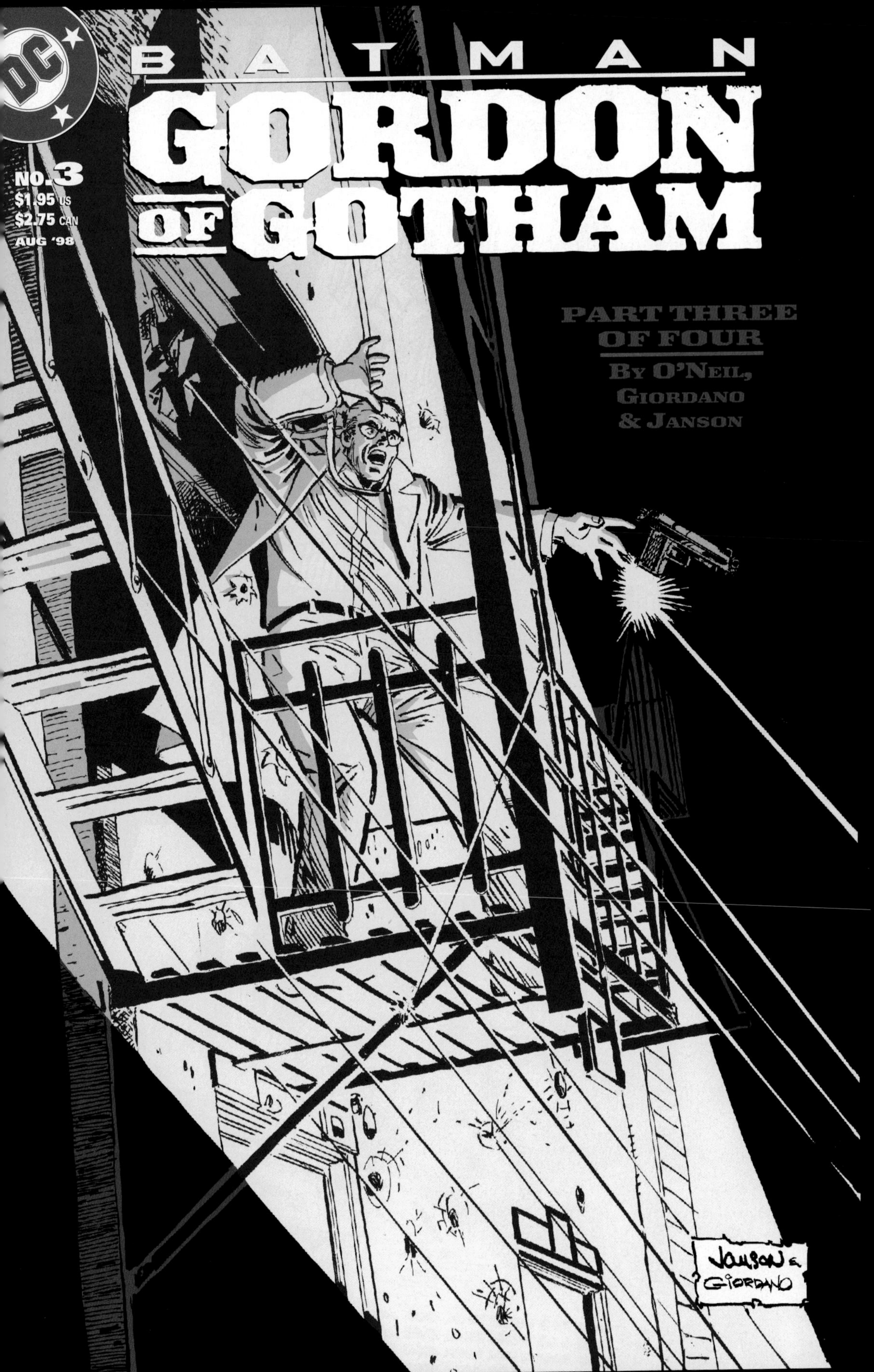

DC
BATMAN
GORDON OF GOTHAM
NO.3
$1.95 US
$2.75 CAN
AUG '98
PART THREE OF FOUR
BY O'NEIL, GIORDANO & JANSON
JANSON & GIORDANO

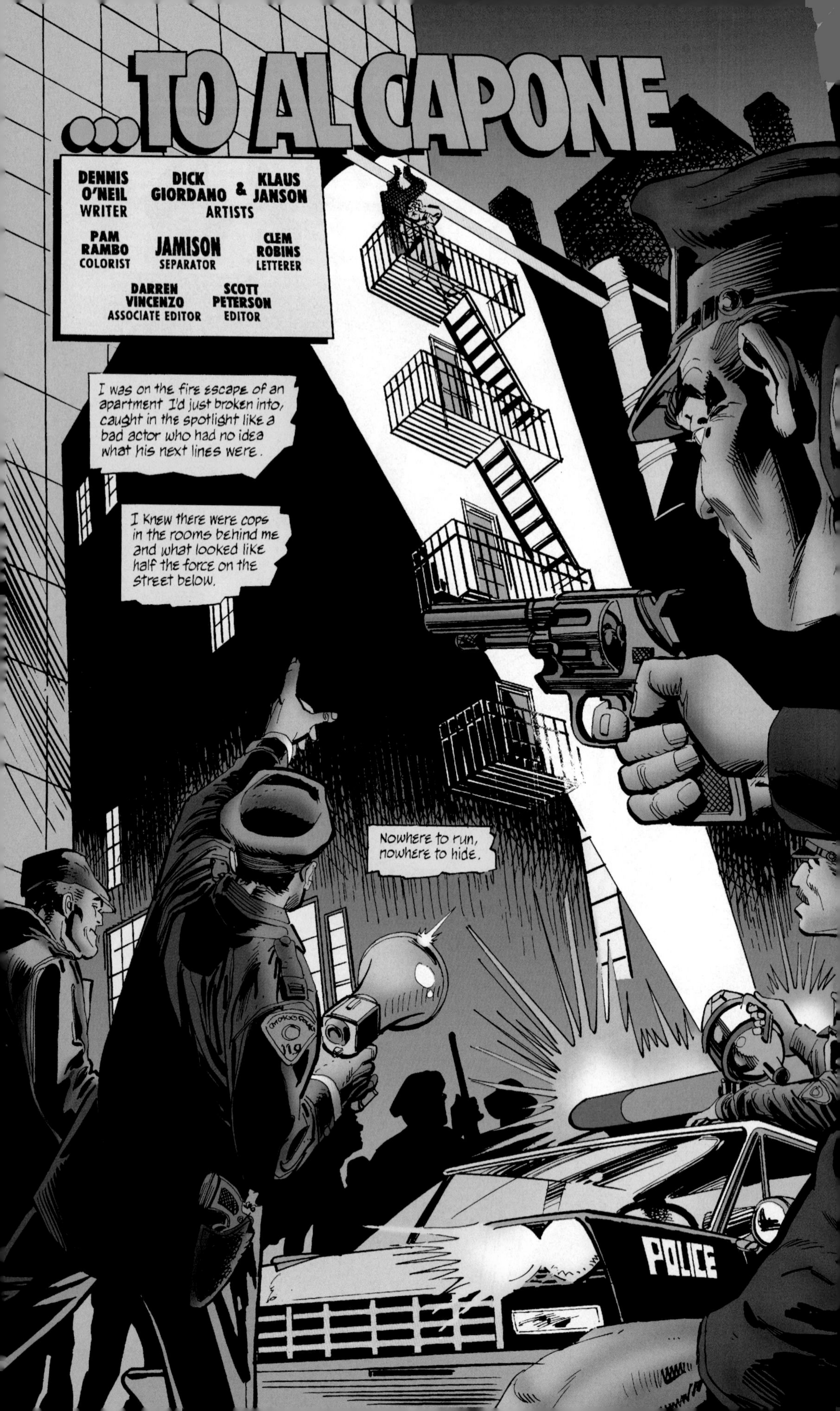
...TO AL CAPONE
DENNIS O'NEIL WRITER
DICK GIORDANO & KLAUS JANSON ARTISTS
PAM RAMBO COLORIST
JAMISON SEPARATOR
CLEM ROBINS LETTERER
DARREN VINCENZO ASSOCIATE EDITOR
SCOTT PETERSON EDITOR
I was on the fire escape of an apartment I'd just broken into, caught in the spotlight like a bad actor who had no idea what his next lines were.
I knew there were cops in the rooms behind me and what looked like half the force on the street below.
Nowhere to run, nowhere to hide.
POLICE

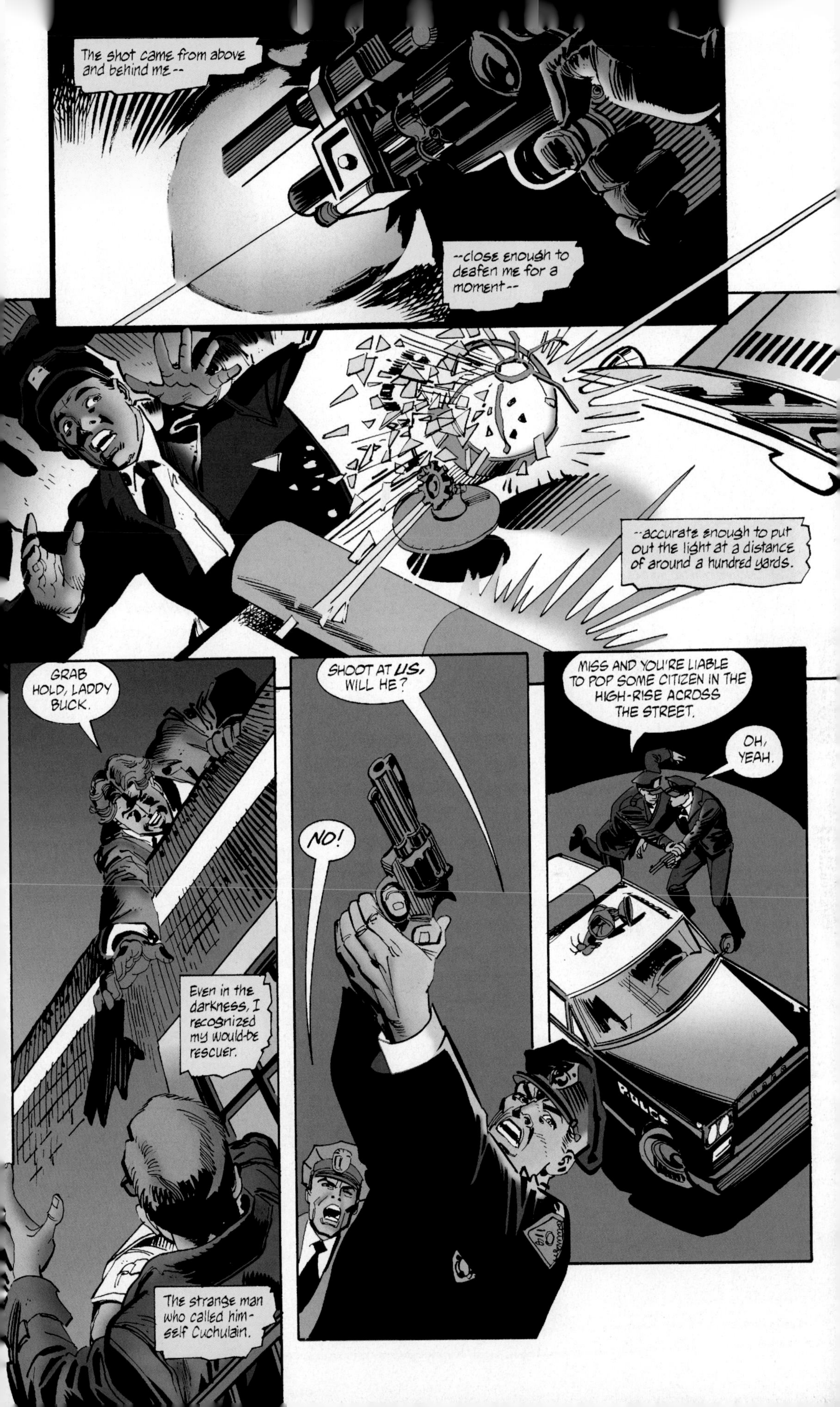

The shot came from above and behind me--
--close enough to deafen me for a moment--
--accurate enough to put out the light at a distance of around a hundred yards.
GRAB HOLD, LADDY BUCK.
Even in the darkness, I recognized my would-be rescuer.
The strange man who called him-self Cuchulain.
SHOOT AT US, WILL HE?
NO!
MISS AND YOU'RE LIABLE TO POP SOME CITIZEN IN THE HIGH-RISE ACROSS THE STREET.
OH, YEAH.
POLICE

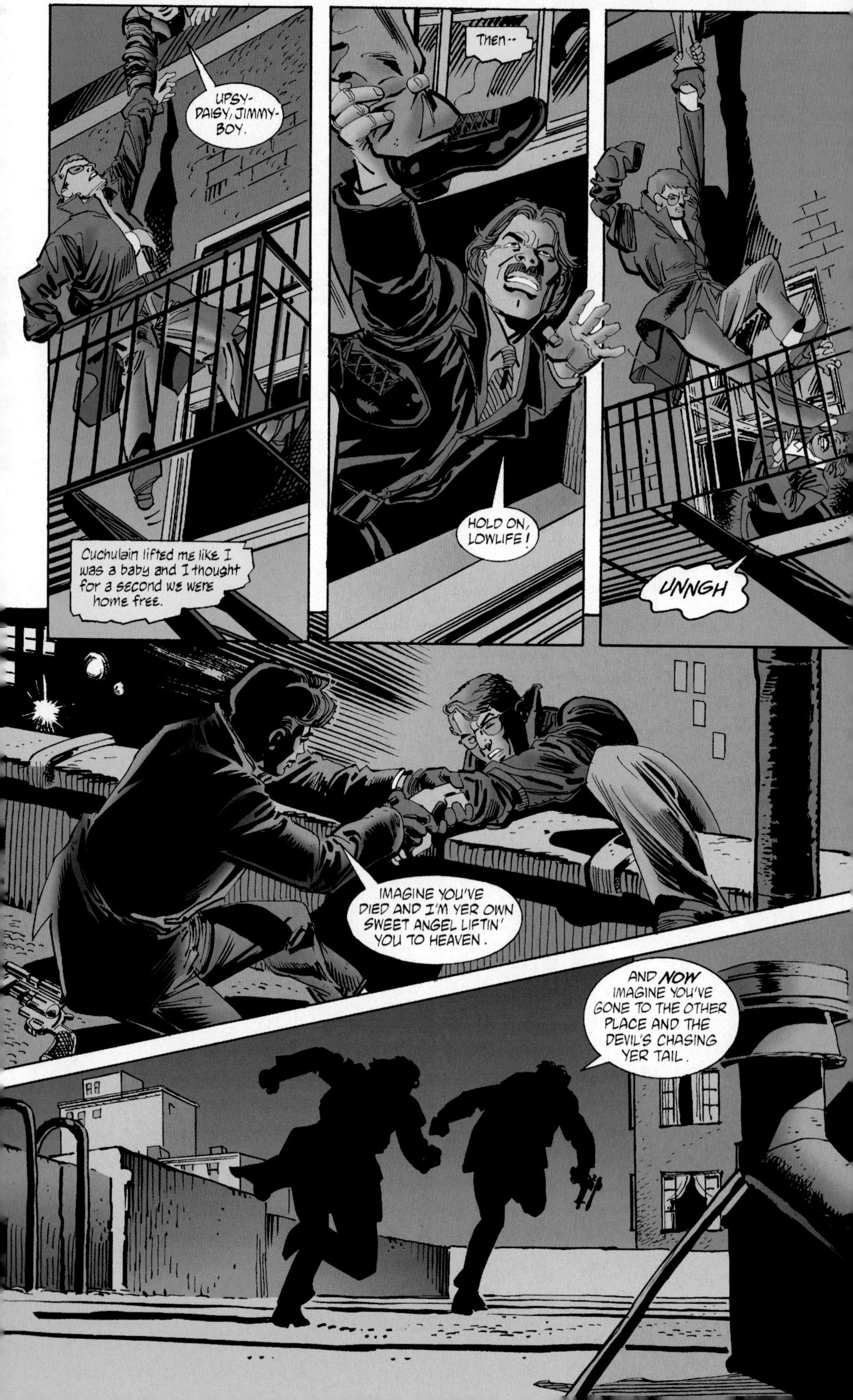
UPSY-DAISY, JIMMY-BOY.
Cuchulain lifted me like I was a baby and I thought for a second we were home free.
Then--
HOLD ON, LOWLIFE!
UNNGH
IMAGINE YOU'VE DIED AND I'M YER OWN SWEET ANGEL LIFTIN' YOU TO HEAVEN.
AND NOW IMAGINE YOU'VE GONE TO THE OTHER PLACE AND THE DEVIL'S CHASING YER TAIL.

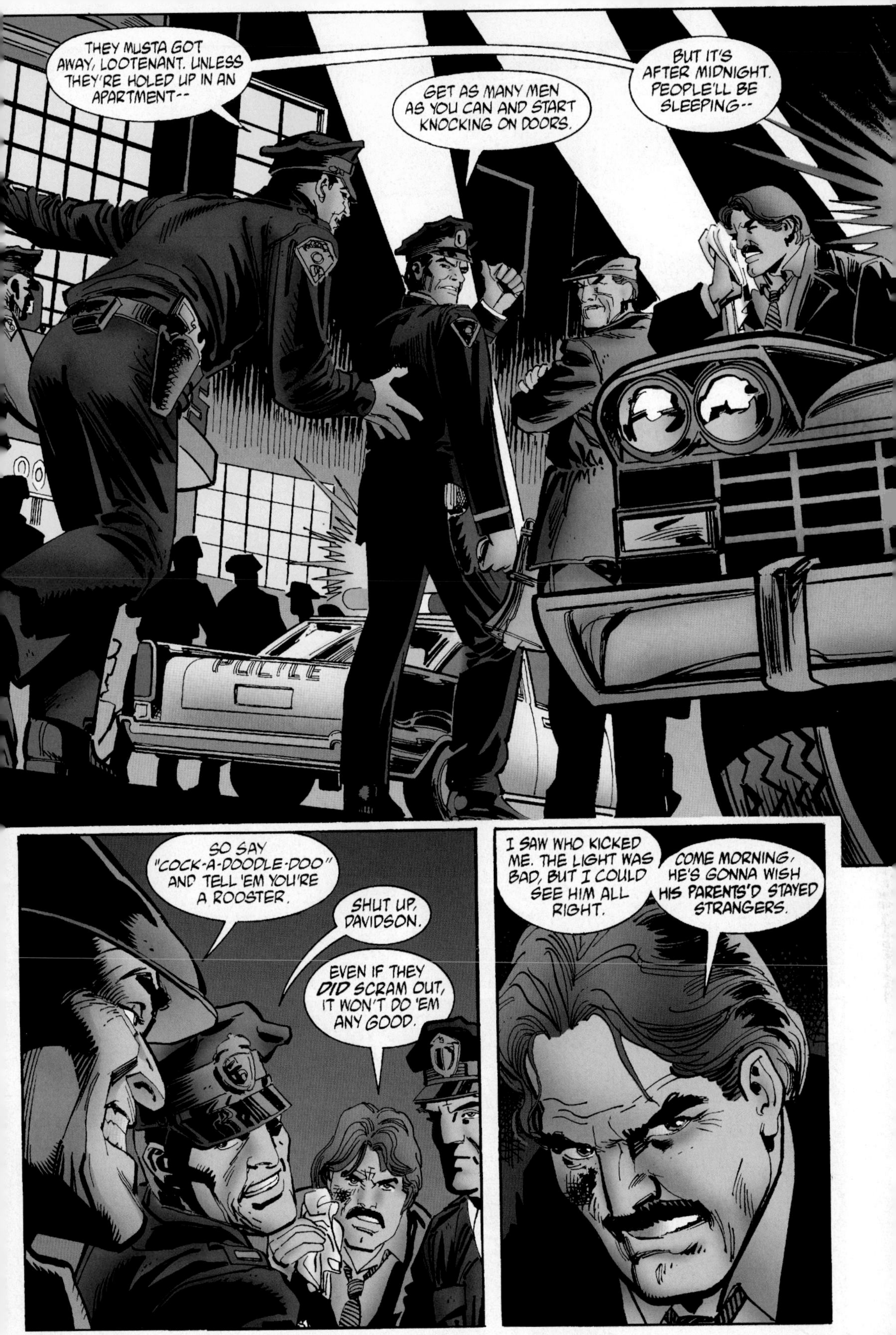
THEY MUSTA GOT AWAY, LOOTENANT. UNLESS THEY'RE HOLED UP IN AN APARTMENT--
GET AS MANY MEN AS YOU CAN AND START KNOCKING ON DOORS.
BUT IT'S AFTER MIDNIGHT. PEOPLE'LL BE SLEEPING--
SO SAY "COCK-A-DOODLE-DOO" AND TELL 'EM YOU'RE A ROOSTER.
SHUT UP, DAVIDSON.
EVEN IF THEY *DID* SCRAM OUT, IT WON'T DO 'EM ANY GOOD.
I SAW WHO KICKED ME. THE LIGHT WAS BAD, BUT I COULD SEE HIM ALL RIGHT.
COME MORNING, HE'S GONNA WISH HIS PARENTS'D STAYED STRANGERS.

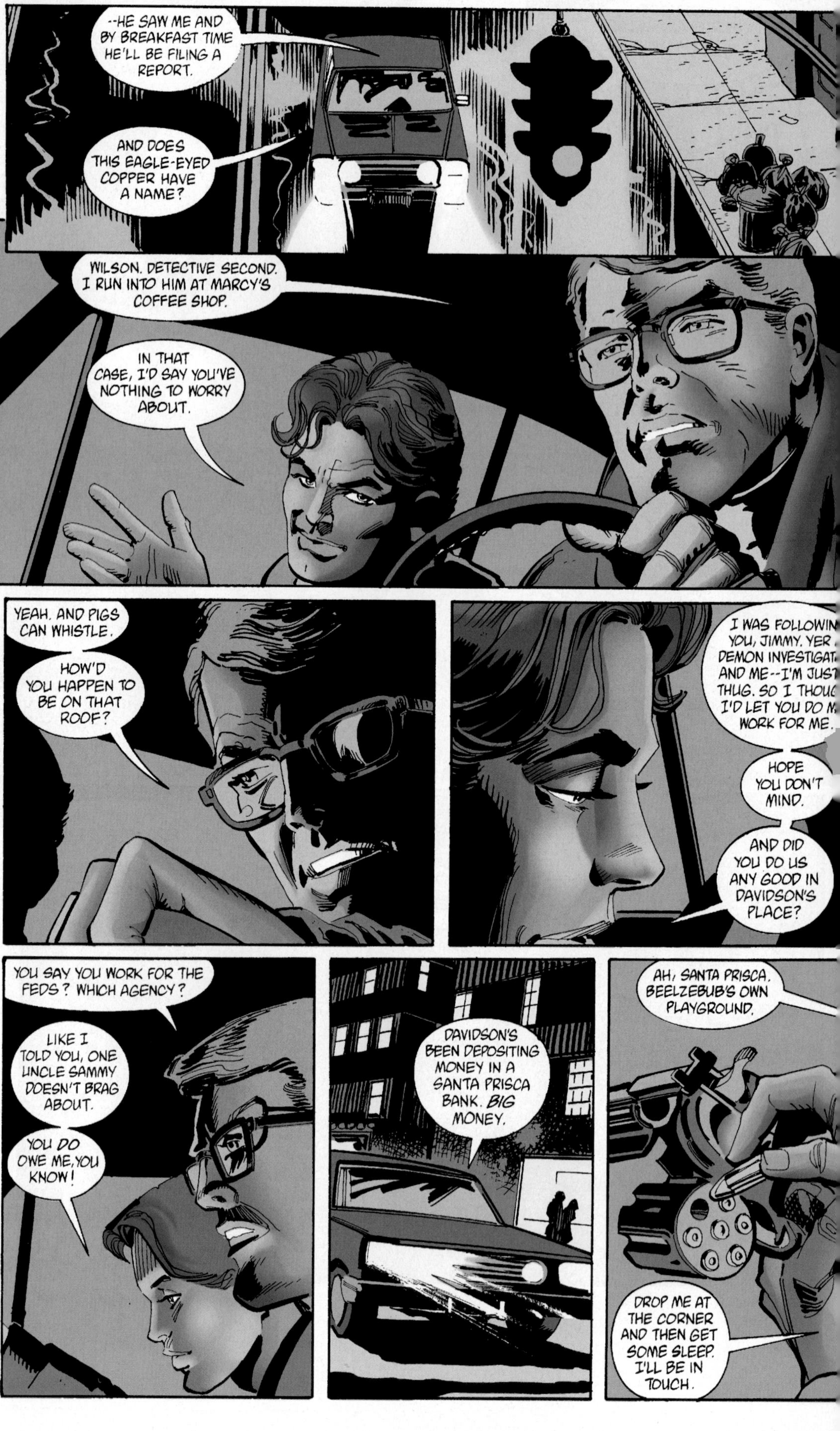
--HE SAW ME AND BY BREAKFAST TIME HE'LL BE FILING A REPORT.
AND DOES THIS EAGLE-EYED COPPER HAVE A NAME?
WILSON. DETECTIVE SECOND. I RUN INTO HIM AT MARCY'S COFFEE SHOP.
IN THAT CASE, I'D SAY YOU'VE NOTHING TO WORRY ABOUT.
YEAH. AND PIGS CAN WHISTLE.
HOW'D YOU HAPPEN TO BE ON THAT ROOF?
I WAS FOLLOWIN YOU, JIMMY. YER DEMON INVESTIGAT AND ME--I'M JUS THUG. SO I THOU I'D LET YOU DO M WORK FOR ME.
HOPE YOU DON'T MIND.
AND DID YOU DO US ANY GOOD IN DAVIDSON'S PLACE?
YOU SAY YOU WORK FOR THE FEDS? WHICH AGENCY?
LIKE I TOLD YOU, ONE UNCLE SAMMY DOESN'T BRAG ABOUT.
YOU DO OWE ME, YOU KNOW!
DAVIDSON'S BEEN DEPOSITING MONEY IN A SANTA PRISCA BANK. BIG MONEY.
AH, SANTA PRISCA. BEELZEBUB'S OWN PLAYGROUND.
DROP ME AT THE CORNER AND THEN GET SOME SLEEP. I'LL BE IN TOUCH.

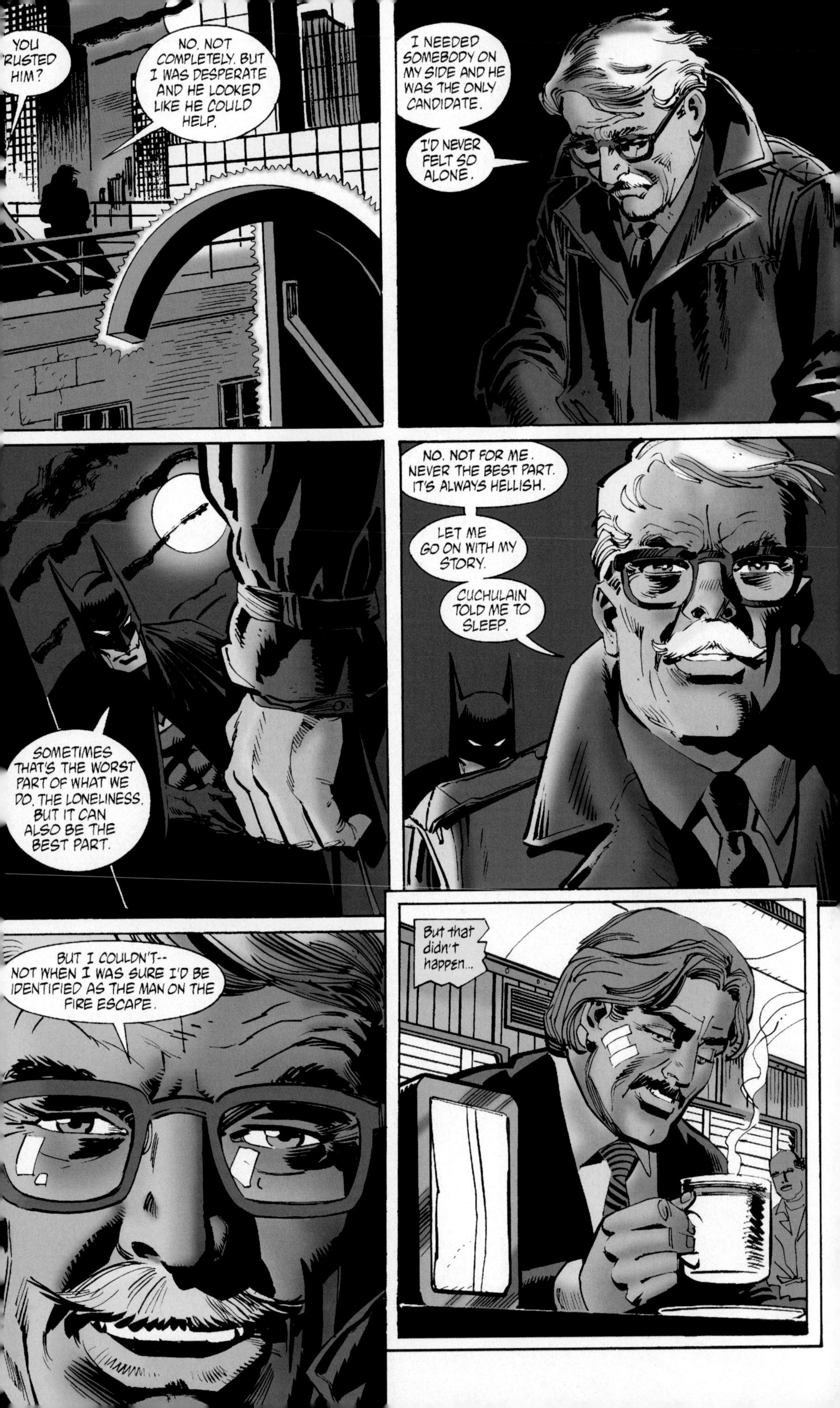
YOU 'RUSTED HIM?
NO. NOT COMPLETELY. BUT I WAS DESPERATE AND HE LOOKED LIKE HE COULD HELP.
I NEEDED SOMEBODY ON MY SIDE AND HE WAS THE ONLY CANDIDATE.
I'D NEVER FELT SO ALONE.
SOMETIMES THAT'S THE WORST PART OF WHAT WE DO. THE LONELINESS. BUT IT CAN ALSO BE THE BEST PART.
NO. NOT FOR ME. NEVER THE BEST PART. IT'S ALWAYS HELLISH.
LET ME GO ON WITH MY STORY.
CUCHULAIN TOLD ME TO SLEEP.
BUT I COULDN'T-- NOT WHEN I WAS SURE I'D BE IDENTIFIED AS THE MAN ON THE FIRE ESCAPE.
But that didn't happen...

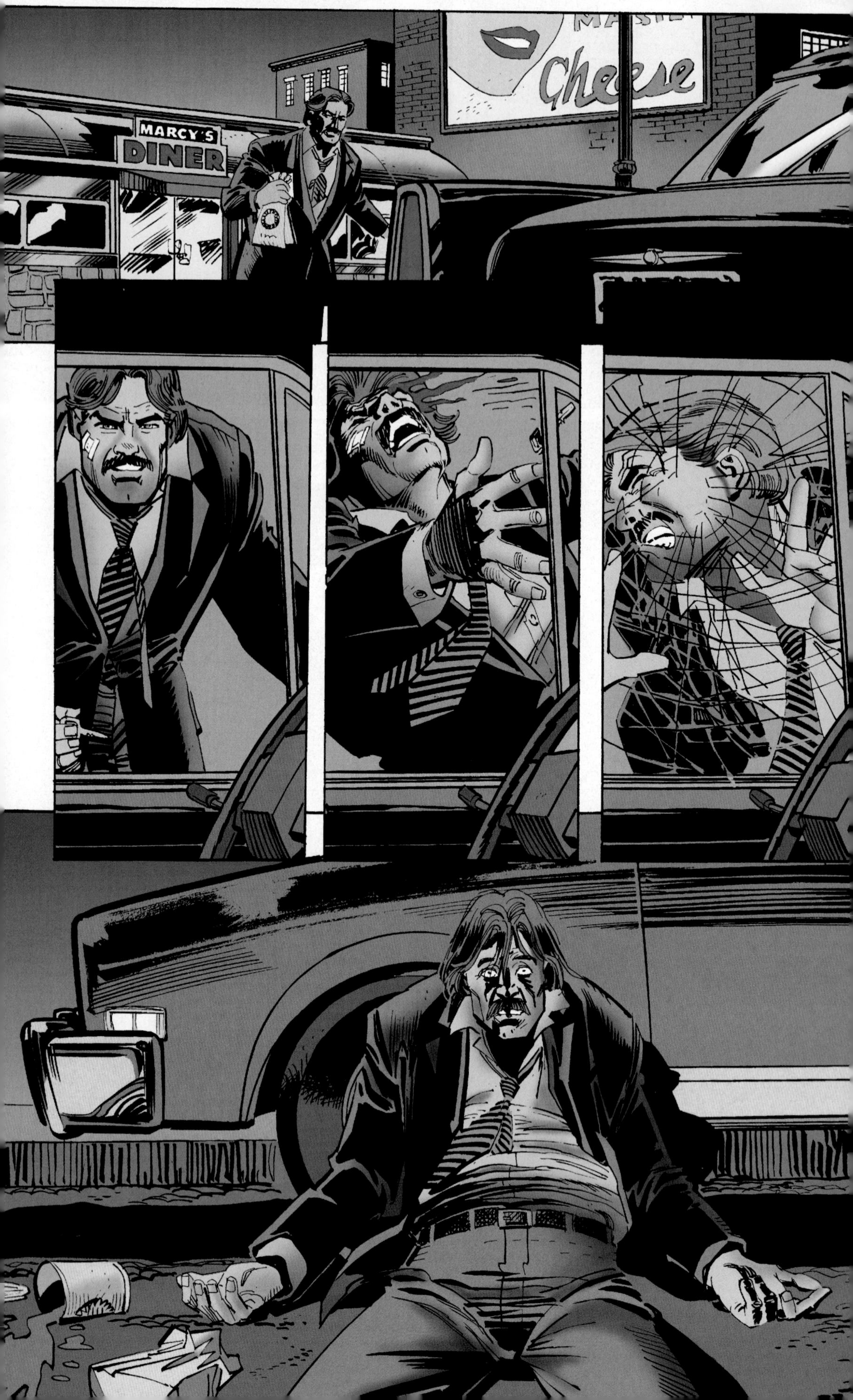
MARCY'S
DINER
Cheese

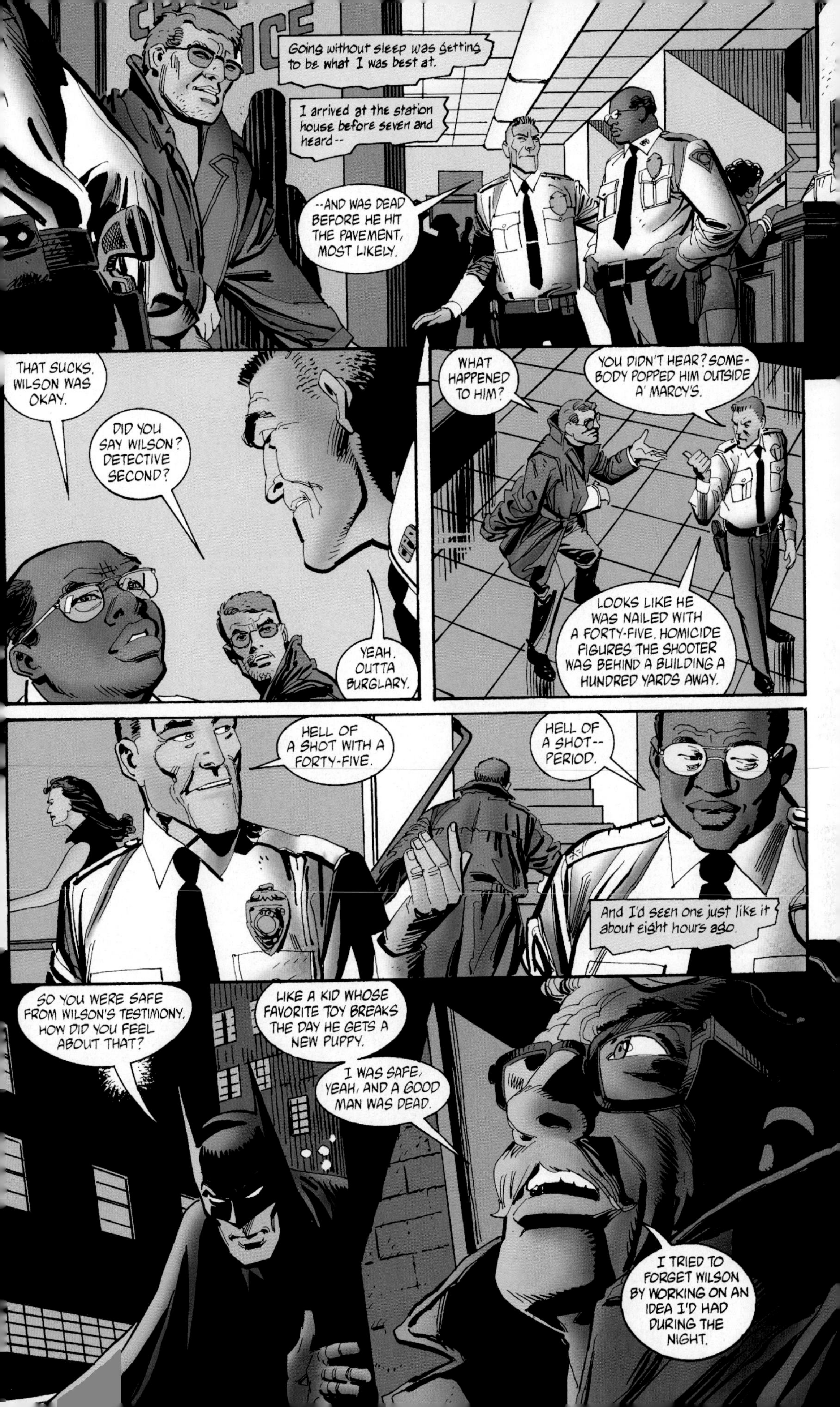

Going without sleep was getting to be what I was best at.
I arrived at the station house before seven and heard--
--AND WAS DEAD BEFORE HE HIT THE PAVEMENT, MOST LIKELY.
THAT SUCKS. WILSON WAS OKAY.
DID YOU SAY WILSON? DETECTIVE SECOND?
YEAH. OUTTA BURGLARY.
WHAT HAPPENED TO HIM?
YOU DIDN'T HEAR? SOMEBODY POPPED HIM OUTSIDE A' MARCY'S.
LOOKS LIKE HE WAS NAILED WITH A FORTY-FIVE. HOMICIDE FIGURES THE SHOOTER WAS BEHIND A BUILDING A HUNDRED YARDS AWAY.
HELL OF A SHOT WITH A FORTY-FIVE.
HELL OF A SHOT--PERIOD.
And I'd seen one just like it about eight hours ago.
SO YOU WERE SAFE FROM WILSON'S TESTIMONY. HOW DID YOU FEEL ABOUT THAT?
LIKE A KID WHOSE FAVORITE TOY BREAKS THE DAY HE GETS A NEW PUPPY.
I WAS SAFE, YEAH, AND A GOOD MAN WAS DEAD.
I TRIED TO FORGET WILSON BY WORKING ON AN IDEA I'D HAD DURING THE NIGHT.

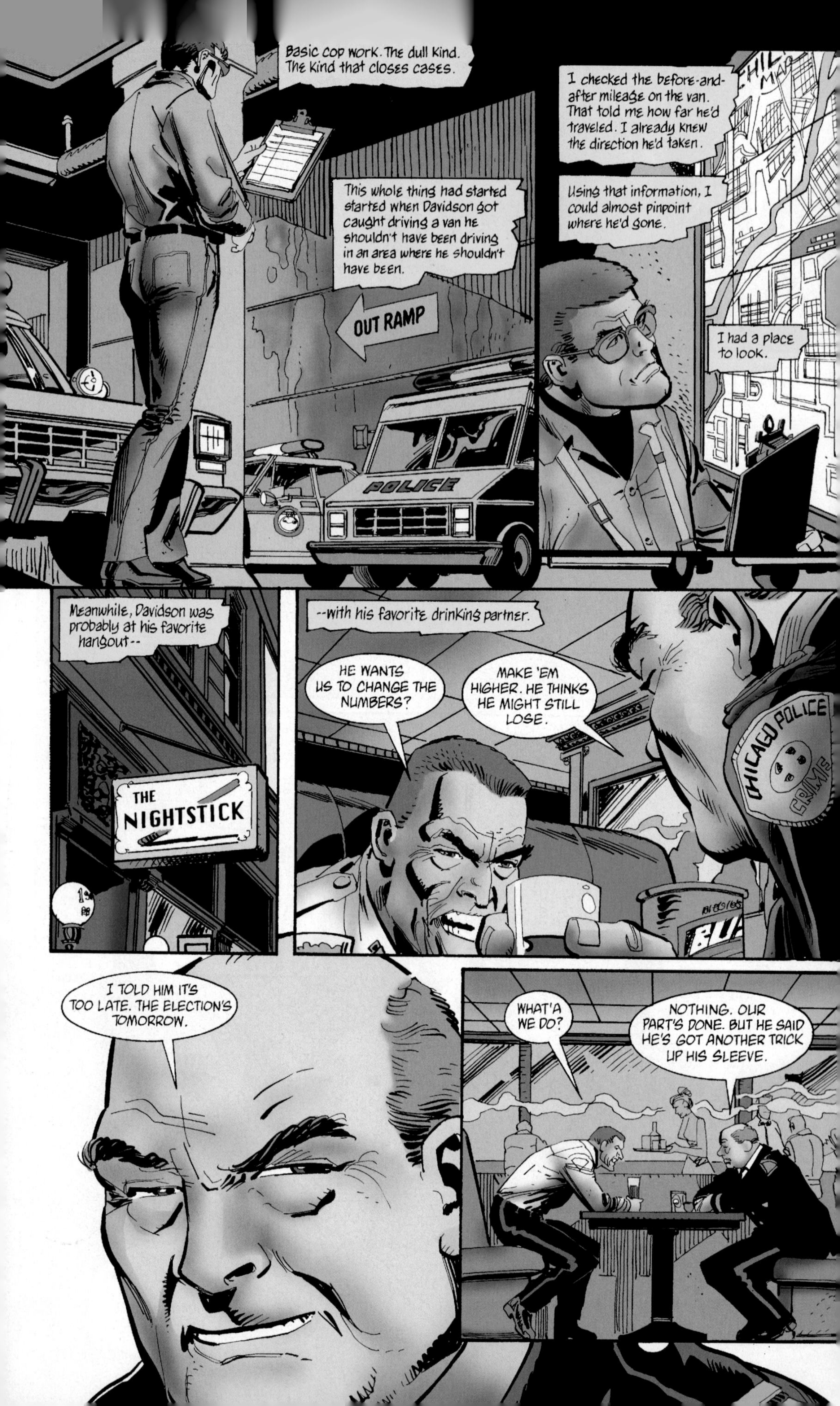

Basic cop work. The dull kind. The kind that closes cases.
This whole thing had started started when Davidson got caught driving a van he shouldn't have been driving in an area where he shouldn't have been.
OUT RAMP
POLICE
I checked the before-and-after mileage on the van. That told me how far he'd traveled. I already knew the direction he'd taken.
Using that information, I could almost pinpoint where he'd gone.
I had a place to look.
Meanwhile, Davidson was probably at his favorite hangout--
THE NIGHTSTICK
--with his favorite drinking partner.
HE WANTS US TO CHANGE THE NUMBERS?
MAKE 'EM HIGHER. HE THINKS HE MIGHT STILL LOSE.
CHICAGO POLICE
I TOLD HIM IT'S TOO LATE. THE ELECTION'S TOMORROW.
WHAT'A WE DO?
NOTHING. OUR PART'S DONE. BUT HE SAID HE'S GOT ANOTHER TRICK UP HIS SLEEVE.

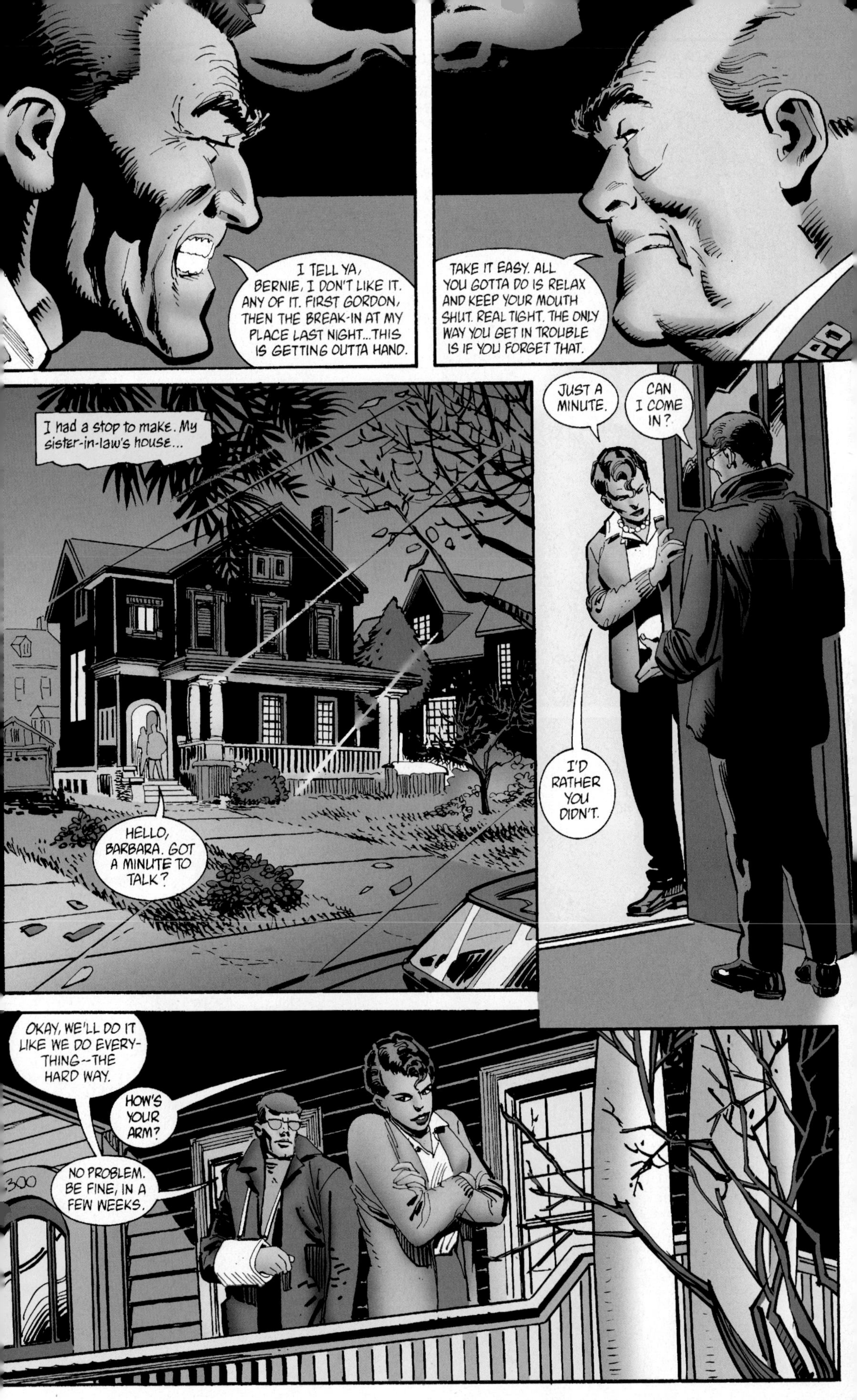
I TELL YA, BERNIE, I DON'T LIKE IT. ANY OF IT. FIRST GORDON, THEN THE BREAK-IN AT MY PLACE LAST NIGHT...THIS IS GETTING OUTTA HAND.
TAKE IT EASY. ALL YOU GOTTA DO IS RELAX AND KEEP YOUR MOUTH SHUT. REAL TIGHT. THE ONLY WAY YOU GET IN TROUBLE IS IF YOU FORGET THAT.
I had a stop to make. My sister-in-law's house...
HELLO, BARBARA. GOT A MINUTE TO TALK?
JUST A MINUTE.
CAN I COME IN?
I'D RATHER YOU DIDN'T.
OKAY, WE'LL DO IT LIKE WE DO EVERYTHING--THE HARD WAY.
HOW'S YOUR ARM?
NO PROBLEM. BE FINE, IN A FEW WEEKS.
300

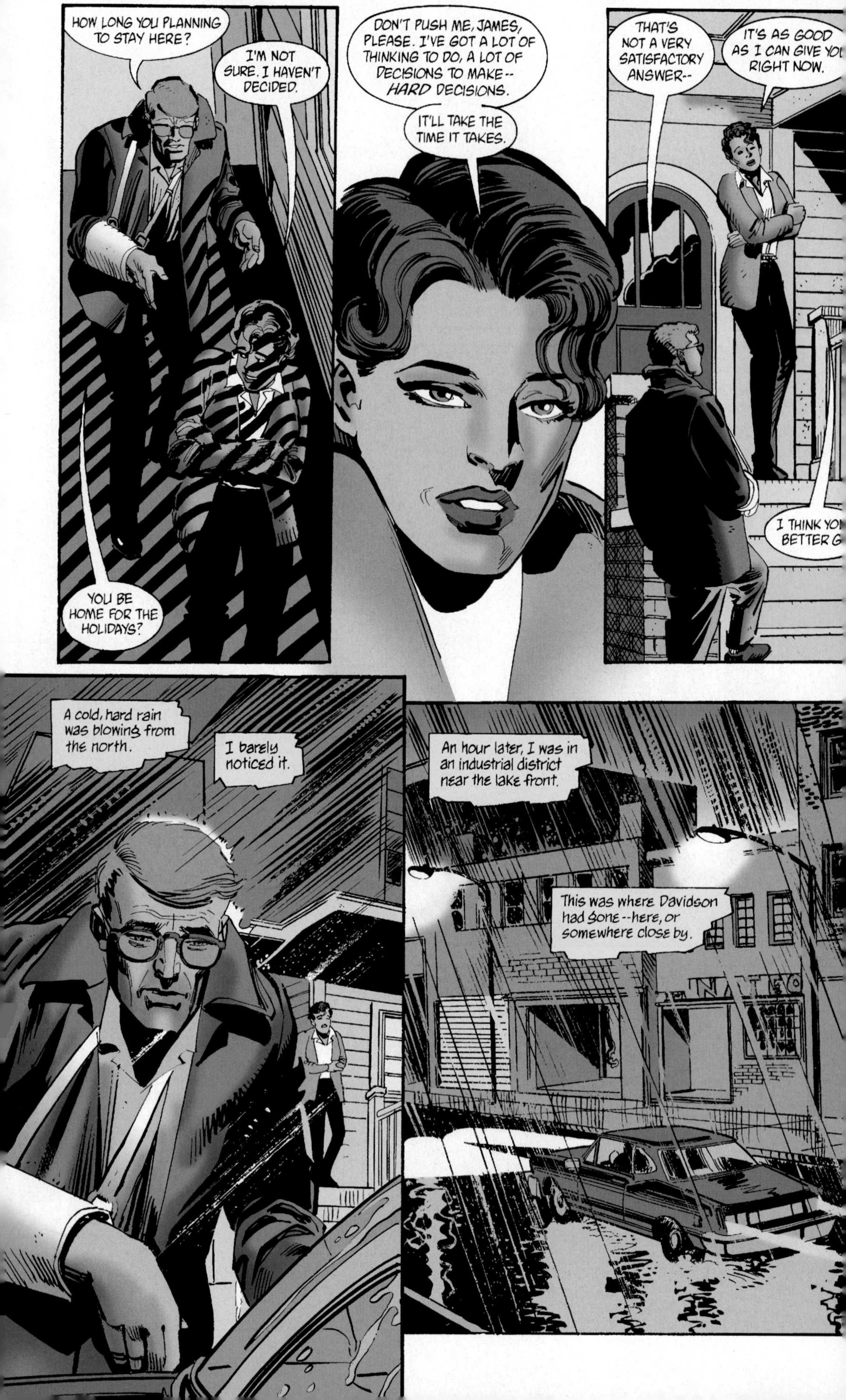
HOW LONG YOU PLANNING TO STAY HERE?
I'M NOT SURE. I HAVEN'T DECIDED.
YOU BE HOME FOR THE HOLIDAYS?
DON'T PUSH ME, JAMES, PLEASE. I'VE GOT A LOT OF THINKING TO DO, A LOT OF DECISIONS TO MAKE-- HARD DECISIONS.
IT'LL TAKE THE TIME IT TAKES.
THAT'S NOT A VERY SATISFACTORY ANSWER--
IT'S AS GOOD AS I CAN GIVE YOU RIGHT NOW.
I THINK YO BETTER G
A cold, hard rain was blowing from the north.
I barely noticed it.
An hour later, I was in an industrial district near the lake front.
This was where Davidson had gone --here, or somewhere close by.

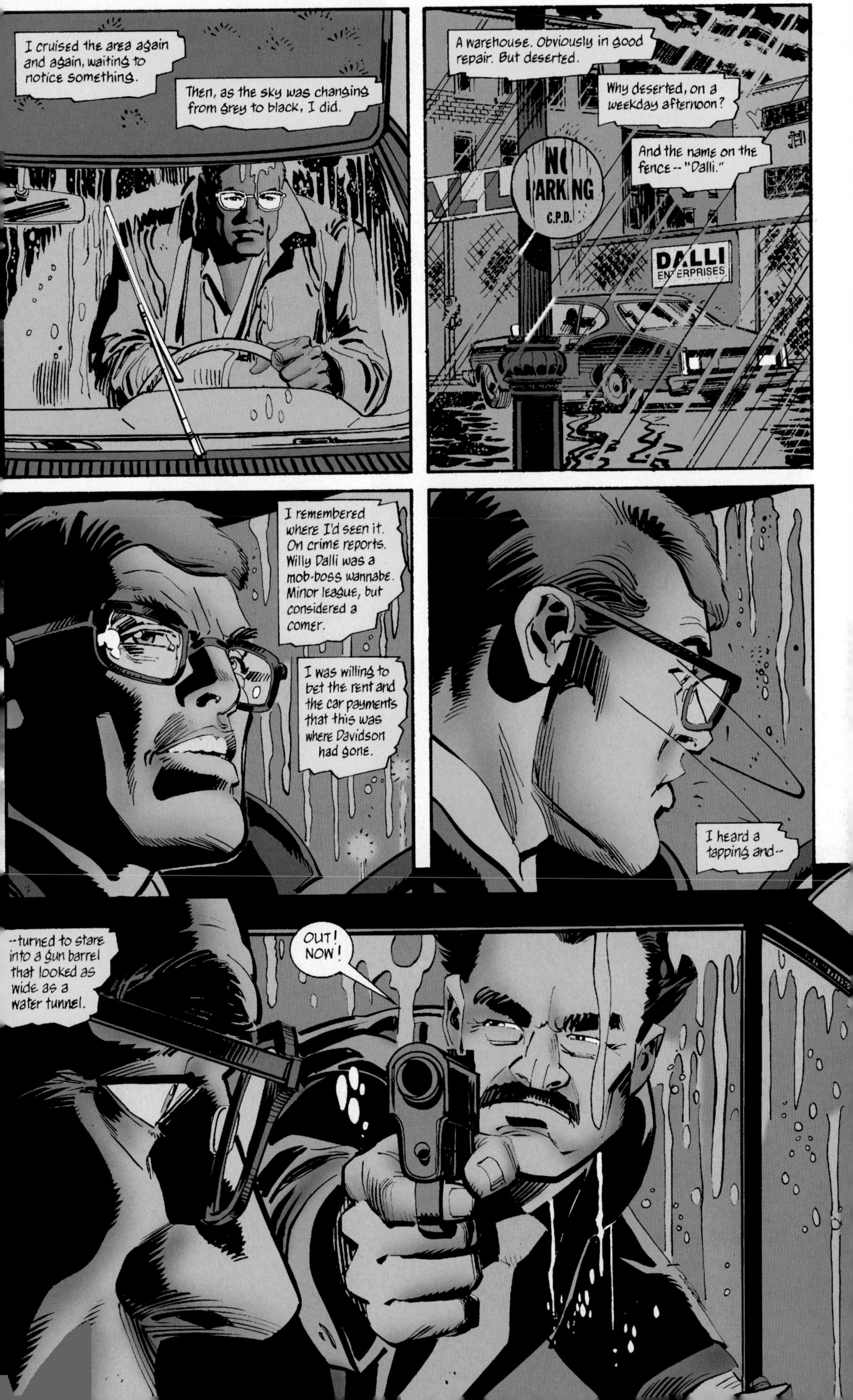
I cruised the area again and again, waiting to notice something.
Then, as the sky was changing from grey to black, I did.
A warehouse. Obviously in good repair. But deserted.
Why deserted, on a weekday afternoon?
And the name on the fence -- "Dalli."
NO PARKING
C.P.D.
DALLI ENTERPRISES
I remembered where I'd seen it. On crime reports. Willy Dalli was a mob-boss wannabe. Minor league, but considered a comer.
I was willing to bet the rent and the car payments that this was where Davidson had gone.
I heard a tapping and--
--turned to stare into a gun barrel that looked as wide as a water tunnel.
OUT! NOW!

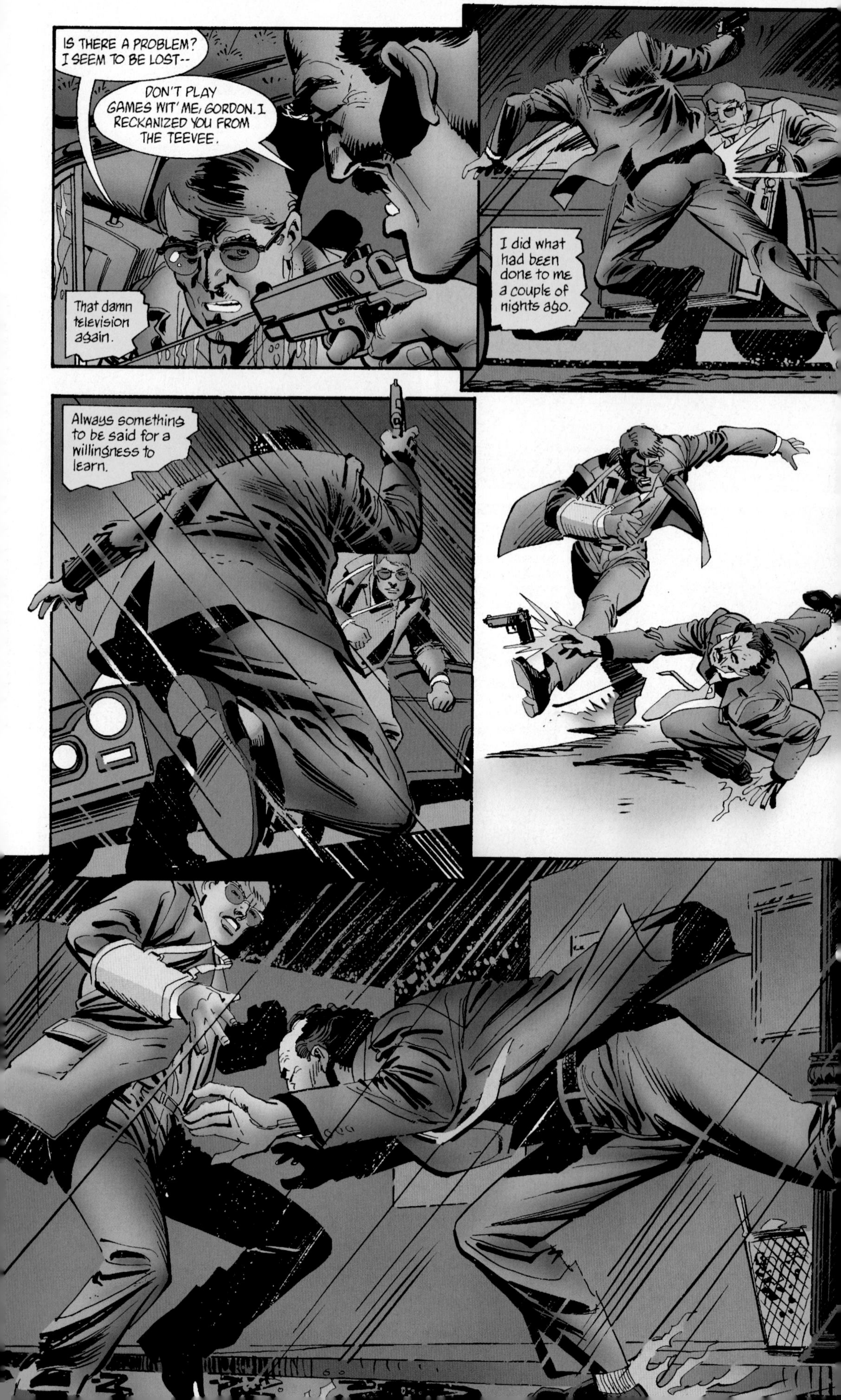
IS THERE A PROBLEM? I SEEM TO BE LOST--
DON'T PLAY GAMES WIT' ME, GORDON. I RECKANIZED YOU FROM THE TEEVEE.
That damn television again.
I did what had been done to me a couple of nights ago.
Always something to be said for a willingness to learn.

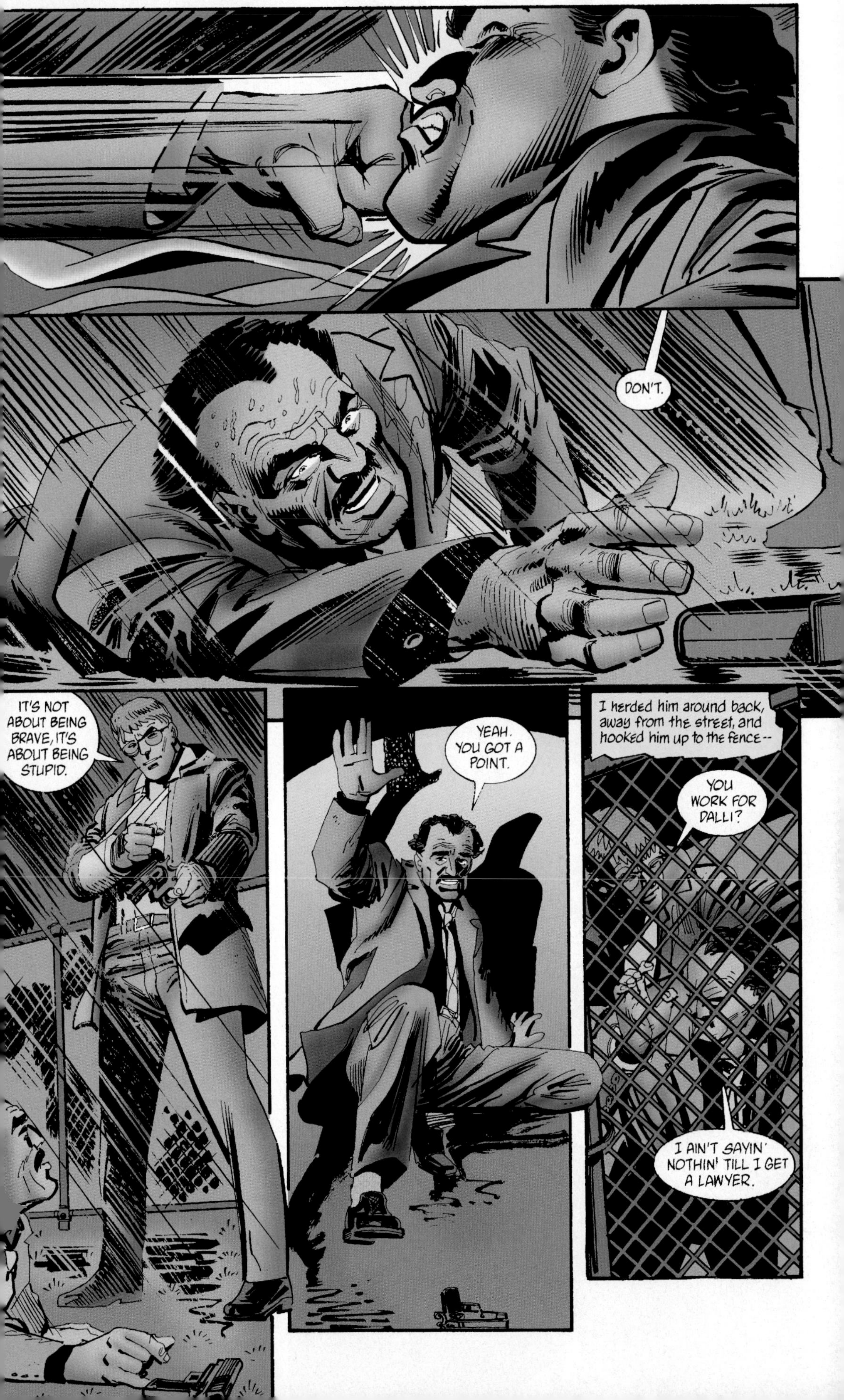
DON'T.
IT'S NOT ABOUT BEING BRAVE, IT'S ABOUT BEING STUPID.
YEAH. YOU GOT A POINT.
I herded him around back, away from the street, and hooked him up to the fence--
YOU WORK FOR DALLI?
I AIN'T SAYIN' NOTHIN' TILL I GET A LAWYER.

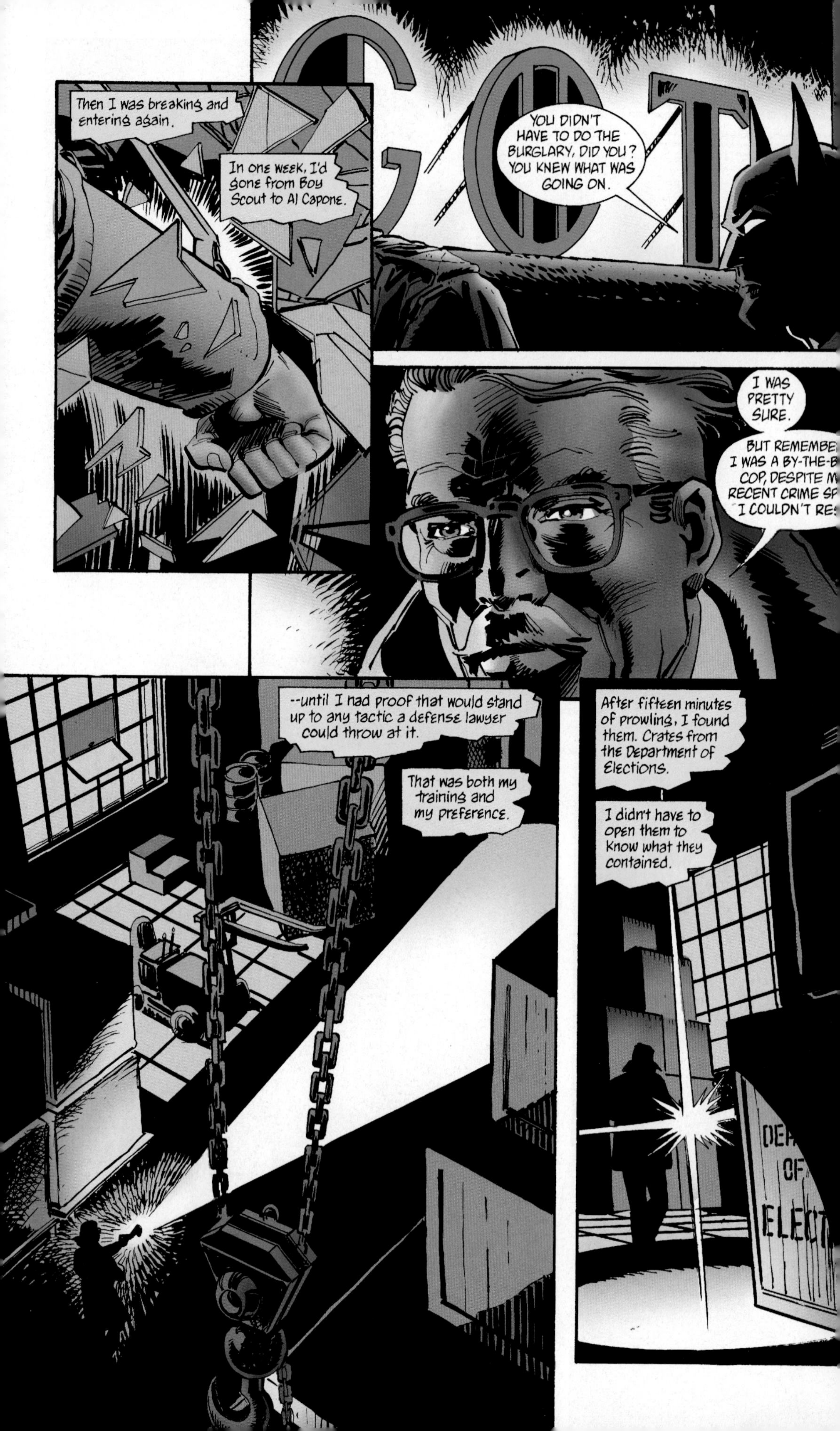
Then I was breaking and entering again.
In one week, I'd gone from Boy Scout to Al Capone.
YOU DIDN'T HAVE TO DO THE BURGLARY, DID YOU? YOU KNEW WHAT WAS GOING ON.
I WAS PRETTY SURE.
BUT REMEMBE
I WAS A BY-THE-B
COP, DESPITE M
RECENT CRIME SP
I COULDN'T RE
--until I had proof that would stand up to any tactic a defense lawyer could throw at it.
That was both my training and my preference.
After fifteen minutes of prowling, I found them. Crates from the Department of Elections.
I didn't have to open them to know what they contained.
DEP
OF
ELECT

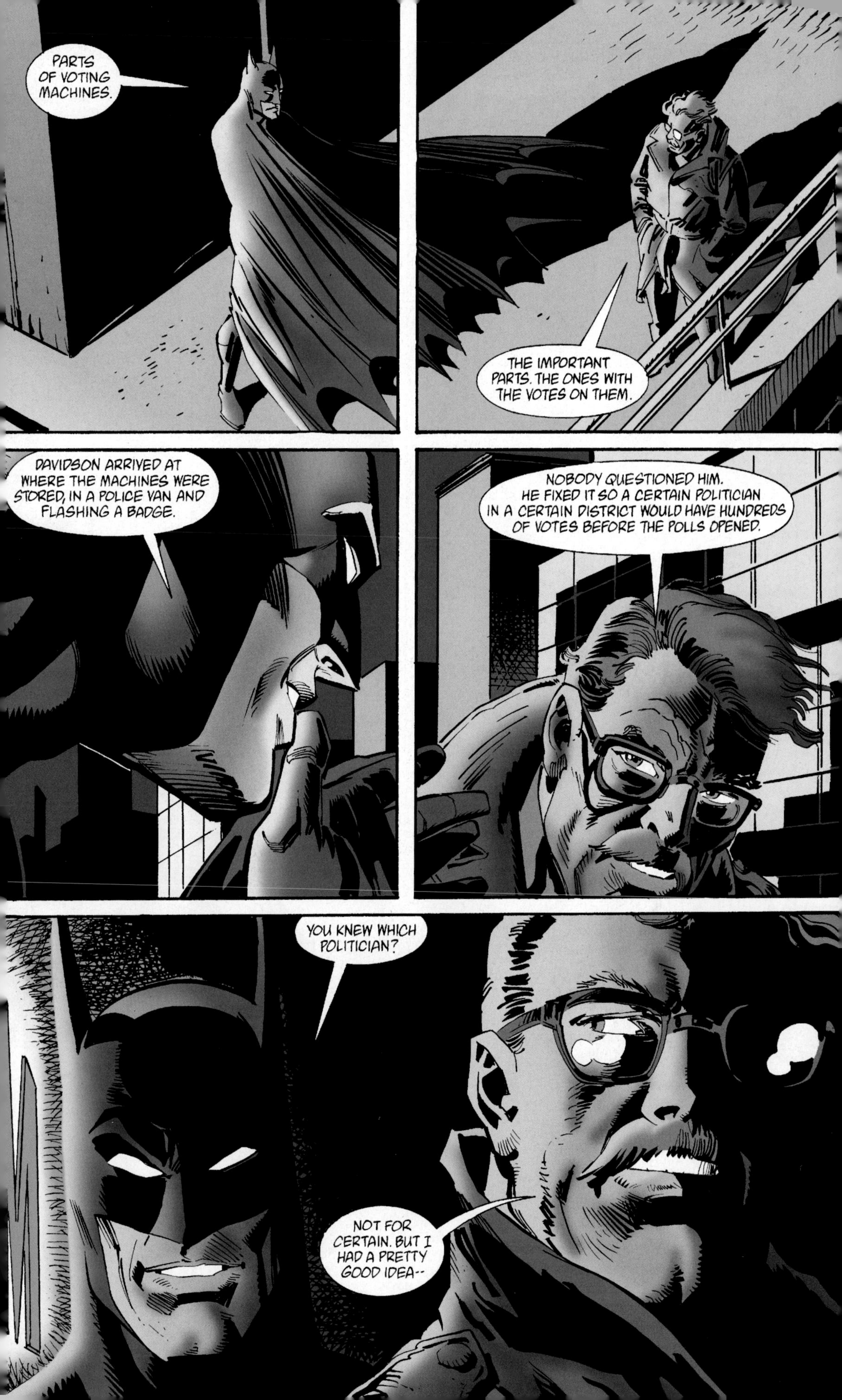
PARTS OF VOTING MACHINES.
THE IMPORTANT PARTS. THE ONES WITH THE VOTES ON THEM.
DAVIDSON ARRIVED AT WHERE THE MACHINES WERE STORED, IN A POLICE VAN AND FLASHING A BADGE.
NOBODY QUESTIONED HIM. HE FIXED IT SO A CERTAIN POLITICIAN IN A CERTAIN DISTRICT WOULD HAVE HUNDREDS OF VOTES BEFORE THE POLLS OPENED.
YOU KNEW WHICH POLITICIAN?
NOT FOR CERTAIN. BUT I HAD A PRETTY GOOD IDEA--

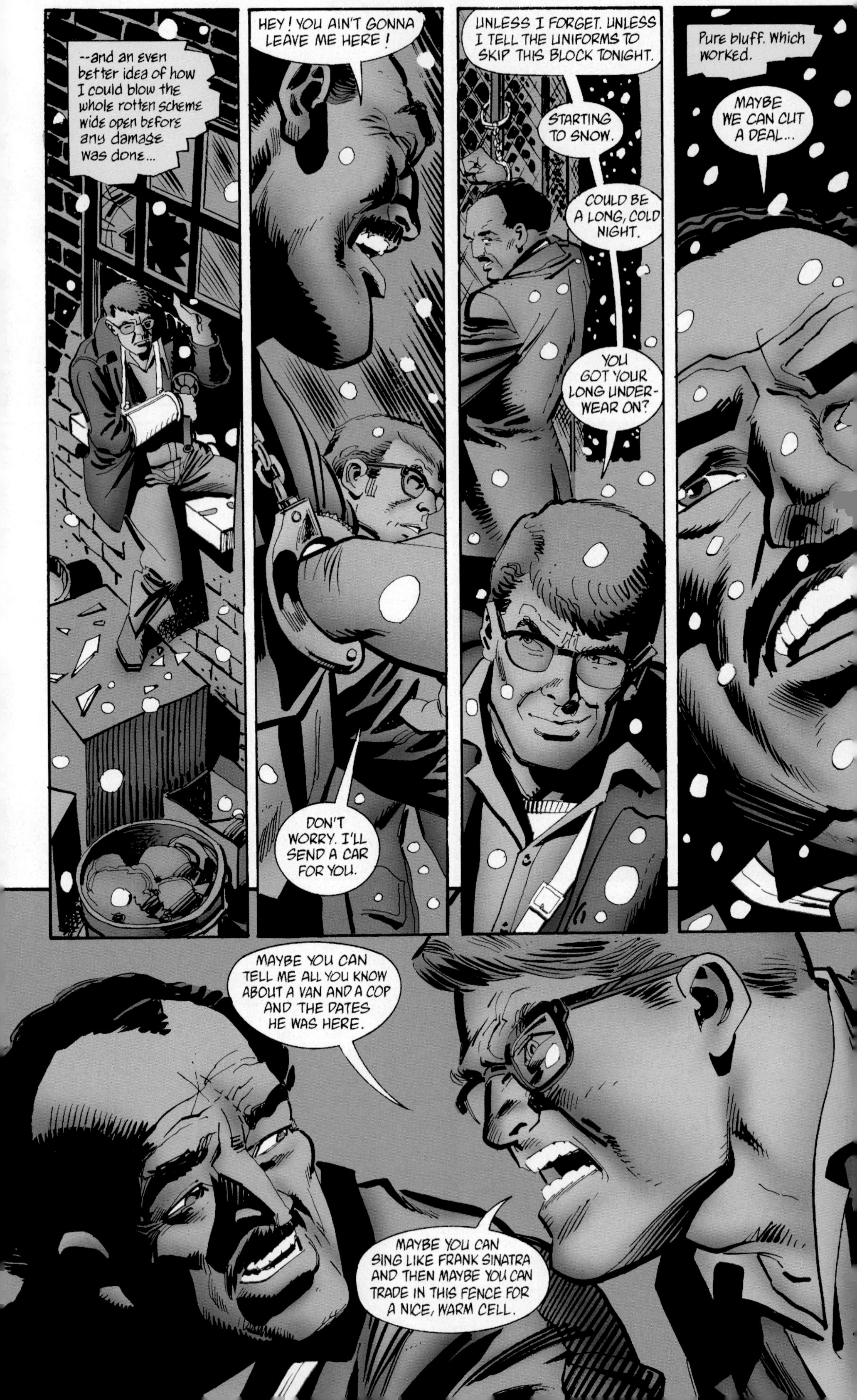
--and an even better idea of how I could blow the whole rotten scheme wide open before any damage was done...
HEY! YOU AIN'T GONNA LEAVE ME HERE!
DON'T WORRY. I'LL SEND A CAR FOR YOU.
UNLESS I FORGET. UNLESS I TELL THE UNIFORMS TO SKIP THIS BLOCK TONIGHT.
STARTING TO SNOW.
COULD BE A LONG, COLD NIGHT.
YOU GOT YOUR LONG UNDER-WEAR ON?
Pure bluff. Which worked.
MAYBE WE CAN CUT A DEAL...
MAYBE YOU CAN TELL ME ALL YOU KNOW ABOUT A VAN AND A COP AND THE DATES HE WAS HERE.
MAYBE YOU CAN SING LIKE FRANK SINATRA AND THEN MAYBE YOU CAN TRADE IN THIS FENCE FOR A NICE, WARM CELL.

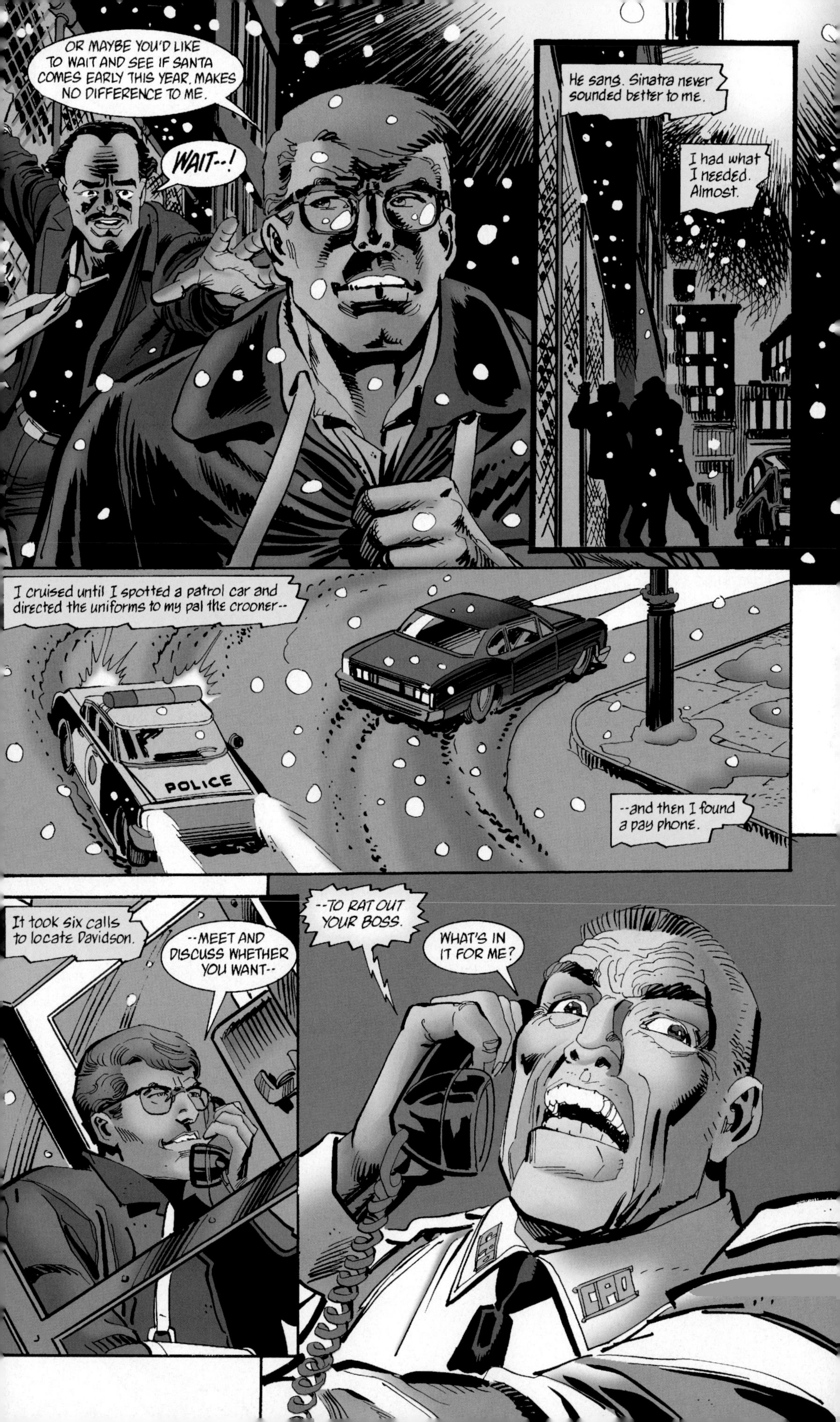
OR MAYBE YOU'D LIKE TO WAIT AND SEE IF SANTA COMES EARLY THIS YEAR. MAKES NO DIFFERENCE TO ME.
WAIT--!
He sang. Sinatra never sounded better to me.
I had what I needed. Almost.
I cruised until I spotted a patrol car and directed the uniforms to my pal the crooner--
POLICE
--and then I found a pay phone.
It took six calls to locate Davidson.
--MEET AND DISCUSS WHETHER YOU WANT--
--TO RAT OUT YOUR BOSS.
WHAT'S IN IT FOR ME?

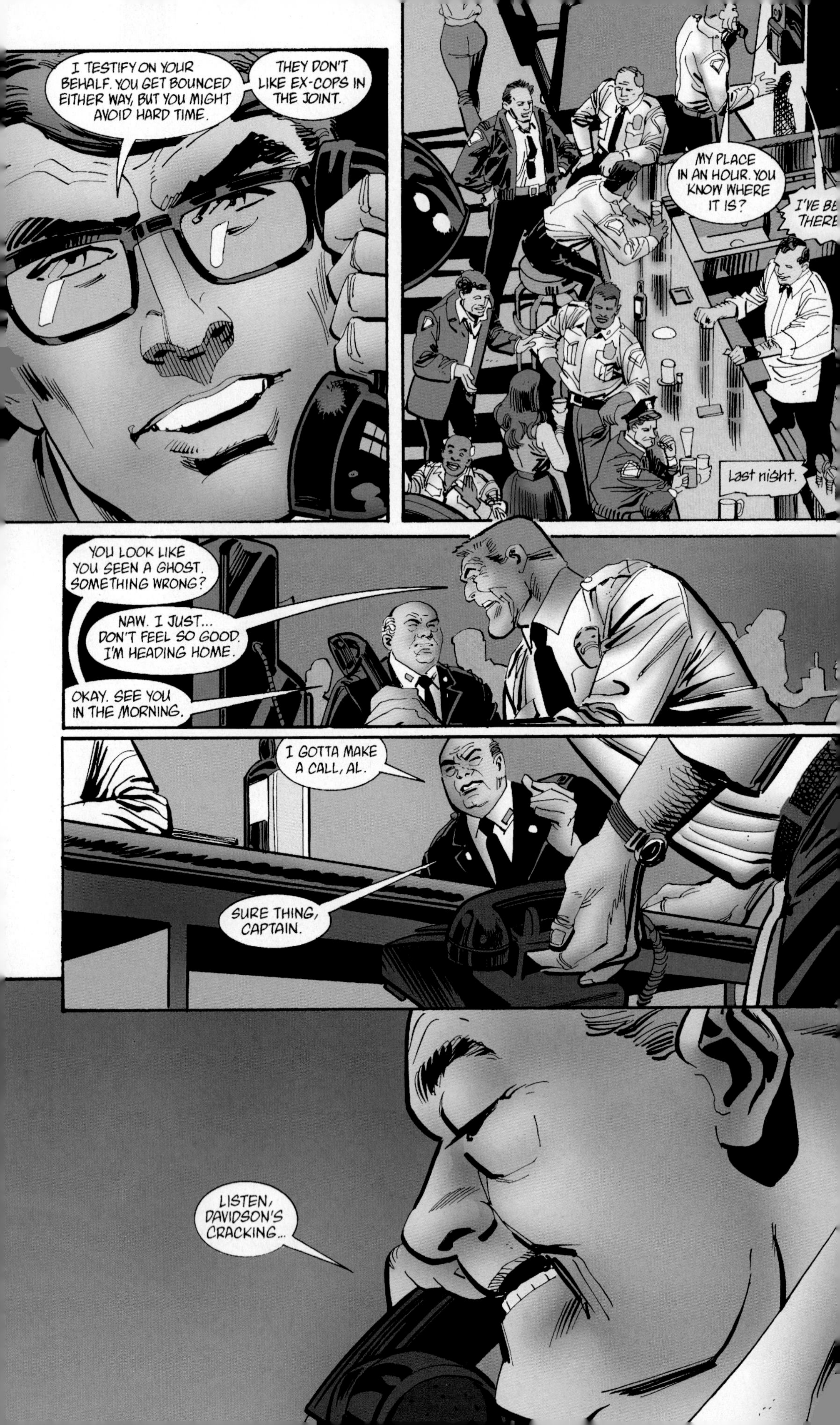
I TESTIFY ON YOUR BEHALF. YOU GET BOUNCED EITHER WAY, BUT YOU MIGHT AVOID HARD TIME.
THEY DON'T LIKE EX-COPS IN THE JOINT.
Last night.
MY PLACE IN AN HOUR. YOU KNOW WHERE IT IS?
YOU LOOK LIKE YOU SEEN A GHOST. SOMETHING WRONG?
NAW. I JUST... DON'T FEEL SO GOOD. I'M HEADING HOME.
OKAY. SEE YOU IN THE MORNING.
I GOTTA MAKE A CALL, AL.
SURE THING, CAPTAIN.
LISTEN, DAVIDSON'S CRACKING...

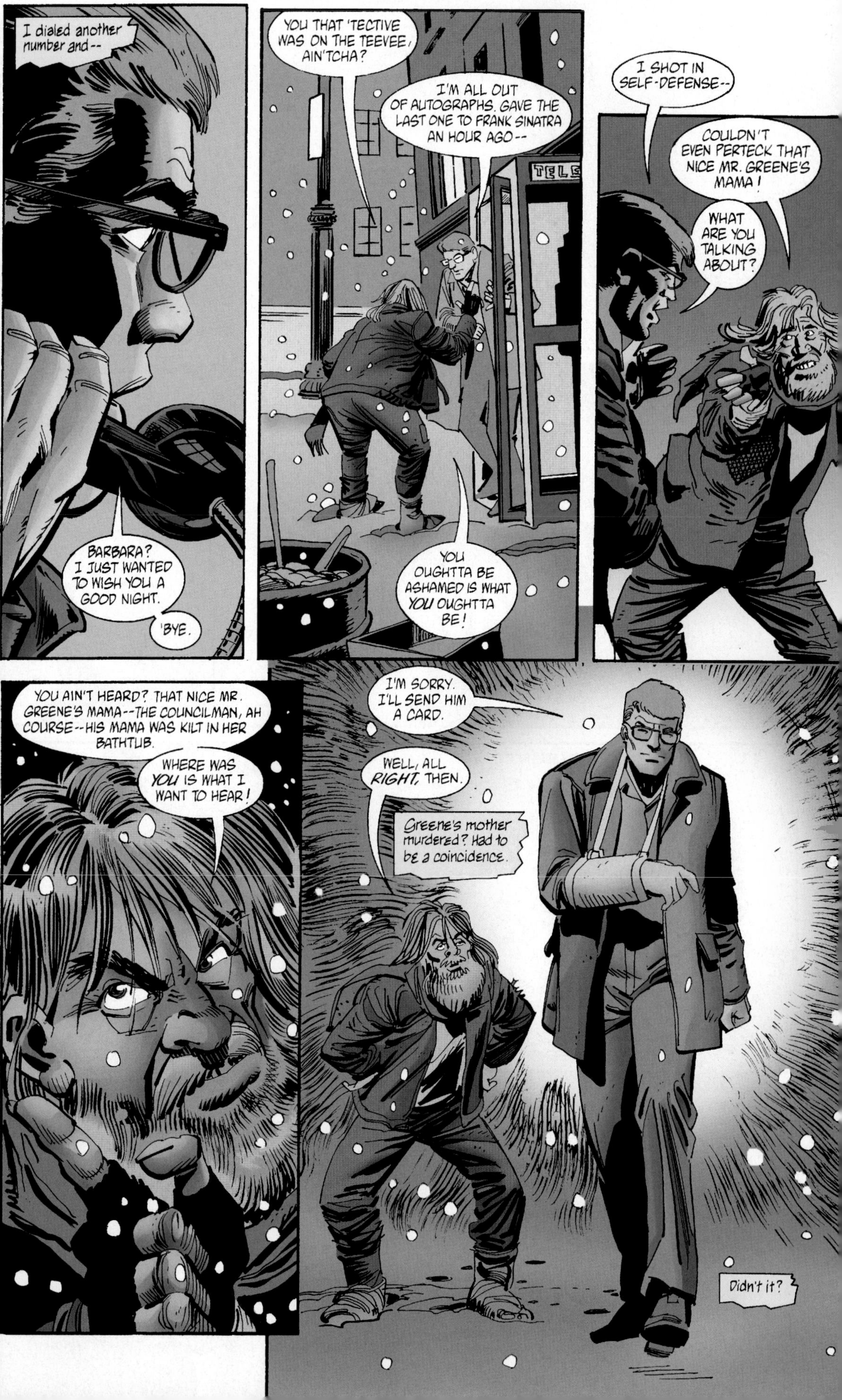
I dialed another number and--
BARBARA? I JUST WANTED TO WISH YOU A GOOD NIGHT.
'BYE.
YOU THAT 'TECTIVE WAS ON THE TEEVEE, AIN'TCHA?
I'M ALL OUT OF AUTOGRAPHS. GAVE THE LAST ONE TO FRANK SINATRA AN HOUR AGO--
YOU OUGHTTA BE ASHAMED IS WHAT YOU OUGHTTA BE!
I SHOT IN SELF-DEFENSE--
COULDN'T EVEN PERTECK THAT NICE MR. GREENE'S MAMA!
WHAT ARE YOU TALKING ABOUT?
YOU AIN'T HEARD? THAT NICE MR. GREENE'S MAMA--THE COUNCILMAN, AH COURSE--HIS MAMA WAS KILT IN HER BATHTUB.
WHERE WAS YOU IS WHAT I WANT TO HEAR!
I'M SORRY. I'LL SEND HIM A CARD.
WELL, ALL RIGHT, THEN.
Greene's mother murdered? Had to be a coincidence.
Didn't it?

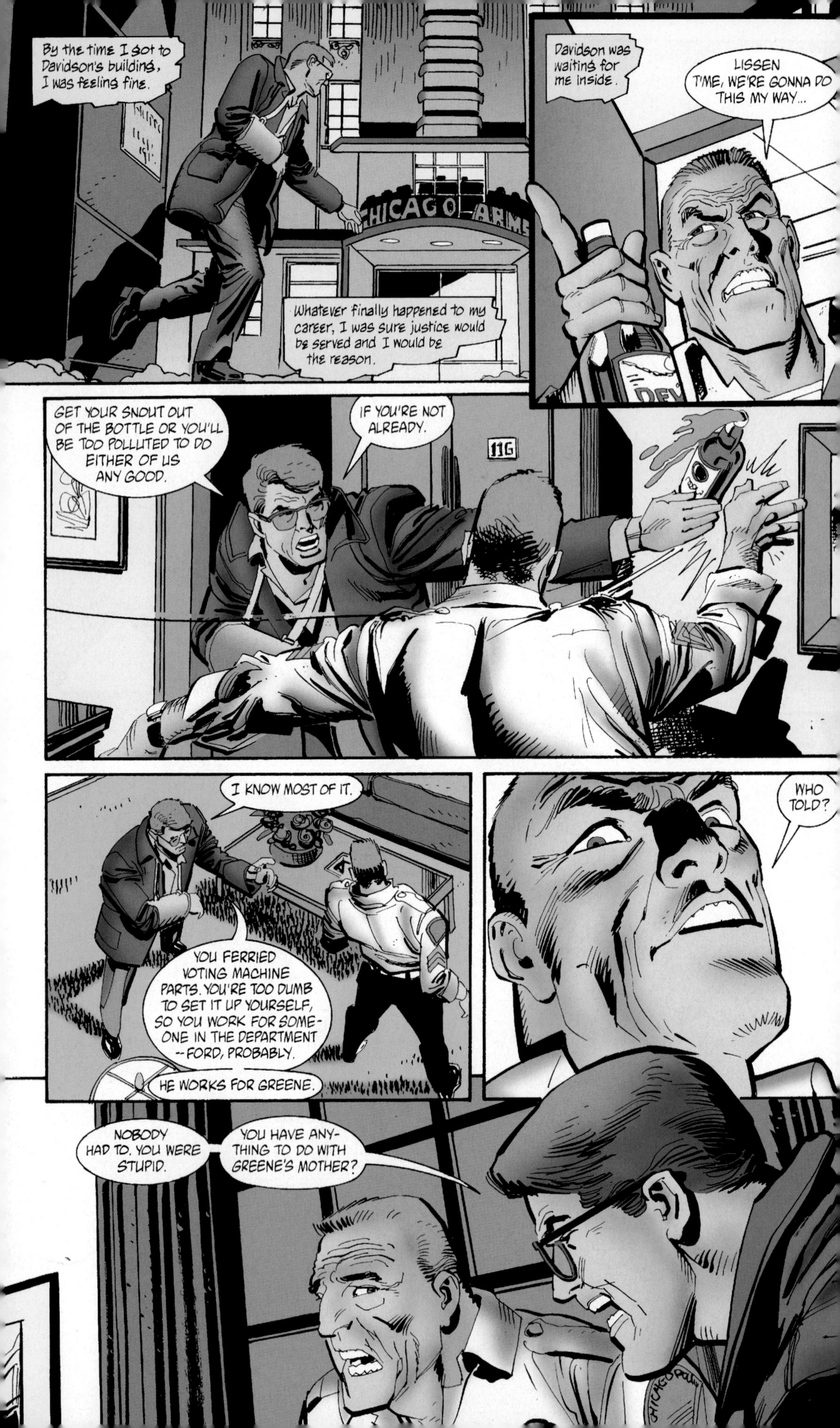

By the time I got to Davidson's building, I was feeling fine.
CHICAGO ARMS
Whatever finally happened to my career, I was sure justice would be served and I would be the reason.
Davidson was waiting for me inside.
LISSEN T'ME, WE'RE GONNA DO THIS MY WAY...
GET YOUR SNOUT OUT OF THE BOTTLE OR YOU'LL BE TOO POLLUTED TO DO EITHER OF US ANY GOOD.
IF YOU'RE NOT ALREADY.
11G
I KNOW MOST OF IT.
YOU FERRIED VOTING MACHINE PARTS. YOU'RE TOO DUMB TO SET IT UP YOURSELF, SO YOU WORK FOR SOME-ONE IN THE DEPARTMENT --FORD, PROBABLY.
HE WORKS FOR GREENE.
WHO TOLD?
NOBODY HAD TO. YOU WERE STUPID.
YOU HAVE ANY-THING TO DO WITH GREENE'S MOTHER?

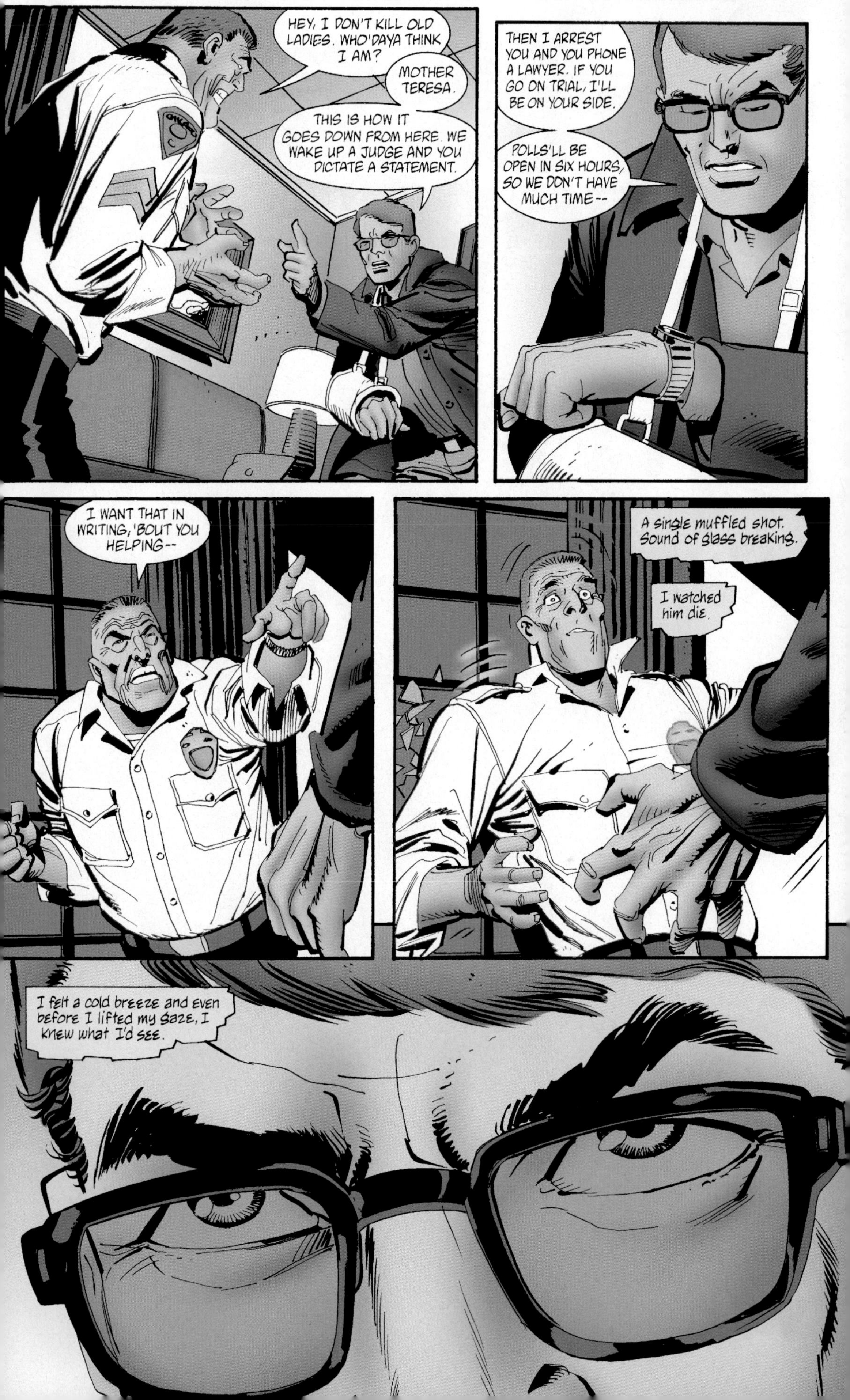
HEY, I DON'T KILL OLD LADIES. WHO'DAYA THINK I AM?
MOTHER TERESA.
THIS IS HOW IT GOES DOWN FROM HERE. WE WAKE UP A JUDGE AND YOU DICTATE A STATEMENT.
THEN I ARREST YOU AND YOU PHONE A LAWYER. IF YOU GO ON TRIAL, I'LL BE ON YOUR SIDE.
POLLS'LL BE OPEN IN SIX HOURS, SO WE DON'T HAVE MUCH TIME--
I WANT THAT IN WRITING, 'BOUT YOU HELPING--
A single muffled shot. Sound of glass breaking.
I watched him die.
I felt a cold breeze and even before I lifted my gaze, I knew what I'd see.

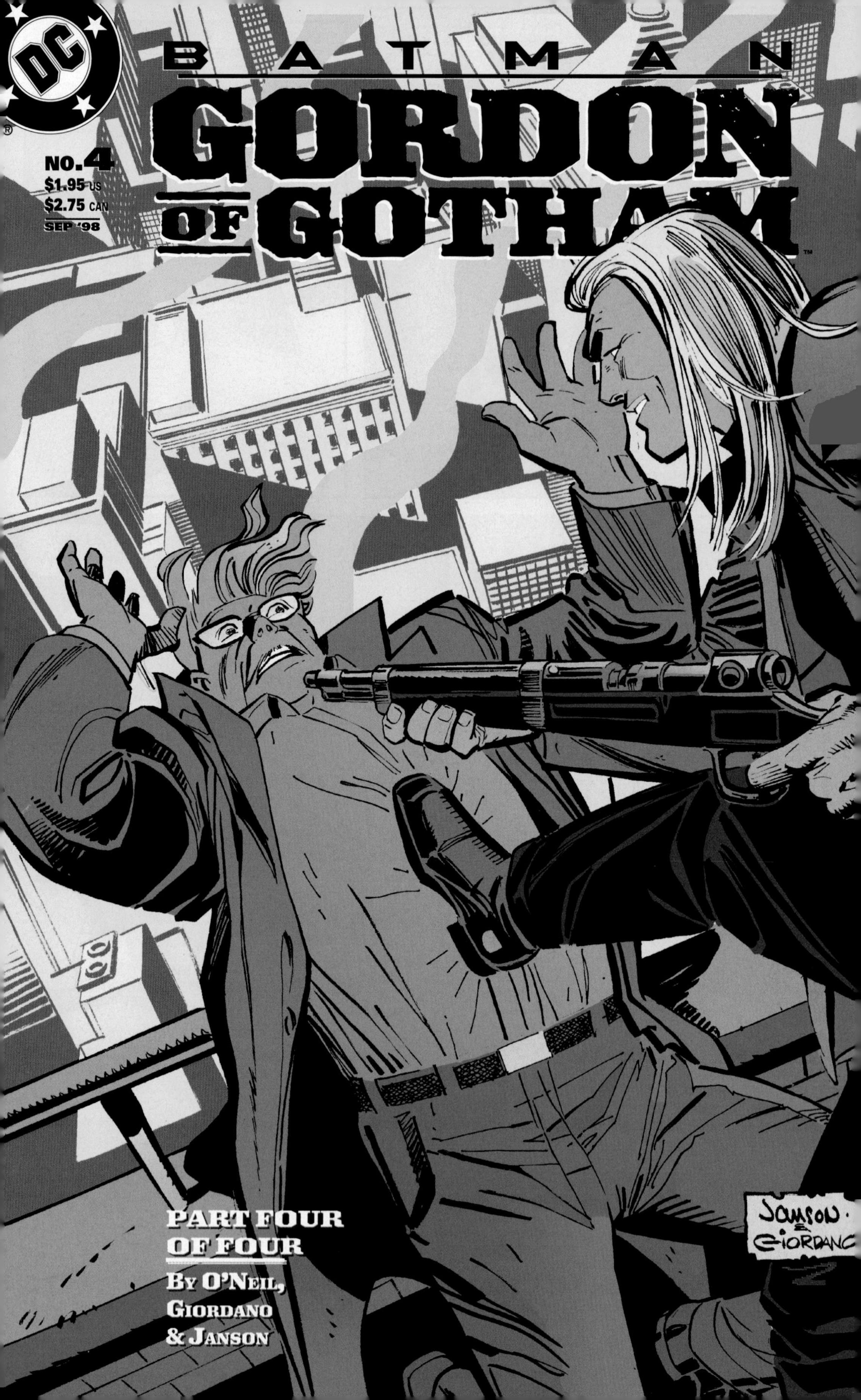
BATMAN
GORDON OF GOTHAM
NO.4
$1.95 US
$2.75 CAN
SEP '98
PART FOUR OF FOUR
BY O'NEIL, GIORDANO & JANSON
JANSON & GIORDANO

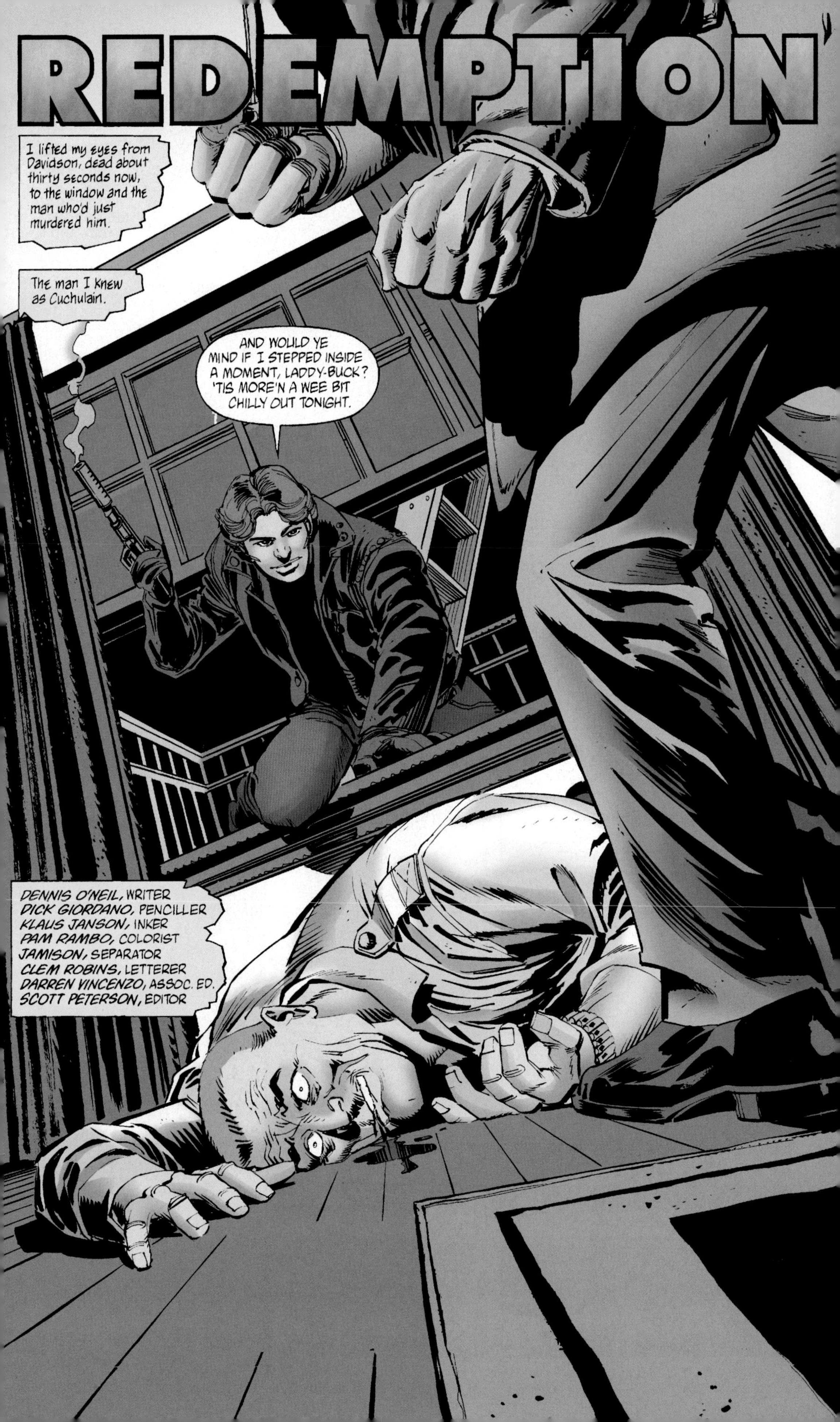
REDEMPTION'
I lifted my eyes from Davidson, dead about thirty seconds now, to the window and the man who'd just murdered him.
The man I knew as Cuchulain.
AND WOULD YE MIND IF I STEPPED INSIDE A MOMENT, LADDY-BUCK? 'TIS MORE'N A WEE BIT CHILLY OUT TONIGHT.
DENNIS O'NEIL, WRITER
DICK GIORDANO, PENCILLER
KLAUS JANSON, INKER
PAM RAMBO, COLORIST
JAMISON, SEPARATOR
CLEM ROBINS, LETTERER
DARREN VINCENZO, ASSOC. ED.
SCOTT PETERSON, EDITOR

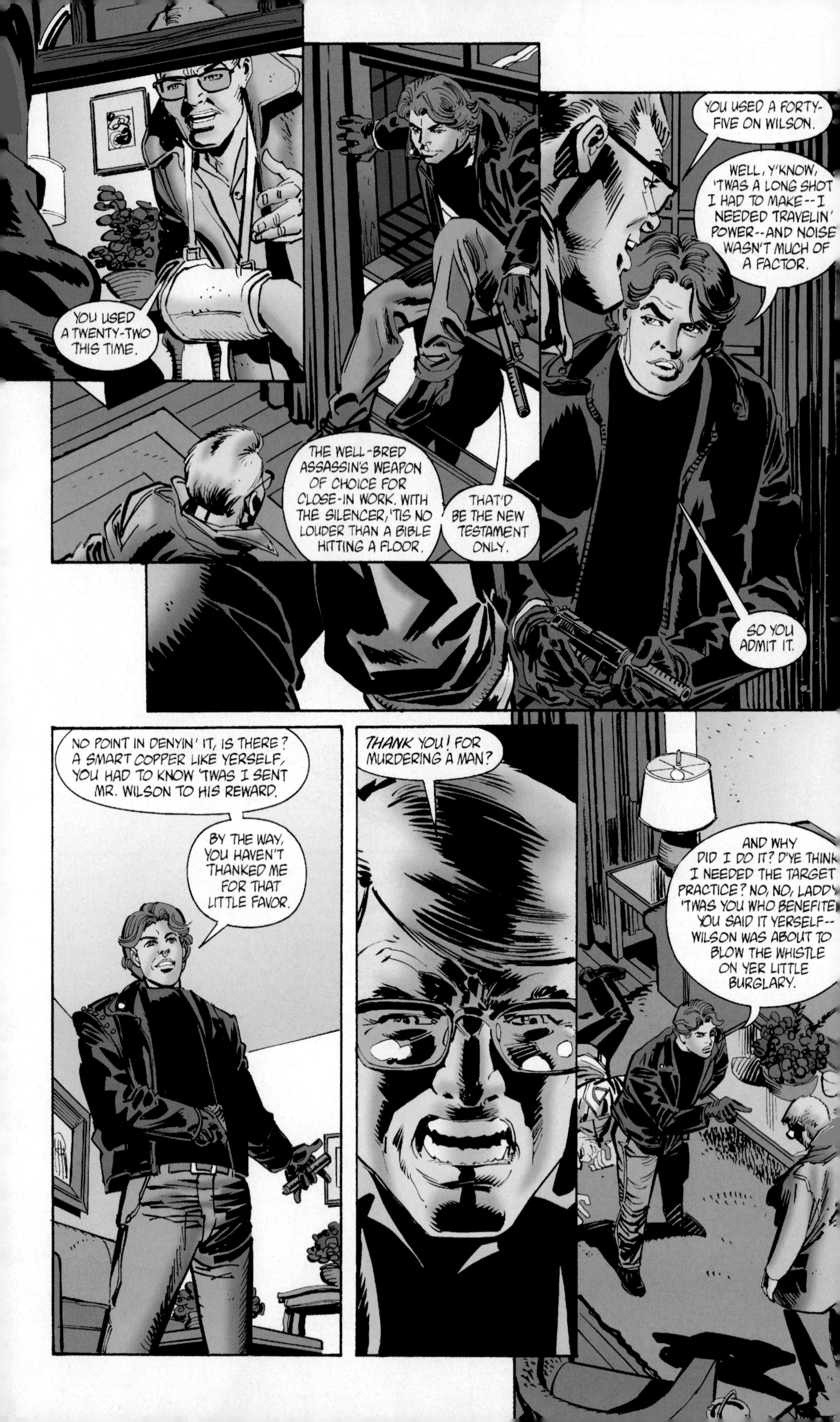
YOU USED A TWENTY-TWO THIS TIME.
YOU USED A FORTY-FIVE ON WILSON.
WELL, Y'KNOW, 'TWAS A LONG SHOT I HAD TO MAKE--I NEEDED TRAVELIN' POWER--AND NOISE WASN'T MUCH OF A FACTOR.
THE WELL-BRED ASSASSIN'S WEAPON OF CHOICE FOR CLOSE-IN WORK. WITH THE SILENCER, 'TIS NO LOUDER THAN A BIBLE HITTING A FLOOR.
THAT'D BE THE NEW TESTAMENT ONLY.
SO YOU ADMIT IT.
NO POINT IN DENYIN' IT, IS THERE? A SMART COPPER LIKE YERSELF, YOU HAD TO KNOW 'TWAS I SENT MR. WILSON TO HIS REWARD.
BY THE WAY, YOU HAVEN'T THANKED ME FOR THAT LITTLE FAVOR.
THANK YOU! FOR MURDERING A MAN?
AND WHY DID I DO IT? D'YE THINK I NEEDED THE TARGET PRACTICE? NO, NO, LADDY 'TWAS YOU WHO BENEFITE YOU SAID IT YERSELF-- WILSON WAS ABOUT TO BLOW THE WHISTLE ON YER LITTLE BURGLARY.

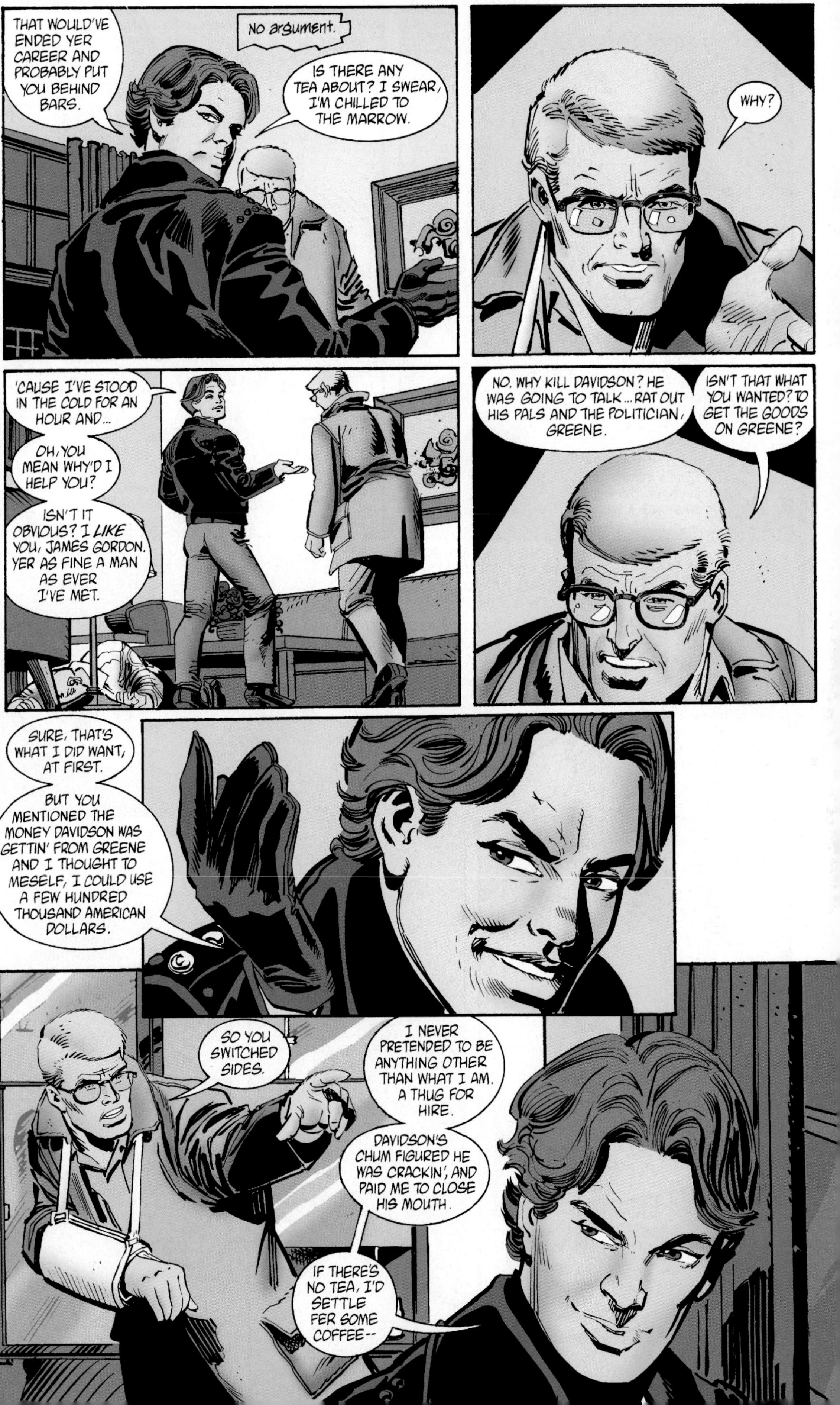
THAT WOULD'VE ENDED YER CAREER AND PROBABLY PUT YOU BEHIND BARS.
No argument.
IS THERE ANY TEA ABOUT? I SWEAR, I'M CHILLED TO THE MARROW.
WHY?
'CAUSE I'VE STOOD IN THE COLD FOR AN HOUR AND...
OH, YOU MEAN WHY'D I HELP YOU?
ISN'T IT OBVIOUS? I *LIKE* YOU, JAMES GORDON. YER AS FINE A MAN AS EVER I'VE MET.
NO. WHY KILL DAVIDSON? HE WAS GOING TO TALK... RAT OUT HIS PALS AND THE POLITICIAN, GREENE.
ISN'T THAT WHAT YOU WANTED? TO GET THE GOODS ON GREENE?
SURE, THAT'S WHAT I DID WANT, AT FIRST.
BUT YOU MENTIONED THE MONEY DAVIDSON WAS GETTIN' FROM GREENE AND I THOUGHT TO MESELF, I COULD USE A FEW HUNDRED THOUSAND AMERICAN DOLLARS.
SO YOU SWITCHED SIDES.
I NEVER PRETENDED TO BE ANYTHING OTHER THAN WHAT I AM. A THUG FOR HIRE.
DAVIDSON'S CHUM FIGURED HE WAS CRACKIN', AND PAID ME TO CLOSE HIS MOUTH.
IF THERE'S NO TEA, I'D SETTLE FER SOME COFFEE--

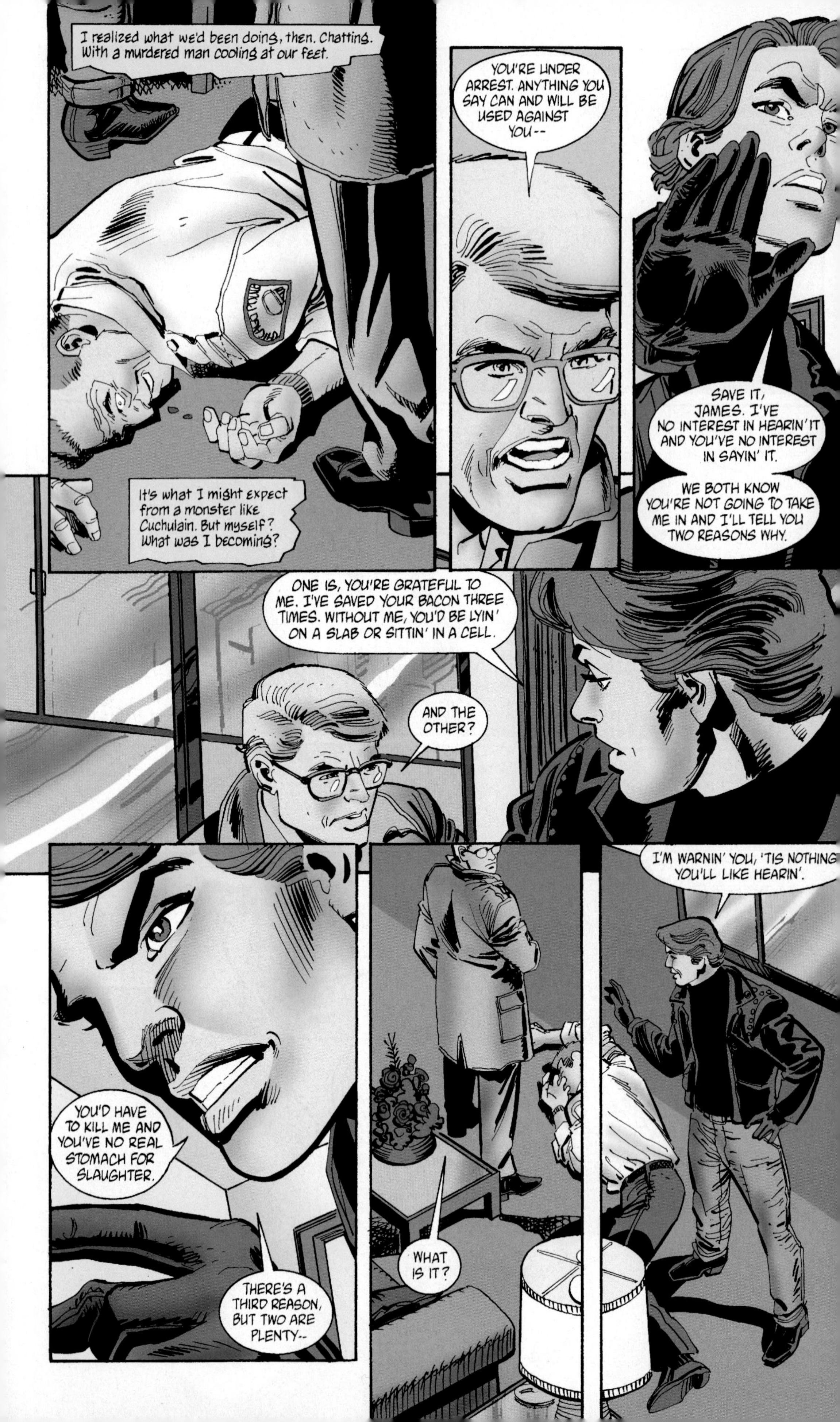
I realized what we'd been doing, then. Chatting. With a murdered man cooling at our feet.
It's what I might expect from a monster like Cuchulain. But myself? What was I becoming?
YOU'RE UNDER ARREST. ANYTHING YOU SAY CAN AND WILL BE USED AGAINST YOU--
SAVE IT, JAMES. I'VE NO INTEREST IN HEARIN' IT AND YOU'VE NO INTEREST IN SAYIN' IT.
WE BOTH KNOW YOU'RE NOT GOING TO TAKE ME IN AND I'LL TELL YOU TWO REASONS WHY.
ONE IS, YOU'RE GRATEFUL TO ME. I'VE SAVED YOUR BACON THREE TIMES. WITHOUT ME, YOU'D BE LYIN' ON A SLAB OR SITTIN' IN A CELL.
AND THE OTHER?
YOU'D HAVE TO KILL ME AND YOU'VE NO REAL STOMACH FOR SLAUGHTER.
THERE'S A THIRD REASON, BUT TWO ARE PLENTY--
WHAT IS IT?
I'M WARNIN' YOU, 'TIS NOTHING YOU'LL LIKE HEARIN'.

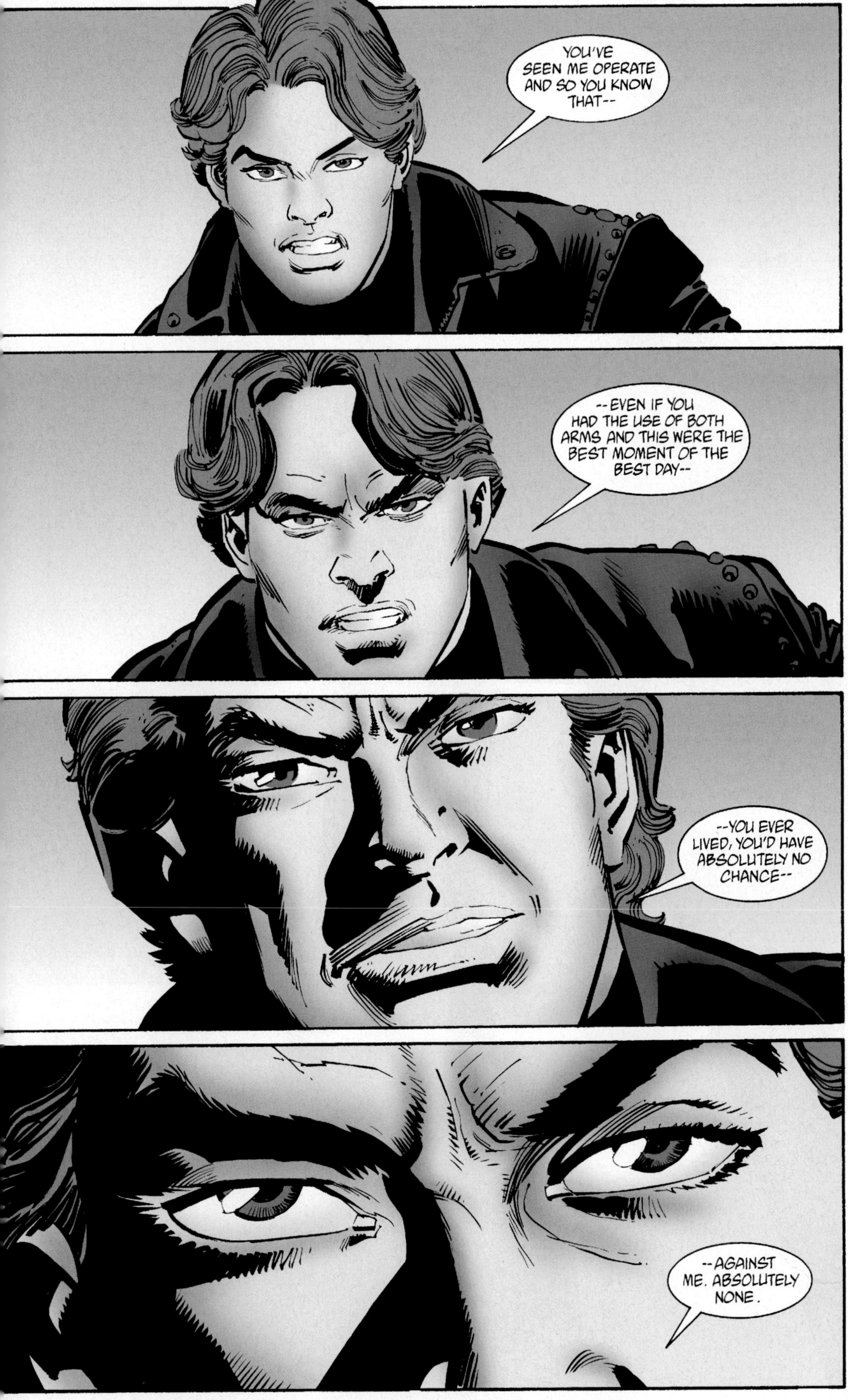
YOU'VE SEEN ME OPERATE AND SO YOU KNOW THAT--
--EVEN IF YOU HAD THE USE OF BOTH ARMS AND THIS WERE THE BEST MOMENT OF THE BEST DAY--
--YOU EVER LIVED, YOU'D HAVE ABSOLUTELY NO CHANCE--
--AGAINST ME. ABSOLUTELY NONE.

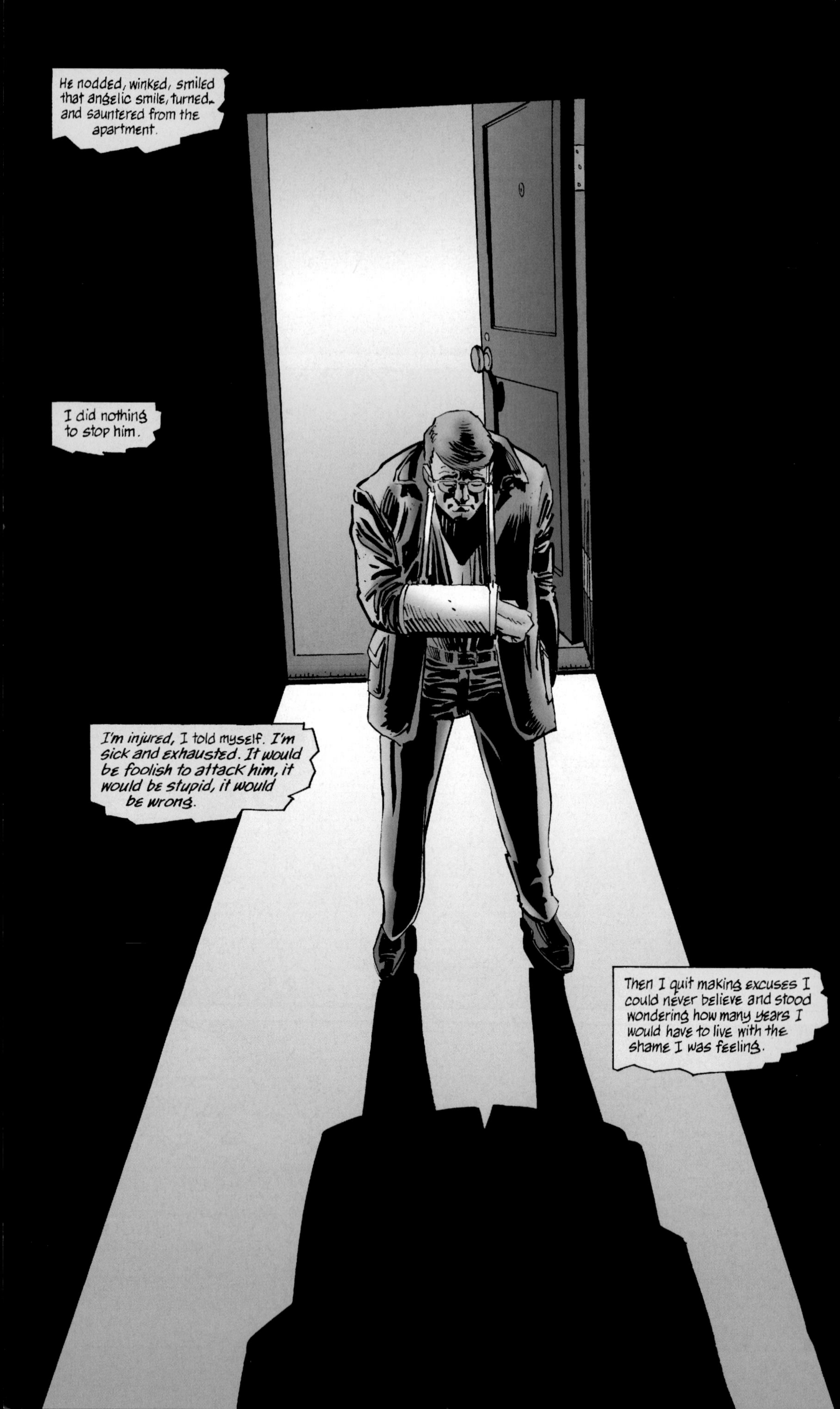
He nodded, winked, smiled that angelic smile, turned and sauntered from the apartment.
I did nothing to stop him.
I'm injured, I told myself. I'm sick and exhausted. It would be foolish to attack him, it would be stupid, it would be wrong.
Then I quit making excuses I could never believe and stood wondering how many years I would have to live with the shame I was feeling.

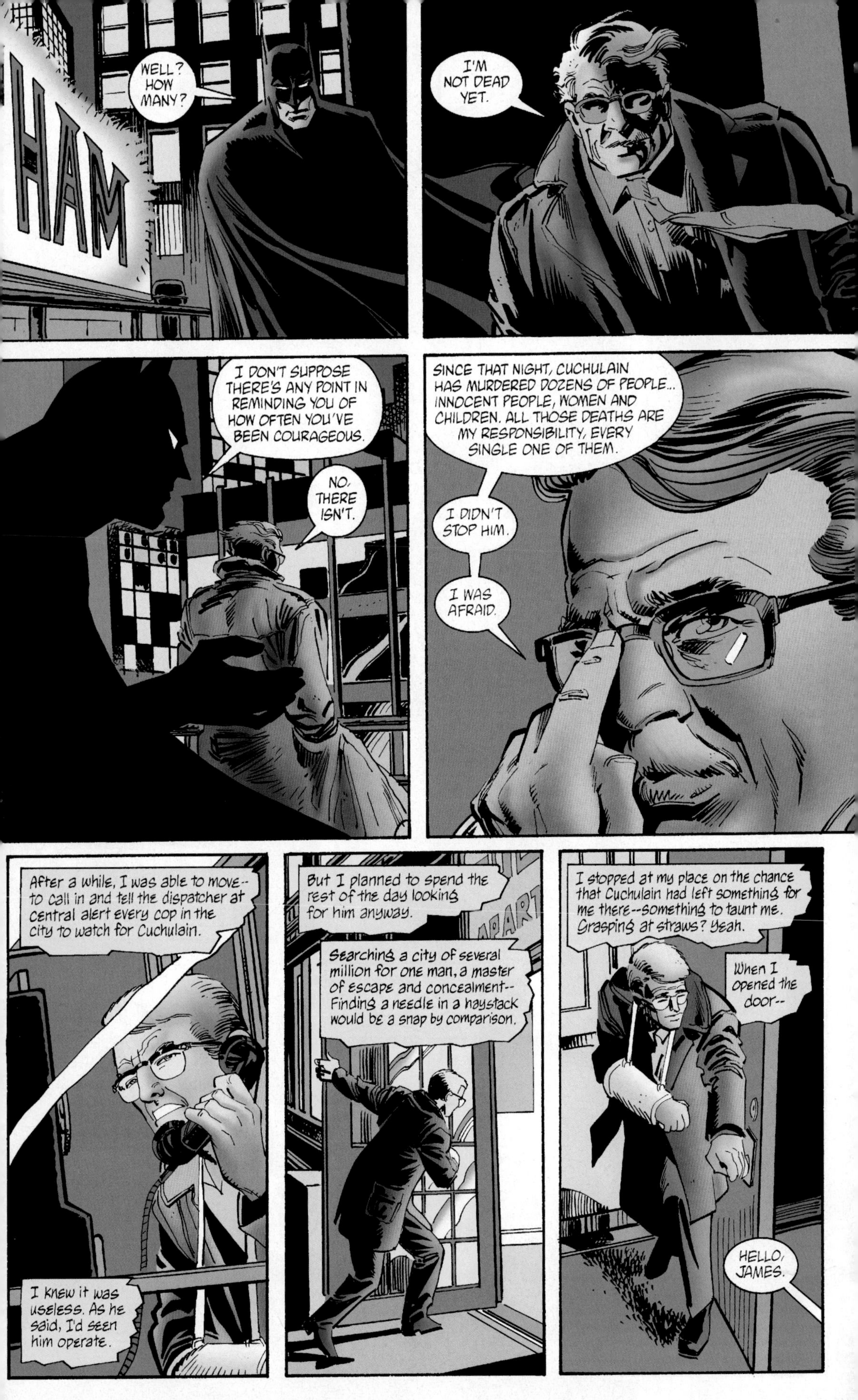
HAM
WELL? HOW MANY?
I'M NOT DEAD YET.
I DON'T SUPPOSE THERE'S ANY POINT IN REMINDING YOU OF HOW OFTEN YOU'VE BEEN COURAGEOUS.
NO, THERE ISN'T.
SINCE THAT NIGHT, CUCHULAIN HAS MURDERED DOZENS OF PEOPLE... INNOCENT PEOPLE, WOMEN AND CHILDREN. ALL THOSE DEATHS ARE MY RESPONSIBILITY, EVERY SINGLE ONE OF THEM.
I DIDN'T STOP HIM.
I WAS AFRAID.
After a while, I was able to move--to call in and tell the dispatcher at Central alert every cop in the city to watch for Cuchulain.
I knew it was useless. As he said, I'd seen him operate.
But I planned to spend the rest of the day looking for him anyway.
Searching a city of several million for one man, a master of escape and concealment--Finding a needle in a haystack would be a snap by comparison.
I stopped at my place on the chance that Cuchulain had left something for me there--something to taunt me. Grasping at straws? Yeah.
When I opened the door--
HELLO, JAMES.

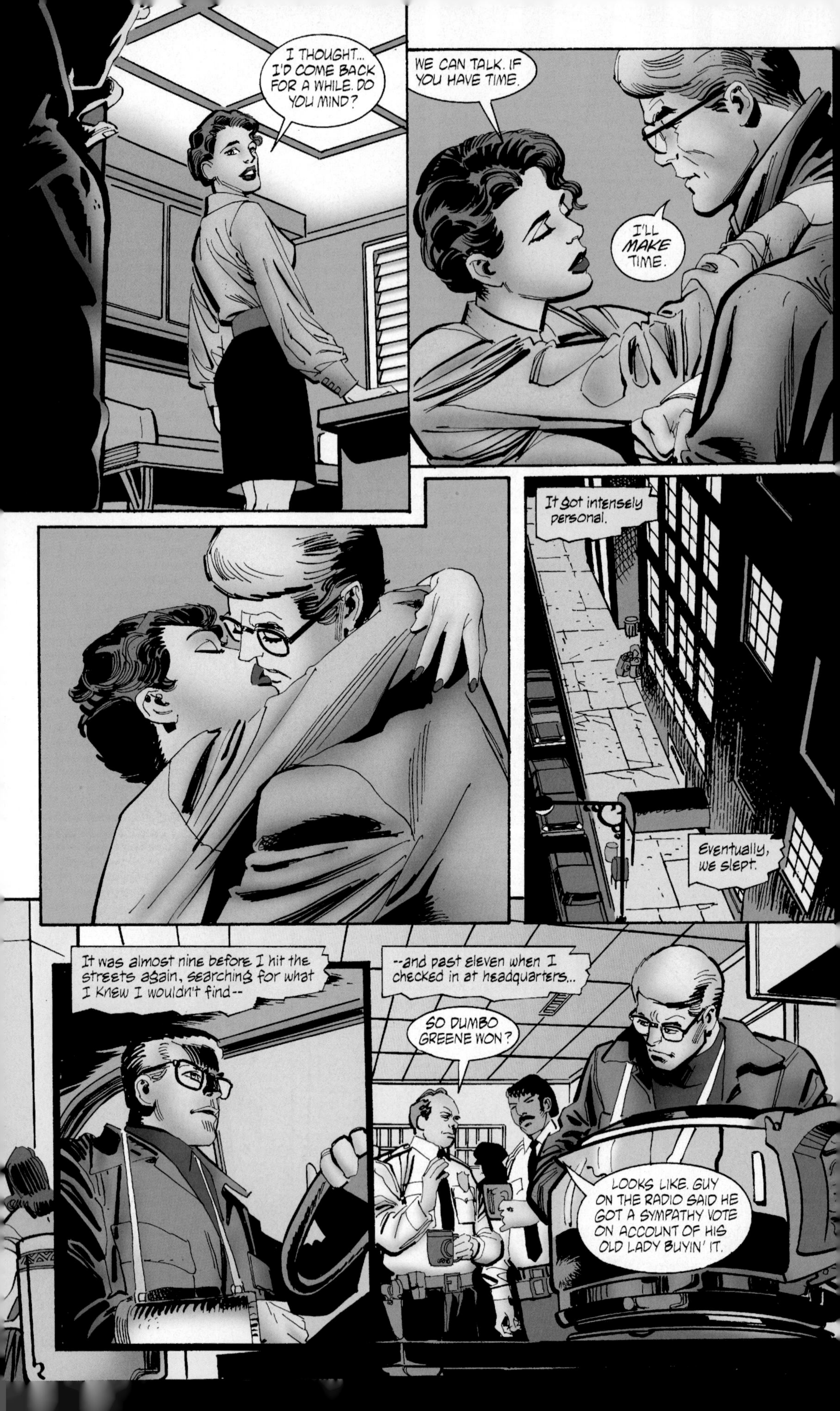
I THOUGHT... I'D COME BACK FOR A WHILE. DO YOU MIND?
WE CAN TALK. IF YOU HAVE TIME.
I'LL MAKE TIME.
It got intensely personal.
Eventually, we slept.
It was almost nine before I hit the streets again, searching for what I knew I wouldn't find--
--and past eleven when I checked in at headquarters...
SO DUMBO GREENE WON?
LOOKS LIKE. GUY ON THE RADIO SAID HE GOT A SYMPATHY VOTE ON ACCOUNT OF HIS OLD LADY BUYIN' IT.

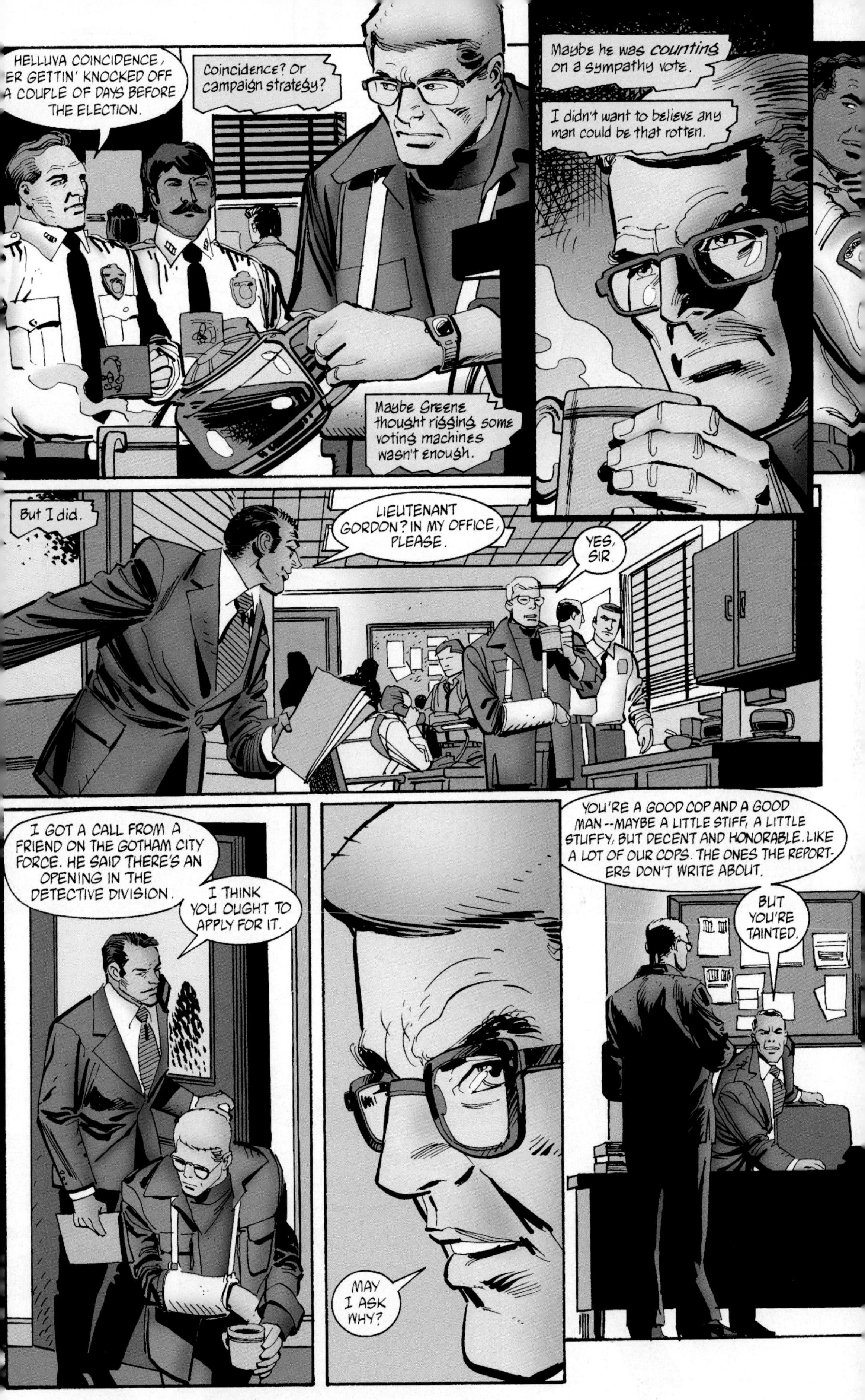

HELLUVA COINCIDENCE, ER GETTIN' KNOCKED OFF A COUPLE OF DAYS BEFORE THE ELECTION.
Coincidence? Or campaign strategy?
Maybe Greene thought rigging some voting machines wasn't enough.
Maybe he was counting on a sympathy vote.
I didn't want to believe any man could be that rotten.
But I did.
LIEUTENANT GORDON? IN MY OFFICE, PLEASE.
YES, SIR.
I GOT A CALL FROM A FRIEND ON THE GOTHAM CITY FORCE. HE SAID THERE'S AN OPENING IN THE DETECTIVE DIVISION.
I THINK YOU OUGHT TO APPLY FOR IT.
MAY I ASK WHY?
YOU'RE A GOOD COP AND A GOOD MAN--MAYBE A LITTLE STIFF, A LITTLE STUFFY, BUT DECENT AND HONORABLE. LIKE A LOT OF OUR COPS. THE ONES THE REPORTERS DON'T WRITE ABOUT.
BUT YOU'RE TAINTED.

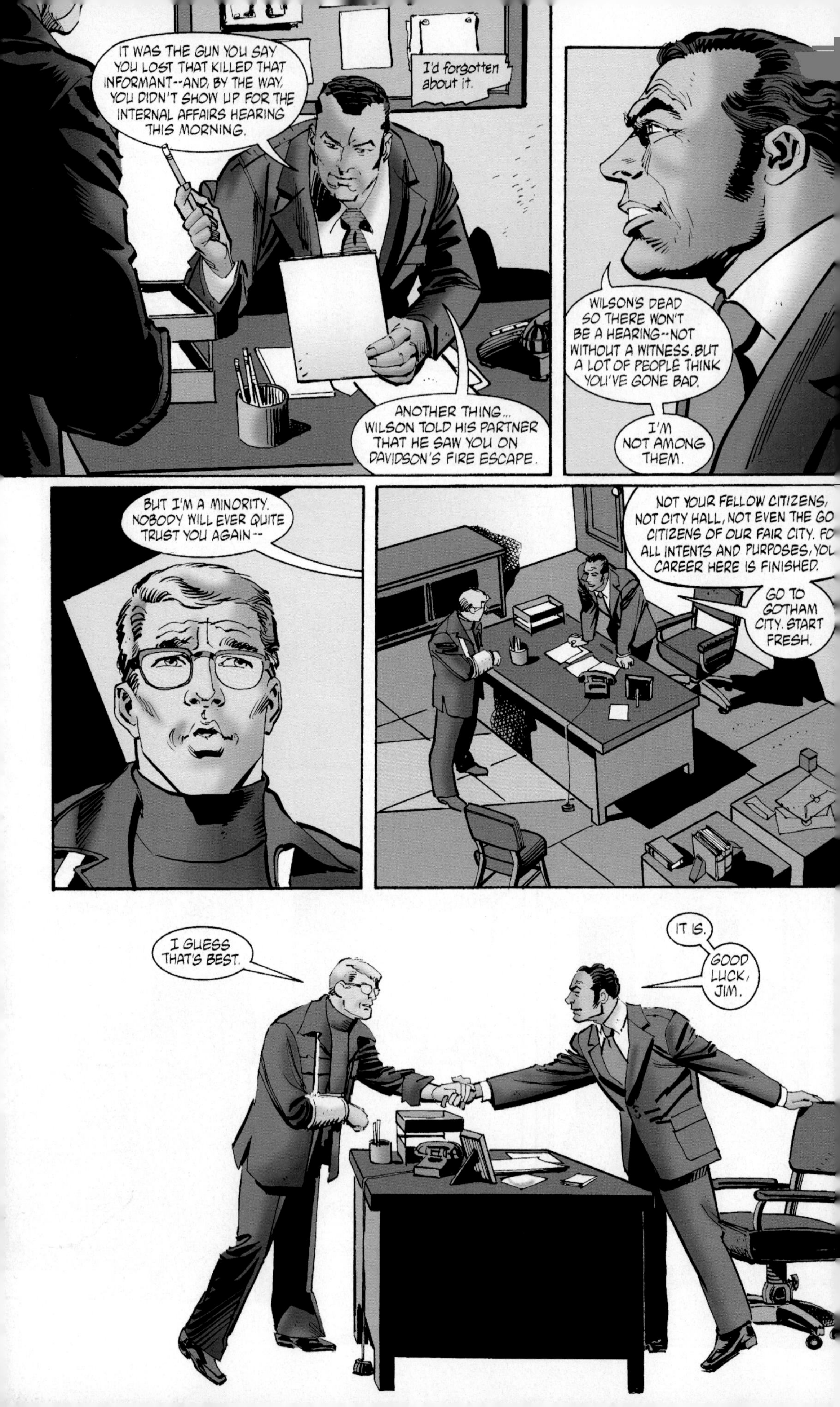
IT WAS THE GUN YOU SAY YOU LOST THAT KILLED THAT INFORMANT--AND, BY THE WAY, YOU DIDN'T SHOW UP FOR THE INTERNAL AFFAIRS HEARING THIS MORNING.
I'd forgotten about it.
ANOTHER THING... WILSON TOLD HIS PARTNER THAT HE SAW YOU ON DAVIDSON'S FIRE ESCAPE.
WILSON'S DEAD SO THERE WON'T BE A HEARING--NOT WITHOUT A WITNESS. BUT A LOT OF PEOPLE THINK YOU'VE GONE BAD.
I'M NOT AMONG THEM.
BUT I'M A MINORITY. NOBODY WILL EVER QUITE TRUST YOU AGAIN--
NOT YOUR FELLOW CITIZENS, NOT CITY HALL, NOT EVEN THE GO CITIZENS OF OUR FAIR CITY. FO ALL INTENTS AND PURPOSES, YOU CAREER HERE IS FINISHED.
GO TO GOTHAM CITY. START FRESH.
I GUESS THAT'S BEST.
IT IS.
GOOD LUCK, JIM.

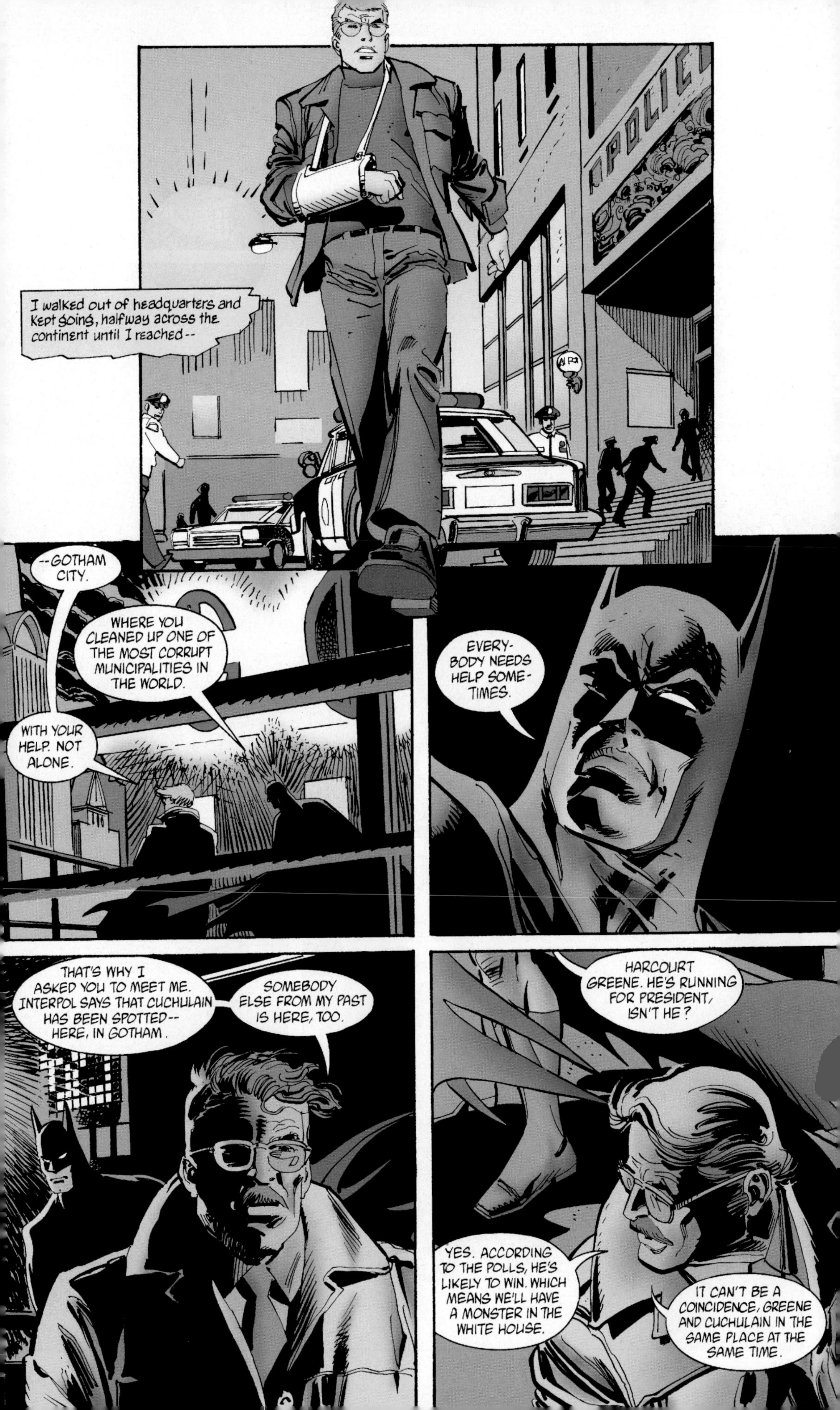

I walked out of headquarters and kept going, halfway across the continent until I reached--
--GOTHAM CITY.
WHERE YOU CLEANED UP ONE OF THE MOST CORRUPT MUNICIPALITIES IN THE WORLD.
WITH YOUR HELP. NOT ALONE.
EVERY-BODY NEEDS HELP SOME-TIMES.
THAT'S WHY I ASKED YOU TO MEET ME. INTERPOL SAYS THAT CUCHULAIN HAS BEEN SPOTTED-- HERE, IN GOTHAM.
SOMEBODY ELSE FROM MY PAST IS HERE, TOO.
HARCOURT GREENE. HE'S RUNNING FOR PRESIDENT, ISN'T HE?
YES. ACCORDING TO THE POLLS, HE'S LIKELY TO WIN. WHICH MEANS WE'LL HAVE A MONSTER IN THE WHITE HOUSE.
IT CAN'T BE A COINCIDENCE, GREENE AND CUCHULAIN IN THE SAME PLACE AT THE SAME TIME.

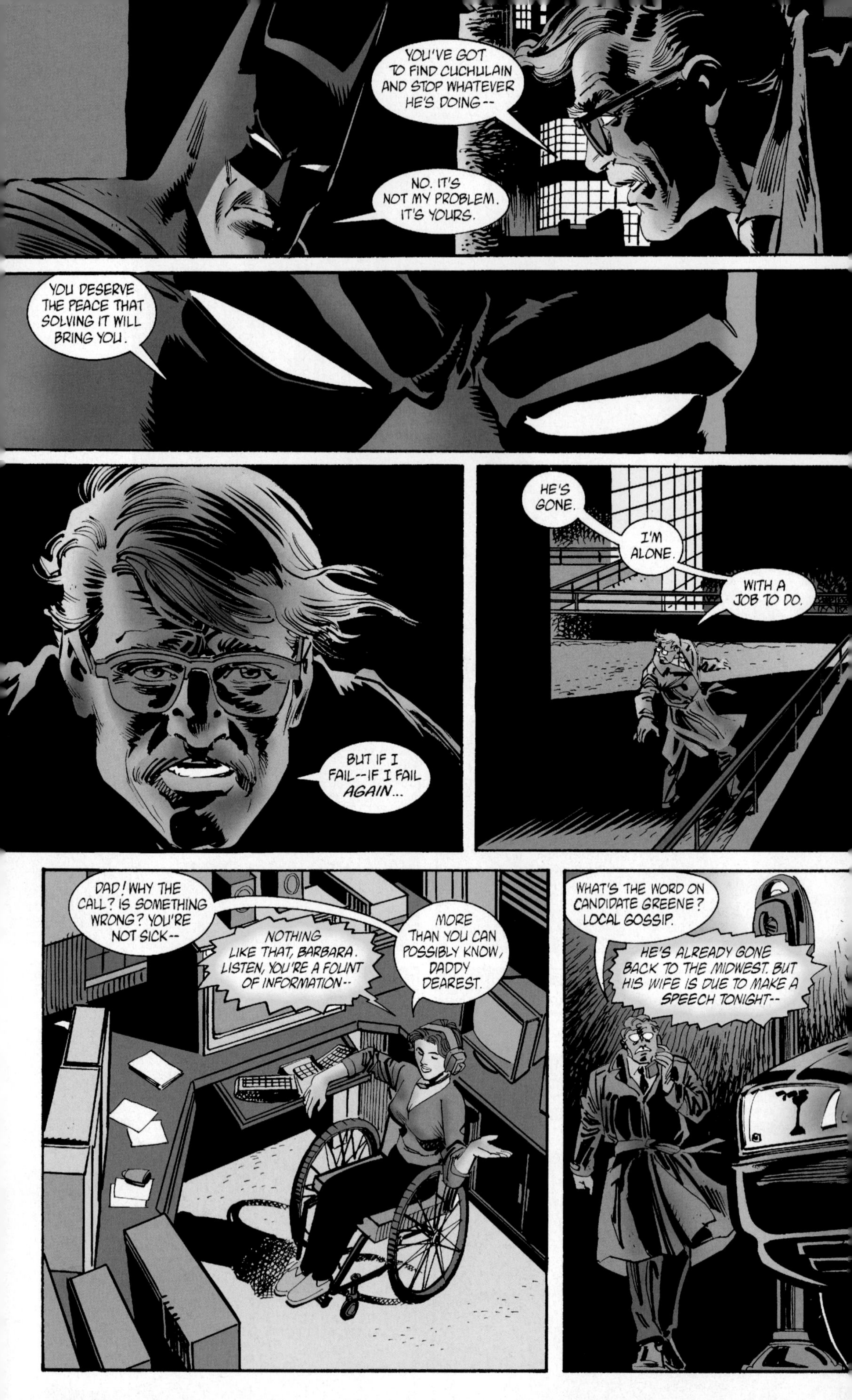
YOU'VE GOT TO FIND CUCHULAIN AND STOP WHATEVER HE'S DOING--
NO. IT'S NOT MY PROBLEM. IT'S YOURS.
YOU DESERVE THE PEACE THAT SOLVING IT WILL BRING YOU.
BUT IF I FAIL--IF I FAIL AGAIN...
HE'S GONE.
I'M ALONE.
WITH A JOB TO DO.
DAD! WHY THE CALL? IS SOMETHING WRONG? YOU'RE NOT SICK--
NOTHING LIKE THAT, BARBARA. LISTEN, YOU'RE A FOUNT OF INFORMATION--
MORE THAN YOU CAN POSSIBLY KNOW, DADDY DEAREST.
WHAT'S THE WORD ON CANDIDATE GREENE? LOCAL GOSSIP.
HE'S ALREADY GONE BACK TO THE MIDWEST. BUT HIS WIFE IS DUE TO MAKE A SPEECH TONIGHT--

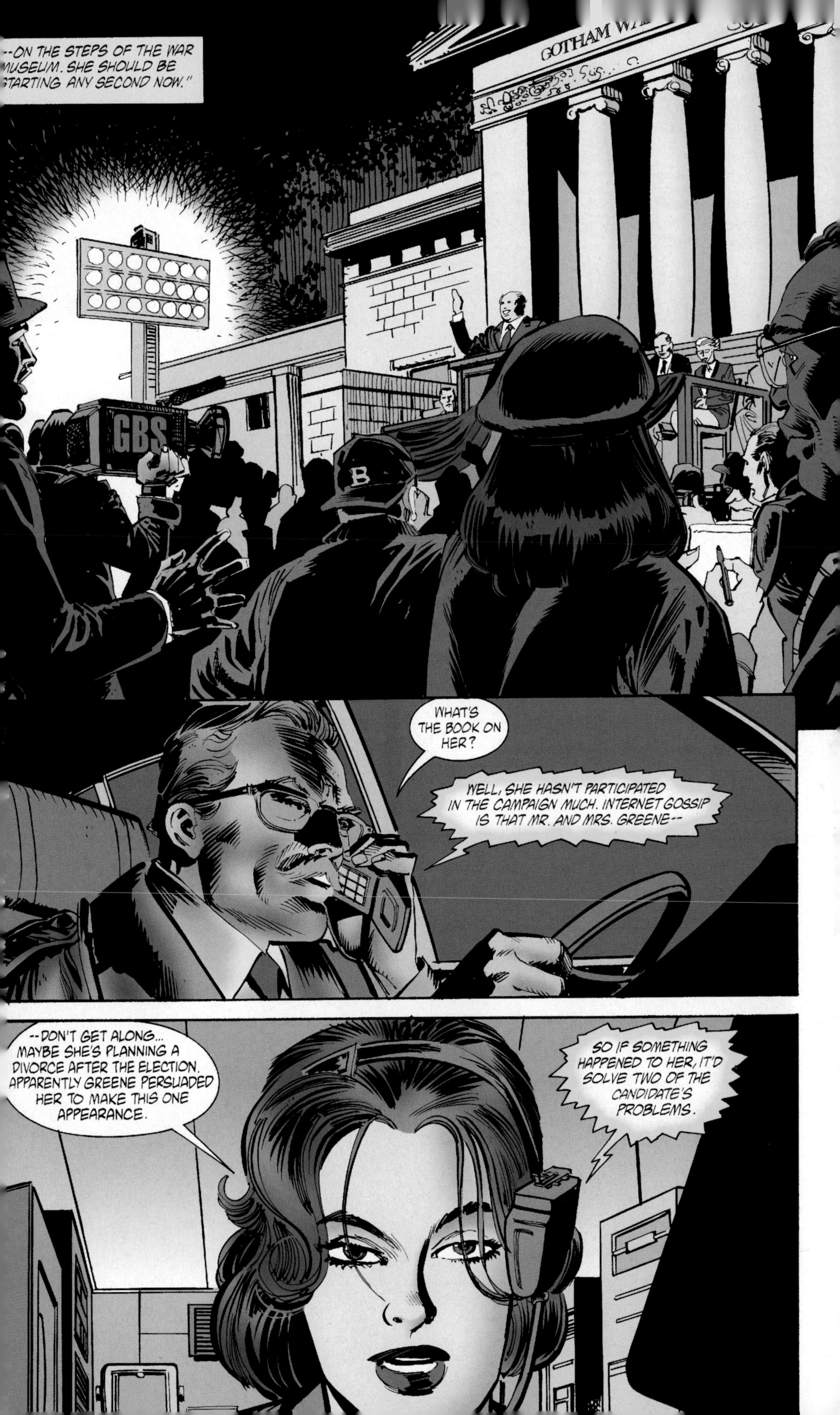
--ON THE STEPS OF THE WAR MUSEUM. SHE SHOULD BE STARTING ANY SECOND NOW."
GOTHAM WA
GBS
B
WHAT'S THE BOOK ON HER?
WELL, SHE HASN'T PARTICIPATED IN THE CAMPAIGN MUCH. INTERNET GOSSIP IS THAT MR. AND MRS. GREENE--
--DON'T GET ALONG... MAYBE SHE'S PLANNING A DIVORCE AFTER THE ELECTION. APPARENTLY GREENE PERSUADED HER TO MAKE THIS ONE APPEARANCE.
SO IF SOMETHING HAPPENED TO HER, IT'D SOLVE TWO OF THE CANDIDATE'S PROBLEMS.

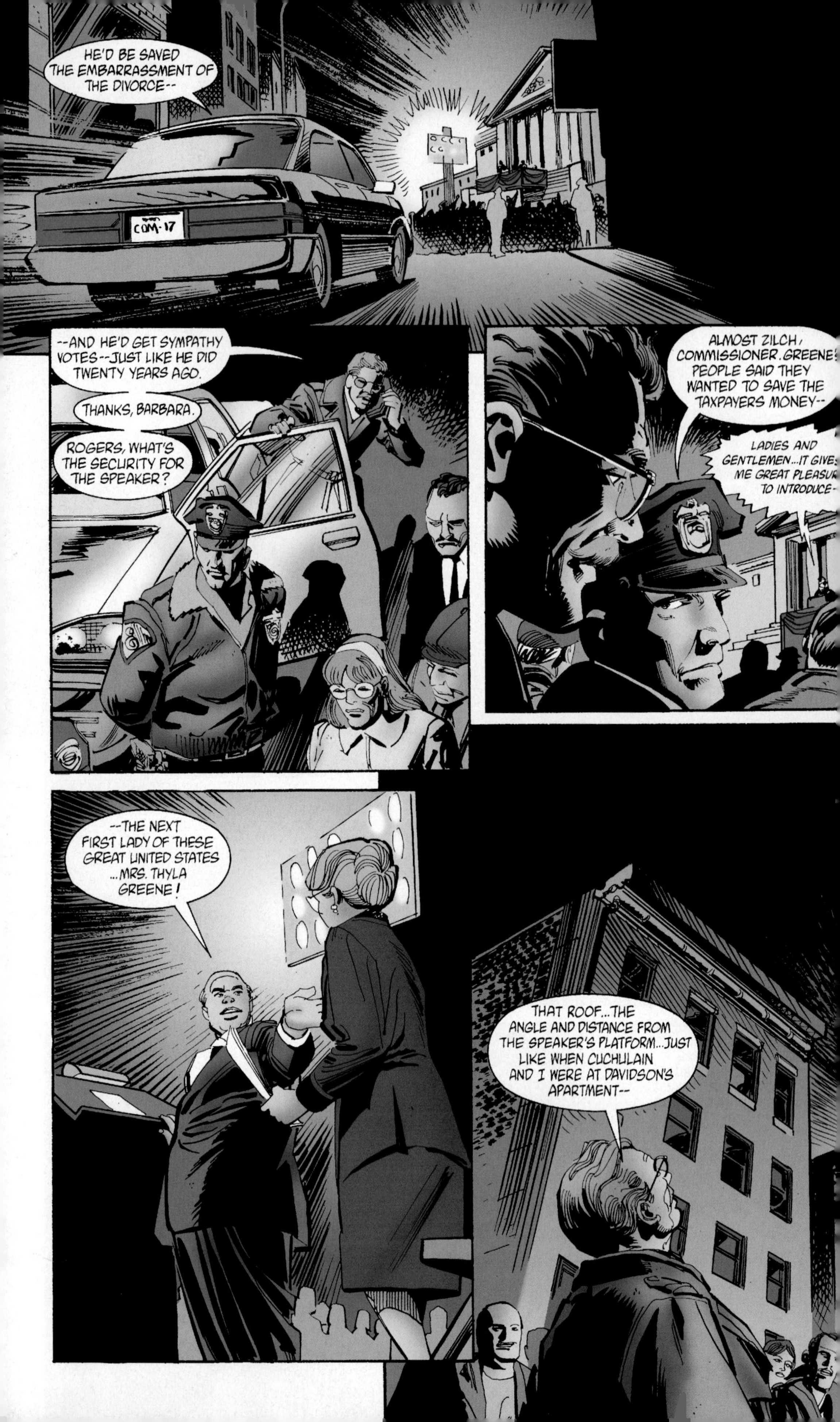
HE'D BE SAVED THE EMBARRASSMENT OF THE DIVORCE--
COM-17
--AND HE'D GET SYMPATHY VOTES--JUST LIKE HE DID TWENTY YEARS AGO.
THANKS, BARBARA.
ROGERS, WHAT'S THE SECURITY FOR THE SPEAKER?
ALMOST ZILCH, COMMISSIONER. GREENE'S PEOPLE SAID THEY WANTED TO SAVE THE TAXPAYERS MONEY--
LADIES AND GENTLEMEN...IT GIVES ME GREAT PLEASURE TO INTRODUCE--
--THE NEXT FIRST LADY OF THESE GREAT UNITED STATES ...MRS. THYLA GREENE!
THAT ROOF...THE ANGLE AND DISTANCE FROM THE SPEAKER'S PLATFORM...JUST LIKE WHEN CUCHULAIN AND I WERE AT DAVIDSON'S APARTMENT--

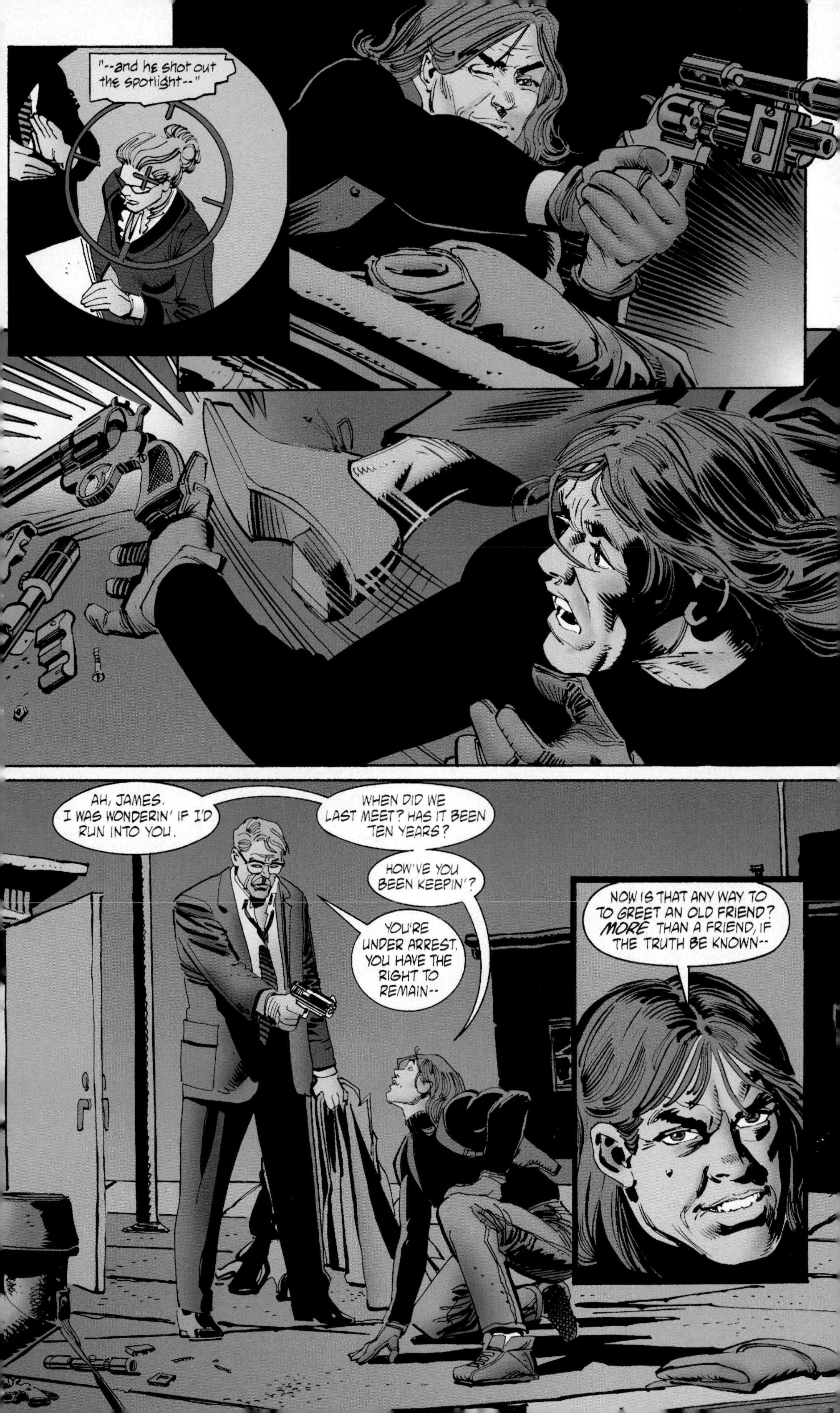
"--and he shot out the spotlight--"
AH, JAMES. I WAS WONDERIN' IF I'D RUN INTO YOU.
WHEN DID WE LAST MEET? HAS IT BEEN TEN YEARS?
HOW'VE YOU BEEN KEEPIN'?
YOU'RE UNDER ARREST. YOU HAVE THE RIGHT TO REMAIN--
NOW IS THAT ANY WAY TO TO GREET AN OLD FRIEND? MORE THAN A FRIEND, IF THE TRUTH BE KNOWN--

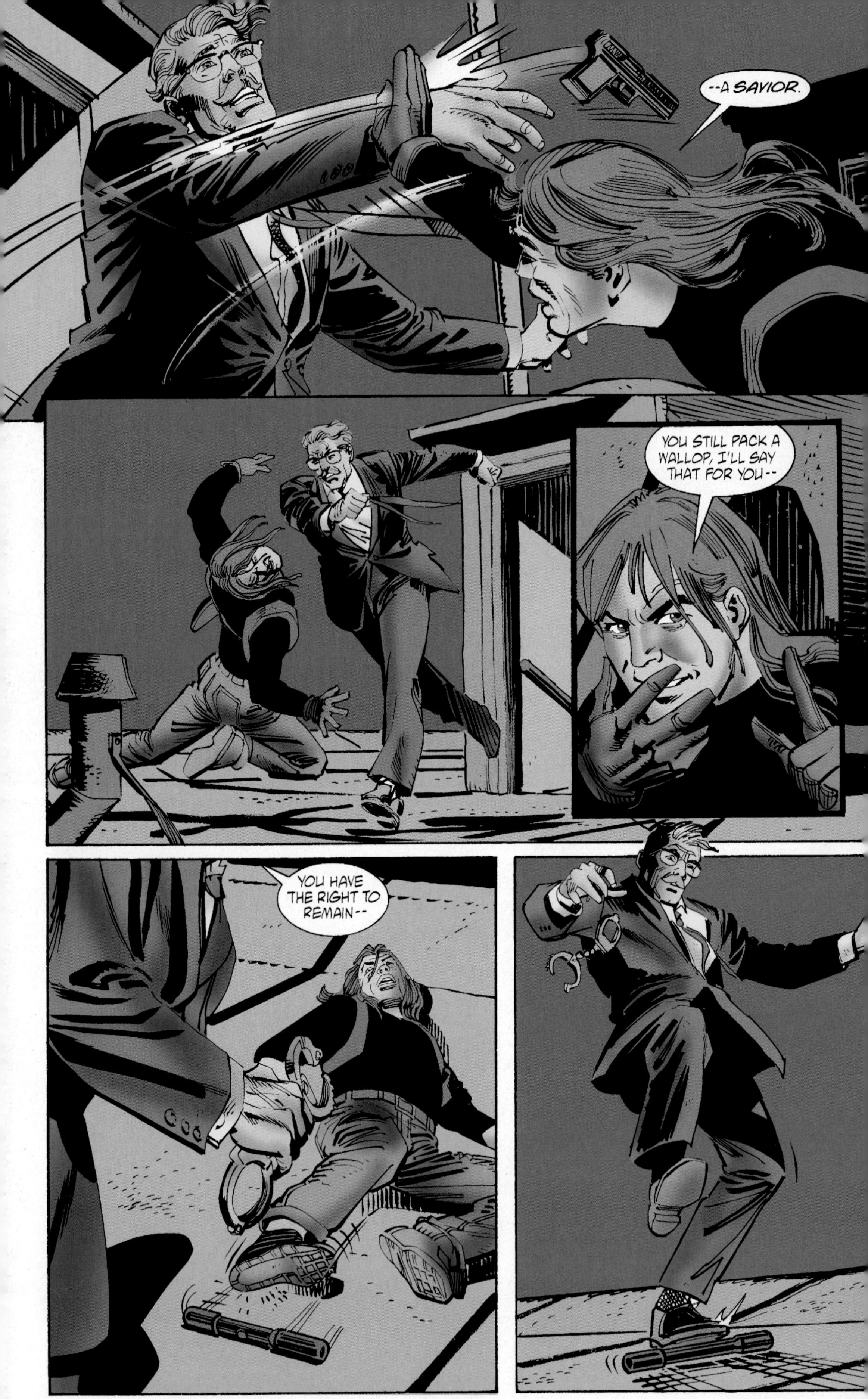
--A SAVIOR.
YOU STILL PACK A WALLOP, I'LL SAY THAT FOR YOU--
YOU HAVE THE RIGHT TO REMAIN--

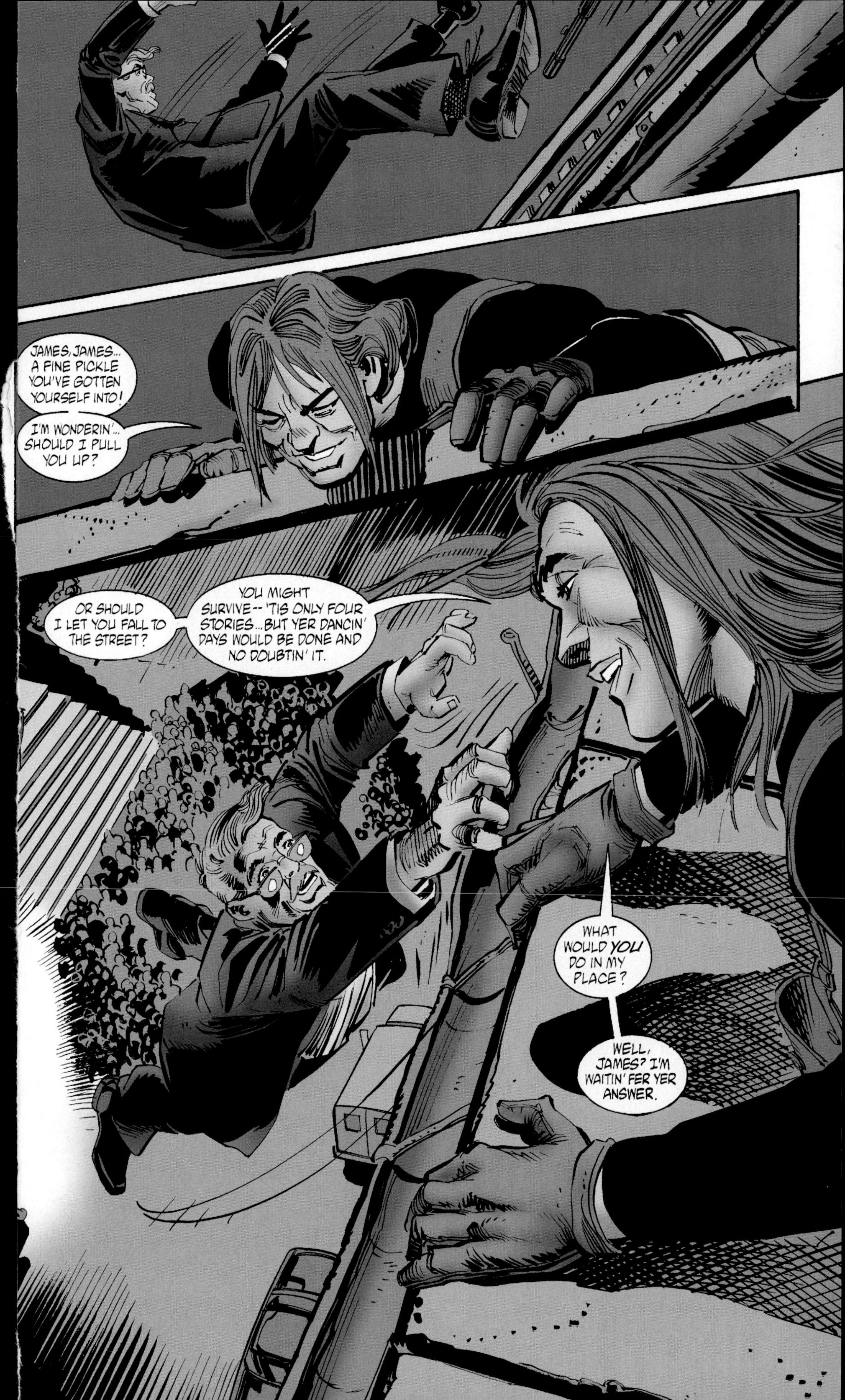
JAMES, JAMES... A FINE PICKLE YOU'VE GOTTEN YOURSELF INTO!
I'M WONDERIN'... SHOULD I PULL YOU UP?
OR SHOULD I LET YOU FALL TO THE STREET?
YOU MIGHT SURVIVE-- 'TIS ONLY FOUR STORIES...BUT YER DANCIN' DAYS WOULD BE DONE AND NO DOUBTIN' IT.
WHAT WOULD YOU DO IN MY PLACE?
WELL, JAMES? I'M WAITIN' FER YER ANSWER.

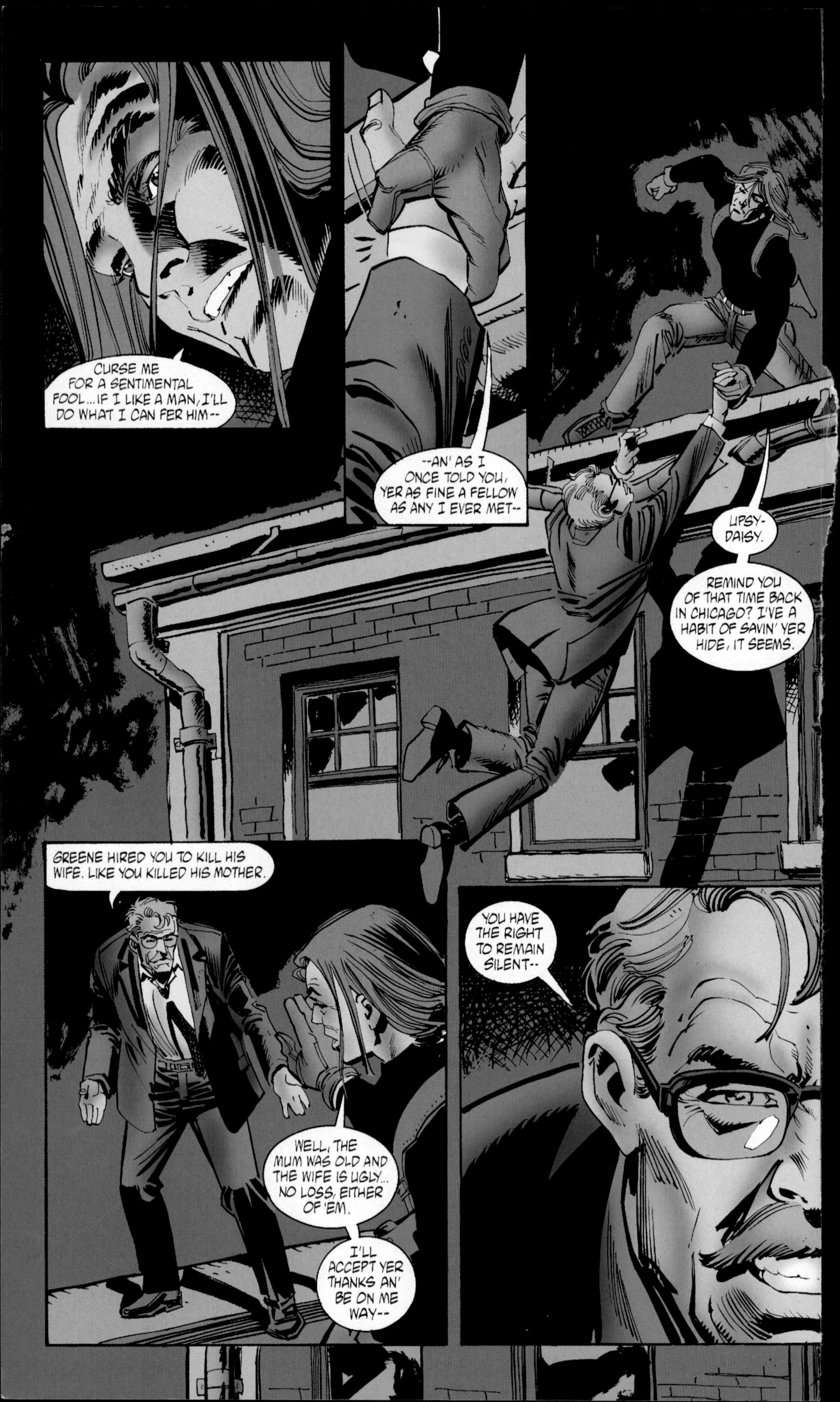
CURSE ME FOR A SENTIMENTAL FOOL... IF I LIKE A MAN, I'LL DO WHAT I CAN FER HIM--
--AN' AS I ONCE TOLD YOU, YER AS FINE A FELLOW AS ANY I EVER MET--
UPSY-DAISY.
REMIND YOU OF THAT TIME BACK IN CHICAGO? I'VE A HABIT OF SAVIN' YER HIDE, IT SEEMS.
GREENE HIRED YOU TO KILL HIS WIFE. LIKE YOU KILLED HIS MOTHER.
WELL, THE MUM WAS OLD AND THE WIFE IS UGLY... NO LOSS, EITHER OF 'EM.
I'LL ACCEPT YER THANKS AN' BE ON ME WAY--
YOU HAVE THE RIGHT TO REMAIN SILENT--

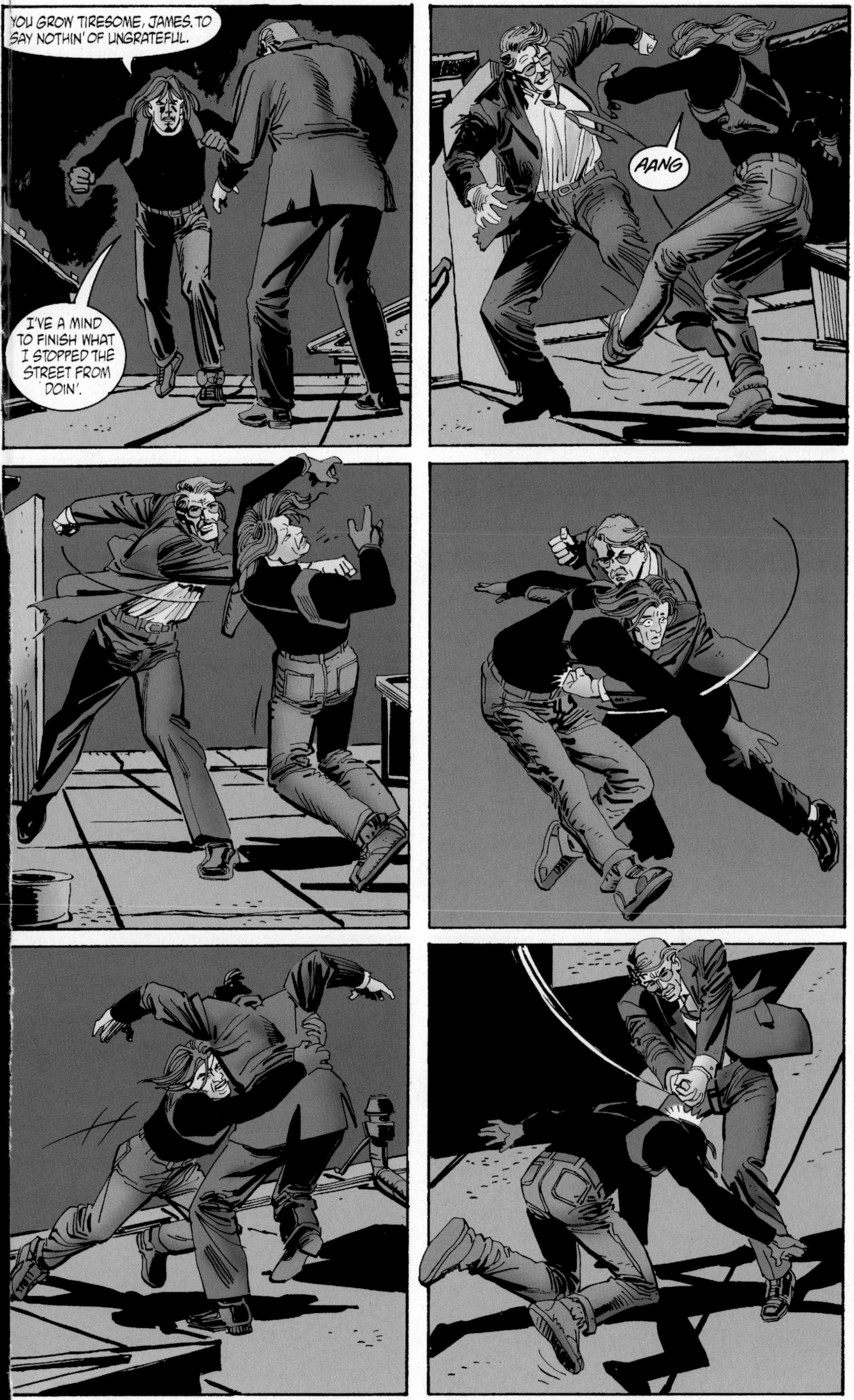
YOU GROW TIRESOME, JAMES. TO SAY NOTHIN' OF UNGRATEFUL.
I'VE A MIND TO FINISH WHAT I STOPPED THE STREET FROM 'DOIN'.
AANG

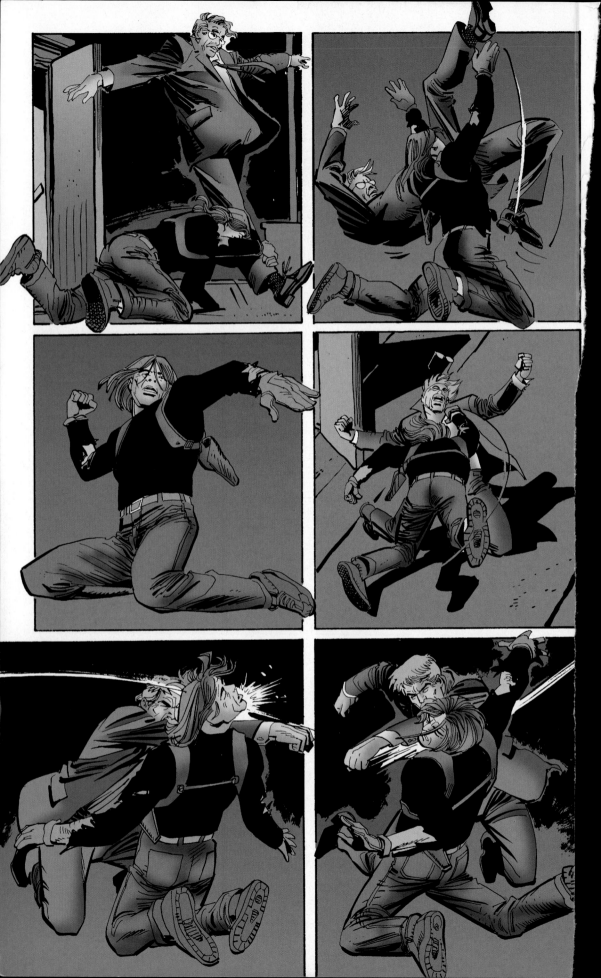

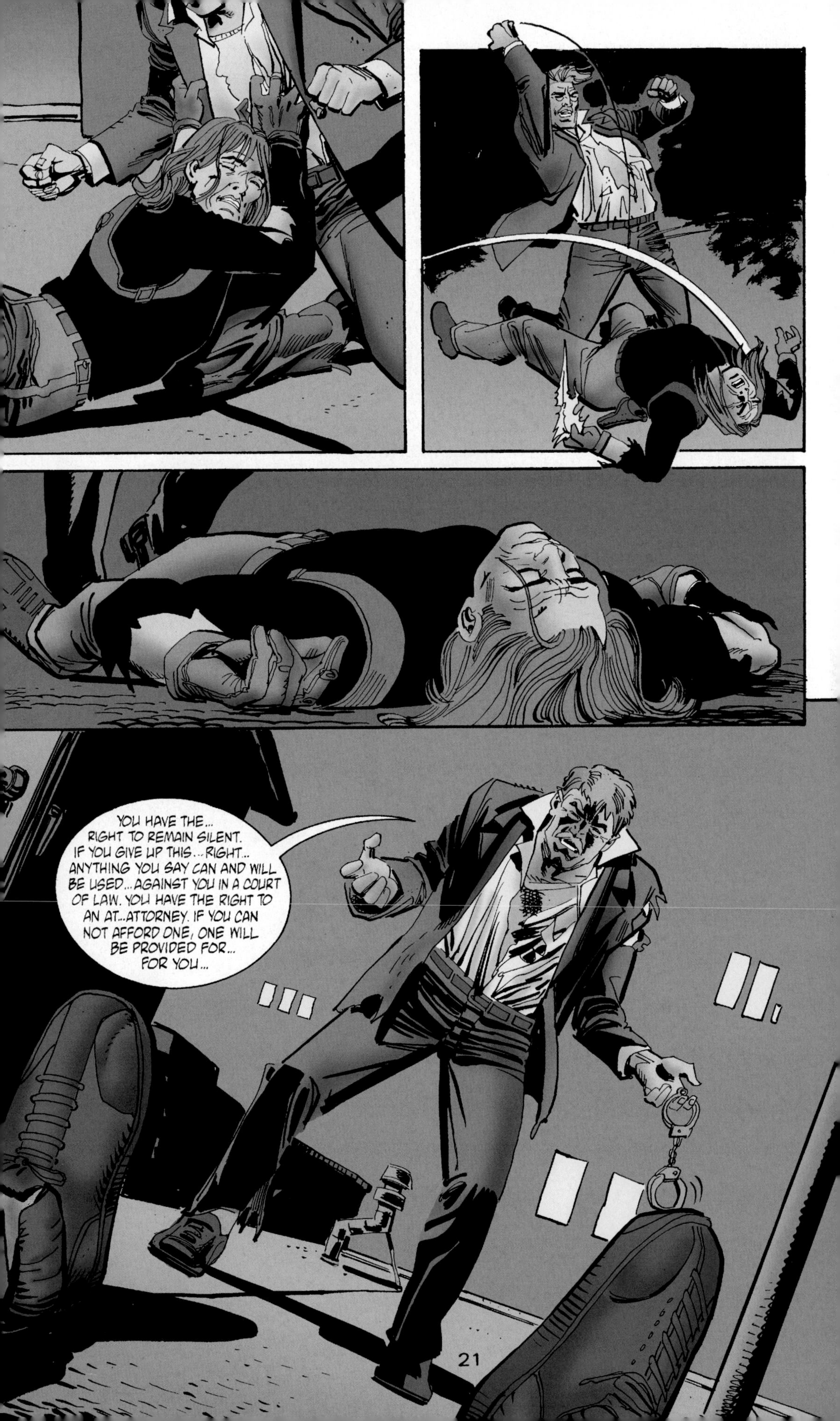
YOU HAVE THE... RIGHT TO REMAIN SILENT. IF YOU GIVE UP THIS... RIGHT... ANYTHING YOU SAY CAN AND WILL BE USED... AGAINST YOU IN A COURT OF LAW. YOU HAVE THE RIGHT TO AN AT...ATTORNEY. IF YOU CAN NOT AFFORD ONE, ONE WILL BE PROVIDED FOR... FOR YOU...

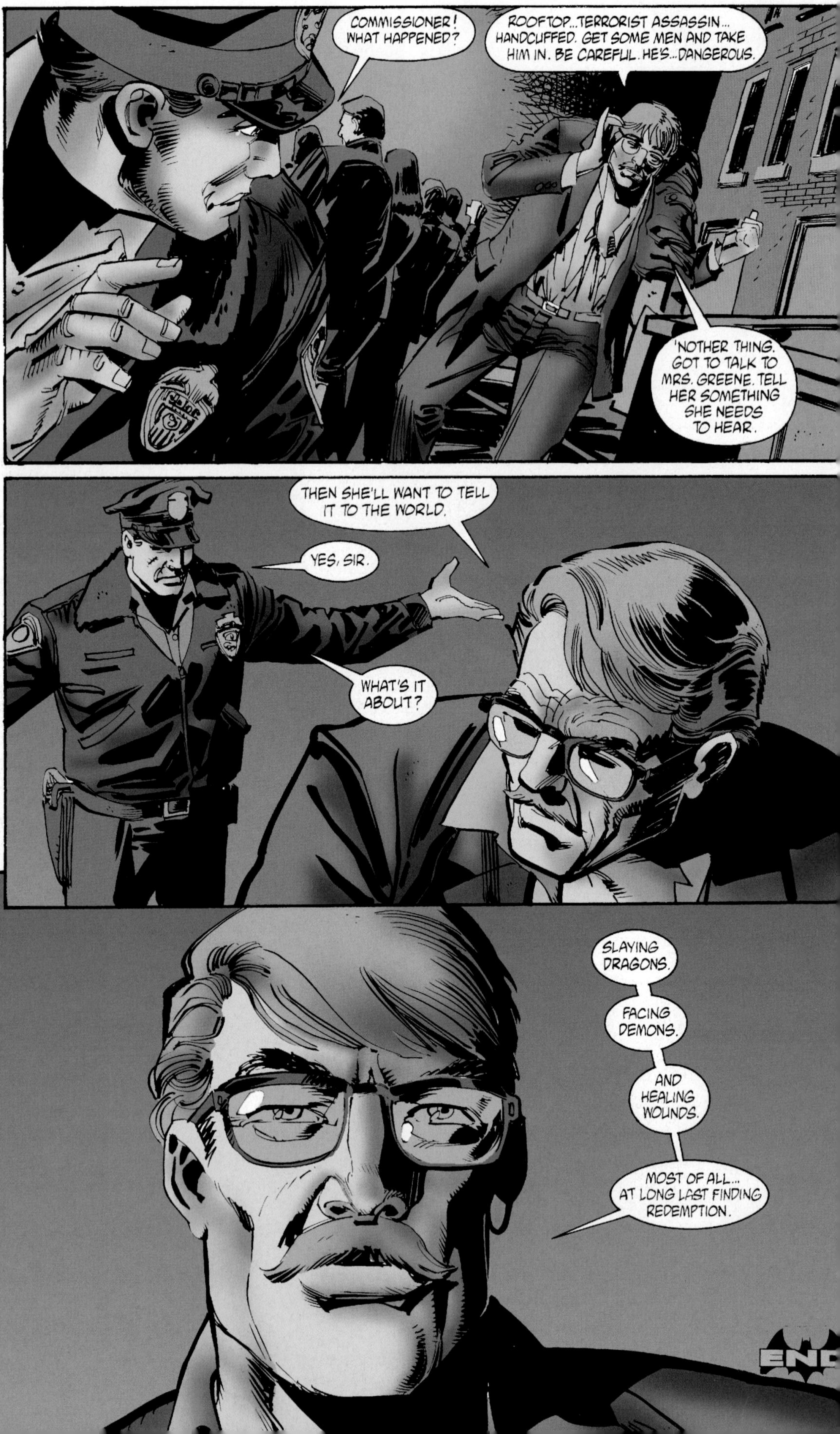
COMMISSIONER! WHAT HAPPENED?
ROOFTOP... TERRORIST ASSASSIN... HANDCUFFED. GET SOME MEN AND TAKE HIM IN. BE CAREFUL. HE'S... DANGEROUS.
'NOTHER THING. GOT TO TALK TO MRS. GREENE. TELL HER SOMETHING SHE NEEDS TO HEAR.
YES, SIR.
WHAT'S IT ABOUT?
THEN SHE'LL WANT TO TELL IT TO THE WORLD.
SLAYING DRAGONS.
FACING DEMONS.
AND HEALING WOUNDS.
MOST OF ALL... AT LONG LAST FINDING REDEMPTION.
END

START AT THE BEGINNING!

BATMAN VOLUME 1: THE COURT OF OWLS

**BATMAN & ROBIN
VOLUME 1:
BORN TO KILL**

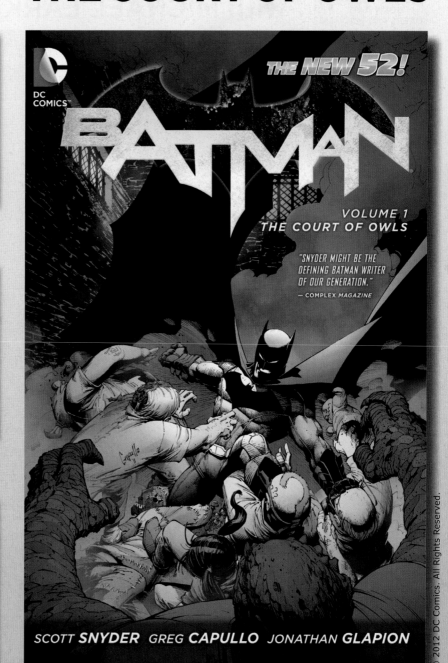

**BATMAN: DETECTIVE
COMICS VOLUME 1:
FACES OF DEATH**

**BATMAN: THE DARK
KNIGHT VOLUME 1:
KNIGHT TERRORS**

FROM THE *NEW YORK TIMES* BEST-SELLING WRITERS

ED BRUBAKER
& GREG RUCKA
with MICHAEL LARK

GOTHAM CENTRAL
BOOK TWO:
JOKERS AND MADMEN

GOTHAM CENTRAL
BOOK THREE:
ON THE FREAK BEAT

GOTHAM CENTRAL
BOOK FOUR:
CORRIGAN

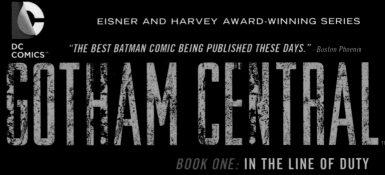

EISNER AND HARVEY AWARD-WINNING SERIES

"THE BEST BATMAN COMIC BEING PUBLISHED THESE DAYS." —*Boston Phoenix*

BOOK ONE: IN THE LINE OF DUTY

ED
GREG
BRUBAKER RUCKA
MICHAEL LARK INTRODUCTION BY
LAWRENCE BLOCK